Microsoft® Office 365™
POWERPOINT® 2016

COMPREHENSIVE

D1566782

SUSAN L. SEBOK

CENGAGE
Learning·

SHELLY CASHMAN SERIES®

Australia • Brazil • Japan • Korea • Mexico • Singapore • Spain • United Kingdom • United States

Microsoft PowerPoint 2016: Comprehensive
Susan L. Sebok

SVP, General Manager: Balraj S. Kalsi

Product Director: Kathleen McMahon

Senior Product Team Manager: Lauren Murphy

Product Team Manager: Andrea Topping

Senior Director, Development: Julia Caballero

Product Development Manager: Leigh Hefferon

Managing Content Developer: Emma F. Newsom

Developmental Editor: Deb Kaufmann

Product Assistant: Erica Chapman

Manuscript Quality Assurance: Jeffrey Schwartz, John Freitas, Serge Palladino, Susan Pedicini, Danielle Shaw, Chris Scriver

Senior Production Director: Wendy Troeger

Production Director: Patty Stephan

Senior Content Project Manager: James Zayicek

Manufacturing Planner: Julio Esperas

Designer: Diana Graham

Text Design: Joel Sadagursky

Cover Template Designer: Diana Graham

Cover image(s): Piotr Zajc/Shutterstock.com; Mrs. Opossum/Shutterstock.com

Compositor: Lumina Datamatics, Inc.

Vice President, Marketing: Brian Joyner

Marketing Director: Michele McTighe

Marketing Manager: Stephanie Albracht

For product information and technology assistance, contact us at
Cengage Learning Customer & Sales Support, 1-800-354-9706

For permission to use material from this text or product, submit all requests online at **www.cengage.com/permissions**
Further permissions questions can be e-mailed to
permissionrequest@cengage.com

Library of Congress Control Number: 2016946795

Soft-cover Edition
ISBN: 978-1-305-87081-9

Loose-leaf Edition
ISBN: 978-1-337-25117-4

Cengage Learning
20 Channel Center Street
Boston, MA 02210
USA

Cengage Learning is a leading provider of customized learning solutions with employees residing in nearly 40 different countries and sales in more than 125 countries around the world. Find your local representative at **www.cengage.com.**

Cengage Learning products are represented in Canada by Nelson Education, Ltd.

To learn more about Cengage Learning, visit **www.cengage.com.**
Purchase any of our products at your local college store or at our preferred online store **www.cengagebrain.com**

Printed in the United States of America
Print Number: 02   Print Year: 2017

Microsoft® Office 365™
POWERPOINT® 2016

COMPREHENSIVE

Contents

Microsoft PowerPoint 2016

Productivity Apps for School and Work

Corinne Hoisington

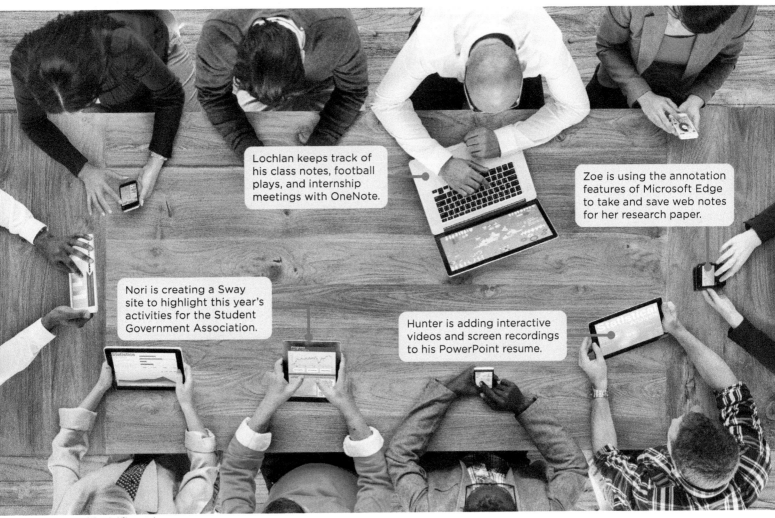

© Rawpixel/Shutterstock.com

Being computer literate no longer means mastery of only Word, Excel, PowerPoint, Outlook, and Access. To become technology power users, Hunter, Nori, Zoe, and Lochlan are exploring Microsoft OneNote, Sway, Mix, and Edge in Office 2016 and Windows 10.

In this Module

Learn to use productivity apps!
Links to companion **Sways**, featuring **videos** with hands-on instructions, are located on www.cengagebrain.com.

Introduction to OneNote 2016

notebook | section tab | To Do tag | screen clipping | note | template | Microsoft OneNote Mobile app | sync | drawing canvas | inked handwriting | Ink to Text

As you glance around any classroom, you invariably see paper notebooks and notepads on each desk. Because deciphering and sharing handwritten notes can be a challenge, Microsoft OneNote 2016 replaces physical notebooks, binders, and paper notes with a searchable, digital notebook. OneNote captures your ideas and schoolwork on any device so you can stay organized, share notes, and work with others on projects. Whether you are a student taking class notes as shown in **Figure 1** or an employee taking notes in company meetings, OneNote is the one place to keep notes for all of your projects.

Figure 1: OneNote 2016 notebook

Each **notebook** is divided into sections, also called **section tabs**, by subject or topic.

Use **To Do tags**, icons that help you keep track of your assignments and other tasks.

Type on a page to add a **note**, a small window that contains text or other types of information.

Personalize a page with a **template**, or stationery.

Write or draw directly on the page using drawing tools.

Pages can include pictures such as **screen clippings**, images from any part of a computer screen.

Attach files and enter equations so you have everything you need in one place.

Creating a OneNote Notebook

OneNote is divided into sections similar to those in a spiral-bound notebook. Each OneNote notebook contains sections, pages, and other notebooks. You can use One-Note for school, business, and personal projects. Store information for each type of project in different notebooks to keep your tasks separate, or use any other organization that suits you. OneNote is flexible enough to adapt to the way you want to work.

When you create a notebook, it contains a blank page with a plain white background by default, though you can use templates, or stationery, to apply designs in categories such as Academic, Business, Decorative, and Planners. Start typing or use the buttons on the Insert tab to insert notes, which are small resizable windows that can contain text, equations, tables, on-screen writing, images, audio and video recordings, to-do lists, file attachments, and file printouts. Add as many notes as you need to each page.

Syncing a Notebook to the Cloud

OneNote saves your notes every time you make a change in a notebook. To make sure you can access your notebooks with a laptop, tablet, or smartphone wherever you are, OneNote uses cloud-based storage, such as OneDrive or SharePoint. **Microsoft OneNote Mobile app**, a lightweight version of OneNote 2016 shown in **Figure 2**, is available for free in the Windows Store, Google Play for Android devices, and the AppStore for iOS devices.

If you have a Microsoft account, OneNote saves your notes on OneDrive automatically for all your mobile devices and computers, which is called **syncing**. For example, you can use OneNote to take notes on your laptop during class, and then open OneNote on your phone to study later. To use a notebook stored on your computer with your OneNote Mobile app, move the notebook to OneDrive. You can quickly share notebook content with other people using OneDrive.

Figure 2: Microsoft OneNote Mobile app

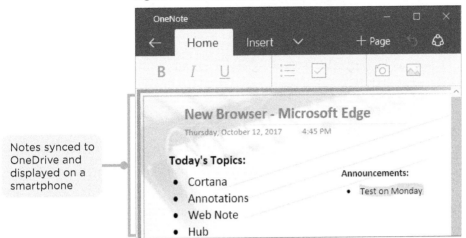

Notes synced to OneDrive and displayed on a smartphone

Taking Notes

Use OneNote pages to organize your notes by class and topic or lecture. Beyond simple typed notes, OneNote stores drawings, converts handwriting to searchable text and mathematical sketches to equations, and records audio and video.

OneNote includes drawing tools that let you sketch freehand drawings such as biological cell diagrams and financial supply-and-demand charts. As shown in **Figure 3**, the Draw tab on the ribbon provides these drawing tools along with shapes so you can insert diagrams and other illustrations to represent your ideas. When you draw on a page, OneNote creates a **drawing canvas**, which is a container for shapes and lines.

On the Job Now

OneNote is ideal for taking notes during meetings, whether you are recording minutes, documenting a discussion, sketching product diagrams, or listing follow-up items. Use a meeting template to add pages with content appropriate for meetings.

Figure 3: Tools on the Draw tab

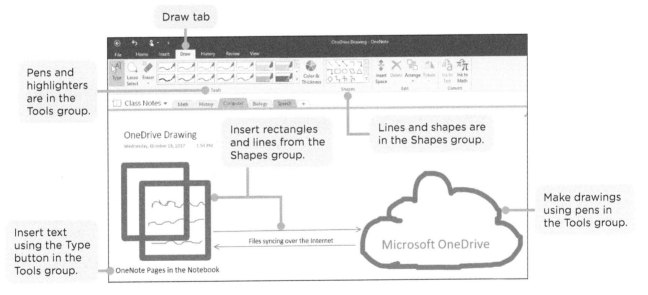

Draw tab

Pens and highlighters are in the Tools group.

Insert rectangles and lines from the Shapes group.

Lines and shapes are in the Shapes group.

Make drawings using pens in the Tools group.

Insert text using the Type button in the Tools group.

Converting Handwriting to Text

When you use a pen tool to write on a notebook page, the text you enter is called **inked handwriting**. OneNote can convert inked handwriting to typed text when you use the **Ink to Text** button in the Convert group on the Draw tab, as shown in **Figure 4**. After OneNote converts the handwriting to text, you can use the Search box to find terms in the converted text or any other note in your notebooks.

Figure 4: Converting handwriting to text

Ink to Text button

Women's Suffrage

Writing inserted with a fingertip

Handwriting converted to searchable text

Suffrage Movement: effort to get right to vote for women

On the Job Now

Use OneNote as a place to brainstorm ongoing work projects. If a notebook contains sensitive material, you can password-protect some or all of the notebook so that only certain people can open it.

Recording a Lecture

If your computer or mobile device has a microphone or camera, OneNote can record the audio or video from a lecture or business meeting as shown in **Figure 5**. When you record a lecture (with your instructor's permission), you can follow along, take regular notes at your own pace, and review the video recording later. You can control the start, pause, and stop motions of the recording when you play back the recording of your notes.

Figure 5: Video inserted in a notebook

Record Video button

Audio & Video Recording tab

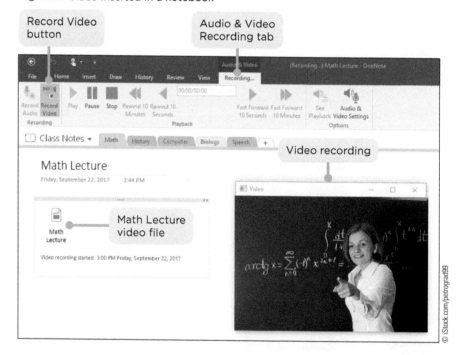

Video recording

Math Lecture video file

© iStock.com/petrograd99

Try This Now

1: Taking Notes for a Week

Learn to use OneNote!
Links to companion **Sways**, featuring **videos** with hands-on instructions, are located on www.cengagebrain.com.

As a student, you can get organized by using OneNote to take detailed notes in your classes. Perform the following tasks:

    a. Create a new OneNote notebook on your Microsoft OneDrive account (the default location for new notebooks). Name the notebook with your first name followed by "Notes," as in **Caleb Notes**.

    b. Create four section tabs, each with a different class name.

    c. Take detailed notes in those classes for one week. Be sure to include notes, drawings, and other types of content.

    d. Sync your notes with your OneDrive. Submit your assignment in the format specified by your instructor.

2: Using OneNote to Organize a Research Paper

You have a research paper due on the topic of three habits of successful students. Use OneNote to organize your research. Perform the following tasks:

    a. Create a new OneNote notebook on your Microsoft OneDrive account. Name the notebook **Success Research**.

    b. Create three section tabs with the following names:

- **Take Detailed Notes**
- **Be Respectful in Class**
- **Come to Class Prepared**

    c. On the web, research the topics and find three sources for each section. Copy a sentence from each source and paste the sentence into the appropriate section. When you paste the sentence, OneNote inserts it in a note with a link to the source.

    d. Sync your notes with your OneDrive. Submit your assignment in the format specified by your instructor.

3: Planning Your Career

Note: This activity requires a webcam or built-in video camera on any type of device.

Consider an occupation that interests you. Using OneNote, examine the responsibilities, education requirements, potential salary, and employment outlook of a specific career. Perform the following tasks:

    a. Create a new OneNote notebook on your Microsoft OneDrive account. Name the notebook with your first name followed by a career title, such as **Kara - App Developer**.

    b. Create four section tabs with the names **Responsibilities, Education Requirements, Median Salary**, and **Employment Outlook**.

    c. Research the responsibilities of your career path. Using OneNote, record a short video (approximately 30 seconds) of yourself explaining the responsibilities of your career path. Place the video in the Responsibilities section.

    d. On the web, research the educational requirements for your career path and find two appropriate sources. Copy a paragraph from each source and paste them into the appropriate section. When you paste a paragraph, OneNote inserts it in a note with a link to the source.

    e. Research the median salary for a single year for this career. Create a mathematical equation in the Median Salary section that multiplies the amount of the median salary times 20 years to calculate how much you will possibly earn.

    f. For the Employment Outlook section, research the outlook for your career path. Take at least four notes about what you find when researching the topic.

    g. Sync your notes with your OneDrive. Submit your assignment in the format specified by your instructor.

Introduction to Sway

Sway site | responsive design | Storyline | card | Creative Commons license | animation emphasis effects | Docs.com

Expressing your ideas in a presentation typically means creating PowerPoint slides or a Word document. Microsoft Sway gives you another way to engage an audience. Sway is a free Microsoft tool available at Sway.com or as an app in Office 365. Using Sway, you can combine text, images, videos, and social media in a website called a **Sway site** that you can share and display on any device. To get started, you create a digital story on a web-based canvas without borders, slides, cells, or page breaks. A Sway site organizes the text, images, and video into a **responsive design**, which means your content adapts perfectly to any screen size as shown in **Figure 6**. You store a Sway site in the cloud on OneDrive using a free Microsoft account.

Figure 6: Sway site with responsive design

You can display a Sway presentation in a web browser.

Sway uses responsive design to make sure pages fit perfectly on any device.

Creating a Sway Presentation

You can use Sway to build a digital flyer, a club newsletter, a vacation blog, an informational site, a digital art portfolio, or a new product rollout. After you select your topic and sign into Sway with your Microsoft account, a **Storyline** opens, providing tools and a work area for composing your digital story. See **Figure 7**. Each story can include text, images, and videos. You create a Sway by adding text and media content into a Storyline section, or **card**. To add pictures, videos, or documents, select a card in the left pane and then select the Insert Content button. The first card in a Sway presentation contains a title and background image.

Design and create
Sway presentations.

Share and play
published Sway sites.

Arrange content in a Storyline,
which contains all the text,
pictures, videos, and other
media in a Sway presentation.

To add content, select a
card, which is designed
to hold a particular type
of information.

After selecting a card,
click the Insert Content
button to add the content
to the Sway presentation.

Adding Content to Build a Story

As you work, Sway searches the Internet to help you find relevant images, videos, tweets, and other content from online sources such as Bing, YouTube, Twitter, and Facebook. You can drag content from the search results right into the Storyline. In addition, you can upload your own images and videos directly in the presentation. For example, if you are creating a Sway presentation about the market for commercial drones, Sway suggests content to incorporate into the presentation by displaying it in the left pane as search results. The search results include drone images tagged with a **Creative Commons license** at online sources as shown in **Figure 8**. A Creative Commons license is a public copyright license that allows the free distribution of an otherwise copyrighted work. In addition, you can specify the source of the media. For example, you can add your own Facebook or OneNote pictures and videos in Sway without leaving the app.

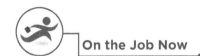

On the Job Now

If you have a Microsoft Word document containing an outline of your business content, drag the outline into Sway to create a card for each topic.

Figure 8: Images in Sway search results

Select the source
of media objects

Information about Creative
Commons licenses

Storyline title

The Market for
Commercial Drones

Drag an image to the
picture placeholder box

Suggested images in
the search results

On the Job Now

If your project team wants to collaborate on a Sway presentation, click the Authors button on the navigation bar to invite others to edit the presentation.

Designing a Sway

Sway professionally designs your Storyline content by resizing background images and fonts to fit your display, and by floating text, animating media, embedding video, and removing images as a page scrolls out of view. Sway also evaluates the images in your Storyline and suggests a color palette based on colors that appear in your photos. Use the Design button to display tools including color palettes, font choices, **animation emphasis effects**, and style templates to provide a personality for a Sway presentation. Instead of creating your own design, you can click the Remix button, which randomly selects unique designs for your Sway site.

Publishing a Sway

Use the Play button to display your finished Sway presentation as a website. The Address bar includes a unique web address where others can view your Sway site. As the author, you can edit a published Sway site by clicking the Edit button (pencil icon) on the Sway toolbar.

Sharing a Sway

When you are ready to share your Sway website, you have several options as shown in **Figure 9**. Use the Share slider button to share the Sway site publically or keep it private. If you add the Sway site to the Microsoft **Docs.com** public gallery, anyone worldwide can use Bing, Google, or other search engines to find, view, and share your Sway site. You can also share your Sway site using Facebook, Twitter, Google+, Yammer, and other social media sites. Link your presentation to any webpage or email the link to your audience. Sway can also generate a code for embedding the link within another webpage.

Figure 9: Sharing a Sway site

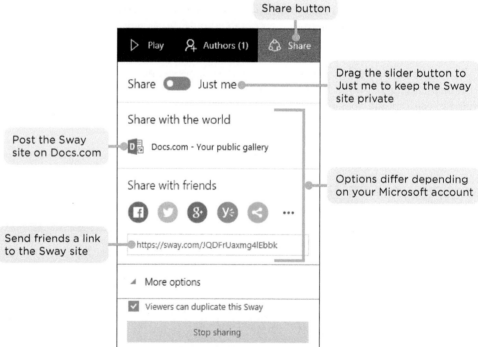

Try This Now

1: Creating a Sway Resume

Sway is a digital storytelling app. Create a Sway resume to share the skills, job experiences, and achievements you have that match the requirements of a future job interest. Perform the following tasks:

    a. Create a new presentation in Sway to use as a digital resume. Title the Sway Storyline with your full name and then select a background image.

    b. Create three separate sections titled **Academic Background, Work Experience**, and **Skills**, and insert text, a picture, and a paragraph or bulleted points in each section. Be sure to include your own picture.

    c. Add a fourth section that includes a video about your school that you find online.

    d. Customize the design of your presentation.

    e. Submit your assignment link in the format specified by your instructor.

2: Creating an Online Sway Newsletter

Newsletters are designed to capture the attention of their target audience. Using Sway, create a newsletter for a club, organization, or your favorite music group. Perform the following tasks:

    a. Create a new presentation in Sway to use as a digital newsletter for a club, organization, or your favorite music group. Provide a title for the Sway Storyline and select an appropriate background image.

    b. Select three separate sections with appropriate titles, such as Upcoming Events. In each section, insert text, a picture, and a paragraph or bulleted points.

    c. Add a fourth section that includes a video about your selected topic.

    d. Customize the design of your presentation.

    e. Submit your assignment link in the format specified by your instructor.

3: Creating and Sharing a Technology Presentation

To place a Sway presentation in the hands of your entire audience, you can share a link to the Sway presentation. Create a Sway presentation on a new technology and share it with your class. Perform the following tasks:

    a. Create a new presentation in Sway about a cutting-edge technology topic. Provide a title for the Sway Storyline and select a background image.

    b. Create four separate sections about your topic, and include text, a picture, and a paragraph in each section.

    c. Add a fifth section that includes a video about your topic.

    d. Customize the design of your presentation.

    e. Share the link to your Sway with your classmates and submit your assignment link in the format specified by your instructor.

Introduction to Office Mix

add-in | clip | slide recording | Slide Notes | screen recording | free-response quiz

Bottom Line

- Office Mix is a free PowerPoint add-in from Microsoft that adds features to PowerPoint.
- The Mix tab on the PowerPoint ribbon provides tools for creating screen recordings, videos, interactive quizzes, and live webpages.

To enliven business meetings and lectures, Microsoft adds a new dimension to presentations with a powerful toolset called Office Mix, a free add-in for PowerPoint. (An **add-in** is software that works with an installed app to extend its features.) Using Office Mix, you can record yourself on video, capture still and moving images on your desktop, and insert interactive elements such as quizzes and live webpages directly into PowerPoint slides. When you post the finished presentation to OneDrive, Office Mix provides a link you can share with friends and colleagues. Anyone with an Internet connection and a web browser can watch a published Office Mix presentation, such as the one in **Figure 10**, on a computer or mobile device.

Figure 10: Office Mix presentation

Learn to use Office Mix!

Links to companion **Sways**, featuring **videos** with hands-on instructions, are located on www.cengagebrain.com.

Adding Office Mix to PowerPoint

To get started, you create an Office Mix account at the website mix.office.com using an email address or a Facebook or Google account. Next, you download and install the Office Mix add-in (see **Figure 11**). Office Mix appears as a new tab named Mix on the PowerPoint ribbon in versions of Office 2013 and Office 2016 running on personal computers (PCs).

Figure 11: Getting started with Office Mix

Capturing Video Clips

A **clip** is a short segment of audio, such as music, or video. After finishing the content on a PowerPoint slide, you can use Office Mix to add a video clip to animate or illustrate the content. Office Mix creates video clips in two ways: by recording live action on a webcam and by capturing screen images and movements. If your computer has a webcam, you can record yourself and annotate the slide to create a **slide recording** as shown in **Figure 12**.

Figure 12: Making a slide recording

When you are making a slide recording, you can record your spoken narration at the same time. The **Slide Notes** feature works like a teleprompter to help you focus on your presentation content instead of memorizing your narration. Use the Inking tools to make annotations or add highlighting using different pen types and colors. After finishing a recording, edit the video in PowerPoint to trim the length or set playback options.

The second way to create a video is to capture on-screen images and actions with or without a voiceover. This method is ideal if you want to show how to use your favorite website or demonstrate an app such as OneNote. To share your screen with an audience, select the part of the screen you want to show in the video. Office Mix captures everything that happens in that area to create a **screen recording**, as shown in **Figure 13**. Office Mix inserts the screen recording as a video in the slide.

Figure 13: Making a screen recording

Inserting Quizzes, Live Webpages, and Apps

To enhance and assess audience understanding, make your slides interactive by adding quizzes, live webpages, and apps. Quizzes give immediate feedback to the user as shown in **Figure 14**. Office Mix supports several quiz formats, including a **free-response quiz** similar to a short answer quiz, and true/false, multiple-choice, and multiple-response formats.

Figure 14: Creating an interactive quiz

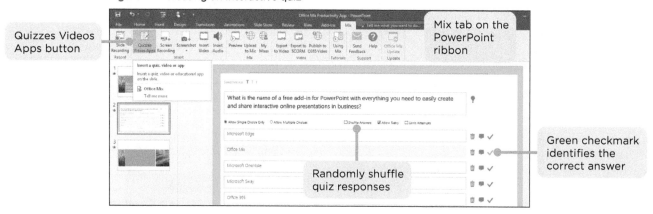

Sharing an Office Mix Presentation

When you complete your work with Office Mix, upload the presentation to your personal Office Mix dashboard as shown in **Figure 15**. Users of PCs, Macs, iOS devices, and Android devices can access and play Office Mix presentations. The Office Mix dashboard displays built-in analytics that include the quiz results and how much time viewers spent on each slide. You can play completed Office Mix presentations online or download them as movies.

Figure 15: Sharing an Office Mix presentation

Try This Now

1: Creating an Office Mix Tutorial for OneNote

Note: This activity requires a microphone on your computer.

Office Mix makes it easy to record screens and their contents. Create PowerPoint slides with an Office Mix screen recording to show OneNote 2016 features. Perform the following tasks:

a. Create a PowerPoint presentation with the Ion Boardroom template. Create an opening slide with the title **My Favorite OneNote Features** and enter your name in the subtitle.

b. Create three additional slides, each titled with a new feature of OneNote. Open OneNote and use the Mix tab in PowerPoint to capture three separate screen recordings that teach your favorite features.

c. Add a fifth slide that quizzes the user with a multiple-choice question about OneNote and includes four responses. Be sure to insert a checkmark indicating the correct response.

d. Upload the completed presentation to your Office Mix dashboard and share the link with your instructor.

e. Submit your assignment link in the format specified by your instructor.

2: Teaching Augmented Reality with Office Mix

Note: This activity requires a webcam or built-in video camera on your computer.

A local elementary school has asked you to teach augmented reality to its students using Office Mix. Perform the following tasks:

a. Research augmented reality using your favorite online search tools.

b. Create a PowerPoint presentation with the Frame template. Create an opening slide with the title **Augmented Reality** and enter your name in the subtitle.

c. Create a slide with four bullets summarizing your research of augmented reality. Create a 20-second slide recording of yourself providing a quick overview of augmented reality.

d. Create another slide with a 30-second screen recording of a video about augmented reality from a site such as YouTube or another video-sharing site.

e. Add a final slide that quizzes the user with a true/false question about augmented reality. Be sure to insert a checkmark indicating the correct response.

f. Upload the completed presentation to your Office Mix dashboard and share the link with your instructor.

g. Submit your assignment link in the format specified by your instructor.

3: Marketing a Travel Destination with Office Mix

Note: This activity requires a webcam or built-in video camera on your computer.

To convince your audience to travel to a particular city, create a slide presentation marketing any city in the world using a slide recording, screen recording, and a quiz. Perform the following tasks:

a. Create a PowerPoint presentation with any template. Create an opening slide with the title of the city you are marketing as a travel destination and your name in the subtitle.

b. Create a slide with four bullets about the featured city. Create a 30-second slide recording of yourself explaining why this city is the perfect vacation destination.

c. Create another slide with a 20-second screen recording of a travel video about the city from a site such as YouTube or another video-sharing site.

d. Add a final slide that quizzes the user with a multiple-choice question about the featured city with five responses. Be sure to include a checkmark indicating the correct response.

e. Upload the completed presentation to your Office Mix dashboard and share your link with your instructor.

f. Submit your assignment link in the format specified by your instructor.

Learn to use Office Mix!

Links to companion **Sways**, featuring **videos** with hands-on instructions, are located on www.cengagebrain.com.

Introduction to Microsoft Edge

Reading view | Hub | Cortana | Web Note | Inking | sandbox

Microsoft Edge is the default web browser developed for the Windows 10 operating system as a replacement for Internet Explorer. Unlike its predecessor, Edge lets you write on webpages, read webpages without advertisements and other distractions, and search for information using a virtual personal assistant. The Edge interface is clean and basic, as shown in **Figure 16**, meaning you can pay more attention to the webpage content.

Figure 16: Microsoft Edge tools

Forward button · New tab button · Web address in the Address bar · Add to favorites or reading list button · Back button · Reading view button · More button · Refresh (F5) button · Hub (Favorites, reading list, history, and downloads) button · Share Web Note button · Make a Web Note button

On the Job Now

Businesses started adopting Internet Explorer more than 20 years ago simply to view webpages. Today, Microsoft Edge has a different purpose: to promote interaction with the web and share its contents with colleagues.

Browsing the Web with Microsoft Edge

One of the fastest browsers available, Edge allows you to type search text directly in the Address bar. As you view the resulting webpage, you can switch to **Reading view**, which is available for most news and research sites, to eliminate distracting advertisements. For example, if you are catching up on technology news online, the webpage might be difficult to read due to a busy layout cluttered with ads. Switch to Reading view to refresh the page and remove the original page formatting, ads, and menu sidebars to read the article distraction-free.

Consider the **Hub** in Microsoft Edge as providing one-stop access to all the things you collect on the web, such as your favorite websites, reading list, surfing history, and downloaded files.

Locating Information with Cortana

Cortana, the Windows 10 virtual assistant, plays an important role in Microsoft Edge. After you turn on Cortana, it appears as an animated circle in the Address bar when you might need assistance, as shown in the restaurant website in **Figure 17**. When you click the Cortana icon, a pane slides in from the right of the browser window to display detailed information about the restaurant, including maps and reviews. Cortana can also assist you in defining words, finding the weather, suggesting coupons for shopping, updating stock market information, and calculating math.

Figure 17: Cortana providing restaurant information

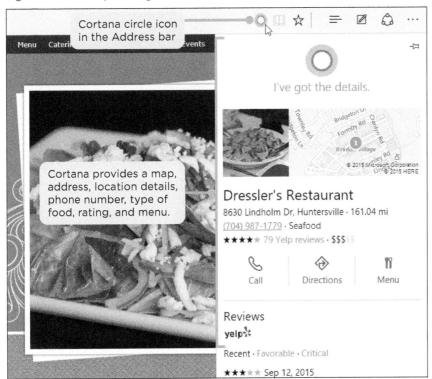

Annotating Webpages

One of the most impressive Microsoft Edge features are the **Web Note** tools, which you use to write on a webpage or to highlight text. When you click the Make a Web Note button, an **Inking** toolbar appears, as shown in **Figure 18**, that provides writing and drawing tools. These tools include an eraser, a pen, and a highlighter with different colors. You can also insert a typed note and copy a screen image (called a screen clipping). You can draw with a pointing device, fingertip, or stylus using different pen colors. Whether you add notes to a recipe, annotate sources for a research paper, or select a product while shopping online, the Web Note tools can enhance your productivity. After you complete your notes, click the Save button to save the annotations to OneNote, your Favorites list, or your Reading list. You can share the inked page with others using the Share Web Note button.

On the Job Now

To enhance security, Microsoft Edge runs in a partial sandbox, an arrangement that prevents attackers from gaining control of your computer. Browsing within the **sandbox** protects computer resources and information from hackers.

Figure 18: Web Note tools in Microsoft Edge

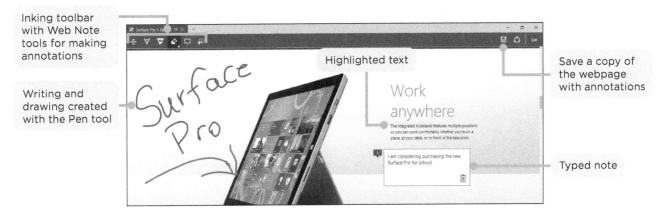

Inking toolbar with Web Note tools for making annotations

Writing and drawing created with the Pen tool

Highlighted text

Save a copy of the webpage with annotations

Typed note

Try This Now

1: Using Cortana in Microsoft Edge

Note: This activity requires using Microsoft Edge on a Windows 10 computer.

Cortana can assist you in finding information on a webpage in Microsoft Edge. Perform the following tasks:

a. Create a Word document using the Word Screen Clipping tool to capture the following screenshots.

- Screenshot A—Using Microsoft Edge, open a webpage with a technology news article. Right-click a term in the article and ask Cortana to define it.
- Screenshot B—Using Microsoft Edge, open the website of a fancy restaurant in a city near you. Make sure the Cortana circle icon is displayed in the Address bar. (If it's not displayed, find a different restaurant website.) Click the Cortana circle icon to display a pane with information about the restaurant.
- Screenshot C—Using Microsoft Edge, type **10 USD to Euros** in the Address bar without pressing the Enter key. Cortana converts the U.S. dollars to Euros.
- Screenshot D—Using Microsoft Edge, type **Apple stock** in the Address bar without pressing the Enter key. Cortana displays the current stock quote.

b. Submit your assignment in the format specified by your instructor.

2: Viewing Online News with Reading View

Note: This activity requires using Microsoft Edge on a Windows 10 computer.

Reading view in Microsoft Edge can make a webpage less cluttered with ads and other distractions. Perform the following tasks:

a. Create a Word document using the Word Screen Clipping tool to capture the following screenshots.

- Screenshot A—Using Microsoft Edge, open the website **mashable.com**. Open a technology article. Click the Reading view button to display an ad-free page that uses only basic text formatting.
- Screenshot B—Using Microsoft Edge, open the website **bbc.com**. Open any news article. Click the Reading view button to display an ad-free page that uses only basic text formatting.
- Screenshot C—Make three types of annotations (Pen, Highlighter, and Add a typed note) on the BBC article page displayed in Reading view.

b. Submit your assignment in the format specified by your instructor.

3: Inking with Microsoft Edge

Note: This activity requires using Microsoft Edge on a Windows 10 computer.

Microsoft Edge provides many annotation options to record your ideas. Perform the following tasks:

a. Open the website **wolframalpha.com** in the Microsoft Edge browser. Wolfram Alpha is a well-respected academic search engine. Type **US$100 1965 dollars in 2015** in the Wolfram Alpha search text box and press the Enter key.
b. Click the Make a Web Note button to display the Web Note tools. Using the Pen tool, draw a circle around the result on the webpage. Save the page to OneNote.
c. In the Wolfram Alpha search text box, type the name of the city closest to where you live and press the Enter key. Using the Highlighter tool, highlight at least three interesting results. Add a note and then type a sentence about what you learned about this city. Save the page to OneNote. Share your OneNote notebook with your instructor.
d. Submit your assignment link in the format specified by your instructor.

Office 2016 and Windows 10: Essential Concepts and Skills

Objectives

You will have mastered the material in this module when you can:

- Use a touch screen
- Perform basic mouse operations
- Start Windows and sign in to an account
- Identify the objects on the Windows 10 desktop
- Identify the apps in and versions of Microsoft Office 2016
- Run an app
- Identify the components of the Microsoft Office ribbon

- Create folders
- Save files
- Change screen resolution
- Perform basic tasks in Microsoft Office apps
- Manage files
- Use Microsoft Office Help and Windows Help

This introductory module uses PowerPoint 2016 to cover features and functions common to Office 2016 apps, as well as the basics of Windows 10.

Roadmap

In this module, you will learn how to perform basic tasks in Windows and PowerPoint. The following roadmap identifies general activities you will perform as you progress through this module:

1. SIGN IN to an account.
2. USE WINDOWS.
3. USE features in PowerPoint that are common across Office APPS.
4. FILE and folder MANAGEMENT.
5. SWITCH between APPS.
6. SAVE and manage FILES.

7. CHANGE SCREEN RESOLUTION.

8. EXIT APPS.

9. USE ADDITIONAL Office APP FEATURES.

10. USE Office and Windows HELP.

At the beginning of the step instructions throughout each module, you will see an abbreviated form of this roadmap. The abbreviated roadmap uses colors to indicate module progress: gray means the module is beyond that activity, blue means the task being shown is covered in that activity, and black means that activity is yet to be covered. For example, the following abbreviated roadmap indicates the module would be showing a task in the USE APPS activity.

1 SIGN IN | 2 USE WINDOWS | 3 USE APPS | 4 FILE MANAGEMENT | 5 SWITCH APPS | 6 SAVE FILES
7 CHANGE SCREEN RESOLUTION | 8 EXIT APPS | 9 USE ADDITIONAL APP FEATURES | 10 USE HELP

Use the abbreviated roadmap as a progress guide while you read or step through the instructions in this module.

Introduction to the Windows 10 Operating System

Windows 10 is the newest version of Microsoft Windows, which is a popular and widely used operating system (Figure 1). An **operating system (OS)** is a set of programs that coordinate all the activities among computer or mobile device hardware.

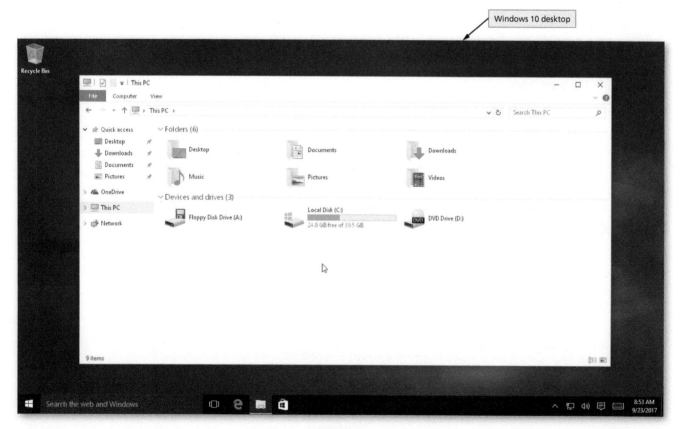

Figure 1

The Windows operating system simplifies the process of working with documents and apps by organizing the manner in which you interact with the computer. Windows is used to run apps. An application, or **app**, consists of programs designed to make users more productive and/or assist them with personal tasks, such as creating presentations or browsing the web.

Using a Touch Screen and a Mouse

Windows users who have computers or devices with touch screen capability can interact with the screen using gestures. A **gesture** is a motion you make on a touch screen with the tip of one or more fingers or your hand. Touch screens are convenient because they do not require a separate device for input. Table 1 presents common ways to interact with a touch screen.

If you are using your finger on a touch screen and are having difficulty completing the steps in this module, consider using a stylus. Many people find it easier to be precise with a stylus than with a finger. In addition, with a stylus you see the pointer. If you still are having trouble completing the steps with a stylus, try using a mouse.

Table 1 Touch Screen Gestures

Motion	Description	Common Uses	Equivalent Mouse Operation
Tap	Quickly touch and release one finger one time.	Activate a link (built-in connection). Press a button. Run a program or an app.	Click
Double-tap	Quickly touch and release one finger two times.	Run a program or an app. Zoom in (show a smaller area on the screen, so that contents appear larger) at the location of the double-tap.	Double-click
Press and hold	Press and hold one finger to cause an action to occur, or until an action occurs.	Display a shortcut menu (immediate access to allowable actions). Activate a mode enabling you to move an item with one finger to a new location.	Right-click
Drag, or slide	Press and hold one finger on an object and then move the finger to the new location.	Move an item around the screen. Scroll.	Drag
Swipe	Press and hold one finger and then move the finger horizontally or vertically on the screen.	Select an object. Swipe from edge to display a bar such as the Action Center, Apps bar, and Navigation bar (all discussed later).	Drag
Stretch	Move two fingers apart.	Zoom in (show a smaller area on the screen, so that contents appear larger).	None
Pinch	Move two fingers together.	Zoom out (show a larger area on the screen, so that contents appear smaller).	None

---

Will the screen look different if you are using a touch screen?

The Windows and Microsoft Office interface varies slightly if you are using a touch screen. For this reason, you might notice that your Windows or PowerPoint screens looks slightly different from the screens in this book.

CONSIDER THIS

Windows users who do not have touch screen capabilities typically work with a mouse that has at least two buttons. For a right-handed user, the left button usually is the primary mouse button, and the right mouse button is the secondary mouse button. Left-handed people, however, can reverse the function of these buttons.

Table 2 explains how to perform a variety of mouse operations. Some apps also use keys in combination with the mouse to perform certain actions. For example, when you hold down the CTRL key while rolling the mouse wheel, text on the screen may become larger or smaller based on the direction you roll the wheel. The function of the mouse buttons and the wheel varies depending on the app.

Table 2   Mouse Operations

Operation	Mouse Action	Example*	Equivalent Touch Gesture
Point	Move the mouse until the pointer on the desktop is positioned on the item of choice.	Position the pointer on the screen.	None
Click	Press and release the primary mouse button, which usually is the left mouse button.	Select or deselect items on the screen or run an app or app feature.	Tap
Right-click	Press and release the secondary mouse button, which usually is the right mouse button.	Display a shortcut menu.	Press and hold
Double-click	Quickly press and release the primary mouse button twice without moving the mouse.	Run an app or app feature.	Double-tap
Triple-click	Quickly press and release the primary mouse button three times without moving the mouse.	Select a paragraph.	Triple-tap
Drag	Point to an item, hold down the primary mouse button, move the item to the desired location on the screen, and then release the mouse button.	Move an object from one location to another or draw pictures.	Drag or slide
Right-drag	Point to an item, hold down the right mouse button, move the item to the desired location on the screen, and then release the right mouse button.	Display a shortcut menu after moving an object from one location to another.	Press and hold, then drag
Rotate wheel	Roll the wheel forward or backward.	Scroll vertically (up and down).	Swipe
Free-spin wheel	Whirl the wheel forward or backward so that it spins freely on its own.	Scroll through many pages in seconds.	Swipe
Press wheel	Press the wheel button while moving the mouse.	Scroll continuously.	None
Tilt wheel	Press the wheel toward the right or left.	Scroll horizontally (left and right).	None
Press thumb button	Press the button on the side of the mouse with your thumb.	Move forward or backward through webpages and/or control media, games, etc.	None

*Note: The examples presented in this column are discussed as they are demonstrated in this module.

Scrolling

A **scroll bar** is a horizontal or vertical bar that appears when the contents of an area may not be visible completely on the screen (Figure 2). A scroll bar contains **scroll arrows** and a **scroll box** that enable you to view areas that currently cannot be seen on the screen. Clicking the up and down scroll arrows moves the screen content up or down one line. You also can click above or below the scroll box to move up or down a section, or drag the scroll box up or down to move to a specific location.

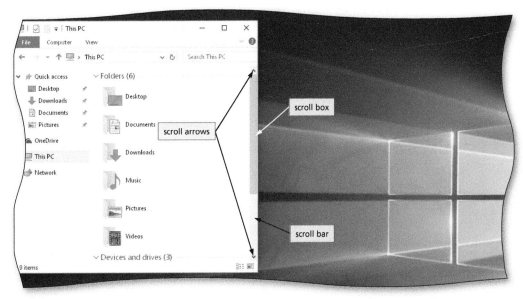

Figure 2

Keyboard Shortcuts

In many cases, you can use the keyboard instead of the mouse to accomplish a task. To perform tasks using the keyboard, you press one or more keyboard keys, sometimes identified as a **keyboard shortcut**. Some keyboard shortcuts consist of a single key, such as the F1 key. For example, to obtain help in many apps, you can press the F1 key. Other keyboard shortcuts consist of multiple keys, in which case a plus sign separates the key names, such as CTRL+ESC. This notation means to press and hold down the first key listed, press one or more additional keys, and then release all keys. For example, to display the Start menu, press CTRL+ESC, that is, hold down the CTRL key, press the ESC key, and then release both keys.

Starting Windows

It is not unusual for multiple people to use the same computer in a work, educational, recreational, or home setting. Windows enables each user to establish a **user account**, which identifies to Windows the resources, such as apps and storage locations, a user can access when working with the computer.

Each user account has a user name and may have a password and an icon, as well. A **user name** is a unique combination of letters or numbers that identifies a specific user to Windows. A **password** is a private combination of letters, numbers, and special characters associated with the user name that allows access to a user's account resources. An icon is a small image that represents an object; thus, a **user icon** is a picture associated with a user name.

When you turn on a computer, Windows starts and displays a **lock screen** consisting of the time and date (Figure 3). To unlock the screen, click the lock screen. Depending on your computer's settings, Windows may or may not display a sign-in screen that shows the user names and user icons for users who have accounts on the computer. This **sign-in screen** enables you to sign in to your user account and makes the computer available for use. Clicking the user icon begins the process of signing in, also called logging on, to your user account.

BTW
Minimize Wrist Injury
Computer users frequently switch between the keyboard and the mouse when developing PowerPoint slides; such switching strains the wrist. To help prevent wrist injury, minimize switching. For instance, if your fingers already are on the keyboard, use keyboard keys to scroll. If your hand already is on the mouse, use the mouse to scroll. If your hand is on the touch screen, use touch gestures to scroll.

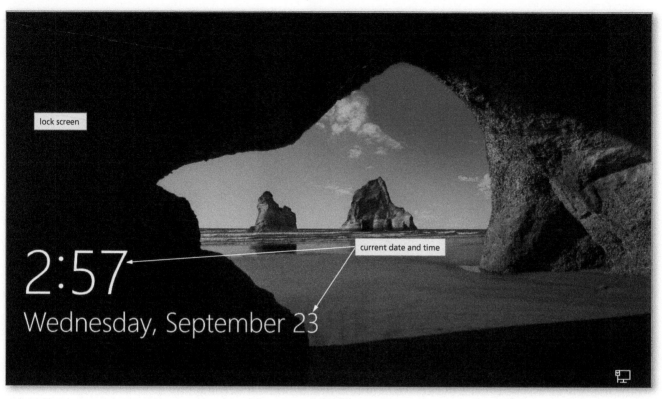

Figure 3

At the bottom of the sign-in screen is the 'Connect to Internet' button, 'Ease of access' button, and a Shut down button. Clicking the 'Connect to Internet' button displays a list of each network connection and its status. You also can connect to or disconnect from a network. Clicking the 'Ease of access' button displays the Ease of access menu, which provides tools to optimize a computer to accommodate the needs of mobility, hearing, and vision impaired users. Clicking the Shut down button displays a menu containing commands related to putting the computer or mobile device in a low-power state, shutting it down, and restarting the computer or mobile device. The commands available on your computer or mobile device may differ.

- The Sleep command saves your work, turns off the computer fans and hard drive, and places the computer in a lower-power state. To wake the computer from sleep mode, press the power button or lift a laptop's cover, and sign in to your account.

- The Shut down command exits running apps, shuts down Windows, and then turns off the computer.

- The Restart command exits running apps, shuts down Windows, and then restarts Windows.

To Sign In to an Account

1 SIGN IN | 2 USE WINDOWS | 3 USE APPS | 4 FILE MANAGEMENT | 5 SWITCH APPS | 6 SAVE FILES
7 CHANGE SCREEN RESOLUTION | 8 EXIT APPS | 9 USE ADDITIONAL APP FEATURES | 10 USE HELP

The following steps, which use SCSeries as the user name, sign in to an account based on a typical Windows installation. *Why? After starting Windows, you might be required to sign in to an account to access the computer or mobile device's resources.* You may need to ask your instructor how to sign in to your account.

1

- Click the lock screen (shown in Figure 3) to display a sign-in screen.
- Click the user icon (for SCSeries, in this case) on the sign-in screen, which depending on settings, either will display a second sign-in screen that contains a Password text box (Figure 4) or will display the Windows desktop (Figure 5).

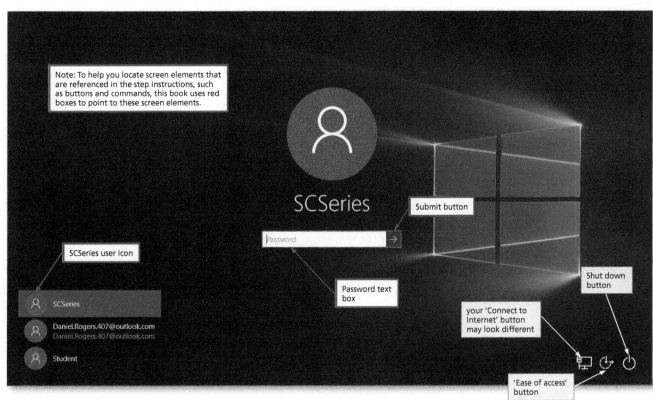

Figure 4

Q&A | Why do I not see a user icon?
Your computer may require you to type a user name instead of clicking an icon.

What is a text box?
A text box is a rectangular box in which you type text.

Why does my screen not show a Password text box?
Your account does not require a password.

- If Windows displays a sign-in screen with a Password text box, type your password in the text box.

2

- Click the Submit button (shown in Figure 4) to sign in to your account and display the Windows desktop (Figure 5).

Q&A | Why does my desktop look different from the one in Figure 5?
The Windows desktop is customizable, and your school or employer may have modified the desktop to meet its needs. Also, your screen resolution, which affects the size of the elements on the screen, may differ from the screen resolution used in this book. Later in this module, you learn how to change screen resolution.

How do I type if my tablet has no keyboard?
You can use your fingers to press keys on a keyboard that appears on the screen, called an on-screen keyboard, or you can purchase a separate physical keyboard that attaches to or wirelessly communicates with the tablet.

Figure 5

The Windows Desktop

The Windows 10 desktop (shown in Figure 5) and the objects on the desktop emulate a work area in an office. Think of the Windows desktop as an electronic version of the top of your desk. You can perform tasks such as placing objects on the desktop, moving the objects around the desktop, and removing items from the desktop.

When you run an app in Windows 10, it appears on the desktop. Some icons also may be displayed on the desktop. For instance, the icon for the **Recycle Bin**, the location of files that have been deleted, appears on the desktop by default. A **file** is a named unit of storage. Files can contain text, images, audio, and video. You can customize your desktop so that icons representing programs and files you use often appear on your desktop.

Introduction to Microsoft Office 2016

Microsoft Office 2016 is the newest version of Microsoft Office, offering features that provide users with better functionality and easier ways to work with the various files they create. This version of Office also is designed to work more optimally on mobile devices and online.

Microsoft Office 2016 Apps

Microsoft Office 2016 includes a wide variety of apps, such as Word, PowerPoint, Excel, Access, Outlook, Publisher, and OneNote:

- **Microsoft Word 2016**, or Word, is a full-featured word processing app that allows you to create professional-looking documents and revise them easily.

- **Microsoft PowerPoint 2016**, or PowerPoint, is a complete presentation app that enables you to produce professional-looking presentations and then deliver them to an audience.

- **Microsoft Excel 2016**, or Excel, is a powerful spreadsheet app that allows you to organize data, complete calculations, make decisions, graph data, develop professional-looking reports, publish organized data to the web, and access real-time data from websites.

- **Microsoft Access 2016**, or Access, is a database management system that enables you to create a database; add, change, and delete data in the database; ask questions concerning the data in the database; and create forms and reports using the data in the database.

- **Microsoft Outlook 2016**, or Outlook, is a communications and scheduling app that allows you to manage email accounts, calendars, contacts, and access to other Internet content.

- **Microsoft Publisher 2016**, or Publisher, is a desktop publishing app that helps you create professional-quality publications and marketing materials that can be shared easily.

- **Microsoft OneNote 2016**, or OneNote, is a note taking app that allows you to store and share information in notebooks with other people.

Microsoft Office 2016 Suites

A **suite** is a collection of individual apps available together as a unit. Microsoft offers a variety of Office suites, including a stand-alone desktop app, Microsoft Office 365, and Microsoft Office Online. **Microsoft Office 365**, or Office 365, provides plans that allow organizations to use Office in a mobile setting while also being able to communicate and share files, depending upon the type of plan selected by the organization. **Microsoft Office Online** includes apps that allow you to edit and share files on the web using the familiar Office interface.

During the Office 365 installation, you select a plan, and depending on your plan, you receive different apps and services. Office Online apps do not require a local installation and can be accessed through OneDrive and your browser. **OneDrive** is a cloud storage service that provides storage and other services, such as Office Online, to computer and mobile device users.

How do you sign up for a OneDrive account?

- Use your browser to navigate to onedrive.live.com.

- Create a Microsoft account by clicking the Sign up button and then entering your information to create the account.

- Sign in to OneDrive using your new account or use it in PowerPoint to save your files on OneDrive.

CONSIDER THIS

Apps in a suite, such as Microsoft Office, typically use a similar interface and share features. Once you are comfortable working with the elements and the interface and performing tasks in one app, the similarity can help you apply the knowledge and skills you have learned to another app(s) in the suite. For example, the process for saving a file in PowerPoint is the same in Word, Excel, and some of the other Office apps. While briefly showing how to use PowerPoint, this module illustrates some of the common functions across the Office apps and identifies the characteristics unique to PowerPoint.

Running and Using an App

To use an app, you must instruct the operating system to run the app. Windows provides many different ways to run an app, one of which is presented in this section (other ways to run an app are presented throughout this module). After an app is running, you can use it to perform a variety of tasks. The following pages use PowerPoint to discuss some elements of the Office interface and to perform tasks that are common to other Office apps.

PowerPoint

PowerPoint is a full-featured presentation app that allows you to produce compelling presentations to deliver and share with an audience. A PowerPoint **presentation** also is called a **slide show**. PowerPoint contains many features to design, develop, and organize slides, including formatting text, adding and editing video and audio clips, creating tables and charts, applying artistic effects to pictures, animating graphics, and collaborating with friends and colleagues. You then can turn your presentation into a video, broadcast your slide show on the web, or create a photo album.

To Run an App Using the Start Menu and Create a Blank Presentation

1 SIGN IN | 2 USE WINDOWS | 3 USE APPS | 4 FILE MANAGEMENT | 5 SWITCH APPS | 6 SAVE FILES
7 CHANGE SCREEN RESOLUTION | 8 EXIT APPS | 9 USE ADDITIONAL APP FEATURES | 10 USE HELP

Across the bottom of the Windows 10 desktop is the taskbar. The taskbar contains the **Start button**, which you use to access apps, files, folders, and settings. A **folder** is a named location on a storage medium that usually contains related documents.

Clicking the Start button displays the Start menu. The **Start menu** allows you to access programs, folders, and files on the computer or mobile device and contains commands that allow you to start programs, store and search for documents, customize the computer or mobile device, and sign out of a user account or shut down the computer or mobile device. A **menu** is a list of related items, including folders, programs, and commands. Each **command** on a menu performs a specific action, such as saving a file or obtaining help. *Why? When you install an app, for example, the app's name will be added to the All apps list on the Start menu.*

The following steps, which assume Windows is running, use the Start menu to run PowerPoint and create a blank presentation based on a typical installation. You may need to ask your instructor how to run PowerPoint on your computer. Although the steps illustrate running the PowerPoint app, the steps to run any Office app are similar.

1

- Click the Start button on the Windows 10 taskbar to display the Start menu (Figure 6).

Figure 6

2

- Click All apps at the bottom of the left pane of the Start menu to display a list of apps installed on the computer or mobile device. If necessary, scroll to display the app you wish to run, PowerPoint 2016, in this case (Figure 7).

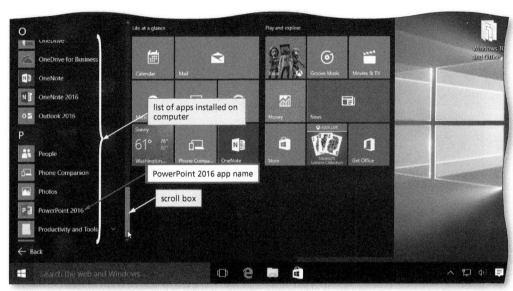

Figure 7

3

- If the app you wish to run is located in a folder, click or scroll to and then click the folder in the All apps list to display a list of the folder's contents.
- Click, or scroll to and then click the app name (PowerPoint 2016, in this case) in the list to run the selected app (Figure 8).

Figure 8

- Click the Blank Presentation thumbnail on the PowerPoint start screen to create a blank PowerPoint presentation in the PowerPoint window (Figure 9).

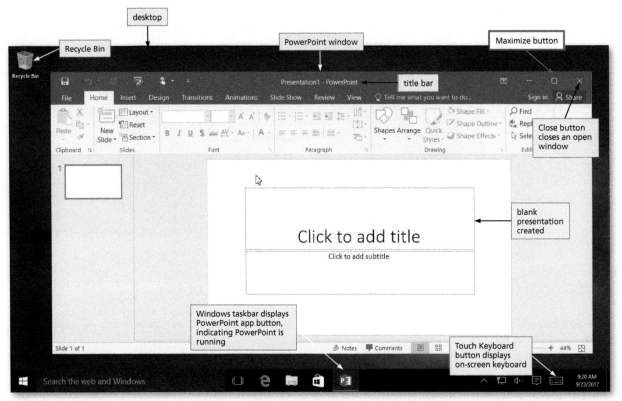

Figure 9

What happens when you run an app?

Some apps provide a means for you to create a blank presentation or document, as shown in Figure 8; others immediately display a blank presentation or document in an app window, such as the PowerPoint window shown in Figure 9. A **window** is a rectangular area that displays data and information. The top of a window has a **title bar**, which is a horizontal space that contains the window's name.

Other Ways

1. Type app name in search box, click app name in results list   2. Double-click file created in app you want to run

To Maximize a Window

Sometimes content is not visible completely in a window. One method of displaying the entire contents of a window is to **maximize** it, or enlarge the window so that it fills the entire screen. The following step maximizes the PowerPoint window; however, any Office app's window can be maximized using this step. *Why? A maximized window provides the most space available for using the app.*

- If the PowerPoint window is not maximized already, click the Maximize button (shown in Figure 9) next to the Close button on the PowerPoint window's title bar to maximize the window (Figure 10).

What happened to the Maximize button?

It changed to a Restore Down button, which you can use to return a window to its size and location before you maximized it.

How do I know
whether a window is
maximized?
A window is
maximized if it fills
the entire display
area and the Restore
Down button is
displayed on the
title bar.

Figure 10

Other Ways

1. Double-click title bar	2. Drag title bar to top of screen

PowerPoint Window, Ribbon, and Elements Common to Office Apps

The PowerPoint window consists of a variety of components to make your work more efficient and presentations more professional: the window, ribbon, Tell Me box, mini toolbar, shortcut menus, Quick Access Toolbar, and Microsoft Account area. Most of these components are common to other Office apps and have been discussed earlier in this module. Other components, discussed in the following paragraphs and later in subsequent modules, are unique to PowerPoint.

The basic unit of a PowerPoint presentation is a **slide**. A slide may contain text and objects, such as graphics, tables, charts, and drawings. When you create a new presentation, the default **Title Slide** layout appears (shown in Figure 11). PowerPoint includes several other built-in standard layouts. All layouts except the Blank slide layout contain placeholders for text or other content such as pictures, charts, or videos. The title slide in Figure 11 has two text placeholders for the main heading, or title, and the subtitle.

Scroll Bars   You use a scroll bar to display different portions of a presentation in the document window. At the right edge of the document window is a vertical scroll bar. If a slide is too wide to fit in the document window, a horizontal scroll bar also appears at the bottom of the document window. On a scroll bar, the position of the scroll box reflects the location of the portion of the slide that is displayed in the document window.

Status Bar   The **status bar**, located at the bottom of the document window above the Windows taskbar, presents information about the presentation, the progress of current tasks, and the status of certain commands and keys; it also provides controls for viewing the presentation. As you type text or perform certain tasks, various indicators and buttons may appear on the status bar.

The left side of the status bar in Figure 11 shows the current slide number followed by the total number of slides in the presentation. The right side of the status bar includes buttons and controls you can use to change the view of a slide and adjust the size of the displayed slide.

BTW

Touch Keyboard
To display the on-screen touch keyboard, click the Touch Keyboard button on the Windows taskbar (shown in Figure 9). When finished using the touch keyboard, click the X button on the touch keyboard to close the keyboard.

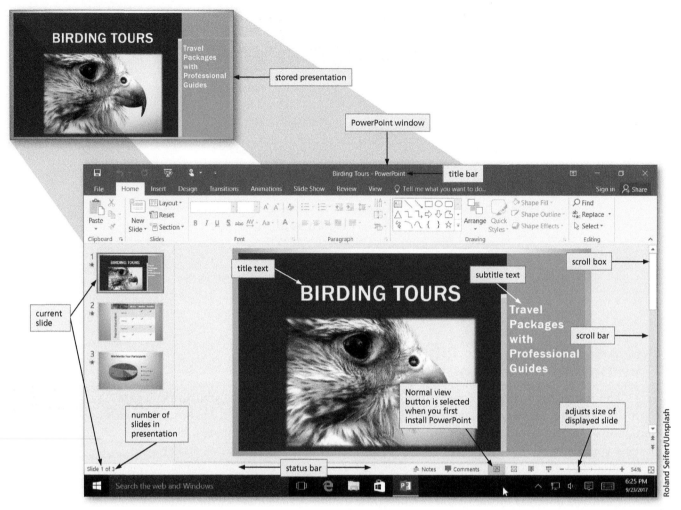

Figure 11

Ribbon   The ribbon, located near the top of the window below the title bar, is the control center in PowerPoint and other Office apps (Figure 12). The ribbon provides easy, central access to the tasks you perform while creating a presentation. The ribbon consists of tabs, groups, and commands. Each **tab** contains a collection of groups, and each **group** contains related commands. When you run an Office app, such as PowerPoint, it initially displays several main tabs, also called default or top-level tabs. All Office apps have a Home tab, which contains the more frequently used commands.

In addition to the main tabs, the Office apps display **tool tabs**, also called contextual tabs (Figure 13), when you perform certain tasks or work with objects such as pictures or tables. If you insert a picture in a PowerPoint presentation for example, the Picture Tools tab and its related subordinate Format tab appear, collectively referred to as the Picture Tools Format tab. When you are finished working with the picture, the Picture Tools Format tab disappears from the ribbon. PowerPoint and other Office apps determine when tool tabs should appear and disappear based on tasks you perform. Some tool tabs, such as the Table Tools tab, have more than one related subordinate tab.

Figure 12

Figure 13

Items on the ribbon include buttons, boxes, and galleries (shown in Figure 12). A **gallery** is a set of choices, often graphical, arranged in a grid or in a list. You can scroll through choices in an in-ribbon gallery by clicking the gallery's scroll arrows. Or, you can click a gallery's More button to view more gallery options on the screen at a time.

Some buttons and boxes have arrows that, when clicked, also display a gallery; others always cause a gallery to be displayed when clicked. Most galleries support **live preview**, which is a feature that allows you to point to a gallery choice and see its effect in the presentation — without actually selecting the choice (Figure 14). Live preview works only if you are using a mouse; if you are using a touch screen, you will not be able to view live previews.

Figure 14

Some commands on the ribbon display an image to help you remember their function. When you point to a command on the ribbon, all or part of the command glows in a shade of gray, and a ScreenTip appears on the screen. A **ScreenTip** is an on-screen note that provides the name of the command, available keyboard shortcut(s), a description of the command, and sometimes instructions for how to obtain help about the command (Figure 15).

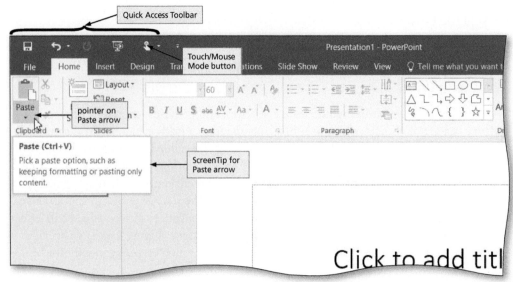

Figure 15

Some groups on the ribbon have a small arrow in the lower-right corner, called a **Dialog Box Launcher**, that when clicked, displays a dialog box or a task pane with additional options for the group (Figure 16). When presented with a dialog box, you make selections and must close the dialog box before returning to the presentation. A **task pane**, in contrast to a dialog box, is a window that can remain open and visible while you work in the presentation.

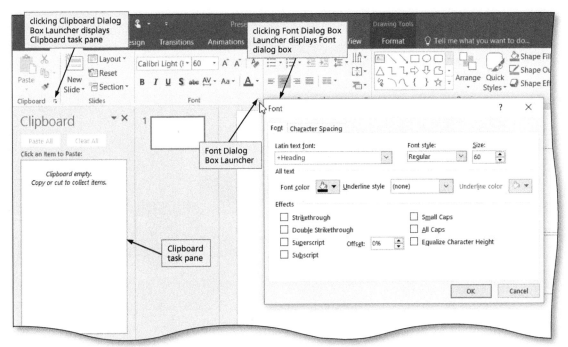

Figure 16

Tell Me Box   The **Tell Me box**, which appears to the right of the tabs on the ribbon, is a type of search box that helps you to perform specific tasks in an Office app (Figure 17). As you type in the Tell Me box, the word-wheeling feature displays search results that are refined as you type. For example, if you want to center text in a slide, you can type "center" in the Tell Me box and then select the appropriate command. The Tell Me box also lists the last five commands accessed from the box.

Figure 17

Mini Toolbar   The **mini toolbar**, which appears automatically based on tasks you perform, contains commands related to changing the appearance of text in a presentation (Figure 18). If you do not use the mini toolbar, it disappears from the screen. The buttons, arrows, and boxes on the mini toolbar vary, depending on whether you are using Touch mode versus Mouse mode. If you right-click an item in the document window, PowerPoint displays both the mini toolbar and a shortcut menu, which is discussed in a later section in this module.

All commands on the mini toolbar also exist on the ribbon. The purpose of the mini toolbar is to minimize hand or mouse movement.

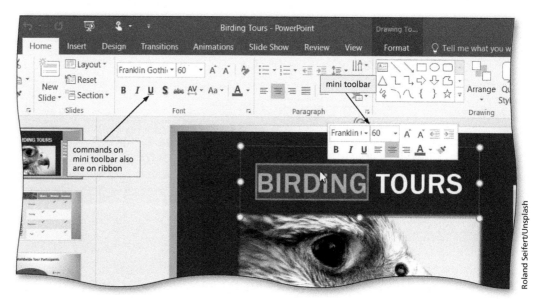

Figure 18

Quick Access Toolbar   The **Quick Access Toolbar**, located initially (by default) above the ribbon at the left edge of the title bar, provides convenient, one-click access to frequently used commands (shown in Figure 15). The commands on the Quick Access Toolbar always are available, regardless of the task you are performing. The Touch/Mouse Mode button on the Quick Access Toolbar allows you to switch between Touch mode and Mouse mode. If you primarily are using touch gestures, Touch mode will add more space between commands on menus and on the ribbon so that they are easier to tap. While touch gestures are convenient ways to interact with Office apps, not all features are supported when you are using Touch mode. If you are using a mouse, Mouse mode will not add the extra space between buttons and commands. The Quick Access Toolbar is discussed in more depth later in the module.

KeyTips   If you prefer using the keyboard instead of the mouse, you can press the ALT key on the keyboard to display **KeyTips**, or keyboard code icons, for certain commands (Figure 19). To select a command using the keyboard, press the letter or number displayed in the KeyTip, which may cause additional KeyTips related to the selected command to appear. To remove KeyTips from the screen, press the ALT key or the ESC key until all KeyTips disappear, or click anywhere in the app window.

Figure 19

Microsoft Account Area   In this area, you can use the Sign in link to sign in to your Microsoft account. Once signed in, you will see your account information, as well as a picture if you have included one in your Microsoft account.

To Display a Different Tab on the Ribbon

1 SIGN IN | 2 USE WINDOWS | 3 USE APPS | 4 FILE MANAGEMENT | 5 SWITCH APPS | 6 SAVE FILES
7 CHANGE SCREEN RESOLUTION | 8 EXIT APPS | 9 USE ADDITIONAL APP FEATURES | 10 USE HELP

When you run PowerPoint, the ribbon displays nine main tabs: File, Home, Insert, Design, Transitions, Animations, Slide Show, Review, and View. The tab currently displayed is called the **active tab**.

The following step displays the Insert tab, that is, makes it the active tab. ***Why?*** *When working with an Office app, you may need to switch tabs to access other options for working with a presentation.*

- Click Insert on the ribbon to display the Insert tab (Figure 20).

🔎 Experiment

- Click the other tabs on the ribbon to view their contents. When you are finished, click Insert on the ribbon to redisplay the Insert tab.

Figure 20

Other Ways

1. Press ALT, press letter corresponding to tab to display   2. Press ALT, press LEFT ARROW or RIGHT ARROW until desired tab is displayed

To Collapse and Expand the Ribbon and Use Full Screen Mode

1 SIGN IN | 2 USE WINDOWS | 3 USE APPS | 4 FILE MANAGEMENT | 5 SWITCH APPS | 6 SAVE FILES
7 CHANGE SCREEN RESOLUTION | 8 EXIT APPS | 9 USE ADDITIONAL APP FEATURES | 10 USE HELP

To display more of a slide or other item in the window of an Office app, some users prefer to collapse the ribbon, which hides the groups on the ribbon and displays only the main tabs, or to use **Full Screen mode**, which hides all the commands and just displays the slide. Each time you run an Office app, such as PowerPoint, the ribbon appears the same way it did the last time you used that Office app. The modules in this book, however, begin with the ribbon appearing as it did at the initial installation of Office or PowerPoint.

The following steps collapse, expand, and restore the ribbon in PowerPoint and then switch to Full Screen mode. *Why? If you need more space on the screen to work with your slide, you may consider collapsing the ribbon or switching to Full Screen mode to gain additional workspace.*

- Click the 'Collapse the Ribbon' button on the ribbon (shown in Figure 20) to collapse the ribbon (Figure 21).

Figure 21

Q&A What happened to the 'Collapse the Ribbon' button?
The 'Pin the ribbon' button replaces the 'Collapse the Ribbon' button when the ribbon is collapsed. You will see the 'Pin the ribbon' button only when you expand a ribbon by clicking a tab.

- Click Home on the ribbon to expand the Home tab (Figure 22).

Figure 22

Q&A Why would I click the Home tab?
If you want to use a command on a collapsed ribbon, click the main tab to display the groups for that tab. After you select a command on the ribbon and resume working in the presentation, the groups will be collapsed once again. If you decide not to use a command on the ribbon, you can collapse the groups by clicking the same main tab or clicking in the app window.

 Experiment

- Click Home on the ribbon to collapse the groups again. Click Home on the ribbon to expand the Home tab.

- Click the 'Pin the ribbon' button on the expanded Home tab to restore the ribbon.
- Click the 'Ribbon Display Options' button to display the Ribbon Display Options menu (Figure 23).

Figure 23

- Click Auto-hide Ribbon to use Full Screen mode, which hides all the commands from the screen (Figure 24).
- Click the ellipsis to display the ribbon temporarily.
- Click the 'Ribbon Display Options' button to display the Ribbon Display Options menu (shown in Figure 23).
- Click 'Show Tabs and Commands' on the Ribbon Display Options menu to exit Full Screen mode.

Figure 24

Other Ways	
1. Double-click a main tab on the ribbon	2. Press CTRL+F1

To Use a Shortcut Menu to Relocate the Quick Access Toolbar

1 SIGN IN │ 2 USE WINDOWS │ 3 USE APPS │ 4 FILE MANAGEMENT │ 5 SWITCH APPS │ 6 SAVE FILES
7 CHANGE SCREEN RESOLUTION │ 8 EXIT APPS │ 9 USE ADDITIONAL APP FEATURES │ 10 USE HELP

When you right-click certain areas of the PowerPoint and other Office app windows, a shortcut menu will appear. A **shortcut menu** is a list of frequently used commands that relate to an object. *Why? You can use shortcut menus to access common commands quickly.* When you right-click the status bar, for example, a shortcut menu appears with commands related to the status bar. When you right-click the Quick Access Toolbar, a shortcut menu appears with commands related to the Quick Access Toolbar. The following steps use a shortcut menu to move the Quick Access Toolbar, which by default is located on the title bar.

- Right-click the Quick Access Toolbar to display a shortcut menu that presents a list of commands related to the Quick Access Toolbar (Figure 25).

Figure 25

- Click 'Show Quick Access Toolbar Below the Ribbon' on the shortcut menu to display the Quick Access Toolbar below the ribbon (Figure 26).

Figure 26

- Right-click the Quick Access Toolbar to display a shortcut menu (Figure 27).

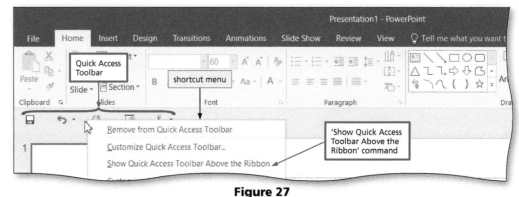

Figure 27

- Click 'Show Quick Access Toolbar Above the Ribbon' on the shortcut menu to return the Quick Access Toolbar to its original position (shown in Figure 25).

Other Ways

1. Click 'Customize Quick Access Toolbar' button on Quick Access Toolbar, click 'Show Below the Ribbon' or 'Show Above the Ribbon'

To Customize the Quick Access Toolbar

1 SIGN IN | 2 USE WINDOWS | 3 USE APPS | 4 FILE MANAGEMENT | 5 SWITCH APPS | 6 SAVE FILES
7 CHANGE SCREEN RESOLUTION | 8 EXIT APPS | 9 USE ADDITIONAL APP FEATURES | 10 USE HELP

The Quick Access Toolbar provides easy access to some of the more frequently used commands in the Office apps. By default, the Quick Access Toolbar contains buttons for the Save, Undo, and Redo commands. If your computer or mobile device has a touch screen, the Quick Access Toolbar also might display the Touch/Mouse Mode button. You can customize the Quick Access Toolbar by changing its location in the window, as shown in the previous steps, and by adding more buttons to reflect commands you would like to access easily. The following steps add the Quick Print button to the Quick Access Toolbar in the PowerPoint window. *Why? Adding the Quick Print button to the Quick Access Toolbar speeds up the process of printing.*

- Click the 'Customize Quick Access Toolbar' button to display the Customize Quick Access Toolbar menu (Figure 28).

Q&A Which commands are listed on the Customize Quick Access Toolbar menu?
It lists commands that commonly are added to the Quick Access Toolbar.

Figure 28

- If it is not selected already, click Quick Print on the Customize Quick Access Toolbar menu to add the Quick Print button to the Quick Access Toolbar (Figure 29).

Figure 29

How would I remove a button from the Quick Access Toolbar?

You would right-click the button you wish to remove and then click 'Remove from Quick Access Toolbar' on the shortcut menu or click the 'Customize Quick Access Toolbar' button on the Quick Access Toolbar and then click the button name in the Customize Quick Access Toolbar menu to remove the check mark.

To Enter Content in a Title Slide

1 SIGN IN | 2 USE WINDOWS | 3 USE APPS | 4 FILE MANAGEMENT | 5 SWITCH APPS | 6 SAVE FILES
7 CHANGE SCREEN RESOLUTION | 8 EXIT APPS | 9 USE ADDITIONAL APP FEATURES | 10 USE HELP

With the exception of a blank slide, PowerPoint assumes every new slide has a title. Many of PowerPoint's layouts have both a title text placeholder and at least one content placeholder. As you begin typing text in the title text placeholder, the title text also is displayed in the Slide 1 thumbnail in the Slides tab. The title for this presentation is Excellent Birding Apps and the subtitle text is Identify Birds Easily. The following step enters a presentation title and subtitle on the title slide. *Why? In general, every presentation should have a title to describe what the presentation will be covering, and the subtitle should support the title text and give additional details.*

- Click the 'Click to add title' label located inside the title text placeholder (shown in Figure 29) to select the placeholder.
- Type **Excellent Birding Apps** in the title text placeholder. Do not press the ENTER key because you do not want to create a new line of text (Figure 30).

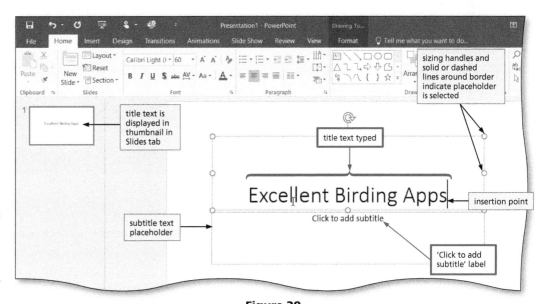

Figure 30

What is the blinking vertical bar to the right of the text?

The blinking bar is the insertion point, which indicates where text, graphics, and other items will be inserted in the document. As you type, the insertion point moves to the right.

What if I make an error while typing?

You can press the BACKSPACE key until you have deleted the text in error and then retype the text correctly.

- Click the 'Click to add subtitle' label located inside the subtitle text placeholder (shown in Figure 30) to select the placeholder.
- Type **Identify Birds Easily** in the subtitle text placeholder. Do not press the ENTER key (Figure 31).

- Click outside the title text and subtitle text placeholders to deselect these slide elements.

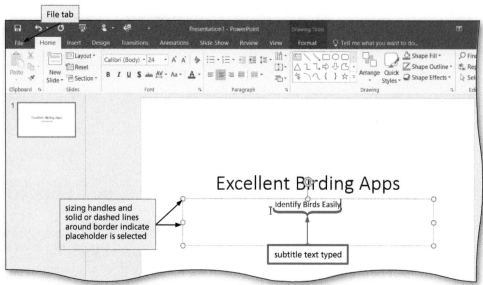

Figure 31

Document Properties

You can organize and identify your files by using **document properties**, which are the details about a file, such as the project author, title, and subject. For example, a class name or presentation topic can describe the file's purpose or content.

CONSIDER THIS

Why would you want to assign document properties to a presentation?

Document properties are valuable for a variety of reasons:

- Users can save time locating a particular file because they can view a file's document properties without opening the file.
- By creating consistent properties for files having similar content, users can better organize their files.
- Some organizations require users to add document properties so that other employees can view details about these files.

To Change Document Properties

1 SIGN IN | 2 USE WINDOWS | 3 USE APPS | 4 FILE MANAGEMENT | 5 SWITCH APPS | 6 SAVE FILES
7 CHANGE SCREEN RESOLUTION | 8 EXIT APPS | 9 USE ADDITIONAL APP FEATURES | 10 USE HELP

You can change the document properties while working with the file in an Office app. When you save the file, the Office app (PowerPoint, in this case) will save the document properties with the file. The following steps change document properties. *Why? Adding document properties will help you identify characteristics of the file without opening it.*

- Click File on the ribbon (shown in Figure 31) to open the Backstage view and then, if necessary, click the Info tab in the Backstage view to display the Info gallery.

Q&A

What is the purpose of the File tab on the ribbon, and what is the Backstage view?

The File tab opens the Backstage view for each Office app, including PowerPoint. The **Backstage view** contains a set of commands that enable you to manage documents and provides data about the documents.

What is the purpose of the Info gallery in the Backstage view?

The Info tab, which is selected by default when you click File on the ribbon, displays the Info gallery, where you can protect a presentation, inspect a presentation, and manage versions of a presentation, as well as view all the file properties, such as when the file was created.

- Click to the right of the Categories property in the Properties list and then type **CIS 101 Assignment** in the Categories text box (Figure 32).

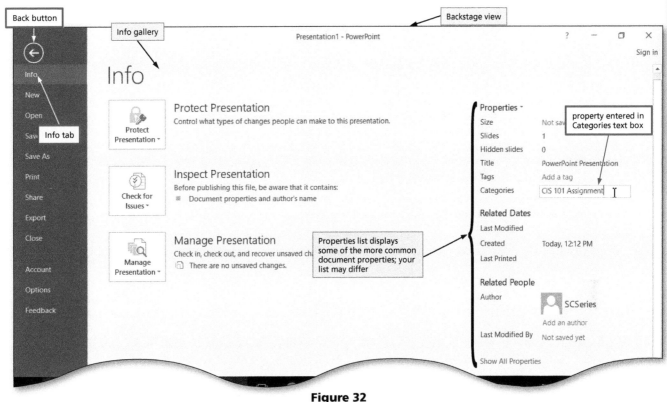

Figure 32

2

- Click the Back button in the upper-left corner of the Backstage view to return to the document window.

Printing, Saving, and Organizing Files

While you are creating a presentation, the computer or mobile device stores it in memory. When you save a presentation, the computer or mobile device places it on a storage medium, such as a hard disk, solid state drive (SSD), USB flash drive, or optical disc. The storage medium can be permanent in your computer, may be portable where you remove it from your computer, or may be on a web server you access through a network or the Internet.

A saved presentation is referred to as a file. A **file name** is the name assigned to a file when it is saved. When saving files, you should organize them so that you easily can find them later. Windows provides tools to help you organize files.

BTW

File Type
Depending on your Windows settings, the file type .pptx may be displayed immediately to the right of the file name after you save the file. The file type .pptx is a PowerPoint 2016 document.

Printing a Presentation

After creating a presentation, you may want to print it. Printing a presentation enables you to distribute it to others in a form that can be read or viewed but typically not edited.

What is the best method for distributing a presentation?

The traditional method of distributing a presentation uses a printer to produce a hard copy. A **hard copy** or **printout** is information that exists on a physical medium, such as paper. Hard copies can be useful for the following reasons:

- Some people prefer proofreading a hard copy of a presentation rather than viewing it on the screen to check for errors and readability.

- Hard copies can serve as a backup reference if your storage medium is lost or becomes corrupted and you need to recreate the presentation.

Instead of distributing a hard copy of a presentation, users can distribute the presentation as an electronic image that mirrors the original document's appearance. The electronic image of the presentation can be sent as an email attachment, posted on a website, or copied to a portable storage medium, such as a USB flash drive. Two popular electronic image formats, sometimes called fixed formats, are PDF by Adobe Systems and XPS by Microsoft. In PowerPoint, you can create electronic image files through the Save As dialog box and the Export, Share, and Print tabs in the Backstage view. Electronic images of documents, such as PDF and XPS, can be useful for the following reasons:

- Users can view electronic images of documents without the software that created the original presentation (e.g., PowerPoint). For example, to view a PDF file you use a program called Adobe Reader, which can be downloaded free from Adobe's website.

- Sending electronic documents saves paper and printer supplies. Society encourages users to contribute to **green computing**, which involves reducing the electricity consumed and environmental waste generated when using computers, mobile devices, and related technologies.

To Print a Presentation

1 SIGN IN | 2 USE WINDOWS | 3 USE APPS | 4 FILE MANAGEMENT | 5 SWITCH APPS | 6 SAVE FILES
7 CHANGE SCREEN RESOLUTION | 8 EXIT APPS | 9 USE ADDITIONAL APP FEATURES | 10 USE HELP

With the presentation opened, you may want to print it. *Why? Because you want to see how the slide will appear on paper; you want to print a hard copy on a printer.* The following steps print a hard copy of the contents of the presentation.

1
- Click File on the ribbon to open the Backstage view.
- Click the Print tab in the Backstage view to display the Print gallery (Figure 33).

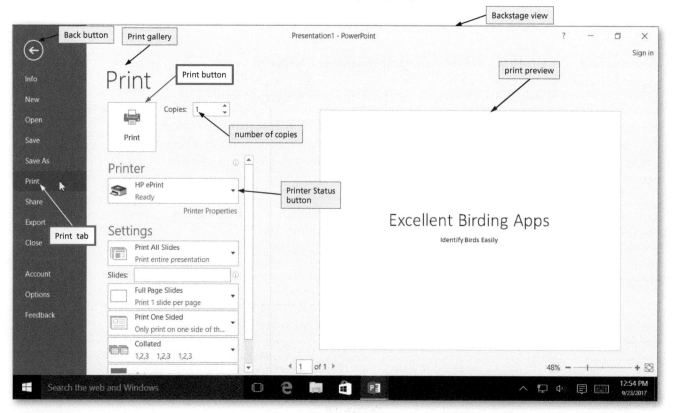

Figure 33

Q&A How can I print multiple copies of my presentation?
Increase the number in the Copies box in the Print gallery.

What if I decide not to print the presentation at this time?
Click the Back button in the upper-left corner of the Backstage view to return to the document window.

2

• Verify that the selected printer will print a hard copy of the presentation. If necessary, click the Printer Status button to display a list of available printer options and then click the desired printer to change the currently selected printer.

3

• Click the Print button in the Print gallery to print the presentation on the currently selected printer.
• When the printer stops, retrieve the hard copy (Figure 34).

Excellent Birding Apps

Identify Birds Easily

Figure 34

Q&A What if I want to print an electronic image of a presentation instead of a hard copy?
You would click the Printer Status button in the Print gallery and then select the desired electronic image option, such as Microsoft XPS Document Writer, which would create an XPS file.

Other Ways

1. Press CTRL+P

Organizing Files and Folders

A file contains data. This data can range from a research paper to an accounting spreadsheet to an electronic math quiz. You should organize and store files in folders to avoid misplacing a file and to help you find a file quickly.

If you are taking an introductory computer class (CIS 101, for example), you may want to design a series of folders for the different subjects covered in the class. To accomplish this, you can arrange the folders in a hierarchy for the class, as shown in Figure 35. The hierarchy contains three levels. The first level contains the storage medium,

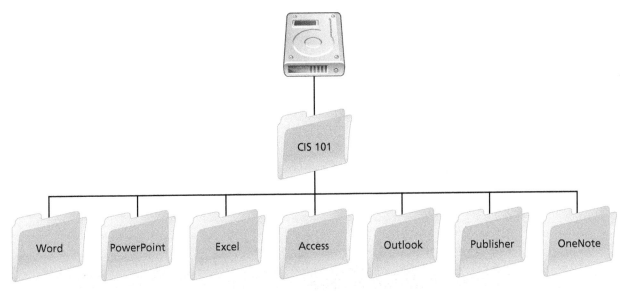

Figure 35

such as a hard drive. The second level contains the class folder (CIS 101, in this case), and the third level contains seven folders, one each for a different Office app that will be covered in the class (Word, PowerPoint, Excel, Access, Outlook, Publisher, and OneNote).

When the hierarchy in Figure 35 is created, the storage medium is said to contain the CIS 101 folder, and the CIS 101 folder is said to contain the separate Office folders (i.e., Word, PowerPoint, Excel, etc.). In addition, this hierarchy easily can be expanded to include folders from other classes taken during additional semesters.

The vertical and horizontal lines in Figure 35 form a pathway that allows you to navigate to a drive or folder on a computer or network. A **path** consists of a drive letter (preceded by a drive name when necessary) and colon, to identify the storage device, and one or more folder names. A hard drive typically has a drive letter of C. Each drive or folder in the hierarchy has a corresponding path.

By default, Windows saves documents in the Documents folder, music in the Music folder, photos in the Pictures folder, videos in the Videos folder, and downloads in the Downloads folder.

The following pages illustrate the steps to organize the folders for this class and save a file in a folder:

1. Create the folder identifying your class.
2. Create the PowerPoint folder in the folder identifying your class.
3. Save a file in the PowerPoint folder.
4. Verify the location of the saved file.

To Create a Folder

1 SIGN IN | 2 USE WINDOWS | 3 USE APPS | 4 FILE MANAGEMENT | 5 SWITCH APPS | 6 SAVE FILES
7 CHANGE SCREEN RESOLUTION | 8 EXIT APPS | 9 USE ADDITIONAL APP FEATURES | 10 USE HELP

When you create a folder, such as the CIS 101 folder shown in Figure 35, you must name the folder. A folder name should describe the folder and its contents. A folder name can contain spaces and any uppercase or lowercase characters, except a backslash (\), slash (/), colon (:), asterisk (*), question mark (?), quotation marks ("), less than symbol (<), greater than symbol (>), or vertical bar (|). Folder names cannot be CON, AUX, COM1, COM2, COM3, COM4, LPT1, LPT2, LPT3, PRN, or NUL. The same rules for naming folders also apply to naming files.

The following steps create a class folder (CIS 101, in this case) in the Documents folder. *Why? When storing files, you should organize the files so that it will be easier to find them later.*

1

- Click the File Explorer button on the taskbar to run File Explorer.
- If necessary, double-click This PC in the navigation pane to expand the contents of your computer.
- Click the Documents folder in the navigation pane to display the contents of the Documents folder in the file list (Figure 36).

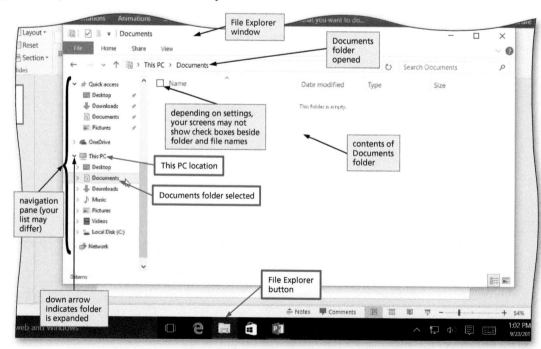

Figure 36

2

- Click the New folder button on the Quick Access Toolbar to create a new folder with the name, New folder, selected in a text box (Figure 37).

Q&A Why is the folder icon displayed differently on my computer or mobile device?
Windows might be configured to display contents differently on your computer or mobile device.

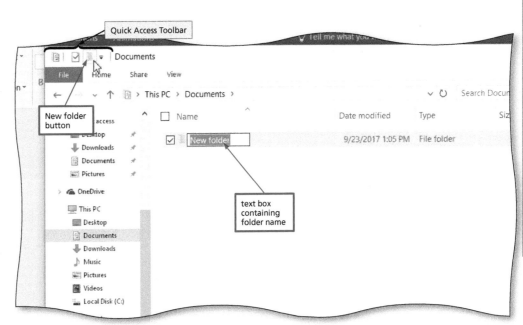

Figure 37

3

- Type **CIS 101** (or your class code) in the text box as the new folder name.

  If requested by your instructor, add your last name to the end of the folder name.

- Press the ENTER key to change the folder name from New folder to a folder name identifying your class (Figure 38).

Q&A What happens when I press the ENTER key?
The class folder (CIS 101, in this case) is displayed in the file list, which contains the folder name, date modified, type, and size.

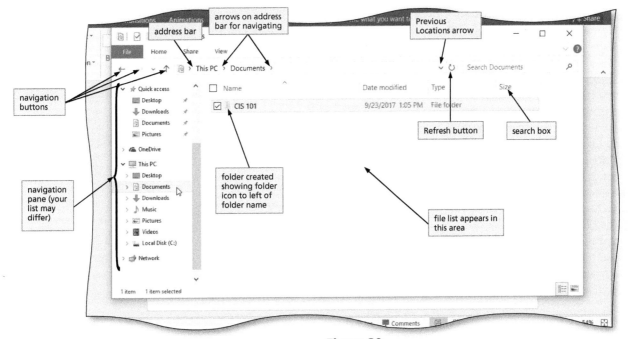

Figure 38

Other Ways

1. Press CTRL+SHIFT+N   2. Click New folder button (Home tab | New group)

Folder Windows

The File Explorer window (shown in Figure 38) is called a folder window. Recall that a folder is a specific named location on a storage medium that contains related files. Most users rely on **folder windows** for finding, viewing, and managing information on their computers. Folder windows have common design elements, including the following (shown in Figure 38).

- The **address bar** provides quick navigation options. The arrows on the address bar allow you to visit different locations on the computer or mobile device.
- The buttons to the left of the address bar allow you to navigate the contents of the navigation pane and view recent pages.
- The **Previous Locations arrow** displays the locations you have visited.
- The **Refresh button** on the right side of the address bar refreshes the contents of the folder list.
- The **Search box** contains the dimmed words, Search Documents. You can type a term in the search box for a list of files, folders, shortcuts, and elements containing that term within the location you are searching.
- The **ribbon** contains four tabs used to accomplish various tasks on the computer or mobile device related to organizing and managing the contents of the open window. This ribbon works similarly to the ribbon in the Office apps.
- The **navigation pane** on the left contains the Quick access area, the OneDrive area, the This PC area, and the Network area.
- The **Quick access area** shows locations you access frequently. By default, this list contains links only to your Desktop, Downloads, Documents, and Pictures.

To Create a Folder within a Folder

With the class folder created, you can create folders that will store the files you create using PowerPoint. The following step creates a PowerPoint folder in the CIS 101 folder (or the folder identifying your class). *Why? To be able to organize your files, you should create a folder structure.*

- Double-click the icon or folder name for the CIS 101 folder (or the folder identifying your class) in the file list to open the folder.
- Click the New folder button on the Quick Access Toolbar to create a new folder with the name, New folder, selected in a text box folder.
- Type **PowerPoint** in the text box as the new folder name.
- Press the ENTER key to rename the folder (Figure 39).

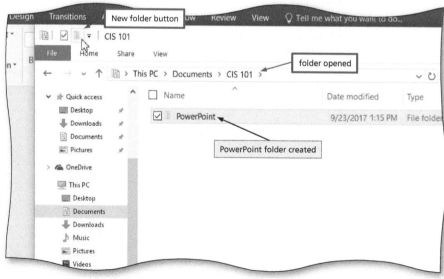

Figure 39

Other Ways

1. Press CTRL+SHIFT+N   2. Click New folder button (Home tab | New group)

To Expand a Folder, Scroll through Folder Contents, and Collapse a Folder

Folder windows display the hierarchy of items and the contents of drives and folders in the file list. You might want to expand a folder in the navigation pane to view its contents, scroll through its contents, and collapse it when you are finished viewing its contents. *Why? When a folder is expanded, you can see all the folders it contains. By contrast, a collapsed folder hides the folders it contains.* The following steps expand, scroll through, and then collapse the folder identifying your class (CIS 101, in this case).

- Double-click the Documents folder in the This PC area of the navigation pane, which expands the folder to display its contents and displays a black down arrow to the left of the Documents folder icon (Figure 40).

Figure 40

- Double-click the CIS 101 folder, which expands the folder to display its contents and displays a black down arrow to the left of the folder icon (Figure 41).

🔍 Experiment

- Drag the scroll box down or click the down scroll arrow on the vertical scroll bar to display additional folders at the bottom of the navigation pane. Drag the scroll box up or click the scroll bar above the scroll box to move the scroll box to the top of the navigation pane. Drag the scroll box down the scroll bar until the scroll box is halfway down the scroll bar.

Figure 41

- Double-click the folder identifying your class (CIS 101, in this case) to collapse the folder (Figure 42).

Q&A Why are some folders indented below others?

A folder contains the indented folders below it.

Figure 42

Other Ways

1. Point to display arrows in navigation pane, click arrow to expand or collapse

2. Select folder to expand or collapse using arrow keys, press RIGHT ARROW to expand; press LEFT ARROW to collapse

To Switch from One App to Another

The next step is to save the PowerPoint file containing the headline you typed earlier. PowerPoint, however, currently is not the active window. You can use the PowerPoint app button on the taskbar and live preview to switch to PowerPoint and then save the presentation in the PowerPoint window.

Why? *By clicking the appropriate app button on the taskbar, you can switch to the running app you want to use.* The following steps switch to the PowerPoint window; however, the steps are the same for any active Office app currently displayed as a button on the taskbar.

1

- Point to the PowerPoint app button on the taskbar to see a live preview of the open presentation(s) or the window title(s) of the open presentation(s), depending on your computer's configuration (Figure 43).

Q&A What if I am using a touch screen?
Live preview will not work if you are using a touch screen. If you are using a touch screen and do not have a mouse, proceed to Step 2.

Figure 43

2

- Click the PowerPoint app button or the live preview to make the app associated with the app button the active window (Figure 44).

Q&A What if multiple documents are open in an app?
Click the desired live preview to switch to the window you want to use.

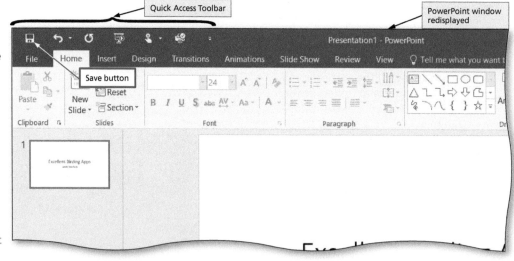

Figure 44

Other Ways

1. Press ALT+TAB until app you wish to display is selected

To Save a File in a Folder

With the PowerPoint folder created, you can save the PowerPoint presentation shown in the document window in the PowerPoint folder. *Why?* *Without saving a file, you may lose all the work you have completed and will be unable to reuse or share it with others later.* The following steps save a file in the PowerPoint folder contained in your class folder (CIS 101, in this case) using the file name, Birding Apps.

1

- Click the Save button (shown in Figure 44) on the Quick Access Toolbar, which, depending on settings, will display either the Save As gallery in the Backstage view (Figure 45) or the Save As dialog box (Figure 46).

Figure 45

Q&A What if the Save As gallery is not displayed in the Backstage view?
Click the Save As tab to display the Save As gallery.

How do I close the Backstage view?
Click the Back button in the upper-left corner of the Backstage view to return to the PowerPoint window.

2

- If your screen displays the Backstage view, click This PC, if necessary, to display options in the right pane related to saving on your computer or mobile device; if your screen already displays the Save As dialog box, proceed to Step 3.

Q&A What if I wanted to save on OneDrive instead?
You would click OneDrive. Saving on OneDrive is discussed in a later section in this module.

- Click the Browse button in the left pane to display the Save As dialog box (Figure 46).

Q&A Why does a file name already appear in the File name box?
PowerPoint automatically suggests a file name the first time you save a presentation. The file name normally consists of the first few words contained in the presentation. Because the suggested file name is selected, you do not need to delete it; as soon as you begin typing, the new file name replaces the selected text.

Figure 46

• Type **Birding Apps** in the File name box (Save As dialog box) to change the file name. Do not press the ENTER key after typing the file name because you do not want to close the dialog box at this time (Figure 47).

Q&A
What characters can I use in a file name?
The only invalid characters are the backslash (\), slash (/), colon (:), asterisk (*), question mark (?), quotation mark ("), less than symbol (<), greater than symbol (>), and vertical bar (|).

Figure 47

• Navigate to the desired save location (in this case, the PowerPoint folder in the CIS 101 folder [or your class folder] in the Documents folder) by performing the tasks in Steps 4a and 4b.

4a

• If the Documents folder is not displayed in the navigation pane, drag the scroll bar in the navigation pane until Documents appears.
• If the Documents folder is not expanded in the navigation pane, double-click Documents to display its folders in the navigation pane.
• If your class folder (CIS 101, in this case) is not expanded, double-click the CIS 101 folder to select the folder and display its contents in the navigation pane (Figure 48).

Q&A
What if I do not want to save in a folder?
Although storing files in folders is an effective technique for organizing files, some users prefer not to store files in folders. If you prefer not to save this file in a folder, select the storage device on which you wish to save the file and then proceed to Step 5.

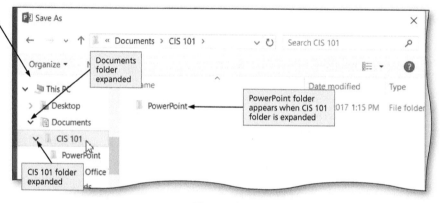

Figure 48

4b

• Click the PowerPoint folder in the navigation pane to select it as the new save location and display its contents in the file list (Figure 49).

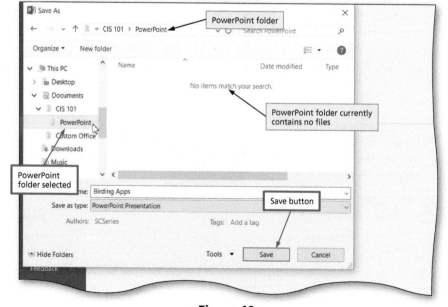

Figure 49

5

- Click the Save button (Save As dialog box) to save the presentation in the selected folder in the selected location with the entered file name (Figure 50).

Q&A
How do I know that the file is saved?
While an Office app such as PowerPoint is saving a file, it briefly displays a message on the status bar indicating the amount of the file saved. In addition, the file name appears on the title bar.

Figure 50

Other Ways

1. Click File on ribbon, click Save As tab in Backstage view, click This PC, click Browse button, type file name (Save As dialog box), navigate to desired save location, click Save button

2. Press F12, type file name (Save As dialog box), navigate to desired save location, click Save button

How often should you save a presentation?
It is important to save a presentation frequently for the following reasons:

- The presentation in memory might be lost if the computer is turned off or you lose electrical power while an app is running.

- If you run out of time before completing a project, you may finish it at a future time without starting over.

CONSIDER THIS

Navigating in Dialog Boxes

Navigating is the process of finding a location on a storage device. While saving the Birding Apps file, for example, Steps 4a and 4b navigated to the PowerPoint folder located in the CIS 101 folder in the Documents folder. When performing certain functions in Windows apps, such as saving a file, opening a file, or inserting a picture in an existing presentation, you most likely will have to navigate to the location where you want to save the file or to the folder containing the file you want to open or insert. Most dialog boxes in Windows apps requiring navigation follow a similar procedure; that is, the way you navigate to a folder in one dialog box, such as the Save As dialog box, is similar to how you might navigate in another dialog box, such as the Open dialog box. If you chose to navigate to a specific location in a dialog box, you would follow the instructions in Steps 4a and 4b.

To Minimize and Restore a Window

1 SIGN IN | 2 USE WINDOWS | 3 USE APPS | 4 FILE MANAGEMENT | 5 SWITCH APPS | 6 SAVE FILES
7 CHANGE SCREEN RESOLUTION | 8 EXIT APPS | 9 USE ADDITIONAL APP FEATURES | 10 USE HELP

Before continuing, you can verify that the PowerPoint file was saved properly. To do this, you will minimize the PowerPoint window and then open the CIS 101 window so that you can verify the file is stored in the CIS 101 folder on the hard drive. A **minimized window** is an open window that is hidden from view but can be displayed quickly by clicking the window's button on the taskbar.

In the following example, PowerPoint is used to illustrate minimizing and restoring windows; however, you would follow the same steps regardless of the Office app you are using. *Why? Before closing an app, you should make sure your file saved correctly so that you can find it later.*

The following steps minimize the PowerPoint window, verify that the file is saved, and then restore the minimized window.

- Click the Minimize button on the PowerPoint window title bar (shown in Figure 50) to minimize the window (Figure 51).

Q&A Is the minimized window still available?
The minimized window, PowerPoint in this case, remains available but no longer is the active window. It is minimized as a button on the taskbar.

- If the File Explorer window is not open on the screen, click the File Explorer button on the taskbar to make the File Explorer window the active window.

Figure 51

- Double-click the PowerPoint folder in the file list to select the folder and display its contents (Figure 52).

Q&A Why does the File Explorer button on the taskbar change?
A selected app button indicates that the app is active on the screen. When the button is not selected, the app is running but not active.

- After viewing the contents of the selected folder, click the PowerPoint app button on the taskbar to restore the minimized window (as shown in Figure 50).

Figure 52

Other Ways

1. Right-click title bar, click Minimize on shortcut menu, click taskbar button in taskbar button area
2. Press WINDOWS+M, press WINDOWS+SHIFT+M
3. Click PowerPoint app button on taskbar to minimize window. Click PowerPoint app button again to restore window.

To Save a File on OneDrive

One of the features of Office is the capability to save files on OneDrive so that you can use the files on multiple computers or mobile devices without having to use an external storage device, such as a USB flash drive. Storing files on OneDrive also enables you to share files more efficiently with others, such as when using Office Online and Office 365.

In the following example, PowerPoint is used to save a file on OneDrive. *Why? Storing files on OneDrive provides more portability options than are available from storing files in the Documents folder.*

You can save files directly on OneDrive from within an Office app. The following steps save the current PowerPoint file on OneDrive. These steps require that you have a Microsoft account and an Internet connection.

- Click File on the ribbon to open the Backstage view.
- Click the Save As tab in the Backstage view to display the Save As gallery.
- Click OneDrive in the left pane to display OneDrive saving options or a Sign In button, if you are not signed in already to your Microsoft account (Figure 53).

Figure 53

2

- If your screen displays a Sign In button (shown in Figure 53), click it to display the Sign in dialog box (Figure 54).

Q&A

What if the Sign In button does not appear?

If you already are signed into your Microsoft account, the Sign In button will not be displayed. In this case, proceed to Step 3.

- Follow the instructions on the screen to sign in to your Microsoft account.

Figure 54

- If necessary, in the Backstage view, click OneDrive in the left pane in the Save As gallery to select OneDrive as the save location.
- Click the Documents, or similar, folder in the right pane to display the Save As dialog box (Figure 55).

Q&A Why does the path in the OneDrive address bar in the Save As dialog box contain various letters and numbers?
The letters and numbers in the address bar uniquely identify the location of your OneDrive files and folders.

Figure 55

- Click the Save button (Save As dialog box) to save the file on OneDrive.

To Sign Out of a Microsoft Account

If you are using a public computer or otherwise wish to sign out of your Microsoft account, you should sign out of the account from the Account gallery in the Backstage view. Signing out of the account is the safest way to make sure that nobody else can access online files or settings stored in your Microsoft account. *Why? For security reasons, you should sign out of your Microsoft account when you are finished using a public or shared computer. Staying signed in to your Microsoft account might enable others to access your files.*

The following steps sign out of a Microsoft account from PowerPoint. You would use the same steps in any Office app. If you do not wish to sign out of your Microsoft account, read these steps without performing them.

1. Click File on the ribbon to open the Backstage view.

2. Click the Account tab to display the Account gallery (Figure 56).

3. Click the Sign out link, which displays the Remove Account dialog box. If a Can't remove Windows accounts dialog box appears instead of the Remove Account dialog box, click the OK button and skip the remaining steps.

Q&A Why does a Can't remove Windows accounts dialog box appear?
If you signed in to Windows using your Microsoft account, then you also must sign out from Windows, rather than signing out from within PowerPoint. When you are finished using Windows, be sure to sign out at that time.

4. Click the Yes button (Remove Account dialog box) to sign out of your Microsoft account on this computer or mobile device.

Q&A Should I sign out of Windows after removing my Microsoft account?
When you are finished using the computer, you should sign out of Windows for maximum security.

5 Click the Back button in the upper-left corner of the Backstage view to return to the presentation.

Figure 56

Screen Resolution

Screen resolution indicates the number of pixels (dots) that the computer uses to display the letters, numbers, graphics, and background you see on the screen. When you increase the screen resolution, Windows displays more information on the screen, but the information decreases in size. The reverse also is true: as you decrease the screen resolution, Windows displays less information on the screen, but the information increases in size.

Screen resolution usually is stated as the product of two numbers, such as 1366 × 768 (pronounced "thirteen sixty-six by seven sixty-eight"). A 1366 × 768 screen resolution results in a display of 1366 distinct pixels on each of 768 lines, or about 1,050,624 pixels. Changing the screen resolution affects how the ribbon appears in Office apps and some Windows dialog boxes. Figure 57, for example, shows the PowerPoint ribbon at screen resolutions of 1366 × 768 and 1024 × 768. All of the same commands are available regardless of screen resolution. The app (PowerPoint, in this case), however, makes changes to the groups and the buttons within the groups to accommodate the various screen resolutions. The result is that certain commands

Figure 57 (a) Ribbon at 1366 × 768 Resolution

Figure 57 (b) Ribbon at 1024 × 768 Resolution

may need to be accessed differently depending on the resolution chosen. A command that is visible on the ribbon and available by clicking a button at one resolution may not be visible and may need to be accessed using its Dialog Box Launcher at a different resolution.

Comparing the two ribbons in Figure 57, notice the changes in content and layout of the groups and galleries. In some cases, the content of a group is the same in each resolution, but the layout of the group differs. For example, the same gallery and buttons appear in the Slides groups in the two resolutions, but the layouts differ. In other cases, the content and layout are the same across the resolution, but the level of detail differs with the resolution.

To Change the Screen Resolution

1 SIGN IN | 2 USE WINDOWS | 3 USE APPS | 4 FILE MANAGEMENT | 5 SWITCH APPS | 6 SAVE FILES
7 CHANGE SCREEN RESOLUTION | 8 EXIT APPS | 9 USE ADDITIONAL APP FEATURES | 10 USE HELP

If you are using a computer to step through the modules in this book and you want your screen to match the figures, you may need to change your screen's resolution. *Why? The figures in this book use a screen resolution of 1366 × 768.* The following steps change the screen resolution to 1366 × 768. Your computer already may be set to 1366 × 768. Keep in mind that many computer labs prevent users from changing the screen resolution; in that case, read the following steps for illustration purposes.

- Click the Show desktop button, which is located at the far-right edge of the taskbar, to display the Windows desktop.
- Right-click an empty area on the Windows desktop to display a shortcut menu that contains a list of commands related to the desktop (Figure 58).

Q&A Why does my shortcut menu display different commands?
Depending on your computer's hardware and configuration, different commands might appear on the shortcut menu.

Figure 58

- Click Display settings on the shortcut menu to open the Settings app window. If necessary, scroll to display the 'Advanced display settings' link (Figure 59).

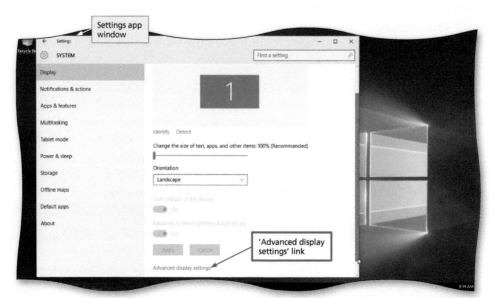

Figure 59

3

- Click 'Advanced display settings' in the Settings app window to display the advanced display settings.
- If necessary, scroll to display the Resolution box (Figure 60).

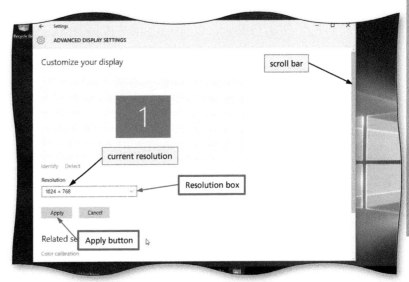

Figure 60

4

- Click the Resolution box to display a list of available screen resolutions (Figure 61).
- If necessary, scroll to and then click 1366 x 768 to select the screen resolution.

◄ Q&A | What if my computer does not support the 1366 x 768 resolution? Some computers do not support the 1366 x 768 resolution. In this case, select a resolution that is close to the 1366 x 768 resolution.

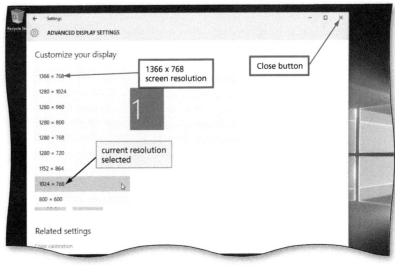

Figure 61

5

- Click the Apply button (Advanced Display Settings window), shown in Figure 60, to change the screen resolution and a confirmation message (Figure 62).
- Click the Keep changes button to accept the new screen resolution.
- Click the Close button (shown in Figure 61) to close the Settings app window.

Figure 62

Other Ways

1. Click Start button, click Settings, click System, click Display, click 'Advanced display settings,' select desired resolution in Resolution box, click Apply button, click Keep changes button

2. Type `screen resolution` in search box, click 'Change the screen resolution,' select desired resolution in Resolution box, click Apply button, click Keep changes button

To Exit an App with One Document Open

When you exit an Office app, such as PowerPoint, if you have made changes to a file since the last time the file was saved, the app displays a dialog box asking if you want to save the changes you made to the file before it closes the app window. *Why? The dialog box contains three buttons with these resulting actions: the Save button saves the changes and then exits the app, the Don't Save button exits the app without saving changes, and the Cancel button closes the dialog box and redisplays the file without saving the changes.*

If no changes have been made to an open presentation since the last time the file was saved, the app will close the window without displaying a dialog box.

The following steps exit PowerPoint. You would follow similar steps in other Office apps.

1

• If necessary, click the PowerPoint app button on the taskbar to display the PowerPoint window on the desktop (Figure 63).

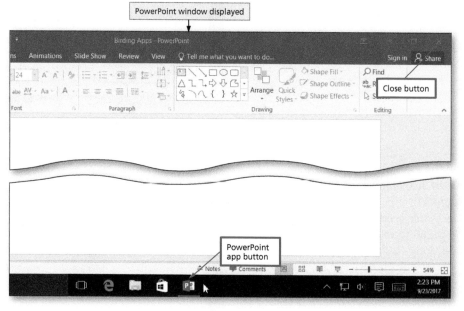

Figure 63

2

• Click the Close button on the right side of the PowerPoint window title bar to close the presentation and exit PowerPoint. If a Microsoft PowerPoint dialog box appears, click the Save button to save any changes made to the presentation since the last save.

Q&A

What if I have more than one presentation open in PowerPoint?
You could click the Close button for each open presentation. When you click the last open document's Close button, you also exit PowerPoint. As an alternative that is more efficient, you could right-click the PowerPoint app button on the taskbar and then click 'Close all windows' on the shortcut menu to close all open documents and exit PowerPoint.

Other Ways

1. Right-click PowerPoint app button on Windows taskbar, click 'Close all windows' on shortcut menu

2. Press ALT+F4

To Copy a Folder to OneDrive

To back up your files or easily make them available on another computer or mobile device, you can copy them to OneDrive. The following steps copy your CIS 101 folder to OneDrive. If you do not have access to a OneDrive account, read the following steps without performing them. *Why? It often is good practice to have a backup of your files so that they are available in case something happens to your original copies.*

1

- Click the File Explorer button on the taskbar to make the folder window the active window.
- Navigate to the CIS 101 folder (or your class folder) in the Documents folder.
- Click Documents in the This PC area of the navigation pane to display the CIS 101 folder in the file list.

Q&A What if my CIS 101 folder is stored in a different location?
Use the navigation pane to navigate to the location of your CIS 101 folder. The CIS 101 folder should be displayed in the file list once you have located it.

- Click the CIS 101 folder in the file list to select it (Figure 64).

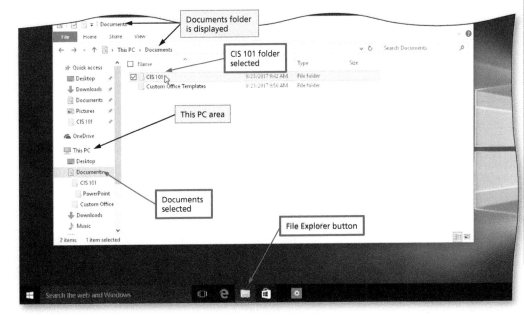

Figure 64

2

- Click Home on the ribbon to display the Home tab.
- Click the Copy to button (Home tab | Organize group) to display the Copy to menu (Figure 65).

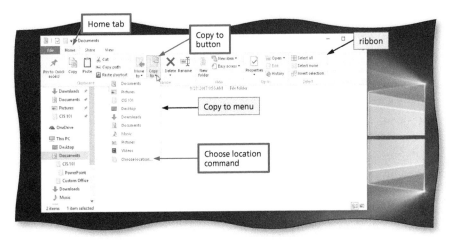

Figure 65

3

- Click Choose location on the Copy to menu to display the Copy Items dialog box.
- Click OneDrive (Copy Items dialog box) to select it (Figure 66).

Figure 66

- Click the Copy button (Copy Items dialog box) to copy the selected folder to OneDrive.
- Click OneDrive in the navigation pane to verify the CIS 101 folder displays in the file list (Figure 67).

Q&A

Why does a Microsoft OneDrive dialog box appear when I click OneDrive in the navigation pane?
If you are not currently signed in to Windows using a Microsoft account, you will manually need to sign in to a Microsoft account to save files to OneDrive. Follow the instructions on the screen to sign in to your Microsoft account.

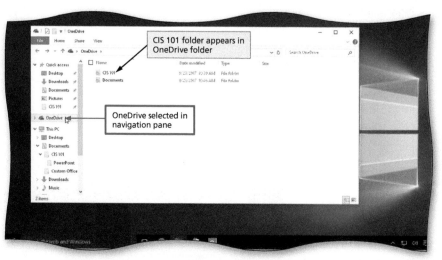

Figure 67

Other Ways

1. In File Explorer, select folder to copy, click Copy button (Home tab | Clipboard group), display contents of OneDrive in file list, click Paste button (Home tab | Clipboard group)

2. In File Explorer, select folder to copy, press CTRL+C, display contents of OneDrive in file list, press CTRL+V

To Unlink a OneDrive Account

1 SIGN IN | 2 USE WINDOWS | 3 USE APPS | **4 FILE MANAGEMENT** | 5 SWITCH APPS | 6 SAVE FILES
7 CHANGE SCREEN RESOLUTION | 8 EXIT APPS | **9 USE ADDITIONAL APP FEATURES** | **10 USE HELP**

If you are using a public computer and are not signed in to Windows with a Microsoft account, you should unlink your OneDrive account so that other users cannot access it. **Why?** *If you do not unlink your OneDrive account, other people accessing the same user account on the computer will be able to view, remove, and add to files stored in your OneDrive account.*

The following steps unlink your OneDrive account. If you do not wish to sign out of your Microsoft account, read these steps without performing them.

- Click the 'Show hidden icons' button on the Windows taskbar to show a menu of hidden icons (Figure 68).

Figure 68

2

- Right-click the OneDrive icon (shown in Figure 68) to display a shortcut menu (Figure 69).

shortcut menu

Settings command

Figure 69

3

- Click Settings on the shortcut menu to display the Microsoft OneDrive dialog box (Figure 70).

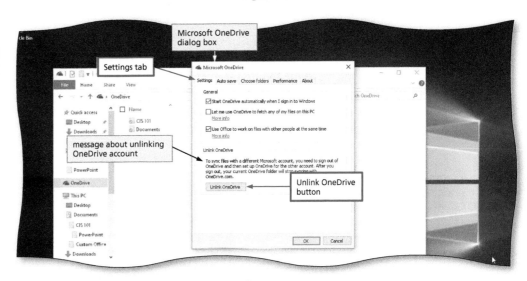

Microsoft OneDrive dialog box

Settings tab

message about unlinking OneDrive account

Unlink OneDrive button

Figure 70

4

- If necessary, click the Settings tab. (Some versions require you click an Account tab instead.)
- Click the Unlink OneDrive button (Microsoft OneDrive dialog box) to unlink the OneDrive account (Figure 71).
- When the Microsoft OneDrive dialog box appears with a Welcome to OneDrive message, click the Close button.
- Minimize the File Explorer window.

Close button

dialog box indicates you no longer are signed in to OneDrive

Figure 71

Break Point: If you wish to take a break, this is a good place to do so. To resume at a later time, continue to follow the steps from this location forward.

Additional Common Features of Office Apps

The previous section used PowerPoint to illustrate common features of Office and some basic elements unique to PowerPoint. The following sections continue to use PowerPoint present additional common features of Office.

In the following pages, you will learn how to do the following:

1. Run PowerPoint using the search box.

2. Open a presentation in PowerPoint.

3. Close the presentation.

4. Reopen the presentation just closed.

5. Create a blank PowerPoint presentation from Windows Explorer and then open the file.

6. Save a presentation with a new file name.

To Run an App Using the Search Box

1 SIGN IN | **2 USE WINDOWS** | 3 USE APPS | 4 FILE MANAGEMENT | 5 SWITCH APPS | 6 SAVE FILES
7 CHANGE SCREEN RESOLUTION | 8 EXIT APPS | **9 USE ADDITIONAL APP FEATURES** | 10 USE HELP

The following steps, which assume Windows is running, use the search box to run PowerPoint based on a typical installation; however, you would follow similar steps to run any app. *Why? Some people prefer to use the search box to locate and run an app, as opposed to searching through a list of all apps on the Start menu.* You may need to ask your instructor how to run PowerPoint on your computer.

- Type **PowerPoint 2016** as the search text in the search box and watch the search results appear in the search results (Figure 72).

Do I need to type the complete app name or use correct capitalization?

No, you need to type just enough characters of the app name for it to appear in the search results. For example, you may be able to type Powerpoint or powerpoint, instead of PowerPoint 2016.

What if the search does not locate the PowerPoint app on my computer?

You may need to adjust the Windows search settings. Search for the word, index; click 'Indexing Options Control panel'; click the Modify button (Indexing Options dialog box); expand the Local Disk, if necessary; place a check mark beside all Program Files entries; and then click the OK button. It may take a few minutes for the index to rebuild. If it still does not work, you may need to click the Advanced button (Indexing Options dialog box) and then click the Rebuild button (Advanced Options dialog box).

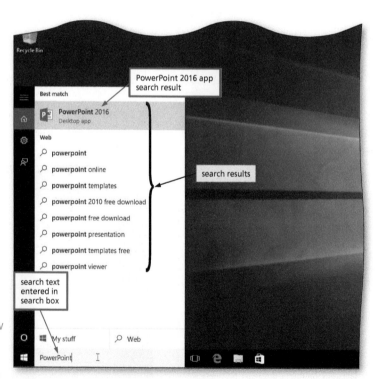

Figure 72

2

- Click the app name, PowerPoint 2016 in this case, in the search results to run PowerPoint and display the PowerPoint start screen.
- Click the Blank Presentation thumbnail on the PowerPoint start screen (shown earlier in this module in Figure 8) to create a blank presentation and display it in the PowerPoint window.
- If the PowerPoint window is not maximized, click the Maximize button on its title bar to maximize the window (Figure 73).

Figure 73

To Open an Existing File

1 SIGN IN | 2 USE WINDOWS | 3 USE APPS | 4 FILE MANAGEMENT | 5 SWITCH APPS | 6 SAVE FILES
7 CHANGE SCREEN RESOLUTION | 8 EXIT APPS | 9 USE ADDITIONAL APP FEATURES | 10 USE HELP

As discussed earlier, the Backstage view contains a set of commands that enable you to manage documents and data about the documents. **Why?** *From the Backstage view in PowerPoint, for example, you can create, open, print, and save documents. You also can share documents, manage versions, set permissions, and modify document properties. In other Office apps, the Backstage view may contain features specific to those apps.* The following steps open a saved file, specifically the Birding Apps file, that recently was saved.

1

- Click File on the ribbon (shown in Figure 73) to open the Backstage view and then click the Open tab in the Backstage view to display the Open gallery in the Backstage view.
- Click This PC to display recent folders accessed on your computer.
- Click the Browse button to display the Open dialog box.
- If necessary, navigate to the location of the file to open (PowerPoint folder in the CIS 101 folder).
- Click the file to open, Birding Apps in this case, to select the file (Figure 74).

Figure 74

- Click the Open button (Open dialog box) to open the file (shown earlier in the module in Figure 50). If necessary, click the Enable Content button.

Q&A Why did a Security Warning appear?

The Security Warning appears when you open an Office file that might contain harmful content. The files you create in this module are not harmful, but you should be cautious when opening files from other people.

Other Ways

1. Press CTRL+O   2. Navigate to file in File Explorer window, double-click file name

To Create a New Document from the Backstage View

1 SIGN IN | 2 USE WINDOWS | 3 USE APPS | 4 FILE MANAGEMENT | 5 SWITCH APPS | 6 SAVE FILES
7 CHANGE SCREEN RESOLUTION | 8 EXIT APPS | **9 USE ADDITIONAL APP FEATURES** | **10 USE HELP**

You can open multiple documents in an Office program, such as PowerPoint, so that you can work on the documents at the same time. The following steps create a file, a blank presentation in this case, from the Backstage view. ***Why?*** *You want to create a new presentation while keeping the current presentation open.*

- Click File on the ribbon to open the Backstage view.
- Click the New tab in the Backstage view to display the New gallery (Figure 75).

Q&A Can I create documents through the Backstage view in other Office apps?

Yes. If the Office app has a New tab in the Backstage view, the New gallery displays various options for creating a new file.

Figure 75

- Click the Blank Presentation thumbnail in the New gallery to create a new presentation (Figure 76).

Figure 76

Other Ways

1. Press CTRL+N

To Enter Text in a Presentation

The next PowerPoint presentation identifies the Best Rates for birding tours. The following step enters the first line of text in a slide.

1 Type **Birding Tours on Sale** in the title text placeholder.

2 Type **Book now for best rates** in the subtitle text placeholder (Figure 77).

3 Click outside the title text and subtitle text placeholders to deselect these slide elements.

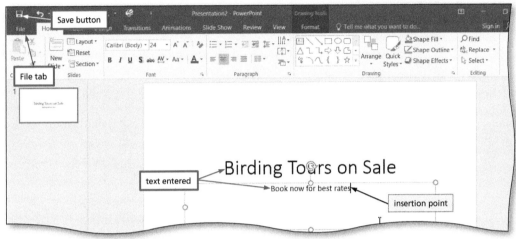

Figure 77

To Save a File in a Folder

The following steps save the second presentation in the PowerPoint folder in the class folder (CIS 101, in this case) in the Documents folder using the file name, Best Rates.

1 Click the Save button on the Quick Access Toolbar, which depending on settings, will display either the Save As gallery in the Backstage view or the Save As dialog box.

2 If your screen displays the Backstage view, click This PC, if necessary, to display options in the right pane related to saving on your computer; if your screen already displays the Save As dialog box, proceed to Step 4.

3 Click the Browse button in the left pane to display the Save As dialog box.

4 Type **Best Rates** in the File name box (Save As dialog box) to change the file name. Do not press the ENTER key after typing the file name because you do not want to close the dialog box at this time.

5 If necessary, navigate to the desired save location (in this case, the PowerPoint folder in the CIS 101 folder [or your class folder] in the Documents folder). For specific instructions, perform the tasks in Steps 4a and 4b in the previous section in this module titled To Save a File in a Folder.

6 Click the Save button (Save As dialog box) to save the presentation in the selected folder on the selected drive with the entered file name.

1 SIGN IN | 2 USE WINDOWS | 3 USE APPS | 4 FILE MANAGEMENT | 5 SWITCH APPS | 6 SAVE FILES
7 CHANGE SCREEN RESOLUTION | 8 EXIT APPS | 9 USE ADDITIONAL APP FEATURES | 10 USE HELP

To Close a File Using the Backstage View

Sometimes, you may want to close an Office file, such as a PowerPoint presentation, entirely and start over with a new file. You also may want to close a file when you are done working with it. ***Why?*** *You should close a file when you are done working with it so that you do not make inadvertent changes to it.* The following steps close the current active PowerPoint file, that is, the Best Rates presentation, without exiting PowerPoint.

①

- Click File on the ribbon to open the Backstage view (Figure 78).

②

- Click Close in the Backstage view to close the open file (Best Rates, in this case) without exiting the active app (PowerPoint).

◁ Q&A ▷ What if PowerPoint displays a dialog box about saving?

Click the Save button if you want to save the changes, click the Don't Save button if you want to ignore the changes since the last time you saved, and click the Cancel button if you do not want to close the presentation.

Figure 78

Can I use the Backstage view to close an open file in other Office apps, such as Excel and Word?
Yes.

Other Ways

1. Press CTRL+F4

To Open a Recent File Using the Backstage View

1 SIGN IN | 2 USE WINDOWS | 3 USE APPS | 4 FILE MANAGEMENT | 5 SWITCH APPS | 6 SAVE FILES
7 CHANGE SCREEN RESOLUTION | 8 EXIT APPS | 9 USE ADDITIONAL APP FEATURES | 10 USE HELP

You sometimes need to open a file that you recently modified. *Why? You may have more changes to make, such as adding more content or correcting errors.* The Backstage view allows you to access recent files easily. The following steps reopen the Best Rates file just closed.

①

- Click File on the ribbon to open the Backstage view.
- Click the Open tab in the Backstage view to display the Open gallery (Figure 79).

②

- Click the desired file name in the Recent list, Best Rates in this case, to open the file.

◁ Q&A ▷ Can I use the Backstage view to open a recent file in other Office apps, such as Word and Excel?
Yes, as long as the file name appears in the list of recent files.

Figure 79

Other Ways

1. Click File on ribbon, click Open tab in Backstage view, click This PC, click Browse button, navigate to file (Open dialog box), click Open button

To Create a New Blank Document from File Explorer

File Explorer provides a means to create a blank Office document without running an Office app. The following steps use File Explorer to create a blank PowerPoint presentation. *Why? Sometimes you might need to create a blank presentation and then return to it later for editing.*

- Click the File Explorer button on the taskbar to make the folder window the active window.
- If necessary, double-click the Documents folder in the navigation pane to expand the Documents folder.
- If necessary, double-click your class folder (CIS 101, in this case) in the navigation pane to expand the folder.
- Click the PowerPoint folder in the navigation pane to display its contents in the file list.
- With the PowerPoint folder selected, right-click an open area in the file list to display a shortcut menu.
- Point to New on the shortcut menu to display the New submenu (Figure 80).

Figure 80

- Click 'Microsoft PowerPoint Presentation' on the New submenu to display an icon and text box for a new file in the current folder window with the file name, New Microsoft PowerPoint Presentation, selected (Figure 81).

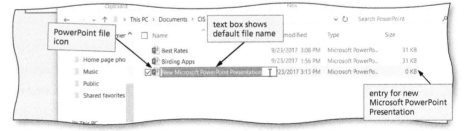

Figure 81

- Type **Recommended Travel Agents** in the text box and then press the ENTER key to assign a new file name to the new file in the current folder (Figure 82).

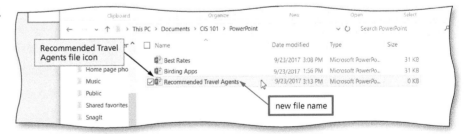

Figure 82

To Run an App from File Explorer and Open a File

Previously in this module, you learned how to run PowerPoint using the Start menu and the search box. The following steps, which assume Windows is running, use File Explorer to run PowerPoint based on a typical installation. *Why? Another way to run an Office app is to open an existing file from File Explorer, which causes the app in which the file was created to run and then open the selected file.* You may need to ask your instructor how to run PowerPoint for your computer.

- If necessary, display the file to open in the folder window in File Explorer (shown in Figure 82).
- Right-click the file icon or file name you want to open (Recommended Travel Agents, in this case) to display a shortcut menu (Figure 83).

Figure 83

- Click Open on the shortcut menu to open the selected file in the app used to create the file, PowerPoint in this case.
- If the window is not maximized, click the Maximize button on the title bar to maximize the window.

Other Ways

1. Double-click file name in file list

To Enter Text in a Slide

The next step is to enter text in the blank PowerPoint slide. The following step enters a line of text.

1 Click anywhere in the rectangle labeled, 'Click to add first slide', and then type **Recommended Travel Agents** in the title text placeholder.

2 Type **Customized birding and nature tours** in the subtitle text placeholder (shown in Figure 84).

To Save an Existing Office File with the Same File Name

1 SIGN IN | 2 USE WINDOWS | 3 USE APPS | 4 FILE MANAGEMENT | 5 SWITCH APPS | 6 SAVE FILES
7 CHANGE SCREEN RESOLUTION | 8 EXIT APPS | 9 USE ADDITIONAL APP FEATURES | 10 USE HELP

Saving frequently cannot be overemphasized. ***Why?*** *You have made modifications to the file (presentation) since you created it. Thus, you should save again. Similarly, you should continue saving files frequently so that you do not lose the changes you have made since the time you last saved the file.* You can use the same file name, such as Recommended Travel Agents, to save the changes made to the presentation. The following step saves a file again with the same file name.

- Click the Save button on the Quick Access Toolbar to overwrite the previously saved file (Recommended Travel Agents, in this case) in the PowerPoint folder (Figure 84).

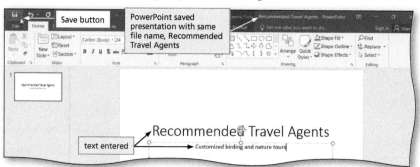

Figure 84

Other Ways

1. Press CTRL+S   2. Press SHIFT+F12

To Save a File with a New File Name

You might want to save a file with a different file name or to a different location. For example, you might start a homework assignment with a data file and then save it with a final file name for submission to your instructor, saving it to a location designated by your instructor. The following steps save a file with a different file name.

1 Click the File tab to open the Backstage view.

2 Click the Save As tab to display the Save As gallery.

3 If necessary, click This PC to display options in the right pane related to saving on your computer.

4 Click the Browse button in the left pane to display the Save As dialog box.

5 Type **Travel Agents** in the File name box (Save As dialog box) to change the file name. Do not press the ENTER key after typing the file name because you do not want to close the dialog box at this time.

6 If necessary, navigate to the desired save location (in this case, the PowerPoint folder in the CIS 101 folder [or your class folder] in the Documents folder). For specific instructions, perform the tasks in Steps 4a and 4b in the previous section titled To Save a File in a Folder.

7 Click the Save button (Save As dialog box) to save the presentation in the selected folder on the selected drive with the entered file name.

To Exit an Office App

You are finished using PowerPoint. The following steps exit PowerPoint.

1 Because you have multiple PowerPoint documents open, right-click the PowerPoint app button on the taskbar and then click 'Close all windows' on the shortcut menu to close all open documents and exit PowerPoint.

2 If a dialog box appears, click the Save button to save any changes made to the file since the last save.

Renaming, Moving, and Deleting Files

Earlier in this module, you learned how to organize files in folders, which is part of a process known as **file management**. The following sections cover additional file management topics including renaming, moving, and deleting files.

To Rename a File

1 SIGN IN | 2 USE WINDOWS | 3 USE APPS | **4 FILE MANAGEMENT** | 5 SWITCH APPS | 6 SAVE FILES
7 CHANGE SCREEN RESOLUTION | 8 EXIT APPS | 9 USE ADDITIONAL APP FEATURES | **10 USE HELP**

In some circumstances, you may want to change the name of, or rename, a file or a folder. *Why? You may want to distinguish a file in one folder or drive from a copy of a similar file, or you may decide to rename a file to better identify its contents.* The following steps change the name of the Birding Apps file in the PowerPoint folder to Birding Apps Presentation.

1

- If necessary, click the File Explorer button on the taskbar to make the folder window the active window.
- Navigate to the location of the file to be renamed (in this case, the PowerPoint folder in the CIS 101 [or your class folder] folder in the Documents folder) to display the file(s) it contains in the file list.
- Click the file to be renamed, the Birding Apps icon or file name in the file list in this case, to select it.
- Right-click the selected file to display a shortcut menu that presents a list of commands related to files (Figure 85).

Figure 85

- Click Rename on the shortcut menu to place the current file name in a text box.
- Type **Birding Apps Presentation** in the text box and then press the ENTER key (Figure 86).

Figure 86

Q&A

Are any risks involved in renaming files that are located on a hard drive?

If you inadvertently rename a file that is associated with certain apps, the apps may not be able to find the file and, therefore, may not run properly. Always use caution when renaming files.

Can I rename a file when it is open?

No, a file must be closed to change the file name.

Other Ways

1. Select file, press F2, type new file name, press ENTER

2. Select file, click Rename (Home tab | Organize group), type new file name, press ENTER

To Move a File

1 SIGN IN | 2 USE WINDOWS | 3 USE APPS | 4 FILE MANAGEMENT | 5 SWITCH APPS | 6 SAVE FILES
7 CHANGE SCREEN RESOLUTION | 8 EXIT APPS | 9 USE ADDITIONAL APP FEATURES | 10 USE HELP

Why? At some time, you may want to move a file from one folder, called the source folder, to another, called the destination folder. When you move a file, it no longer appears in the original folder. If the destination and the source folders are on the same media, you can move a file by dragging it. If the folders are on different media, you will need to right-drag the file and then click Move here on the shortcut menu. The following step moves the Recommended Travel Agents file from the PowerPoint folder to the CIS 101 folder.

- If necessary, in File Explorer, navigate to the location of the file to be moved (in this case, the PowerPoint folder in the CIS 101 folder [or your class folder] in the Documents folder).
- If necessary, click the PowerPoint folder in the navigation pane to display the files it contains in the right pane.
- Drag the file to be moved, the Recommended Travel Agents file in the right pane in this case, to the CIS 101 folder in the navigation pane (Figure 87).

Experiment

- Click the CIS 101 folder in the navigation pane to verify that the file was moved.

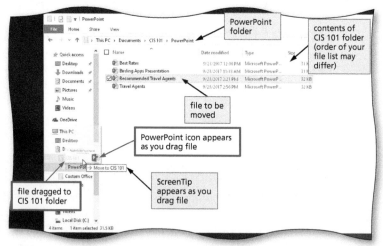

Figure 87

Other Ways

1. Right-click file to move, click Cut on shortcut menu, right-click destination folder, click Paste on shortcut menu

2. Select file to move, press CTRL+X, select destination folder, press CTRL+V

To Delete a File

1 SIGN IN | 2 USE WINDOWS | 3 USE APPS | 4 FILE MANAGEMENT | 5 SWITCH APPS | 6 SAVE FILES
7 CHANGE SCREEN RESOLUTION | 8 EXIT APPS | 9 USE ADDITIONAL APP FEATURES | 10 USE HELP

A final task you may want to perform is to delete a file. Exercise extreme caution when deleting a file or files. When you delete a file from a hard drive, the deleted file is stored in the Recycle Bin where you can recover it until you empty the Recycle Bin. If you delete a file from removable media, such as a USB flash drive, the file is deleted permanently. The next steps delete the Recommended Travel Agents file from the CIS 101 folder. *Why?* When a file no longer is needed, you can delete it to conserve space on your storage location.

- If necessary, in File Explorer, navigate to the location of the file to be deleted (in this case, the CIS 101 folder [or your class folder] in the Documents folder).
- Click the file to be deleted, the Recommended Travel Agents icon or file name in the right pane in this case, to select the file.
- Right-click the selected file to display a shortcut menu (Figure 88).

Figure 88

- Click Delete on the shortcut menu to delete the file.
- If a dialog box appears, click the Yes button to delete the file.

Q&A

Can I use this same technique to delete a folder?

Yes. Right-click the folder and then click Delete on the shortcut menu. When you delete a folder, all of the files and folders contained in the folder you are deleting, together with any files and folders on lower hierarchical levels, are deleted as well. For example, if you delete the CIS 101 folder, you will delete all folders and files inside the CIS 101 folder.

Other Ways

1. Select file, press DELETE key

Microsoft Office and Windows Help

At any time while you are using one of the Office apps, such as PowerPoint, you can use Office Help to display information about all topics associated with the app. Help in other Office apps operates in a similar fashion.

In Office, Help is presented in a window that has browser-style navigation buttons. Each Office app has its own Help home page, which is the starting Help page that is displayed in the Help window. If your computer is connected to the Internet, the contents of the Help page reflect both the local help files installed on the computer and material from Microsoft's website.

To Open the Help Window in an Office App

1 SIGN IN | 2 USE WINDOWS | 3 USE APPS | 4 FILE MANAGEMENT | 5 SWITCH APPS | 6 SAVE FILES
7 CHANGE SCREEN RESOLUTION | 8 EXIT APPS | 9 USE ADDITIONAL APP FEATURES | **10 USE HELP**

The following step opens the PowerPoint Help window. *Why? You might not understand how certain commands or operations work in PowerPoint, so you can obtain the necessary information using help.*

- Run PowerPoint.
- Click the Blank Presentation thumbnail to display a blank presentation.
- Press F1 to open the PowerPoint Help window (Figure 89).

Figure 89

Moving and Resizing Windows

At times, it is useful, or even necessary, to have more than one window open and visible on the screen at the same time. You can resize and move these open windows so that you can view different areas of and elements in the window. In the case of the Help window, for example, it could be covering text in the PowerPoint window that you need to see.

To Move a Window by Dragging

1 SIGN IN | **2 USE WINDOWS** | 3 USE APPS | 4 FILE MANAGEMENT | 5 SWITCH APPS | 6 SAVE FILES
7 CHANGE SCREEN RESOLUTION | 8 EXIT APPS | 9 USE ADDITIONAL APP FEATURES | 10 USE HELP

You can move any open window that is not maximized to another location on the desktop by dragging the title bar of the window. *Why? You might want to have a better view of what is behind the window or just want to move the window so that you can see it better.* The following step drags the PowerPoint Help window to the upper-left corner of the desktop.

- Drag the window title bar (the PowerPoint Help window title bar, in this case) so that the window moves to the upper-left corner of the desktop, as shown in Figure 90.

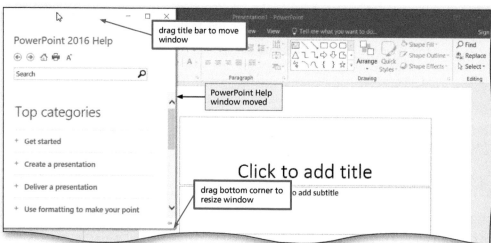

Figure 90

To Resize a Window by Dragging

1 SIGN IN | **2 USE WINDOWS** | 3 USE APPS | 4 FILE MANAGEMENT | 5 SWITCH APPS | 6 SAVE FILES
7 CHANGE SCREEN RESOLUTION | 8 EXIT APPS | 9 USE ADDITIONAL APP FEATURES | 10 USE HELP

A method used to change the size of a window is to drag the window borders. The following step changes the size of the PowerPoint Help window by dragging its borders. *Why? Sometimes, information is not visible completely in a window, and you want to increase the size of the window.*

- Point to the lower-right corner of the window (the PowerPoint Help window, in this case) until the pointer changes to a two-headed arrow.
- Drag the bottom border downward to display more of the active window (Figure 91).

Q&A Can I drag other borders on the window to enlarge or shrink the window?
Yes, you can drag the left, right, and top borders and any window corner to resize a window.

Will Windows remember the new size of the window after I close it?
Yes. When you reopen the window, Windows will display it at the same size it was when you closed it.

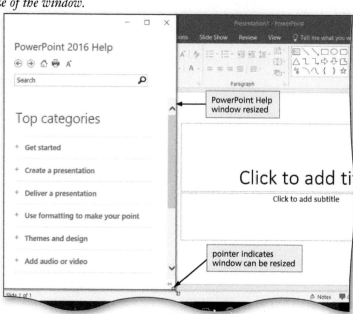

Figure 91

Using Office Help

Once an Office app's Help window is open, several methods exist for navigating Help. You can search for help by using any of the three following methods from the Help window:

1. Enter search text in the Search text box.
2. Click the links in the Help window.
3. Use the Table of Contents.

To Obtain Help Using the Search Text Box

1 SIGN IN | 2 USE WINDOWS | 3 USE APPS | 4 FILE MANAGEMENT | 5 SWITCH APPS | 6 SAVE FILES
7 CHANGE SCREEN RESOLUTION | 8 EXIT APPS | 9 USE ADDITIONAL APP FEATURES | 10 USE HELP

Assume for the following example that you want to know more about fonts. The following steps use the Search text box to obtain useful information about fonts by entering the word, fonts, as search text. *Why? You may not know the exact help topic you are looking to find, so using keywords can help narrow your search.*

- Type **fonts** in the Search text box at the top of the PowerPoint Help window to enter the search text.
- Press the ENTER key to display the search results (Figure 92).

Q&A Why do my search results differ?
If you do not have an Internet connection, your results will reflect only the content of the Help files on your computer. When searching for help online, results also can change as content is added, deleted, and updated on the online Help webpages maintained by Microsoft.

Why were my search results not very helpful?
When initiating a search, be sure to check the spelling of the search text; also, keep your search specific to return the most accurate results.

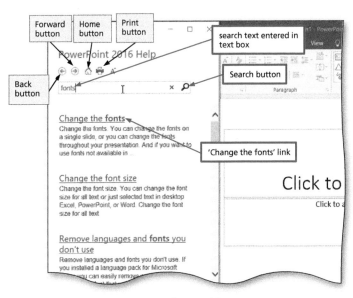

Figure 92

- Click the 'Change the fonts', or a similar, link to display the Help information associated with the selected topic (Figure 93).

Figure 93

- Click the Home button in the Help window to clear the search results and redisplay the Help home page (Figure 94).
- Click the Close button in the PowerPoint 2016 Help window to close the window.

Figure 94

BTW

Customizing the Ribbon

In addition to customizing the Quick Access Toolbar, you can add items to and remove items from the ribbon. To customize the ribbon, click File on the ribbon to open the Backstage view, click the Options tab in the Backstage view, and then click Customize Ribbon in the left pane of the Options dialog box. More information about customizing the ribbon is presented in a later module.

Obtaining Help while Working in an Office App

Help in the Office apps, such as PowerPoint, provides you with the ability to obtain help directly, without opening the Help window and initiating a search. For example, you may be unsure about how a particular command works, or you may be presented with a dialog box that you are not sure how to use.

Figure 95 shows one option for obtaining help while working in an Office app. If you want to learn more about a command, point to its button and wait for the ScreenTip to appear. If the Help icon and 'Tell me more' link appear in the ScreenTip, click the 'Tell me more' link or press the F1 key while pointing to the button to open the Help window associated with that command.

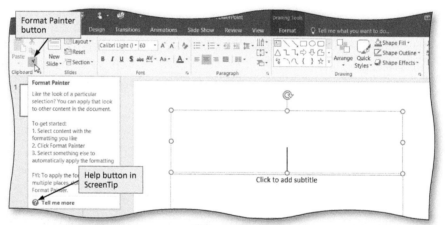

Figure 95

Figure 96 shows a dialog box that contains a Help button. Clicking the Help button or pressing the F1 key while the dialog box is displayed opens a Help window. The Help window contains help about that dialog box, if available. If no help file is available for that particular dialog box, then the main Help window opens.

Figure 96

As mentioned previously, the Tell Me box is available in most Office apps and can perform a variety of functions. One of these functions is to provide easy access to commands by typing a description of the command.

To Obtain Help Using the Tell Me Box

1 SIGN IN | 2 USE WINDOWS | 3 USE APPS | 4 FILE MANAGEMENT | 5 SWITCH APPS | 6 SAVE FILES
7 CHANGE SCREEN RESOLUTION | 8 EXIT APPS | 9 USE ADDITIONAL APP FEATURES | 10 USE HELP

If you are having trouble finding a command in an Office app, you can use the Tell Me box to search for the function you are trying to perform. As you type, the Tell Me box will suggest commands that match the search text you are entering. *Why? You can use the Tell Me box to access commands quickly that you otherwise may be unable to find on the ribbon.* The following steps find information about margins.

- Type **border** in the Tell Me box and watch the search results appear.
- Point to Border Style to display a submenu displaying the various border designs (Figure 97).
- Click an empty area of the presentation window to close the search results.

- Exit Microsoft PowerPoint.

Figure 97

Using the Windows Search Box

One of the more powerful Windows features is the Windows search box. The search box is a central location from where you can type search text and quickly access related Windows commands or web search results. In addition, **Cortana** is a new search tool in Windows that you can access using the search box. It can act as a personal assistant by performing functions such as providing ideas; searching for apps, files, and folders; and setting reminders. In addition to typing search text in the search box, you also can use your computer or mobile device's microphone to give verbal commands.

To Use the Windows Search Box

1 SIGN IN | 2 USE WINDOWS | 3 USE APPS | 4 FILE MANAGEMENT | 5 SWITCH APPS | 6 SAVE FILES
7 CHANGE SCREEN RESOLUTION | 8 EXIT APPS | 9 USE ADDITIONAL APP FEATURES | 10 USE HELP

The following step uses the Windows search box to search for a Windows command. *Why? Using the search box to locate apps, settings, folders, and files can be faster than navigating windows and dialog boxes to search for the desired content.*

- Type **notification** in the search box to display the search results. The search results include related Windows settings, Windows Store apps, and web search results (Figure 98).
- Click an empty area of the desktop to close the search results.

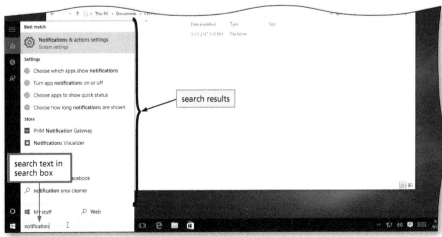

Figure 98

Summary

In this module, you learned how to use the Windows interface, several touch screen and mouse operations, and file and folder management. You also learned some basic features of PowerPoint and discovered the common elements that exist among Microsoft Office apps. Topics covered included signing in, using Windows, using apps, file management, switching between apps, saving files, changing screen resolution, exiting apps, using additional app features, and using Help.

CONSIDER THIS: PLAN AHEAD

What guidelines should you follow to plan your projects?

The process of communicating specific information is a learned, rational skill. Computers and software, especially Microsoft Office 2016, can help you develop ideas and present detailed information to a particular audience and minimize much of the laborious work of drafting and revising projects. No matter what method you use to plan a project, it is beneficial to follow some specific guidelines from the onset to arrive at a final product that is informative, relevant, and effective. Use some aspects of these guidelines every time you undertake a project, and others as needed in specific instances.

1. Determine the project's purpose.

   a) Clearly define why you are undertaking this assignment.

   b) Begin to draft ideas of how best to communicate information by handwriting ideas on paper; composing directly on a laptop, tablet, or mobile device; or developing a strategy that fits your particular thinking and writing style.

2. Analyze your audience.

   a) Learn about the people who will read, analyze, or view your work.

   b) Determine their interests and needs so that you can present the information they need to know and omit the information they already possess.

   c) Form a mental picture of these people or find photos of people who fit this profile so that you can develop a project with the audience in mind.

3. Gather possible content.

   a) Locate existing information that may reside in spreadsheets, databases, or other files.

   b) Conduct a web search to find relevant websites.

   c) Read pamphlets, magazine and newspaper articles, and books to gain insights of how others have approached your topic.

   d) Conduct personal interviews to obtain perspectives not available by any other means.

   e) Consider video and audio clips as potential sources for material that might complement or support the factual data you uncover.

4. Determine what content to present to your audience.

   a) Write three or four major ideas you want an audience member to remember after reading or viewing your project.

   b) Envision your project's endpoint, the key fact you wish to emphasize, so that all project elements lead to this final element.

   c) Determine relevant time factors, such as the length of time to develop the project, how long readers will spend reviewing your project, or the amount of time allocated for your speaking engagement.

   d) Decide whether a graph, photo, or artistic element can express or enhance a particular concept.

   e) Be mindful of the order in which you plan to present the content, and place the most important material at the beginning or end of the presentation, because readers and audience members generally remember the first and last pieces of information they see and hear.

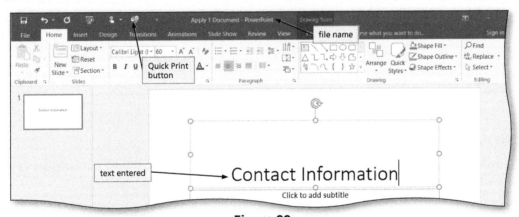
Apply Your Knowledge

Reinforce the skills and apply the concepts you learned in this module.

Creating a Folder and a Presentation

Instructions: You will create a PowerPoint Assignments folder and then create a PowerPoint presentation and save it in the folder.

Perform the following tasks:
1. Open the File Explorer window and then double-click to open the Documents folder.
2. Click the New folder button on the Quick Access Toolbar to display a new folder icon and text box for the folder name.
3. Type **PowerPoint Assignments** in the text box to name the folder. Press the ENTER key to create the folder in the Documents folder.
4. Run PowerPoint and create a new blank presentation.
5. Type **Contact Information** in the title text placeholder (Figure 99).

Figure 99

6. If requested by your instructor, enter your name, phone number, and email address in the subtitle placeholder.
7. Click the Save button on the Quick Access Toolbar. Navigate to the PowerPoint Assignments folder in the Documents folder and then save the presentation using the file name, Apply 1 Document (Figure 99).
8. If your Quick Access Toolbar does not show the Quick Print button, add the Quick Print button to the Quick Access Toolbar. Print the presentation using the Quick Print button on the Quick Access Toolbar. When you are finished printing, remove the Quick Print button from the Quick Access Toolbar.
9. Submit the printout to your instructor.
10. Exit PowerPoint.
11. ✻ What other commands might you find useful to include on the Quick Access Toolbar?

STUDENT ASSIGNMENTS

Extend Your Knowledge

Extend the skills you learned in this module and experiment with new skills. You will use Help to complete the assignment.

Using Help

Instructions: Use PowerPoint Help to perform the following tasks.

Perform the following tasks:

1. Run PowerPoint.

2. Press F1 to open the PowerPoint Help window (shown in Figure 89).

3. Search PowerPoint Help to answer the following questions.

    a. What are three new features of PowerPoint 2016?

    b. What type of training is available through PowerPoint Help for PowerPoint 2016?

    c. What are the steps to customize the ribbon?

    d. What is the purpose of the Office Clipboard?

    e. What is the purpose of Slide Sorter view?

    f. How do you change a slide layout?

    g. How do you insert pictures?

    h. How do you change the size of text?

    i. What are the steps to zoom in and out of a slide?

    j. What is the purpose of the Insights pane? How do you display it?

4. Type the answers from your searches in a new blank PowerPoint presentation. Save the presentation with a new file name and then submit it in the format specified by your instructor.

5. If requested by your instructor, enter your name in the PowerPoint slide.

6. Exit PowerPoint.

7. ☀ What search text did you use to perform the searches above? Did it take multiple attempts to search and locate the exact information for which you were searching?

Expand Your World

Create a solution that uses cloud or web technologies by learning and investigating on your own from general guidance.

Creating Folders on OneDrive and Using the PowerPoint Online App

Instructions: You will create the folders shown in Figure 100 on OneDrive. Then, you will use the PowerPoint Online app to create a small file and save it in a folder on OneDrive.

Perform the following tasks:

1. Sign in to OneDrive in your browser.

2. Use the New button to create the folder structure shown in Figure 100.

Figure 100

3. In the Upcoming Events folder, use the New button to create a PowerPoint presentation with the file name, Expand 1 Task List, that contains the text, Prepare agenda for Tuesday's meeting.

4. If requested by your instructor, add your name to the PowerPoint slide.

5. Save the presentation in the Upcoming Events folder and then exit the app.

6. Submit the assignment in the format specified by your instructor.

7. ✳ Based on your current knowledge of OneDrive, do you think you will use it? What about the PowerPoint Online app?

In the Labs

Design, create, modify, and/or use files following the guidelines, concepts, and skills presented in this module. Labs 1 and 2, which increase in difficulty, require you to create solutions based on what you learned in the module; Lab 3 requires you to apply your creative thinking and problem-solving skills to design and implement a solution.

Lab 1: **Creating Folders for a Bookstore**

Problem: Your friend works for a local bookstore. He would like to organize his files in relation to the types of books available in the store. He has seven main categories: fiction, biography, children, humor, social science, nonfiction, and medical. You are to create a folder structure similar to Figure 101.

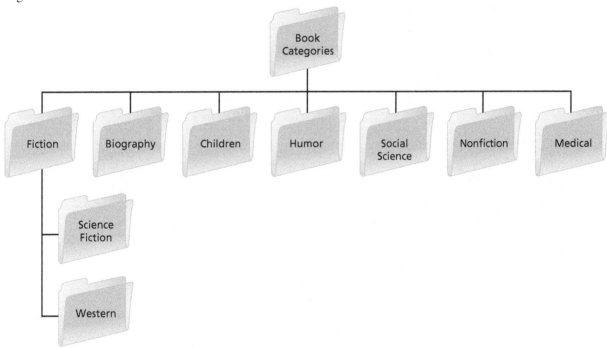

Figure 101

Perform the following tasks:

1. Click the File Explorer button on the taskbar and display the contents of the Documents folder.

2. In the Documents folder, create the main folder and name it Book Categories.

3. Navigate to the Book Categories folder.

4. Within the Book Categories folder, create a folder for each of the following: Fiction, Biography, Children, Humor, Social Science, Nonfiction, and Medical.

5. Within the Fiction folder, create two additional folders, one for Science Fiction and the second for Western.

Continued >

In the Labs *continued*

6. If requested by your instructor, add another folder using your last name as the folder name.

7. Submit the assignment in the format specified by your instructor.

8. ✳ Think about how you use your computer for various tasks (consider personal, professional, and academic reasons). What folders will be required to store the files you save?

Lab 2: **Creating PowerPoint Presentations and Saving Them in Appropriate Folders**

Problem: You are taking a class that requires you to complete three PowerPoint modules. You will save the work completed in each module in a different folder (Figure 102).

Perform the following tasks:

1. Create the folders shown in Figure 102.

2. Create a PowerPoint presentation containing the text, Module 1 Notes.

3. In the Backstage view, click Save As and then click This PC.

4. Click the Browse button to display the Save As dialog box. Click Documents to open the Documents folder. Navigate to the Module 1 folder and then save the file in the PowerPoint folder using the file name, Lab 2 Module 1 Notes.

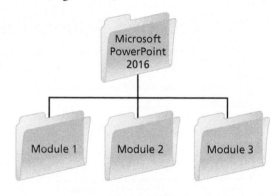

Figure 102

5. Create another PowerPoint presentation containing the text, Module 2 Notes, and then save it in the Module 2 folder using the file name, Lab 2 Module 2 Notes.

6. Create a third PowerPoint presentation containing the text, Module 3 Notes, and then save it in the Module 3 folder using the file name, Lab 2 Module 3 Notes.

7. If requested by your instructor, add your name to each of the three PowerPoint documents.

8. Submit the assignment in the format specified by your instructor.

9. ✳ Based on your current knowledge of Windows and PowerPoint, how will you organize folders for assignments in this class? Why?

Lab 3: **Consider This: Your Turn**

Performing Research about Malware

Problem: You have just installed a new computer with the Windows operating system. Because you want to be sure that it is protected from the threat of malware, you decide to research malware, malware protection, and removing malware.

Perform the following tasks:

Part 1: Research the following three topics: malware, malware protection, and removing malware. Use the concepts and techniques presented in this module to use the search box to find information regarding these topics. Create a PowerPoint presentation that contains steps to safeguard a computer properly from malware, ways to prevent malware, as well as the different ways to remove malware or a virus should your computer become infected. Submit your assignment and the answers to the following critical thinking questions in the format specified by your instructor.

Part 2: ✳ You made several decisions while searching for this assignment. What decisions did you make? What was the rationale behind them? How did you locate the information about malware?

1 Creating and Editing a Presentation with Pictures

Objectives

You will have mastered the material in this module when you can:

- Select and change a document theme and variant
- Create a title slide and a text slide with a multilevel bulleted list
- Add new slides and change slide layouts
- Insert pictures into slides with and without content placeholders
- Move and resize pictures

- Change font size and color
- Bold and italicize text
- Duplicate a slide
- Arrange slides
- Select slide transitions
- View a presentation in Slide Show view

Introduction

A PowerPoint **presentation**, also called a **slide show**, can help you deliver a dynamic, professional-looking message to an audience. PowerPoint allows you to produce slides to use in an academic, business, or other environment. The collection of slides in a presentation is called a **deck**, resembling a deck of cards that are stacked on top of each other. A common use of slide decks is to enhance an oral presentation. A speaker might desire to convey information, such as urging students to volunteer at a fund-raising event, explaining changes in employee compensation packages, or describing a new laboratory procedure. The PowerPoint slides should reinforce the speaker's message and help the audience retain the information presented. Custom slides can fit your specific needs and contain diagrams, charts, tables, pictures, shapes, video, sound, and animation effects to make your presentation more effective. An accompanying handout gives audience members reference notes and review material for your presentation.

Project — Presentation with a Bulleted List and Pictures

In this module's project, you will follow proper design guidelines and learn to use PowerPoint to create, save, and view the slides shown in Figures 1–1a through 1–1e. The objective is to produce a presentation, titled Tall Oaks, to promote three programs at the nature center. This slide show has a variety of pictures and visual elements to add interest and give facts about the events. Some of the text has formatting and color enhancements. Transitions help one slide flow gracefully into the next during a slide show.

(a) Slide 1 (Title Slide with Picture)

(b) Slide 2 (Multilevel Bulleted List with Picture)

(c) Slide 3 (Comparison Layout and Pictures)

(d) Slide 4 (Title and Illustration)

(e) Slide 5 (Closing Slide)

Figure 1–1

In this module, you will learn how to perform basic tasks using PowerPoint. The following roadmap identifies general activities you will perform as you progress through this module:

1. INSERT the four PRESENTATION SLIDES, using various layouts.
2. ENTER the TEXT for the slides.
3. FORMAT the TEXT on each slide.
4. INSERT GRAPHICAL ELEMENTS, including pictures.
5. SIZE AND POSITION the graphical elements.
6. ENHANCE the SLIDE SHOW by adding a closing slide and transition.
7. DISPLAY the SLIDES.

For an introduction to Office and instructions about how to perform basic tasks in Office apps, read the Office and Windows module at the beginning of this book, where you can learn how to run an application, use the ribbon, save a file, open a file, print a file, exit an application, use Help, and much more.

Choosing a Document Theme and Variant

You easily can give the slides in a presentation a professional and integrated appearance by using a theme. A document **theme** is a specific design with coordinating colors, fonts, and special effects such as shadows and reflections. Several themes are available when you run PowerPoint, each with a specific name. Using one of the formatted themes makes creating a professional-looking presentation easier and quicker than using the Blank Presentation template, where you would need to make all design decisions.

Each theme has a set of four alternate designs, called **variants**. Each variant has the same overall composition, but the colors, fonts, and design elements differ. Once you select a theme, you then can select a variation that best fits your overall design needs. If you later decide that another theme or variant would better fit the presentation's general theme, you can change these elements while you are developing slides.

For an introduction to Windows and instructions about how to perform basic Windows tasks, read the Office and Windows module at the beginning of this book, where you can learn how to resize windows, change screen resolution, create folders, move and rename files, use Windows Help, and much more.

To Choose a Document Theme and Variant

1 INSERT PRESENTATION SLIDES | 2 ENTER TEXT | 3 FORMAT TEXT | 4 INSERT GRAPHICAL ELEMENTS
5 SIZE & POSITION | 6 ENHANCE SLIDE SHOW | 7 DISPLAY SLIDES

When you begin creating a new PowerPoint presentation, you need to select a theme. You either can start with no design elements by using the Blank Presentation, or you can select one of the available professionally designed themes. The following steps apply the Berlin theme and then change the variant. *Why? The title slide will have text and a picture, so you want to select a theme, like Berlin, with an uncluttered background. The presentation discusses three events occurring at the nature center, and green is the color commonly associated with nature's forests and grasslands. The default Berlin theme is predominantly orange and black, but one of its variants is green and is an appropriate choice to relate to the nature concept.*

BTW
The PowerPoint Window
The modules in this book begin with the PowerPoint window appearing as it did at the initial installation of the software. Your PowerPoint window may look different depending on your screen resolution and other PowerPoint settings.

- Run PowerPoint and point to the Berlin theme on the Recent screen (Figure 1–2).

Q&A

I do not see the Berlin theme. What should I do?

Your list of available templates may differ from those shown in the figure. You may need to scroll down to locate the Berlin theme or enter "Berlin" in the Search box.

Figure 1–2

- Click the Berlin theme to display a theme preview dialog box with a thumbnail view of the theme and its variants (Figure 1–3).

Q&A

Can I see previews of other themes?

Yes. Click the right or left arrows on the sides of the theme preview dialog box.

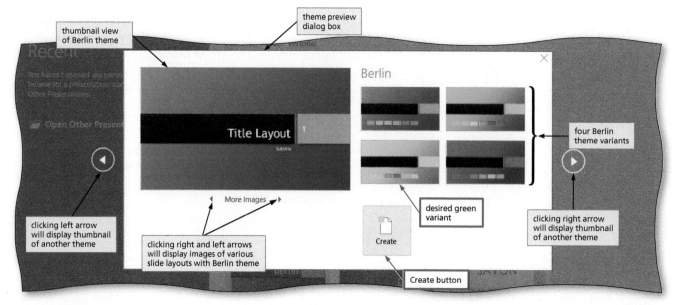

Figure 1–3

3
- Click the lower-left (green) variant to view a preview of that style applied to the thumbnail.

Q&A Can I see previews of the Berlin theme and green variant applied to layouts other than the title slide?
Yes. Click the right or left arrows beside the words, More Images, below the thumbnail. Three other layouts will be displayed: Title and Content, Two Content, and Photo.

- Click the Create button to apply the Berlin theme and green variant to the presentation and to display Slide 1 (Figure 1–4).

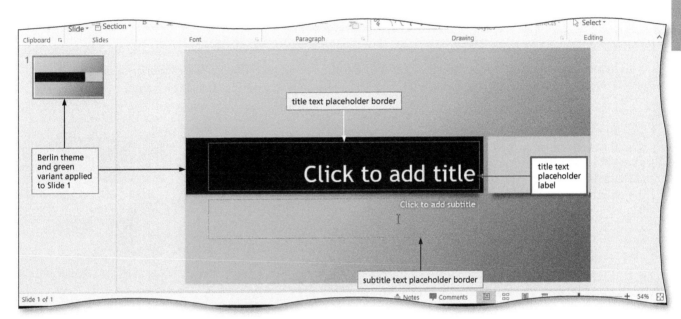

Figure 1–4

Creating a Title Slide

When you open a new presentation, the default **Title Slide** layout appears. The purpose of this layout is to introduce the presentation to the audience. PowerPoint includes other standard layouts for each of the themes. The slide layouts are set up in **landscape orientation**, where the slide width is greater than its height. In landscape orientation, the slide size is preset to 10 inches wide and 7.5 inches high when printed on a standard sheet of paper measuring 11 inches wide and 8.5 inches high.

    Placeholders are boxes with dotted or hatch-marked borders that are displayed when you create a new slide. Most layouts have both a title text placeholder and at least one content placeholder. Depending on the particular slide layout selected, title and subtitle placeholders are displayed for the slide title and subtitle; a content text placeholder is displayed for text, art, or a table, chart, picture, graphic, or movie. The title slide has two text placeholders where you can type the main heading, or title, of a new slide and the subtitle.

    With the exception of the Blank slide layout, PowerPoint assumes every new slide has a title. To make creating a presentation easier, any text you type after a new slide appears becomes title text in the title text placeholder. The following steps create the title slide for this presentation.

BTW
PowerPoint Screen Resolution
If you are using a computer or mobile device to step through the project in this module and you want your screens to match the figures in this book, you should change your screen's resolution to 1366 x 768. For information about how to change a computer's resolution, refer to the Office and Windows module at the beginning of this book.

How do I choose the words for the slide?

All presentations should follow the 7 × 7 rule, which states that each slide should have a maximum of seven lines, and each line should have a maximum of seven words. PowerPoint designers must choose their words carefully and, in turn, help viewers read the slides easily.

Avoid line wraps. Your audience's eyes want to stop at the end of a line. Thus, you must plan your words carefully or adjust the font size so that each point displays on only one line.

To Enter the Presentation Title

1 INSERT PRESENTATION SLIDES | 2 ENTER TEXT | 3 FORMAT TEXT | 4 INSERT GRAPHICAL ELEMENTS
5 SIZE & POSITION | 6 ENHANCE SLIDE SHOW | 7 DISPLAY SLIDES

The presentation title for Project 1 is Autumn Family Programs. *Why? The presentation discusses three programs that will be held during the fall months.* The following steps create the slide show's title.

1

- Click the label, 'Click to add title', located inside the title text placeholder to select the placeholder (Figure 1–5).

Figure 1–5

2

- Type **Autumn Family Programs** in the title text placeholder. Do not press the ENTER key (Figure 1–6).

Figure 1–6

Correcting a Mistake When Typing

If you type the wrong letter, press the BACKSPACE key to erase all the characters back to and including the one that is incorrect. If you mistakenly press the ENTER key after typing the title and the insertion point is on the new line, simply press the BACKSPACE key to return the insertion point to the right of the last letter in the word, Programs.

By default, PowerPoint allows you to reverse up to the last 20 changes by clicking the Undo button on the Quick Access Toolbar. The ScreenTip that appears when you point to the Undo button changes to indicate the type of change just made. For example, if you type text in the title text placeholder and then point to the Undo button, the ScreenTip that appears is Undo Typing. For clarity, when referencing the Undo button in this project, the name displaying in the ScreenTip is used. You can reapply a change that you reversed with the Undo button by clicking the Redo button on the Quick Access Toolbar. Clicking the Redo button reverses the last undo action. The ScreenTip name reflects the type of reversal last performed.

BTW
**Touch Screen
Differences**
The Office and Windows interfaces may vary if you are using a touch screen. For this reason, you might notice that the function or appearance of your touch screen differs slightly from this module's presentation.

Paragraphs

Text in the subtitle text placeholder supports the title text. It can appear on one or more lines in the placeholder. To create more than one subtitle line, you press the ENTER key after typing some words. PowerPoint creates a new line, which is the second paragraph in the placeholder. A **paragraph** is a segment of text with the same format that begins when you press the ENTER key and ends when you press the ENTER key again. This new paragraph is the same level as the previous paragraph. A **level** is a position within a structure, such as an outline, that indicates the magnitude of importance. PowerPoint allows for five paragraph levels.

How do you use the touch keyboard with a touch screen?
To display the on-screen keyboard, tap the Touch Keyboard button on the Windows taskbar. When finished using the touch keyboard, tap the X button on the touch keyboard to close the keyboard.

CONSIDER THIS

To Enter the Presentation Subtitle Paragraph

1 INSERT PRESENTATION SLIDES | 2 ENTER TEXT | 3 FORMAT TEXT | 4 INSERT GRAPHICAL ELEMENTS
5 SIZE & POSITION | 6 ENHANCE SLIDE SHOW | 7 DISPLAY SLIDES

The first subtitle paragraph is related to the title. *Why?* *The subtitle gives an additional detail, the nature center's name.* The following steps enter the presentation subtitle.

1
• Click the label, 'Click to add subtitle', located inside the subtitle text placeholder to select the placeholder (Figure 1–7).

Figure 1–7

- Type **Tall Oaks Nature Center** but do not press the ENTER key (Figure 1–8).

Figure 1–8

To Zoom a Slide

You can **zoom** the view of the slide on the screen so that the text or other content is enlarged or shrunk. When you zoom in, you get a close-up view of your slide; when you zoom out, you see more of the slide at a reduced size. You will be modifying the text and other slide components as you create the presentation, so you can enlarge the slide on the screen. *Why? Zooming the slide can help you see slide elements more clearly so that you can position them precisely where desired.* The following step changes the zoom to 70 percent.

🔍 **Experiment**

- Repeatedly click the Zoom In and Zoom Out buttons on the status bar and watch the size of the slide change in the Slide pane.

- Click the Zoom In or Zoom Out button as many times as necessary until the Zoom button on the status bar displays 70% on its face (Figure 1–9).

Q&A If I change the zoom percentage, will the slide display differently when I run the presentation?
No. Changing the zoom helps you develop the slide content and does not affect the slide show.

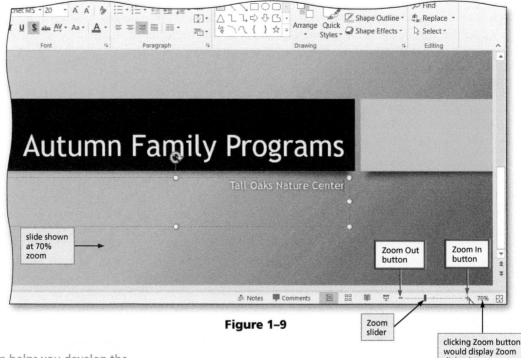

Figure 1–9

Other Ways

1. Drag Zoom slider on status bar	2. Click Zoom level button on status bar, select desired zoom percent or type (Zoom dialog box), click OK button	3. Click Zoom button (View tab | Zoom group), select desired zoom percent or type (Zoom dialog box), click OK button	4. For touch screens: Pinch two fingers together in Slide pane (zoom out) or stretch two fingers apart (zoom in)

Formatting Characters in a Presentation

Recall that each document theme determines the color scheme, font set, and layout of a presentation. You can use a specific document theme and then change the characters' formats any time before, during, or after you type the text.

Fonts and Font Styles

Characters that appear on the screen are a specific shape and size. Examples of how you can modify the appearance, or **format**, of these typed characters on the screen and in print include changing the font, style, size, and color. The **font**, or typeface, defines the appearance and shape of the letters, numbers, punctuation marks, and symbols. **Style** indicates how the characters are formatted. PowerPoint's text font styles include regular, italic, bold, and bold italic. **Size** specifies the height of the characters and is gauged by a measurement system that uses points. A **point** is 1/72 of an inch in height. Thus, a character with a font size of 36 is 36/72 (or 1/2) of an inch in height. **Color** defines the hue of the characters.

This presentation uses the Berlin document theme, which has particular font styles and font sizes. The Berlin document theme default title text font is named Trebuchet MS. It has no special effects, and its size is 54 point. The Berlin default subtitle text font also is Trebuchet MS with a font size of 20 point.

1 INSERT PRESENTATION SLIDES | 2 ENTER TEXT | 3 FORMAT TEXT | 4 INSERT GRAPHICAL ELEMENTS

5 SIZE & POSITION | 6 ENHANCE SLIDE SHOW | 7 DISPLAY SLIDES

To Select a Paragraph

You can use many techniques to format characters. When you want to apply the same formats to multiple words or paragraphs, it is helpful to select these words. **Why?** *It is efficient to select the desired text and then make the desired changes to all the characters simultaneously.* The first formatting change you will make will apply to the title slide subtitle. The following step selects this paragraph.

- Triple-click the paragraph, Tall Oaks Nature Center, in the subtitle text placeholder to select the paragraph (Figure 1–10).

mini toolbar appears whenever you select text

subtitle text paragraph to be formatted is selected

Figure 1–10

Other Ways

1. Position pointer to left of first paragraph and drag to end of line

To Italicize Text

Different font styles often are used on slides. *Why?* *These style changes make the words more appealing to the reader and emphasize particular text.* **Italic** text has a slanted appearance. Used sparingly, it draws the readers' eyes to these characters. The following step adds emphasis to the line of the subtitle text by changing regular text to italic text.

- With the subtitle text still selected, click the Italic button on the mini toolbar to italicize that text on the slide (Figure 1–11).

Q&A
If I change my mind and decide not to italicize the text, how can I remove this style?
Immediately click the Undo button on the Quick Access Toolbar, click the Italic button a second time, or press CTRL+Z.

Figure 1–11

Other Ways			
1. Right-click selected text, click Italic button in mini toolbar near shortcut menu	2. Select text, click Italic button (Home tab | Font group)	3. Click Font dialog box launcher (Home tab | Font group), click Font tab (Font dialog box), click Italic in Font style list, click OK button	4. Select text, press CTRL+I

To Increase Font Size

Why? *To add emphasis, you increase the font size for the subtitle text.* The 'Increase Font Size' button on the mini toolbar increases the font size in preset increments. The following step uses this button to increase the font size.

- With the text, Tall Oaks Nature Center, selected, click the 'Increase Font Size' button on the mini toolbar four times to increase the font size of the selected text from 20 to 36 point (Figure 1–12).

Figure 1–12

Other Ways			
1. Click Font Size arrow on mini toolbar, click desired font size in Font Size gallery	2. Click 'Increase Font Size' button (Home tab | Font group)	3. Click Font Size arrow (Home tab | Font group), click desired font size in Font size gallery	4. Press CTRL+SHIFT+>

To Select a Word

PowerPoint designers use many techniques to emphasize words and characters on a slide. To accentuate the word, Autumn, on your slide, you want to increase the font size and change the font color to orange for this word in the title text. To make these changes, you should begin by selecting the word, Autumn. *Why? You could perform these actions separately, but it is more efficient to select the word and then change the font attributes.* The following step selects a word.

- Position the pointer somewhere in the word to be selected (in this case, in the word, Autumn).

- Double-click the word to select it (Figure 1–13).

Figure 1–13

Other Ways

1. Position pointer before first character, press CTRL+SHIFT+RIGHT ARROW   2. Position pointer before first character, drag right to select word

To Change the Text Color

PowerPoint allows you to use one or more text colors in a presentation. You decide to change the color of the word you selected, Autumn. *Why? The color, orange, is associated with that season, and you want to add more emphasis, subtly, to this word in your title slide text.* The following steps add emphasis to this word by changing the font color from white to orange.

- With the word, Autumn, selected, click the Font Color arrow on the mini toolbar to display the Font Color gallery, which includes Theme Colors and Standard Colors (Figure 1–14).

Q&A If the mini toolbar disappears from the screen, how can I display it once again?
Right-click the text, and the mini toolbar should appear.

🔍 **Experiment**

- Point to various colors in the gallery and watch the word's font color change.

Figure 1–14

• Click Orange in the Standard Colors row on the mini toolbar (third color from left) to change the font color to Orange (Figure 1–15).

Q&A Why did I select the color Orange?
Orange is one of the 10 standard colors associated with every document theme, and it is a universal color representing the fall colors. The new color will emphasize the fact that the presentation focuses on programs suited for this time of year.

What is the difference between the colors shown in the Theme Colors area and the Standard Colors?
The 10 colors in the top row of the Theme Colors area are two text, two background, and six accent colors in the Berlin theme; the five colors in each column under the top row display different transparencies. The Standard Colors are available in every document theme.

Figure 1–15

3

• Click outside the selected area to deselect the word.

4

• Save the presentation on your hard disk, OneDrive, or other storage location using Tall Oaks as the file name.

Q&A Why should I save the presentation at this time?
You have performed many tasks while creating this presentation and do not want to risk losing work completed thus far.

Other Ways

1. Right-click selected text, click Font on shortcut menu, click Font Color button, click desired color

2. Click Font Color arrow (Home tab | Font group), click desired color

BTW
Organizing Files and Folders
You should organize and store files in folders so that you easily can find the files later. For example, if you are taking an introductory technology class called CIS 101, a good practice would be to save all PowerPoint files in a PowerPoint folder in a CIS 101 folder. For a discussion of folders and detailed examples of creating folders, refer to the Office and Windows module at the beginning of this book.

Adding a New Slide to a Presentation

With the text for the title slide for the presentation created, the next step is to add the first text slide immediately after the title slide. Usually, when you create a presentation, you add slides with text, pictures, graphics, or charts. Some placeholders allow you to double-click the placeholder and then access other objects, such as videos, charts, diagrams, and organization charts. You can change the layout for a slide at any time during the creation of a presentation.

To Add a New Text Slide with a Bulleted List

1 INSERT PRESENTATION SLIDES | 2 ENTER TEXT | 3 FORMAT TEXT | **4 INSERT GRAPHICAL ELEMENTS**
5 SIZE & POSITION | 6 ENHANCE SLIDE SHOW | 7 DISPLAY SLIDES

When you add a new slide, PowerPoint uses the Title and Content slide layout. This layout provides a title placeholder and a content area for text, art, charts, and other graphics. A vertical scroll bar appears in the Slide pane when you add the second slide. *Why? The scroll bar allows you to move from slide to slide easily.* A small image of this slide also appears in the Slides tab. The following step adds a new slide with the Title and Content slide layout.

1

- Click the New Slide button (Home tab | Slides group) to insert a new slide with the Title and Content layout (Figure 1–16).

Q&A

Why does the bullet character display a white dot?
The Berlin document theme determines the bullet characters. Each paragraph level has an associated bullet character.

I clicked the New Slide arrow instead of the New Slide button. What should I do?
Click the Title and Content slide thumbnail in the Berlin layout gallery.

How do I know which slide number I am viewing?
The left edge of the status bar shows the current slide number followed by the total number of slides in the document. In addition, the slide number is displayed to the left of the slide thumbnail.

What are those six icons grouped in the middle of the Slide pane?
You can click one of the icons to insert a specific type of content: table, chart, SmartArt graphic, pictures, online pictures, or video.

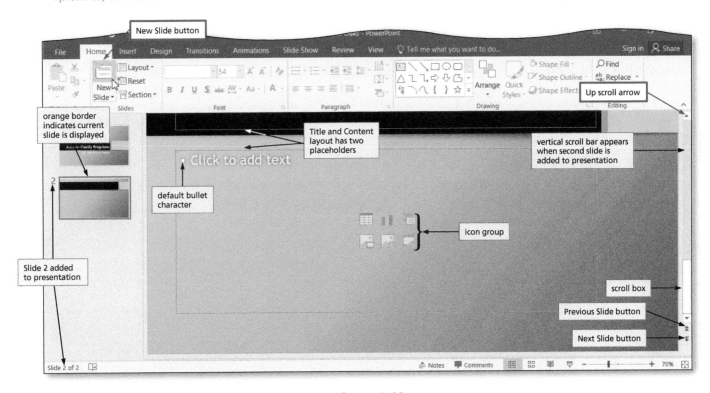

Figure 1–16

Other Ways

1. Click New Slide button (Insert tab | Slides group)   2. Press CTRL+M

Creating a Text Slide with a Multilevel Bulleted List

The information in the Slide 2 text placeholder is presented in a bulleted list with three levels. A **bulleted list** is a list of paragraphs, each of which may be preceded by a bullet character, such as a dot, arrow, or checkmark. Most themes display a bullet character at the start of a paragraph by default. A slide that consists of more than one

BTW
The Ribbon and Screen Resolution
PowerPoint may change how the groups and buttons within the groups appear on the ribbon, depending on the computer or mobile device's screen resolution. Thus, your ribbon may look different from the ones in this book if you are using a screen resolution other than 1366 x 768.

level of bulleted text is called a **multilevel bulleted list slide**. In a multilevel bulleted list, a lower-level paragraph is a subset of a higher-level paragraph. It usually contains information that supports the topic in the paragraph immediately above it.

BTW
File Type
Depending on your Windows settings, the file type .pptx may be displayed on the title bar immediately to the right of the file name after you save the file. The file type .pptx identifies a PowerPoint document.

As you can see in Figure 1–1b, two of the Slide 2 paragraphs appear at the same level, called the first level: Enjoy a hike on natural surface trails, and 9 a.m. every Saturday. Beginning with the second level, each paragraph indents to the right of the preceding level and is pushed down to a lower level. For example, if you increase the indent of a first-level paragraph, it becomes a second-level paragraph. The second and fourth paragraphs on Slide 2 are second-level paragraphs. The last paragraph, Extra supplies will be available, is a third-level paragraph.

Creating a text slide with a multilevel bulleted list requires several steps. Initially, you enter a slide title in the title text placeholder. Next, you select the content text placeholder. Then, you type the text for the multilevel bulleted list, increasing and decreasing the indents as needed. The next several sections add a slide with a multilevel bulleted list.

To Enter a Slide Title

1 INSERT PRESENTATION SLIDES | 2 ENTER TEXT | 3 FORMAT TEXT | 4 INSERT GRAPHICAL ELEMENTS
5 SIZE & POSITION | 6 ENHANCE SLIDE SHOW | 7 DISPLAY SLIDES

PowerPoint assumes every new slide has a title. **Why?** *The audience members read the title and then can begin to focus their attention on the information being presented on that slide.* The title for Slide 2 is Morning Bird Walks. The following step enters this title.

- If necessary, click the Up scroll arrow several times until the entire title text placeholder is visible.

- Click the label 'Click to add title', to select it and then type **Morning Bird Walks** in the title text placeholder. Do not press the ENTER key (Figure 1–17).

Figure 1–17

To Select a Text Placeholder

Why? *Before you can type text into a content placeholder, you first must select it.* The following step selects the text placeholder on Slide 2.

- Click the label, 'Click to add text', to select the content placeholder (Figure 1–18).

Q&A Why does my pointer have a different shape? If you move the pointer away from the bullet, it will change shape.

Figure 1–18

Other Ways

1. Press CTRL+ENTER

To Type a Multilevel Bulleted List

The content placeholder provides an area for the text characters. When you click inside a placeholder, you then can type or paste text. As discussed previously, a bulleted list is a list of paragraphs, each of which is preceded by a bullet. A paragraph is a segment of text ended by pressing the ENTER key. The theme determines the bullets for each level. ***Why?*** *The bullet variations are determined by the specific paragraph levels, and they generally vary in size, shape, and color.*

The content text placeholder is selected, so the next step is to type the multilevel bulleted list that consists of six paragraphs, as shown in Figure 1–1b. Creating a lower-level paragraph is called **demoting** text; creating a higher-level paragraph is called **promoting** text. The following steps create a multilevel bulleted list consisting of three levels.

- Type **Enjoy a hike on natural surface trails** and then press the ENTER key (Figure 1–19).

Figure 1–19

2

- Click the 'Increase List Level' button (Home tab | Paragraph group) to indent the second paragraph below the first and create a second-level paragraph (Figure 1–20).

Q&A Why does the bullet for this paragraph have a different size?
A different bullet is assigned to each paragraph level.

Figure 1–20

3

- Type **Approximately 1.5 miles** and then press the ENTER key (Figure 1–21).

Figure 1–21

4

- Click the 'Decrease List Level' button (Home tab | Paragraph group) so that the second-level paragraph becomes a first-level paragraph (Figure 1–22).

Q&A Can I delete bullets on a slide?
Yes. If you do not want bullets to display in a particular paragraph, click the Bullets button (Home tab | Paragraph group) or right-click the paragraph and then click the Bullets button on the shortcut menu.

Figure 1–22

Other Ways

1. Press TAB to promote paragraph; press SHIFT+TAB to demote paragraph

To Type the Remaining Text for Slide 2

The following steps complete the text for Slide 2.

1 Type **9 a.m. every Saturday** and then press the ENTER key.

2 Click the 'Increase List Level' button (Home tab | Paragraph group) to demote the paragraph to the second level.

3 Type **Bring binoculars and a field guide** and then press the ENTER key to add a new paragraph at the same level as the previous paragraph.

4 Click the 'Increase List Level' button (Home tab | Paragraph group) to demote the paragraph to the third level.

5 Type **Extra supplies will be available** but do not press the ENTER key (Figure 1–23).

Q&A I pressed the ENTER key in error, and now a new bullet appears after the last entry on this slide. How can I remove this extra bullet?
Press the BACKSPACE key twice.

remaining text for slide

Figure 1–23

BTW
Automatic Spelling Correction
As you type, PowerPoint automatically corrects some misspelled words. For example, if you type availalbe, PowerPoint automatically corrects the misspelling and displays the word, available, when you press the SPACEBAR or type a punctuation mark. To see a complete list of automatically corrected words, click File on the ribbon to open the Backstage view, click the Options tab in the Backstage view, click Proofing in the left pane (PowerPoint Options dialog box), click the AutoCorrect Options button, and then scroll through the list near the bottom of the dialog box.

To Select a Group of Words

1 INSERT PRESENTATION SLIDES | 2 ENTER TEXT | 3 FORMAT TEXT | **4 INSERT GRAPHICAL ELEMENTS**
5 SIZE & POSITION | **6 ENHANCE SLIDE SHOW** | **7 DISPLAY SLIDES**

PowerPoint designers use many techniques to emphasize words and characters on a slide. To highlight the day of the week when the walks are held, you want to bold and increase the font size of the words, every Saturday, in the body text. The following steps select two words. **Why?** *You could perform these actions separately, but it is more efficient to select the words and then change the font attributes.*

1
- Position the pointer immediately to the left of the first character of the text to be selected (in this case, the e in the word, every) (Figure 1–24).

pointer

words to select

Figure 1–24

- Drag the pointer through the last character of the text to be selected (in this case, the y in the word, Saturday) (Figure 1–25).

Figure 1–25

Other Ways

1. Press CTRL+SHIFT+RIGHT ARROW repeatedly until desired words are selected

To Bold Text

1 INSERT PRESENTATION SLIDES | 2 ENTER TEXT | 3 FORMAT TEXT | 4 INSERT GRAPHICAL ELEMENTS

5 SIZE & POSITION | 6 ENHANCE SLIDE SHOW | 7 DISPLAY SLIDES

Why? Bold characters display somewhat thicker and darker than those that display in a regular font style. Clicking the Bold button on the mini toolbar is an efficient method of bolding text. To add more emphasis to the fact that the body needs nature for cooling purposes, you want to bold the words, every Saturday. The following step bolds this text.

- With the words, every Saturday, selected, click the Bold button on the mini toolbar to bold the two words (Figure 1–26).

Figure 1–26

Other Ways

1. Right-click selected text, click Font on shortcut menu, click Font tab (Font dialog box), click Bold in Font style list, click OK button

2. Select text, click Bold button (Home tab | Font group)

3. Click Font dialog box launcher (Home tab | Font group), click Font tab (Font dialog box), click Bold in Font style list, click OK button

4. Select text, press CTRL+B

To Increase Font Size

The following steps increase the font size from 24 to 28 point. *Why? To add emphasis, you increase the font size for the words, every Saturday.*

1 With the words, every Saturday, still selected, click the 'Increase Font Size' button on the mini toolbar once (Figure 1–27).

2 Click outside the selected area to deselect the two words.

Figure 1–27

Adding New Slides, Changing Slide Layouts, and Changing the Theme

Slide 3 in Figure 1–1c contains two pictures: a grasshopper and a dragonfly. Slide 4 in Figure 1–1d contains an illustration of a firefly and does not contain a bulleted list. When you add a new slide, PowerPoint applies the Title and Content layout. This layout and the Title Slide layout for Slide 1 are the default styles. A **layout** specifies the arrangement of placeholders on a slide. These placeholders are arranged in various configurations and can contain text, such as the slide title or a bulleted list, or they can contain content, such as SmartArt graphics, pictures, charts, tables, and shapes. The placement of the text, in relationship to content, depends on the slide layout. You can specify a particular slide layout when you add a new slide to a presentation or after you have created the slide.

Using the **layout gallery**, you can choose a slide layout. The nine layouts in this gallery have a variety of placeholders to define text and content positioning and formatting. Three layouts are for text: Title Slide, Section Header, and Title Only. Five are for text and content: Title and Content, Two Content, Comparison, Content with Caption, and Picture with Caption. The Blank layout has no placeholders. If none of these standard layouts meets your design needs, you can create a **custom layout**. A custom layout specifies the number, size, and location of placeholders, background content, and optional slide and placeholder-level properties.

When you change the layout of a slide, PowerPoint retains the text and objects and repositions them into the appropriate placeholders. Using slide layouts eliminates the need to resize objects and the font size because PowerPoint automatically sizes the objects and text to fit the placeholders. At any time when creating the slide content, you can change the theme and variant to give the presentation a different look and feel.

BTW

Customizing a Slide Layout

PowerPoint provides a wide variety of slide layouts for each theme, but you can customize the layouts to make your deck unique. Display the View tab, click Slide Master (View tab | Master Views group), select the thumbnail below the slide master in the left pane that you would like to customize, and then make the desired modifications.

To Add a New Slide and Enter a Slide Title and Headings

1 INSERT PRESENTATION SLIDES | 2 ENTER TEXT | 3 FORMAT TEXT | **4 INSERT GRAPHICAL ELEMENTS**

5 SIZE & POSITION | 6 ENHANCE SLIDE SHOW | 7 DISPLAY SLIDES

The text on Slide 3 in Figure 1–1c consists of a title and two headings. The appropriate layout for this slide is named Comparison. *Why?* *The Comparison layout has two headings and two text placeholders adjacent to each other, so an audience member easily can compare and contrast the items shown side by side.* The following steps add Slide 3 to the presentation with the Comparison layout and then enter the title and heading text for this slide.

1

- Click the New Slide arrow in the Slides group to display the Berlin layout gallery (Figure 1–28).

Figure 1–28

2

- Click Comparison to add Slide 3 and apply that layout (Figure 1–29).

Figure 1–29

- Type **Afternoon Insect Identification** in the title text placeholder.
- Click the left heading placeholder with the label, 'Click to add text', to select this placeholder (Figure 1–30).

Figure 1–30

- Type **Grasshoppers** and then press the ENTER key.
- Type **(also known as locusts)** but do not press the ENTER key.
- Select the right heading placeholder and then type **Dragonflies** and press the ENTER key.

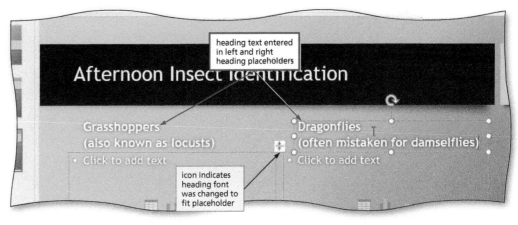

Figure 1–31

- Type **(often mistaken for damselflies)** but do not press the ENTER key (Figure 1–31).

Q&A What is the white box with the arrow between the placeholders?

The text is too large to fit in the placeholder using the default font and paragraph attributes, so PowerPoint adjusts the text so it displays properly. That icon informs you that the font was altered.

To Add a Slide with the Title Only Layout

1 INSERT PRESENTATION SLIDES | 2 ENTER TEXT | 3 FORMAT TEXT | **4 INSERT GRAPHICAL ELEMENTS**
5 SIZE & POSITION | 6 ENHANCE SLIDE SHOW | 7 DISPLAY SLIDES

The following steps add Slide 4 to the presentation with the Title Only slide layout style. *Why? The only text on the slide is the title, and the majority of the slide content is the illustration.*

- If necessary, click Home on the ribbon to display the Home tab.

- Click the New Slide arrow (Home tab | Slides group) to display the Berlin layout gallery (Figure 1–32).

Figure 1–32

- Click Title Only to add a new slide and apply that layout to Slide 4 (Figure 1–33).

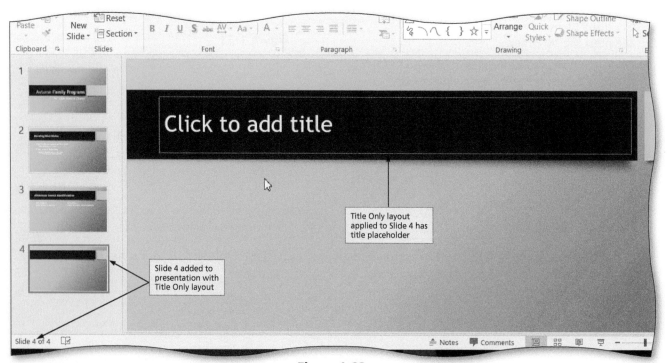

Figure 1–33

To Enter a Slide Title

The only text on Slide 4 is the title. The following step enters the title text for this slide.

1 Type **Twilight Firefly Hikes** as the title text but do not press the ENTER key (Figure 1–34).

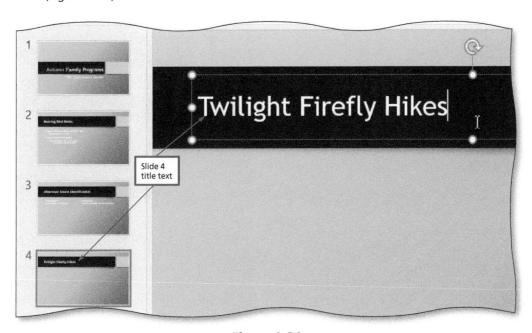

Figure 1–34

To Change the Theme

1 INSERT PRESENTATION SLIDES | 2 ENTER TEXT | 3 FORMAT TEXT | **4 INSERT GRAPHICAL ELEMENTS**
5 SIZE & POSITION | 6 ENHANCE SLIDE SHOW | 7 DISPLAY SLIDES

A theme provides consistency in design and color throughout the entire presentation by setting the color scheme, font set, and layout of a presentation. This collection of formatting choices includes a set of colors (the Theme Colors group), a set of heading and content text fonts (the Theme Fonts group), and a set of lines and fill effects (the Theme Effects group). These groups allow you to choose and change the appearance of all the slides or individual slides in your presentation. *Why? At any time while creating the slide deck, you may decide to switch the theme so that the slides have a totally different appearance.* The following steps change the theme for this presentation from Berlin to Main Event.

- Click Design on the ribbon to display the Design tab (Figure 1–35).

Figure 1–35

2

- Click the More button (Design tab | Themes group) to expand the gallery, which shows more theme gallery options. If necessary, scroll down to the bottom of the gallery to view the Main Event thumbnail (Figure 1–36).

Experiment

- Point to various document themes in the Themes gallery and watch the colors and fonts change on the title slide.

Figure 1–36

Q&A Are the themes displayed in a specific order?
No. Your themes might be in a different order than shown here.

How can I determine the theme names?
If you point to a theme, a ScreenTip with the theme's name appears on the screen.

3

- Click the Main Event theme to apply this theme to all four slides (Figure 1–37).

Q&A If I decide at some future time that this design does not fit the theme of my presentation, can I apply a different design?
Yes. You can repeat these steps at any time while creating your presentation.

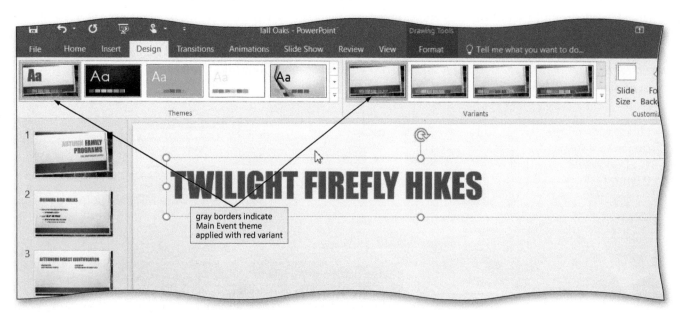

Figure 1–37

To Change the Variant

When you began creating this presentation, you selected the Berlin theme and then chose a green variant. You can change the color variation at any time for any theme. *Why? The new Main Event theme has a default red color, but you want to emphasize the green color associated with nature, just like you initially did when you chose the green variant for the Berlin theme.* The following steps change the variant from red to green.

- Point to the green variant (Design tab | Variants group) to see a preview of the green variant on Slide 4 (Figure 1–38).

🔍 **Experiment**

- Point to the orange, green, and blue variants and watch the colors change on the slide.

Figure 1–38

- Click the green variant to apply this color to all four slides (Figure 1–39).

Q&A If I decide at some future time that this color variation does not fit the theme of my presentation, can I apply a different variant?
Yes. You can repeat these steps at any time.

Figure 1–39

- Save the presentation again on the same storage location with the same file name.

Q&A Why should I save the presentation again?
You have made several modifications to the presentation since you last saved it. Thus, you should save it again.

Break Point: If you wish to take a break, this is a good place to do so. You can exit PowerPoint now. To resume at a later time, run PowerPoint, open the file called Tall Oaks, and continue following the steps from this location forward. For a detailed example of exiting PowerPoint, running PowerPoint, and opening a file, refer to the Office and Windows module at the beginning of the book.

PowerPoint Views

The PowerPoint window display varies depending on the view. A **view** is the mode in which the presentation appears on the screen. You will use some views when you are developing slides and others when you are delivering your presentation. When creating a presentation, you most likely will use Normal, Slide Sorter, Notes Pane, and Outline views. When presenting your slides to an audience, you most likely will use Slide Sorter, Presenter, and Reading views.

The default view is **Normal view**, which is composed of three areas that allow you to work on various aspects of a presentation simultaneously. The large area in the middle, called the **Slide pane**, displays the slide you currently are developing and allows you to enter text, tables, charts, graphics, pictures, video, and other elements. As you create the slides, miniature views of the individual slides, called thumbnails, are displayed in the **Slides tab** on the left of the screen. You can rearrange the thumbnails in this pane. The **Notes pane**, by default, is hidden at the bottom of the window. If you want to type notes to yourself or remarks to share with your audience, you can click the Notes button in the status bar to open the Notes pane. After you have created at least two slides, a **scroll bar** containing **scroll arrows** and **scroll boxes** will appear on the right edge of the window.

To Move to Another Slide in Normal View

1 INSERT PRESENTATION SLIDES | 2 ENTER TEXT | 3 FORMAT TEXT | **4 INSERT GRAPHICAL ELEMENTS**
5 SIZE & POSITION | **6 ENHANCE SLIDE SHOW** | **7 DISPLAY SLIDES**

Why? *When creating or editing a presentation in Normal view (the view you are currently using), you often want to display a slide other than the current one.* Before continuing with developing this project, you want to display the title slide. You can click the desired slide in the Slides tab or drag the scroll box on the vertical scroll bar; if you are using a touch screen, you can tap the desired slide in the Slides tab. When you drag the scroll box, the **slide indicator** shows the number and title of the slide you are about to display. Releasing shows the slide. The following steps move from Slide 4 to Slide 1 using the scroll box in the Slide pane.

- Position the pointer on the scroll box.

- Press and hold down the mouse button so that Slide: 4 of 4 Twilight Firefly Hikes appears in the slide indicator (Figure 1–40).

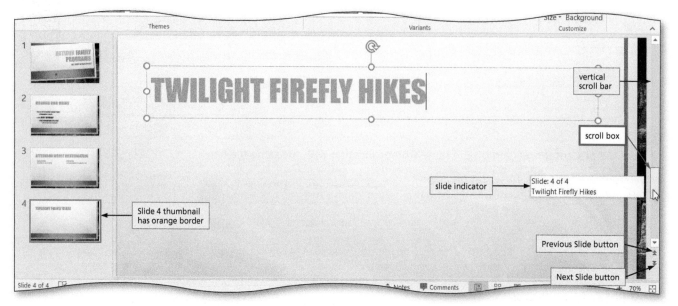

Figure 1–40

2

- Drag the scroll box up the vertical scroll bar until Slide: 1 of 4 Autumn Family Programs appears in the slide indicator (Figure 1–41).

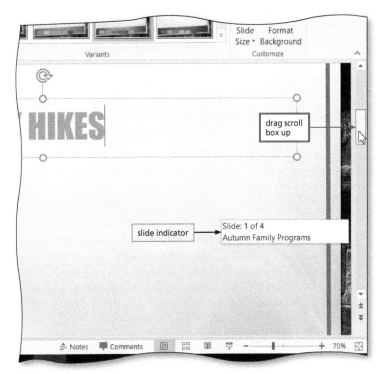

Figure 1–41

3

- Release so that Slide 1 appears in the Slide pane and the Slide 1 thumbnail has an orange border in the Slides tab (Figure 1–42).

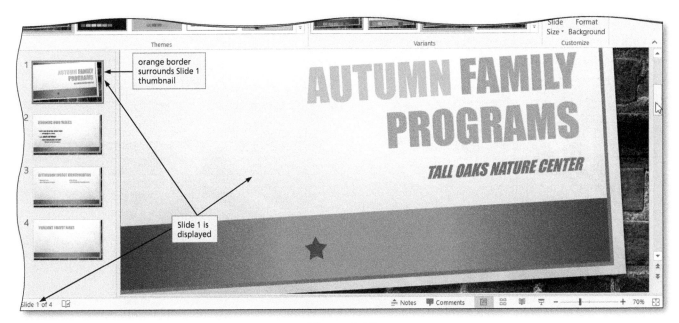

Figure 1–42

Other Ways

1. Click Next Slide button or Previous Slide button to move forward or back one slide

2. Click slide in Slides tab

3. Press PAGE DOWN or PAGE UP to move forward or back one slide

BTW
Microsoft Clip Organizer
Previous versions of Microsoft Office stored photos, illustrations, animations, videos, and other media in the Clip Organizer. Office 2016 has replaced this feature with the Insert Pictures dialog box, which is displayed when you click the Online Pictures button (Insert tab | Images group). You then can search for and insert files using Bing Image Search.

Inserting Pictures into Slides

Adding pictures can help increase the visual and audio appeal of many slides. These images may include photographs, illustrations, and other artwork. If you have a Microsoft account, you can add pictures from websites, including Flickr and OneDrive.

You can add pictures to your presentation in two ways. One way is by selecting one of the slide layouts that includes a content placeholder with a Pictures button. A second method is by clicking the Pictures button in the Images area on the Insert tab. Clicking the Pictures button opens the Insert Picture dialog box. The **Insert Picture dialog box** allows you to search for picture files that are stored on your computer or a storage device. Contact your instructor if you need the pictures used in the following steps.

CONSIDER THIS

How can you design a title slide that holds your audience's attention?

Develop a slide that reflects the content of your presentation but does so in a thought-provoking way. A title, at the very least, should prepare your audience for the material they are about to see and hear. Look for ways to focus attention on your theme and the method in which you plan to present this theme. A unique photograph or graphic can help generate interest. You may decide to introduce your topic with a startling fact, a rhetorical question, or a quotation. The device you choose depends upon your audience, the occasion, and the presentation's purpose.

To Insert a Picture into the Title Slide

1 INSERT PRESENTATION SLIDES | 2 ENTER TEXT | 3 FORMAT TEXT | **4 INSERT GRAPHICAL ELEMENTS**
5 SIZE & POSITION | 6 ENHANCE SLIDE SHOW | 7 DISPLAY SLIDES

Slide 1 uses the Title Slide layout, which has two placeholders for text but none for graphical content. You desire to place a graphic on Slide 1. *Why? It is likely that your viewers will see an image on this slide before they read any text, so you want to include a picture to create interest in the presentation and introduce your audience to the topic.* For this presentation, you will insert a photograph of several leaves that have changed colors. Later in this module, you will resize and position the picture in an appropriate location. The following steps add a picture to Slide 1.

1
- Click Insert on the ribbon to display the Insert tab.
- Click the Pictures button (Insert tab | Images group) to display the Insert Picture dialog box.

Q&A What should I do if no pictures are displayed when I click the Pictures button?
You may need to click the Online Pictures button instead of the Pictures button.

2
- Navigate to the Data Files and the Module 01 folder. Click the Autumn Leaves picture to select that file (Figure 1–43).

Q&A Why do I see only a list of file names and not thumbnails of the pictures in my folder?
Your view is different from the view shown in Figure 1–43.

Figure 1–43

3

- Click the Insert button (Insert Picture dialog box) to insert the picture into Slide 1 (Figure 1–44).

Q&A Can I double-click the picture or file name instead of selecting it and clicking the Insert button?
Yes. Either method inserts the picture.

Why is this picture displayed in this location on the slide?
The slide layout does not have a content placeholder, so PowerPoint inserts the file in an area of the slide. You will move and resize the picture later in this module.

Figure 1–44

To Insert a Picture into a Slide without a Content Placeholder

The next step is to add an owl picture to Slide 2. This slide has a bulleted list in the text placeholder, so the icon group does not display in the center of the placeholder. Later in this module, you will resize the inserted picture. The following steps add one picture to Slide 2.

1 Click the Slide 2 thumbnail in the Slides tab to display Slide 2.

2 Click Insert on the ribbon to display the Insert tab and then click the Pictures button (Insert tab | Images group) to display the Insert Picture dialog box.

3 If necessary, scroll down the list of files, click Owl to select the file, and then click the Insert button to insert the picture into Slide 2 (Figure 1–45).

Q&A Why is my picture a different size from the one shown in Figure1-1b?
The clip was inserted into the slide and not into a content placeholder. You will resize the picture later in this module.

BTW
Wrapping Text around a Photo
PowerPoint does not allow you to wrap text around a picture or other graphics, such as tables, shapes, and charts. This feature, however, is available in Word.

Figure 1–45

To Insert a Picture
into a Content Placeholder

Slide 3 uses the Comparison layout, which has a content placeholder below each of the two headings. You desire to insert pictures into both content placeholders. ***Why?*** *You want to display two insects that participants likely will identify during the program at the nature center.* The following steps insert a picture of a grasshopper into the left content placeholder and a dragonfly into the right content placeholder on Slide 3.

- Click the Slide 3 thumbnail in the Slides tab to display Slide 3 (Figure 1–46).

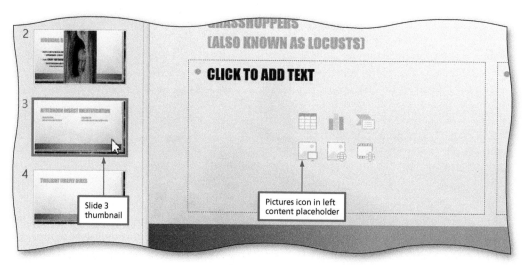

Figure 1–46

2

- Click the Pictures icon in the left content placeholder to select that placeholder and to open the Insert Picture dialog box.

- If necessary, scroll down the list of files, click Grasshopper to select the file, and then double-click to insert the picture into the left content placeholder (Figure 1–47).

Figure 1–47

Q&A Do I need to select the file name before double-clicking to insert the picture?

No. You just can double-click the file name.

3

- Click the Pictures icon in the right content placeholder to select that placeholder and to open the Insert Picture dialog box.

- If necessary, scroll down the list to display the Dragonfly file name and then insert this picture into the right content placeholder (Figure 1–48).

Skitter Photo/StockSnap.io

Figure 1–48

To Insert a Picture into a Slide without a Content Placeholder

Next, you will add a picture to Slide 4. This picture is an illustration, not an actual photograph, of a firefly. You will not insert this file into a content placeholder, so it will display in the center of the slide. Later in this module, you will resize this picture. You locate and insert illustrations in the same manner you used to insert photos. The following steps add an illustration picture to Slide 4.

1 Click the Slide 4 thumbnail in the Slides tab.

2 Display the Insert tab, click the Pictures button, and then insert the Firefly file into Slide 4 (Figure 1–49).

Figure 1–49

Break Point: If you wish to take a break, this is a good place to do so. You can save your presentation and then exit PowerPoint now. To resume at a later time, run PowerPoint, open the file called Tall Oaks, and continue following the steps from this location forward.

Resizing Photos and Illustrations

Sometimes it is necessary to change the size of pictures and illustrations. **Resizing** includes enlarging or reducing the size of a graphic. You can resize these images using a variety of techniques. One method involves changing the size of a picture by specifying exact dimensions in a dialog box. Another method involves sliding or dragging one of the graphic's sizing handles to the desired location. A selected graphic appears surrounded by a **selection rectangle**, which has small circles, called **sizing handles** or move handles, at each corner and middle location.

To Proportionally Resize Pictures

1 INSERT PRESENTATION SLIDES | 2 ENTER TEXT | 3 FORMAT TEXT | 4 INSERT GRAPHICAL ELEMENTS
5 SIZE & POSITION | **6 ENHANCE SLIDE SHOW** | **7 DISPLAY SLIDES**

Why? On Slides 1, 2, and 4, the picture and illustration sizes are too large to display aesthetically on the slides. At times it is important to maintain the proportions of a picture, such as when a person is featured prominently. To change the size of a picture and keep the width and height in proportion to each other, drag the corner sizing handles to view how the image will look on the slide. Using these corner handles maintains the graphic's original proportions. If, however, the proportions do not need to be maintained precisely, as with the owl picture on Slide 2, drag the side sizing handles to alter the proportions so that the graphic's height and width become larger or smaller. The following steps proportionally decrease the size of the Slide 1 picture using a corner sizing handle.

- Click the Slide 1 thumbnail in the Slides tab to display Slide 1.

- Click the leaves picture to select it and display the selection rectangle.

- Point to the lower-right corner sizing handle on the picture so that the pointer changes to a two-headed arrow (Figure 1–50).

Q&A I am using a touch screen and do not see a two-headed arrow when I press and hold the lower-right sizing handle. Why?
Touch screens may not display pointers; you can just press and slide sizing handles to resize.

Figure 1–50

2

- Drag the sizing handle diagonally toward the upper-left corner of the slide until the lower-right sizing handle or the crosshair is positioned approximately as shown in Figure 1–51.

Q&A What if the picture is not the same size as the one shown in Figure 1–51?
Repeat Steps 1 and 2.

Can I drag any corner sizing handle diagonally inward toward the opposite corner to resize the picture?
Yes.

Figure 1–51

3

- Release to resize the picture.

To Nonproportionally Resize the Photograph on Slide 2

1 INSERT PRESENTATION SLIDES | 2 ENTER TEXT | 3 FORMAT TEXT | 4 INSERT GRAPHICAL ELEMENTS

5 SIZE & POSITION | **6 ENHANCE SLIDE SHOW** | 7 DISPLAY SLIDES

Why? *The height of the owl picture in Slide 2 extends from the top to the bottom of the slide. The width, however, will cover some of the text when the picture is positioned on the right side of the slide.* The width of this picture can be decreased slightly without negatively distorting the original image. You can decrease the width of a picture by sliding or dragging one of the sizing handles on the sides of the image. The following steps resize the width of the nature bottle picture using a sizing handle along the side of the image.

1

- Display Slide 2 and then click the owl picture to select it and display the selection rectangle.

- Click the Zoom Out button as many times as necessary until the Zoom level is 50%.

- Point to the middle sizing handle on the bottom edge of the picture so that the pointer changes to a two-headed arrow (Figure 1–52).

Figure 1–52

- Drag the sizing handle upward until the sizing handle or crosshair is positioned on the top of the green bar, as shown in Figure 1–53.

Q&A What if the picture is not the same size as the one shown in Figure 1–53?
Repeat Steps 1 and 2.

Figure 1–53

- Release to resize the picture.
- Click outside the picture to deselect it (Figure 1–54).

Q&A What if I want to return the picture to its original size and start again?
With the picture selected, click the Reset Picture arrow (Picture Tools Format tab | Adjust group) and then click Reset Picture & Size in the Reset Picture gallery.

What happened to the Picture Tools Format tab?
When you click outside the picture, PowerPoint deselects the object and removes the Picture Tools Format tab from the screen.

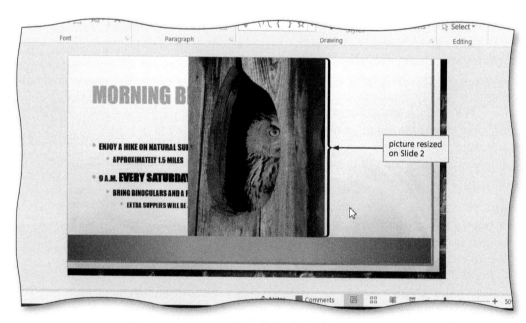

Figure 1–54

To Resize the Illustration on Slide 4

The firefly picture illustration on Slide 4 can be reduced slightly to fit entirely on the slide. You resize an illustration in the same manner that you resize a photograph. You want to maintain the proportions of the character and nature in this illustration, so you will drag one of the corner sizing handles. The following steps resize this illustration using a corner sizing handle.

1 Display Slide 4 and then click the firefly illustration to select it.

2 Drag any corner sizing handle on the illustration diagonally inward until the illustration is positioned and resized approximately as shown in Figure 1–55.

Figure 1–55

To Move Pictures

1 INSERT PRESENTATION SLIDES | 2 ENTER TEXT | 3 FORMAT TEXT | 4 INSERT GRAPHICAL ELEMENTS
5 SIZE & POSITION | **6 ENHANCE SLIDE SHOW** | 7 DISPLAY SLIDES

Why? After you insert a photo or an illustration on a slide, you might want to reposition it. The leaves picture on Slide 1 could be moved to the lower-left side of the slide, the owl on Slide 2 could be moved to the right side of the slide, and the illustration on Slide 4 could be positioned in the center of the slide. PowerPoint displays **Smart Guides** automatically when a picture, shape, or other object is moved and is close to lining up with another slide element. These layout guides, which display as dashed lines, help you align slide elements vertically and horizontally. They display when aligning to the left, right, top, bottom, and middle of placeholders and other objects on a slide. For example, a Smart Guide will display to help you align the right or left edge of a picture in relation to a text placeholder or to another picture. The following steps center the illustration on Slide 4 and move the pictures on Slides 2 and 1.

1

- If necessary, click the firefly illustration on Slide 4 to select it.

- With the four-headed arrow displaying, drag the illustration downward and toward the left until the horizontal Smart Guide is displayed under the title text placeholder and the vertical Smart Guide is displayed through the center of the slide, as shown in Figure 1–56, and then release.

- If necessary, select the illustration and then use the ARROW keys to position it precisely as shown in Figure 1–56.

 Q&A The firefly still is not located exactly where I want it to display. What can I do to align the image?
Press the CTRL key while you press the ARROW keys. This key combination moves the illustration in smaller increments than when you press only an ARROW key.

Figure 1–56

- Display Slide 2 and then click the owl picture to select it.
- Drag the picture downward and to the right until the horizontal Smart Guide is displayed above the title text placeholder and the right edge is aligned with the vertical gray bar on the right side of the slide (Figure 1–57).

Figure 1–57

- Display Slide 1 and then click the leaves picture to select it.
- Drag the picture downward until the horizontal Smart Guide is displayed under the title text placeholder and the vertical Smart Guide is displayed near the left side of the slide, as shown in Figure 1–58, and then release.

Can I move the picture in small increments?

Yes. To move or nudge the picture in very small increments, hold down the CTRL key with the picture selected while pressing the ARROW keys. You cannot perform this action using a touch screen.

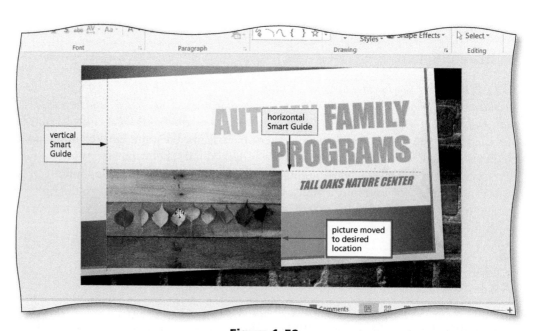

Figure 1–58

To Rotate a Picture

1 INSERT PRESENTATION SLIDES | 2 ENTER TEXT | 3 FORMAT TEXT | 4 INSERT GRAPHICAL ELEMENTS
5 SIZE & POSITION | 6 ENHANCE SLIDE SHOW | 7 DISPLAY SLIDES

Why? *The Main Event Title Slide layout is angled, so the picture would complement the design by being angled, too.* Dragging the **rotation handle** above a selected object allows you to rotate an object in any direction. The following steps rotate the leaves picture.

1
- With the leaves picture selected, position the mouse pointer over the rotation handle so that it changes to a Free Rotate pointer (Figure 1–59).

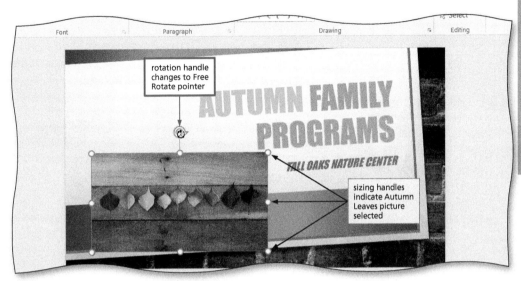

Figure 1–59

2
- Drag the rotation handle counterclockwise and then move the picture so that it is displayed as shown in Figure 1–60.

Figure 1–60

Ending a Slide Show with a Closing Slide

All the text for the slides in the Tall Oaks slide show has been entered. This presentation thus far consists of a title slide, one text slide with a multilevel bulleted list, a third slide with a Comparison layout, and a fourth slide for an illustration. A closing slide that resembles the title slide is the final slide to create.

What factors should you consider when developing a closing slide for the presentation?
After the last slide appears during a slide show, the default PowerPoint setting is to end the presentation with a **black slide**. This black slide appears only when the slide show is running and concludes the slide show, so your audience never sees the PowerPoint window. It is a good idea, however, to end your presentation with a final closing slide to display at the end of the presentation. This slide ends the presentation gracefully and should be an exact copy, or a very similar copy, of your title slide. The audience will recognize that the presentation is drawing to a close when this slide appears. It can remain on the screen when the audience asks questions, approaches the speaker for further information, or exits the room.

CONSIDER THIS

To Duplicate a Slide

Why? *When two slides contain similar information and have the same format, duplicating one slide and then making minor modifications to the new slide saves time and increases consistency.* Slide 5 will have the same layout and design as Slide 1. The most expedient method of creating this slide is to copy Slide 1 and then make minor modifications to the new slide. The following steps duplicate the title slide.

1

• With Slide 1 selected, click the New Slide arrow (Home tab | Slides group) to display the Main Event layout gallery (Figure 1–61).

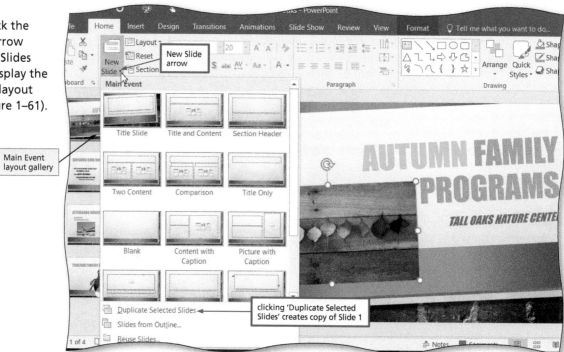

Figure 1–61

2

• Click 'Duplicate Selected Slides' in the Main Event layout gallery to create a new Slide 2, which is a duplicate of Slide 1 (Figure 1–62).

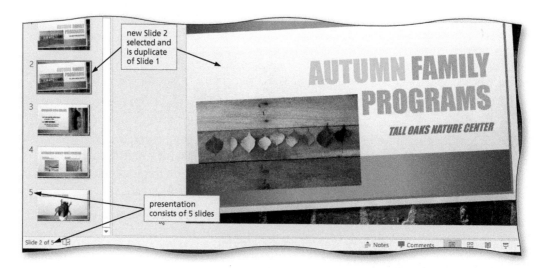

Figure 1–62

To Arrange a Slide

The new Slide 2 was inserted directly below Slide 1 because Slide 1 was the selected slide. This duplicate slide needs to display at the end of the presentation directly after the final title and content slide. *Why? It is a closing slide that reinforces the concept presented in Slide 1 and indicates to your audiences that your presentation is ending.*

Changing slide order is an easy process and is best performed in the Slides tab. When you click the thumbnail and begin to drag it to a new location, the remaining thumbnails realign to show the new sequence. When you release, the slide drops into the desired location. Hence, this process of sliding or dragging and then dropping the thumbnail in a new location is called **drag and drop**. You can use the drag-and-drop method to move any selected item, including text and graphics. The following step moves the new Slide 2 to the end of the presentation so that it becomes a closing slide.

- With Slide 2 selected, drag the Slide 2 slide thumbnail below the last slide in the Slides tab so that it becomes the new Slide 5 (Figure 1–63).

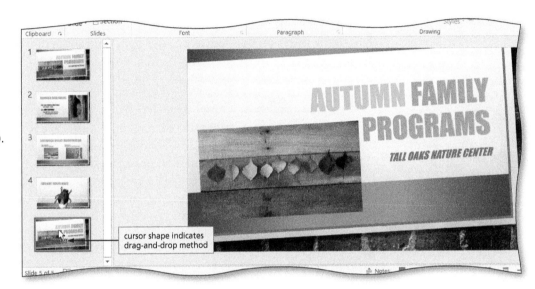

Figure 1–63

Other Ways

1. Click Slide Sorter button on status bar, drag thumbnail to new location

2. Click Slide Sorter button (View tab | Presentation Views group), click slide thumbnail, drag thumbnail to new location

Break Point: If you wish to take a break, this is a good place to do so. Be sure to save the Tall Oaks file again and then you can exit PowerPoint. To resume at a later time, run PowerPoint, open the file called Tall Oaks, and continue following the steps from this location forward.

Making Changes to Slide Text Content

After creating slides in a presentation, you may find that you want to make changes to the text. Changes may be required because a slide contains an error, the scope of the presentation shifts, or the style is inconsistent. This section explains the types of changes that commonly occur when creating a presentation.

You generally make three types of changes to text in a presentation: additions, replacements, and deletions.

- Additions are necessary when you omit text from a slide and need to add it later. You may need to insert text in the form of a sentence, word, or single character. For example, you may want to add the presenter's middle name on the title slide.

- Replacements are needed when you want to revise the text in a presentation. For example, you may want to substitute the word, *their*, for the word, *there*.

• Deletions are required when text on a slide is incorrect or no longer is relevant to the presentation. For example, a slide may look cluttered. Therefore, you may want to remove one of the bulleted paragraphs to add more space.

Editing text in PowerPoint basically is the same as editing text in a word processing program. The following sections illustrate the most common changes made to text in a presentation.

Replacing Text in an Existing Slide

When you need to correct a word or phrase, you can replace the text by selecting the text to be replaced and then typing the new text. As soon as you press any key on the keyboard, the selected text is deleted and the new text is displayed.

PowerPoint inserts text to the left of the insertion point. The text to the right of the insertion point moves to the right (and shifts downward if necessary) to accommodate the added text.

Deleting Text

You can delete text using one of many methods. One is to use the BACKSPACE key to remove text just typed. The second is to position the insertion point to the left of the text you want to delete and then press the DELETE key. The third method is to drag through the text you want to delete and then click the Cut button on the mini toolbar, press DELETE or BACKSPACE key, or press CTRL+X. Use the third method when deleting large sections of text.

To Delete Text in a Placeholder

1 INSERT PRESENTATION SLIDES | 2 ENTER TEXT | **3 FORMAT TEXT** | 4 INSERT GRAPHICAL ELEMENTS
5 SIZE & POSITION | 6 ENHANCE SLIDE SHOW | **7 DISPLAY SLIDES**

Why? *To keep the ending slide clean and simple, you want to edit a few words in the slide title and subtitle text.* The following steps change Autumn to Register For and then change Tall Oaks Nature Center to Call 555-8928 today! in the placeholders.

1

• With Slide 5 selected, position the pointer immediately to the left of the first character of the text to be selected in the title text placeholder (in this case, the A in the word, Autumn).

• Drag the pointer through the last character of the text to be selected (in this case, the n in the word, Autumn) (Figure 1–64).

Q&A Can I drag from left to right or right to left?
Yes. Either direction will select the letters.

Could I also have selected the word, Autumn, by double-clicking it?
Yes. Either method works to select a word.

Figure 1–64

2

- Press the DELETE key to delete the selected text.
- Type **Register for** as the first words in the title text placeholder (Figure 1–65).

Q&A Could I have typed these words while the word, Autumn, was selected without cutting the text first?
Yes. Either method works to replace words. You will use this alternate method in the next step.

Why does the text display with all capital letters despite the fact that I am typing uppercase and lowercase letters?
The Main Event theme uses the All Caps effect for the title and subtitle text. This effect converts lowercase letters to uppercase letters.

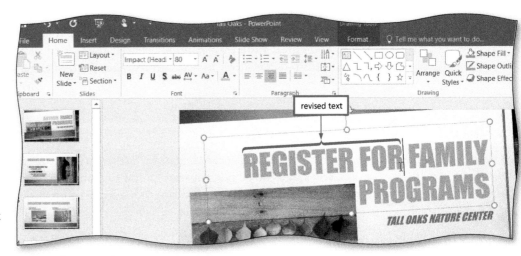

Figure 1–65

3

- Position the pointer anywhere in the subtitle text placeholder other than on the picture and then triple-click to select all the text, Tall Oaks Nature Center (Figure 1–66).

Figure 1–66

4

- Type **Call 816-555-8928 today!** as the new subtitle text (Figure 1-67).
- If requested by your instructor, change the last four digits of the phone number in the subtitle text placeholder, 8928, to the last four digits of your phone number.

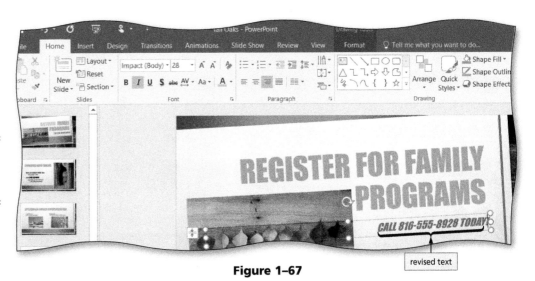

Figure 1–67

Other Ways

1. Right-click selected text, click Cut on shortcut menu | 2. Select text, press DELETE or BACKSPACE key | 3. Select text, press CTRL+X

Adding a Transition

PowerPoint includes a wide variety of visual and sound effects that can be applied to text or content. A **slide transition** is a special effect used to progress from one slide to the next in a slide show. You can control the speed of the transition effect and add a sound.

To Add a Transition between Slides

1 INSERT PRESENTATION SLIDES | 2 ENTER TEXT | 3 FORMAT TEXT | 4 INSERT GRAPHICAL ELEMENTS
5 SIZE & POSITION | 6 ENHANCE SLIDE SHOW | 7 DISPLAY SLIDES

Why? *Transitions add interest when you advance the slides in a presentation and make a slide show presentation look professional.* In this presentation, you apply the Wind transition in the Exciting category to all slides and change the transition speed from 2 seconds to 3 seconds. The following steps apply this transition to the presentation.

- Click the Transitions tab on the ribbon and then point to the More button (Transitions tab | Transition to This Slide group) in the Transition to This Slide gallery (Figure 1–68).

Q&A Is a transition applied now?
No. None, the first slide icon in the Transition to This Slide group, is selected, which indicates no transition has been applied.

Figure 1–68

- Click the More button to expand the Transitions gallery.
- Point to the Wind transition in the Exciting category in the Transitions gallery (Figure 1–69).

Figure 1–69

3

- Click Wind in the Exciting category in the Transitions gallery to view a preview of this transition and to apply this transition to the closing slide.

Q&A Why does a star appear next to Slide 5 in the Slides tab? The star indicates that a transition animation effect is applied to that slide.

- Click the Duration up arrow (Transitions tab | Timing group) four times to change the transition speed from 02.00 seconds to 03.00 seconds (Figure 1–70).

Figure 1–70

Q&A Why did the time change from the default 02.00 to 03.00?
Each transition has a default duration time. The default Wind transition time is 02.00 seconds.

4

- Click the Preview Transitions button (Transitions tab | Preview area) to view the transition and the new transition time (Figure 1–71).

Q&A Can I adjust the duration time I just set?
Yes. Click the Duration up or down arrows or type a speed in the Duration box and preview the transition until you find the time that best fits your presentation.

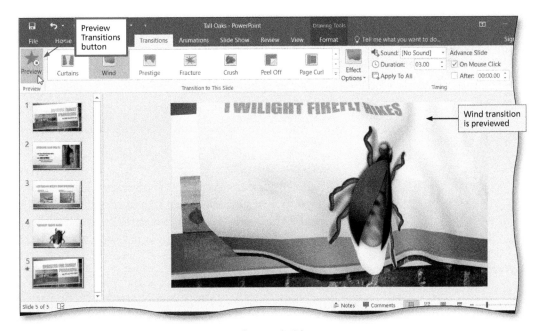

Figure 1–71

5

- Click the 'Apply To All' button (Transitions tab | Timing group) to apply the Wind transition and the increased transition time to Slides 1 through 4 in the presentation (Figure 1–72).

Q&A What if I want to apply a different transition and duration to each slide in the presentation? Repeat Steps 2 and 3 for each slide individually.

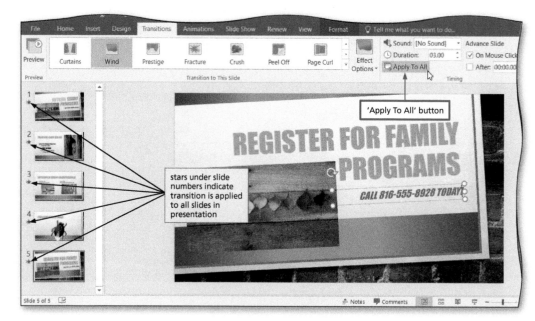

'Apply To All' button

stars under slide numbers indicate transition is applied to all slides in presentation

Figure 1–72

Document Properties

PowerPoint helps you organize and identify your files by using **document properties**, which are the details about a file such as the project author, title, and subject. For example, a class name or presentation topic can describe the file's purpose or content.

Why would you want to assign document properties to a presentation?

Document properties are valuable for a variety of reasons:

- Users can save time locating a particular file because they can view a file's document properties without opening the presentation.

- By creating consistent properties for files having similar content, users can better organize their presentations.

- Some organizations require PowerPoint users to add document properties so that other employees can view details about these files.

The more common document properties are standard and automatically updated properties. **Standard properties** are associated with all Microsoft Office files and include author, title, and subject. **Automatically updated properties** include file system properties, such as the date you create or change a file, and statistics, such as the file size.

BTW

Printing Document Properties

PowerPoint 2016 does not allow you to print document properties. This feature, however, is available in other Office 2016 apps, including Word and Excel.

TO CHANGE DOCUMENT PROPERTIES

To change document properties, you would follow these steps.

1. Click File on the ribbon to open the Backstage view and then, if necessary, click the Info tab in the Backstage view to display the Info gallery.

2. If the property you wish to change is displayed in the Properties list in the right pane of the Info gallery, try to click that property. If a text box with that property is displayed, type the text for the property in the box, and then click the Back button in the upper-left corner of the Backstage view to return to the PowerPoint window. Skip the remaining steps.

3. If the property you wish to change is not displayed in the Properties list in the right pane of the Info gallery or you cannot change it in the Info gallery, click the Properties button in the right pane to display the Properties menu, and then click Advanced Properties on the Properties menu to display the Summary tab in the Properties dialog box.

Q&A Why are some of the document properties in my Document Information Panel already filled in?
The person who installed Office 2016 on your computer or network may have set or customized the properties.

4. Type the desired text in the appropriate property boxes.

5. Click the OK button (Properties dialog box) to close the dialog box

6. Click the Back button in the upper-left corner of the Backstage view to return to the PowerPoint presentation window.

BTW
PowerPoint Help
At any time while using PowerPoint, you can find answers to questions and display information about various topics through PowerPoint Help. Used properly, this form of assistance can increase your productivity and reduce your frustrations by minimizing the time you spend learning how to use PowerPoint. For instructions about PowerPoint Help and exercises that will help you gain confidence in using it, read the Office and Windows module at the beginning of this book.

Viewing the Presentation in Slide Show View

The 'Start From Beginning' button, located in the Quick Access Toolbar, allows you to show a presentation using a computer. As the name implies, the first slide to be displayed always will be Slide 1. You also can run a presentation starting with the slide currently displaying when you click the Slide Show button on the status bar. In either case, PowerPoint displays the slides on the full screen without any of the PowerPoint window objects, such as the ribbon. The full-screen slide hides the toolbars, menus, and other PowerPoint window elements.

To Start Slide Show View

1 INSERT PRESENTATION SLIDES | 2 ENTER TEXT | 3 FORMAT TEXT | 4 INSERT GRAPHICAL ELEMENTS
5 SIZE & POSITION | 6 ENHANCE SLIDE SHOW | **7 DISPLAY SLIDES**

Why? *You run a presentation for your audience so they can see the slides in their entirety and view any transitions or other effects added to the slides.* When making a presentation, you use **Slide Show view**. You can start Slide Show view from Normal view or Slide Sorter view. Slide Show view begins when you click the 'Start From Beginning' button or the Slide Show button. The following steps start Slide Show view starting with Slide 1.

• Point to the 'Start From Beginning' button (Figure 1–73).

Q&A What would have displayed if I had clicked the Slide Show button instead of the 'Start From Beginning' button?
When you click the Slide Show button to start the presentation, PowerPoint begins the show with the currently displayed slide, which in this case is Slide 5. Only Slide 5 would display during the slide show.

Figure 1–73

- Click the 'Start From Beginning' button to display the transition and the title slide (Figure 1–74).

Q&A Where is the PowerPoint window? When you run a slide show, the PowerPoint window is hidden. It will reappear once you end your slide show.

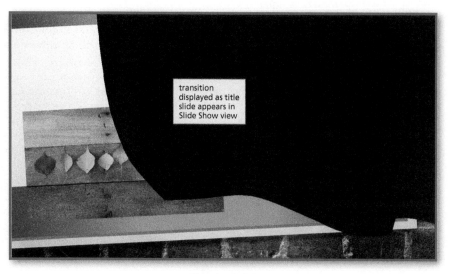

transition displayed as title slide appears in Slide Show view

Figure 1–74

Other Ways

1. Display Slide 1, click Slide Show button on status bar	2. Click 'Start From Beginning' button (Slide Show tab | Start Slide Show group)	3. Press F5

To Move Manually through Slides in a Slide Show

1 INSERT PRESENTATION SLIDES | 2 ENTER TEXT | 3 FORMAT TEXT | 4 INSERT GRAPHICAL ELEMENTS
5 SIZE & POSITION | 6 ENHANCE SLIDE SHOW | **7 DISPLAY SLIDES**

After you begin Slide Show view, you can move forward or backward through the slides. PowerPoint allows you to advance through the slides manually or automatically. During a slide show, each slide in the presentation shows on the screen, one slide at a time. Each time you click, the next slide appears. The following steps move manually through the slides. *Why? You can control the length of time each slide is displayed and change the preset order if you need to review a slide already shown or jump ahead to another slide designed to display later in the presentation.*

- Click each slide until Slide 5 (Register for Family Programs) is displayed (Figure 1–75).

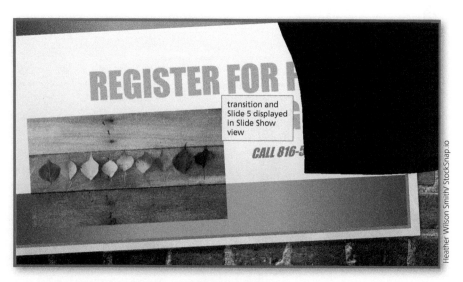

REGISTER FOR F

transition and Slide 5 displayed in Slide Show view

CALL 816-5

Heather Wilson Smith/ StockSnap.io

Figure 1–75

• Click Slide 5 so that the black slide appears with a message announcing the end of the slide show (Figure 1–76).

Q&A I see a small toolbar in the lower-left corner of my slide. What is this toolbar?

You may see the Slide Show toolbar when you begin running a slide show and then click a slide or move the pointer. The buttons on this toolbar allow you to navigate to the next slide or the previous slide, to mark up the current slide, or to change the current display. If you do not see the toolbar, hover the mouse near the lower-left corner of the screen.

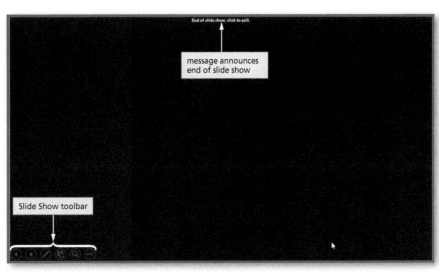

Figure 1–76

❸

• Click the black slide to return to Normal view in the PowerPoint window.

Other Ways

1. Press PAGE DOWN to advance one slide at a time, or press PAGE UP to go back one slide at a time

2. Press RIGHT ARROW or DOWN ARROW to advance one slide at a time, or press LEFT ARROW or UP ARROW to go back one slide at a time

3. If Slide Show toolbar is displayed, click Next Slide or Previous Slide button on toolbar

---

To Save and Print the Presentation

It is a good practice to save a presentation before printing it, in the event you experience difficulties printing. For a detailed example of the procedure summarized below for saving and printing a presentation, refer to the Office and Windows module at the beginning of this book.

❶ Save the presentation again on the same storage location with the same file name.

❷ Print the presentation.

Q&A Do I have to wait until my presentation is complete to print it?

No, you can print a presentation at any time while you are creating it.

❸ Because the project now is complete, you can exit PowerPoint.

BTW
Conserving Ink and Toner
If you want to conserve ink or toner, you can instruct PowerPoint to print draft quality documents by clicking File on the ribbon to open the Backstage view, clicking the Options tab in the Backstage view to display the PowerPoint Options dialog box, clicking Advanced in the left pane (PowerPoint Options dialog box), scrolling to the Print area in the right pane, not placing a check mark in the High quality check box, and then clicking the OK button. Then, use the Backstage view to print the document as usual.

BTW
Distributing a Document
Instead of printing and distributing a hard copy of a document, you can distribute the document electronically. Options include sending the document via email; posting it on cloud storage (such as OneDrive) and sharing the file with others; posting it on social media, a blog, or other website; and sharing a link associated with an online location of the document. You also can create and share a PDF or XPS image of the document, so that users can view the file in Acrobat Reader or XPS Viewer instead of in PowerPoint.

Summary

In this module, you learned how to use PowerPoint to create and enhance a presentation. Topics covered included applying and changing a document theme and variant, creating a title slide and text slides with a bulleted list, inserting pictures and then resizing and moving them on a slide, formatting and editing text, adding a slide transition, and viewing the presentation in Slide Show view.

CONSIDER THIS: PLAN AHEAD

What decisions will you need to make when creating your next presentation?
Use these guidelines as you complete the assignments in this module and create your own slide show decks outside of this class.

1. Determine the content you want to include on your slides.

2. Determine which theme and variant are appropriate.

3. Identify the slide layouts that best communicate your message.

4. Format various text elements to emphasize important points.

    a) Select appropriate font sizes.

    b) Emphasize important words with bold or italic type and color.

5. Locate graphical elements, such as pictures, that reinforce your message.

    a) Size and position them aesthetically on slides.

6. Determine a storage location for the presentation.

7. Determine the best method for distributing the presentation.

Apply Your Knowledge

Reinforce the skills and apply the concepts you learned in this module.

Modifying Character Formats and Paragraph Levels and Moving an Illustration

Note: To complete this assignment, you will be required to use the Data Files. Please contact your instructor for information about accessing the Data Files.

Instructions: Run PowerPoint. Open the presentation called Apply 1-1 Email Fraud, which is located in the Data Files.

The two slides in the presentation discuss phishing, which is a scam in which a perpetrator attempts to obtain an individual's personal and/or financial information. The document you open is an unformatted presentation. You are to modify the document theme, indent the paragraphs, resize and move the image, and format the text so the slides look like Figure 1–77.

Perform the following tasks:

1. Change the document theme to Droplet. Select the blue (third) variant.
2. On the title slide, use your name in place of Student Name and bold and italicize your name.
3. If requested by your instructor, change your first name to your grandmother's first name on the title slide.
4. Increase the title text font size to 60 point and then bold this text. Resize and position the illustration using the Smart Guides to align the image with the bottom of the subtitle placeholder and the right edge of the placeholders, as shown in Figure 1–77a.
5. On Slide 2, increase the indent of the second, third, and fourth paragraphs to second-level paragraphs. Then combine paragraphs six and seven (Work related and Personal) to read, **Work and personal messages can contain threats**, as shown in Figure 1–77b. Increase the indent of this paragraph to second level.

(a) Slide 1 (Title Slide with a Picture)

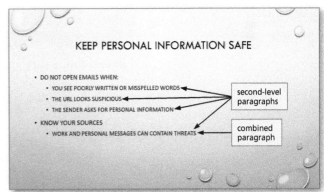

(b) Slide 2 (Multilevel Bulleted List)

Figure 1–77

6. Apply the Ripple transition in the Exciting category to both slides. Change the duration to 3.00 seconds. Click the 'Start From Beginning' button to start the show from the first slide. Then click to display each slide and again to end the presentation.

Continued >

Apply Your Knowledge *continued*

7. Save the presentation using the file name, Apply 1-1 Phishing.

8. Submit the revised document in the format specified by your instructor.

9. ✳ In Step 5 you combined two paragraphs and added text. How did this action improve the slide content?

Extend Your Knowledge

Extend the skills you learned in this module and experiment with new skills. You may need to use Help to complete the assignment.

Changing Slide Theme, Layout, and Text

Note: To complete this assignment, you will be required to use the Data Files. Please contact your instructor for information about accessing the Data Files.

Instructions: Run PowerPoint. Open the presentation called Extend 1-1 Waterfalls, which is located in the Data Files. Slide 1 is shown in Figure 1-78. You are aware that geologists have classified many types of waterfalls, including cascade and cataract, and the three slides in this file are part of a presentation you are developing for your geology class on this topic. Choose a theme, format the slides, and create a closing slide.

Perform the following tasks:

1. Change the document theme to Slice and the variant to green.

2. On Slide 1, format the text using techniques you learned in this module, such as changing the font size and color and bolding and italicizing words.

3. Replace the text, Student Name, with your name. In addition, delete the bullet preceding your name because, in most cases, a bullet is displayed as the first character in a list consisting of several paragraphs, not just one line of text. To delete the bullet, position the insertion point in the paragraph and then click the Bullets button (Home tab | Paragraph group).

4. Resize the picture and move it to an appropriate area on the slide.

5. On Slide 2, add bullets to the three paragraphs. To add bullets, select the paragraphs and then click the Bullets button (Home tab | Paragraph group). Insert the picture called Cascade, which is located in the Data Files, resize it, and then move it to an appropriate area on the slide.

6. On Slide 3, add bullets to the two paragraphs. Insert the picture called Cataract, which is located in the Data Files, resize it, and then move it to an appropriate area on the slide.

7. Create a closing slide using the title slide as a guide. Change the subtitle text to Natural Wonders and then underline this text. Insert the two waterfall pictures, Cascade and Cataract, and then size and move all three pictures to appropriate places on the slide.

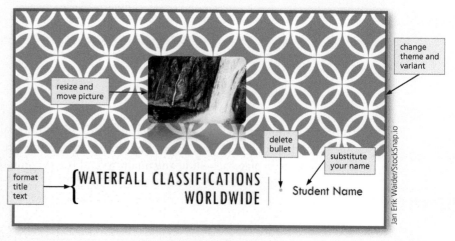

Figure 1–78

8. Apply the Drape transition in the Exciting category to all slides and then change the duration for Slide 1 to 3.50 seconds. Click the 'Start From Beginning' button to start the show from the first slide. Then click to display each slide and again to end the presentation.

9. Save the presentation using the file name, Extend 1-1 Natural Wonders.

10. Submit the revised document in the format specified by your instructor.

11. If requested by your instructor, replace your last name on Slide 1 with the name of your hometown.

12. ✸ How did you determine the appropriate size and location of the three pictures on the closing slide?

Expand Your World

Create a solution that uses cloud and web technologies by learning and investigating on your own from general guidance.

Modifying and Exporting a Presentation

Note: To complete this assignment, you will be required to use the Data Files. Please contact your instructor for information about accessing the Data Files.

Instructions: Run PowerPoint. Open the presentation called Expand 1-1 Youth Group, which is located in the Data Files. The local youth group in your community is sponsoring a talent show, and you are part of a committee to publicize the event. You want to share the one slide you developed with some of the participants, so you have decided to store the file on OneDrive. You are going to modify the slide you have created, shown in Figure 1–79, and save it to OneDrive.

Perform the following tasks:

1. Insert the pictures called Musician and Singers, which are located in the Data Files. Size and then move them to the areas indicated in Figure 1–79. Use the guides to help you position the pictures.

2. If requested to do so by your instructor, change the words, Phoenix, AZ, to the town and state where you were born.

3. Save the presentation using the file name, Expand 1-1 Talent Show.

4. Export the file to your OneDrive account.

5. Submit the assignment in the format specified by your instructor.

6. ✸ When would you save one of your files for school or your job to OneDrive? Do you think using OneDrive enhances collaboration efforts? Why?

Figure 1–79

In the Labs

Design, create, modify, and/or use a presentation following the guidelines, concepts, and skills presented in this module. Labs 1 and 2, which increase in difficulty, require you to create solutions based on what you learned in the module; Lab 3 requires you to apply your creative thinking and problem-solving skills to design and implement a solution.

Lab 1: **Creating a Presentation with Pictures**

Note: To complete this assignment, you will be required to use the Data Files. Please contact your instructor for information about accessing the Data Files.

Problem: Your friend, Bobby, has expanded her Bake Shoppe and wants to publicize new offerings. She has asked you to help her create a presentation that showcases pastries and breads. You prepare the PowerPoint presentation shown in Figure 1–80.

Perform the following tasks:

1. Run PowerPoint. Create a new presentation using the Retrospect document theme. Do not change the variant.

2. Using Figure 1–80a, create the title slide. Type the title text and subtitle text shown in the figure. Decrease the font size of the title text to 60 point and bold this text. Change the font color to Orange, Accent 1 (in Theme Colors row).

(a) Slide 1 (Title Slide)

(b) Slide 2

(c) Slide 3

(d) Slide 4 (Closing Slide)

Figure 1–80

3. On Slide 1, insert the illustration called Bakery, which is located in the Data Files. Move the illustration up to the top of the slide and then use the Smart Guides to align its left and right edges with the sides of the text placeholders. Use the lower-center sizing handle to resize this illustration so that it fits above the title text.

4. Replace the words, Anytown, USA, with your hometown city and state.

5. Create Slide 2 using the Title Only layout. Type the title text, Fresh Daily, bold this text, and then change the font color to Orange, Accent 1 (in Theme Colors row). Insert the picture called Doughnut, which is located in the Data Files, resize it as shown in Figure 1–80b, and then move it to the left side of the slide. Insert the picture called Muffin, which is located in the Data Files, and then resize and move it to the right side of the slide, as shown in the figure.

6. Using Figure 1–80c as a guide, create Slide 3 using the Picture with Caption layout. Insert the picture called Bread, which is located in the Data Files. Type the title text, Artisan Breads, increase the font size to 48 point, and then bold this text. Type `All natural ingredients` as the subtitle text, press the Tab key four times, and then type `No preservatives` in the placeholder. Increase this subtitle text size to 28 point.

7. Create a closing slide by duplicating Slide 1. Change the subtitle text using Figure 1–80d as a guide.

8. Apply the Clock transition in the Exciting category to all slides. Change the duration to 2.00 seconds.

9. Click the 'Start From Beginning' button to start the show from the first slide. Then click to display each slide and again to end the presentation.

10. Save the presentation using the file name, Lab 1-1 Bake. Submit the document in the format specified by your instructor.

11. ⊛ What is the significance of changing the font color on Slides 1 and 2 but not Slide 3?

Lab 2: **Creating a Presentation with Bulleted Lists and Pictures**

Note: To complete this assignment, you will be required to use the Data Files. Please contact your instructor for information about accessing the Data Files.

Problem: The history museum in your town is a popular destination for residents, tourists, and researchers. Among the more popular exhibits are the dinosaurs, mummies, and antiques. You want to highlight these three attractions, so you create the presentation shown in Figure 1–81.

Perform the following tasks:

1. Run PowerPoint. Create a new presentation using the Quotable document theme.

2. Using Figure 1–81, create the title slide. Use your name in place of Student Name.

3. If requested by your instructor, substitute the name of your hometown in place of your last name.

4. On Slide 1 (Figure 1–81a), italicize the text, History Museum. Increase the font size of the subtitle text, Popular Exhibits, to 32 point and the font size of your name to 24 point. Change the font color of the title text to Dark Blue (in Standard Colors row).

5. Create the three slides shown in Figures 1-81b, 1-81c, and 1-81d. Use the Comparison layout for Slide 2, the Section Header layout for Slide 3, and the Two Content layout for Slide 4. Change the color of the title text on these three text slides to Dark Blue. Increase the font size of the subtitle text on Slides 2 and 3 to 24 point.

Continued >

In the Labs *continued*

(a) Slide 1 (Title Slide)

(b) Slide 2

(c) Slide 3

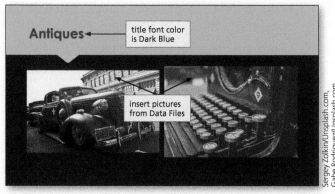

(d) Slide 4

Sergey Zolkin/Unsplash.com, Gabe Rodriguez/Unsplash.com

Figure 1–81

6. Add the pictures shown in Figures 1-81a through 1-81d using the guides on Slides 1 and 3 to help align them. The pictures to be inserted are called Museum Icon, Girls in Museum, T-rex Skeleton, T-rex 3D, Pharaoh, Car, and Typewriter, and they are located in the Data Files. Zoom the slides and then resize the pictures when necessary.

7. Apply the Gallery transition in the Exciting category to all slides. Change the duration to 2.25 seconds.

8. Click the 'Start From Beginning' button to start the show from the first slide. Then click to display each slide and again to end the presentation.

9. Save the presentation using the file name, Lab 1-2 History Museum.

10. Submit the revised document in the format specified by your instructor.

11. ✳ How does changing the title text font color to Dark Blue complement the theme color?

Lab 3: **Consider This: Your Turn**

Design and Create a Presentation about the Building Construction Technology Program

Note: To complete this assignment, you will be required to use the Data Files. Please contact your instructor for information about accessing the Data Files.

Part 1: Your school is expanding the courses offered in the Building Construction Technology Program, and the department chair has asked you to help promote the program. He informs you that students obtain hands-on experience using the latest methods of construction, and they receive instruction in the classroom and in the lab. The capstone courses are held in the field, where students build an actual energy-efficient home from the ground up. The skills learned and experience gained prepare students for careers in carpentry, masonry, plumbing, electrical, project supervision, cost estimating, and drafting. Use the concepts and techniques presented in this module to prepare a presentation with a minimum of four slides that showcase the Building Construction Technology program. Select a suitable theme, and include a title slide, bulleted list, closing slide, and transition. The presentation should contain pictures and illustrations resized appropriately. Several pictures are available in the Data Files: Backhoe, Concrete, Hammer, Hard Hat, Measuring Tape, Nail, and Tool Belt. Review and revise your presentation as needed. Submit your assignment in the format specified by your instructor.

Part 2: ✷ You made several decisions while creating the presentation in this assignment: what theme to use, where to place text, how to format the text (font, font size, paragraph alignment, bulleted paragraphs, italics, bold, color). You decided which images to use and where to position them. You also chose a transition. What was the rationale behind each of these decisions? When you reviewed the slides, what further revisions did you make and why? Where would you recommend showing this slide show?

2 | Enhancing a Presentation with Pictures, Shapes, and WordArt

Objectives

You will have mastered the material in this module when you can:

- Search for and download an online theme
- Insert and format pictures
- Insert and size a shape
- Apply effects to a shape
- Add text to a shape

- Change the text font
- Insert a picture to create a background
- Insert and format WordArt
- Format slide backgrounds
- Find and replace text and check spelling
- Add and print speaker notes

Introduction

In our visually oriented culture, audience members enjoy viewing effective graphics. Whether reading a document or viewing a PowerPoint presentation, people increasingly want to see photographs, artwork, graphics, and a variety of typefaces. Researchers have known for decades that documents with visual elements are more effective than those that consist of only text because the illustrations motivate audiences to study the material. People remember at least one-third more information when the document they are seeing or reading contains visual elements. These graphics help clarify and emphasize details, so they appeal to audience members with differing backgrounds, reading levels, attention spans, and motivations.

Project — Presentation with Pictures, Shapes, and WordArt

The project in this module focuses on publicizing a basketball camp held each summer for children living in the park district. Professionals teach boys and girls a variety of offensive and defensive skills during this fun and educational event. The presentation shown in Figure 2–1 follows graphical guidelines and has a variety of illustrations and visual elements that are colorful and appealing to child athletes and their parents. For example, the pictures have particular shapes and effects. The enhanced type has a style that blends well with the formatted background and illustrations. Pictures and type are formatted using picture styles and WordArt, which give the presentation a professional look. You plan to present the material during winter and spring sports tournaments, so you want to add notes explaining concepts you will be discussing during these events.

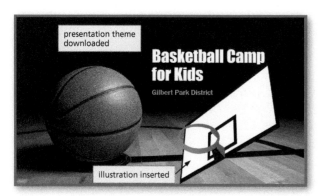

(a) Slide 1 (Title Slide)

(b) Slide 2 (Formatted Picture)

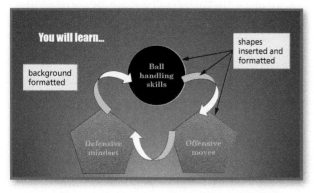

(c) Slide 3 (Shapes Inserted and Formatted)

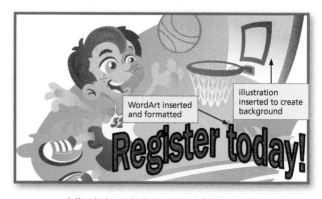

(d) Slide 4 (Picture Background)

Figure 2–1

For an introduction to Windows and instructions about how to perform basic Windows tasks, read the Office and Windows module at the beginning of this book, where you can learn how to resize windows, change screen resolution, create folders, move and rename files, use Windows Help, and much more.

In this module, you will learn how to create the slides shown in Figure 2–1. The following roadmap identifies general activities you will perform as you progress through this module:

1. DOWNLOAD a theme and SELECT SLIDES for the presentation.
2. INSERT and FORMAT PICTURES for the slides.
3. INSERT and FORMAT SHAPES on one slide.
4. FORMAT SLIDE BACKGROUNDS with a gradient, texture, and picture fill.
5. INSERT and FORMAT WORDART by changing the shape, fill, and outline.
6. REVIEW, REVISE, and PRINT SLIDES by finding a synonym, checking spelling, and adding speaker notes.

Downloading a Theme and Editing Slides

In Module 1, you selected a theme and then typed the content for the title and text slides. In this module, you will type the slide content for the title and text slides, select a background, insert and format pictures and shapes, and then insert and format WordArt. To begin creating the four slides in this presentation, you will download a theme, delete unneeded slides in this downloaded presentation, and then enter text in three of the four slides.

To Search for and Download an Online Theme

1 DOWNLOAD & SELECT SLIDES | 2 INSERT & FORMAT PICTURES | 3 INSERT & FORMAT SHAPES
4 FORMAT SLIDE BACKGROUNDS | 5 INSERT & FORMAT WORDART | 6 REVIEW, REVISE, & PRINT SLIDES

PowerPoint displays many themes that are varied and appealing and give you an excellent start at designing a presentation. At times, however, you may have a specific topic and design concept and could use some assistance in starting to develop the presentation. Microsoft offers hundreds of predesigned themes and templates that could provide you with an excellent starting point. *Why? You can search for one of these ready-made presentations, or you can browse one of the predefined categories, such as business and education. The themes and templates can save you time and help you develop content.* The following steps search for a theme with a basketball concept.

- Run PowerPoint and then type `basketball` in the 'Search for online templates and themes' box (Figure 2–2).

Q&A Why are my theme thumbnails displaying in a different order?
The order changes as you choose themes for presentations. In addition, Microsoft occasionally adds and modifies the themes, so the order may change.

Can I choose one of the keywords listed below the 'Search for online templates and themes' box?
Yes. Click one of the terms in the Suggested searches list to display a variety of templates and themes relating to those topics.

Figure 2–2

- Click the Start searching button (the magnifying glass) or press the ENTER key to search for and display all themes with the keyword, basketball.

- Click the 'Basketball presentation (widescreen)' theme to display a theme preview dialog box with a thumbnail view of the theme (Figure 2–3).

Figure 2–3

Q&A Can I see previews of the slides in this theme?
Yes. Click the right or left arrows beside the words, More Images, below the thumbnail. On some devices, a preview of all slides starts automatically after you tap the theme.

- Click the Create button to download the theme and open a presentation with that theme in PowerPoint.

To Delete a Slide

1 DOWNLOAD & SELECT SLIDES | 2 INSERT & FORMAT PICTURES | 3 INSERT & FORMAT SHAPES
4 FORMAT SLIDE BACKGROUNDS | 5 INSERT & FORMAT WORDART | 6 REVIEW, REVISE, & PRINT SLIDES

The downloaded theme has nine slides with a variety of layouts. You will use four different layouts in your Basketball Camp presentation, so you can delete the slides you downloaded that you will not need. *Why? Deleting the extra slides now helps reduce clutter and helps you focus on the layouts you will use.* The following steps delete the extra slides.

- Click the Slide 3 thumbnail in the Slides tab to select this slide.

- Press and hold the SHIFT key, scroll down, and then click the thumbnail for Slide 7 to select slides 3 through 7 (Figure 2–4).

Q&A Do I need to select consecutive slides?
No. You can select an individual slide to delete. You also can select nonconsecutive slides by pressing and holding the CTRL key down and then clicking the thumbnails of the slides you want to delete.

Why did I press and hold down the SHIFT key instead of the CTRL key?
Holding down the SHIFT key selects consecutive slides between the first and last selected slides, whereas holding the CTRL key selects only the slides you click.

Figure 2–4

2
- Right-click any selected slide to display the shortcut menu (Figure 2–5).

Figure 2–5

3
- Click Delete Slide to delete the selected slides from the presentation (Figure 2–6).

Figure 2–6

Other Ways

1. Select slide(s), press DELETE
2. Select slide(s), press BACKSPACE

To Create a Title Slide

Recall from Module 1 that the title slide introduces the presentation to the audience. In addition to introducing the presentation, this project uses the title slide to capture the audience's attention by using title text and an illustration. *Why? The presentation focuses on basketball, so the picture of a ball and court on the title slide can be supplemented with a backboard illustration that you will insert later on this slide.* The following steps create the slide show's title slide.

 Display Slide 1, select the text in the title text placeholder, and then type **Basketball Camp for Kids** as the title text.

Q&A Why do I have to select the text in the placeholder before typing?
This downloaded template includes text in some of the placeholders that must be replaced with your own text.

BTW

PowerPoint Screen Resolution
If you are using a computer or mobile device to step through the project in this module and you want your screens to match the figures in this book, you should change your screen's resolution to 1366 x 768. For information about how to change a computer's resolution, refer to the Office and Windows module at the beginning of this book.

For an introduction to Office and instructions about how to perform basic tasks in Office apps, read the Office and Windows module at the beginning of this book, where you can learn how to run an application, use the ribbon, save a file, open a file, print a file, exit an application, use Help, and much more.

2 Click the subtitle text placeholder, select the text in that placeholder, and then type `Gilbert Park District` as the subtitle text (Figure 2–7).

- If requested by your instructor, type the name of the city or county in which you were born instead of the word, Gilbert.

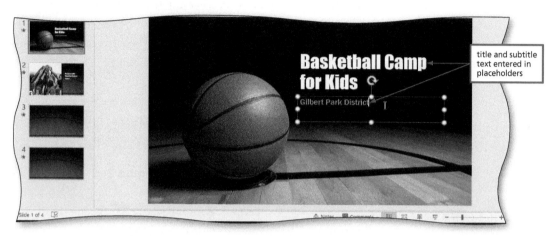

Figure 2–7

BTW
Touch Screen Differences
The Office and Windows interfaces may vary if you are using a touch screen. For this reason, you might notice that the function or appearance of your touch screen differs slightly from this module's presentation..

To Create the First Text Slide

The first text slide you create in Module 2 emphasizes two benefits of attending the weekly camp: receiving professional instruction and developing friendships. The following steps create the Slide 2 text slide using the Picture with Caption layout.

1 Display Slide 2, select the text in the title text placeholder, and then type `Learn from pros and make acquaintances` in the placeholder.

2 Select the text in the caption placeholder and then type `Classes meet weekday mornings throughout the summer` in this placeholder (Figure 2–8).

BTW
The Ribbon and Screen Resolution
PowerPoint may change how the groups and buttons within the groups appear on the ribbon, depending on the computer or mobile device's screen resolution. Thus, your ribbon may look different from the ones in this book if you are using a screen resolution other than 1366 × 768.

Figure 2–8

To Create the Second Text Slide

The second text slide you create shows three skills that will be taught: ball handling, offensive moves, and defensive strategies. The following steps add a title to Slide 3, which uses the Title Only layout, and save the presentation.

1 Display Slide 3 and then type **You will lern…** in the title text placeholder. The word, lern, is misspelled intentionally; the red wavy line indicates the misspelling (Figure 2-9).

2 Save the presentation using **Basketball Camp** as the file name.

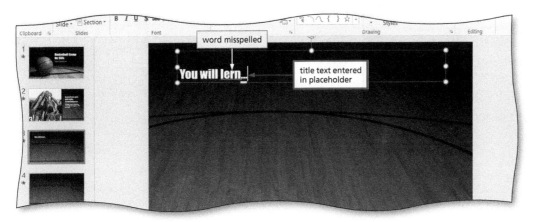

Figure 2-9

Inserting and Formatting Pictures in a Presentation

With the text entered in three of the four slides, the next step is to insert pictures into Slides 1 and 2 and then format the pictures. These graphical images draw the viewers' eyes to the slides and help them retain the information presented.

In the following pages, you will perform these tasks:

1. Insert an illustration into Slide 1.
2. Resize the illustration.
3. Change the Slide 2 photo.
4. Change the photo's brightness and contrast.
5. Change the photo's style and effect.
6. Add and modify the photo's border.

BTW
Organizing Files and Folders
You should organize and store files in folders so that you easily can find the files later. For example, if you are taking an introductory technology class called CIS 101, a good practice would be to save all PowerPoint files in a PowerPoint folder in a CIS 101 folder. For a discussion of folders and detailed examples of creating folders, refer to the Office and Windows module at the beginning of this book.

To Insert a Picture into a Slide without a Content Placeholder

1 DOWNLOAD & SELECT SLIDES | 2 INSERT & FORMAT PICTURES | 3 INSERT & FORMAT SHAPES
4 FORMAT SLIDE BACKGROUNDS | 5 INSERT & FORMAT WORDART | 6 REVIEW, REVISE, & PRINT SLIDES

In Module 1, you inserted photos and an illustration into slides without a content placeholder. *Why? Some slide layouts do not have a content placeholder, so you must insert and move the pictures to appropriate locations on the slide.* The illustration for Slide 1 is available in the Data Files. Contact your instructor if you need the pictures used in the following steps. The instructions in this module show the required files in the Module 02 folder in the Data Files folder. The following steps insert an illustration into the title slide.

1

- Display Slide 1 and then click Insert on the ribbon to display the Insert tab.
- Click the Pictures button (Insert tab | Images group) to display the Insert Picture dialog box.

2

- If necessary, navigate to the PowerPoint Module 02 folder and then click Backboard to select the file name (Figure 2–10).

Q&A

What if Backboard is not displayed in the navigation pane?
Drag the navigation pane scroll bar (Insert Picture dialog box) until Backboard appears. If this file is not in the list, see your instructor.

Why do I see just file names and not thumbnails of the pictures in my folder?
Your view is different from the view shown in Figure 2–10.

Figure 2–10

3

- Click the Insert button (Insert Picture dialog box) to insert the illustration into Slide 1.
- Drag the upper-left sizing handle diagonally toward the lower-right corner of the slide until the crosshair is positioned approximately as shown in Figure 2–11.

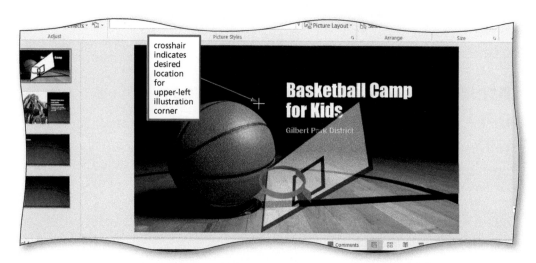

Figure 2–11

4

- Release to resize the illustration.
- Drag the illustration to the right until the vertical Smart Guide is displayed near the right side of the slide, as shown in Figure 2–12, and then release.

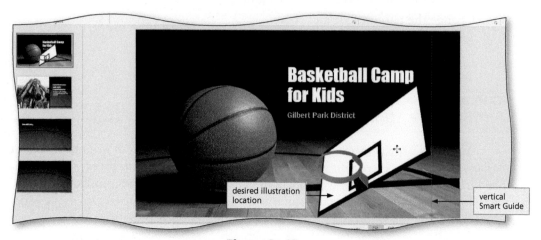

Figure 2–12

To Change a Picture

Why? *The downloaded theme included the photo of several team members on Slide 2. You need to change the photo because those players are wearing green uniforms, which are not the clothes your camp participants will wear.* The next task in the presentation is to change the default picture on Slide 2 to one of the pictures in the Data Files. The following steps change the Slide 2 photo to the Teamwork photo, which, in this example, is located in the Module 02 folder in the Data Files folder.

- Display Slide 2 and then right-click the picture to display the shortcut menu (Figure 2–13).

Q&A Why are the Style and Crop buttons displayed near the shortcut menu on my screen?
These two buttons display either above or below the shortcut menu depending upon where you right-click on the screen.

Figure 2–13

- Click Change Picture to display the Insert Pictures dialog box (Figure 2–14).

Figure 2–14

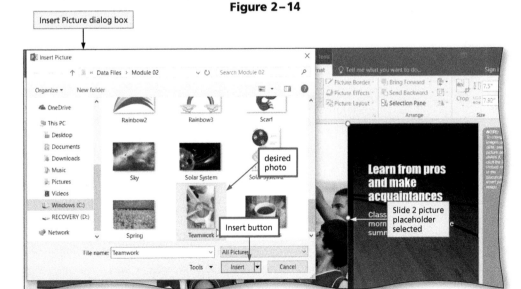

- Click the Browse button in the 'From a file' area to display the Insert Picture dialog box.
- If necessary, navigate to the PowerPoint Module 02 folder, scroll down, and then click Teamwork to select the file (Figure 2–15).

Figure 2–15

- Click the Insert button (Insert Picture dialog box) to insert the photo into the Slide 2 picture placeholder.
- Click the gray text box on the right side of the slide to select this object (Figure 2–16).

Q&A Why should I select and then delete this gray text box?

When you delete the box, the slide will expand to the right to fill that space and you will be able to view a larger slide image.

Figure 2–16

- Press the DELETE key to delete this text box.

Q&A Could I have followed the directions in the gray box on the right to change the image?

Yes, either method works. You also could have selected the gray box and then clicked the Cut button (Home tab | Clipboard group) button to delete the text box.

Other Ways

1. Click Change Picture button (Picture Tools Format tab | Adjust group)

To Correct a Picture

1 DOWNLOAD & SELECT SLIDES | 2 INSERT & FORMAT PICTURES | 3 INSERT & FORMAT SHAPES
4 FORMAT SLIDE BACKGROUNDS | 5 INSERT & FORMAT WORDART | 6 REVIEW, REVISE, & PRINT SLIDES

A photo's color intensity can be modified by changing the brightness and contrast. **Brightness** determines the overall lightness or darkness of the entire image, whereas **contrast** is the difference between the darkest and lightest areas of the image. The brightness and contrast are changed in predefined percentage increments. The following step decreases the brightness and increases the contrast. *Why? Altering the photo's brightness will coordinate with the dark colors on the basketball court while increasing the contrast will sharpen the image. It is important for the audience to recognize the basketball and the players' overlapping hands but not focus on each aspect of this photo.*

1

- Select the Teamwork photo on Slide 2 and then click Format on the ribbon to display the Picture Tools Format tab.

- Click the Corrections button (Picture Tools Format tab | Adjust group) to display the Corrections gallery.

- Scroll down to display the last row of images in the Corrections gallery and then

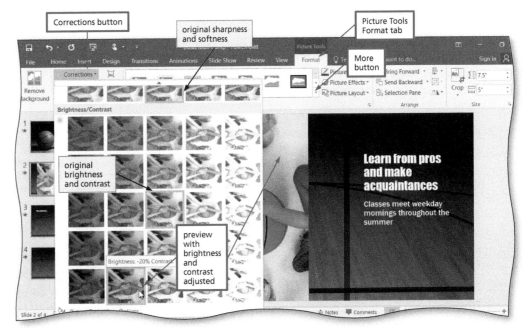

point to Brightness: −20% Contrast: +40% (second picture in last Brightness/Contrast row) to display a live preview of these corrections on the picture (Figure 2–17).

Figure 2–17

Q&A Can I use live preview on a touch screen?
Live preview is not available on a touch screen.

Why is a gray border surrounding the pictures in the center of the Sharpen/Soften and Brightness/Contrast areas of the gallery?
The image on Slide 2 currently has normal sharpness, brightness, and contrast (0%), which is represented by these center images in the gallery.

Experiment

- Point to various pictures in the Brightness/Contrast area and watch the brightness and contrast change on the picture in Slide 2.

- Click Brightness: −20% Contrast: +40% to apply this correction to the Teamwork photo.

Q&A How can I remove all effects from the picture?
Click the Reset Picture button (Picture Tools Format tab | Adjust group).

Other Ways

1. Click Picture Corrections Options (Corrections gallery), move Brightness or Contrast sliders or enter number in box next to slider (Format Picture pane)

To Apply a Picture Style

1 DOWNLOAD & SELECT SLIDES | 2 INSERT & FORMAT PICTURES | 3 INSERT & FORMAT SHAPES
4 FORMAT SLIDE BACKGROUNDS | 5 INSERT & FORMAT WORDART | 6 REVIEW, REVISE, & PRINT SLIDES

A **style** is a named group of formatting characteristics. The picture on Slide 2 emphasizes the concept of teamwork in this sport, and you can increase its visual appeal by applying a style. *Why? PowerPoint provides more than 25 picture styles that enable you easily to change a picture's look to a more visually appealing style, including a variety of shapes, angles, borders, and reflections.* You want to use a style that applies a shadow to the Teamwork photo. The following steps apply a picture style to the Slide 2 photo.

- With the Slide 2 picture selected and the Picture Tools Format tab displaying, click the More button in the Picture Styles gallery (Picture Tools Format tab | Picture Styles group) (shown in Figure 2–17) to expand the gallery.
- Point to Bevel Rectangle in the Picture Styles gallery (last style in third row) to display a live preview of that style applied to the picture in the document (Figure 2–18).

Figure 2–18

Experiment

- Point to various picture styles in the Picture Styles gallery and watch the style of the picture change in the document window.

- Click Bevel Rectangle in the Picture Styles gallery to apply the style to the selected picture.

To Add a Picture Border

1 DOWNLOAD & SELECT SLIDES | 2 INSERT & FORMAT PICTURES | 3 INSERT & FORMAT SHAPES
4 FORMAT SLIDE BACKGROUNDS | 5 INSERT & FORMAT WORDART | 6 REVIEW, REVISE, & PRINT SLIDES

The next step is to add a border to the Slide 2 picture. *Why? Some picture styles do not have a border; others, such as the Bevel Rectangle style you applied to this picture, do have this edging. This border is small, and you want a larger edge around the photo to draw attention to the graphic.* The following steps add a border to the Teamwork picture.

- With the Slide 2 picture still selected, click the Picture Border arrow (Picture Tools Format tab | Picture Styles group) to display the Picture Border gallery.

Q&A What if the Picture Tools Format tab no longer is displayed on my ribbon?

Click the picture to display the Picture Tools Format tab.

2

- Point to Weight on the Picture Border gallery to display the Weight gallery.

- Point to 6 pt to display a live preview of this line weight on the picture (Figure 2–19).

Can I make the line width more than 6 pt?
Yes. Click More Lines, Click Solid line in the Line section of the Format Picture pane, and then increase the amount in the Width box.

Figure 2–19

Experiment

- Point to various line weights in the Weight gallery and watch the line thickness change.

- Click 6 pt to add this line weight to the picture.

To Change a Picture Border Color

1 DOWNLOAD & SELECT SLIDES | **2 INSERT & FORMAT PICTURES** | **3 INSERT & FORMAT SHAPES**
4 FORMAT SLIDE BACKGROUNDS | **5 INSERT & FORMAT WORDART** | **6 REVIEW, REVISE, & PRINT SLIDES**

The default color for the border you added to the Slide 2 picture is white, but you will change the border color to black. *Why? The black color coordinates with other elements on the slide, especially the lines on the basketball and the court.* The following steps change the Slide 2 picture border color.

1

- With the Slide 2 photo still selected, click the Picture Border arrow (Picture Tools Format tab | Picture Styles group) to display the Picture Border gallery again.

2

- Point to Black, Background 1 (first color in first row) in the Picture Border gallery to display a live preview of that border color on the picture (Figure 2–20).

Figure 2–20

Experiment

• Point to various colors in the Picture Border gallery and watch the border on the picture change in the slide.

3

• Click Black, Background 1 in the Picture Border gallery to change the picture border color.

To Apply Picture Effects

1 DOWNLOAD & SELECT SLIDES | 2 INSERT & FORMAT PICTURES | 3 INSERT & FORMAT SHAPES
4 FORMAT SLIDE BACKGROUNDS | 5 INSERT & FORMAT WORDART | 6 REVIEW, REVISE, & PRINT SLIDES

Why? Picture effects allow you to further customize a picture. PowerPoint provides a variety of picture effects, including shadows, reflections, glow, soft edges, bevel, and 3-D rotation. The difference between the effects and the styles is that each effect has several options, providing you with more control over the exact look of the image.

In this presentation, the photo on Slide 2 has a brown glow effect and a bevel applied to its edges. The following steps apply picture effects to the selected picture.

1

• With the Slide 2 picture still selected, click the Picture Effects button (Picture Tools Format tab | Picture Styles group) to display the Picture Effects menu.

Q&A | What if the Picture Tools Format tab no longer is displayed on my ribbon?
Click the picture to display the Picture Tools Format tab.

• Point to Glow on the Picture Effects menu to display the Glow gallery.

• Point to Brown, 18 pt glow, Accent color 3 in the Glow Variations area (third glow in last row) to display a live preview of the selected glow effect applied to the picture in the document window (Figure 2–21).

Figure 2–21

 Experiment

• Point to various glow effects in the Glow gallery and watch the picture change in the document window.

2

- Click Brown, 18 pt glow, Accent color 3 in the Glow gallery to apply the selected picture effect.

3

- Click the Picture Effects button (Picture Tools Format tab | Picture Styles group) to display the Picture Effects menu again.

- Point to Bevel on the Picture Effects menu to display the Bevel gallery.

- Point to Angle (first bevel in second Bevel row) to display a live preview of the selected bevel effect applied to the Slide 2 picture (Figure 2–22).

Figure 2–22

Experiment

- Point to various bevel effects in the Bevel gallery and watch the picture change in the slide.

4

- Click Angle in the Bevel gallery to apply the selected picture effect.

Other Ways

1. Right-click picture, click Format Picture on shortcut menu, select desired options (Format Picture pane), click Close button

2. Click Format Shape pane launcher (Picture Tools Format tab | Picture Styles group), select desired options (Format Picture pane), click Close button

Break Point: If you wish to take a break, this is a good place to do so. Be sure to save the Basketball Camp file again and then you can exit PowerPoint. To resume at a later time, run PowerPoint, open the file called Basketball Camp, and continue following the steps from this location forward.

Inserting and Formatting a Shape

One method of getting the audience's attention and reinforcing the major concepts being presented is to have graphical elements on the slide. PowerPoint provides a wide variety of predefined shapes that can add visual interest to a slide. Shape elements include lines, basic geometrical shapes, arrows, equation shapes, flowchart symbols, stars, banners, and callouts. After adding a shape to a slide, you can change its default characteristics by adding text, bullets, numbers, and styles. You also can combine multiple shapes to create a more complex graphic.

The predefined shapes are found in the Shapes gallery. This collection is found on the Home tab | Drawing group and the Insert tab | Illustrations group. Once you have inserted and selected a shape, the Drawing Tools Format tab is displayed, and the Shapes gallery also is displayed in the Insert Shapes group.

BTW

Inserting Special Characters
Along with adding shapes to a slide, you can insert characters not found on your keyboard, such as the section sign (§), the copyright sign (©), and Greek capital letters (e.g., Δ, Ω, and ß). To insert these characters, click the Insert tab and then click the Symbol button (Insert tab | Symbols group). When the Symbol dialog box is displayed, you can use the same font you currently are using in your presentation, or you can select another font. The Webdings, Wingdings, Wingdings 2, and Wingdings 3 fonts have a variety of symbols.

Slide 3 in this presentation is enhanced in a variety of ways. First, an oval, an arrow, and a pentagon shape are inserted on the slide and formatted. Then, text is added to the oval and pentagon and formatted. The pentagon is copied, and the text is modified in this new shape. Finally, the arrow shape is duplicated twice and moved into position.

To Add a Shape

1 DOWNLOAD & SELECT SLIDES | 2 INSERT & FORMAT PICTURES | 3 INSERT & FORMAT SHAPES
4 FORMAT SLIDE BACKGROUNDS | 5 INSERT & FORMAT WORDART | 6 REVIEW, REVISE, & PRINT SLIDES

Many of the shapes included in the Shapes gallery can direct the viewer to important aspects of the presentation. The following steps add an oval shape, which displays as a circle, to Slide 3. *Why? A circle shape complements the basketball photo on Slide 1 and helps reinforce the presentation's basketball theme.*

- Display Slide 3 and then, if necessary, click the Home tab (Figure 2–23).

Figure 2–23

- Click the Shapes More button (Home tab | Drawing group) shown in Figure 2–23 to display the Shapes gallery (Figure 2–24).

Q&A

I do not see a Shapes More button and the three rows of the shapes shown in Figure 2–24. Instead, I have a Shapes button. Why?
Monitor dimensions and resolution affect how buttons display on the ribbon. Click the Shapes button to display the entire Shapes gallery.

Figure 2–24

- Click the Oval shape in the Basic Shapes area of the Shapes gallery.

Q&A Why did my pointer change shape?
The pointer changed to a plus shape to indicate the Oval shape has been added to the Clipboard.

- Position the pointer (a crosshair) near the center of the slide, as shown in Figure 2–25.

Figure 2–25

- Click Slide 3 to insert the Oval shape.

Other Ways

1. Click Shapes button (Insert tab | Illustrations group)

To Resize a Shape

1 DOWNLOAD & SELECT SLIDES | 2 INSERT & FORMAT PICTURES | 3 INSERT & FORMAT SHAPES
4 FORMAT SLIDE BACKGROUNDS | 5 INSERT & FORMAT WORDART | 6 REVIEW, REVISE, & PRINT SLIDES

The next step is to resize the Oval shape. **Why?** *The oval should be enlarged so that it is a focal point in the middle area of the slide.* The following steps resize the selected shape.

- Press and hold down the SHIFT key and then drag the upper-left corner sizing handle until the shape is resized approximately as shown in Figure 2–26 and the top is aligned with a horizontal Smart Guide.

Q&A Why did I need to press the SHIFT key while enlarging the shape?
Holding down the SHIFT key while dragging keeps the proportions of the original shape.

What if my shape is not selected?
To select a shape, click it.

If I am using a touch screen, how can I maintain the shape's original proportion?
If you drag one of the corner sizing handles, the object should stay in proportion.

Figure 2–26

2

- Release to resize the shape.
- Drag the shape until the vertical Smart Guide is displayed in the middle of the oval and the horizontal Smart Guide is displayed at the top of the oval, as shown in Figure 2–27, and then release.

Q&A

What if I want to move the shape to a precise location on the slide?

With the shape selected, press the ARROW keys or the CTRL+ARROW keys to move the shape to the desired location.

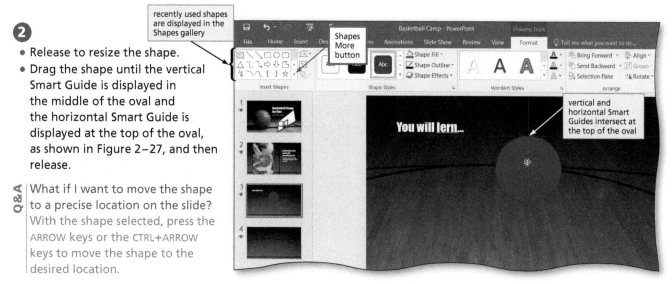

Figure 2–27

Other Ways

1. Enter shape height and width in Height and Width boxes (Drawing Tools Format tab | Size group)
2. Click Size and Position pane launcher (Drawing Tools Format tab | Size group), click Size tab, enter desired height and width values in boxes, click Close button

To Add Other Shapes

1 DOWNLOAD & SELECT SLIDES | 2 INSERT & FORMAT PICTURES | 3 INSERT & FORMAT SHAPES
4 FORMAT SLIDE BACKGROUNDS | 5 INSERT & FORMAT WORDART | 6 REVIEW, REVISE, & PRINT SLIDES

Ovals, squares, arrows, stars, and equation shapes are among the items included in the Shapes gallery. These shapes can be combined to show relationships among the elements, and they can help illustrate the basic concepts presented in your slide show. ***Why?*** *Arrows are especially useful in showing the relationship among slide elements and guiding the viewer's eyes to move from one shape to the next.* More than two dozen arrow shapes are displayed in the Block Arrows section of the Shapes gallery. The following steps add one of these arrows and the pentagon shapes to Slide 3.

1

- Click the Shapes More button (Drawing Tools Format tab | Insert Shapes group) shown in Figure 2–27 to display the Shapes gallery (Figure 2–28).

Q&A

When I inserted the Oval shape, I selected it on the Home tab. Is the same Shapes gallery also displayed on the Drawing Tools Format tab?

Yes. The Shapes gallery is displayed on this tab once an object is inserted and selected on the slide.

Figure 2–28

- Click the Curved Left Arrow shape in the Block Arrows area of the Shapes gallery.
- Position the pointer to the right of the oval shape in Slide 3 and then click to insert the Curved Left Arrow shape.

- Press and hold down the SHIFT key and then drag a corner sizing handle until the arrow shape is approximately the size shown in Figure 2–29.

Q&A

If I am using a touch screen, how can I maintain the Oval shape's original proportion?
The object should stay in proportion when you drag one of the corner sizing handles.

- If necessary, drag the Curved Left Arrow shape to the right side of the oval, as shown in Figure 2–29, and then release.

Figure 2–29

- Display the Shapes gallery and then click the Regular Pentagon shape in the Basic Shapes area of the gallery (shown in Figure 2–28).
- Position the pointer toward the lower-left side of the Curved Left Arrow shape and then click to insert the Regular Pentagon shape.

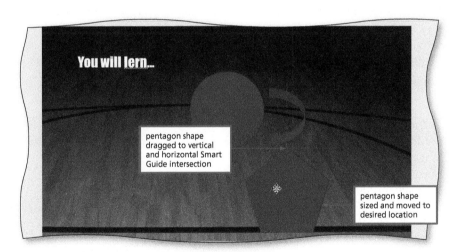

- Press and hold down the SHIFT key and then drag a corner sizing handle to resize the pentagon shape so that it is the size shown in Figure 2–30.
- Drag the pentagon shape so that its tip is placed at the intersection of the horizontal Smart Guide above the pentagon and the vertical Smart Guide in the middle of the shape, as shown in Figure 2–30, and then release.

Figure 2–30

To Apply a Shape Style

1 DOWNLOAD & SELECT SLIDES | 2 INSERT & FORMAT PICTURES | **3 INSERT & FORMAT SHAPES**
4 FORMAT SLIDE BACKGROUNDS | 5 INSERT & FORMAT WORDART | 6 REVIEW, REVISE, & PRINT SLIDES

Formatting text in a shape follows the same techniques as formatting text in a placeholder. You can change font, font color and size, and alignment. You later will add information about a skill to the Oval shape, but first you want to apply a shape style. *Why?* *The style will give depth and dimension to the object.* The Quick Styles gallery has a variety of styles that change depending upon the theme applied to the presentation. The following steps apply a style to the oval.

1

- Display the Home tab, click the oval to select it, and then click the Quick Styles button (Home tab | Drawing group) (Figure 2–31).

Figure 2–31

2

- Point to Light 1 Outline, Colored Fill – Black, Dark 1 in the Quick Styles gallery (first shape in third Theme Styles row) to display a live preview of that style applied to the oval in the slide (Figure 2–32).

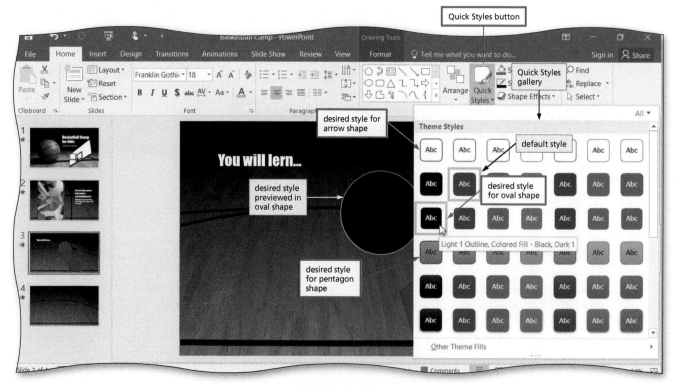

Figure 2–32

Experiment

- Point to various styles in the Quick Styles gallery and watch the style of the shape change.

3

- Click Light 1 Outline, Colored Fill – Black, Dark 1 in the Quick Styles gallery to apply the selected style to the oval.

Other Ways

1. Click Shape Styles More button (Drawing Tools Format tab | Shape Styles group), select style
2. Right-click shape, click Style button on mini toolbar, select desired style

To Apply Another Style

You later will add text to the oval and pentagon about particular skills taught at the camp, but now you want to format the arrow and pentagon shapes. *Why? You can apply shape styles to the arrow and pentagon that will coordinate with the oval's style. A light style color in the arrow shape will help join darker style colors of the oval and rectangle. This formatting will add interest and emphasize the relationship between basketball playing skills.* The following steps apply styles to the arrow and pentagon shapes.

1 Click the arrow shape to select it.

2 Click the Quick Styles button (Home tab | Drawing group) to display the Quick Styles gallery and then apply the Colored Outline – Black, Dark 1 style (first style in first Theme Styles row) to the arrow shape.

3 Click the pentagon shape to select it and then click the Quick Styles button.

4 Click Subtle Effect – Black, Dark 1 (first style in fourth Theme Styles row) to apply that style to the pentagon shape (Figure 2–33).

BTW

Deleting a Shape
If you want to delete a shape you have added to a slide, click that shape to select it and then press the delete key. If you want to DELETE multiple shapes, press the CTRL key while clicking the undesired shapes and then press the DELETE key.

Figure 2–33

To Add Text to a Shape

The three shapes on Slide 3 help call attention to the key aspects of your presentation. *Why? Your goal is to emphasize key skills the campers will learn.* The next step is to add this information to Slide 3. The following steps add text to the oval and pentagon shapes.

- With the pentagon selected, type `Offensive moves` to add the text in the shape.

- Click the oval to select it and then type `Ball handling skills` to add the text in the shape (Figure 2–34).

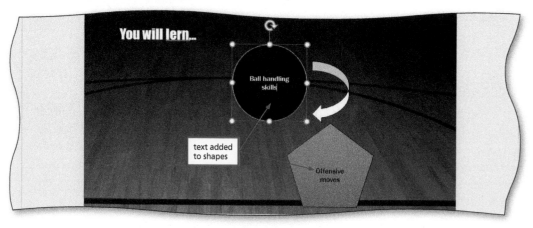

Figure 2–34

To Change the Font

The default theme font is Franklin Gothic Medium. To draw more attention to text in the shapes and to help differentiate these slide elements from the title text, you want to change the font to Century Schoolbook. *Why? Century Schoolbook is a serif typeface, meaning the ends of some of the letter are adorned with small decorations, called serifs. These adornments slow down the viewer's reading speed, which might help them retain the information they saw.* To change the font, you must select the letters you want to format. In Module 1, you selected a paragraph and then formatted the characters, and you follow the same procedure to change the font. The following steps change the text font in the shape.

- With the oval selected, triple-click the text to select all the characters and display the mini toolbar (Figure 2–35).

Figure 2–35

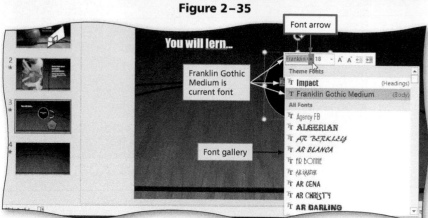

- Click the Font arrow to display the Font gallery (Figure 2–36).

Q&A Will the fonts in my Font gallery be the same as those shown in Figure 2–36?
Your list of available fonts may differ, depending on what fonts you have installed and the type of printer you are using.

Figure 2–36

3

- Drag or scroll through the Font gallery and then point to Century Schoolbook (or a similar font) to display a live preview of the title text in the Century Schoolbook font (Figure 2–37).

🔍 **Experiment**

- Point to various fonts in the Font gallery and watch the subtitle text font change in the slide.

- Click Century Schoolbook (or a similar font) to change the font of the selected text to Century Schoolbook.

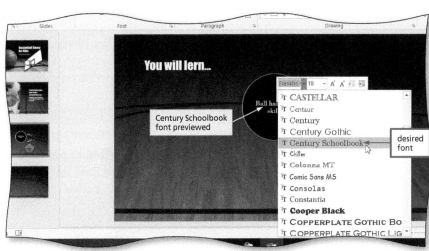

Figure 2–37

Other Ways

1. Click Font arrow (Home tab | Font group), click desired font in Font gallery
2. Right-click selected text, click Font on shortcut menu (Font dialog box), click Font tab, select desired font in Font list, click OK button
3. Click Font dialog box launcher (Home tab | Font group), click Font tab (Font dialog box), select desired font in Font list, click OK button
4. Press CTRL+SHIFT+F, click Font tab (Font dialog box), select desired font in the Font list, click OK button
5. Right-click selected text, click Font arrow on mini toolbar, select desired font

To Format the Text

To increase readability, you can format the oval text by increasing the font size, bolding the characters, and changing the font color to orange. The following steps format the oval text.

BTW

Text in a Shape
When you add text to a shape, it becomes part of the shape. If you rotate or flip the shape, the text also rotates or flips.

1 With the oval text selected, click the Increase Font Size button (Home tab | Font group) two times to increase the font size to 24 pt.

2 Click the Bold button (Home tab | Font group) to bold the text.

3 Click the Font Color arrow and change the color to Orange (third color in Standard Colors row) (Figure 2–38).

Q&A What should I do if one or more letters of the word, handling, wrap to the third line in the shape?
Press and hold down the SHIFT key and then drag a corner sizing handle outward slightly to resize the oval shape.

Figure 2–38

Could I also add a shadow behind the text to add depth and help the letters display prominently?
Yes. Select the text and then click the Text Shadow button (Home tab | Font group).

Other Ways

1. Right-click selected text, click desired text format button on mini toolbar

Format Painter

To save time and avoid formatting errors, you can use the Format Painter to apply custom formatting to other places in your presentation quickly and easily. You can use this feature in three ways:

- To copy only character attributes, such as font and font effects, select text that has these qualities.
- To copy both character attributes and paragraph attributes, such as alignment and indentation, select the entire paragraph.
- To apply the same formatting to multiple words, phrases, or paragraphs, double-click the Format Painter button and then select each item you want to format. You then can press the ESC key or click the Format Painter button to turn off this feature.

To Format Text Using the Format Painter

1 DOWNLOAD & SELECT SLIDES | 2 INSERT & FORMAT PICTURES | 3 INSERT & FORMAT SHAPES
4 FORMAT SLIDE BACKGROUNDS | 5 INSERT & FORMAT WORDART | 6 REVIEW, REVISE, & PRINT SLIDES

Why? *To save time and duplicated effort, you quickly can use the Format Painter to copy formatting attributes from the oval shape text and apply them to pentagon shape text.* The following steps use the Format Painter to copy formatting features.

- With the oval text still selected, double-click the Format Painter button (Home tab | Clipboard group).
- Move the pointer off the ribbon (Figure 2–39).

Q&A Why does the Format Painter button on my screen display only a paint brush and not the words, Format Painter?
Monitor dimensions and resolution affect how buttons display on the ribbon.

Why did my pointer change shape?
The pointer changed shape by adding a paintbrush to indicate that the Format Painter function is active.

Figure 2–39

- Triple-click the pentagon text to apply the format to all characters (Figure 2–40).
- Click the Format Painter button or press the ESC key to turn off the Format Painter feature.

Q&A What should I do if one or more letters of the word, Offensive, wrap to a second line in the shape?
Press and hold down the SHIFT key and then drag a corner sizing handle outward slightly to resize the pentagon shape.

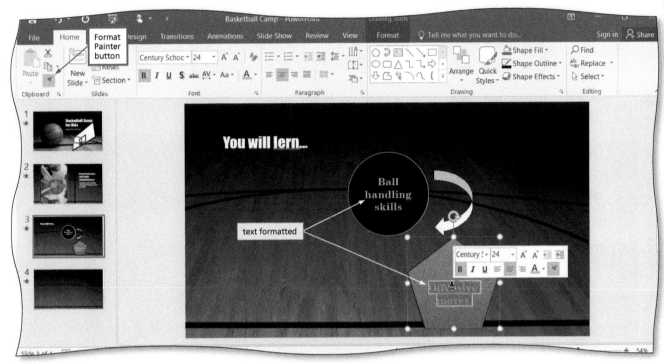

Figure 2–40

Other Ways

1. Select text, double-click Format Painter button on mini toolbar

To Copy and Paste a Shape

1 DOWNLOAD & SELECT SLIDES | 2 INSERT & FORMAT PICTURES | 3 INSERT & FORMAT SHAPES
4 FORMAT SLIDE BACKGROUNDS | 5 INSERT & FORMAT WORDART | 6 REVIEW, REVISE, & PRINT SLIDES

Good basketball players have both offensive and defensive skills. You already have created the shape stating the campers will work on refining their offensive talents. You now need to create a second shape with information about defensive instruction that will be provided at the camp. The following steps copy the pentagon shape and then change the text. *Why? You could repeat all the steps you performed to create the first pentagon, but it is much more efficient to duplicate the shape and then edit the text.*

- With the pentagon shape selected, click the Copy button (Home tab | Clipboard group) (Figure 2–41).

Figure 2–41

②
- Click the Paste button (Home tab | Clipboard group) to insert a duplicate Regular Pentagon shape on Slide 3.
- Drag the new pentagon shape to the left of the original pentagon shape, as shown in Figure 2–42.
- In the left pentagon shape, select the text, Offensive moves, and then type **Defensive mindset** as the replacement text (Figure 2–42).

◄ | What should I do if one or more letters of the word, Defensive, wrap to a second line in the shape?

Q&A | Press and hold down the SHIFT key and then drag a corner sizing handle outward slightly to resize the pentagon shape.

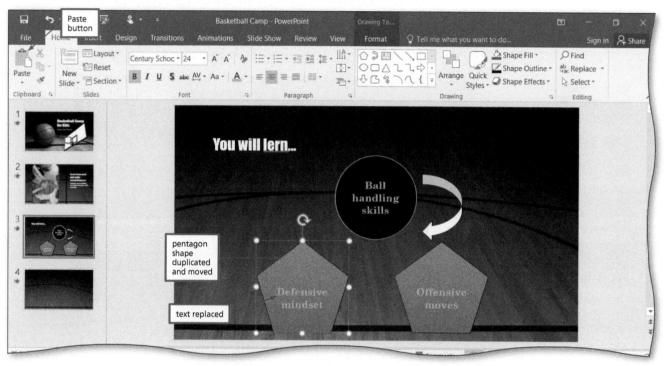

Figure 2–42

③
- Select the arrow shape and then click the Copy button (Home tab | Clipboard group) (Figure 2–43).

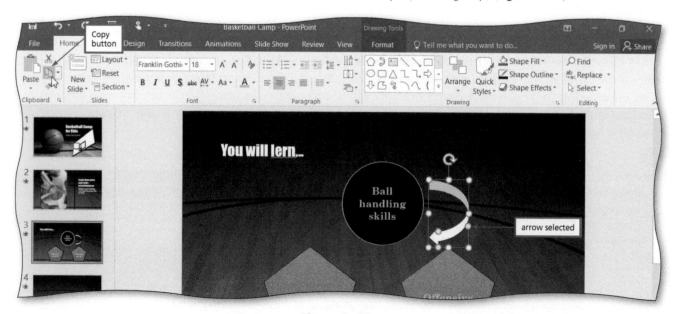

Figure 2–43

4

- Click the Paste button (Home tab | Clipboard group) two times to insert two duplicate arrow shapes on Slide 3.
- Drag one of the duplicate arrow shapes between the two pentagon shapes and then drag the other duplicate arrow shape between the left pentagon shape and the oval shape (Figure 2–44).

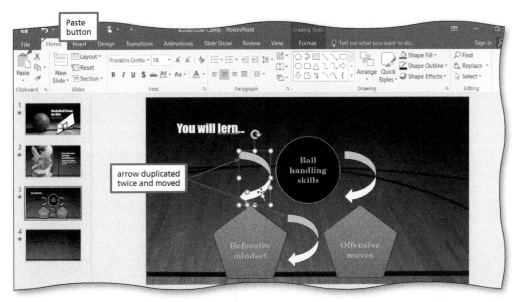

Figure 2–44

5

- With the left arrow selected, drag its rotation handle clockwise or counterclockwise so that it is displayed as shown in Figure 2–45. Repeat this procedure for the other two arrows, and then adjust the shapes' locations on Slide 3 so that the arrows touch their adjacent shapes (Figure 2–45).

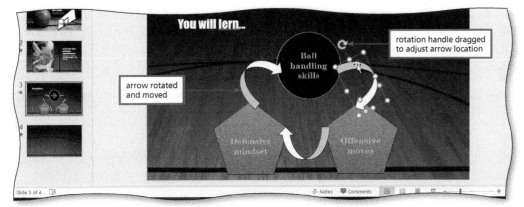

Figure 2–45

- If the end of an arrow is underneath an oval or a pentagon shape, select the arrow, click the Drawing Tools Format tab, and then click the Bring Forward button (Drawing Tools Format tab | Arrange group) to bring the arrow on top of the shape.

Other Ways

1. Right-click selected shape, click Copy on shortcut menu, right-click blank area, click Paste on shortcut menu
2. Select shape, press CTRL+C, press CTRL+V

Break Point: If you wish to take a break, this is a good place to do so. Be sure to save the Basketball Camp file again and then you can exit PowerPoint. To resume at a later time, run PowerPoint, open the file called Basketball Camp, and continue following the steps from this location forward.

Formatting Slide Backgrounds

A slide's background is an integral part of a presentation because it can generate audience interest. Every slide can have the same background, or different backgrounds can be used in a presentation. This background is considered **fill**, which is the content that makes up the interior of a shape, line, or character. Four fills are available: solid, gradient, picture or texture, and pattern. **Solid fill** is one color used throughout the entire slide. **Gradient fill** is one color shade gradually progressing to another shade of the same color or one color progressing to another color. **Picture or texture fill** uses a specific file or an image that simulates a material, such as cork, granite, marble, or canvas. **Pattern fill** adds designs, such as dots or dashes, which repeat in rows across the slide.

Once you add a fill, you can adjust its appearance. For example, you can adjust its **transparency**, which allows you to see through the background, so that any text on the slide is visible. You also can select a color that is part of the theme or a custom color. You can use an **offset**, another background feature, to move the background away from the slide borders in varying distances by percentage. A **tiling option** repeats the background image many times vertically and horizontally on the slide; the smaller the tiling percentage, the greater the number of times the image is repeated.

To Insert a Texture Fill

1 DOWNLOAD & SELECT SLIDES | **2** INSERT & FORMAT PICTURES | **3** INSERT & FORMAT SHAPES
4 FORMAT SLIDE BACKGROUNDS | **5** INSERT & FORMAT WORDART | **6** REVIEW, REVISE, & PRINT SLIDES

Why? *Various texture fills are available to give your background a unique look.* The 24 pictures in the Texture gallery give the appearance of a physical object, such as water drops, sand, tissue paper, and a paper bag. You also can use your own texture pictures for custom backgrounds. The following steps insert the Brown marble texture fill on Slide 2 in the presentation.

• Display Slide 2. Click the Design tab and then click the Format Background button (Design tab | Customize group) to display the Format Background pane (Figure 2–46).

Figure 2–46

2

- With the Fill section displaying (Format Background pane), if necessary, click 'Picture or texture fill' and then click the Texture button to display the Texture gallery (Figure 2–47).

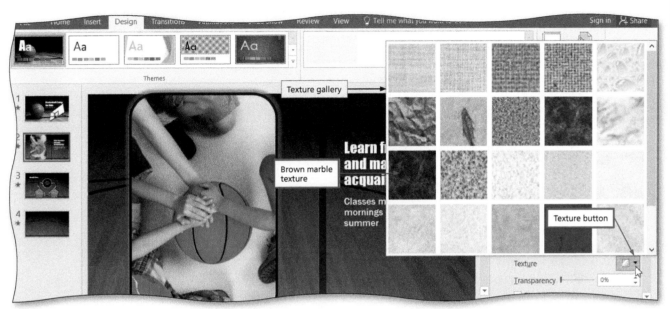

Figure 2–47

3

- Click the Brown marble texture (first texture in third row) to insert this texture fill as the background on Slide 2 (Figure 2–48).

  Is a live preview available to see the various textures on this slide?
No. Live preview is not an option with the background textures and fills.

Could I insert this background on all four slides simultaneously?
Yes. You would click the 'Apply to All' button to insert the Brown marble background on all slides.

Figure 2–48

Other Ways

1. Right-click background, click Format Background on shortcut menu, select desired options (Format Background pane)

To Format the Background Texture Fill Transparency

Why? The Brown marble texture on Slide 2 is dark, and its pattern may detract from the photo and text. One method of reducing this darkness is to change the transparency. The **Transparency slider** indicates the amount of opaqueness. The default setting is 0, which is fully opaque. The opposite extreme is 100%, which is fully transparent. To change the transparency, you can move the Transparency slider or enter a number in the box next to the slider. The following step adjusts the texture transparency to 15%.

• Click the Transparency slider (Format Background pane) and drag it to the right until 15% is displayed in the Transparency box (Figure 2–49).

Q&A Can I move the slider in small increments so that I can get a precise percentage easily?
Yes. Click the up or down arrows in the Transparency box to move the slider in 1% increments.

Figure 2–49

To Insert a Gradient Fill

Although you selected Brown marble texture fill on Slide 2 and changed the transparency, you decide that another type of background may be more suitable for Slide 3. *Why? The Brown marble texture does not offer sufficient contrast with the oval symbol and may detract from the messages presented in the three symbols.* For each theme, PowerPoint provides 30 preset **gradient fills** with five designs for each of the six major theme colors. Each fill has one dark color shade that gradually lightens to either another shade of the same color or another color. The following steps replace the background on Slide 3 to a preset gradient fill.

• Display Slide 3. With the Fill section displaying (Format Background pane), click Gradient fill in the Format Background pane (shown in Figure 2–49) and then click the Preset gradients button to display the Preset gradients gallery (Figure 2–50).

Q&A Are the backgrounds displayed in a specific order?
Yes. The first row has light colors at the top of the background; the middle rows have darker fills at the bottom; the bottom row has overall dark fills on all edges.

Is a live preview available to see the various gradients on this slide?
No. Live preview is not an option with the background textures and fills.

Figure 2–50

2

- Click Bottom Spotlight – Accent 3 (third fill in fourth row) to apply that style to Slide 3 (Figure 2–51).

Q&A If I decide later that this background gradient does not fit the theme of my presentation, can I apply a different background?
Yes. You can repeat these steps at any time while creating your presentation.

Figure 2–51

Other Ways

1. Click Design tab on ribbon, click Format Background button (Customize group), select desired options (Format Background pane)
2. Right-click background, click Format Background on shortcut menu, select desired options (Format Background pane)

To Insert a Picture to Create a Background

Why? *For variety and interest, you want to use an illustration as the Slide 4 background.* This picture is stored in the Data Files folder. PowerPoint will stretch the height and width of this picture to fill the slide area. The following steps insert the illustration, Basketball Boy, on Slide 4 only.

- Display Slide 4. With the Fill section displaying (Format Background pane), if necessary, click 'Picture or texture fill' and then click the File button (Format Background pane) to display the Insert Picture dialog box. If necessary, navigate to the Module 02 folder in the Data Files folder or the location where your data files are located.
- Click Basketball Boy to select the file name (Figure 2–52).

Figure 2–52

2

- Click the Insert button (Insert Picture dialog box) to insert the Basketball Boy illustration as the Slide 4 background (Figure 2–53).

Q&A What if I do not want to use this picture?
Click the Undo button on the Quick Access Toolbar or click the Reset Background button at the bottom of the Format Background pane.

Figure 2–53

To Format the Background Picture Fill Transparency

1 DOWNLOAD & SELECT SLIDES | 2 INSERT & FORMAT PICTURES | 3 INSERT & FORMAT SHAPES
4 FORMAT SLIDE BACKGROUNDS | 5 INSERT & FORMAT WORDART | 6 REVIEW, REVISE, & PRINT SLIDES

Why? The Basketball Boy illustration on Slide 4 has vibrant colors that will conflict with the WordArt you will add later in this project. You can adjust the transparency of picture in the same manner that you change the transparency of a slide texture. The following steps adjust the transparency of the background picture to 30% and then close the Format Background pane.

1

- Click the Transparency slider and drag it to the right until 30% is displayed in the Transparency box (Figure 2–54).

2

- Click the Close button (Format Background pane) to close the pane and return to Slide 4.

Figure 2–54

Inserting and Formatting WordArt

One method of adding appealing visual elements to a presentation is by using **WordArt** styles. This feature is found in other Microsoft Office applications, including Word and Excel. This gallery of decorative effects allows you to type new text or convert existing text to WordArt. You then can add elements such as fills, outlines, and effects.

WordArt **fill** in the interior of a letter can consist of a solid color, texture, picture, or gradient. The WordArt **outline** is the exterior border surrounding each letter or symbol. PowerPoint allows you to change the outline color, weight, and style. You also can add an **effect**, which helps add emphasis or depth to the characters. Some effects are shadows, reflections, glows, bevels, and 3-D rotations.

1 DOWNLOAD & SELECT SLIDES | 2 INSERT & FORMAT PICTURES | 3 INSERT & FORMAT SHAPES
4 FORMAT SLIDE BACKGROUNDS | 5 INSERT & FORMAT WORDART | 6 REVIEW, REVISE, & PRINT SLIDES

To Insert WordArt

The basketball camp is a very popular event among boys and girls in the community, and the sessions fill every year. Parents need to register their student early to reserve a place. You want to emphasize this concept, and the last slide in the presentation is an excellent location to urge your audience to take action. *Why? Audience members remember the first and last things they see and hear.* You quickly can add a visual element to the slide by selecting a WordArt style from the WordArt Styles gallery and then applying it to some text. The following steps insert WordArt.

- Display the Insert tab and then click the WordArt button (Insert tab | Text group) to display the WordArt gallery (Figure 2–55).

Figure 2–55

- Click 'Fill – Red, Accent 2, Outline – Accent 2' (third style in first row) to insert the WordArt object (Figure 2–56).

Figure 2–56

- Type **Register today!** in the object as the WordArt text (Figure 2–57).

Q&A Why did the Drawing Tools Format tab appear automatically in the ribbon?
It appears when you select text to which you could add a WordArt style or other effect.

Figure 2–57

To Change the WordArt Shape

Why? *The WordArt text is useful to emphasize the need to register children early for camp. You further can emphasize this text by changing its shape.* PowerPoint provides a variety of graphical shapes that add interest to WordArt text. The following steps change the WordArt shape to Chevron Up.

1

- With the WordArt object still selected, click the Text Effects button (Drawing Tools Format tab | WordArt Styles group) to display the Text Effects menu (Figure 2–58).

Figure 2–58

2

- Point to Transform in the Text Effects menu to display the WordArt Transform gallery (Figure 2–59).

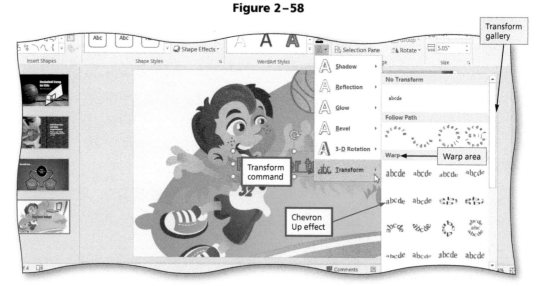

Figure 2–59

3

- Point to the Chevron Up effect in the Warp area (first effect in second row in Warp area) to display a live preview of that text effect applied to the WordArt object (Figure 2–60).

Figure 2–60

Experiment

- Point to various effects in the Transform gallery and watch the format of the text and borders change.

◄ How can I see the preview of a Transform effect if the gallery overlays the WordArt letters?
Ⓠ Move the WordArt box to the left or right side of the slide and then repeat Steps 1 and 2.

4

- Click the Chevron Up shape to apply this text effect to the WordArt object.

◄ Can I change the shape I applied to the WordArt?
Ⓠ Yes. Position the insertion point in the box and then repeat Steps 1 and 2.

5

- Drag the lower-right sizing handle diagonally toward the lower-right corner of the slide until the crosshair is positioned approximately as shown in Figure 2–61.

crosshair indicates lower-right WordArt location

Figure 2–61

6

- Release to resize the WordArt object.
- Drag the WordArt object toward the right side of the slide until it is positioned approximately as shown in Figure 2–62.

WordArt object moved to desired location

Figure 2–62

To Apply a WordArt Text Fill

1 DOWNLOAD & SELECT SLIDES | 2 INSERT & FORMAT PICTURES | 3 INSERT & FORMAT SHAPES
4 FORMAT SLIDE BACKGROUNDS | 5 INSERT & FORMAT WORDART | 6 REVIEW, REVISE, & PRINT SLIDES

Various texture fills are available to give your WordArt characters a unique look. You used a texture fill to add interest to the Slide 3 background. The following steps add the Medium wood texture as a fill for the WordArt characters. *Why? The brown fill coordinates well with the red WordArt outline and is similar to the color of the basketball court in the Slide 1 and Slide 2 backgrounds.*

1

- With the WordArt object selected, click the Text Fill arrow (Drawing Tools Format tab | WordArt Styles group) to display the Text Fill gallery.
- Point to Texture in the Text Fill gallery to display the Texture gallery.

2

- If necessary, scroll down and then point to the Medium wood texture (last texture in last row) to display a live preview of that texture applied to the WordArt object (Figure 2–63).

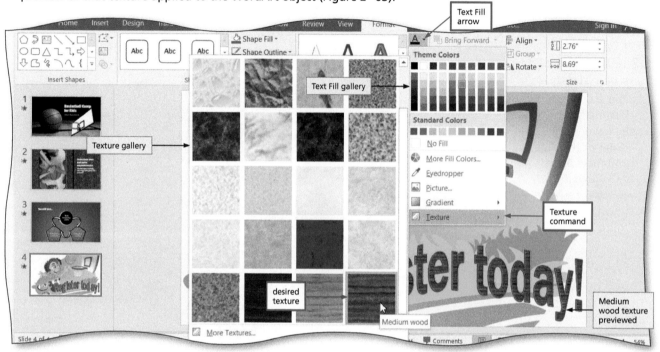

Figure 2–63

🔍 **Experiment**

- Point to various styles in the Texture gallery and watch the fill change.

3

- Click the Medium wood texture to apply this texture as the fill for the WordArt object.

◀ **Q&A**   Can I apply this texture simultaneously to text that appears in more than one place on my slide?
Yes. You can select one area of text, press and then hold the CTRL key while you select the other text, and then apply the texture.

To Change the Weight of the WordArt Outline

1 DOWNLOAD & SELECT SLIDES | 2 INSERT & FORMAT PICTURES | 3 INSERT & FORMAT SHAPES
4 FORMAT SLIDE BACKGROUNDS | 5 INSERT & FORMAT WORDART | **6 REVIEW, REVISE, & PRINT SLIDES**

The letters in the WordArt style applied have an outline around the edges. You can increase the width of the outlines. *Why? The thicker line will emphasize this characteristic and add another visual element.* As with fonts, lines also are measured in points, and PowerPoint gives you the option to change the line **weight**, or thickness, starting with ¼ point (pt) and increasing in ¼-point increments. Other outline options include modifying the color and the line style, such as changing to dots or dashes or a combination of dots and dashes. The following steps change the WordArt outline weight to 6 pt.

1

- With the WordArt object still selected, click the Text Outline arrow (Drawing Tools Format tab | WordArt Styles group) to display the Text Outline gallery.
- Point to Weight in the gallery to display the Weight list.
- Point to 6 pt to display a live preview of this line weight on the WordArt text outline (Figure 2–64).

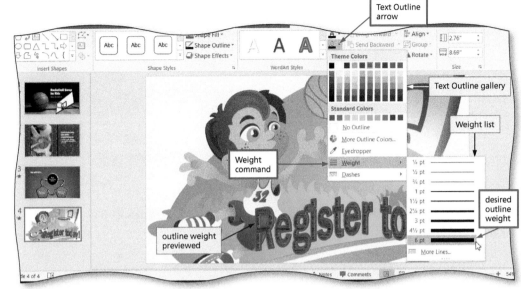

Figure 2–64

Q&A Can I make the line width more than 6 pt?
Yes. Click More Lines and increase the amount in the Width box.

Experiment

- Point to various line weights in the Weight list and watch the line thickness change.

2

- Click 6 pt to apply this line weight to the WordArt text outline.

Q&A Must my text have an outline?
No. To delete the outline, click No Outline in the Text Outline gallery.

To Change the Color of the WordArt Outline

1 DOWNLOAD & SELECT SLIDES | 2 INSERT & FORMAT PICTURES | 3 INSERT & FORMAT SHAPES
4 FORMAT SLIDE BACKGROUNDS | 5 INSERT & FORMAT WORDART | **6 REVIEW, REVISE, & PRINT SLIDES**

Why? *The WordArt outline color and the boy's shorts are similar, so you can add contrast by changing one of these slide elements.* The following steps change the WordArt outline color.

1

- With the WordArt object still selected, display the Text Outline gallery.
- Point to Black, Background 1 (first color in Theme Colors row) to display a live preview of this outline color (Figure 2–65).

Figure 2–65

Experiment

• Point to various colors in the gallery and watch the outline colors change.

2

• Click Black, Background 1 to apply this color to the WordArt outline.

• Click outside of the WordArt box to deselect this slide element (Figure 2–66).

WordArt object formatted

Figure 2–66

Reviewing and Revising Individual Slides

The text, pictures, and shapes for all slides in the Basketball Camp presentation have been entered. Once you complete a slide show, you might decide to change elements. PowerPoint provides several tools to assist you with making changes. They include finding and replacing text, inserting a synonym, checking spelling, and printing speaker notes. The following pages discuss these tools.

BTW

Finding and Replacing Text

When finding and replacing text, you do not need to display the slide that contains the word for which you are searching. You can perform this action when any slide is displayed. To see the results of the search and replace action, however, you need to display the slide where the change occurred.

Replace Dialog Box

At times, you might want to change all occurrences of a word or phrase to another word or phrase. For example, an instructor may have one slide show to accompany a lecture for several introductory classes, and he wants to update slides with the particular class name and section that appear on several slides. He manually could change the characters, but PowerPoint includes an efficient method of replacing one word with another. The Find and Replace feature automatically locates specific text and then replaces it with desired text.

In some cases, you may want to replace only certain occurrences of a word or phrase, not all of them. To instruct PowerPoint to confirm each change, click the Find Next button in the Replace dialog box instead of the Replace All button. When PowerPoint locates an occurrence of the text, it pauses and waits for you to click either the Replace button or the Find Next button. Clicking the Replace button changes the text; clicking the Find Next button instructs PowerPoint to disregard that particular instance and look for the next occurrence of the Find what text.

To Find and Insert a Synonym

1 DOWNLOAD & SELECT SLIDES | 2 INSERT & FORMAT PICTURES | 3 INSERT & FORMAT SHAPES
4 FORMAT SLIDE BACKGROUNDS | 5 INSERT & FORMAT WORDART | 6 REVIEW, REVISE, & PRINT SLIDES

Why? *When reviewing your slide show, you may decide that a particular word does not express the exact usage you intended or that you used the same word on multiple slides.* In these cases, you could find a **synonym**, or word similar in meaning, to replace the inappropriate or duplicate word. PowerPoint provides a **thesaurus**, which is a list of synonyms and antonyms, to help you find a replacement word.

In this project, you want to find a synonym to replace the word, acquaintances, on Slide 2. The following steps locate an appropriate synonym and replace the word.

1

- Display Slide 2 and then place the insertion point in the word, acquaintances.

- Right-click to display a shortcut menu related to the word, acquaintances. Then, point to Synonyms on the shortcut menu to display a list of synonyms for this word (Figure 2–67).

Q&A How do I locate a synonym for multiple words?
You need to select all the words and then right-click to display the shortcut menu.

If I am using a touch screen, how do I find a synonym?
Tap the Thesaurus button (Review tab | Proofing group) to display the Thesaurus pane for the selected word. Then, in the pane, tap the arrow next to the word to display a shortcut menu.

Figure 2–67

2

- Click the synonym you want (friends) on the Synonyms submenu to replace the word, acquaintances, in the presentation with the word, friends (Figure 2–68).

Q&A What if a suitable word does not display in the Synonyms submenu?
You can display the Thesaurus pane by clicking Thesaurus on the Synonyms submenu. A complete thesaurus with synonyms displays in the pane along with an antonym, which is a word with an opposite meaning.

Figure 2–68

Other Ways

1. Click Thesaurus (Review tab | Proofing group)   2. Press SHIFT+F7

1 DOWNLOAD & SELECT SLIDES | 2 INSERT & FORMAT PICTURES | 3 INSERT & FORMAT SHAPES
4 FORMAT SLIDE BACKGROUNDS | 5 INSERT & FORMAT WORDART | 6 REVIEW, REVISE, & PRINT SLIDES

To Add Notes

Why? As you create slides, you may find material you want to state verbally and do not want to include on the slide. After adding these comments, you can print a set of speaker notes that will print below a small image of the slide. You can type and format comments in the **Notes pane** as you work in Normal view and then print this information as **notes pages**. The Notes pane is hidden until you click the Notes button on the status bar to open the pane. If you want to close the Notes pane, click the Notes button again. Charts, tables, and pictures added to the Notes pane also print on these pages. The following steps add text to the Notes pane on Slides 2, 3, and 4.

Note: In the following step, the word, skills, has been misspelled intentionally as skils to illustrate the use of PowerPoint's spell check feature. Your slides may contain different misspelled words, depending upon the accuracy of your typing.

①

- If necessary, click the Notes button on the status bar to display the Notes pane for Slide 2.

Q&A | Why might I need to click the Notes button?
By default, the Notes pane is closed when you begin a new presentation. Once you display the Notes pane for any slide, the Notes pane will remain open unless you click the Notes button to close it.

- Click the Notes pane and then type **Every morning begins with a group session that covers the day's agenda. The coaches then separate the campers into groups to cover fundamental skils. Each morning ends with a contest designed to be fun and competitive.** (Figure 2–69).

Figure 2–69

Q&A | What if I cannot see all the lines I typed?
You can drag the splitter bar up to enlarge the Notes pane. Clicking the Notes pane scroll arrows or swiping up or down on the Notes pane allows you to view the entire text.

②

- Display Slide 3, click the Notes pane, and then type **Campers will gain confidence while learning sportsmanship and strategies.** (Figure 2–70).

Figure 2–70

③

- Display Slide 4 and then type **Space is limited. Every camper will receive a t-shirt, snacks, and water. Parents are encouraged to attend the awards ceremony at the end of the camp session.** in the Notes pane (Figure 2–71).

Figure 2–71

To Find and Replace Text

1 DOWNLOAD & SELECT SLIDES | 2 INSERT & FORMAT PICTURES | 3 INSERT & FORMAT SHAPES
4 FORMAT SLIDE BACKGROUNDS | 5 INSERT & FORMAT WORDART | **6 REVIEW, REVISE, & PRINT SLIDES**

While reviewing your slides, you realize that the camp will be held in the afternoon, not in the morning. To change this word throughout a presentation, you could view each slide, look for the word, morning, delete the word, and then type the replacement word, afternoon. A more efficient and effective method of performing this action is to use PowerPoint's Find and Replace feature. *Why? This method locates each occurrence of a word or phrase automatically and then replaces it with specified text.* The word, morning, displays three times in the slides and notes. The following steps use Find and Replace to replace all occurrences of the word, morning, with the word, afternoon.

1

- If necessary, display the Home tab and then click the Replace button (Home tab | Editing group) to display the Replace dialog box.

- Type **morning** in the Find what box (Replace dialog box).

- Click the Replace with box and then type **afternoon** in the box (Figure 2–72).

Figure 2–72

2

- Click the Replace All button (Replace dialog box) to instruct PowerPoint to replace all occurrences of the Find what word, morning, with the Replace with word, afternoon (Figure 2–73).

Q&A If I accidentally replaced the wrong text, can I undo this replacement?
Yes. Press CTRL+Z or click the Undo button on the Quick Access Toolbar to undo all replacements. If you had clicked the Replace button instead of the Replace All button, PowerPoint would undo only the most recent replacement.

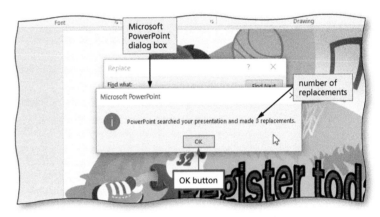

Figure 2–73

3

- Click the OK button (Microsoft PowerPoint dialog box).

- Click the Close button (Replace dialog box).

Other Ways

1. Press CTRL+H

Checking Spelling

After you create a presentation, you should check it visually for spelling errors and style consistency. In addition, you can use PowerPoint's Spelling tool to identify possible misspellings on the slides and in the notes. You should proofread your presentation carefully by pointing to each word and saying it aloud as you point to it. Be mindful of commonly misused words such as its and it's, through and though, and to and too.

PowerPoint checks the entire presentation for spelling mistakes using a standard dictionary contained in the Microsoft Office group. This dictionary is shared with the other Microsoft Office applications such as Word and Excel. A custom dictionary is available if you want to add special words such as proper names, cities, and acronyms.

BTW
Formatting Notes Pane Text
You can format text in the Notes pane in the same manner you format text on a slide. To add emphasis, for example, you can italicize key words or change the font color and size.

When checking a presentation for spelling errors, PowerPoint opens the standard dictionary and the custom dictionary file, if one exists. When a word appears in the Spelling pane, you can perform one of several actions, as described in Table 2–1.

The standard dictionary contains commonly used English words. It does not, however, contain many proper names, abbreviations, technical terms, poetic contractions, or antiquated terms. PowerPoint treats words not found in the dictionaries as misspellings.

Table 2–1 Spelling Pane Buttons and Actions

Button Name/Action	When to Use	Action
Ignore	Word is spelled correctly but not found in dictionaries	PowerPoint continues checking rest of the presentation but will flag that word again if it appears later in document.
Ignore All	Word is spelled correctly but not found in dictionaries	PowerPoint ignores all occurrences of the word and continues checking rest of presentation.
Add	Add word to custom dictionary	PowerPoint opens custom dictionary, adds word, and continues checking rest of presentation.
Change	Word is misspelled	Click proper spelling of the word in Suggestions list. PowerPoint corrects word, continues checking rest of presentation, but will flag that word again if it appears later in document.
Change All	Word is misspelled	Click proper spelling of word in Suggestions list. PowerPoint changes all occurrences of misspelled word and continues checking rest of presentation.
Listen to the pronunciation	To hear the pronunciation of a word	Click the audio speaker icon next to the properly spelled word near the bottom of the Spelling pane.
View synonyms	See some synonyms for the correctly spelled word	View the bullet list of synonyms below the correctly spelled word near the bottom of the Spelling pane.
Close	Stop spelling checker	PowerPoint closes spelling checker and returns to PowerPoint window.

To Check Spelling

1 DOWNLOAD & SELECT SLIDES | 2 INSERT & FORMAT PICTURES | 3 INSERT & FORMAT SHAPES
4 FORMAT SLIDE BACKGROUNDS | 5 INSERT & FORMAT WORDART | 6 REVIEW, REVISE, & PRINT SLIDES

Why? *Although PowerPoint's spelling checker is a valuable tool, it is not infallible. You should not rely on the spelling checker to catch all your mistakes.* The following steps check the spelling on all slides in the Basketball Camp presentation.

1

- Click Review on the ribbon to display the Review tab.

- Click the Spelling button (Review Tab | Proofing group) to start the spelling checker and display the Spelling pane (Figure 2–74).

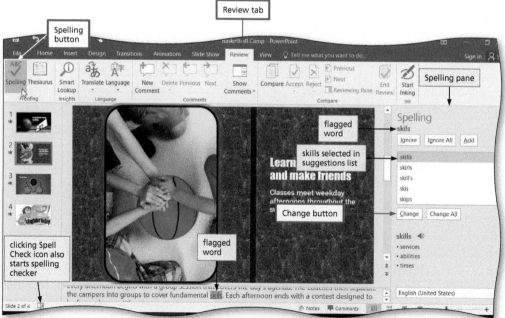

Figure 2–74

2

- With the word, skils, selected in the list and in the Notes pane, click the Change button (Spelling pane) to replace the misspelled flagged word, skils, with the selected correctly spelled word, skills, and then continue the spelling check (Figure 2–75).

Figure 2–75

Could I have clicked the Change All button instead of the Change button?
Yes. When you click the Change All button, you change the current and future occurrences of the misspelled word. The misspelled word, skils, appears only once in the presentation, so clicking the Change or the Change All button in this instance produces identical results.

Occasionally a correctly spelled word is flagged as a possible misspelled word. Why?
Your custom dictionary does not contain the word, so it is seen as spelled incorrectly. You can add this word to a custom dictionary to prevent the spelling checker from flagging it as a mistake.

3

- Replace the misspelled word, lern, with the word, learn.
- Continue checking all flagged words in the presentation. When the Microsoft PowerPoint dialog box appears, click the OK button (Microsoft PowerPoint dialog box) to close the spelling checker and return to the slide where a possible misspelled word appeared.

Other Ways

1. Click Spell Check icon on status bar   2. Right-click flagged word, click correct word   3. Press F7

To Insert a Slide Number

PowerPoint can insert the slide number on your slides automatically to indicate where the slide is positioned within the presentation. The number location on the slide is determined by the presentation theme. You have the option to not display this slide number on the title slide. To insert a slide number on all slides except the title slide, you would follow these steps.

1. Display the Insert tab and then click the Slide Number button (Insert tab | Text group) to display the Header and Footer dialog box.
2. Click the Slide number check box (Header and Footer dialog box) to place a check mark in it.

Can I prevent the slide number from being displayed on the title slide?
Yes. Click the 'Don't show on title slide' check box (Header and Footer dialog box) to place a check mark in it.

3. Click the 'Apply to All' button (Header and Footer dialog box) to close the dialog box and insert the slide number.

How does clicking the 'Apply to All' button differ from clicking the Apply button?
The Apply button inserts the slide number only on the currently displayed slide, whereas the 'Apply to All' button inserts the slide number on every slide.

BTW
PowerPoint Help
At any time while using PowerPoint, you can find answers to questions and display information about various topics through PowerPoint Help. Used properly, this form of assistance can increase your productivity and reduce your frustrations by minimizing the time you spend learning how to use PowerPoint. For instructions about PowerPoint Help and exercises that will help you gain confidence in using it, read the Office and Windows module at the beginning of this book.

Other Ways

1. Click 'Header & Footer' button (Insert tab | Text group), click Slide tab, if necessary (Header and Footer dialog box), click Slide number and 'Don't show on title slide' check boxes, click 'Apply to All' button

To Add a Transition between Slides

A final enhancement you will make in this presentation is to change the transition from Fade to Wipe for all slides and increase the transition duration. The following steps apply this transition to the presentation.

1 Click Transitions on the ribbon and then click the Wipe transition (Transitions tab | Transition to This Slide group) to apply this transition.

2 Click the Duration up arrow in the Timing group four times to change the transition speed from 01.00 to 02.00.

3 Click the Preview Transitions button (Transitions tab | Preview area) to view the new transition and time.

4 Click the 'Apply To All' button (Transitions tab | Timing group) to apply this transition and speed to all four slides in the presentation (Figure 2–76).

Q&A Can I apply a particular transition or duration to one slide and then change the transition or timing for a different slide in the presentation?
Yes. Select a slide and then select a transition and duration. Do not click the 'Apply To All' button. Repeat this process to apply the transition and duration to individual slides.

Figure 2–76

CONSIDER THIS

How can I use handouts to organize my speech?
As you develop a lengthy presentation with many visuals, handouts can help you organize your material. Print handouts with the maximum number of slides per page. Use scissors to cut each thumbnail and then place these miniature slide images adjacent to each other on a flat surface. Any type on the thumbnails will be too small to read, so the images will need to work with only the support of the verbal message you provide. You can rearrange these thumbnails as you organize your speech. When you return to your computer, you can rearrange the slides on your screen to match the order of your thumbnail printouts. Begin speaking the actual words you want to incorporate in the body of the talk. This process of glancing at the thumbnails and hearing yourself say the key ideas of the speech is one of the best methods of organizing and preparing for the actual presentation. Ultimately, when you deliver your speech in front of an audience, the images on the slides or on your note cards should be sufficient to remind you of the accompanying verbal message.

Enhancing a Presentation with Pictures, Shapes, and WordArt   **PowerPoint Module 2   PPT 101**

1 DOWNLOAD & SELECT SLIDES | 2 INSERT & FORMAT PICTURES | 3 INSERT & FORMAT SHAPES
4 FORMAT SLIDE BACKGROUNDS | 5 INSERT & FORMAT WORDART | **6 REVIEW, REVISE, & PRINT SLIDES**

PowerPoint Module 2

To Print Speaker Notes

Why? Comments added to slides in the Notes pane give the speaker information that supplements the text on the slide. They will print with a small image of the slide at the top and the comments below the slide. The following steps print the speaker notes.

1

• Display Slide 1, click File on the ribbon to open the Backstage view, and then click the Print tab in the Backstage view to display Slide 1 in the Print gallery.

• Click 'Full Page Slides' in the Settings area to display the Print gallery (Figure 2–77).

Q&A Why does the preview of my slide appear in black and white?
Your printer determines how the preview appears. If your printer is not capable of printing color images, the preview will not appear in color.

Figure 2–77

2

• Click Notes Pages in the Print Layout area to select this option and then click the Next Page button three times to display a preview of Slide 4 (Figure 2–78).

Q&A Can I preview Slides 1, 2, or 3 now?
Yes. Click the Previous Page button to preview the other slides.

Figure 2–78

- Verify that the printer listed on the Printer Status button will print a hard copy of the presentation. If necessary, click the Printer Status button to display a list of available printer options and then click the desired printer to change the currently selected printer.

- Click the Print button in the Print gallery to print the notes pages on the currently selected printer.

- When the printer stops, retrieve the hard copy.

Q&A I am not using a color printer, so why do the background images display in the figures but not in my printout?
Graphics are displayed depending upon the settings in the Print gallery. For example, the background will print if Color is specified whereas it will not with a Grayscale or Pure Black and White setting.

Other Ways

1. Press CTRL+P, select desired options

To Save and Print the Presentation

It is a good practice to save a presentation before printing it, in the event you experience difficulties printing. For a detailed example of the procedure summarized below for saving and printing a presentation, refer to the Office and Windows module at the beginning of this book.

1 Save the presentation again on the same storage location with the same file name.

2 Print the presentation.

Q&A Do I have to wait until my presentation is complete to print it?
No, you can follow these steps to print a presentation at any time while you are creating it.

3 Because the project now is complete, you can exit PowerPoint.

BTW
Conserving Ink and Toner
If you want to conserve ink or toner, you can instruct PowerPoint to print draft quality documents by clicking File on the ribbon to open the Backstage view, clicking the Options tab in the Backstage view to display the PowerPoint Options dialog box, clicking Advanced in the left pane (PowerPoint Options dialog box), scrolling to the Print area in the right pane, not placing a check mark in the High quality check box, and then clicking the OK button. Then, use the Backstage view to print the document as usual.

BTW
Distributing a Document
Instead of printing and distributing a hard copy of a document, you can distribute the document electronically. Options include sending the document via email; posting it on cloud storage (such as OneDrive) and sharing the file with others; posting it on social media, a blog, or other website; and sharing a link associated with an online location of the document. You also can create and share a PDF or XPS image of the document, so that users can view the file in Acrobat Reader or XPS Viewer instead of in PowerPoint.

BTW
Printing Document Properties
PowerPoint 2016 does not allow you to print document properties. This feature, however, is available in other Office 2016 apps, including Word and Excel.

Summary

In this module, you have learned how to insert and format pictures, add and format shapes, insert and format WordArt, add and format slide backgrounds, find and replace text, check spelling, add notes, and print speaker notes.

What decisions will you need to make when creating your next presentation?
Use these guidelines as you complete the assignments in this module and create your own slide show decks outside of this class.

1. Determine if an online theme can help you design and develop the presentation efficiently and effectively.

2. Identify personal pictures that would create interest and promote the message being presented.

3. Consider modifying pictures.

    a) Add corrections.
    b) Add styles.
    c) Add effects.
    d) Add and format borders.

4. Locate shapes that supplement the verbal and written message.

    a) Size and position them aesthetically on slides.
    b) Add styles.

5. Develop WordArt that emphasizes major presentation messages.

    a) Modify the shape.
    b) Change the weight and color to coordinate with slide elements.

6. Format individual slide backgrounds.

    a) Add and modify fills.
    b) Insert a picture background.

7. Change fonts to emphasize particular slide components.

8. Search for synonyms that help express your thoughts.

9. Create speaker notes.

10. Check spelling.

Apply Your Knowledge

Reinforce the skills and apply the concepts you learned in this module.

Changing the Background and Adding Photos and WordArt

Note: To complete this assignment, you will be required to use the Data Files. Please contact your instructor for information about accessing the Data Files.

Instructions: Run PowerPoint. Open the presentation called Apply 2–1 Bees, which is located in the Data Files. The four slides in the presentation discuss bee stings. The document you open is an unformatted presentation. You are to add pictures, apply picture styles, add WordArt, change slide layouts, and apply a transition so the slides look like Figure 2–79.

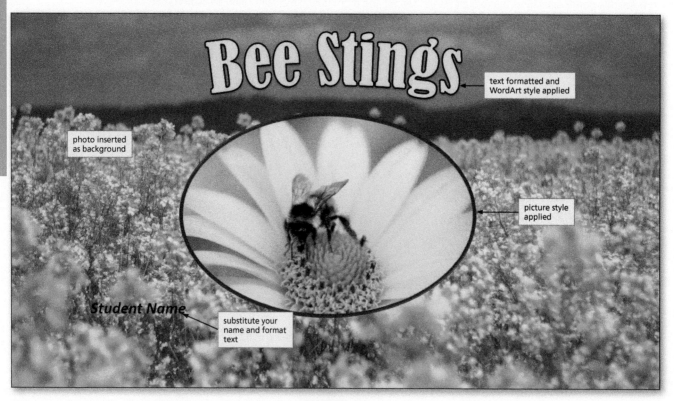

(a) Slide 1

Figure 2–79

Perform the following tasks:

1. On the title slide, use your name in place of Student Name and then bold and italicize this text (Figure 2–79a).

2. If requested to do so by your instructor, change your first name to your mother's first name on the title slide.

3. Increase the title text font size to 96 point and change the font to Bernard MT Condensed. Apply the WordArt style, Fill – White, Outline – Accent 1, Shadow (in first row). Change text fill color to Yellow (in Standard Colors row). Change text outline to Black, Text 1 (in first Theme Colors row) and then change the outline weight to 2¼ pt. Apply the Transform text effect, Arch Up (in Follow Path row) to this text.

4. Apply the Beveled Oval, Black picture style to the picture on Slide 1 and then move the picture to the center of the slide as shown in Figure 2–79a. Use the vertical Smart Guide to align the picture in this location.

5. Create a background on Slide 1 by inserting the photo, Spring, which is located in the Data Files.

6. On Slide 2, change the layout to Title and Content. Increase the title text font to 54 point, change the font color to Green (in Standard Colors row), and then bold this text. Increase the list font size to 32 point, as shown in Figure 2–79b.

7. Create a background on Slides 2 and 3 by inserting the Light Gradient – Accent 4 gradient fill (in first Preset gradients row).

8. On Slide 2, insert the picture, Bee2, move it to the right side of the slide, and then apply the Soft Edge Rectangle picture style to the picture.

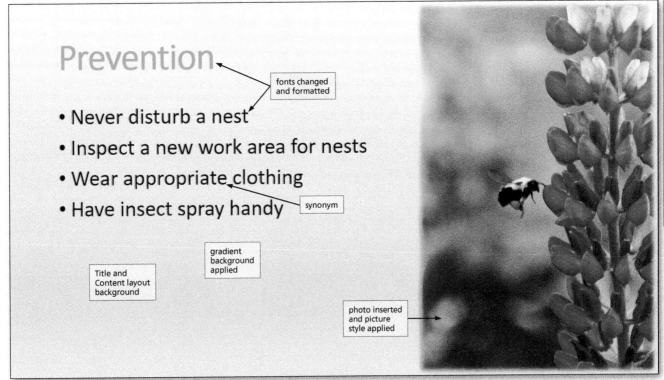

(b) Slide 2

Figure 2–79

9. On Slide 2, type `Wear long pants and a long-sleeved shirt when hiking or working outside.` in the Notes pane.

10. Replace the word, proper, with the synonym, appropriate.

11. On Slide 3 (Figure 2–79c), increase the title text font to 54 point, change the font color to Green (in Standard Colors row), and then bold this text. Increase the list font size to 24 point. Insert the photo, Bee3, and then apply the Reflected Bevel, Black picture style and change the picture brightness to Brightness: +20% Contrast: 0% (Normal) (in Brightness/Contrast area).

12. Type `Apply ice to control swelling.` in the Notes pane.

13. Create a new Slide 4 with the blank layout. Create a background on Slide 4 by inserting the photo, Hiking. Insert the illustration, Bee4. Resize this illustration and move it to the woman's right arm, as shown in Figure 2–79d.

14. On Slide 4, insert the Oval Callout shape (in first row in Callouts area) and then move it to the right side of the woman's head. Apply the Subtle Effect – Gold, Accent 4 (in fourth row) shape style to the callout. Size the shape as shown in the figure. Type `I am glad I have insect repellent in my backpack` in the shape. Bold and italicize this text and then change the font size to 20 point, as shown in Figure 2–79d.

15. Apply the Wind transition in the Exciting category to all slides. Change the duration to 2.50 seconds.

Continued >

Apply Your Knowledge *continued*

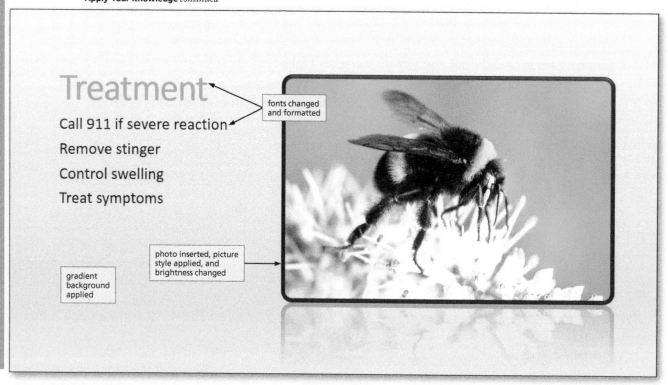

(c) Slide 3

Figure 2–79

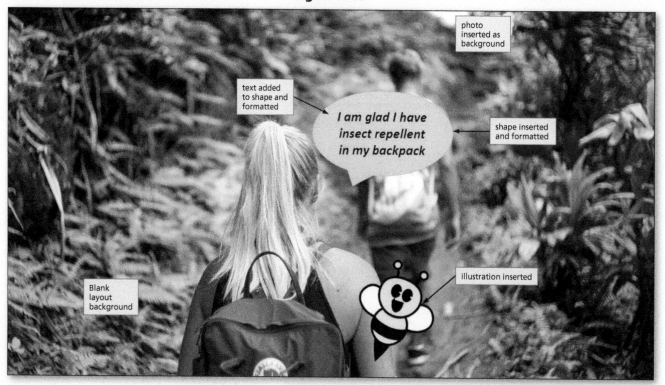

(d) Slide 4

Figure 2–79

16. Save the presentation using the file name, Apply 2–1 Bee Stings.

17. Submit the revised document in the format specified by your instructor.

18. ✳ In Step 4 you applied the Beveled Oval, Black picture style to the photo on Slide 1. How did this style enhance the photo and the slide?

Extend Your Knowledge

Extend the skills you learned in this module and experiment with new skills. You may need to use Help to complete the assignment.

Changing Slide Backgrounds, Inserting Shapes and WordArt, and Finding and Replacing Text

Note: To complete this assignment, you will be required to use the Data Files. Please contact your instructor for information about accessing the Data Files.

Instructions: Run PowerPoint. Open the presentation, Extend 2–1 Monarch, which is located in the Data Files. You will create backgrounds including inserting a photo to create a background, apply a WordArt Style and effect, add shapes, and find and replace text to create the presentation.

Perform the following tasks:

1. Change the document theme to Basis and choose the orange variant (third variant).

2. Find and replace the words, stay alive, with the word, survive, on all slides.

3. On all slides, create a background by inserting the photo, Sky. Change the transparency to 25%.

4. On the title slide (Figure 2–80a), apply the WordArt style, Fill - Black, Text 1, Outline – Background 1, Hard Shadow – Accent 1 (second style in third row), to the title text, and then increase the font size to 72 point. Apply the WordArt Glow text effect, Red, 18 pt glow, Accent color 3 (in Glow Variations area), and then italicize this text. Also, align the text in the middle of the text box by clicking the Align Text button (Home tab | Paragraph group) and then selecting Middle in the Align Text gallery. You may need to use Help for assistance in aligning this text.

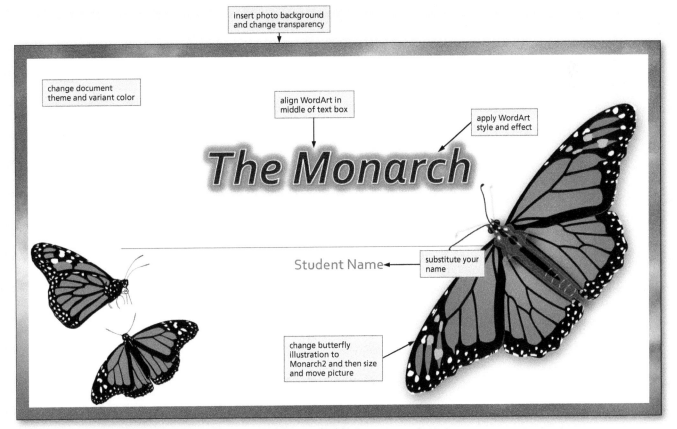

(a) Slide 1

Figure 2–80

Continued >

Extend Your Knowledge *continued*

5. If requested to do so by your instructor, add your current or previous pet's name as the Slide 1 subtitle text in place of Student Name.

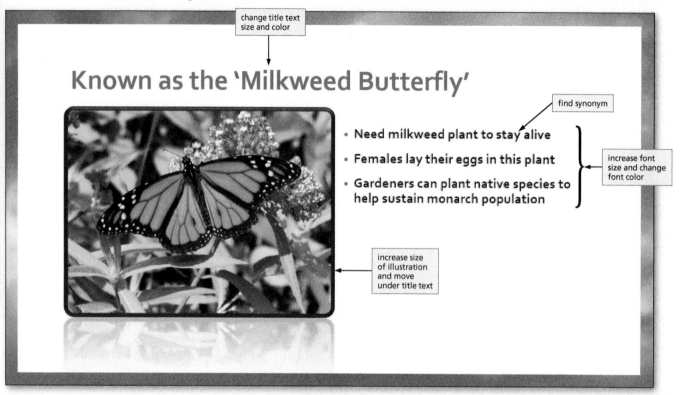

(b) Slide 2

Figure 2–80

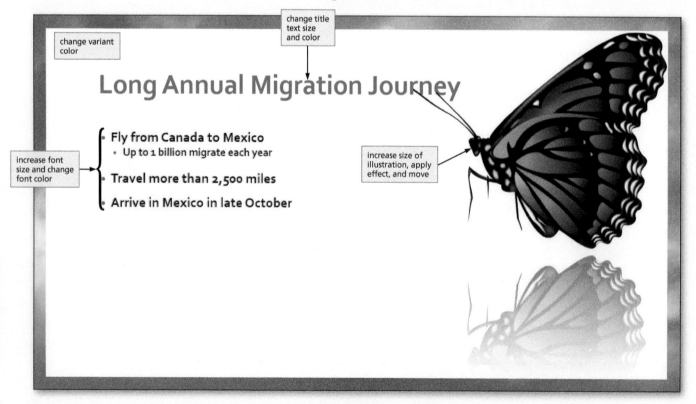

(c) Slide 3

Figure 2–80

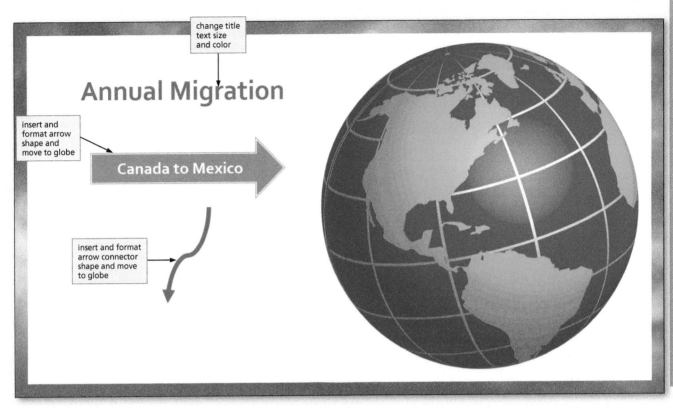

(d) Slide 4

Figure 2–80

6. On Slide 1, move the butterfly illustration in the upper-left corner to the lower-left corner of the slide. Change the butterfly illustration in the upper-right corner of the slide to the illustration, Monarch2. Increase the size of this illustration to approximately 6.26" × 5.44" and move it to the lower-right side of the slide as shown in Figure 2–80a. *Hint*: Use the Size group on the Picture Tools Format tab to enter these measurements for the illustration.

7. On Slides 2 and 3, increase the font size of the first-level paragraphs to 20 point and the one second-level paragraph on Slide 3 to 16 point. Also, change the color of this text to Black, Text 1 (in first Theme Colors row) and then bold this text.

8. On Slide 2 (Figure 2–80b), increase the size of the illustration to approximately 4.14" × 5.53", apply the Reflected Bevel, Black picture style, and then move it under the title text.

9. On Slide 3 (Figure 2–80c), increase the size of the illustration to approximately 4.35" × 5.2", apply the Half Reflection, 8 pt offset reflection picture effect (Reflection Variations area), and then move this illustration to the upper-right corner of the slide.

10. On Slides 2, 3, and 4, decrease the size of the title text to 40 point and then bold this text.

11. On Slide 4 (Figure 2–80d), insert the Right Arrow shape (in Block Arrows area) and position it on the globe illustration near the Canada–United States border. Size the shape as shown in the figure. Type **Canada to Mexico** in the shape. Bold this text and then change the font size to 24 point. Apply the Light 1 Outline, Colored Fill – Orange, Accent 4 shape style (in third Theme Styles row) to the shape.

12. On Slide 4, insert a Curved Arrow Connector shape by displaying the Shapes gallery, clicking this shape (in Lines area), and then positioning the pointer over central Canada in the globe illustration. Then, click and drag the pointer to central Mexico. Size this arrow so it is approximately 0.84" × 1.91". Hint: You can size a shape in the same manner as you size a picture or illustration.

Continued >

Extend Your Knowledge *continued*

13. With the Curved Arrow Connector selected, click the Shape Outline button (Drawing Tools Format tab | Shape Styles group) to display the Shape Outline gallery and then click the Red, Accent 1 style (in first Theme Styles row) to apply this style to this arrow shape. Change the shape outline weight to 6 pt.

14. Apply an appropriate transition to all slides.

15. Save the presentation using the file name, Extend 2–1 Monarch Migration.

16. Submit the revised document in the format specified by your instructor.

17. ✸ In this assignment, you changed the transparency of the inserted background picture on all the slides to 25%. How did this transparency change enhance your slides?

Expand Your World

Create a solution that uses cloud and web technologies by learning and investigating on your own from general guidance.

Modifying a Presentation Using PowerPoint Online

Note: To complete this assignment, you will be required to use the Data Files. Please contact your instructor for information about accessing the Data Files.

Instructions: The park district director in your community is planning a basketball camp for next summer. He has asked you to help him promote this event, and he wants to focus on the skills boys and girls will learn and develop. You inform him that you have created a Basketball Camp presentation for your computer class, and he would like you to customize the content of these slides slightly to promote the summer camp.

Perform the following tasks:

1. Run a browser. Search for the text, PowerPoint Online, using a search engine. Visit several websites to learn about PowerPoint Online. Navigate to the Office Online website. You will need to sign in to your Microsoft account. Run PowerPoint Online.

2. Locate the Basketball Camp presentation in the Recent list and then click the file name to open the file. Click the Edit Presentation button and then click 'Edit in PowerPoint Online' and display the ribbon. Modify the presentation you created for the Basketball Camp presentation by adding the name and address of the nearest park district headquarters on the title slide. In addition, add the date that is the first Saturday in June next year and a starting time of 1 p.m.

3. If requested by your instructor, add the name of one of your high school teachers as the park district director's name on the title slide.

4. Save the presentation using the file name, Expand 2–1 Basketball Camp.

5. Submit the assignment in the format specified by your instructor.

6. ✸ Other than the content the director asked you to include on the title slide, how does the presentation you created using PowerPoint Online differ from the presentation you created in the Module 2 project? Which tabs are not available in PowerPoint Online? View the Home, Design, and Transitions tabs. Do you think the formatting functions, themes, and transitions are adequate to develop effective presentations? Why or why not?

In the Labs

Design, create, modify, and/or use a presentation following the guidelines, concepts, and skills presented in this module. Labs 1 and 2, which increase in difficulty, require you to create solutions based on what you learned in the module; Lab 3 requires you to apply your creative thinking and problem-solving skills to design and implement a solution.

Lab 1: Creating a Presentation, Inserting Photos, Applying Picture Styles, and Inserting Shapes

Note: To complete this assignment, you will be required to use the Data Files. Please contact your instructor for information about accessing the Data Files.

Problem: Your astronomy class is studying the dwarf planet, Pluto, and the New Horizon probe that has been taking photographs of this planet. Prepare the PowerPoint presentation shown in Figure 2–81.

Perform the following tasks:
1. Run PowerPoint. Create a new presentation using the Celestial theme.
2. On Slide 1, insert the photo, Pluto1, as shown in Figure 2–81a. Apply the Metal Oval picture style to the picture, decrease the size of the picture slightly, and then move it to the left side of the slide as shown in the figure.
3. Type **Pluto Up Close** as the Slide 1 title text. Press the ENTER key after the words, PLUTO and UP, so the text is displayed on three lines. Change the font to Britannic Bold and increase the font size to 88 point. Apply the WordArt style Gradient Fill – Gray (first style in

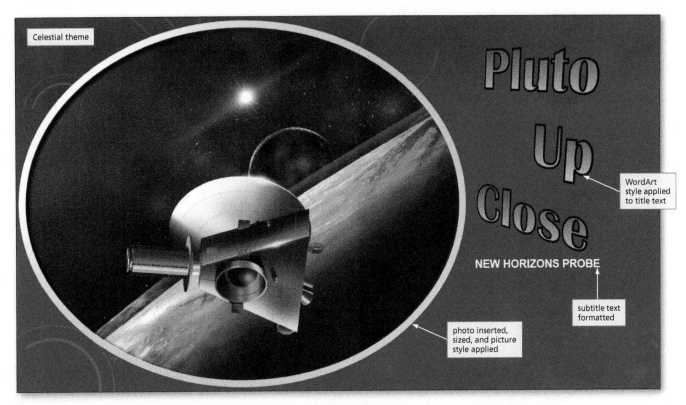

(a) Slide 1

Figure 2–81

Continued >

In the Labs *continued*

second row). Change the text outline color to Black, Background 1 (in Theme Colors row) and the text outline weight to 3 pt. Also, apply the Perspective Heroic Extreme Left 3-D Rotation (in Perspective area) to this text. Type **New Horizons Probe** as the subtitle text. Change the font to Arial, decrease the font size to 16 point, and then bold this text.

4. Insert four new slides. Create Slides 2 and 5 with the Two Content layout, Slide 3 with the Panoramic Picture with Caption layout, and Slide 4 with the Title Only layout.

5. Using Figures 2–81b through 2–81e as a guide, type the title and content text. On Slide 2, change the title font to Arial, increase the font size to 44 point, and then change the font color to Red (in Standard Colors row). Use the Format Painter to apply these formatting changes to the title text on Slides 4 and 5.

6. On Slide 3, change the font size of the two paragraphs to 24 point and then bold this text.

7. On Slide 5, change the bulleted list font size to 28 point and then bold this text.

8. Using Figures 2–81b through 2–81e as a guide, insert all illustrations on Slides 2 through 5. The pictures and illustration to be inserted, which are available in the Data Files, are called Pluto2 (for Slide 2), Solar System (for Slide 3), Pluto3 (for Slide 4), and Solar System2 (for Slide 5).

9. Size the pictures and then use the Smart Guides to position these images. You may want to zoom the slides to help you align these graphic elements.

10. On Slide 2, apply the Bevel Perspective picture style to the picture, change the picture border color to Red, and then change the border weight to 3 pt, as shown in Figure 2–81b.

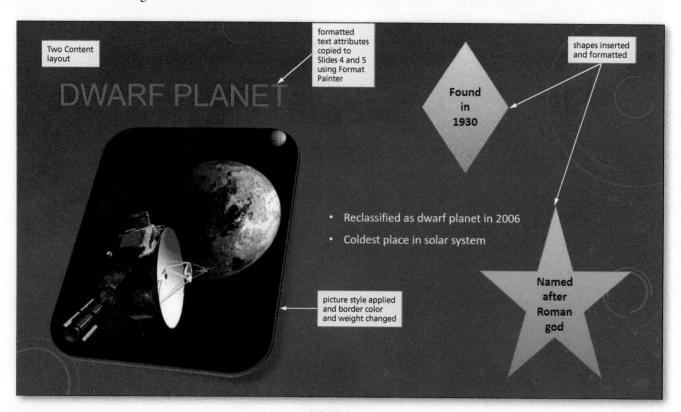

(b) Slide 2

Figure 2–81

11. On Slide 2, insert the Diamond shape located in the Basic Shapes area to the right of the title text. Apply the Subtle Effect – Olive Green, Accent 4 shape style (in Theme Styles area) to the shape, type **Found in 1930** in the shape, and then bold this text. Insert the 5-Point Star shape located in the Stars and Banners area in the lower-right corner of the slide. Apply the Subtle Effect – Blue, Accent 2 shape style (in Theme Styles area) to the shape, type **Named after Roman god** in the shape, and then bold this text. Adjust the size and position of these two shapes, as shown in the figure.

12. On Slide 3, insert the Sun shape located in the Basic Shapes area on the lower-right corner of the slide. Apply the Intense Effect – Gold, Accent 5 shape style (in Theme Styles area) to the shape. Size the shape as shown in the figure. Type the text, **Pluto takes 248 earth years to orbit the sun** in the shape and then bold this text, as shown in Figure 2–81c.

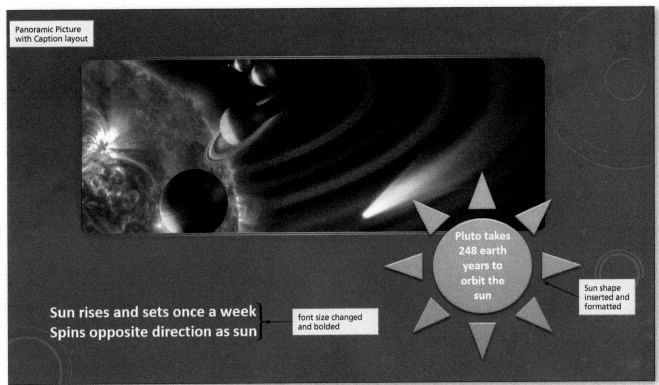

(c) Slide 3

Figure 2–81

13. On Slide 4, insert the Oval shape. Select this shape, hold down the SHIFT key, and then draw a circle .75" × .75", as shown in Figure 2–81d. *Hint*: Use the Size group in the Drawing Tools Format tab to enter the exact measurement of the shape. Change the shape fill gradient to Linear Down (in first Light Variations area). Then copy and paste this shape four times. Move the five shapes around the Pluto illustration, as shown in the figure.

14. On Slide 5, apply the Simple Frame, White picture style to the illustration. Insert the Left Arrow shape located in the Block Arrows area to the right of the illustration. Change the shape fill to Red. Size the shape as shown in the figure. Type **Pluto** in the shape and then bold this text, as shown in Figure 2–81e.

15. On Slide 2, type **Pluto was discovered on February 18, 1930, by Clyde Tombaugh of the Lowell Observatory.** in the Notes pane.

16. On Slide 3, type **It takes five hours for the sun's rays to reach Pluto. It takes only eight minutes for the sun's rays to reach Earth.** in the Notes pane.

Continued >

STUDENT ASSIGNMENTS

In the Labs *continued*

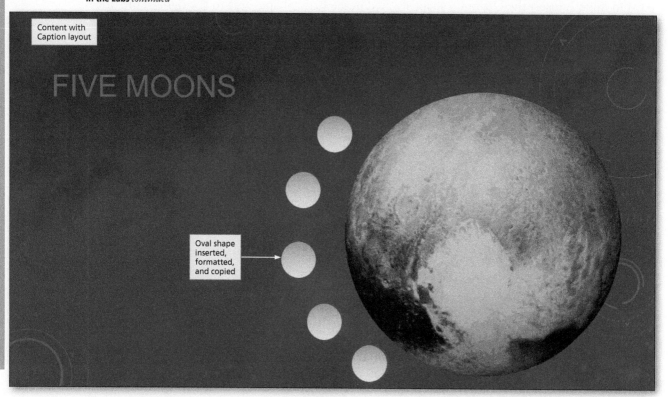

(d) Slide 4

Figure 2–81

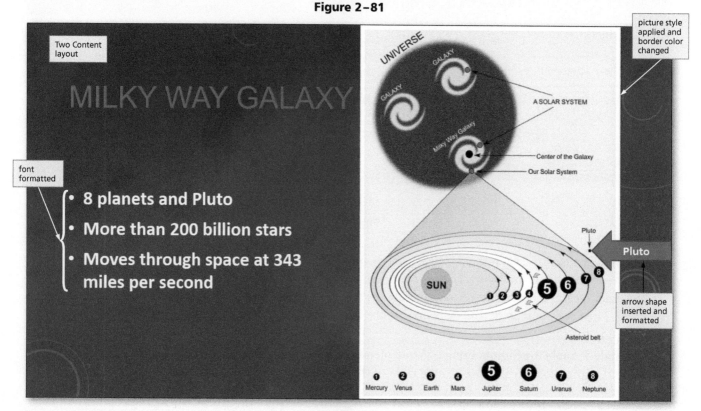

(e) Slide 5

Figure 2–81

17. If requested by your instructor, type the name of the city or county in which you were born into the title placeholder on Slide 3.

18. Apply the Vortex transition in the Exciting category to all slides. Change the duration to 3.0 seconds.

19. Check the spelling and correct any errors. Save the presentation using the file name, Lab 2–1 Pluto Up Close.

20. Print the notes pages.

21. Submit the document in the format specified by your instructor.

22. ✸ In Step 2, you applied the Metal Oval picture style to the picture. How did this improve the design of the slide? Why did you put a 3 pt red border on the picture on Slide 2?

Lab 2: Creating a Presentation Using an Online Theme Template, Shapes, and WordArt

Note: To complete this assignment, you will be required to use the Data Files. Please contact your instructor for information about accessing the Data Files.

Problem: Your local library has hired a singer for the summer reading program. Her weekly show is centered around music and art, and one of her songs is about the colors of the rainbow. In addition to her backdrop of rainbow colors, you decide to develop a presentation to teach the children more about rainbows. You create the presentation shown in Figure 2–82.

Perform the following tasks:

1. Run PowerPoint and then search for an online template by typing **nature** in the 'Search for online templates and themes' box. Choose the template called Nature presentation, illustrated landscape design (widescreen).

2. Delete Slides 12 and 13, delete Slides 6 through 10, and then delete Slides 3 and 4. Duplicate Slide 2 and then move Slide 4 to the end of the presentation.

3. Type the title and text content for all slides, as shown in Figures 2–82a through 2–82e.

(a) Slide 1

Figure 2–82

Continued >

In the Labs continued

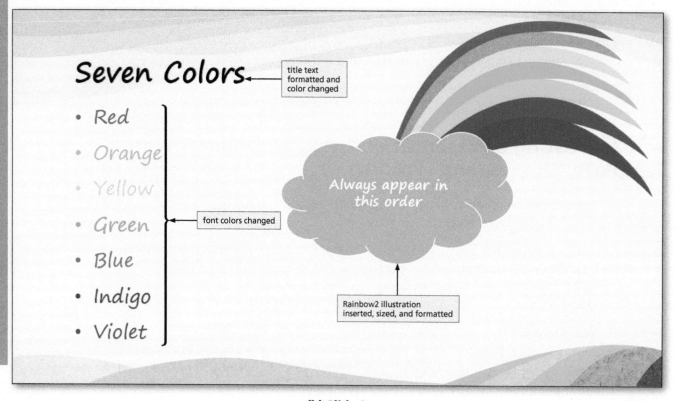

(b) Slide 2

Figure 2–82

(c) Slide 3

Figure 2–82

4. Insert the illustrations shown in Figures 2–82b through 2–82d from the Data Files. The illustrations are called Rainbow1 (for Slide 1), Rainbow2 (for Slide 2), Rainbow3 (for Slide 3), and People (for Slide 4). Size the illustrations using Figure 2–82 as a guide.

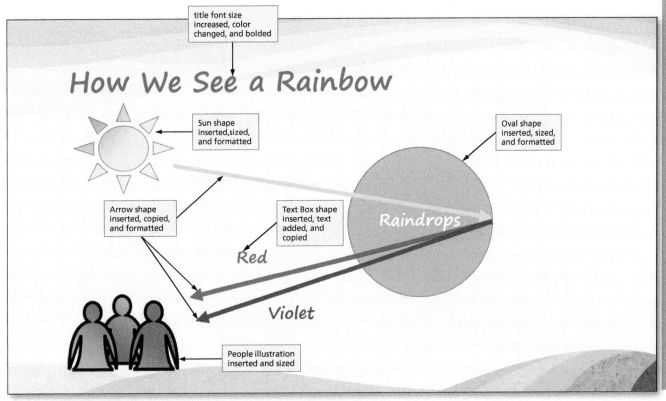

(d) Slide 4

Figure 2–82

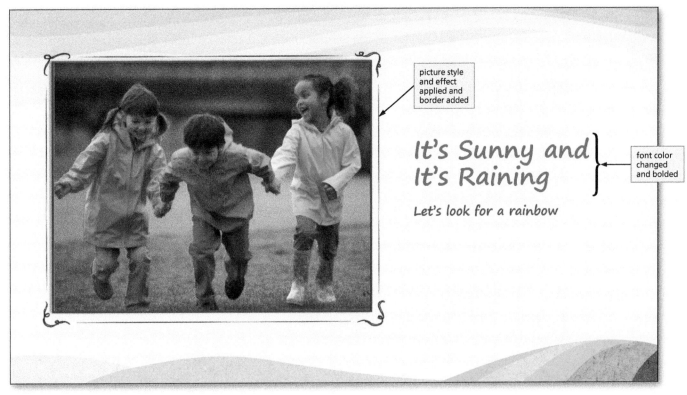

(e) Slide 5

Figure 2–82

5. On the title slide, select the title text and then apply the WordArt style Fill – White, Outline – Accent 1, Shadow (fourth style in first row). Increase the font size to 72 point. Change the text fill to Red (in Standard Colors row), the text outline color to Purple (in Standard Colors row),

Continued >

In the Labs *continued*

and the text outline weight to 3 pt. Also, apply the Arch Up transform effect (Follow Path area), to this text. Position this WordArt, as shown in Figure 2–82a.

6. If requested by your instructor, add the name of your hometown in the subtitle placeholder.

7. On Slide 2, increase the font size of the title to 40 point, change the font color to Black, Text 2 (in first Theme Colors row), and then bold this text. Increase the font size of the bulleted list to 28 point. Change the font color for each bulleted paragraph to the color that is named. For example, the first bulleted paragraph is Red, so change the font color to Red. Use Blue for the Blue text and Dark Blue for the Indigo text, as shown in Figure 2–82b.

8. On Slide 2, insert the Cloud shape, located in the Basic Shapes area, at the bottom of the rainbow illustration. Change the shape style to Light 1, Outline, Colored Fill – Light Blue, Accent 2 (in third Theme Styles row). Size the shape as shown in the figure. Type `Always appear in this order` in the shape, increase the font size to 20 point, and then bold this text, as shown in Figure 2–82b.

9. On Slide 3, increase the font size of the title text to 40 point, change the font color to Red, and then bold this text. Change the font color of the bulleted list text to Dark Blue (in Standard Colors row). For the illustration, apply the Brightness: +20% Contrast: +40% (in Brightness/Contrast area), as shown in Figure 2–82c.

10. On Slide 4, increase the font size of the title text to 40 point, change the font color to Red, and then bold this text, as shown in Figure 2–82d. Insert the Sun shape, located in the Basic Shapes area, in the upper left area of the slide below the title text. Change the shape fill color to Yellow (in Standard Colors row) and then apply the From Top Left Corner gradient (in Dark Variations area) to the shape. Size and position the shape as shown in the figure.

11. On Slide 4, insert the Oval shape located in the Basic Shapes area, resize the shape so that it is approximately 3" × 3", and then change the Shape Fill color to Light Blue, Accent 2 (in Theme Colors row). Move this shape to the area shown in the figure. Type `Raindrops` in the shape, increase the font size to 24 point, and then bold this text.

12. On Slide 4, insert the Arrow shape, located in the Lines area, from the edge of the sun shape to the right side of the blue shape, as shown in Figure 2–82d. Change the weight to 6 pt. Copy and paste this arrow two times and use the sizing handles to position the arrows, as shown in the figure. Change the upper Arrow shape outline color to Yellow, the middle Arrow shape to Red, and the lower Arrow shape to Purple.

13. On Slide 4, insert the Text Box shape, located in the Basic Shapes area, type `Red` in the shape, change the font color to Red, increase the font size to 24 point, and then bold this text. Copy and paste this shape one time, change the text to `Violet,` and then change the font color to Purple. Move these two text box shapes to the areas shown in the figure.

14. On Slide 5, change the title text font color to Red and then bold this text, as shown in Figure 2–82e. Change the font color of the text to Purple and then bold this text. Apply the Simple Frame, White picture style to the picture. Add a 3 pt Purple border and then apply the Offset Left shadow (in Outer area) picture effect.

15. Change the transition to Origami in the Exciting category to all slides. Change the duration to 2.5 seconds.

16. Check spelling and correct all errors. Save the presentation using the file name, Lab 2–2 About Rainbows.

17. Submit the revised document in the format specified by your instructor.

18. ✹ You searched for an online rainbow theme. Do you think any of the other themes would have worked well for your presentation? Does choosing specific slide layouts while beginning the exercise help save time creating the presentation?

Lab 3: **Consider This: Your Turn**

Design and Create a Presentation about Learning to Knit and Crochet

Note: To complete this assignment, you will be required to use the Data Files. Please contact your instructor for information about accessing the Data Files.

Part 1: More than 50 million people knit or crochet to create fun and useful items, to relax, or to exchange ideas with fellow hobbyists at a regional guild or group. The local craft store in your community is offering a series of classes on knitting and crocheting techniques, and the manager has asked you to help promote the event. The introductory course includes instruction on selecting yarn, hooks, and needles; reading patterns; and making basic stitches. The intermediate and advanced courses include knitting in the round; making sleeves, button holes, and cables; and bead and filet crocheting. Classes are scheduled for four weeks on consecutive Saturdays beginning the first week of every month. All students will learn new skills and complete a fashionable project, which could include creating afghans, hats, and scarves for community residents in need. Use the concepts and techniques presented in this module to prepare a presentation to promote the classes. Select a suitable theme, and include a title slide, bulleted lists, shapes, and WordArt. The presentation should contain photos and illustrations appropriately resized. Six photos and illustrations are available in the Data Files: Green Yarn, Mitten, Two Mittens, Penguin, Quilt, and Scarf. Apply picture styles and effects. Add a title slide and closing slide to complete your presentation. Format the title slide with a shape. Format the background with at least one picture and apply a background texture to at least one slide. Review and revise your presentation as needed. Submit your assignment in the format specified by your instructor.

Part 2: ✹ You made several decisions while creating the presentation in this assignment: where to place text, how to format the text (such as font, font size, and where to use WordArt), which graphical image(s) to use, what styles and effects to apply, where to position the graphical images, how to format the graphical images, and which shapes to use to add interest to the presentation. What was the rationale behind each of these decisions? When you reviewed the document, what further revisions did you make and why? Where would you recommend showing this slide show?

3 Reusing a Presentation and Adding Media and Animation

Objectives

You will have mastered the material in this module when you can:

- Color a photo
- Add an artistic effect to a photo
- Align paragraph text
- Change views
- Ungroup, change the color of, and regroup an illustration
- Copy a slide element from one slide to another
- Insert and edit a video clip

- Insert an audio clip
- Control audio and video clips
- Insert entrance, emphasis, and exit effects
- Control animation timing
- Change theme colors
- Change a theme and variant on one slide
- Print handouts

BTW

Media in Presentations
Well-produced video and audio clips add value to a presentation when they help explain a concept that cannot be captured in a photo or illustration. Before you insert these files on a slide, however, consider whether they really add any value to your overall slide show. Audiences quickly tire of extraneous movement and sounds on slides, and they will find such media clips annoying. The audience's attention should focus primarily on the presenter; extraneous or inappropriate media files may divert their attention and, in turn, decrease the quality of the presentation.

Introduction

At times, you will need to revise a PowerPoint presentation. Changes may include inserting and adding effects to photos, altering the colors of photos and illustrations, and updating visual elements displayed on a slide. Applying a different theme, changing fonts, and substituting graphical elements can give a slide show an entirely new look. Adding media, including sounds, video, and music, can enhance a presentation and help audience members retain the information being presented. Adding animation can reinforce important points and enliven a presentation.

Project — Presentation with Video, Audio, Animation, and Photos with Effects

The project in this module follows graphical guidelines and uses PowerPoint to create the presentation shown in Figure 3–1. The slides in this revised presentation, which discusses the Spokes Bike Club, have a variety of audio and visual elements. For example, the photos in the slides' backgrounds have artistic effects applied that soften the images and help the audience focus on other elements on the slides. The bicycle wheel photo has colors that blend well with the background. The bullet list is animated with entrance, emphasis, and exit effects. The video has been edited to play only one portion and has effects to add audience interest. Bicycle riding sounds integrate with the visual elements.

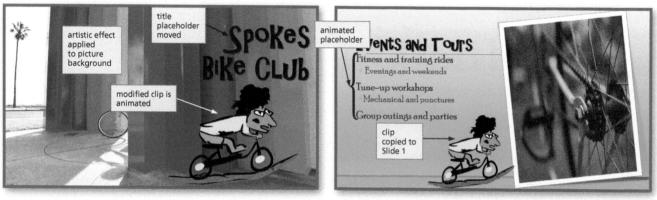

(a) Slide 1 (Title Slide with Picture Background, Modified Clip, and Animated Clip)

(b) Slide 2 (Bulleted List)

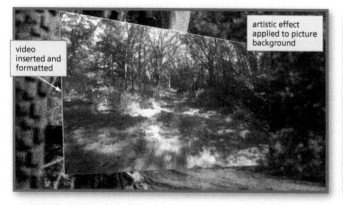

(c) Slide 3 (Picture Background and Video Clip)

(d) Slide 4 (Video Playing Full Screen)

Figure 3–1

For an introduction to Windows and instructions about how to perform basic Windows tasks, read the Office and Windows module at the beginning of this book, where you can learn how to resize windows, change screen resolution, create folders, move and rename files, use Windows Help, and much more.

Overall, the slides have myriad media elements and effects that are exciting for your audience to watch and hear.

In this module, you will learn how to create the slides shown in Figure 3–1. The following roadmap identifies general activities you will perform as you progress through this module:

1. INSERT and ADD EFFECTS to photos, including changing colors and styles.

2. MODIFY PLACEHOLDERS on the slides by moving and changing sizes.

3. MODIFY and COPY an ILLUSTRATION to customize its appearance.

4. ADD MEDIA files to slides.

5. ANIMATE SLIDE CONTENT with entrance, emphasis, and exit effects.

6. CUSTOMIZE SLIDE ELEMENTS by changing a theme and variant on one slide and changing the theme colors.

Inserting Photos and Adding Effects

The Spokes Bike Club presentation consists of three slides that have some text, a clip art image, a formatted background, and a transition applied to all slides. You will insert a photo into one slide and then modify it and another photo by adding artistic effects and recoloring. You also will copy the clip art from Slide 2 to Slide 1 and modify the objects in this clip. In Module 2, you inserted photos, made corrections, and added styles and effects; the new effects you apply in this module will add to your repertoire of photo enhancements that increase interest in your presentation.

In the following pages, you will perform these tasks:

1. Insert the first photo into Slide 1.

2. Recolor the Slide 1 photo.

3. Add an artistic effect to the Slide 3 photo.

4. Send the Slide 1 photo back behind all other slide objects.

To Insert and Resize a Photo into a Slide without Content Placeholders

The first step is to insert a photo into Slide 1. This photo is available in the Data Files. Please contact your instructor for information about accessing the required file. The following steps insert a photo into Slide 1.

1 Run PowerPoint and then open the presentation, Spokes, from the Data Files.

2 Save the presentation using the file name, Spokes Bike Club.

3 With Slide 1 displaying, click Insert on the ribbon to display the Insert tab and then click the Pictures button (Insert tab | Images group) to display the Insert Picture dialog box.

4 If necessary, navigate to the photo location (in this case, the Module 03 folder in the Data Files folder).

5 Click Hidden Bike to select the file.

6 Click the Insert button (Insert Picture dialog box) to insert the photo into Slide 1.

7 Drag the sizing handles to resize the photo so that it covers the entire slide. You can click the Height and Width arrows (Picture Tools Format tab | Size group) to adjust the picture size so that it is approximately 7.5" x 13.33" (Figure 3–2).

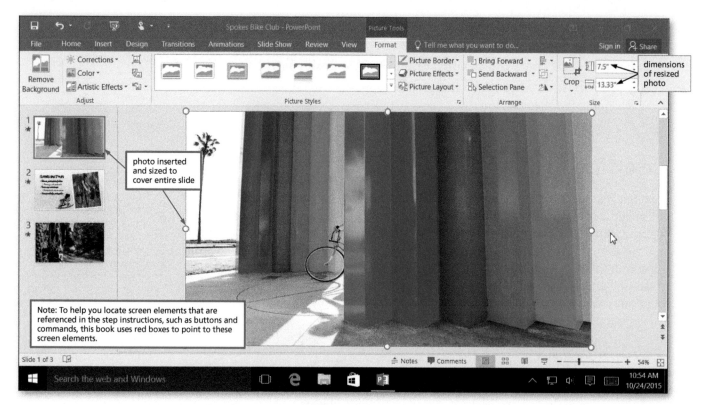

Figure 3–2

BTW
**Touch Screen
Differences**
The Office and Windows
interfaces may vary if you are
using a touch screen. For this
reason, you might notice that
the function or appearance
of your touch screen differs
slightly from this module's
presentation.

Adjusting Photo Colors

PowerPoint allows you to adjust colors to match or add contrast to slide elements by coloring photos. The Color gallery has a wide variety of preset formatting combinations. The thumbnails in the gallery display the more common color saturation, color tone, and recolor adjustments. **Color saturation** changes the intensity of colors. High saturation produces vivid colors; low saturation produces gray tones. **Color tone** affects the coolness, called blue, or the warmness, called orange, of photos. When a digital camera does not measure the tone correctly, a **color cast** occurs, and, as a result, one color dominates the photo. **Recolor** effects convert the photo into a wide variety of hues. The more common are **grayscale**, which changes the color photo into black, white, and shades of gray, and **sepia**, which changes the photo colors into brown, gold, and yellow, reminiscent of a faded photo. You also can fine-tune the color adjustments by clicking the Picture Color Options and More Variations commands in the Color gallery.

To Color a Photo

1 INSERT & ADD EFFECTS | 2 MODIFY PLACEHOLDERS | 3 MODIFY & COPY ILLUSTRATIONS
4 ADD MEDIA | 5 ANIMATE SLIDE CONTENT | 6 CUSTOMIZE SLIDE ELEMENTS

The Office theme and text on Slides 1 and 2 are simple and fulfill the need to communicate the presentation's bicycling message. The photos on Slides 1 and 3 help set the tone of riding on an open road and enjoying the freedom that biking brings. You may want to add an effect to photos. *Why? An effect adds variety to the presentation and helps enhance ordinary photos.* The following steps recolor the Slide 1 photo to intensify the bright colors.

1

- With Slide 1 displaying and the Hidden Bike photo selected, click the Color button (Picture Tools Format tab | Adjust group) to display the Color gallery (Figure 3–3).

Q&A Why does the Adjust group look different on my screen?
Your monitor is set to a different resolution. See the Office 2016 and Windows 10 module for an explanation of screen resolution and the appearance of the ribbon.

Why are gray borders surrounding the thumbnails in the Color Saturation, Color Tone, and Recolor areas in the gallery?
The gray borders show the color saturation, tone, and recolor settings currently in effect for the image on Slide 1.

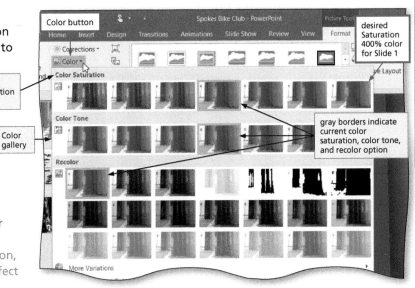

Figure 3–3

2

- Point to Saturation: 400% (last thumbnail in Color Saturation row) to display a live preview of this adjustment on the photo.

 Experiment

- Point to various thumbnails in the Color Saturation area and watch the saturation change on the photo in Slide 1.

- Click Saturation: 400% to apply this saturation to the Hidden Bike photo (Figure 3–4).

Q&A Could I have applied this recoloring to the photo if it had been a background instead of a file inserted into the slide?
No. Artistic effects and recoloring cannot be applied to backgrounds.

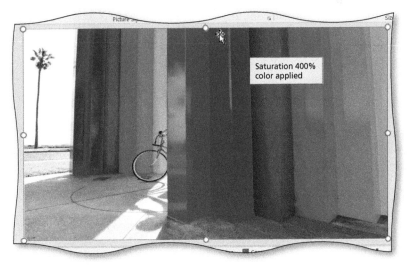

Figure 3–4

Other Ways

1. Click Format Picture on shortcut menu, click Picture icon, click Picture Color, use Saturation slider (Format Picture pane)

To Add an Artistic Effect to a Photo

1 INSERT & ADD EFFECTS | **2 MODIFY PLACEHOLDERS** | **3 MODIFY & COPY ILLUSTRATIONS**
4 ADD MEDIA | **5 ANIMATE SLIDE CONTENT** | **6 CUSTOMIZE SLIDE ELEMENTS**

Artists use a variety of techniques to create effects in their paintings. They can vary the amount of paint on their brushstroke, use fine bristles to add details, mix colors to increase or decrease intensity, and smooth their paints together to blend the colors. You, likewise, can add similar effects to your photos using PowerPoint's built-in artistic effects. **Why?** *The completed Slide 3 will have both a photo and a video, so applying an artistic effect to the photo will provide a contrast between the two images.* The following steps add an artistic effect to the Slide 3 photo.

1

- Display Slide 3 and select the photo.
- Click the Artistic Effects button (Picture Tools Format tab | Adjust group) to display the Artistic Effects gallery (Figure 3–5).

Figure 3–5

2

- Point to Cement (first thumbnail in fourth row) to display a live preview of this effect on the photo.

Experiment

- Point to various artistic effects and watch the hues change on the photo in Slide 3.
- Click Cement to apply this artistic effect to the photo (Figure 3–6).

Figure 3–6

Q&A Can I adjust a photo by recoloring and applying an artistic effect?

Yes. You can apply both a color and an effect. You may prefer at times to mix these adjustments to create a unique image.

Other Ways

1. Click Format Picture on shortcut menu, click Effects icon, click Artistic Effects

---

To Change the Stacking Order

1 INSERT & ADD EFFECTS | 2 MODIFY PLACEHOLDERS | 3 MODIFY & COPY ILLUSTRATIONS
4 ADD MEDIA | 5 ANIMATE SLIDE CONTENT | 6 CUSTOMIZE SLIDE ELEMENTS

The objects on a slide stack on top of each other, much like individual cards in a deck. To change the order of these objects, you use the Bring Forward and Send Backward commands. **Bring Forward** moves an object toward the top of the stack, and **Send Backward** moves an object underneath another object. When you click the Bring Forward arrow, PowerPoint displays a menu with additional command, **Bring to Front**, which moves a selected object to the top of the stack. Likewise, when you click the Send Backward arrow, the **Send to Back** command moves the selected object underneath all objects on the slide. The following steps arrange the Slide 1 photo. *Why? On this slide, the photo is on top of the placeholders, so you no longer can see the text. If you send the photo to the bottom of the stack on the slide, the letters will become visible.*

1

- Display Slide 1 and then select the Hidden Bike photo.
- Click the Picture Tools Format tab and then click the Send Backward arrow (Picture Tools Format tab | Arrange group) to display the Send Backward menu (Figure 3–7).

Q&A How can I see objects that are not on the top of the stack?
Press TAB or SHIFT+TAB to display each slide object.

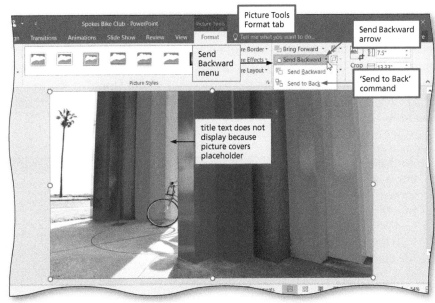

Figure 3–7

2

- Click 'Send to Back' to move the photo underneath all slide objects (Figure 3–8).

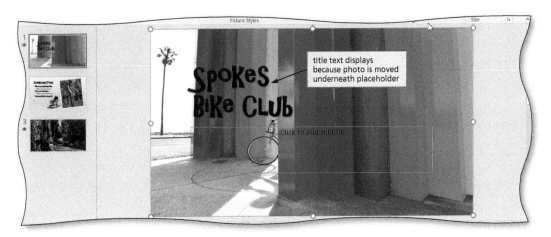

Figure 3–8

Other Ways

1. Click Send Backward arrow (Picture Tools Format tab | Arrange group), press K
2. Right-click photo, point to 'Send to Back' on shortcut menu, click 'Send to Back'

Modifying Placeholders

You have become familiar with inserting text and graphical content in the three types of placeholders: title, subtitle, and content. These placeholders can be moved, resized, and deleted to meet desired design requirements. In addition, placeholders can be added to a slide when needed. After you have modified the placeholder locations, you can view thumbnails of all your slides simultaneously by changing views.

In the following pages, you will perform these tasks:

1. Resize the Slide 1 title text placeholder.
2. Align the Slide 1 title text.
3. Move the Slide 1 title text placeholder.
4. Delete the Slide 1 subtitle text placeholder.
5. Change views.

BTW
The Ribbon and Screen Resolution
PowerPoint may change how the groups and buttons within the groups appear on the ribbon, depending on the computer or mobile device's screen resolution. Thus, your ribbon may look different from the ones in this book if you are using a screen resolution other than 1366 x 768.

PowerPoint Module 3

To Resize a Placeholder

When the Slide 1 title placeholder is selected, the AutoFit button displays on the left side of the placeholder because the two lines of text exceed the placeholder's borders. PowerPoint attempts to reduce the font size when the text does not fit, and you can click this button to resize the existing text in the placeholder so the spillover text will fit within the borders. The following step increases the Slide 1 title text placeholder size. *Why? The two lines of text exceed the placeholder's borders, so you can resize the placeholder and fit the letters within the rectangle.*

- With Slide 1 displaying, click somewhere in the title text paragraphs to position the insertion point in the placeholder. Click the border of the title text placeholder to select it and then point to the top-middle sizing handle.
- Drag the top title text placeholder border upward to enlarge the placeholder (Figure 3–9).

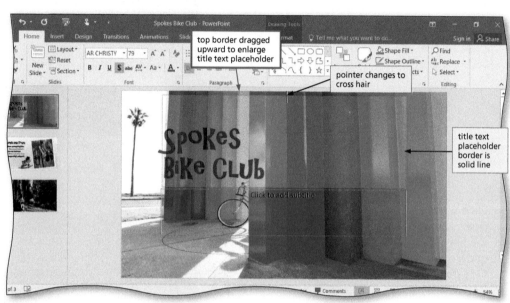

Figure 3–9

Q&A Can I drag other sizing handles to enlarge or shrink the placeholder?
Yes, you also can drag the left, right, top, and corner sizing handles to resize a placeholder. When you drag a corner sizing handle, the box keeps the same proportion and simply enlarges or shrinks the overall shape.

To Align Paragraph Text

The presentation theme determines the formatting characteristics of fonts and colors. It also establishes paragraph formatting, including the alignment of text. Some themes **center** the text paragraphs between the left and right placeholder borders, while others **left-align** the paragraph so that the first character of a text line is near the left border or **right-align** the paragraph so that the last character of a text line is near the right border. The paragraph also can be **justified** so that the text is aligned to both the left and right borders. When PowerPoint justifies text, it adds extras spaces between the words to fill the entire line.

The words, Spokes Bike Club, are left-aligned in the Slide 1 title text placeholder. Later, you will add an illustration on the right side of the slide below this text, so you desire to right-align the paragraph. *Why? Both the text and the picture will be located on the right side of the slide, so the alignments complement each other.* The following steps change the alignment of the Slide 1 title text placeholder.

- With the Home tab displayed, click somewhere in the title text paragraph of Slide 1 to position the insertion point in the text to be formatted (Figure 3–10).

Figure 3–10

- Click the Align Right button (Home tab | Paragraph group) to move the text to the right side of the title text placeholder (Figure 3–11).

Q&A What if I want to return the paragraph to left-alignment?
Click the Align Left button (Home tab | Paragraph group).

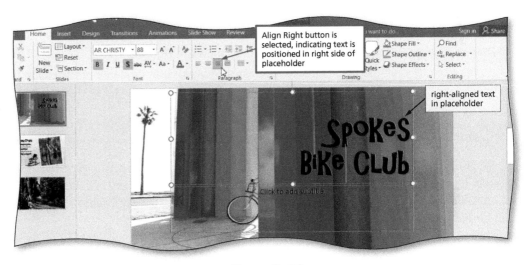

Figure 3–11

Other Ways

1. Right-click paragraph, click Align Right button on mini toolbar	2. Right-click paragraph, click Paragraph on shortcut menu, click Alignment arrow (Paragraph dialog box), click Right, click OK button	3. Click Paragraph dialog box launcher (Home tab | Paragraph group), click Alignment arrow (Paragraph dialog box), click Right, click OK button	4. Press CTRL+R

1 INSERT & ADD EFFECTS | 2 MODIFY PLACEHOLDERS | **3 MODIFY & COPY ILLUSTRATIONS**
4 ADD MEDIA | 5 ANIMATE SLIDE CONTENT | 6 CUSTOMIZE SLIDE ELEMENTS

To Move a Placeholder

Why? *If you desire to have a placeholder appear in a different area of the slide, you can move it to a new location.* The theme layouts determine where the text and content placeholders display on the slide. The Slide 1 title text placeholder currently displays in the middle third of the slide, but the text in this placeholder would be more aesthetically pleasing if it were moved to the upper-right corner of the slide. The following step moves the Slide 1 title text placeholder.

- Click the border of the Slide 1 title text placeholder to select it.
- With the title text placeholder border displaying as a solid line or fine dots, point to an area of the left border between the middle and lower sizing handles so that the pointer changes to a four-headed arrow.

Figure 3–12

Q&A Can I click any part of the border to select it?
Yes. You can click any of the four border lines.

How do I know if the placeholder is selected?
The selection handles are displayed.

- Drag the placeholder upward and to the right, as shown in Figure 3–12.
- If requested by your instructor, replace with word, Spokes, with the name of the city in which you were born.

To Delete a Placeholder

1 INSERT & ADD EFFECTS | **2 MODIFY PLACEHOLDERS** | **3 MODIFY & COPY ILLUSTRATIONS**
4 ADD MEDIA | 5 ANIMATE SLIDE CONTENT | 6 CUSTOMIZE SLIDE ELEMENTS

When you run a slide show, empty placeholders do not display. You may desire to delete unused placeholders from a slide. *Why? So they are not a distraction when you are designing slide content.* The subtitle text placeholder on Slide 1 is not required for this presentation, so you can remove it. The following steps remove the Slide 1 subtitle text placeholder.

- Click a border of the subtitle text placeholder so that it displays as a solid or finely dotted line (Figure 3–13).

- Press the DELETE key to remove the subtitle text placeholder.

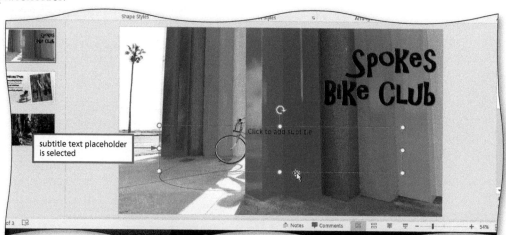

Figure 3–13

Q&A Can I also click the Cut button to delete the placeholder?
Yes. Generally, however, the Cut button is used when you desire to remove a selected slide element, place it on the Clipboard, and then paste it in another area. The DELETE key is used when you do not want to reuse that particular slide element.

Other Ways

1. Select placeholder, press BACKSPACE

2. Right-click placeholder border, click Cut on shortcut menu

To Add a Text Box

You occasionally may need to insert a small amount of text in an area of a slide where no content placeholder is located. A text box allows you to emphasize or set off text that you consider important for your audience to read. To add a text box to a slide, you would perform the following steps.

1. Click the Text Box button (Insert tab | Text group), click the slide, and then drag the object to the desired location on the slide.

2. Click inside the text box to add or paste text.

3. If necessary, change the look and style of the text box characters by using formatting features (Home tab | Font group).

Changing Views

You have been using **Normal view** to create and edit your slides. Once you completed your slides in projects for previous modules, you reviewed the final products by displaying each slide in **Slide Show view**, which occupies the full computer screen. You were able to view how the transitions, graphics, and effects will display in an actual presentation before an audience.

PowerPoint has other views to help review a presentation for content, organization, and overall appearance. **Slide Sorter view** allows you to look at several slides at one time. **Reading view** is similar to Slide Show view because each slide displays individually, but the slides do not fill the entire screen. Using this view, you easily can progress through the slides forward or backward with simple controls at the bottom of the window. Switching between Slide Sorter, Reading, and Normal views helps you review your presentation, assess whether the slides have an attractive design and adequate content, and make sure they are organized for the most impact. After reviewing the slides, you can change the view to Normal so that you may continue working on the presentation.

To Change Views

1 INSERT & ADD EFFECTS | 2 MODIFY PLACEHOLDERS | 3 MODIFY & COPY ILLUSTRATIONS
4 ADD MEDIA | 5 ANIMATE SLIDE CONTENT | 6 CUSTOMIZE SLIDE ELEMENTS

Why? *You have made several modifications to the slides, so you should check for balance and consistency.* The following steps change the view from Normal view to Slide Sorter view, then Reading view, and back to Normal view.

- Click the Slide Sorter view button on the right side of the status bar to display the presentation in Slide Sorter view (Figure 3–14).

Q&A Why is Slide 1 selected?
It is the current slide in the Slides tab.

Figure 3–14

- Click the Reading View button on the right side of the status bar to display Slide 1 of the presentation in Reading view (Figure 3–15).

Figure 3–15

- Click the Next button two times to advance through the presentation.
- Click the Previous button two times to display Slide 2 and then Slide 1.
- Click the Menu button to display commonly used commands (Figure 3–16).

- Click End Show to return to Slide Sorter view, which is the view you were using before Reading view.
- Click the Normal view button to display the presentation in Normal view.

Figure 3–16

Modifying and Copying an Illustration

Slides 1 and 2 (shown in Figures 3–1a and 3–1b) contain an illustration of a biker that was inserted and then modified. You may want to modify an illustration for various reasons. Many times, you cannot find an illustration that precisely represents your topic. For example, you want a picture of a red flower with red petals, but the only available picture has yellow petals.

Occasionally, you may want to remove or change a portion of an illustration or you might want to combine two or more illustrations. For example, you can use one illustration for the background and another photo as the foreground. Other times, you may want to combine an illustration with another type of object. In this presentation, the biker has a brown shirt, and you want to change the color to yellow. In addition, the bike hubs are black, and you want to change them to yellow. The illustration has a blue background, which is not required to display on the slide. You will ungroup the illustration, change the color of the shirt and hubs, and remove the blue background.

Modifying the clip on Slide 2 and then copying it to Slide 1 requires several steps. In the following pages, you will perform these tasks:

1. Zoom Slide 2 to examine the illustration.

2. Ungroup the illustration.

3. Change objects' color.
4. Delete objects.
5. Regroup the illustration.
6. Copy the illustration from Slide 2 to Slide 1.

To Zoom a Slide

You will be modifying small areas of the illustration, so it will help you select the relevant pieces if the graphic is enlarged. The following step changes the zoom to 90 percent.

1 Display Slide 2 and then drag the Zoom slider or click the Zoom level button or the Zoom In button to change the zoom level to 90%. If necessary, click the Down scroll arrow several times so that the entire graphic is visible (Figure 3–17).

Figure 3–17

To Ungroup an Illustration

1 INSERT & ADD EFFECTS | 2 MODIFY PLACEHOLDERS | 3 MODIFY & COPY ILLUSTRATIONS
4 ADD MEDIA | 5 ANIMATE SLIDE CONTENT | 6 CUSTOMIZE SLIDE ELEMENTS

The next step is to ungroup the biker illustration, also called a clip, on Slide 2. When you **ungroup** an illustration, PowerPoint breaks it into its component objects. A clip may be composed of a few individual objects or several complex groups of objects. These groups can be ungrouped repeatedly until they decompose into individual objects. *Why? Because an illustration is a collection of complex groups of objects, you may need to ungroup a complex object into less complex objects before being able to modify a specific object.* When you ungroup a clip and click the Yes button in the Microsoft PowerPoint dialog box, PowerPoint converts the clip to a PowerPoint object. The following steps ungroup an illustration.

1

- Click the biker clip to select it and then click Format on the ribbon to display the Picture Tools Format tab.
- Click the Group Objects button (Picture Tools Format tab | Arrange group) to display the Group Objects menu (Figure 3–18).

 Q&A Why does the Group Objects button look different on my screen?
Your monitor is set to a different resolution. See the Office 2016 and Windows 10 module for an explanation of screen resolution and the appearance of the ribbon.

Figure 3–18

- Click Ungroup on the Group Objects menu to display the Microsoft PowerPoint dialog box (Figure 3–19).

Figure 3–19

- Click the Yes button (Microsoft PowerPoint dialog box) to convert the clip to a Microsoft Office drawing.

Q&A What happens if I click the No button?
The clip will remain displayed on the slide as an illustration and will not ungroup.

- Click Format on the ribbon to display the Drawing Tools Format tab. Click the Group Objects button (Drawing Tools Format tab | Arrange group) and then click Ungroup again to display the objects that form the biker clip (Figure 3–20).

Q&A Why does the ribbon change from the Picture Tools Drawing tab to the Drawing Tools Format tab and show different options this time?
The illustration has become a drawing object, so tools related to drawing now display.

Why do all those circles display in the clip?
The circles are sizing handles for each of the clip's objects, which resemble pieces of a jigsaw puzzle.

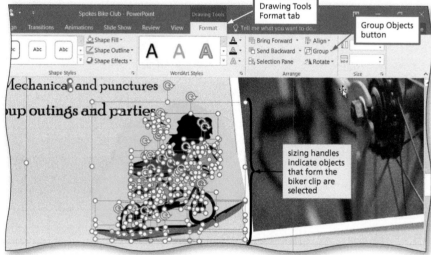

Figure 3–20

Other Ways

1. Right-click clip, point to Group on shortcut menu, click Ungroup   2. Press CTRL+SHIFT+G

To Change the Color of a Clip Object

Now that the biker illustration is ungrouped, you can change the color of the objects. You must exercise care when selecting the correct object to modify. **Why?** *A clip might be composed of hundreds of objects.* The following steps change the color of the biker's shirt from brown to yellow.

- Click an area of the slide that is not part of the clip to deselect all the clip pieces.
- Click the biker's shirt to display sizing handles around the brown colored area (Figure 3–21).

Q&A What if I selected a different area by mistake?
Click outside the clip and retry.

Figure 3–21

2

- Click the Shape Fill arrow (Drawing Tools Format tab | Shape Styles group) to display the Shape Fill gallery.
- Point to Yellow (fourth color in Standard Colors row) to display a live preview of the shirt color (Figure 3–22).

 Experiment

- Point to various colors and watch the biker's shirt color change.

Figure 3–22

3

- Click the color Yellow to change the biker's shirt color (Figure 3–23).

Q&A Why is the bar under the Shape Fill button now yellow?
The button displays the last fill color selected.

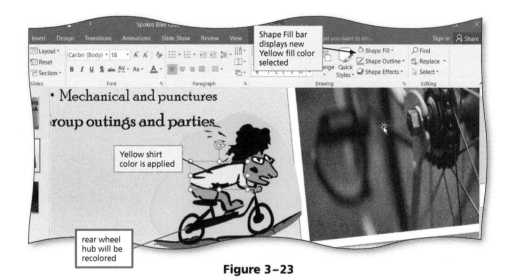

Figure 3–23

4

- Click the rear wheel hub to select it.
- Click the Shape Fill button (Drawing Tools Format tab | Shape Styles group) to change the wheel hub color to Yellow (Figure 3–24).

Q&A Why did I not need to click the Shape Fill arrow to select this color?
PowerPoint uses the last fill color selected. This color displays in the bar under the bucket icon on the button.

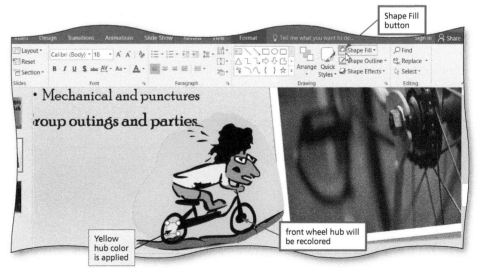

Figure 3–24

5

- Change the front wheel hub color to Yellow (Figure 3–25).

Q&A Can I select multiple objects so I can color them simultaneously?
Yes. While pressing the SHIFT key, click the desired elements to select them.

Figure 3–25

Other Ways

1. Click Shape Fill arrow (Home tab | Drawing group)	2. Right-click object, click Fill button below shortcut menu	3. Right-click object, click Format Shape on shortcut menu, click 'Fill & Line' icon

To Delete a Clip Object

1 INSERT & ADD EFFECTS | 2 MODIFY PLACEHOLDERS | 3 MODIFY & COPY ILLUSTRATIONS
4 ADD MEDIA | 5 ANIMATE SLIDE CONTENT | 6 CUSTOMIZE SLIDE ELEMENTS

With the biker's shirt and hub colors changed, you want to delete the blue background object. ***Why?*** *This object clutters the slide and is not a necessary element of the clip.* The following steps delete this object.

1

- Click the background in any area where the blue color displays to select this object (Figure 3–26).

Q&A Can I select multiple objects so I can delete them simultaneously?
Yes. While pressing the SHIFT key, click the unwanted elements to select them.

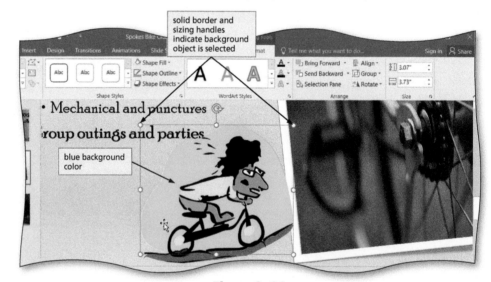

Figure 3–26

2

- Press the DELETE key to delete this object (Figure 3–27).

Figure 3–27

3

- Click one black sweat droplet, press the SHIFT key, and then click the other five sweat droplets to select all six objects (Figure 3–28).

Q&A What can I do if I am having difficulty selecting just these six objects?
Try increasing the zoom, or select a few objects at a time and then delete them.

- Press the DELETE key to delete these objects.

Figure 3–28

To Regroup Objects

1 INSERT & ADD EFFECTS | 2 MODIFY PLACEHOLDERS | 3 MODIFY & COPY ILLUSTRATIONS
4 ADD MEDIA | 5 ANIMATE SLIDE CONTENT | 6 CUSTOMIZE SLIDE ELEMENTS

When you ungrouped the biker clip, you eliminated the embedding data or linking information that tied all the individual pieces together. If you attempt to move or size this clip now, you might encounter difficulties because it consists of multiple objects and is no longer one unified piece. Dragging or sizing affects only a selected object, not the entire collection of objects, so you must use caution when objects are not completely regrouped. You can **regroup** all of the ungrouped objects so they are reassembled into a single unit. The individual pieces of the biker clip now will be regrouped. *Why? When they are regrouped, they cannot be accidentally moved or manipulated.* The following steps regroup these objects into one object.

1

- Position the selection pointer (the left-pointing arrow) in the lower-left corner of the biker illustration and then drag diagonally to the upper-right corner of the illustration so that the entire illustration is covered with a gray box (Figure 3–29).

Q&A Must I drag diagonally from left to right?
No. You can drag in any direction as long as the gray box covers all the clip.

Figure 3–29

- Release the mouse to display all the selected pieces of the illustration.
- Click the Drawing Tools Format tab, and then click the Group Objects button (Drawing Tools Format tab | Arrange group) to display the Group Objects menu (Figure 3–30).

- Click Regroup to recombine all the clip objects.

Figure 3–30

- Use the Zoom slider to change the zoom level to 60%.

Other Ways
1. Right-click selected clip, point to Group on shortcut menu, click Regroup

To Copy a Clip from One Slide to Another

1 INSERT & ADD EFFECTS | 2 MODIFY PLACEHOLDERS | 3 MODIFY & COPY ILLUSTRATIONS
4 ADD MEDIA | 5 ANIMATE SLIDE CONTENT | 6 CUSTOMIZE SLIDE ELEMENTS

The biker clip on Slide 2 also can display in its modified form on the title slide. You first must copy it using the Office Clipboard and then paste it in the desired location. The **Office Clipboard** is a temporary storage location that can hold a maximum of 24 text or graphics items copied from any Office program. *Why? You have made modifications to the illustration that you would like to duplicate on the title slide.* The same procedure of copying and pasting objects works for copying and pasting text from one placeholder to another. The following steps copy this slide element from Slide 2 to Slide 1.

- With the biker illustration on Slide 2 selected, display the Home tab and then click the Copy button (Home tab | Clipboard group) (Figure 3–31).

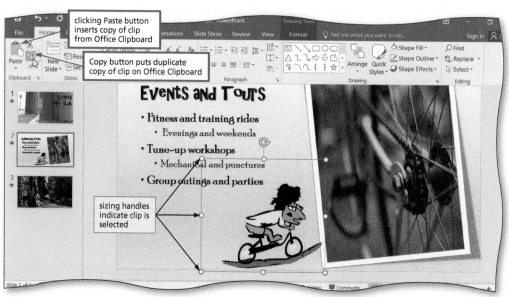

- Display Slide 1 and then click the Paste button (Home tab | Clipboard group), shown in Figure 3–31, to insert the biker illustration into the title slide.

Figure 3–31

Q&A Is the clip deleted from the Office Clipboard when I paste it into the slide?
No.

● Increase the biker illustration size by dragging one of the corner sizing handles outward until the biker is the size shown in Figure 3–32 (approximately 5.24" x 6.55" as indicated on the Drawing Tools Format tab). Drag the biker to the location shown in this figure.

Figure 3–32

Break Point: If you wish to take a break, this is a good place to do so. Be sure to save the Spokes Bike Club file again and then you can quit PowerPoint. To resume at a later time, start PowerPoint, open the file called Spokes Bike Club, and continue following the steps from this location forward.

Adding Media to Slides

Media files can enrich a presentation if they are used correctly. Video files can be produced with a camera and editing software, and sound files can come from the Internet, files stored on your computer, or an audio track on a CD. To hear the sounds, you need a sound card and speakers or headphones on your system.

Once an audio or video clip is inserted into a slide, you can specify options that affect how the file is displayed and played. For example, you can have the video play automatically when the slide is displayed, or you can click the video frame when you are ready to start the playback. You also can have the video fill the entire slide, which is referred to as **full screen**. If you decide to play the slide show automatically and have it display full screen, you can drag the video frame to the gray area off the slide so that it does not display briefly before going to full screen. You can select the 'Loop until Stopped' option to have the video repeat until you click the next slide, or you can choose to not have the video frame display on the slide until you click the slide.

If your video clip has recorded sounds, the volume controls give you the option to set how loudly this audio will play. They also allow you to mute the sound so that your audience will hear no background noise or music.

In the following pages, you will perform these tasks:

1. Insert a video file into Slide 3.

2. Trim the video file to shorten the play time.

3. Add video options that determine the clip's appearance and playback.

4. Insert an audio file into Slide 1.

5. Add audio options that determine the clip's appearance and playback.

6. Resize the Slide 3 video clip.

7. Add a video style to the Slide 3 clip.

8. Add a border to the Slide 3 clip and then change the border weight and color.

BTW

Using Codecs
Video and audio content developers use a codec (**co**mpressor/**dec**ompressor) to reduce the file size of digital media. The reduced file size helps transfer files across the Internet quickly and smoothly and helps save space on storage media. Your computer can play any compressed file if the specific codec used to compress the file is available on your computer. If the codec is not installed or is not recognized, your computer attempts to download this file from the Internet. Many codec files are available to download from the Internet at no cost.

To Insert a Video File

Slide 3 has another photo of a biker, and you have a video clip of a person riding a bike through a wooded area. You want to use a majority of the clip and eliminate a few seconds from the beginning and end. PowerPoint allows you to insert this clip into your slide and then trim the file. ***Why? You want to play just a portion of the video when you preview the clip or run the slide show.*** This clip is available in the Data Files. The following steps insert this video clip into Slide 3.

1

- Display Slide 3 and then display the Insert tab. Click the Insert Video button (Insert tab | Media group) to display the Insert Video menu (Figure 3–33).

Figure 3–33

2

- Click 'Video on My PC' on the Insert Video menu to display the Insert Video dialog box.
- If the list of files for Module 03 is not displayed in the Insert Video dialog box, navigate to the location where the files are located.
- Click Mountain Bike Video to select the file (Figure 3–34).

Figure 3–34

3

- Click the Insert button (Insert Video dialog box) to insert the video clip into Slide 3 (Figure 3–35).

Q&A

Can I adjust the color of a video clip? Yes. You can correct the brightness and contrast, and you also can recolor a video clip using the same methods you learned in this module to color a photo.

Figure 3–35

To Trim a Video File

Why? The Mountain Bike Video file has a running time of slightly more than 32 seconds. Much of the video is the same view of the bike path through the woods, so you decide to delete a few seconds from the beginning and the end to shorten the duration. PowerPoint's **Trim Video** feature allows you to trim the beginning and end of your clip by designating your desired Start Time and End Time. These precise time measurements are accurate to one-thousandth of a second. The start point is indicated by a green marker, and the end point is indicated by a red marker. The following steps trim the Mountain Bike Video clip.

1

• With the video clip selected on Slide 3, click the Play/Pause button in the video controls underneath the video to play the entire video.

Q&A Can I play the video by clicking the Play button in the Preview group?
Yes. This Play button plays the entire clip. You may prefer to click the Play/Pause button displayed in the video controls to stop the video and examine one of the frames.

Figure 3–36

• Click Playback on the ribbon to display the Video Tools Playback tab.
• Click the Trim Video button (Video Tools Playback tab | Editing group) to display the Trim Video dialog box (Figure 3–36).

2

• Point to the start point, which is indicated by the green marker on the right side, so that the pointer changes to a two-headed arrow.
• Slide or drag the green marker to the right until the Start Time is approximately 00:05.991 (Figure 3–37).

Figure 3–37

- Point to the end point, which is indicated by the red marker on the right side, so that the pointer changes to a two-headed arrow.
- Slide or drag the red marker to the left until the End Time is 00:29.100 (Figure 3–38).

Q&A Can I specify the start or end times without dragging the markers?
Yes. You can enter the time in the Start Time or End Time boxes, or you can click the Start Time or End Time box arrows. You also can click the Next Frame and Previous Frame buttons (Trim Video dialog box).

Figure 3–38

- Click the Play/Pause button (Trim Video dialog box) to review the shortened video clip.
- Click the OK button (Trim Video dialog box) to set the Start Time and End Time and to close the Trim Video dialog box.

Other Ways

1. Right-click clip, click Trim on shortcut menu

To Add Video Options

1 INSERT & ADD EFFECTS | 2 MODIFY PLACEHOLDERS | 3 MODIFY & COPY ILLUSTRATIONS
4 ADD MEDIA | 5 ANIMATE SLIDE CONTENT | 6 CUSTOMIZE SLIDE ELEMENTS

Once the video clip is inserted into Slide 3, you can specify that the video plays automatically when the slide is displayed. **Why?** *When you are giving your presentation, you do not want to click the mouse to start the video.* You also can adjust the volume of the sound recorded on the file. The following steps add the option of playing the video full screen automatically and also decrease the volume of the clip.

- With the Video Tools Playback tab displaying, click the Start arrow (Video Tools Playback tab | Video Options group) to display the Start menu (Figure 3–39).

Q&A What does the On Click option do?
The video clip would begin playing when a presenter clicks the frame during the slide show.

Figure 3–39

- Click Automatically in the Start menu to run the video clip automatically when the slide is displayed.

- Click the 'Play Full Screen' check box (Video Tools Playback tab | Video Options group) to place a check mark in it.
- Click the Volume button (Video Tools Playback tab | Video Options group) to display the Volume menu (Figure 3–40).

- Click Medium on the Volume menu to set the audio volume.

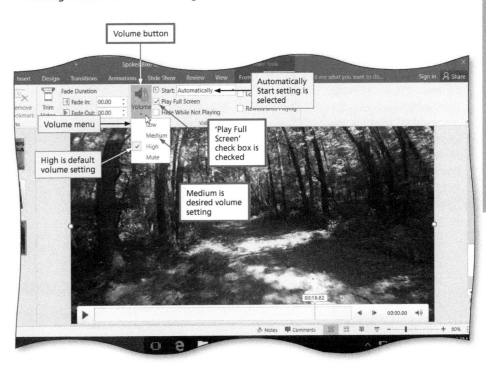

Figure 3–40

Q&A Will the Mute option silence the video's background sounds?
Yes. Click Mute if you do not want your audience to hear any recorded sounds.

To Insert an Audio File

1 INSERT & ADD EFFECTS | 2 MODIFY PLACEHOLDERS | 3 MODIFY & COPY ILLUSTRATIONS
4 ADD MEDIA | 5 ANIMATE SLIDE CONTENT | 6 CUSTOMIZE SLIDE ELEMENTS

If you have a digital audio recorder or an app on your smartphone or mobile device, you can record sounds to insert into your presentation. The following steps insert an audio clip into Slide 1. *Why? An audio clip of pedaling sounds adds interest to the start of your presentation when Slide 1 is displayed.*

- Display Slide 1 and then click Insert on the ribbon to display the Insert tab.
- Click the Insert Audio button (Insert tab | Media group) to display the Insert Audio menu (Figure 3–41).

Figure 3–41

- Click 'Audio on My PC' on the Insert Audio menu to open the Insert Audio dialog box.
- If the list of files for Module 03 is not displayed in the Insert Audio dialog box, navigate to the location where the files are located.
- Click Pedaling Sounds to select the file (Figure 3–42).

Figure 3–42

- Click the Insert button (Insert Audio dialog box) to insert the audio clip into Slide 1 (Figure 3–43).

Q&A Why does a sound icon display on the slide?
The icon indicates an audio file is inserted.

Do the audio control buttons have the same functions as the video control buttons that displayed when I inserted the Mountain Bike Video clip?
Yes. The controls include playing and pausing the sound, moving back or forward 0.25 seconds, audio progress, elapsed time, and muting or unmuting the sound.

Figure 3–43

4

- Drag the sound icon to the lower-left corner of the slide (Figure 3–44).

Must I move the icon on the slide?
No. Although your audience will not see the icon when you run the slide show, it is easier for you to see the audio controls in this area of this slide.

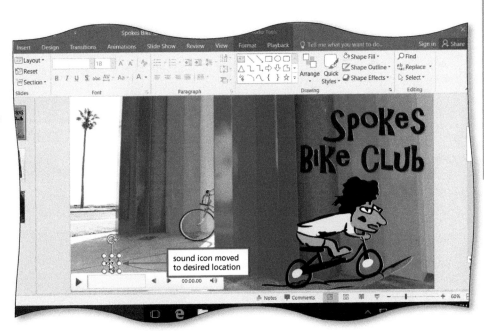

Figure 3–44

To Add Audio Options

1 INSERT & ADD EFFECTS | 2 MODIFY PLACEHOLDERS | 3 MODIFY & COPY ILLUSTRATIONS
4 ADD MEDIA | 5 ANIMATE SLIDE CONTENT | 6 CUSTOMIZE SLIDE ELEMENTS

Once an audio clip is inserted into a slide, you can specify options that control playback and appearance. As with the video options you applied to the Mountain Bike Video clip, the audio clip can play either automatically or when clicked, it can repeat the clip while a particular slide is displayed, and you can drag the sound icon off the slide and set the volume. The following steps add the options of starting automatically, playing until the slide no longer is displayed, and hiding the sound icon on the slide. *Why? You do not want to click the screen to start the sound, so you do not need to see the icon. In addition, you want the pedaling sound to repeat while the slide is displayed to coordinate with the bicycle picture prominently shown and to keep the audience's attention focused on the topic of riding a bike.*

1

- If necessary, click Playback on the ribbon to display the Audio Tools Playback tab. Click the Start arrow (Audio Tools Playback tab | Audio Options group) to display the Start menu (Figure 3–45).

2

- Click Automatically in the Start menu.

Does the On Click option function the same way for an audio clip as On Click does for a video clip?
Yes. If you were to select On Click, the sound would begin playing only after the presenter clicks Slide 1 during a presentation.

Figure 3–45

- Click the 'Loop until Stopped' check box (Audio Tools Playback tab | Audio Options group) to place a check mark in it.

Q&A

What is the difference between the 'Loop until Stopped' option and the 'Play Across Slides' option?
The audio clip in the 'Loop until Stopped' option repeats for as long as one slide is displayed. In contrast, the 'Play Across Slides' option would play the clip only once, but it would continue to play while other slides in the presentation are displayed. Once the end of the clip is reached, the sound would end and not repeat.

- Click the 'Hide During Show' check box (Audio Tools Playback tab | Audio Options group) to place a check mark in it (Figure 3–46).

Q&A

Why would I want the icon to display during the show?
If you had selected the On Click option, you would need to find this icon on the slide and click it to start playing the clip.

Can I adjust the sound's volume?
Yes. You can adjust the volume or mute the sound by clicking the Volume button (Audio Tools Playback tab | Audio Options group) or by clicking the Mute/Unmute button on the Media Controls bar and using the volume slider.

Figure 3–46

BTW
Ideal Decibels for Creativity
When you need to be creative, move to an environment filled with moderate background noise, such as a coffee shop. Researchers at the University of British Columbia state that a noise level of approximately 70 decibels, which is the sound of a quiet conversation or highway noise from afar, fosters original ideas. Anything louder than this ambient noise level decreases the thought process.

TO TRIM AN AUDIO FILE

PowerPoint's **Trim Audio** feature allows you to set the beginning and end of a clip. You select the desired sound to play by designating a Start Time and End Time, which are accurate to one-thousandth of a second. As with the video file markers, the Start Time is indicated by a green marker and the End Time is indicated by a red marker. To trim an audio file, you would perform the following steps.

1. Select the sound icon on the slide and then click the Trim Audio button (Audio Tools Playback tab | Editing group).
2. Drag the green marker to the right until the desired Start Time is displayed.
3. Drag the red marker to the left until the desired End Time is displayed.
4. Click the Play/Pause button (Trim Audio dialog box) to review the shortened audio clip.
5. Click the OK button to set the Start Time and End Time and to close the Trim Audio dialog box.

To Resize a Video

The default Mountain Bike Video frame size can be changed. You resize a video clip in the same manner that you resize photos and illustrations. The following steps will decrease the Mountain Bike Video frame using a sizing handle. *Why? You want to fit the video near the center of the slide.*

- Display Slide 3 and select the video frame. Click Format on the ribbon to display the Video Tools Format tab (Figure 3–47).

Figure 3–47

2

- With the video selected, drag any corner sizing handle diagonally inward until the frame is resized to approximately 5.5" x 9.78".
- Drag the clip to the location shown in Figure 3–48.

Figure 3–48

To Add a Video Style

The video styles are similar to the photo styles you applied in Module 2 and include various shapes, angles, borders, and reflections. The following steps apply a video style to the Mountain Bike Video clip on Slide 3. *Why? The Mountain Bike Video clip on Slide 3 displays full screen when it is playing, but you decide to increase the visual appeal of the clip when it is not playing by applying a video style.*

1

- With the video selected and the Video Tools Format tab displaying, click the More button in the Video Styles gallery (Video Tools Format tab | Video Styles group) (shown in Figure 3–48) to expand the gallery.
- Point to Reflected Perspective Right in the Intense area of the Video Styles gallery (sixth style in first row) to display a live preview of that style applied to the video frame on the slide (Figure 3–49).

Figure 3–49

Experiment

- Point to various photo styles in the Video Styles gallery and watch the style of the video frame change in the document window.

3

- Click Reflected Perspective Right in the Video Styles gallery to apply the style to the selected video and then move the video to the location displayed in Figure 3–50.

Q&A Can I preview the movie clip?
Yes. Point to the clip and then click the Play button on the ribbon (Preview group) or the Play/Pause button on the video controls below the video.

Figure 3–50

To Add a Video Border

You have added borders to photos, and this design element can be added to video frames. The following steps apply a border to the Mountain Bike Video clip. *Why? A border adds visual interest and distinguishes the video frame from the photo background.*

1

- With the video clip selected, click the Video Border button (Video Tools Format tab | Video Styles group) and then point to Weight on the Video Border gallery to display the Weight gallery.

- Point to 2¼ pt to display a live preview of this line weight on the video frame (Figure 3–51).

🔍 **Experiment**

- Point to various line weights in the Weight gallery and watch the line thickness change.

- Click 2¼ pt to add this line weight to the video.

Figure 3–51

To Change a Video Border Color

Once you have added a border to a video, you can modify the default color. The following steps change the video border color to yellow. *Why? Yellow is used as an accent color in many components of the Spokes Bike Club slides.*

- With the video clip selected, click the Video Border button (Video Tools Format tab | Video Styles group) and then point to Yellow (fourth color in Standard Colors row) to display a live preview of this border color on the video frame (Figure 3–52).

🔍 **Experiment**

- Point to various colors in the gallery and watch the line colors change.

- Click Yellow to change the video border color.

Figure 3–52

Other Ways

1. Click Format Video on shortcut menu, click Fill & Line icon, click Color button

Break Point: If you wish to take a break, this is a good place to do so. Be sure to save the Spokes Bike Club file again and then you can quit PowerPoint. To resume at a later time, start PowerPoint, open the file called Spokes Bike Club, and continue following the steps from this location forward.

Animating Slide Content

Animation includes special visual and sound effects applied to text or other content. You already are familiar with one form of animation: transitions between slides. To add visual interest and clarity to a presentation, you can animate various parts of an individual slide, including pictures, shapes, text, and other slide elements. For example, each paragraph on the slide can spin as it is displayed. Individual letters and shapes also can spin or move in various motions. PowerPoint has a variety of built-in animations that will fade, wipe, or fly-in text and graphics.

Custom Animations

BTW
Animation Effect Icon Colors
Animation effects allow you to control how objects enter, move on, and exit slides. Using a traffic signal analogy may help you remember the sequence of events. Green icons indicate when the animation effect starts on the slide. Yellow icons represent the object's motion; use them with caution so they do not distract from the message you are conveying to your audience. Red icons indicate when the object stops appearing on a slide.

You can create your own **custom animations** to meet your unique needs. Custom animation effects are grouped in categories: entrance, exit, emphasis, and motion paths. **Entrance effects**, as the name implies, determine how slide elements first appear on a slide. **Exit effects** work in the opposite manner as entrance effects: They determine how slide elements disappear. **Emphasis effects** modify text and objects displayed on the screen. For example, letters may darken or increase in font size. The entrance, exit, and emphasis animations are grouped into categories: Basic, Subtle, Moderate, and Exciting. You can set the animation speed to Very Fast, Fast, Medium, Slow, or Very Slow.

The Slide 2 illustration shows a person riding a bike. When the slide is displayed, the audience will see this biker enter from the lower-left corner, move across the slide, stop beside the bicycle picture, rock slightly, and then continue across the slide toward the right corner.

In the following pages, you will perform these tasks:

1. Apply an entrance effect to the biker illustration and then change the direction.
2. Apply emphasis and exit effects.
3. Change the exit effect direction.
4. Preview the animation sequence.
5. Modify the entrance, emphasis, and exit effects' timing.
6. Animate text paragraphs.

To Animate an Illustration Using an Entrance Effect

1 INSERT & ADD EFFECTS | 2 MODIFY PLACEHOLDERS | 3 MODIFY & COPY ILLUSTRATIONS
4 ADD MEDIA | 5 ANIMATE SLIDE CONTENT | **6 CUSTOMIZE SLIDE ELEMENTS**

The biker you modified will not appear on Slide 2 when you display the slide. Instead, it will enter the slide from the lower-left corner. *Why? The biker is facing right, so he will appear to be pedaling forward.* It will then continue across the slide until it reaches the lower-right side of the photo. Entrance effects are colored green in the Animation gallery. The following step applies an entrance effect to the biker illustration in Slide 2.

- Display Slide 2, select the biker clip, and then click Animations on the ribbon to display the Animations tab.
- Click the Fly In animation in the Animation gallery (Animations tab | Animation group) to display a live preview of this animation and to apply this entrance animation to the biker illustration (Figure 3–53).

Q&A | Are more entrance animations available?
Yes. Click the More button in the Animation gallery to see additional animations. You can select one of the 13 entrance animations that are displayed, or you can click the 'More Entrance Effects' command to expand the selection. You can click any animation to see a preview of the effect.

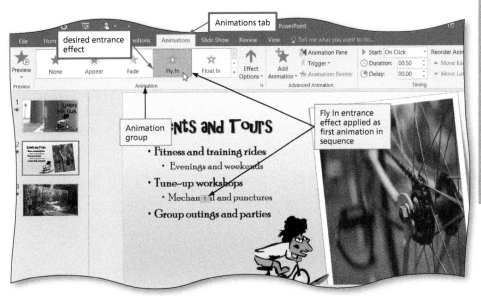

Figure 3–53

Q&A Why does the number 1 appear in a box on the left side of the clip?
The 1 is a sequence number and indicates Fly In is the first animation that will appear on the slide when you click the slide.

To Change Animation Direction

1 INSERT & ADD EFFECTS | 2 MODIFY PLACEHOLDERS | 3 MODIFY & COPY ILLUSTRATIONS
4 ADD MEDIA | 5 ANIMATE SLIDE CONTENT | 6 CUSTOMIZE SLIDE ELEMENTS

Why? *By default, the illustration appears on the slide by entering from the bottom edge, and you want it to enter from the left.* You can modify this direction and specify that it enters from another side or from a corner. The following steps change the biker entrance animation to enter from the left.

1

- Click the Effect Options button (Animations tab | Animation group) to display the Direction gallery (Figure 3–54).

Q&A Why does a pink box appear around the From Bottom arrow?
From Bottom is the default entrance direction applied to the animation.

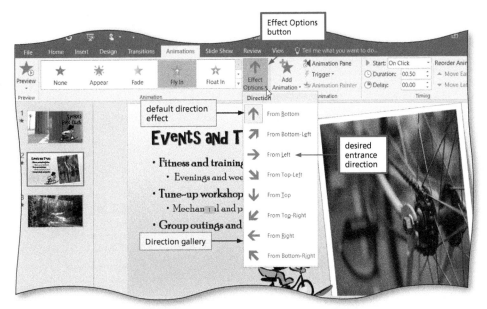

Figure 3–54

2

- Click the From Left arrow to see a preview of this animation and apply this direction to the entrance animation.

Q&A Can I change this entrance effect?
Yes. Repeat Step 1 to select another direction.

To Animate an Illustration Using an Emphasis Effect

Why? *The biker will enter the slide from the left corner and stop beside the bicycle photo. You then want it to rock slightly.* PowerPoint provides several effects that you can apply to a picture once it appears on a slide. These movements are categorized as emphasis effects, and they are colored yellow in the Animation gallery. You already have applied an entrance effect to the biker, so you want to add another animation to this illustration. The following steps apply an emphasis effect to the biker after the entrance effect.

①

- Select the biker illustration and then click the Add Animation button (Animations tab | Advanced Animation group) to display the Animation gallery (Figure 3–55).

Q&A Are more emphasis effects available in addition to those shown in the Animation gallery?
Yes. To see additional emphasis effects, click 'More Emphasis Effects' in the lower portion of the Animation gallery. The effects are arranged in the Basic, Subtle, Moderate, and Exciting categories.

Figure 3–55

②

- Click Teeter (third effect in the first Emphasis row) to see a preview of this animation and to apply this emphasis effect to the biker illustration (Figure 3–56).

Q&A Do I need to use both an entrance and an emphasis effect, or can I use only an emphasis effect?
You can use one or the other effect, or both effects.

Why does the number 2 appear in a box below the number 1 on the left side of the illustration?
The 2 in the numbered tag indicates a second animation is applied in the animation sequence.

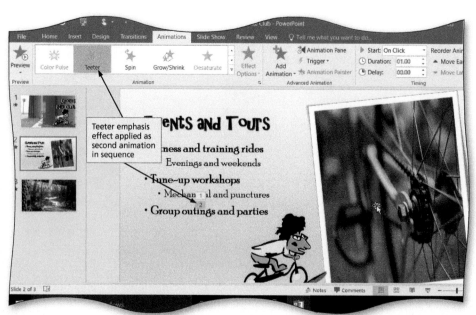

Figure 3–56

To Animate an Illustration Using an Exit Effect

The animated biker will enter the slide from the lower-left corner, stop beside the bicycle photo, and then teeter. It then will continue across the slide and exit in the lower-right corner. To continue this animation sequence, you first need to apply an exit effect. As with the entrance and emphasis effects, PowerPoint provides a wide variety of effects that you can apply to remove an illustration from a slide. These exit effects are colored red in the Animation gallery. You already have applied the Fly In entrance effect, so you will apply the Fly Out exit effect. *Why? It would give continuity to the animation sequence.* The following steps add this exit effect to the biker illustration after the emphasis effect.

1

- Select the biker illustration and then click the Add Animation button (Animations tab | Advanced Animation group) again to display the Animation gallery.
- Scroll down to display all the exit effects in the gallery (Figure 3–57).

◄ Are more exit effects
Q&A available in addition to those shown in the Animation gallery?
Yes. To see additional exit effects, click 'More Exit Effects' in the lower portion of the Animation gallery. The effects are arranged in the Basic, Subtle, Moderate, and Exciting categories.

Figure 3–57

2

- Click Fly Out to see a preview of this animation and to add this exit effect to the sequence of biker illustration animations (Figure 3–58).

◄ How can I tell that this exit
Q&A effect has been applied?
The Fly Out effect is displayed in the Animation gallery (Animations tab | Animation group), and the number 3 is displayed to the left of the biker illustration.

How can I delete an animation effect?
Click the number associated with the animation you wish to delete and then press the DELETE key.

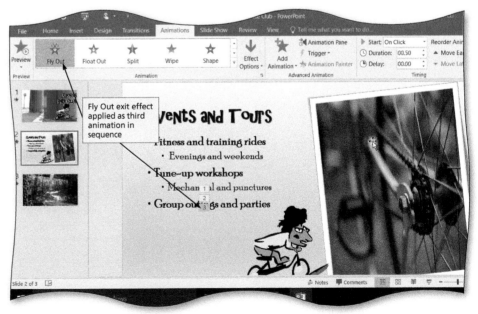

Figure 3–58

To Change Exit Animation Direction

The default direction for a picture to exit a slide is To Bottom. In this presentation, you want the biker to exit in the lower-right corner. *Why? To give the impression it is continuing down a bike path across the slide.* The following steps change the exit animation direction from To Bottom to To Right.

1 Click the Effect Options button (Animations tab | Animation group) to display the Direction gallery (Figure 3–59).

2 Click the To Right arrow to apply this direction to the exit animation effect.

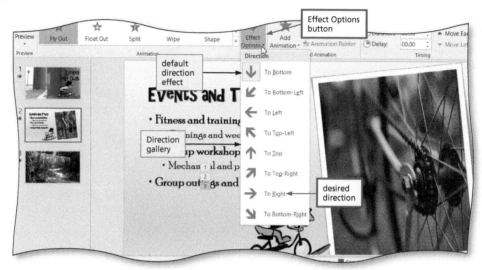

Figure 3–59

To Preview an Animation Sequence

1 INSERT & ADD EFFECTS | 2 MODIFY PLACEHOLDERS | 3 MODIFY & COPY ILLUSTRATIONS
4 ADD MEDIA | 5 ANIMATE SLIDE CONTENT | 6 CUSTOMIZE SLIDE ELEMENTS

Why? Although you have not completed developing the presentation, you should view the animation you have added to check for continuity and verify that the animation is displaying as you expected. By default, the entrance, emphasis, and exit animations will be displayed when you run the presentation and click the slide. The following step runs the presentation and displays the three animations.

1

• Click the Preview button (Animations tab | Preview group) to view all the Slide 2 animations (Figure 3–60).

Q&A Why does a red square appear in the middle of the circle on the Preview button when I click that button?
The red square indicates the animation sequence is in progress. Ordinarily, a green arrow is displayed in the circle.

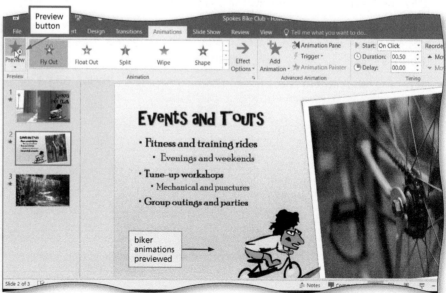

Figure 3–60

To Modify Entrance Animation Timing

The three animation effects are displayed quickly. To create a dramatic effect, you can change the timing. The default setting is to start each animation with a click, but you can change this setting so that the entrance effect is delayed until a specified number of seconds has passed. The following steps modify the start, delay, and duration settings for the entrance animation. *Why? You want the slide title text to display and then, a few seconds later, the biker to start to move across the slide slowly.*

- Click the tag numbered 1 on the left side of the biker illustration and then click the Start arrow (Animations tab | Timing group) to display the Start menu (Figure 3–61).

- Click After Previous to change the start option.

Q&A Why did the numbered tags change from 1, 2, 3 to 0, 1, 2?
The first animation now occurs automatically without a click. The first and second clicks now will apply the emphasis and exit animations.

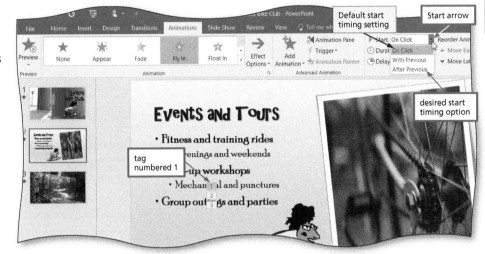

Figure 3–61

What is the difference between the With Previous and After Previous settings?
The With Previous setting starts the effect simultaneously with any prior animation; the After Previous setting starts the animation after a prior animation has ended. If the prior animation is fast or a short duration, it may be difficult for a viewer to discern the difference between these two settings.

- Click the Duration up arrow (Animations tab | Timing group) several times to increase the time from 00.50 second to 02.00 seconds (Figure 3–62).
- Click the Preview button to view the animations.

Q&A What is the difference between the duration time and the delay time?
The duration time is the length of time in which the animation occurs; the delay time is the length of time that passes before the animation begins.

Can I type the speed in the Duration box instead of clicking the arrow to adjust the speed?
Yes. Typing the numbers allows you to set a precise timing.

Figure 3–62

4

- Click the Delay up arrow (Animations tab | Timing group) several times to increase the delay time from 00.00 seconds to 03.00 seconds (Figure 3–63).
- Click the Preview button to view the animations.

Q&A Can I adjust the delay time I just set? Yes. Click the Delay up or down arrows and run the slide show to display Slide 2 until you find the time that best fits your presentation.

Figure 3–63

To Modify Emphasis and Exit Timings

Now that the entrance animation settings have been modified, you can change the emphasis and exit effects for the biker illustration. The emphasis effect can occur once the entrance effect has concluded, and then the exit effect can commence. The biker will start moving slowly, but he will increase his speed after he pauses briefly. You, consequently, will shorten the duration of the exit effect compared with the duration of the entrance effect. The animation sequence should flow without stopping, so you will not change the default delay timing of 00.00 seconds for the emphasis and exit effects. The following steps modify the start and duration settings for the emphasis and exit animations.

1 Click the tag numbered 1, which represents the emphasis effect, on the left side of the biker illustration.

2 Click the Start arrow (Animations tab | Timing group) to display the Start menu and then click After Previous to change the start option.

3 Click the Duration up arrow (Animations tab | Timing group) several times to increase the time to 02.00 seconds.

4 Click the tag numbered 1, which now represents the exit effect, click the Start arrow, and then click After Previous.

5 Click the Duration up arrow twice to increase the time to 01.00 seconds.

6 Preview the Slide 2 animation (Figure 3–64).

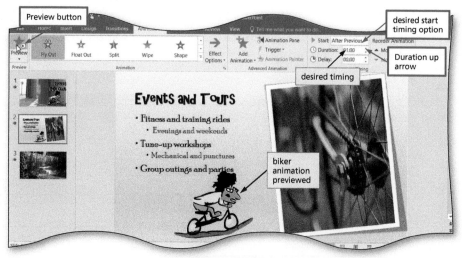

Figure 3–64

To Animate Content Placeholder Paragraphs

The biker illustration on Slide 2 has one entrance, one emphasis, and one exit animation. You decide to add similar animations to the five bulleted paragraphs in the Slide 2 content placeholder. *Why? For a special effect, you can add several emphasis animations to one slide element.* The following steps add one entrance and two emphasis animations to the bulleted list paragraphs.

- Double-click the Slide 2 content placeholder border so that it displays as a solid line (Figure 3–65).

Figure 3–65

- Click the More button (shown in Figure 3–65) in the Animation group (Animations tab | Animation group) to expand the Animation gallery (Figure 3–66).

Figure 3–66

- Click the Fade entrance effect in the Animation gallery (second effect in first row) to add and preview this animation.
- Change the Start option to With Previous.
- Change the Duration time to 02.00 seconds (Figure 3–67).

Q&A Do I need to change the delay time?

No. The paragraphs can start appearing on the slide when the biker exit effect is beginning.

Figure 3–67

- Click the Add Animation button (Animations tab | Advanced Animation group), scroll down to display the entire Emphasis area, and then click the Font Color emphasis animation effect (last effect in third row).
- Change the Start option to After Previous (Figure 3–68).
- Preview the Slide 2 animation.

Figure 3–68

- Click the Add Animation button, scroll down to display the entire Emphasis area again, and then click the Underline emphasis animation effect (first effect in the fourth row).

Q&A Why do the animation effects display differently in the Animation gallery on my screen?
The width of the Animation gallery and the order of the animations may vary, especially if you are using a tablet.

- Change the Start option to With Previous (Figure 3–69).

Q&A Why is a second set of animation numbered tags starting with 0 displaying on the left side of the content placeholder?
They represent the three animations associated with the paragraphs in that placeholder.

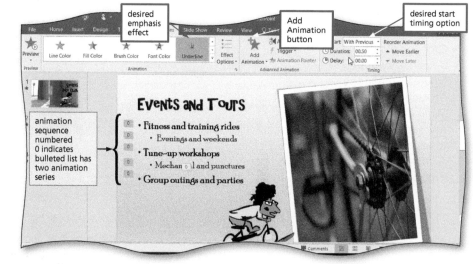

Figure 3–69

BTW

PowerPoint Help
At any time while using PowerPoint, you can find answers to questions and display information about various topics through PowerPoint Help. Used properly, this form of assistance can increase your productivity and reduce your frustrations by minimizing the time you spend learning how to use PowerPoint. For instructions about PowerPoint Help and exercises that will help you gain confidence in using it, read the Office and Windows module at the beginning of this book.

Customizing Slide Elements

PowerPoint's varied themes and layouts help give presentations a unified and aesthetically pleasing look. You may, however, desire to modify the default settings to give your slides a unique quality. One of the easier methods of developing a custom show is to change a theme for one or more slides, not an entire presentation. Similarly, you can change the variant for one or more slides to give a coordinating look to the slides in your deck. One other method of altering your slides slightly is to change the default colors associated with a particular theme.

The animated elements on Slide 2 help emphasize the events and tours that members of the Spokes Bike Club can experience. Changing the theme colors for that slide to yellow coordinates with the yellow slide elements.

To Change the Theme and Variant on One Slide

The Office theme applied to the presentation is appropriate for this topic. The font and placeholder locations are simple and add variety without calling attention to the design elements. The following steps change the theme and variant for Slide 2. **Why?** *To call attention to the material in the bulleted list on Slide 2, you can apply an equally effective theme that has a design element on the bottom that resembles a bike path. You then can modify this new theme by changing the variant on one slide.*

1

- With Slide 2 displaying, display the Design tab and then click the More button (Design tab | Themes group) to expand the Theme gallery.
- Point to the Retrospect theme to see a preview of that theme on Slide 2 (Figure 3–70).

Experiment

- Point to various document themes in the Themes gallery and watch the colors and fonts change on Slide 2.

Figure 3–70

2

- Right-click the Retrospect theme to display a shortcut menu (Figure 3–71).

Figure 3–71

3

- Click 'Apply to Selected Slides' to apply the Retrospect theme to Slide 2.
- Right-click the green variant (second variant in row) to display a shortcut menu (Figure 3–72).

Figure 3–72

4

- Click 'Apply to Selected Slides' to apply the green variant to Slide 2 (Figure 3–73).

Figure 3–73

To Change the Theme Colors

1 INSERT & ADD EFFECTS | 2 MODIFY PLACEHOLDERS | 3 MODIFY & COPY ILLUSTRATIONS
4 ADD MEDIA | 5 ANIMATE SLIDE CONTENT | 6 CUSTOMIZE SLIDE ELEMENTS

Every theme has 10 standard colors: two for text, two for backgrounds, and six for accents. The following steps change the theme colors for the Spokes Bike Club slides. *Why? You can change the look of your presentation and add variety by applying the colors from one theme to another theme.*

1

- Click the More button (shown in Figure 3–73) in the Variants group to expand the gallery.
- Point to Colors in the menu to display the Colors gallery (Figure 3–74).

🔑 **Experiment**

- Point to various color rows in the gallery and watch the colors change on Slide 2.

Figure 3–74

2

- Click Green in the gallery to change the Slide 2 theme colors (Figure 3–75).

BTW

Printing Document Properties
PowerPoint 2016 does not allow you to print document properties. This feature, however, is available in other Office 2016 apps, including Word and Excel.

Figure 3–75

To Run a Slide Show with Media

All changes are complete, so you now can view the Spokes Bike Club presentation. The following steps start Slide Show view.

1 Click the 'Start From Beginning' button on the Show tab to display the title slide and listen to the bicycle engine sound. Allow the audio clip to repeat several times.

2 Press the SPACEBAR to display Slide 2. Watch the biker and bulleted list animations.

3 Press the SPACEBAR to display Slide 3. Watch the video clip.

4 Press the SPACEBAR to end the slide show and then press the SPACEBAR again to exit the slide show.

To Preview and Print a Handout

1 INSERT & ADD EFFECTS | 2 MODIFY PLACEHOLDERS | 3 MODIFY & COPY ILLUSTRATIONS
4 ADD MEDIA | 5 ANIMATE SLIDE CONTENT | 6 CUSTOMIZE SLIDE ELEMENTS

Printing handouts is useful for reviewing a presentation. You can analyze several slides displayed simultaneously on one page. Additionally, many businesses distribute handouts of the slide show before or after a presentation so attendees can refer to a copy. Each page of the handout can contain reduced images of one, two, three, four, six, or nine slides. The three-slides-per-page handout includes lines beside each slide so that your audience can write notes conveniently. The following steps preview and print a presentation handout with two slides per page. **Why?** *Two of the slides are predominantly pictures, so your audience does not need full pages of those images. The five bulleted paragraphs on Slide 2 can be read easily on one-half of a sheet of paper.*

1

- Click File on the ribbon to open the Backstage view and then click the Print tab.
- Click the Previous Page button to display Slide 1 in the Print gallery.
- Click 'Full Page Slides' in the Settings area to display the Full Page Slides gallery (Figure 3–76).

Q&A Why does the preview of my slide appear in black and white?
Your printer determines how the preview appears. If your printer is not capable of printing color images, the preview will appear in black and white.

Figure 3–76

- Click 2 Slides in the Handouts area to select this option and display a preview of the handout (Figure 3–77).

Q&A

The current date displays in the upper-right corner of the handout, and the page number displays in the lower-right corner of the footer. Can I change their location or add other information to the header and footer?
Yes. Click the 'Edit Header & Footer' link at the bottom of the Print gallery, click the Notes and Handouts tab (Header and Footer dialog box), and then decide what content to include on the handout page.

Figure 3–77

- Click the Next Page and Previous Page buttons to display previews of the two pages in the handout.
- Click the Print button in the Print gallery to print the handout.
- When the printer stops, retrieve the printed handout.
- Save the presentation again in the same storage location with the same file name.
- Because the project now is complete, you can exit PowerPoint.

Summary

In this module, you have learned how to adjust photo colors and effects, modify placeholders, modify and copy illustrations, add and format media, animate slide content, customize slides, and print a handout.

BTW
Distributing a Document
Instead of printing and distributing a hard copy of a document, you can distribute the document electronically. Options include sending the document via email; posting it on cloud storage (such as OneDrive) and sharing the file with others; posting it on social media, a blog, or other website; and sharing a link associated with an online location of the document. You also can create and share a PDF or XPS image of the document, so that users can view the file in Acrobat Reader or XPS Viewer instead of in PowerPoint.

What decisions will you need to make when creating your next presentation?

Use these guidelines as you complete the assignments in this module and create your own slide show decks outside of this class.

1. Determine if adjusting photo colors and effects can increase visual appeal.

    a) Change color saturation.

    b) Change tones.

    c) Recolor the image.

2. Vary paragraph alignment.

    a) Themes dictate whether paragraph text is aligned left, center, or right in a placeholder, but you can modify these design decisions when necessary. Moving placeholders and changing paragraph alignment can help create a unique slide.

    b) Different effects are achieved when text alignment shifts in a presentation.

3. Use multimedia selectively.

    a) Locate video, music, and sound files that are appropriate for your audience and that you have permission to use.

    b) Use media files only when necessary, however, because they draw the audience's attention away from the presenter and toward the slides.

    c) Using too many multimedia files can be overwhelming.

4. Use animation sparingly.

    a) PowerPoint audience members usually take notice the first time an animation is displayed on the screen, so be certain the animation will help focus on the precise points being presented during a particular time of the presentation.

    b) Avoid using animation for the sake of using animation. Use animation only when necessary to add emphasis.

    c) Animation overuse annoys and desensitizes audience members.

    d) Carefully decide how text or a slide element enters and exits a slide and how it is displayed once it is present on the slide.

5. Use handouts to organize your speech and to distribute to audiences.

    a) Determine if a handout with two slides per page will help unify your message when you distribute copies to an audience.

Apply Your Knowledge

Reinforce the skills and apply the concepts you learned in this module.

Resizing a Photo by Entering Exact Measurements, Formatting a Video Border, Trimming a Video File, Resizing and Moving a Placeholder, and Animating a Photo and Title

Note: To complete this assignment, you will be required to use the Data Files. Please contact your instructor for information about accessing the Data Files.

Instructions: Run PowerPoint. Open the presentation called Apply 3-1 Cats, which is located in the Data Files. The four slides in the presentation, shown in Figure 3–78, discuss the factors you should consider when adopting a cat. The local pet store is holding a special event for cat adoptions. The document you open is composed of slides containing pictures and a video. You will apply artistic effects or modify some of these graphic elements. You also will move placeholders. In addition, you will animate photos and a title using an entrance effect.

Continued >

Apply Your Knowledge *continued*

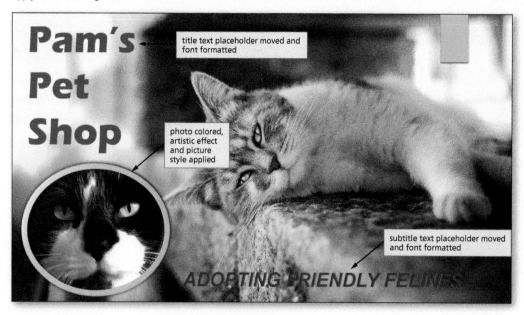

(a) Slide 1

Figure 3–78a

Perform the following tasks:

1. On Slide 1 (Figure 3–78a), move the title text placeholder to the upper area of the slide, the subtitle text placeholder to the lower area of the slide, and the green-eyed cat picture to the bottom left corner of the slide, as shown in the figure. Color the green-eyed cat picture by selecting Saturation: 200% from the Color Saturation area, and apply the Paint Brush artistic effect to the picture, as shown in figure. Decrease the picture size to 3.35"×3.88" and apply the Metal Oval picture style to the picture. Apply the Float In animation entrance effect, change the duration to 2.50, and then change the Start timing setting to With Previous.

2. On Slide 1, change the title font to Eras Bold ITC, increase the font size to 72 point, and then change the font color to Dark Blue, Background 2 (in Theme Colors row). Change the size of the title text placeholder to 3.73"×3.75" and then move it to the left area of the slide using the Smart Guides to line it up with the left edge of the picture, as shown in the figure. Apply the Fly In animation and then change the direction to From Right to the title text font and change the duration to 2.00. Change the Start timing setting to After Previous.

3. On Slide 1, change the subtitle font to Arial, increase the font size to 36 point, change the font color to Dark Blue (in Standard Colors row), and then bold and italicize this text.

4. On Slide 2 (Figure 3–78b), change the title text font to Arial, increase the font size to 44 point, bold this text, and then change the font color to Light Green (in Standard Colors row). Align this text left. Use the Format Painter to format the title text font on Slides 3 and 4 with the same features as the title text font on Slide 2.

5. Increase the size of the bulleted list font on Slide 2 to 24 point and then bold this text. Apply the Grow & Turn entrance effect to the bulleted list and then change the duration to 1.75. Change the Start timing setting to After Previous.

6. On Slide 2, increase the size of the right cat picture to approximately 4.12"×4.29" and then apply the Bevel Rectangle picture style to the cat picture. Decrease the size of the kitten picture in the center of the slide to approximately 4.24"×4.98" and then apply the Soft Edge Oval picture style to the kitten picture. Move the cat and kitten pictures to the locations shown in the figure.

7. On Slide 3 (Figure 3–78c), increase the size of the video to 5"×8.88". Apply the Rotated, Gradient video style in the Moderate area to the video, change the border weight to 6 pt, and

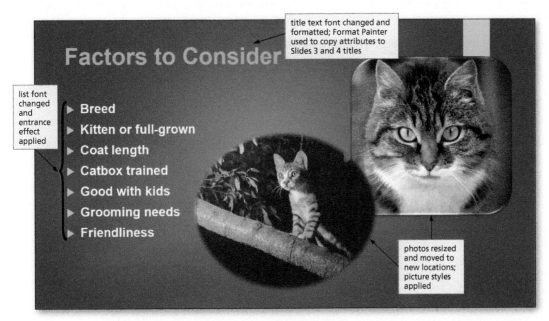

title text font changed and formatted; Format Painter used to copy attributes to Slides 3 and 4 titles

list font changed and entrance effect applied

photos resized and moved to new locations; picture styles applied

(b) Slide 2

Figure 3–78b

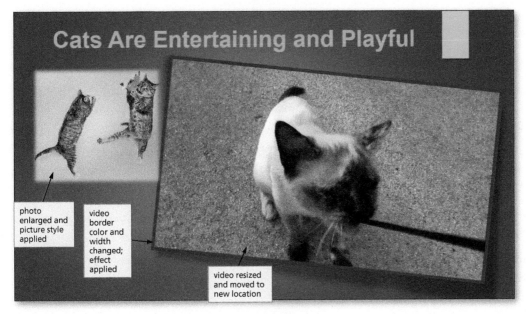

photo enlarged and picture style applied

video border color and width changed; effect applied

video resized and moved to new location

(c) Slide 3

Figure 3–78c

then change the border color to Dark Blue (in Standard Colors row). Move the video to the location shown in the figure. Trim the video so that the Start Time is 00:15.073. Start this video automatically.

8. Increase the size of the picture to approximately 3.1"×3.51" on Slide 3. Apply the Soft Edge Rectangle picture style to the picture.

9. On Slide 4 (Figure 3–78d), reset the picture to its original color and style by clicking the Reset Picture button (Picture Tools Format tab | Adjust group). Increase the size of the picture to approximately 5.75"×10.21", apply the Beveled Oval, Black picture style, and then move the picture to the location shown in the figure.

Continued >

Apply Your Knowledge *continued*

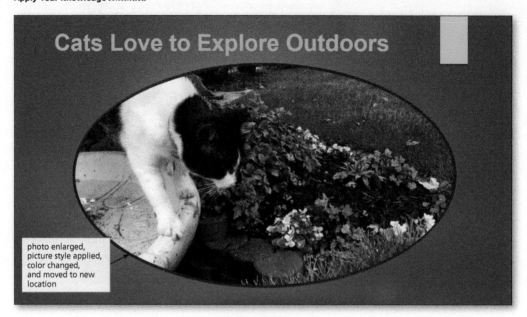

(d) Slide 4

Figure 3–78d

10. If requested by your instructor, add your mother's first name as a second line under the subtitle on Slide 1.

11. Apply the Clock transition in the Exciting category to all the slides. Change the duration to 3.00 seconds.

12. View the presentation and then save the file using the file name, Apply 3–1 Adopt a Cat.

13. Submit the revised document in the format specified by your instructor.

14. ☀ In Step 2, you changed the size of the title text placeholder and then moved it to the upper left area of the slide. How did this style improve the slide? On Slide 3, you trimmed the start time of the video. Why?

Extend Your Knowledge

Extend the skills you learned in this module and experiment with new skills. You may need to use Help to complete the assignment.

Changing Theme Colors, Coloring a Picture, Inserting and Trimming a Video File, Adding a Text Box, and Animating an Illustration

Note: To complete this assignment, you will be required to use the Data Files. Please contact your instructor for information about accessing the Data Files.

Instructions: Run PowerPoint. Open the presentation called Extend 3-1 Swimming, which is located in the Data Files. You will change theme colors, insert a video file, trim a video file, and insert a text box to create the presentation shown in Figure 3–79.

Perform the following tasks:

1. Change the theme variant to Black on Slide 1 only. Change the theme color to Blue II on Slide 3 only.

2. On Slide 1 (Figure 3–79a), change the title text font to Britannic Bold, increase the font size to 48 point, change the font color to Yellow (in Standard Colors row), and then center the text.

(a) Slide 1

Figure 3–79a

Change the font case to UPPERCASE. (*Hint*: The Change Case button is located in the Font group (Home tab | Font group).) Move the title text placeholder to the top of the slide, as shown in the figure. Delete the subtitle text placeholder.

3. Increase the size of the picture on Slide 1 to approximately 6.19" × 11", apply the Moderate Frame, White picture style, and then move the picture to the center of the slide, using the vertical Smart Guide to help you align this picture. Recolor the picture using the Blue, Accent color 3 Dark color (in Recolor area). Adjust the title text placeholder so that the text is below the picture border.

4. On Slide 1, apply the Grow/Shrink Emphasis effect to the Teardrop shape and then change the duration to 3.00. Change the Start timing setting to After Previous.

5. On Slide 2 (Figure 3–79b), change the title text font to Franklin Gothic Heavy, increase the font size to 40 point, change the font color to Dark Blue (in Standard Colors row), and then center the text. Use the Format Painter to apply these attributes to the title text font on Slide 4.

6. Apply the Bevel Perspective picture style to the picture. Increase the size of the picture to approximately 5.01" × 7.63" and then position it on the right side of the slide.

7. On Slide 2, apply the Zoom Entrance effect to the bulleted list, change the duration to 2:00, and then change the Start timing setting to After Previous.

8. On Slide 3 (Figure 3–79c), insert the video file called Swim, which is located in the Data Files. Increase the size of the video to approximately 6.41" × 8.74" and move the video to the location shown in the figure. Apply the Simple Frame, White video style and then change the Video Border color to Yellow (in Standard Colors row). Trim the video so that the End Time is 00:14.151. Start this video automatically.

9. Insert a text box on the left side of Slide 3 and type `Video highlights from one of our swim meets` in the text box, change the font to Arial, change font size to 24 point, and then bold and italicize this text. Adjust the size of the text box so that it measures approximately 2.52" × 2.01", and then use the horizontal Smart Guide to center the text box between the left end of the slide and the left edge of the video file.

Continued >

Extend Your Knowledge *continued*

(b) Slide 2

Figure 3–79b

(c) Slide 3

Figure 3–79c

10. On Slide 4 (Figure 3–79d), increase the size of the swimmer picture to approximately 3.88" × 6.29" and apply the Beveled Oval, Black picture style to the picture. Change the border color to Light Green (in Standard Colors row) and then change the border weight to 6 pt. Position this picture on the left side of the slide under the title using the Smart Guides to align the picture with the left, right, and bottom edges of the placeholder.

11. On Slide 4, apply the Float Out exit effect to the flippers illustration and then change the duration to 5.00. Change the Start timing setting to After Previous.

12. If requested by your instructor, insert a text box on Slide 3 under the text box and add the time of day you were born.

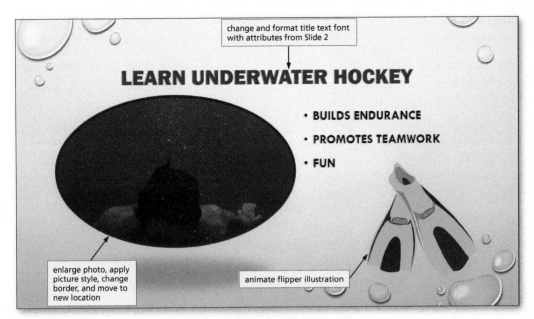

(d) Slide 4

Figure 3–79d

13. Apply an appropriate transition to all slides.

14. View the presentation and then save the file using the file name, Extend 3-1 Galaxy Aquatic Center.

15. Submit the revised document in the format specified by your instructor.

16. ✹ In this assignment, you inserted a video file and trimmed it. How did this enhance the presentation?

Expand Your World

Create a solution that uses cloud or web technologies by learning and investigating on your own from general guidance.

Inserting Video Files from the Web

Instructions: The Spokes Bike Club presentation you created in the module has a video you inserted from the Data Files. The bicyclist in this video mounted a camera on his helmet and recorded his ride through the forest. Using a helmet can help reduce head and brain injury risk and increase rider visibility to motorists and other cyclists. Many organizations promoting bicycling safety have created videos describing how to select and fit a bicycle helmet, and these videos are posted to online websites. PowerPoint allows you to insert online videos easily in a manner similar to how you inserted the Mountain Bike Video clip. You are going to search for and then insert one of these online videos into the Spokes Bike Club presentation.

Perform the following tasks:

1. In PowerPoint, open the Spokes Bike Club file, insert a new Slide 4 with the Title and Content layout, and then type `Helmet Safety Tips` as the title text. Use the Format Painter to copy the title text font formatting from Slide 2 to the new Slide 4 title. Center this title text.

2. Format the Slide 4 background with a gradient or texture fill.

3. Click the Insert Video icon in the content placeholder to display the Insert Video dialog box. Click the YouTube button in the dialog box and then type `bicycling helmet safety` as the search text in the Search YouTube search box.

Continued >

Expand Your World *continued*

4. When the search results are displayed, browse the video frames and click one that appears to fit the theme of this presentation. View the title of the video and its source in the lower-left corner of the dialog box. Then, click the View Larger (magnifying glass) icon in the lower-right corner of the video frame to view a preview of the video.

5. Click the Insert button to insert the video on Slide 4.

6. Add a style to the video and then resize the frame. Start this file automatically during the presentation and have it play full screen, if possible. If necessary, trim the video to the length you desire.

7. If requested to do so by your instructor, add the city where you were born to the Slide 4 title text.

8. View the presentation and then save the file using the file name, Expand 3-1 Spokes.

9. Submit the assignment in the format specified by your instructor.

10. ✸ What criteria did you use to select a particular YouTube video? What decisions did you make to choose a background and video style?

In the Labs

Design, create, modify, and/or use a presentation following the guidelines, concepts, and skills presented in this module. Labs 1 and 2, which increase in difficulty, require you to create solutions based on what you learned in the module; Lab 3 requires you to apply your creative thinking and problem-solving skills to design and implement a solution.

Lab 1: Changing the Stacking Order, Inserting an Audio File, and Animating a Photo, Illustration, and Title

Note: To complete this assignment, you will be required to use the Data Files. Please contact your instructor for information about accessing the Data Files.

Problem: Your local library is featuring information about national parks. Your travel club is planning to visit Yellowstone National Park next year, and you decide to gather some general information to present to the club. You create the slides shown in Figure 3–80.

Perform the following tasks:

1. Run PowerPoint. Open the presentation called Lab 3-1 Yellowstone, which is located in the Data Files. On Slide 1, increase the size of the waterfall picture to 7.5" × 11.54" and then move the picture to the left side of the slide, as shown in Figure 3–80a.

2. On Slide 1, select the title text placeholder. Display the Animation gallery, click 'More Entrance Effects,' and then apply the Expand entrance effect (in Subtle area) to the title text. Change the Start timing option to With Previous and the duration to 03.00 seconds. Bring the title text Forward so that the eagle's wings do not block the title.

3. On Slide 1, decrease the size of the eagle illustration to approximately 4.43" × 5.3" and then move it to the position shown in the figure. Apply the Fly In entrance effect with the From Bottom-Right direction to the illustration and then change the start timing option to After Previous and the duration to 02.50 seconds. Add the Fly Out exit animation with the To Left direction to the eagle illustration and then change the Start timing option to After Previous and the duration to 3.00 seconds.

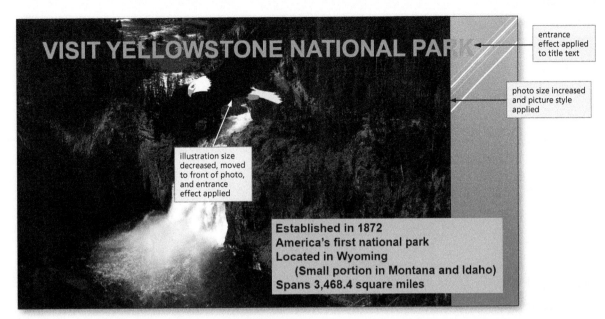

(a) Slide 1

Figure 3–80a

4. On Slide 2 (Figure 3–80b), change the size of the video so that it measures approximately 5.93" × 8.9". Change the video style to the Canvas, White style (in Intense area) and then change the border weight to 6 pt. Have the video start Automatically. Trim the video by changing the Start Time to 00:28.008 and changing the End Time to 00:50.55. Move the video to the location shown in the figure.

5. On Slide 3 (Figure 3–80c), increase the size of the picture to approximately 6.26" × 8.23" and then apply the Moderate Frame, Black picture style to the picture. Move the picture to the location shown in the figure. Start the audio file Automatically and hide this file during the show. Trim the audio file so that the Start Time is at 01:00 and the End Time is at 02:00.

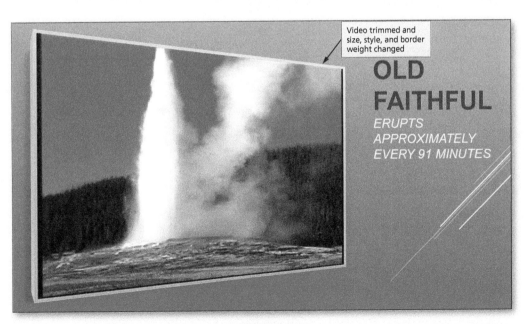

(b) Slide 2

Figure 3–80b

Continued >

In the Labs *continued*

picture style applied to resized photo

TWO GEYSERS ERUPTING TOGETHER

Old Faithful Geyser

Beehive Geyser

audio file trimmed, volume changed, and sound icon hidden during show

(c) Slide 3

Figure 3–80c

6. On Slide 4 (Figure 3–80d), apply the Moderate Frame, Black picture style to the bear picture. Apply the Metal Oval picture style to the wolf picture. Move the two pictures to the locations shown, and bring the wolf picture forward, as shown in the figure.

7. Apply the Fade entrance effect to the two pictures. Change the Start timing option to After Previous and the duration to 02.50.

8. Insert the audio file called Wolves, which is located in the Data Files. Change the volume to Medium, start Automatically, and hide the audio file during the show.

9. On Slide 5 (Figure 3–80e) apply the Metal Oval picture style to the four fish pictures. Apply the Bounce entrance effect to the upper left picture and then change the Start timing option to After Previous and the duration to 5.25. Apply these same animation effects to the remaining three pictures in a clockwise order.

picture styles applied to photos and entrance effects added

▸ Wolves
▸ Grizzly bears
▸ Herds of bison
▸ Elk
▸ And much more

audio file inserted and hidden during show

YELLOWSTONE HAS ABUNDANT WILDLIFE

(d) Slide 4

Figure 3–80d

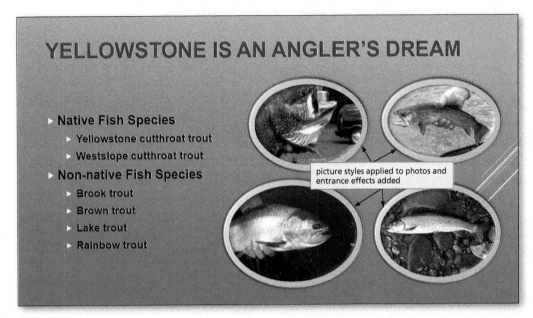

(e) Slide 5

Figure 3–80e

10. Apply the Wind transition in the Exciting category to all the slides. Change the duration to 2.50 seconds.

11. If requested by your instructor, insert a text box on Slide 2 and add the name of the street where you lived as a child.

12. View the presentation and then save the file using the file name, Lab 3–1 Visiting Yellowstone.

13. Submit the document in the format specified by your instructor.

14. ⊛ On Slide 1, why did you bring the title text to the front of the eagle illustration? Why did you choose the Bounce entrance effect with a 05.25 duration on the four fish pictures on Slide 5?

Lab 2: Adding Audio Options, Ungrouping a Clip, Changing the Color of a Clip Object, Deleting a Clip Object, and Regrouping Objects

Note: To complete this assignment, you will be required to use the Data Files. Please contact your instructor for information about accessing the Data Files.

Problem: You work at a nature center and are asked to do a PowerPoint presentation on how to attract hummingbirds to your yard. You create the presentation shown in Figure 3–81.

Perform the following tasks:
1. Run PowerPoint. Open the presentation called Lab 3-2 Hummingbirds, which is located in the Data Files. On Slide 1 (Figure 3–81a), change the volume of the audio file to High and then select Start Automatically, 'Play Across Slides', 'Loop until Stopped', 'Rewind after Playing', and 'Hide During Show'.

2. Copy the hummingbird illustration from Slide 2 (Figure 3–81b) to Slide 1 and then delete it from Slide 2. Decrease the size of this illustration so that it measures approximately

Continued >

In the Labs *continued*

1.71" × 1.87" and then move it to the location shown in Figure 3–81a. Apply the Fly In 'From Top–Right' entrance effect to the illustration, change the Start timing setting to After Previous, and then change the duration to 02.50.

3. Increase the title text font on Slide 1 to 72 point, bold the text, and then change the color of the title text font to Red (in Standard Colors). Decrease the size of the title text placeholder to approximately 1.65" × 7.62" and then position the title on top of the red rectangle. Apply the Fly In entrance effect with the From Top direction to the title, change the Start timing option to After Previous, and then change the duration to 02.50.

4. On Slide 1, change the shape fill color of the red rectangle to Lime, Accent 1 (in first Theme Colors row). Decrease the size of the rectangle shape to approximately 1.7" × 6.96", as shown in the figure. Increase the font size of the three paragraphs in the rectangle shape to 28 point and then bold this text.

5. On Slide 1, apply the Appear entrance effect to the first paragraph in the list and then change the start timing option to After Previous and the duration to 02.50. Apply the same animation settings for the second and third paragraphs in the list.

6. On Slide 2 (Figure 3–81b), move the video to the right side of the slide, increase the size to approximately 5.84" × 8.2", apply the Beveled Oval, Black video style (in Moderate area) to the video, change the video border color to Red (in Standard Colors), and then change the border weight to 3 pt. Trim the video so that the End Time is 00:17.88. Change the volume to High and then start the video automatically.

7. On Slide 2 (Figure 3–81b), apply the Float In entrance effect to the title text and then change the direction to Float Down. Change the start timing option to With Previous and the duration to 03.00.

8. On Slide 3 (Figure 3–81c), apply the Shape entrance effect to the title text and then change the Start timing option to With Previous and the duration to 3.00.

9. On Slide 3, select the hummingbird and flowers illustration and zoom in to view the three pink flowers. Ungroup this illustration. Select the three pink flowers and change their fill color to Red (in Standard Colors). Delete the three green leaves in the middle of the dark green stem.

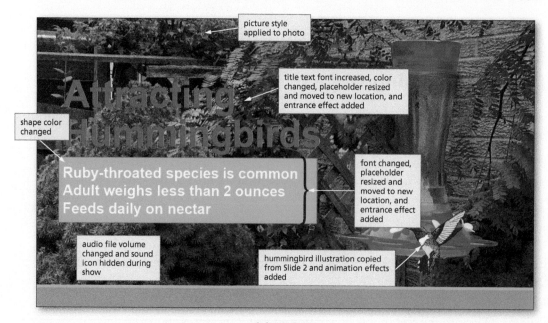

(a) Slide 1

Figure 3–81a

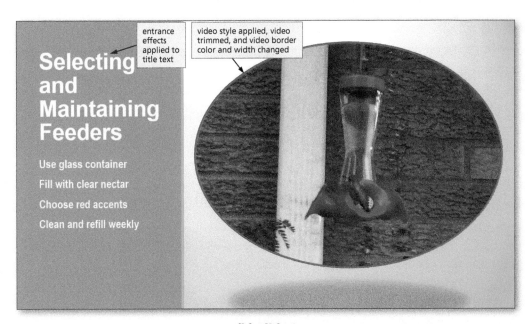

(b) Slide 2

Figure 3–81b

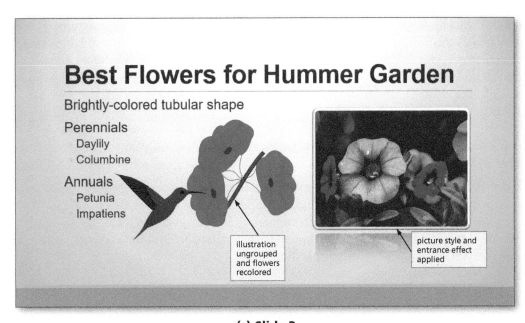

(c) Slide 3

Figure 3–81c

Regroup the illustration, increase the size to approximately 3.14" × 4.85", and then zoom out and move it to the area shown in the figure.

10. On Slide 3, apply the Reflected Bevel, White picture style to the flower picture. Resize the picture to approximately 3.1" × 4.17" and then move it to the right side of the slide, as shown in the figure. Apply the Zoom entrance effect to this picture. Change the Start timing option to On Click and the duration to 2.00.

11. If requested by your instructor, insert a text box at the lower-right corner of Slide 2 and type the color of your eyes in the text box.

12. Change the transition to None for all slides.

Continued >

In the Labs *continued*

13. View the presentation and then save the file using the file name, Lab 3–2 Attracting Hummingbirds.

14. Submit the revised document in the format specified by your instructor.

15. ✹ In Step 9, you changed the color of the three flowers from pink to red. Why? Why did you change the volume of the audio file to High?

Lab 3: **Consider This: Your Turn**

Design and Create a Presentation about Winter Bird Feeding

Note: To complete this assignment, you will be required to use the Data Files. Please contact your instructor for information about accessing the Data Files.

Part 1: Winter storms in cold climates can affect wild birds. Ice and deep snow reduce the natural food supply, and birds, consequently, have a difficult time surviving and thriving. People can help the birds by buying or making feeders, hanging them in the backyard, and keeping them clean and full. Nutritious winter seed foods include mixes of black oil sunflowers, hulled peanuts, and white millet. Suet and peanut butter are high-energy foods that help the birds stay warm. Providing water also helps the birds from becoming dehydrated. Place the feeders at least 10 feet from shrubs and compact the snow beneath them. Use the concepts and techniques presented in this module to create a presentation with this information to show at your local garden center. Select a suitable theme, change the theme colors, and then include a title slide, photos, and illustration. The Data Files contain a video called Birds in Winter and photos and illustrations called Bird Feeder, Red Jay, and Birds in Tree. Trim the video file and add a style. The illustration can be ungrouped, and you can change the color of it and the photos to add some visual interest to the presentation. Add animation to the slide content using effects and timing. Review and revise your presentation as needed and then save the file using the file name, Lab 3-3 Winter Bird Feeding. Submit your assignment in the format specified by your instructor.

Part 2: ✹ You made several decisions while creating the presentation in this assignment: selecting a theme and changing the theme colors, coloring and adding effects to the illustration and photos, trimming the video and adding a style, and adding animation. What was the rationale behind each of these decisions? When you reviewed the document, what further revisions did you make and why? Where would you recommend showing this slide show?

4 Creating and Formatting Information Graphics

Objectives

You will have mastered the material in this module when you can:

- Insert a SmartArt graphic
- Insert images from a file into a SmartArt graphic
- Format a SmartArt graphic
- Convert text to a SmartArt graphic
- Create and format a chart
- Rotate a chart

- Change the chart title and legend
- Separate a pie chart slice
- Create and format a table
- Insert a symbol in a table
- Change table text alignment and orientation
- Add an image to a table

Introduction

Audiences generally focus first on the visual elements displayed on a slide. Graphical elements increase **visual literacy**, which is the ability to examine and assess these images. They can be divided into two categories: images and information graphics. Images are the illustrations and photos you have used in Modules 1, 2, and 3, and information graphics are tables, charts, graphs, and diagrams. Both sets of visuals help audience members interpret and retain material, so they should be designed and presented with care.

Project — Presentation with SmartArt, a Chart, and a Table

On average, a person generates more than four pounds of trash every day. This waste includes aluminum cans, plastic and glass bottles, and various metals. Recycling efforts are increasing as communities provide dedicated areas for collecting materials, but the U.S. Environmental Protection Agency estimates that only 30 percent of recyclable materials actually make their way to recycling bins instead of landfills. Your community has three areas in town where residents can drop off cans, bottles, and metals, and you want to prepare a presentation that publicizes these locations and the need for everyone to take action. The project in this module follows visual content guidelines and uses PowerPoint to create the presentation shown in Figure 4–1. The slide show uses several visual elements to help audience members understand how recycling benefits the environment and where products can be recycled. The first two slides are enhanced with SmartArt graphics and pictures. The three-dimensional pie chart on Slide 3 depicts the amount of glass, metal, paper, and plastic recycled in your town, and the five-column table on Slide 4 lists the locations of three recycling centers and the types of materials accepted at each site.

(a) Slide 1 (Title Slide with SmartArt Enhanced with Photos)

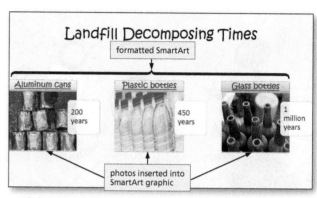

(b) Slide 2 (SmartArt Enhanced with Photos)

(c) Slide 3 (3-D Chart)

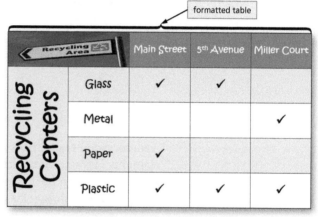

(d) Slide 4 (Five-column Chart)

Figure 4–1

In this module, you will learn how to create the slides shown in Figure 4–1. The following roadmap identifies general activities you will perform as you progress through this module:

1. INSERT and MODIFY a SMARTART graphic.
2. ADD SMARTART STYLES and EFFECTS.
3. CONVERT TEXT TO a SMARTART graphic and FORMAT the content.
4. CREATE a CHART to show proportions.
5. FORMAT a CHART by changing style and layout.
6. CREATE a TABLE to compare and contrast data.
7. CHANGE TABLE content STYLE and ALIGNMENT.

Creating and Formatting a SmartArt Graphic

An illustration often can help convey relationships between key points in your presentation. Microsoft Office 2016 includes **SmartArt graphics**, which are visual representations of your ideas. The SmartArt layouts have a variety of shapes, arrows, and lines to correspond to the major points you want your audience to remember.

You can create a SmartArt graphic in two ways: Select a SmartArt graphic type and then add text and pictures, or convert text or pictures already present on a slide to a SmartArt graphic. Once the SmartArt graphic is present, you can customize its look. Table 4–1 lists the SmartArt types and their uses.

BTW
Updated Layouts
Some of the items in the SmartArt Styles gallery may be updates; Microsoft periodically adds layouts to the Office.com and corresponding categories.

Table 4–1 SmartArt Graphic Layout Types and Purposes

Type	Purpose
List	Show nonsequential information
Process	Show steps in a process or timeline
Cycle	Show a continual process
Hierarchy	Create an organizational chart
Relationship	Illustrate connections
Matrix	Show how parts relate to a whole
Pyramid	Show proportional relationships with the largest component at the top or bottom
Picture	Include a placeholder for pictures within the graphic
Office.com	Use addition layouts available from Office.com

To Insert a SmartArt Graphic

1 INSERT & MODIFY SMARTART | 2 ADD SMARTART STYLES & EFFECTS | 3 CONVERT TEXT TO SMARTART & FORMAT
4 CREATE CHART | 5 FORMAT CHART | 6 CREATE TABLE | 7 CHANGE TABLE STYLE & ALIGNMENT

Several SmartArt layouts have placeholders for one or more pictures, and they are grouped in the Picture category. The 'Circular Picture Callout' graphic is appropriate for this presentation. *Why? It has one large area for a picture and three other areas for smaller pictures. These images would allow you to insert pictures of recycling possibilities, which should create interest among community residents considering participating in these efforts.* The following steps open the Recycling presentation, save the file with a new name, and then insert the 'Circular Picture Callout' SmartArt graphic on Slide 1.

1

- Run PowerPoint and then open the presentation, Recycling, from the Data Files.

- Save the presentation using the file name, Area Recycling.

- With Slide 1 selected, display the Insert tab and then click the SmartArt button (Insert tab | Illustrations group) to display the Choose a SmartArt Graphic dialog box.

- Click Picture in the left pane to display the Picture gallery.

- Click the 'Circular Picture Callout' graphic (second graphic in first row) to display a preview of this layout in the right pane (Figure 4–2).

 Experiment

- Click various categories and graphics in the SmartArt Styles gallery and view the various layouts.

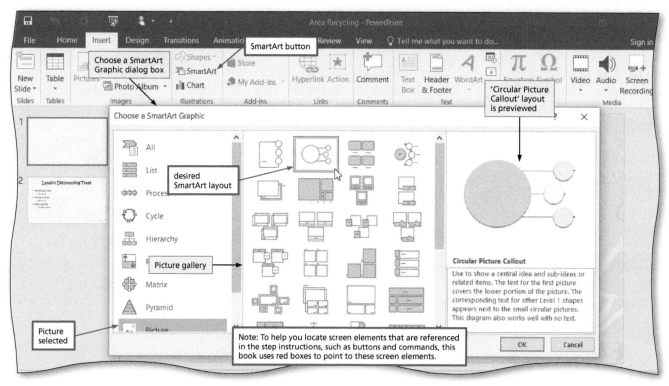

Figure 4–2

2

- Click the OK button to insert this SmartArt layout on Slide 1.

- If necessary, click the Text Pane button (SmartArt Tools Design tab | Create Graphic group) or the arrow icon in the center-left edge of the graphic to open the Text Pane if it does not display automatically (Figure 4–3).

Q&A Can I click either the Text Pane button or the arrow icon to close the Text Pane? Yes.

Figure 4–3

Other Ways

1. Click 'Insert a SmartArt graphic' icon in placeholder

Text Pane

The **Text Pane** assists you in creating a graphic because you can direct your attention to developing and editing the message without being concerned with the actual graphic. The Text Pane consists of two areas: The top portion has the text that will appear in the SmartArt layout and the bottom portion gives the name of the graphic and suggestions of what type of information is best suited for this type of visual. Each SmartArt graphic has an associated Text Pane with bullets that function as an outline and map directly to the image. You can create new lines of bulleted text and then indent and demote these lines. You also can check spelling. Table 4–2 shows the keyboard shortcuts you can use with the Text Pane.

Table 4–2 Text Pane Keyboard Shortcuts	
Activity	**Shortcut**
Indent text	TAB or ALT+SHIFT+RIGHT ARROW
Demote text	SHIFT+TAB or ALT+SHIFT+LEFT ARROW
Add a tab character	CTRL+TAB
Create a new line of text	ENTER
Check spelling	F7
Merge two lines of text	DELETE at the end of the first text line
Display the shortcut menu	SHIFT+F10
Switch between the SmartArt drawing canvas and the Text Pane	CTRL+SHIFT+F2
Close the Text Pane	ALT+F4
Switch the focus from the Text Pane to the SmartArt graphic border	ESC

BTW
Touch Screen Differences
The Office and Windows interfaces may vary if you are using a touch screen. For this reason, you might notice that the function or appearance of your touch screen differs slightly from this module's presentation.

To Enter Text in a SmartArt Graphic

1 INSERT & MODIFY SMARTART | 2 ADD SMARTART STYLES & EFFECTS | 3 CONVERT TEXT TO SMARTART & FORMAT
4 CREATE CHART | 5 FORMAT CHART | 6 CREATE TABLE | 7 CHANGE TABLE STYLE & ALIGNMENT

Why? *You want to add text that shows the topic of the presentation and labels the images you will add on this slide.* The 'Circular Picture Callout' graphic has placeholders for text that can supplement the visuals. The following steps insert four lines of text in the Text Pane and in the corresponding SmartArt shapes on Slide 1.

- If necessary, position the insertion point beside the first bullet in the Text Pane. Type **Reduce, Reuse, Recycle** in the first bullet paragraph and then click the second bullet line or press the DOWN ARROW key to move the insertion point to the second bullet paragraph (Figure 4–4).

Figure 4–4

- Type **At home** in the second bullet paragraph and then click the third bullet line or press the DOWN ARROW key to move the insertion point to the third bullet paragraph.

- Type **At work** in the third bullet paragraph and then click the fourth bullet line or press the DOWN ARROW key to move the insertion point to the fourth bullet paragraph.

- Type **On the road** in the fourth bullet paragraph. Do not press the DOWN ARROW or ENTER keys (Figure 4–5).

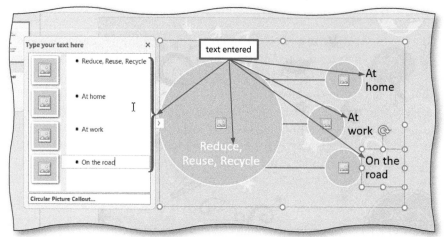

Figure 4–5

Q&A I mistakenly pressed the DOWN ARROW or ENTER key. How can I delete the bullet paragraph I just added?
Press the BACKSPACE key to delete the paragraph.

When I mistakenly pressed the TAB key to move to the next paragraph, the current paragraph's level is changed. How can I fix it?
Press SHIFT+TAB to return to the previous level.

Other Ways

1. Right-click SmartArt graphic, click Show Text Pane on shortcut menu, enter text in Text Pane

To Format Text Pane Characters

1 INSERT & MODIFY SMARTART | 2 ADD SMARTART STYLES & EFFECTS | 3 CONVERT TEXT TO SMARTART & FORMAT
4 CREATE CHART | 5 FORMAT CHART | 6 CREATE TABLE | 7 CHANGE TABLE STYLE & ALIGNMENT

Once the desired characters are entered in the Text Pane, you can change the font size and apply formatting features, such as bold, italic, and underlined text. *Why? Changing the font and adding effects can help draw the audience members to the varied slide content and coordinate with the visual content.* The following steps format the text by changing the font and bolding the letters.

- With the Text Pane open, drag through all four bullet paragraphs to select the text and display the mini toolbar.

Q&A If my Text Pane no longer is displayed, how can I get it to appear?
Click the control, which is the tab with a left-pointing arrow, on the left side of the SmartArt graphic.

2

- Display the Font gallery and change the font to Kristen ITC.

- Bold the text (Figure 4–6).

Q&A These formatting changes did not appear in the Text Pane. Why?
Not all the formatting changes are evident in the Text Pane, but they appear in the corresponding shape.

Figure 4–6

3

- Click the Close button in the SmartArt Text Pane so that it no longer is displayed.

To Insert a Picture from a File into a SmartArt Graphic

The picture icons in the middle of the four circles in the 'Circular Picture Callout' SmartArt layout indicate that the shapes are designed to hold images. These images can add a personalized touch to your presentation. *Why? The purpose of this presentation is to show the wide variety of recycling possibilities, and audience members would be familiar with the three topics shown in these SmartArt circles.* You can select files from the Internet or from images you have obtained from other sources, such as a photograph taken with your digital camera. The following steps insert images located in the Data Files into the large SmartArt circle.

1

- Click the 'Insert Picture from File' icon in the SmartArt large circle picture placeholder (shown in Figure 4–6) to display the Insert Picture dialog box.

- Click the Browse button in the From a file area to display the Insert Picture dialog box.

- If necessary, navigate to the desired picture location (in this case, the Module 04 folder in the Data Files folder) and then click Globe to select the file (Figure 4–7).

Q&A What if the illustration is not in the Data Files folder?
Use the same process, but be certain to select the location containing the picture in the file list.

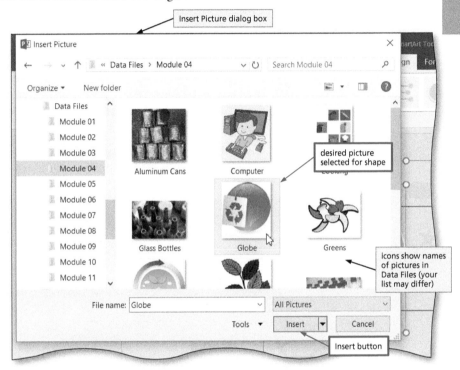

Figure 4–7

2

- Click the Insert button (Insert Picture dialog box) to insert the Globe picture into the SmartArt large circle picture placeholder (Figure 4–8).

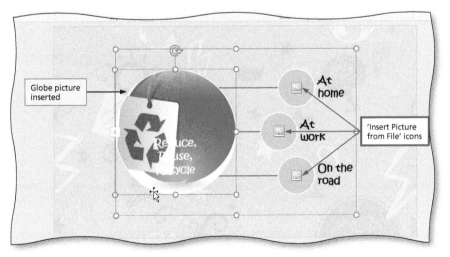

Figure 4–8

Other Ways

1. Click Shape Fill button (SmartArt Tools Format tab | Shape Styles group), click Picture

2. Right-click SmartArt shape, click Fill button, click Picture

BTW
The Ribbon and Screen Resolution
PowerPoint may change how the groups and buttons within the groups appear on the ribbon, depending on the computer or mobile device's screen resolution. Thus, your ribbon may look different from the ones in this book if you are using a screen resolution other than 1366 x 768.

To Insert Additional Pictures from a File into a SmartArt Graphic

The Globe illustration fills the left shape in the SmartArt graphic, and you want to insert additional recycling photos in the three circles in the right portion of the graphic. These images are located in the Data Files. The following steps insert photos into the three smaller SmartArt graphic circles.

1 Click the 'Insert Picture from File' icon in the top circle to the left of the words, At home, to display the Insert Pictures dialog box.

2 Click the Browse button in the 'From a file' area, scroll down and then click Home in the list of picture files, and then click the Insert button (Insert Picture dialog box) to insert the photo into the top-right SmartArt circle picture placeholder.

3 Click the center 'Insert Picture from File' icon to the left of the words, At work, click the Browse button in the Insert Pictures dialog box, and then insert the photo with the file name, Work, into the placeholder.

4 Click the bottom 'Insert Picture from File' icon to the left of the words, On the road, and then insert the photo with the file name, Road, into the placeholder (Figure 4–9).

Figure 4–9

To Apply a SmartArt Style

1 INSERT & MODIFY SMARTART | 2 ADD SMARTART STYLES & EFFECTS | 3 CONVERT TEXT TO SMARTART & FORMAT
4 CREATE CHART | 5 FORMAT CHART | 6 CREATE TABLE | 7 CHANGE TABLE STYLE & ALIGNMENT

You can change the look of your SmartArt graphic easily by applying a **SmartArt style**. *Why? You can use these professionally designed effects to customize the appearance of your presentation with a variety of shape fills, edges, shadows, line styles, gradients, and three-dimensional styles.* The following steps add the Cartoon style to the 'Circular Picture Callout' SmartArt graphic.

1

- With the SmartArt graphic still selected, click the SmartArt Styles More button (SmartArt Tools Design tab | SmartArt Styles group) (shown in Figure 4–9) to expand the SmartArt Styles gallery (Figure 4–10)

Q&A How do I select the graphic if it no longer is selected?
Click the graphic anywhere except the pictures you just added.

Figure 4–10

2

- Point to the Cartoon style in the 3-D area (third style in first 3-D row) in the SmartArt Styles gallery to display a live preview of this style (Figure 4–11).

🔍 **Experiment**

- Point to various styles in the SmartArt Styles gallery and watch the 'Circular Picture Callout' graphic change styles.

3

- Click Cartoon to apply this style to the graphic.

Figure 4–11

Other Ways

1. Right-click SmartArt graphic in an area other than a picture, click Style button

---

To Change SmartArt Color

1 INSERT & MODIFY SMARTART | 2 ADD SMARTART STYLES & EFFECTS | 3 CONVERT TEXT TO SMARTART & FORMAT
4 CREATE CHART | 5 FORMAT CHART | 6 CREATE TABLE | 7 CHANGE TABLE STYLE & ALIGNMENT

Another modification you can make to your SmartArt graphic is to change its color. As with the WordArt Style gallery, PowerPoint provides a gallery of color options you can preview and evaluate. The following steps change the SmartArt graphic color to a Colorful range. *Why? The styles in the Colorful range have different colors for the text and other slide elements. The images in your SmartArt have green accents and the globe land and oceans are dark green and blue, so you want SmartArt elements that coordinate and are visible with these colors.*

- With the SmartArt graphic still selected, click the Change Colors button (SmartArt Tools Design tab | SmartArt Styles group) to display the Change Colors gallery (Figure 4–12).

Figure 4–12

- Point to 'Colored Outline – Accent 3' in the Accent 3 area to display a live preview of these colors (Figure 4–13).

Experiment

- Point to various colors in the Change Colors gallery and watch the shapes change colors.

Figure 4–13

- Click 'Colored Outline – Accent 3' to apply this color variation to the graphic (Figure 4–14).

Figure 4–14

Other Ways

1. Right-click SmartArt graphic in an area other than a picture, click Color button

To Resize a SmartArt Graphic

1 INSERT & MODIFY SMARTART | 2 ADD SMARTART STYLES & EFFECTS | 3 CONVERT TEXT TO SMARTART & FORMAT
4 CREATE CHART | 5 FORMAT CHART | 6 CREATE TABLE | 7 CHANGE TABLE STYLE & ALIGNMENT

When you view the completed graphic, you may decide that individual shapes or the entire piece of art needs to be enlarged or reduced. If you change the size of one shape, the other shapes also may change size to maintain proportions. Likewise, the font size may change in all the shapes if you increase or decrease the font size of one shape. On Slide 1, you want to change the SmartArt graphic size. *Why? A larger graphic size will fill the empty space on the slide and add readability.* All the shapes will enlarge proportionally when you adjust the graphic's height and width. The following step resizes the SmartArt graphic.

- With the SmartArt graphic still selected, drag the upper-left sizing handle to the upper-left corner of the slide.

- Drag the lower-right sizing handle to the lower-right corner of the slide, as shown in Figure 4–15.

Figure 4–15

Other Ways

1. Right-click SmartArt graphic, click Size and Position on shortcut menu

To Change the Font Size and Move a Text Box

1 INSERT & MODIFY SMARTART | 2 ADD SMARTART STYLES & EFFECTS | 3 CONVERT TEXT TO SMARTART & FORMAT
4 CREATE CHART | 5 FORMAT CHART | 6 CREATE TABLE | 7 CHANGE TABLE STYLE & ALIGNMENT

Why? The text box in the large SmartArt circle is covering the recycling tag. The letters would be more readable if they were displayed in the dark blue and green areas of the globe and enlarged slightly. The following steps increase the font size and then move the text box.

- Select the three words in the large SmartArt circle text box and then click the 'Increase Font Size' button on the mini toolbar menu twice to increase the font size to 48 point.

- Click any of the letters in the large SmartArt circle to select the text box.

- Drag the text box upward to the location shown in Figure 4–16.

Figure 4–16

To Convert Text to a SmartArt Graphic

You quickly can convert small amounts of slide text and pictures into a SmartArt graphic. Once you determine the type of graphic, such as process or cycle, you then have a wide variety of styles from which to choose in the SmartArt Graphics gallery. As with other galleries, you can point to the samples and view a live preview if you are using a mouse. The following steps convert the six bulleted text paragraphs on Slide 2 to the 'Titled Picture Blocks' graphic, which is part of the Picture category. *Why? This SmartArt style is a good match for the content of Slide 2. It has three large areas for photos, placeholders for the Level 1 text above each photo, and placeholders for the Level 2 text beside each photo.*

1

- Display Slide 2.

- With the Home tab displayed, select the six bulleted list items and then click the 'Convert to SmartArt' button (Home tab | Paragraph group) to display the SmartArt Graphics gallery (Figure 4–17).

Figure 4–17

2

- Click 'More SmartArt Graphics' in the SmartArt Graphics gallery to display the Choose a SmartArt Graphic dialog box.

- Click Picture in the left pane to display the Picture gallery.

- Click the 'Titled Picture Blocks' graphic (first graphic in fourth row) to display a preview of this graphic in the right pane (Figure 4–18).

Figure 4–18

3

- Click the OK button (Choose a SmartArt Graphic dialog box) to apply this shape and convert the text (Figure 4–19).

How can I edit the text that displays in the three shapes?

You can click the text and then make the desired changes. Also, if you display the Text Pane on the left side of the graphic, you can click the text you want to change and make your edits.

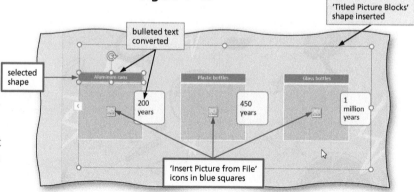

Figure 4–19

Other Ways

1. Select text, click 'Convert to SmartArt' on shortcut menu

To Insert Pictures from a File into a SmartArt Graphic

The picture icon in each of the three blue boxes in the SmartArt graphic indicates the shape is designed to hold an image. In this presentation, you will add images located in the Data Files. The following steps insert photos into the SmartArt graphic.

1 Click the 'Insert Picture from File' icon in the left blue box under the words, Aluminum cans, to display the Insert Pictures dialog box.

2 Click the Browse button in the 'From a file' area, click the Aluminum Cans icon in the list of picture files, and then click the Insert button (Insert Picture dialog box) to insert the picture into the left SmartArt square picture placeholder.

3 Click the 'Insert Picture from File' icon in the center blue box under the words, Plastic bottles, to display the Insert Picture dialog box, click the Browse button to display the Insert Picture dialog box, and then insert the picture with the file name, Plastic Bottles, into the placeholder.

4 Click the 'Insert Picture from File' icon in the right blue box under the words, Glass bottles, and then insert the picture with the file name, Glass Bottles, into the placeholder (Figure 4–20).

Figure 4–20

To Add a SmartArt Style to the Graphic

To enhance the appearance of the group of squares, you can add a three-dimensional style. The following steps add the Subtle Effect to the 'Titled Picture Blocks' graphic.

1 With the SmartArt graphic still selected, if necessary, display the SmartArt Tools Design tab and then click the SmartArt Styles More button (SmartArt Tools Design tab | SmartArt Styles) to expand the SmartArt Styles gallery.

BTW
Building Speaker Confidence
As you rehearse your speech, keep in mind that your audience will be studying the visual elements during your actual presentation and will not be focusing on you. Using information graphics in a presentation should give you confidence as a presenter because they support your verbal message and help reinforce the message you are trying to convey.

2 Click Subtle Effect in the Best Match for Document area (third graphic) to apply this style to the graphic (Figure 4–21).

Figure 4–21

BTW
Preparation Time
Be certain to begin developing a presentation well in advance of assignment deadlines when incorporating information graphics. Create a schedule so that you have adequate time to prepare clear visuals. Developing a presentation incorporating SmartArt, charts, and tables generally requires extra preparation time because you need to gather data from reputable and current sources to incorporate into these visual elements.

To Change the SmartArt Color

Adding more colors to the SmartArt graphic would enhance its visual appeal. The following steps change the SmartArt graphic color to a Colorful range.

1 With the SmartArt graphic still selected, click the Change Colors button (SmartArt Tools Design tab | SmartArt Styles group) to display the Change Colors gallery.

2 Click 'Colorful Range – Accent Colors 5 to 6' (last color in Colorful row) to apply this color variation to the graphic (Figure 4–22).

Figure 4–22

To Resize a SmartArt Graphic

Although white space on a slide generally is good to have, Slide 2 has sufficient space to allow the SmartArt graphic size to increase slightly. When you adjust the graphic's height and width, all the squares will enlarge proportionally. The following step resizes the SmartArt graphic.

1 With the SmartArt graphic still selected, drag the top-left sizing handle diagonally upward to the left edge of the slide and below the title text placeholder. Then drag the bottom-right sizing handle diagonally to the bottom-right edge of the slide, as shown in Figure 4–23.

Q&A Can I drag other sizing handles to resize the graphic?
You can drag the upper-right and lower-left sizing handles. If you drag the middle-left handle, however, you will display the Text Pane.

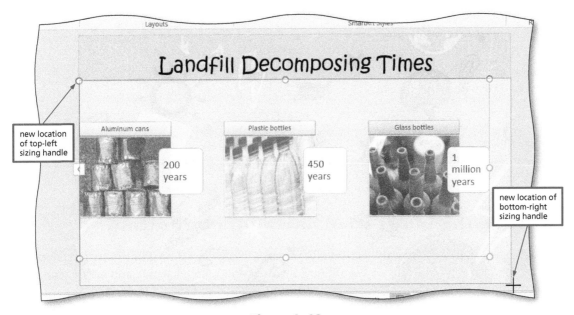

Figure 4–23

To Format SmartArt Graphic Text

1 INSERT & MODIFY SMARTART | 2 ADD SMARTART STYLES & EFFECTS | 3 CONVERT TEXT TO SMARTART & FORMAT
4 CREATE CHART | 5 FORMAT CHART | 6 CREATE TABLE | 7 CHANGE TABLE STYLE & ALIGNMENT

The text in the three rectangles above the photos can be reformatted. You can select all three rectangles and then change the text. *Why? Changing the size, color, and other aspects will make the text more readable.* For consistency and efficiency, it is best to format the same items on a slide simultaneously. These rectangles are separate items in the SmartArt graphic. Select these objects by selecting one rectangle, pressing and holding down the SHIFT key, and then selecting the second and third rectangles. The following steps simultaneously bold and underline the rectangle text, change the font color to Dark Blue, increase the font size, and change the font.

1

- Click the rectangle labeled Aluminum cans to select it. Press and hold down the SHIFT key and then click the Plastic bottles and Glass bottles rectangles (Figure 4–24).

Figure 4–24

2

- Display the Home tab and then click the Bold button (Home tab | Font group).

- Click the Underline button (Home tab | Font group) to add an underline to the text.

- Click the Font Color arrow and then click Dark Blue (ninth color in Standard Colors row) to change the font color to Dark Blue.

- Click the 'Increase Font Size' button several times to increase the font size to 24 point.

- Change the font to Kristen ITC (Figure 4–25).

Figure 4–25

Q&A
Can I make other formatting changes to the graphics' text?
Yes. You can format the text by making any of the modifications in the Font group.

If I am using a touch screen, can I modify all three rectangles simultaneously?
No. You need to repeat Step 2 for each of the rectangles.

Break Point: If you wish to take a break, this is a good place to do so. Be sure to save the Area Recycling file again and then you can exit PowerPoint. To resume at a later time, run PowerPoint, open the file called Area Recycling, and continue following the steps from this location forward.

Adding a Chart to a Slide and Formatting

On average, people discard three pounds of garbage each day. Much of this material can be recycled and can be divided into four categories: glass, metal, paper, and plastic. Some communities offer curbside recycling, and many schools and offices have recycling programs, particularly for paper. The chart on Slide 3, shown in earlier in Figure 4–1c, shows the proportion of the four categories of materials that commonly are recycled.

Microsoft Excel and Microsoft Graph

PowerPoint uses one of two programs to develop a chart. It opens Microsoft Excel if that software is installed on your system. If Excel is not installed, PowerPoint opens Microsoft Graph and displays a chart with its associated data in a table called a datasheet. Microsoft Graph does not have the advanced features found in Excel. In this module, the assumption is made that Excel has been installed. When you start to create a chart, Excel opens and displays a chart in the PowerPoint slide. The default chart type is a **Clustered Column chart**. The Clustered Column chart is appropriate when comparing two or more items in specified intervals, such as comparing how inflation has risen during the past 10 years. Other popular chart types are line, bar, and pie. You will use a pie chart in Slide 3.

The figures for the chart are entered in a corresponding **Microsoft Excel worksheet,** which is a rectangular grid containing vertical columns and horizontal rows. Column letters display above the grid to identify particular **columns**, and row numbers display on the left side of the grid to identify particular **rows. Cells** are the intersections of rows and columns, and they are the locations for the chart data and text labels. For example, cell A1 is the intersection of column A and row 1. Numeric and text data are entered in the **active cell**, which is the one cell surrounded by a heavy border. You will replace the sample data in the worksheet by typing entries in the cells, but you also can import data from a text file, import an Excel worksheet or chart, or paste data obtained from another program. Once you have entered the data, you can modify the appearance of the chart using menus and commands.

In the following pages, you will perform these tasks:

1. Insert a chart and then replace the sample data.
2. Change the line and shape outline weights.
3. Change the chart layout.
4. Resize the chart and then change the title and legend font size.
5. Rotate the chart.
6. Separate a pie slice.
7. Insert a text box and format text.

How can I choose an appropriate chart type?

General adult audiences are familiar with bar and pie charts, so those chart types are good choices. Specialized audiences, such as engineers and architects, are comfortable reading scatter and bubble charts.

Common chart types and their purposes are as follows:

- Column — Vertical bars compare values over a period of time.

- Bar — Horizontal bars compare two or more values to show how the proportions relate to each other.

- Line — A line or lines show trends, increases and decreases, levels, and costs during a continuous period of time.

- Pie — A pie chart divides a single total into parts to illustrate how the segments differ from each other and the whole.

- Scatter — A scatterplot displays the effect on one variable when another variable changes.

In general, three-dimensional charts are more difficult to comprehend than two-dimensional charts. The added design elements in a three-dimensional chart add clutter and take up space. A chart may include a **legend**, which is a box that identifies each slice of the pie chart and coordinates with the colors assigned to the slice categories. A legend may help to unclutter the chart, so consider using one prominently on the slide.

1 INSERT & MODIFY SMARTART | 2 ADD SMARTART STYLES & EFFECTS | 3 CONVERT TEXT TO SMARTART & FORMAT

To Insert a Chart

4 CREATE CHART | **5 FORMAT CHART** | 6 CREATE TABLE | 7 CHANGE TABLE STYLE & ALIGNMENT

The next step in developing the presentation is to insert a pie chart. *Why? The pie chart is a useful tool to show proportional amounts. In this presentation, you want to show how much content is recycled, and the slices of pie will show that paper is the most commonly recovered material.* The following steps insert a chart with sample data into Slide 3.

- Click the New Slide button (Home tab | Slides group) to add Slide 3 to the presentation (Figure 4–26).

Figure 4–26

- Click the Insert Chart icon in the content placeholder to display the Insert Chart dialog box.

- Click Pie in the left pane to display the Pie gallery and then click the 3-D Pie button (second chart) to select that chart type (Figure 4–27).

Experiment

- Point to the 3-D Pie chart to see a large preview of this type.

Q&A Can I change the chart type after I have inserted a chart?
Yes. Click the 'Change Chart Type' button in the Type group on the Chart Tools Design tab to display the Change Chart Type dialog box and then make another selection.

Figure 4–27

- Click the OK button (Insert Chart dialog box) to start the Microsoft Excel program and open a worksheet on the top of the Area Recycling presentation (Figure 4–28).

Q&A What do the numbers in the worksheet and the chart represent?
Excel places sample data in the worksheet and charts the sample data in the default chart type.

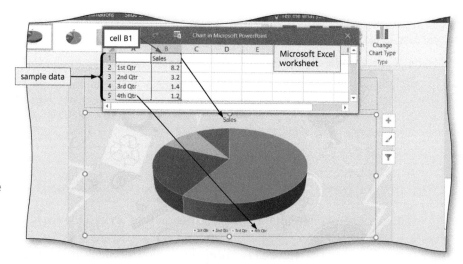

Figure 4–28

Other Ways

1. Click Chart button (Insert tab | Illustrations group)

CONSIDER THIS

How do I locate credible sources to obtain information for the graphic?

At times, you are familiar with the data for your chart or table because you have conducted in-the-field, or primary, research by interviewing experts or taking measurements. Other times, however, you must gather the data from secondary sources, such as magazine articles, newspaper articles, or websites. General circulation magazines and newspapers, such as *Newsweek* and the *Wall Street Journal*, use experienced journalists and editors to verify their information. Also, online databases, such as EBSCO-host, OCLC FirstSearch, LexisNexis Academic, and NewsBank contain articles from credible sources.

Some sources have particular biases, however, and they present information that supports their causes. Political, religious, and social publications and websites often are designed for specific audiences who share a common point of view. You should, therefore, recognize that data from these sources can be skewed.

If you did not conduct the research yourself, you should give credit to the source of your information. You are acknowledging that someone else provided the data and giving your audience the opportunity to obtain the same materials you used. Type the source at the bottom of your chart or table, especially if you are distributing handouts of your slides. At the very least, state the source during the body of your speech.

To Replace Sample Data

The next step in creating the chart is to replace the sample data, which will redraw the chart. *Why? The worksheet displays sample data in two columns and five rows, but you want to change this data to show the specific recycling categories and the amount of material recovered.* The first row and left column contain text labels and will be used to create the chart title and legend. The other cells contain numbers that are used to determine the size of the pie slices. The steps on the next page replace the sample data in the worksheet.

- Click cell B1, which is the intersection of column B and row 1, to select it.

Q&A Why did my pointer change shape?

The pointer changes to a block plus sign to indicate a cell is selected.

- Type **Recycled Materials** in cell B1 to replace the sample chart title (Figure 4–29).

Figure 4–29

- Click cell A2 to select that cell.

- Type **Glass** in cell A2 (Figure 4–30).

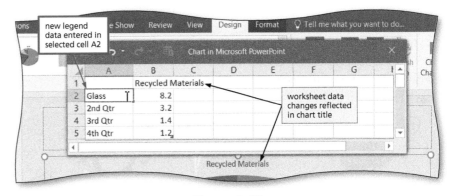

Figure 4–30

- Move the pointer to cell A3.

- Type **Paper** in cell A3 and then move the pointer to cell A4.

- Type **Metal** in cell A4 and then move the pointer to cell A5.

- Type **Plastic** in cell A5 (Figure 4–31).

Figure 4–31

4

- Click cell B2, type **24** in that cell, and then move the pointer to cell B3.

- Type **40** in cell B3 and then move the pointer to cell B4.

- Type **10** in cell B4 and then move the pointer to cell B5.

- Type **6** in cell B5.

- Press the ENTER key to move the pointer to cell B6 (Figure 4–32).

Q&A Why do the slices in the PowerPoint pie chart change locations?
As you enter data in the Excel worksheet, the chart slices rotate to reflect these new figures.

Figure 4–32

 5

- Close Excel by clicking its Close button.

Q&A Can I open the Excel spreadsheet once it has been closed?
Yes. Click the chart to select it and then click the Edit Data button (Chart Tools Design tab | Data group).

To Change the Shape Outline Weight

1 INSERT & MODIFY SMARTART | 2 ADD SMARTART STYLES & EFFECTS | 3 CONVERT TEXT TO SMARTART & FORMAT
4 CREATE CHART | **5 FORMAT CHART** | **6 CREATE TABLE** | **7 CHANGE TABLE STYLE & ALIGNMENT**

The chart has a thin white outline around each pie slice and around each color square in the legend. You can change the weight of these lines. ***Why?*** *A thicker line can accentuate each slice and add another strong visual element to the slide.* The following steps change the outline weight.

1

- Click the center of the pie chart to select it and display the sizing handles around each slice.

- Click the Chart Tools Format tab to display the Chart Tools Format ribbon (Figure 4–33).

Figure 4–33

- Click the Shape Outline arrow (Chart Tools Format tab | Shape Styles group) to display the Shape Outline gallery.
- Point to Weight in the Shape Outline gallery to display the Weight gallery.
- Point to 4½ pt to display a live preview of this outline line weight (Figure 4–34).

Experiment

- Point to various weights on the submenu and watch the border weights on the pie slices change.

3

- Click 4½ pt to increase the border around each slice to that width.

Figure 4–34

Other Ways

1. Right-click chart, click Outline button, click Weight

To Change the Shape Outline Color

1 INSERT & MODIFY SMARTART | 2 ADD SMARTART STYLES & EFFECTS | 3 CONVERT TEXT TO SMARTART & FORMAT
4 CREATE CHART | 5 FORMAT CHART | 6 CREATE TABLE | 7 CHANGE TABLE STYLE & ALIGNMENT

Why? At this point, it is difficult to see the borders around the legend squares and around each pie slice because they are white. You can change this color to add contrast to each slice and legend color square. The following steps change the border color.

- With the pie chart selected, click the Shape Outline arrow (Chart Tools Format tab | Shape Styles group) to display the Shape Outline gallery.
- Point to Green (sixth color in Standard Colors row) to display a live preview of that border color on the pie slice shapes and legend squares (Figure 4–35).

Experiment

- Point to various colors in the Shape Outline gallery and watch the border colors on the pie slices change.

2

- Click Green to add green borders around each slice and also around the color squares in the legend.

Figure 4–35

Other Ways

1. Right-click chart, click Outline button, click desired color

To Change a Chart Layout

Once you have selected a chart type, you can modify the look of the chart elements by changing its layout. The various layouts move the legend above or below the chart, or they move some or all of the legend data directly onto the individual chart pieces. For example, in the pie chart type, seven different layouts display various combinations of percentages and identifying information on the chart, and show or do not show the chart title. The following steps apply a chart layout with a title and legend that displays on the pie slices. *Why?* *Your data consists of category names and percentages, so you need a layout that shows the proportion of each category along with a chart title.*

- With the chart still selected, click the Chart Tools Design tab to display the Chart Tools Design ribbon and then click the Quick Layout button to display the Quick Layout gallery.

- Point to Layout 5 (second chart in second row) to display a live preview of that style on the pie slice shapes (Figure 4–36).

Experiment

- Point to various layouts in the Quick Layout gallery and watch the layouts on the chart change.

Figure 4–36

- Click Layout 5 in the Quick Layout gallery to apply the selected layout to the chart.

To Resize a Chart

You resize a chart the same way you resize a SmartArt graphic or any other graphical object. When designing a slide, you may want to delete the slide title text placeholder. *Why? Removing the title text placeholder increases the white space on the slide, so you are able to enlarge the chart and aid readability. In addition, the chart layout displays a title that provides sufficient information to describe the chart's purpose.* The following steps delete the title text placeholder and resize the chart to fill Slide 3.

- Click a border of the title text placeholder so that it displays as a solid line and then press the DELETE key to remove the placeholder.

Q&A

If I am using a touch screen, how do I delete the placeholder?
Press and hold on a border of the title text placeholder and then tap Delete on the shortcut menu to remove the placeholder.

- Select the chart and then drag the upper-left sizing handle to the upper-left corner of the slide.

- Drag the lower-right sizing handle to the lower-right corner of the slide, as shown in Figure 4–37.

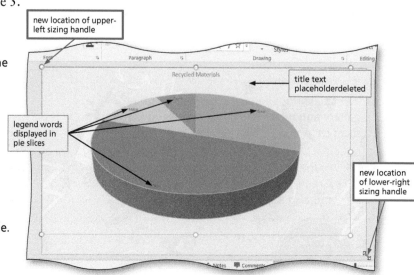

Figure 4–37

To Change the Title and Legend Font and Font Size

Depending upon the complexity of the chart and the overall slide, you may want to increase the font size of the chart title and legend. *Why? The larger font size increases readability.* The following steps change the font size of both of these chart elements.

1

- Click the chart title, Recycled Materials, to select the text box.

- Click the 'Increase Font Size' button (Home tab | Font group) repeatedly until the font size is 48 point.

- Change the font of the chart title to Kristen ITC (Figure 4–38).

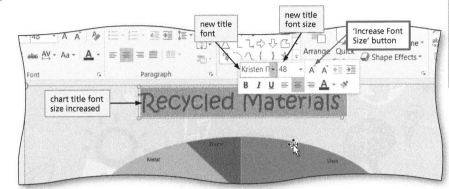

Figure 4–38

2

- Click one of the legends to select all the legends simultaneously.

- Click the 'Increase Font Size' button (Home tab | Font group) repeatedly until the font size of the legend text is 24 point.

- Change the legend font to Kristen ITC.

- Click the Bold button (Home tab | Font group) to bold the legend text (Figure 4–39).

Q&A What are the functions of the three buttons on the right side of the slide?

The Chart Elements button allows you to display the chart title, data labels, and legends; the Chart Styles button shows chart styles and color options; the Chart Filters button allows you to show, hide, edit, or rearrange data.

Figure 4–39

To Rotate a Chart

Excel determines where each slice of pie is positioned in the chart. You may desire to have a specific slice display in a different location, such as at the top or bottom of the circle. You can rotate the entire chart clockwise until a particular part of the chart displays where you desire. A circle's circumference is 360 degrees, so if you want to move a slice from the top of the chart to the bottom, you would rotate it halfway around the circle, or 180 degrees. Similarly, if you a want a slice to move one-quarter of the way around the slide, you would rotate it either 90 degrees or 270 degrees. The steps on the next page rotate the chart so that the purple Plastic slice displays at the bottom of the chart. *Why? Consumers use many plastic products, so you want to call attention to the fact that this material should be recycled.*

❶

- Click the purple Plastic slice of the pie chart to select it. Click the Chart Tools Format tab to display the Chart Tools Format ribbon.

- Click the Format Selection button (Chart Tools Format tab | Current Selection group) to display the Format Data Point pane (Figure 4–40).

Figure 4–40

❷

- Click the 'Angle of first slice' slider and drag it to the right until 150 is displayed in the 'Angle of first slice' box to rotate the Plastic slice 150 degrees to the right (Figure 4–41).

Q&A Can I move the slider in small increments so that I can get a precise angle degree easily?

Yes. Click the up or down arrows in the 'Angle of first slice' box to move the slider in one-degree increments or select the box and type the desired degree.

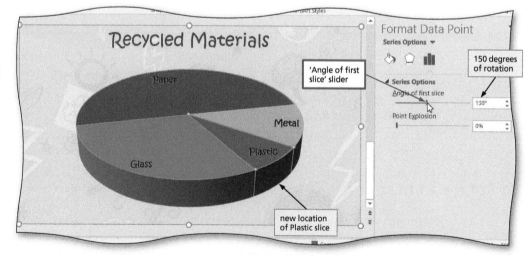

Figure 4–41

Other Ways

1. Right-click selection, click 'Format Data Point' on shortcut menu

To Separate a Pie Slice

Why? *At times, you may desire to draw the viewers' attention to a particular area of the pie chart. To add this emphasis, you can separate, or explode, one or more slices.* For example, you can separate the purple Plastic slice of the chart to stress that it is important to recycle this material. The following steps separate a chart slice.

- Click the Point Explosion slider and drag it to the right until 15 is displayed in the Point Explosion box to separate the slice from the pie chart (Figure 4–42).

Q&A Can I move the slider in small increments so that I can get a precise percentage easily?

Yes. Click the up or down arrows in the Point Explosion box to move the slider in one-percent increments or select the box and type the desired percentage.

Figure 4–42

- Click the Close button in the Format Data Point pane to close the pane.

Q&A Can I specify a precise position where the chart will display on the slide?

Yes. Right-click the edge of the chart, click 'Format Chart Area' on the shortcut menu, click 'Size & Properties' in Format Chart Area task pane, enter measurements in the Position section, and then specify from the Top Left Corner or the Center of the slide.

Other Ways

1. Right-click selection, click 'Format Data Point' on shortcut menu, set Point Explosion percentage

To Insert a Text Box and Format Text

A text box can contain information that is separate from the title or content placeholders. You can place this slide element anywhere on the slide and format the letters using any style and effect. You also can change the text box shape by moving the sizing handles. The steps on the next page insert a text box, add text, and then format these characters. *Why?* *You want to add an interesting fact about recycling paper.*

- Display the Insert tab, click the Text Box button (Insert tab | Text group), and then click below the Paper label (Figure 4–43).

Figure 4–43

- If necessary, click the text box and then type **One ton of recycled paper can save 17 trees** in the text box (Figure 4–44).

Figure 4–44

- Select the text in the text box and then increase the font size to 20 point and change the font to Kristen ITC.

- Drag a border of the text box to center the text in the Paper slice, as shown in Figure 4–45.

Q&A Can I change the shape of the text box?
Yes. Drag the sizing handles to the desired dimensions.

- Click outside the pie chart to deselect the text.

Figure 4–45

Break Point: If you wish to take a break, this is a good place to do so. Be sure to save the Area Recycling file again and then you can exit PowerPoint. To resume at a later time, run PowerPoint, open the file called Area Recycling, and continue following the steps from this location forward.

Adding a Table to a Slide and Formatting

One effective method of organizing information on a slide is to use a **table**, which is a grid consisting of rows and columns. You can enhance a table with formatting, including adding colors, lines, and backgrounds, and changing fonts.

In the following pages, you will perform these tasks:

1. Insert a table and then enter data and symbols.
2. Apply a table style.
3. Add table borders and an effect.
4. Resize the table.
5. Merge table cells and then display text in the cell vertically.
6. Add an image.
7. Align text in cells.
8. Format table data.

Tables

The table on Slide 4 (shown earlier in Figure 4–1d) contains information about the three recycling centers in the community and the types of materials accepted at each location. This data is listed in five columns and five rows.

To begin developing this table, you first must create an empty table and insert it into the slide. You must specify the table's **dimension**, which is the total number of rows and columns. This table will have a 5 × 5 dimension: the first number indicates the number of columns and the second specifies the number of rows. You will fill the cells with data pertaining to the types of materials permitted. Then you will format the table using a table style.

To Insert an Empty Table

1 INSERT & MODIFY SMARTART | 2 ADD SMARTART STYLES & EFFECTS | 3 CONVERT TEXT TO SMARTART & FORMAT
4 CREATE CHART | 5 FORMAT CHART | **6 CREATE TABLE** | **7 CHANGE TABLE STYLE & ALIGNMENT**

The following steps insert an empty table with five columns and five rows into Slide 4. *Why? The first row will contain the column headings, and the additional rows will have information about four recycling categories. The five columns will contain the table title and the locations of the recycling centers.*

- Add a new slide to the presentation (Figure 4–46).

Figure 4–46

- Click the Insert Table icon in the content placeholder to display the Insert Table dialog box.

- Click the up arrow to the right of the 'Number of rows' box three times so that the number 5 appears in the box (Figure 4–47).

Figure 4–47

- Click the OK button (Insert table dialog box) to insert the table into Slide 4 (Figure 4–48).

Figure 4–48

Other Ways

1. Click Table button (Insert tab | Tables group), drag to select columns and rows, click or press ENTER

To Enter Data in a Table

1 INSERT & MODIFY SMARTART | 2 ADD SMARTART STYLES & EFFECTS | 3 CONVERT TEXT TO SMARTART & FORMAT
4 CREATE CHART | 5 FORMAT CHART | 6 CREATE TABLE | 7 CHANGE TABLE STYLE & ALIGNMENT

Before formatting or making any changes in the table style, you enter the data in the table. *Why? It is easier to see formatting and style changes applied to existing data.* The second column will have the four material categories types, and the three columns to the right of these categories will contain data with check mark symbols representing the type of products accepted at each location. The next step is to enter data in the cells of the empty table. To place data in a cell, you click the cell and then type text. The following steps enter the data in the table.

- Click the second cell in the second column to place the insertion point in this cell. Type **Glass** and then click the cell below or press the DOWN ARROW key to advance the insertion point to the next cell in this column.

- Type **Metal** and then advance the insertion point to the next cell in this column.

- Type **Paper** and then advance the insertion point to the next cell in this column.

- Type **Plastic** and click the empty cell to the right or press the TAB key (Figure 4–49).

◄ **Q&A** What if I pressed the ENTER key after filling in the last cell?
Press the BACKSPACE key.

How would I add more rows to the table?
Press the TAB key when the insertion point is positioned in the bottom-right cell.

If I am using a touch screen, how do I add rows to the table?
Press and hold the bottom-right cell, tap Insert on the shortcut menu, and then tap Insert Rows Below.

Figure 4–49

- Click the third cell in the first row to place the insertion point in this cell. Type **Main Street** and then advance the insertion point to the adjacent right cell in this row.

- Type **5th Avenue** and then advance the insertion point to the adjacent right cell.

- Type **Miller Court** as the cell content (Figure 4–50).

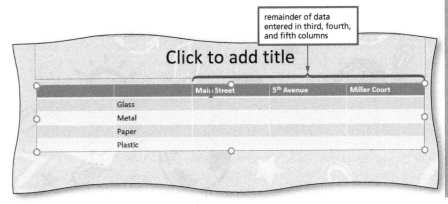

Figure 4–50

- If requested by your instructor, type the name of the street you grew up on instead of the name, Miller Court.

Q&A | How do I correct cell contents if I make a mistake?
Click the cell and then correct the text.

To Insert a Symbol

1 INSERT & MODIFY SMARTART | 2 ADD SMARTART STYLES & EFFECTS | 3 CONVERT TEXT TO SMARTART & FORMAT
4 CREATE CHART | 5 FORMAT CHART | 6 CREATE TABLE | 7 CHANGE TABLE STYLE & ALIGNMENT

The data in tables frequently consists of words. At times, however, the cells can contain characters and pictures that depict specific meanings. *Why? Audience members easily can identify these images, such as mathematical symbols and geometric shapes.* You can add illustrations and photos to the table cells and also can insert special symbols. Many symbols are found in the Webding and Wingding fonts. You insert symbols, such as mathematical characters and dots, by changing the font using the Symbol dialog box. The following steps insert a check mark symbol in several table cells.

- Click the second cell in the third column to place the insertion point in this cell.

- Display the Insert tab.

- Click the Symbol button (Insert tab | Symbols group) to display the Symbol dialog box (Figure 4–51).

Q&A | What if the symbol I want to insert already appears in the Symbol dialog box?
You can click any symbol shown in the dialog box to insert it in the slide.

Figure 4–51

Why does my 'Recently used symbols' list display different symbols from those shown in Figure 4–51?
As you insert symbols, PowerPoint places them in the 'Recently used symbols' list.

• Click the Symbol dialog box title bar and then drag the dialog box to the lower-left edge of the slide so that the some of the second column of the table is visible.

Figure 4-52

• If Wingdings is not the font displayed in the Font box, click the Font arrow (Symbol dialog box) and then drag or scroll to Wingdings and click this font.

• Drag or scroll down until the last row of this font is visible.

• Click the check mark symbol as shown in Figure 4-52.

• Click the Insert button (Symbol dialog box) to place the check mark symbol in the selected table cell (Figure 4-53).

Q&A
Why is the Symbol dialog box still open?
The Symbol dialog box remains open, allowing you to insert additional symbols in the selected cell.

• Click the Close button (Symbol dialog box).

Figure 4-53

To Copy a Symbol

1 INSERT & MODIFY SMARTART | 2 ADD SMARTART STYLES & EFFECTS | 3 CONVERT TEXT TO SMARTART & FORMAT
4 CREATE CHART | 5 FORMAT CHART | 6 CREATE TABLE | 7 CHANGE TABLE STYLE & ALIGNMENT

The Recycling Centers chart will contain check marks for the types of material accepted. To add the check marks to specific cells, you would need to repeat the process you used to insert the first check mark. Rather than inserting this symbol from the Symbol dialog box, you can copy the symbol and then paste it in the appropriate cells. *Why? This process can be accomplished more quickly with copy and paste when using the same symbol multiple times.* The following steps copy the check mark symbol to cells in the Slide 4 table.

• Select the check mark symbol in the table, display the Home tab, and then click the Copy button (Home tab | Clipboard group) to copy the check mark symbol to the Office Clipboard (Figure 4-54).

Figure 4-54

- Click the third cell in the third column to place the insertion point in this cell and then click the Paste button (Home tab | Clipboard group) (Figure 4–55).

- Press the BACKSPACE key to delete the extra row that is displayed in the cell when the symbol is pasted.

Q&A | If I am using a touch screen, how do I delete the extra row?
Display the onscreen keyboard and then press the BACKSPACE key.

Figure 4–55

- Using Figure 4–56 as a guide, continue pasting the check mark symbols in the table cells.

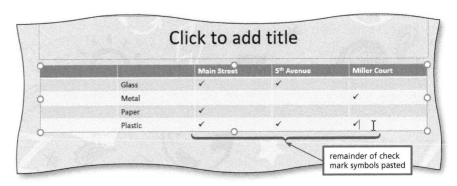

Figure 4–56

To Apply a Table Style

1 INSERT & MODIFY SMARTART | 2 ADD SMARTART STYLES & EFFECTS | 3 CONVERT TEXT TO SMARTART & FORMAT
4 CREATE CHART | 5 FORMAT CHART | 6 CREATE TABLE | **7 CHANGE TABLE STYLE & ALIGNMENT**

When you inserted the table, PowerPoint automatically applied a style. Thumbnails of this style and others are displayed in the Table Styles gallery. These styles use a variety of colors and shading and are grouped in the categories of Best Match for Document, Light, Medium, and Dark. The following steps apply a table style in the Best Match for Document area to the Slide 4 table. **Why?** *The styles in the Best Match for Document use the theme colors applied to the presentation, so they coordinate nicely with the colors you have been using in the first three slides in this presentation.*

- With the insertion point in the table, display the Table Tools Design tab (Figure 4–57).

Figure 4–57

- Click the More button in the Table Styles gallery (Table Tools Design tab | Tables Styles group) to expand the Table Styles gallery.

- Scroll down and then point to 'Medium Style 3 – Accent 1' in the Medium area (second style in third Medium row) to display a live preview of that style applied to the table (Figure 4–58).

Figure 4–58

 Experiment

- Point to various styles in the Table Styles gallery and watch the colors and format change on the table.

- Click 'Medium Style 3 – Accent 1' in the Table Styles gallery to apply the selected style to the table (Figure 4–59).

Q&A

Can I resize the columns and rows or the entire table?
Yes. To resize columns or rows, drag a **column boundary** (the border to the right of a column) or the **row boundary** (the border at the bottom of a row) until the column or row is the desired width or height. To resize the entire table, drag a **table sizing handle**.

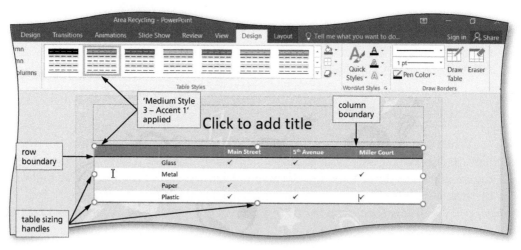

Figure 4–59

To Add Borders to a Table

1 INSERT & MODIFY SMARTART | 2 ADD SMARTART STYLES & EFFECTS | 3 CONVERT TEXT TO SMARTART & FORMAT
4 CREATE CHART | 5 FORMAT CHART | 6 CREATE TABLE | 7 CHANGE TABLE STYLE & ALIGNMENT

The Slide 4 table does not have borders around the entire table or between the cells. The following steps add borders to the entire table. **Why?** *These details will give the chart some dimension and add to its visual appeal.*

1

- Click the edge of the table so that the insertion point does not appear in any cell.

- Click the Borders arrow (Table Tools Design tab | Table Styles group) to display the Borders gallery (Figure 4–60).

Q&A Why is the button called No Border in the ScreenTip and Borders on the ribbon?
The ScreenTip name for the button will change based on the type of border, if any, present in the table. Currently no borders are applied.

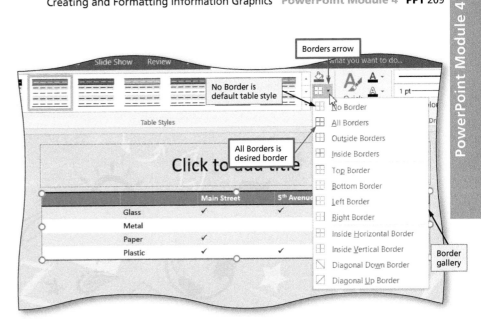

Figure 4–60

2

- Click All Borders in the Borders gallery to add borders around the entire table and to each table cell (Figure 4–61).

Q&A Why is the border color black?
PowerPoint's default border color is black. This color is displayed on the Pen Color button (Table Tools Design tab | Draw Borders group).

Can I apply any of the border options in the Border gallery?
Yes. You can vary the look of your table by applying borders only to the cells, around the table, to the top, bottom, left or right edges, or a combination of these areas.

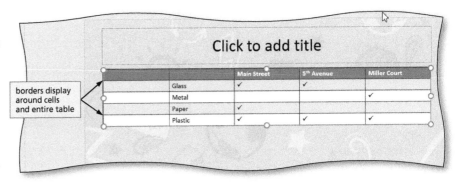

Figure 4–61

To Add an Effect to a Table

1 INSERT & MODIFY SMARTART | 2 ADD SMARTART STYLES & EFFECTS | 3 CONVERT TEXT TO SMARTART & FORMAT
4 CREATE CHART | 5 FORMAT CHART | 6 CREATE TABLE | 7 CHANGE TABLE STYLE & ALIGNMENT

Why? Adding an effect will enhance the table design. PowerPoint gives you the option of applying a bevel to specified cells so they have a three-dimensional appearance. You also can add a shadow or reflection to the entire table. The following steps add a shadow and give a three-dimensional appearance to the entire table.

1

- With the table selected, click the Effects button (Table Tools Design tab | Table Styles group) to display the Effects menu.

Q&A What is the difference between a shadow and a reflection?
A shadow gives the appearance that light is falling on the table, which causes a shadow behind the graphic. A reflection gives the appearance that the table is shiny, so a mirror image appears below the actual graphic.

2

- Point to Shadow to display the Shadow gallery (Figure 4–62).

Q&A

How do the shadows differ in the Outer, Inner, and Perspective categories?

The Outer shadows are displayed on the outside of the table, whereas the Inner shadows are displayed in the interior cells. The Perspective shadows give the illusion that a light is shining from the right or left side of the table or from above, and the table is casting a shadow.

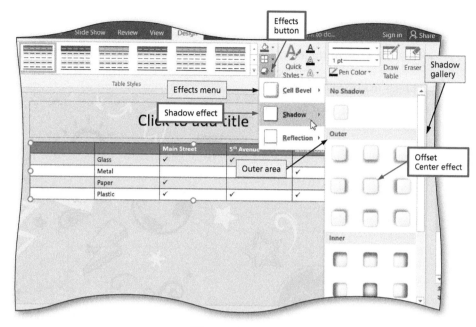

Figure 4–62

3

- Point to Offset Center in the Outer category (second shadow in second row) to display a live preview of this shadow (Figure 4–63).

Experiment

- Point to the various shadows in the Shadow gallery and watch the shadows change in the table.

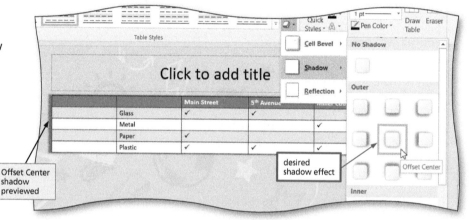

Figure 4–63

4

- Click Offset Center to apply this shadow to the table.
- Click outside the table so it no longer is selected (Figure 4–64).

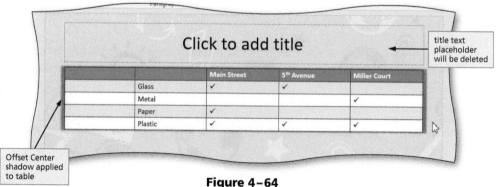

Figure 4–64

To Resize a Table

Why? On Slide 4, you can remove the title text placeholder because the table will have the title, Recycling Centers, in the first column. If you resize the table to fill the slide it will be more readable. You resize a table the same way you resize a chart, a SmartArt graphic, or any other graphical object. The following steps resize the table to fill Slide 4.

1
- Click a border of the title text placeholder so that it displays as a solid line and then press the DELETE key to remove the placeholder (Figure 4–65).

Q&A If I am using a touch screen, how do I remove the placeholder?
Press and hold a border of the title text placeholder and then tap Delete on the shortcut menu.

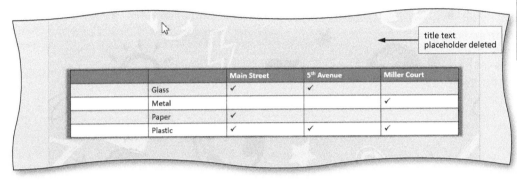

Figure 4–65

2
- Select the table and then drag the upper-left sizing handle diagonally to the upper-left corner of the slide.

- Drag the lower-right sizing handle diagonally to the lower-right corner of the slide, as shown in Figure 4–66.

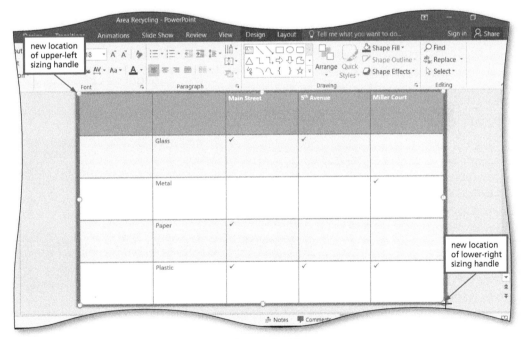

Figure 4–66

To Merge Cells

You want to insert a photo of a recycling sign in the area where the first two cells reside in the first row, so you need to make room for this picture. In addition, you want to merge cells in the first column to fit a chart title. ***Why?*** *To provide space for graphics and text, you can merge two or more cells to create one large cell.* The Slide 4 table title will display vertically in the first column. The following steps merge two cells in the first table row into a single cell and merge four cells in the first column into a single cell.

• Drag through the first and second column cells in the first table row to select these two cells (Figure 4–67).

Figure 4–67

• Click the Table Tools Layout tab to display the Table Tools Layout ribbon.

• Click the Merge Cells button (Table Tools Layout tab | Merge group) to merge the two cells into one cell (Figure 4–68).

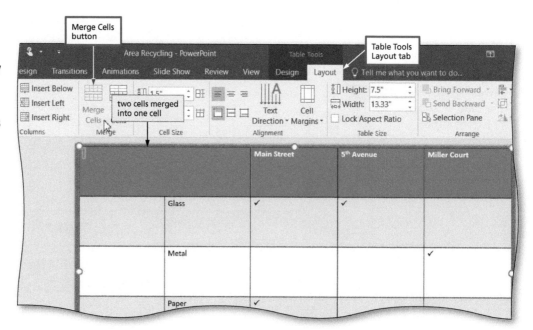

Figure 4–68

3

- Drag through the second, third, fourth, and fifth cells in the first table column to select these cells (Figure 4–69).

cells to merge are selected

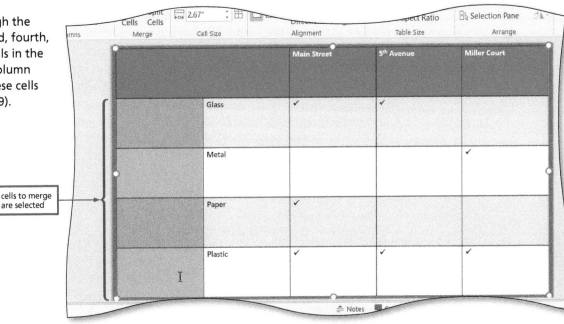

Figure 4–69

4

- Click the Merge Cells button to merge these cells (Figure 4–70).

Merge Cells button

Q&A Could I have merged the four cells in the first column before merging the two cells in the first row? Yes.

four cells merged into one cell

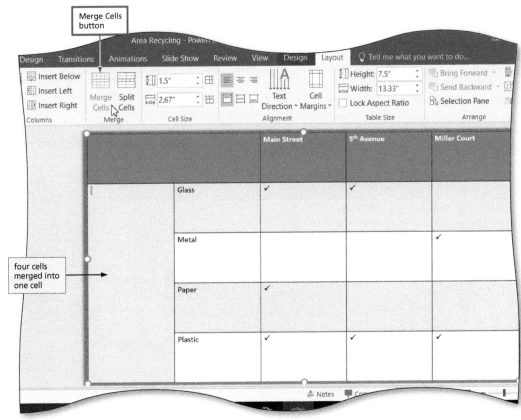

Figure 4–70

Other Ways

1. Right-click selected cells, click Merge Cells on shortcut menu

To Change Table Column Height and Width

The font size of the text in a table cell determines that cell's minimum height. You occasionally, however, may need to change the default height or width of a table column or row. To resize a column or row, you would perform the following steps.

1. Select the table. To change the height, position the pointer over the inside border of the column you want to resize and then drag the column to the right or left.

2. To change the width, position the pointer over the inside border of the row you want to resize and then click and drag the row up or down.

Other Ways

1. Enter desired measurements in Height and Width boxes (Table Tools Layout tab | Cell Size group)

To Display Text in a Cell Vertically

1 INSERT & MODIFY SMARTART | 2 ADD SMARTART STYLES & EFFECTS | 3 CONVERT TEXT TO SMARTART & FORMAT
4 CREATE CHART | 5 FORMAT CHART | 6 CREATE TABLE | 7 CHANGE TABLE STYLE & ALIGNMENT

You want the Slide 4 table title to display vertically in the first column. *Why? To add variety to your slides, you can display text in a nonstandard manner.* By rotating text 270 degrees, you call attention to these letters. The default orientation of table cell text is horizontal. You can change this direction to stack the letters so they display above and below each other, or you can rotate the direction in 90-degree increments. The following steps rotate the text in the first column cell.

- With the Table Tools Layout tab displayed and the column 1 cell selected, type **Recycling Centers** in the table cell.

- Click the Text Direction button (Table Tools Layout tab | Alignment group) to display the Text Direction gallery (Figure 4–71).

Experiment

- Point to the three other direction options in the Text Direction gallery and watch the text change in the cell.

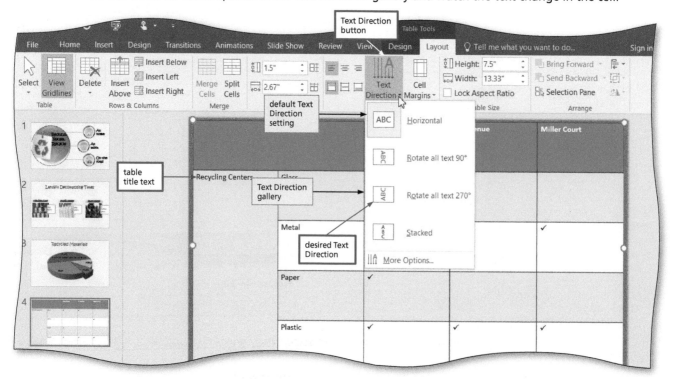

Figure 4–71

2
- Click 'Rotate all text 270°' to rotate the text in the cell (Figure 4–72).

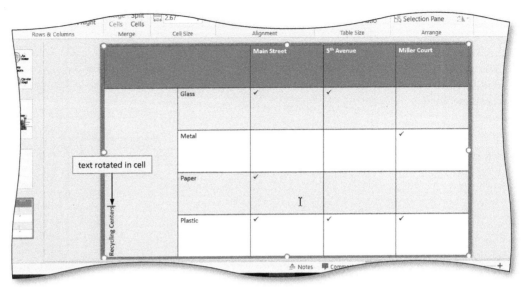

Figure 4–72

Other Ways

1. Right-click selected cells, click Format Shape on shortcut menu, click Text Options tab, click Textbox icon, click Text direction arrow

To Add an Image to a Table and Change the Transparency

1 INSERT & MODIFY SMARTART | 2 ADD SMARTART STYLES & EFFECTS | 3 CONVERT TEXT TO SMARTART & FORMAT

4 CREATE CHART | 5 FORMAT CHART | 6 CREATE TABLE | **7 CHANGE TABLE STYLE & ALIGNMENT**

Another table enhancement you can make is to add a photo or illustration to a table cell. The following steps add a picture of a recycling center sign to the upper-left table cell and then decrease the transparency so the picture is displayed with the full color intensity. *Why? This illustration is another graphical element that reinforces the purpose of the table.*

1
- Right-click the first cell in the first row to display the shortcut menu and mini toolbar (Figure 4–73).

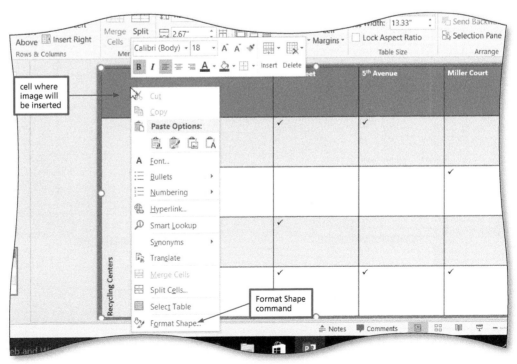

Figure 4–73

2

- Click Format Shape to display the Format Shape pane and then, if necessary, click Fill to expand the Fill section.

- Click 'Picture or texture fill' to select this option (Figure 4–74).

3

- Click the File button to display the Insert Picture dialog box.

- Click the Recycling Sign picture located in the Data Files and then click the Insert button (Insert Picture dialog box) to insert the Recycling Sign picture into the table cell.

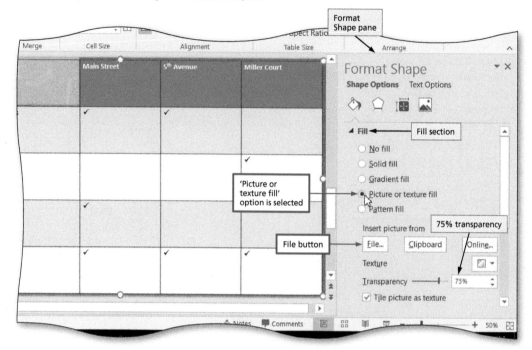

Figure 4–74

4

- If the Transparency is more than 0%, drag slider to the left until 0% is displayed in the Transparency text box (Figure 4–75).

Figure 4–75

5

- Click the Close button (Format Shape pane).

Other Ways

1. Right-click selected cell, click Shape Fill arrow on mini toolbar, click Picture

To Align Text in Cells

The data in each cell can be aligned horizontally and vertically. You change the horizontal alignment of each cell in a similar manner as you center, left-align, or right-align text in a placeholder. You also can change the vertical alignment so that the data displays at the top, middle, or bottom of each cell. The following steps center the text both horizontally and vertically in each table cell. *Why? Having the text centered vertically and horizontally helps balance the cells by distributing the empty space evenly around the cell contents.*

1
- Click the Select button (Table Tools Layout tab |Table group) to display the Select menu (Figure 4–76).

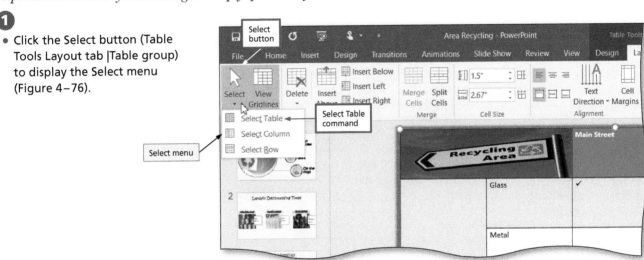

Figure 4–76

2
- Click Select Table in the Select menu to select the entire table.

- Click the Center button (Table Tools Layout tab | Alignment group) to center the text between the left and right borders of each cell in the table (Figure 4–77).

Figure 4–77

• Click the Center Vertically button (Table Tools Layout tab | Alignment group) to center the text between the top and bottom borders of each cell in the table (Figure 4–78).

Q&A Must I center all the table cells, or can I center only specific cells?
You can center as many cells as you desire at one time by selecting one or more cells.

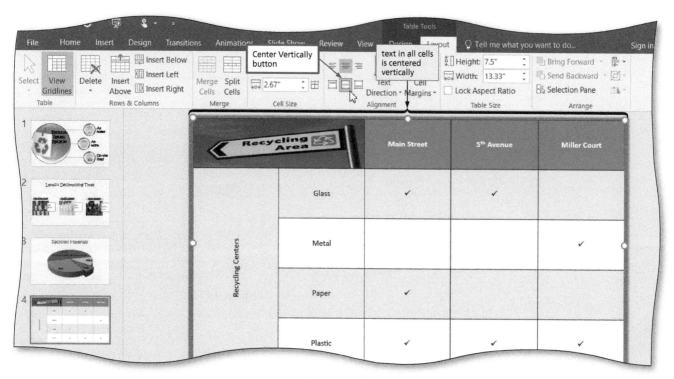

Figure 4–78

Other Ways

1. Right-click selected cells, click Format Shape on shortcut menu, click Text Options tab, click Textbox icon, click Vertical alignment arrow

---

BTW
Clearing Table Formatting
The table you create on Slide 4 has five columns and five rows. Many times, however, you may need to create larger tables and then enter data into many cells. In these cases, experienced PowerPoint designers recommend clearing all formatting from the table so that you can concentrate on the numbers and letters and not be distracted by the colors and borders. To clear formatting, click the Clear Table command at the bottom of the Table Styles gallery (Table Tools Design tab | Table Styles group). Then, add a table style once you have verified that all table data is correct.

To Format Table Data

The final table enhancement is to bold the text in all cells and increase the font size of the title and the symbols. The entire table is selected, so you can bold all text simultaneously. The title and symbols will have different font sizes. The following steps format the data.

1 Display the Home tab and then click the Bold button (Home tab | Font group) to bold all text in the table.

2 Select the table title text in the first column and then increase the font size to 72 point and change the font to Kristen ITC.

3 Select the three column headings and then increase the font size to 28 point and change the font to Kristen ITC.

④ Select the four cells with the recycling category names in the second column and then increase the font size to 32 point and change the font to Kristen ITC.

⑤ Select all the table cells below the column headings and then increase the font size of the check marks to 40 point (Figure 4–79).

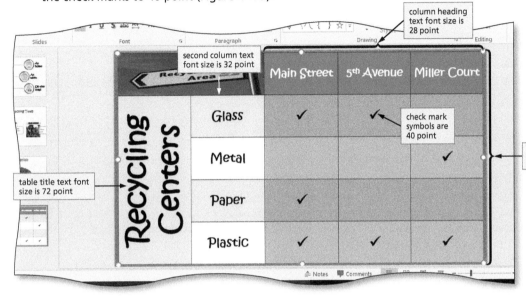

Figure 4–79

To Add a Transition between Slides

A final enhancement you will make in this presentation is to apply the Crush transition in the Exciting category to all slides and change the transition duration to 3.00. The following steps apply this transition to the presentation.

① Apply the Crush transition in the Exciting category (Transitions tab | Transition to This Slide group) to all four slides in the presentation.

② Change the transition duration from 02.00 to 03.00 for all slides.

To Save and Print the Presentation

With the presentation completed, you should save the file and print handouts for your audience. The following steps save the file and then print a presentation handout with two slides per page.

① Save the presentation again in the same storage location with the same file name.

② Open the Backstage view, click the Print tab, click 'Full Page Slides' in the Settings area, click 2 Slides in the Handouts area to display a preview of the handout, and then click the Print button in the Print gallery to print the presentation.

③ Because the project now is complete, you can exit PowerPoint.

Summary

In this module you have learned how to insert a SmartArt graphic and then add pictures and text, convert text to a SmartArt graphic, create and format a chart and a table, change table text alignment and orientation, and insert symbols.

CONSIDER THIS: PLAN AHEAD

What decisions will you need to make when creating your next presentation?
Use these guidelines as you complete the assignments in this module and create your own slide show decks outside of this class.

1. Audiences recall visual concepts more quickly and accurately than when viewing text alone, so consider using graphics in your presentation.

   a) Decide the precise message you want to convey to your audience.

   b) Determine if a SmartArt graphic, chart, or table is the better method of presenting the information.

2. Choose an appropriate SmartArt layout.

   a) Determine which layout best represents the concept you are attempting to present. Some of the layouts, such as Matrix, Pyramid, and Relationship, offer outstanding methods of showing how ideas are connected to each other, while other layouts, such as Cycle, List, and Process, are best at showing steps to complete a task.

   b) Use Table 4–1 to help you select a layout.

3. Choose an appropriate chart type.

   a) Charts are excellent visuals to show relationships between groups of data, especially numbers.

   b) Decide which chart type best conveys the points you are attempting to make in your presentation. PowerPoint provides a wide variety of styles within each category of chart, so determine which one is most effective in showing the relationships.

4. Obtain information for the graphic from credible sources.

   a) Text or numbers should be current and correct.

   b) Verify the sources of the information.

   c) Be certain you have typed the data correctly.

   d) Acknowledge the source of the information on the slide or during your presentation.

5. Test your visual elements.

   a) Show your slides to several friends or colleagues and ask them to interpret what they see.

   b) Have your test audience summarize the information they perceive on the tables and charts and compare their analyses to what you are attempting to convey.

Apply Your Knowledge

Reinforce the skills and apply the concepts you learned in this module.

Converting Text to a SmartArt Graphic

Note: To complete this assignment, you will be required to use the Data Files. Please contact your instructor for information about accessing the Data Files.

Instructions: Run PowerPoint. Open the presentation called Apply 4–1 Camping, which is located in the Data Files.

The slide in the presentation presents information about tent or RV camping or renting a cabin at a campground. The document you open is a partially formatted presentation. You are to convert the list to SmartArt and format the graphic so the slide looks like Figure 4–80.

Perform the following tasks:
1. Select the WordArt title, Camp Bullfrog, and increase the font size to 60 point. Also change the font case to UPPERCASE, and then add the 'Orange, 18 pt glow, Accent color 1' glow text effect (in Glow Variations area), as shown in Figure 4–80.

2. Convert the list to SmartArt by applying the Vertical Box List layout (in List category). Change the colors to 'Colorful Range – Accent Colors 5 to 6'. Apply the Cartoon 3-D Style.

3. Resize this SmartArt graphic to approximately 3.52" × 8".

4. With the Text Pane open, select the three Level 1 bullet paragraphs, change the font to Arial, increase the font size to 24 point, change the font color to 'Black, Text 1' (in first Theme Colors row), and then bold this text.

5. With the Text Pane open, select the four Level 2 bullet paragraphs, change the font to Arial and increase the font size to 20 point.

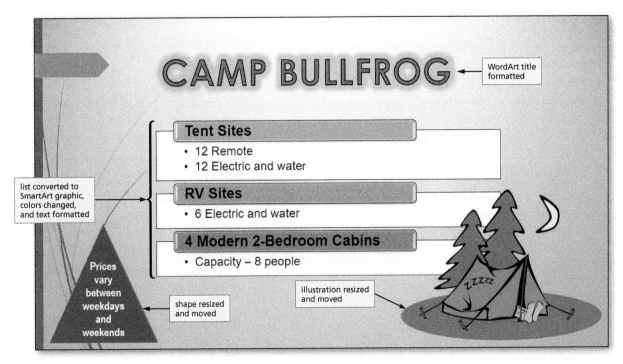

Figure 4–80

Continued >

Apply Your Knowledge *continued*

6. Increase the size of the camping illustration to approximately 3.42" × 4.72" and then move the illustration to the lower-right corner of the slide, as shown in the figure. Adjust the size of the triangle shape to approximately 2.67" × 2.49" and then move this shape to the lower-left corner of the slide, as shown.

7. If requested by your instructor, add your grandfather's first name after the word, people, on the last line of the Level 2 bullet paragraph.

8. Apply the Window transition in the Dynamic Content category to the slide. Change the duration to 4.00 seconds.

9. View the presentation and then save the file using the file name, Apply 4–1 Camp Bullfrog.

10. Submit the revised document in the format specified by your instructor.

11. �ख In Step 2, you chose the Vertical Box List and changed the colors of the SmartArt graphic. How did this style improve the slide and increase the audience's attention to the content?

Extend Your Knowledge

Extend the skills you learned in this module and experiment with new skills. You may need to use Help to complete the assignment.

Changing the Chart Type and Style and Formatting a SmartArt Graphic

Note: To complete this assignment, you will be required to use the Data Files. Please contact your instructor for information about accessing the Data Files.

Instructions: Run PowerPoint. Open the presentation called Extend 4–1 Fishing, which is located in the Data Files. You will format a chart by applying a type and style and then you will convert text to a SmartArt graphic to create the presentation shown in Figure 4–81.

Perform the following tasks:
1. On Slide 1 (Figure 4–81a), change the chart type from a Line chart to a Column chart, and then change the chart style to Style 8 (eighth style). *Hint:* Click the chart to select it, click the Change Chart Type button (Chart Tools Design tab | Type group), and then select the Column chart type. Increase the size of the chart to 5.56" × 7.4" and then move the chart to the location shown in the figure. Add a Yellow shape outline to the chart and then change the outline weight to 3 pt. Delete the chart title, Total Fish Caught. Increase the font size of the legend to 14 point and then bold this text.

2. On Slide 2 (Figure 4–81b), convert the list to SmartArt by applying the Converging Radial graphic (in Relationship category). Change the colors to 'Colored Fill - Accent 2', located in the Accent 2 area. Apply the Polished 3-D style. Resize the SmartArt graphic to approximately 4.84" × 7.97". If necessary, move the graphic so that it is centered between the left edge of the slide and the angler.

3. On Slide 2, increase the size of the center circle of the SmartArt graphic to approximately 2.75" × 2.75" and then change the font color to Dark Blue (in Standard Colors).

(a) Slide 1

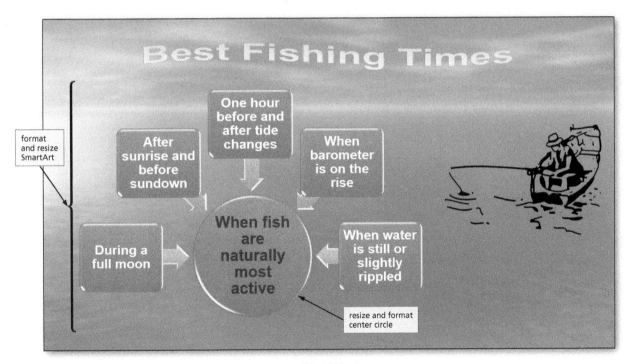

(b) Slide 2
Figure 4–81 (Continued)

Continued >

Extend Your Knowledge *continued*

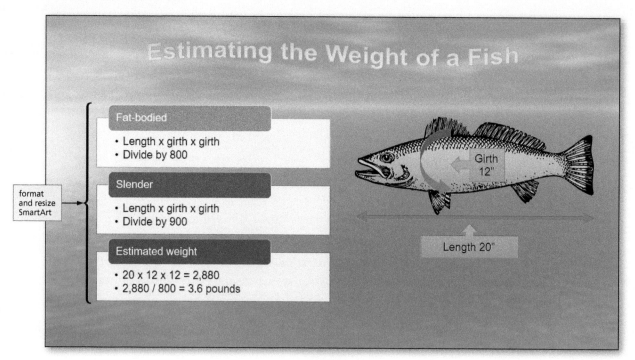

(c) Slide 3
Figure 4–81

4. On Slide 3 (Figure 4–81c), convert the list to SmartArt by applying the Vertical Box List graphic (in List category). Change the colors to 'Colorful Range - Accent Colors 3 to 4'. Apply the Brick Scene 3-D style. Select the text in the three colored rectangle shapes in the SmartArt graphic and then increase the font size to 22 point and bold this text.

5. If requested by your instructor, insert a text box on Slide 2 in the lower-right area of the slide and add the name of the first school you attended.

6. Apply the Ripple transition in the Exciting category to all slides and then change the duration to 3.00 seconds.

7. View the presentation and then save the file using the file name, Extend 4–1 Best Fishing Times.

8. Submit the revised document in the format specified by your instructor.

9. ✳ In this assignment, you changed the chart style on Slide 1 and changed the text to SmartArt graphics on Slides 2 and 3. How did these edits enhance the presentation?

Expand Your World

Create a solution that uses cloud or web technologies by learning and investigating on your own from general guidance.

Creating Charts and Graphs Using Websites

Instructions: PowerPoint presents a wide variety of chart and table layouts, and you must decide which one is effective in presenting the relationships between data and indicating important trends.

Several websites offer opportunities to create graphics that help explain concepts to your audience. Many of these websites are easy to use and allow you to save the chart or graph you create and then import it into your PowerPoint presentation.

Perform the following tasks:

1. Visit one of the following websites, or locate other websites that help you create a chart or graph: ChartGo (chartgo.com), Chartle (chartle.net), Rich Chart Live (richchartlive.com), Online Charts Builder (charts.hohli.com), or Lucidchart (lucidchart.com).
2. Create a chart using the same data supplied for Slide 3 in the Area Recycling presentation.
3. Save the new chart and then insert it into a new Slide 3 in the Area Recycling presentation. Delete the original Slide 3 in the presentation.
4. If requested to do so by your instructor, add your grandmother's first name to the chart title.
5. Save the presentation using the file name, Expand 4–1 Area Recycling.
6. Submit the assignment in the format specified by your instructor.
7. ✸ Which features do the websites offer that help you create charts and graphs? How does the graphic you created online compare to the chart you created using PowerPoint? How do the websites allow you to share your graphics using social networks?

In the Labs

Design, create, modify, and/or use a presentation following the guidelines, concepts, and skills presented in this module. Labs 1 and 2, which increase in difficulty, require you to create solutions based on what you learned in the module; Lab 3 requires you to apply your creative thinking and problem-solving skills to design and implement a solution.

Lab 1: Inserting and Formatting SmartArt and Formatting a Table

Note: To complete this assignment, you will be required to use the Data Files. Please contact your instructor for information about accessing the Data Files.

Problem: You have an interest in composting and thought this topic would be appropriate for an informative speech assignment in your communication class. Create the slides shown in Figure 4–82.

Perform the following tasks:

1. Run PowerPoint. Open the presentation called Lab 4–1 Compost, which is located in the Data Files. On Slide 1 (Figure 4–82a), insert the Hexagon Cluster SmartArt graphic (in seventh Picture row).
2. In the SmartArt Text Pane, type **Browns** as the first Level 1 text that will appear in the lower-left hexagon shape. Type **Greens** as the second Level 1 text that will appear to the right of the first hexagon shape on the right, **Air** as the third Level 1 text for the upper left hexagon shape, and **Water** as the fourth Level 1 text for the fourth hexagon shape, as shown in the figure.

Continued >

In the Labs continued

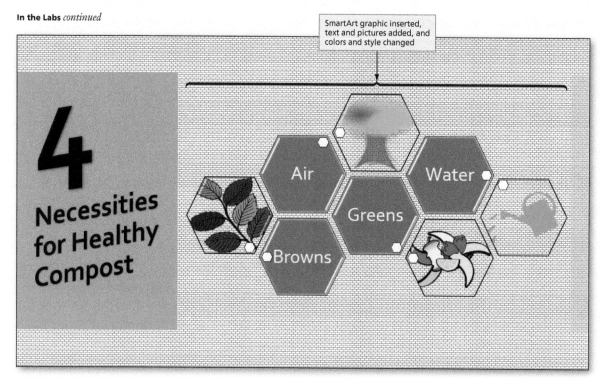

SmartArt graphic inserted, text and pictures added, and colors and style changed

(a) Slide 1

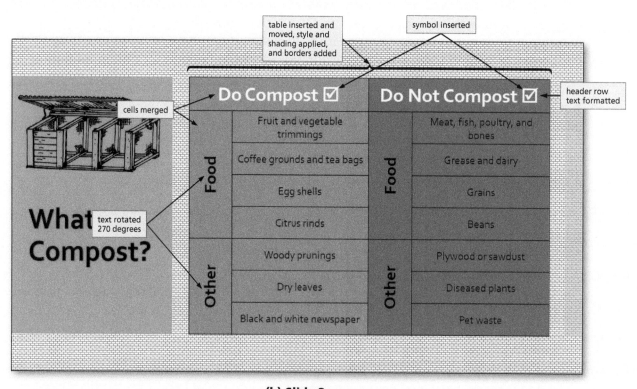

table inserted and moved, style and shading applied, and borders added

symbol inserted

cells merged

header row text formatted

text rotated 270 degrees

(b) Slide 2
Figure 4–82

3. Insert the picture called Leaves, which is available in the Data Files, in the left hexagon shape. Insert the picture called Tree, which is available in the Data Files, in the top hexagon shape. Insert the picture called Water, which is available in the Data Files, in the right hexagon shape. Insert the picture called Greens, which is available in the Data files, in the bottom hexagon shape.

4. Change the colors of the SmartArt graphic to 'Colored Fill - Accent 6' (second color in Accent 6 row). Apply the Cartoon 3-D style. Adjust the size of the SmartArt graphic to approximately 6.58" × 8.84" and then move it to the area shown in the figure.

5. On Slide 2 (Figure 4–82b), insert a table with 4 columns and 8 rows. Increase the size of the table to 5.82" × 8.5" and then move the table to the area shown in the figure. In row 1, merge cells 1 and 2 and then merge cells 3 and 4. In column 1, select rows 2, 3, 4, and 5 and then merge them. In column 3, select rows 2, 3, 4, and 5 and then merge them. In column 1, select rows 6, 7, and 8 and then merge them. In column 3, select rows 6, 7, and 8 and then merge them.

6. Change the width of the two vertically merged cells in column 1 to 1" by typing **1** in the Table Column Width text box (Table Tools Layout tab | Cell Size). Repeat this process to change the width of the two vertically merged cells in column 3.

7. Change the width of rows 2 through 8 in column 2 to 3.2". Repeat this process for rows 2 through 8 in column 4.

8. Enter the data in the table shown in Table 4–3 What to Compost?

Table 4–3 What to Compost?			
Do Compost		**Do Not Compost**	
Food	Fruit and vegetable trimmings	Food	Meat, fish, poultry, and bones
	Coffee grounds and tea bags		Grease and dairy
	Egg shells		Grains
	Citrus rinds		Beans
Other	Woody prunings	Other	Plywood or sawdust
	Dry leaves		Diseased plants
	Black and white newspaper		Pet waste

9. Change the font size for the words, Food, and Other, in both columns 1 and 3 to 28 point and then bold this text. Rotate these four words 270°. Select the table, center the table text, and then center the text vertically, as shown in the figure.

10. Change the font size of the table header text to 32 point and then center this text. Insert the Wingdings 254 symbol (checked box in the last row of the gallery) after the text, Do Compost. Copy this symbol after the text, Do Not Compost, as shown in the figure.

Continued >

In the Labs *continued*

11. Apply the 'Themed Style 1 – Accent 5' (in first Best Match for Document row) to the table. Change the shading of the left side of the table under the heading, Do Compost, to 'Brown, Accent 4' (first Theme Colors row). Change the shading of the right side of the table under the heading, Do Not Compost, to 'Orange, Accent 6' (first Theme Colors row).

12. Add borders to all table cells.

13. If requested by your instructor, insert a text box with the name of your grade school under the SmartArt diagram on Slide 1.

14. Apply the Fade transition in the Subtle category to both slides and then change the duration to 2.25 seconds.

15. View the presentation and then save the file using the file name, Lab 4–1 Compost Necessities.

16. Submit the document in the format specified by your instructor.

17. ✺ On Slide 1, you used the Hexagon Cluster SmartArt graphic. Is this style appropriate for this presentation content? Why? Why did you select the style of the table on Slide 2?

Lab 2: Creating a Presentation with SmartArt, a Chart, and a Table

Note: To complete this assignment, you will be required to use the Data Files. Please contact your instructor for information about accessing the Data Files.

Problem: For a special project, you surveyed students attending your culinary school about searching for recipes on the Internet. You had a positive response and decided to share the results of your study with school administrators and fellow students by creating the slides shown in Figure 4–83.

Perform the following tasks:

1. Run PowerPoint. Open the presentation called Lab 4–2 Recipes, which is located in the Data Files.

2. On Slide 1 (Figure 4–83a), insert the Pyramid List SmartArt graphic (in List group). Enter the text shown in the figure and then bold this text. Change the colors of the graphic to 'Gradient Loop – Accent 2' (Accent 2 row) and then change the style to Inset (first 3-D row). Send the graphic backward and move it to the right so the illustration will display as shown in the figure.

3. On Slide 2, insert a 3-D Pie chart, as shown in Figure 4–83b. Use the data in Table 4–4 Important Features to replace the sample data in the worksheet. Change the Quick Layout to Layout 1. Change the chart style to Style 3. Select the chart title text, Column 1, and then press the DELETE key to delete this text.

4. Increase the legend font size to 20 point and then bold this text. Select the chart, and then rotate it approximately 75 degrees so that the Fresh ingredients slice is at the bottom-right. Separate the Fresh ingredients slice 20%, add a 6 pt border to this slice, and then change its border color to Light Green (Standard Colors row).

(a) Slide 1

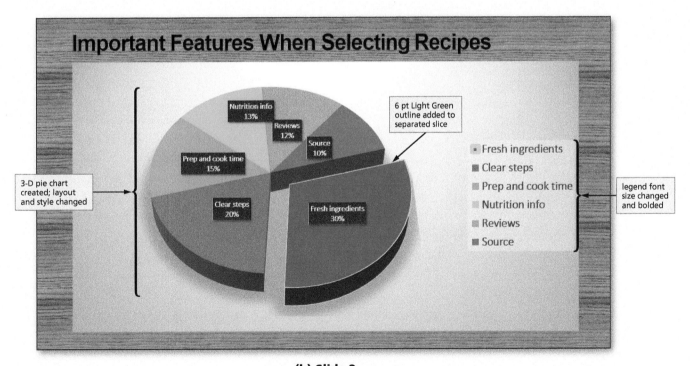

(b) Slide 2
Figure 4–83 (Continued)

Continued >

In the Labs *continued*

Table 4–4 Important Features	
Fresh ingredients	30%
Clear steps	20%
Prep and cook time	15%
Nutrition info	13%
Reviews	12%
Source	10%

5. Increase the size of the chart to 6.11" × 11.76" and then move it to the location shown on Slide 2.

6. On Slide 3 (Figure 4–82c), in the header row of the table, split the upper-left and upper-right cells to 2 columns and 1 row. Increase the font size of the header row text to 36 point and then bold this text.

7. Increase the size of the table to approximately 5.31" × 12.06" and then move the table to the location shown in the figure. Change the table style to 'Themed Style 2 - Accent 1' (second row in Best Match for Document area). Change the borders to All Borders. Insert the picture called Computer, which is located in the Data Files, in the second cell of the table's first row. Insert the picture called Cooking, which is located in the Data Files, in the fourth cell of the table's first row.

8. If requested by your instructor, enter the name of the last TV program you watched as the second line of the subtitle text on Slide 1.

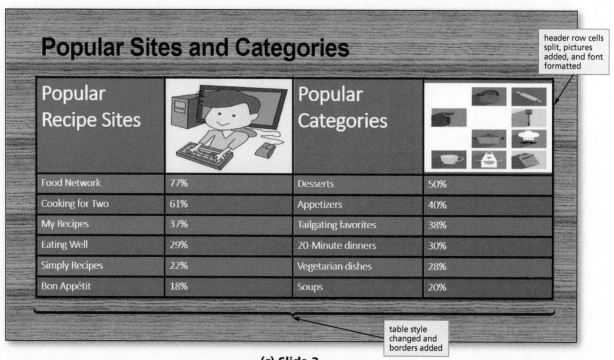

(c) Slide 3
Figure 4–83

9. Apply the Uncover transition in the Subtle category to all slides and then change the duration to 3.25 seconds.

10. View the presentation and then save the file using the file name, Lab 4–2 Recipes Online Survey.

11. Submit the revised document in the format specified by your instructor.

12. ✹ How did adding a SmartArt graphic to the title slide enhance the presentation?

Lab 3: **Consider This: Your Turn**

Design and Create a Presentation about Recycling Materials

Note: To complete this assignment, you will be required to use the Data Files. Please contact your instructor for information about accessing the Data Files.

Part 1:   The Area Recycling presentation you created in this module addresses issues community residents may have regarding the types of materials consumers can recycle, how long these products take to decompose in landfills, and where recycling centers are located in town. Questions may remain, however, on which materials are safe to recycle and which should be placed in trash receptacles. Aluminum cans, for example, are fine for recycling, but aluminum foil, metal coat hangers, and scrap metal are not. Plastic bottles are allowed, but their caps, lids, and sprayers must be removed. Newspapers, magazines, and brown paper bags are fine, but saturated pizza boxes, waxy ice cream containers, and paper towel rolls are not. Finally, glass food containers can be recycled, but window glass, dishware, and ceramics cannot. Open the Area Recycling file you created and then use the concepts and techniques presented in this module to add a new Slide 5 with a table containing information regarding products that can and cannot be recycled. Review websites for additional recycling guidelines. Apply a table style, add borders, an effect, and a symbol, change colors where appropriate, and add a recycling icon. Review and revise your presentation as needed and then save the file using the file name, Lab 4–3 Recycling Materials. Submit your assignment in the format specified by your instructor.

Part 2:   ✹ You made several decisions while creating the presentation in this assignment: applying a table style, adding borders and an effect, changing the table colors, and adding a picture and symbol. What was the rationale behind each of these decisions? When you reviewed the document, what further revisions did you make and why? Where would you recommend showing this slide show?

5 | Collaborating on and Delivering a Presentation

Objectives

You will have mastered the material in this module when you can:

- Combine PowerPoint files
- Accept and reject a reviewer's proposed changes
- Delete, reply to, and insert comments
- Reuse slides from an existing presentation
- Insert slide footer content
- Set slide size and presentation resolution

- Save files as a PowerPoint show
- Package a presentation for storage on a compact disc
- Save a presentation in a previous PowerPoint format
- Inspect and protect files
- Use presentation tools to navigate and annotate slide shows

Introduction

Often presentations are enhanced when individuals collaborate to fine-tune text, visuals, and design elements on the slides. A **review cycle** occurs when a slide show designer shares a file with multiple reviewers so they can make comments and changes to their copies of the slides and then return the file to the designer. A **comment** is a description that normally does not display as part of the slide show. It can be used to clarify information that may be difficult to understand, to pose questions, or to communicate suggestions. The designer then can display the comments, modify their content, and ask the reviewers to again review the presentation, and continue this process until the slides are satisfactory. Once the presentation is complete, the designer can protect the file so no one can open it without a password, remove comments and other information, and assure that slide content has not been altered. The designer also can save the presentation to a CD, DVD, or flash drive, or as a PowerPoint show that will run without opening PowerPoint. In addition, a presenter can use PowerPoint's variety of tools to run the show effectively and emphasize various elements on the screen.

Project — Presentation with Comments, Inserted Slides, Protection, and Annotation

BTW

Pixels

Screen resolution specifies the amount of pixels displayed on your screen. The word, pixel, combines pix (for "pictures") and el (for "element").

The seven slides in the Chicago presentation (Figure 5–1) give information and provide images of that Midwestern city's skyline, famous building, and attractions. All slides in the presentation were developed using versions of PowerPoint used prior to the current PowerPoint 2016. In these previous versions, the slides used a 4:3 width-to-height ratio, which was the standard proportion of computer monitors at that time. Today, however, most people use PowerPoint 2016's default 16:9 ratio, which is the proportion of most widescreen monitors today. You will change the slide size in your Chicago presentation after all the slides are created.

When you are developing a presentation, it often is advantageous to ask a variety of people to review your work in progress. These individuals can evaluate the wording, art, and design, and experts in the subject can check the slides for accuracy. They can add comments to the slides in specific areas, such as a paragraph, a graphic, or a table. You then can review their comments and use them to modify and enhance your work. You also can insert slides from other presentations into your presentation.

Once you develop the final set of slides, you can complete the file by removing any comments and personal information, adding a password so that unauthorized people cannot see the file contents without your permission, saving the file as a PowerPoint show so it runs automatically when you open a file, and saving the file to a CD, DVD, or flash drive.

When running your presentation, you may decide to show the slides nonsequentially. For example, you may need to review a slide you discussed already, or you may want to skip some slides and jump forward. You also may want to emphasize, or **annotate**, material on the slides by highlighting text or writing on the slides. You can save your annotations to review during or after the presentation.

In this module, you will learn how to create the slides shown in Figure 5–1. The following roadmap identifies general activities you will perform as you progress through this module:

1. COLLABORATE on a presentation by using comments.
2. FORMAT SLIDES and SET SLIDE SHOW RESOLUTION.
3. SAVE and PACKAGE a PRESENTATION.
4. PROTECT and SECURE a PRESENTATION.
5. USE PRESENTATION TOOLS to navigate and annotate slides during a presentation.

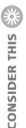

CONSIDER THIS

What are some tips for collaborating successfully?

Working with your classmates can yield numerous benefits. Your peers can assist in brainstorming, developing key ideas, revising your project, and keeping you on track so that your presentation meets the assignment goals.

The first step when collaborating with peers is to define success. What, ultimately, is the goal? For example, are you developing a persuasive presentation to school administrators in an effort to fund a new club? Next, you can set short-term and long-term goals that help lead you to completing the project successfully. These goals can be weekly tasks to accomplish, such as interviewing content experts, conducting online research, or compiling an annotated bibliography. After that, you can develop a plan to finish the project by outlining subtasks that each member must accomplish. Each collaborator should inform the group members when the task is complete or if problems are delaying progress. When collaborators meet, whether in person or online, they should establish an agenda and have one member keep notes of topics discussed.

(a) Slide 1 (Title Slide Enhanced from Reviewer)

(b) Slide 2 (SmartArt from Reviewer)

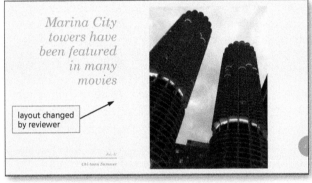

(c) Slide 3 (Enhanced from Reviewer)

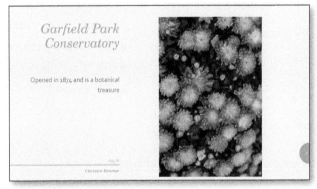

(d) Slide 4 (Reused from Existing Presentation)

(e) Slide 5 (Reused from Existing Presentation)

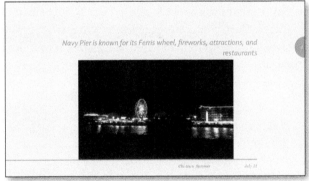

(f) Slide 6 (Inserted from Reviewer's Presentation)

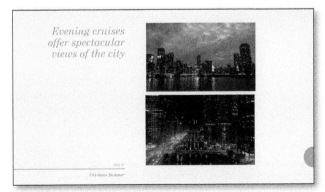

(g) Slide 7 (Inserted from Reviewer's Presentation)

Figure 5–1

Collaborating on a Presentation

PowerPoint provides several methods to collaborate with friends or coworkers who can view your slide show and then provide feedback. When you **collaborate**, you work together on a document with other PowerPoint users who are cooperating jointly and assisting willingly with the endeavor. You can distribute your slide show physically to others by exchanging a compact disc or a flash drive. You also can share your presentation through the Internet by sending the file as an email attachment or saving the file to a storage location, such as Microsoft OneDrive or Microsoft Office SharePoint.

In the following pages, you will follow these general steps to collaborate with Bernie Halen, who has analyzed a presentation you created after visiting Chicago for a weekend this past summer:

1. Combine (merge) presentations.
2. Print slides and comments.
3. Review and accept or reject changes.
4. Reply to a comment.
5. Insert a comment.
6. Delete a comment.

To Merge a Presentation

1 COLLABORATE | 2 FORMAT SLIDES & SET SLIDE SHOW RESOLUTION | 3 SAVE & PACKAGE A PRESENTATION
4 PROTECT & SECURE PRESENTATION | 5 USE PRESENTATION TOOLS

Why? Bernie Halen reviewed your Chicago presentation and made several comments, so you want to combine (merge) his changes with your file to see if they improve the original design and slide content. Bernie's changes to the initial presentation include adding a subtitle, converting the Slide 1 title and subtitle text to WordArt, and changing the Slide 2 bulleted list to a SmartArt graphic. A transition is added to all slides, the theme is changed, paragraphs are edited, and two slides are added. The following steps merge this reviewer's file with your Chicago Final presentation.

- Run PowerPoint and then open the presentation, Chicago, from the Data Files.
- Save the presentation using the file name, Chicago Final.
- Display the Review tab (Figure 5–2).

Q&A
Why do the slides have a different size than the slides I have seen in previous presentations?
The slides in the Chicago presentation use a 4:3 ratio, which was the default setting in PowerPoint versions prior to PowerPoint 2013.

Figure 5–2

- Click the Compare button (Review tab | Compare group) to display the Choose File to Merge with Current Presentation dialog box.

- With the list of your Data Files displaying, click Chicago - Bernie to select the file name (Figure 5–3).

Figure 5–3

- Click the Merge button (Choose File to Merge with Current Presentation dialog box) to merge Bernie Halen's presentation with the Chicago presentation and to display the Revisions pane.

- If necessary, click the Show Comments button (Review tab | Comments group) to display the Comments pane (Figure 5–4).

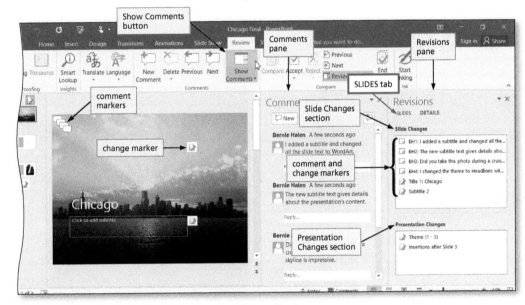

Figure 5–4

Q&A

When does the Comments pane display automatically?

It displays when left open during a previous PowerPoint session. Clicking the Show Comments button or the Comments button on the status bar displays or hides the Comments pane.

How do I display the Revisions pane if it does not display automatically?

Click the Reviewing Pane button (Review tab | Compare group) to display the Revisions pane.

If several reviewers have made comments and suggestions, can I merge their files, too?

Yes. Repeat Steps 1, 2, and 3. Each reviewer's initials display in a color-coded comment box.

To Print Comments

1 COLLABORATE | **2 FORMAT SLIDES & SET SLIDE SHOW RESOLUTION** | **3 SAVE & PACKAGE A PRESENTATION**
4 PROTECT & SECURE PRESENTATION | **5 USE PRESENTATION TOOLS**

You can print each slide and the comments a reviewer has made before you begin to accept and reject each suggestion. *Why? As owner of the original presentation, you want to review the comments and modifications on a hard copy before making decisions about whether to accept these suggestions.* PowerPoint can print these slides and comments on individual pages. The following steps print the slides with comments.

- Open the Backstage view and then click the Print tab to display the Print gallery.

- Click 'Full Page Slides' in the Print gallery to display print layouts.

- If necessary, click 'Print Comments and Ink Markup' to place a check mark by this option and turn on printing comment pages (Figure 5–5).

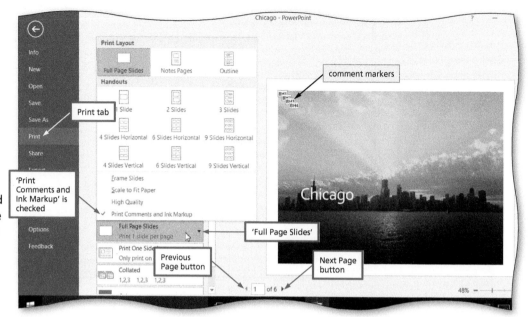

Figure 5–5

Q&A If I want to print only the slides and not the comments, would I click 'Print Comments and Ink Markup' to remove the check mark?
Yes. Tapping or clicking the command turns on and turns off printing the notes pages.

2

- Click the Next Page and Previous Page buttons to scroll through the previews of the three slides and the three comment pages.

- Click the Print button to print the six pages (Figure 5–6).

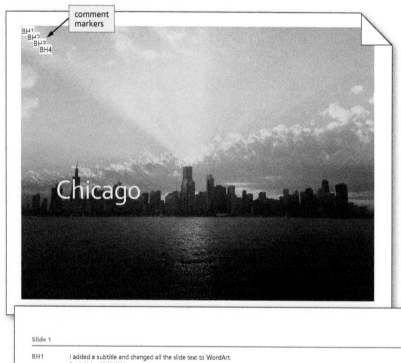

(a) Page 1 (Title Slide)

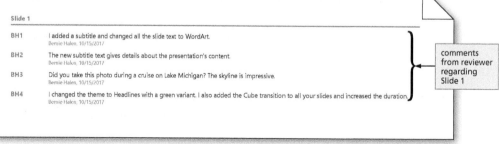

(b) Page 2 (Comments from Reviewer)

Figure 5–6 (Continued)

BH5

comment marker

Chicago

- Third largest city in United States
- Incorporated in 1865
- World's first skyscraper built in 1885

(c) Page 3 (Slide 2)

Slide 2

BH5   I converted your Slide 2 text to SmartArt.
Bernie Halen, 10/15/2017

comment from reviewer regarding Slide 2

(d) Page 4 (Comments from Reviewer)

BH6
BH7

comment markers

Marina City towers have been featured in many movies

(e) Page 5 (Slide 3)

Slide 3

BH6   These identical towers are considered some of the most photographed buildings in Chicago. It must be amazing to live in a condo on the upper floors.
Bernie Halen, 10/15/2017

BH7   I changed your bulleted text to title text.
Bernie Halen, 10/15/2017

comments from reviewer regarding Slide 3

(f) Page 6 (Comments from Reviewer)

Figure 5–6

Other Ways

1. Press CTRL+P, click 'Full Page Slides' in the Print gallery, if necessary check 'Print Comments and Ink Markup', click Print button

To Preview the Presentation Changes

The reviewer made several changes to the overall presentation and then edited your three slides. You can preview his modifications to obtain an overview of his suggestions. *Why? Seeing his edits now can help you decide later whether to accept or reject each change as you step through each revision.* The changes that apply to the entire presentation are displayed in the Presentation Changes section of the Revisions pane, and changes to each individual slide are displayed in the Slide Changes section of this pane. Vertical rectangular icons indicate change markers, and horizontal rectangular icons represent comment markers. Each reviewer's revisions are color-coded. The following steps preview the merged presentation.

- If necessary, display the Review tab. With Slide 1 displaying, click the SLIDES tab in the Revisions pane to display a thumbnail of merged Slide 1 (Figure 5–7).

Figure 5–7

- Click the Bernie Halen check box above the Slide 1 thumbnail (Revisions pane) to view the proposed text changes in the main slide pane (Figure 5–8).

- Click the Bernie Halen check box again to undo the changes.

Can I make some, but not all, of the reviewer's changes on Slide 1?

Yes. PowerPoint allows you to view each proposed change individually and then either accept or reject the modification.

Figure 5–8

How do I accept and evaluate criticism positively?

Receiving feedback from others ultimately should enhance your presentation. If several of your reviewers make similar comments, such as too much text appears on one slide or that a chart would help present your concept, then you should heed their criticism and modify your slides. Criticism from a variety of people, particularly if they are from different cultures or vary in age, gives a wide range of viewpoints. Some reviewers might focus on the font size, others on color and design choices, while others might single out the overall message. These individuals should evaluate and comment on your work, such as saying that the overall presentation is good or that a particular paragraph is confusing, and then give specific information of what elements are effective or how you can edit the paragraph.

When you receive these comments, do not get defensive. Ask yourself why your reviewers would have made these comments. Perhaps they lack a background in the subject matter. Or they may have a particular interest in this topic and can add their expertise.

To Review, Accept, and Reject Presentation Changes

1 COLLABORATE | 2 FORMAT SLIDES & SET SLIDE SHOW RESOLUTION | 3 SAVE & PACKAGE A PRESENTATION
4 PROTECT & SECURE PRESENTATION | 5 USE PRESENTATION TOOLS

Changes that affect the entire presentation are indicated in the Presentation Changes section of the Revisions pane. These changes can include transitions, color schemes, fonts, and backgrounds. They also can include slide insertions. Bernie inserted three slides in his review; two have identical text and different photos of the city's popular tourist attraction, Navy Pier. After inserting these slides in the presentation, you can view each slide and then delete, or reject, a slide insertion. The following steps display and accept the reviewer's three slides and then delete one of the inserted slides. *Why? You want to see all the slides and then evaluate how they add value to the presentation. Two of the slides have similar photos of Navy Pier, and you want to use the slide that shows the most buildings and attractions on that structure.*

1

- Click the DETAILS tab in the Revisions pane.

- Click the first presentation change marker, Theme (1 - 3), in the Presentation Changes section of the Revisions pane to display the Theme box with an explanation of the proposed change for all slides in the presentation (Figure 5–9).

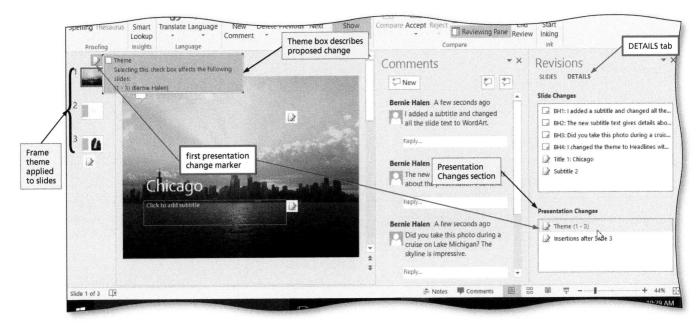

Figure 5–9

2

- Click the Theme check box to view the new Headlines theme on all slides (Figure 5–10).

Q&A

Can I also apply the change by tapping or clicking the Accept Change button (Review tab | Compare group)?
Yes. Either method applies the Headlines theme.

If I decide to not apply the new theme, can I reverse this change?
Yes. Click the Reject Change button (Review tab | Compare group) or click the check box to remove the check and reject the reviewer's theme modification.

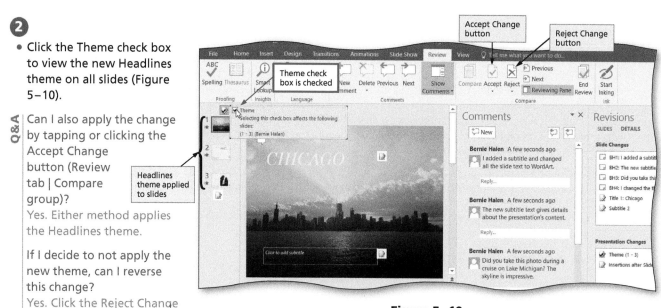

Figure 5–10

3

- Click the second presentation change marker, Insertions after Slide 3, in the Presentation Changes section to display an insertion box with a list of the three proposed new slides to insert into the presentation, two with no title text and one with the title text, 'Evening cruises offer spectacular views of the city' (Figure 5–11).

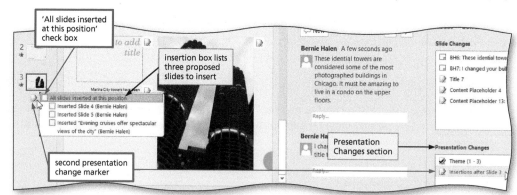

Figure 5–11

Q&A

What is the significance of the check boxes in the insertion box?
You can click the first check box to insert all three slides in your presentation. You can elect to insert one or two slides by clicking the check mark to the left of each slide title.

4

- Click the 'All slides inserted at this position' check box to insert the three new slides (Figure 5–12).

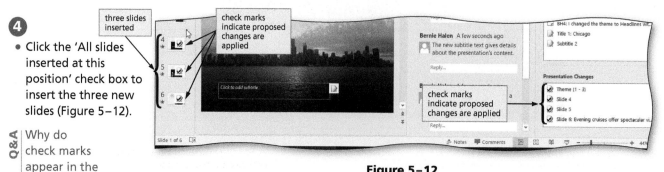

Figure 5–12

Q&A

Why do check marks appear in the Slides 4, 5, and 6 thumbnails in the Slides tab and in the Presentation Changes section?
The check marks indicate you have applied the proposed change.

5

- Display Slide 4 and review the slide contents. Then, display Slide 5 and compare the photo on this slide to the photo on Slide 4.

- Display Slide 4 again and then read the comment Bernie made about Slides 4 and 5 (Figure 5–13).

Figure 5–13

6

- Display Slide 5 and then click the change marker on the Slide 5 thumbnail to display the insertion box (Figure 5–14).

Figure 5–14

7

- Click the 'Inserted Slide 5' check box to clear this check box and delete Slide 5 from the presentation (Figure 5–15).

Q&A If I decide to insert the original Slide 5, how can I perform this task?
Click the change marker above the current Slide 5 to insert the slide you deleted.

Figure 5–15

Other Ways

1. Click Next Change or Previous Change button (Review tab | Compare group), click Accept Change button or Reject Change button

2. Right-click proposed change, click Accept Change or Reject Change on shortcut menu

To Review, Accept, and Reject Slide Changes

Changes that affect only the displayed slide are indicated in the Slide Changes section of the DETAILS tab on the Revisions pane. A reviewer can modify many aspects of the slide, such as adding and deleting pictures and clips, editing text, and moving placeholders. The following steps display and accept the reviewer's revisions to Slide 1. *Why? You agree with the changes Bernie suggested because they enhance your slides.*

1

- With Slide 1 displaying, click the slide change, 'Title 1: Chicago,' in the Slide Changes section of the Revisions pane to display the Title 1 box with Bernie Halen's five proposed changes for the Chicago text in the rectangle (Figure 5–16).

Figure 5–16

2

- Click the 'All changes to Title 1' check box to preview all proposed changes to the Chicago text (Figure 5–17).

Figure 5–17

3

- Click to uncheck the Text settings check box to preview only the other changes to the title text, not the alignment of the title SmartArt (Figure 5–18).

Q&A Can I select any combination of the check boxes to modify the text in the rectangle?
Yes. You can click the individual check boxes to preview the reviewer's modifications.

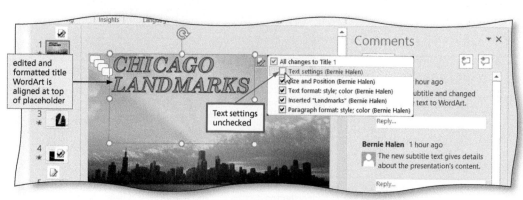

Figure 5–18

4

- Click the slide change, Subtitle 2, in the Slide Changes section to display the insertion box showing the changes to the Slide 2 subtitle.

- Click the 'All changes to Subtitle 2' check box to view the proposed changes (Figure 5–19).

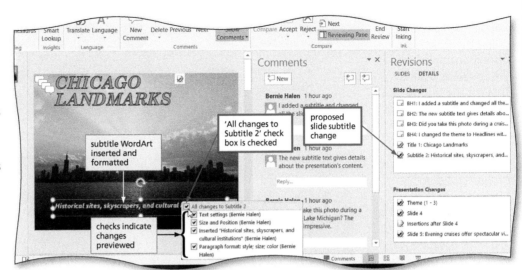

Figure 5–19

Other Ways

1. Click Next Change or Previous Change button (Review tab | Compare group), click Accept Change button or Reject Change button
2. Right-click proposed change, click Accept Change or Reject Change on shortcut menu

To Review Comments

1 COLLABORATE | 2 FORMAT SLIDES & SET SLIDE SHOW RESOLUTION | 3 SAVE & PACKAGE A PRESENTATION
4 PROTECT & SECURE PRESENTATION | 5 USE PRESENTATION TOOLS

Why? *You want to look at each comment before deciding to accept or reject the changes.* The Comments pane displays the reviewer's name above each comment, and an associated comment marker is displayed on the slide and in the Slide Changes section of the Revisions pane. The following steps review comments for Slide 1.

1

- Click the BH1 comment in the Slide Changes section to select the comment and the associated comment marker on the slide (Figure 5–20).

Q&A Why does the number 1 display after the commenter's initials in the Slide Changes section of the Revisions pane?
The number indicates it is the first comment the reviewer inserted.

Figure 5–20

- Read the comment and then click the Next button in the Comments pane to select the second comment and the associated comment marker on the slide (Figure 5–21).

Q&A Can I click the buttons on the Review tab instead of the buttons in the Comments pane?
Yes. Either method allows you to review comments.

Figure 5–21

- Click the Next button to review the third comment and click it again to review the fourth comment.

Other Ways

1. Click Next button or Previous button (Review tab | Comments group)

To Reply to a Comment

1 COLLABORATE | 2 FORMAT SLIDES & SET SLIDE SHOW RESOLUTION | 3 SAVE & PACKAGE A PRESENTATION
4 PROTECT & SECURE PRESENTATION | 5 USE PRESENTATION TOOLS

Bernie asked a question in his third comment. One method of responding is by replying to the comment he made. You want to provide feedback to him by responding to his query. *Why? Giving feedback helps the reviewer realize his efforts in improving the presentation were useful and encourages him to continue to participate in collaboration efforts.* The following steps reply to a comment on Slide 1.

- With Slide 1 displaying, select the third comment.

- Click the Reply box to place the insertion point in the Reply box (Figure 5–22).

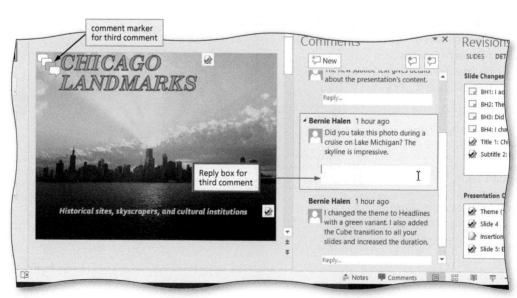

Figure 5–22

2

• Type **When I was in Chicago this past summer, I took a sightseeing cruise that began on the Chicago River and then went out on Lake Michigan.** in the Reply box and then press the ENTER key (Figure 5–23).

Why does my name differ from that shown in the figure, which is Marianne?
The name reflects the information that was entered when Microsoft Office 2016 was installed on your computer.

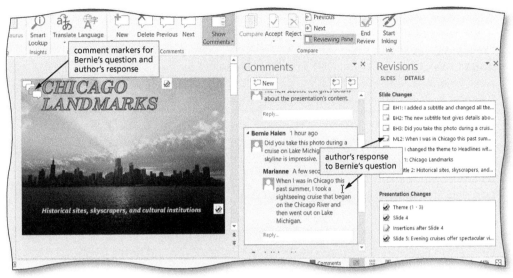

Figure 5–23

To Insert a Comment

1 COLLABORATE | 2 FORMAT SLIDES & SET SLIDE SHOW RESOLUTION | 3 SAVE & PACKAGE A PRESENTATION

4 PROTECT & SECURE PRESENTATION | 5 USE PRESENTATION TOOLS

Bernie Halen's comments and changes greatly enhanced your slide show, and you would like to thank him for taking the time to review your original slides and to respond to his questions. *Why? He will be able to see what modifications you accepted.* The following steps insert a comment on Slide 1.

1

• With Slide 1 displaying, click the Insert Comment button, which has the label New (Comments pane), to open a comment box in the Comments pane (Figure 5–24).

Why is my comment box displayed at the top of the Comments pane? Depending upon your computer, PowerPoint will display the new box either at the beginning or the end of the list of comments in the Comments pane.

Figure 5–24

2

- Click the comment box, type **Your comments and modifications are great, Bernie. I really appreciate the work you did to improve my slides.** in the box, and then press the ENTER key (Figure 5–25).

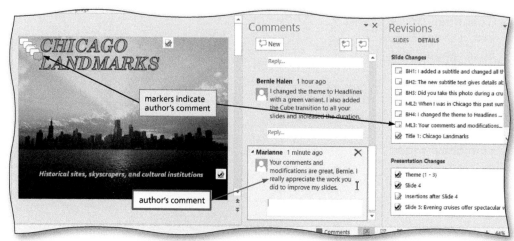

Figure 5–25

Q&A | Can I move the comment on the slide?

Yes. Select the comment icon on the slide and then drag it to another location on the slide.

Other Ways

1. Click New Comment button (Review tab | Comments group)

To Delete a Comment

1 COLLABORATE | **2 FORMAT SLIDES & SET SLIDE SHOW RESOLUTION** | 3 SAVE & PACKAGE A PRESENTATION
4 PROTECT & SECURE PRESENTATION | 5 USE PRESENTATION TOOLS

Once you have reviewed comments, you may no longer want them to be a part of your slides. You can delete comments that you have read and considered as you are preparing your slides. The following steps delete three of Bernie's comments. *Why? They are not necessary now because you have incorporated the changes into your initial presentation.*

1

- With Slide 1 displaying, scroll up and then click Bernie Halen's first comment in the Comments pane to select it (Figure 5–26).

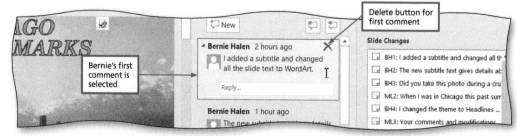

Figure 5–26

Q&A | The Delete button is not displayed in this first comment. What should I do?

Position the pointer up slightly beside Bernie's comment so that it appears as an I-beam.

2

- Click the Delete button (Comments pane) to delete Bernie's first comment and to select the new first comment, which previously was the second comment in the list (Figure 5–27).

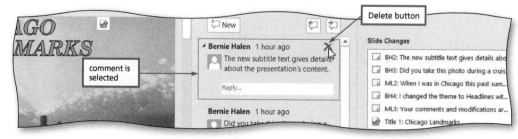

Figure 5–27

3

- Delete the selected comment about the new subtitle.

- Skip the next comment.

- Select the last Bernie Halen comment regarding the theme, variant, and transition and then delete this comment (Figure 5–28).

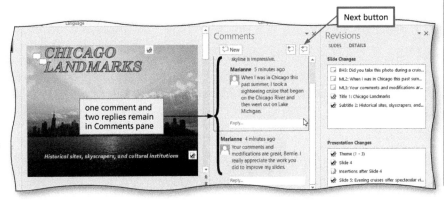

Figure 5–28

Other Ways

1. Click Delete Comment button (Review tab | Comments group)   2. Right-click comment, click Delete Comment on shortcut menu

---

To Review and Accept Slide Changes on the Remaining Slides

You have accepted most of Bernie Halen's presentation and Slide 1 changes. He also inserted comments in and made changes to other slides. The following steps review his comments and accept his modifications.

1 Click the Next button (Comments pane) several times until Slide 2 displays.

2 Read the comment labeled BH5 and then delete this comment.

3 Click the SLIDES tab in the Revisions pane to show a thumbnail of Slide 2 in the Revisions pane.

4 Click the check box above the Slide 2 thumbnail (Revisions pane) to display a preview of the Slide 2 revisions.

5 Click the Next button (Comments pane) to display Slide 3. Read and then delete the two comments on this slide.

6 Click the check box above the Slide 3 thumbnail (Revisions pane) to display a preview of the Slide 3 revisions.

7 Click the Next button (Comments pane) to display Slide 4. Read the comment and then type **I chose Slide 4 because it displayed more buildings and attractions.** as a reply.

8 Click the Next button to display Slide 5 (Figure 5–29).

BTW

Reviewers' Technology Limitations
People who receive copies of your presentation to review may not be able to open a PowerPoint 2016 file saved in the default .pptx format because they have a previous version of this software or may not have Internet access available readily. For these reasons, you need to know their software and hardware limitations and distribute your file or handouts accordingly.

Figure 5–29

To Run the Revised Presentation in Reading View

Bernie's changes modified the original presentation substantially, so it is a good idea to review the new presentation. The following steps review the slides in Reading view. *Why? This view helps you see large images of the slides so you can evaluate their content without needing to start Slide Show view.*

- Display Slide 1 and then click the Reading View button on the status bar to display Slide 1 in this view (Figure 5–30).

- Click the Next and Previous buttons to review the changes on each slide.

- Click the black 'End of slide show' screen to end the slide show and return to Normal view.

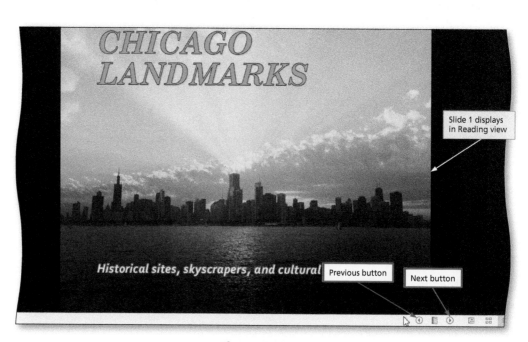

Figure 5–30

Other Ways

1. Click Reading View button (View tab | Presentation Views group)

How should I give constructive criticism when I am reviewing a presentation?

If you are asked to critique a presentation, begin and end with positive comments. Give specific details about a few key areas that can be improved. Be honest, but be tactful. Avoid using the word, you. For example, instead of writing, "You need to give some statistics to support your viewpoint," write "I had difficulty understanding which departments' sales have increased in the past six months. Perhaps a chart with specific figures would help depict how dramatically revenues have improved."

To End the Review and Hide Markup

You have analyzed all of the reviewer's proposed changes and replied to some of his questions. Your review of the merged presentation is complete, so you can accept and apply all the changes and then close the Comments and Revisions panes. You also can hide the comments that are present on Slide 1. *Why? You do not need to see the comments when you are developing the remainder of the presentation, so you can hide them.* The following steps end the review of the merged slides (which closes the Revisions pane), close the Comments pane, and hide the comment markers.

1

- Click the End Review button (Review tab | Compare group) to display the Microsoft PowerPoint dialog box (Figure 5–31).

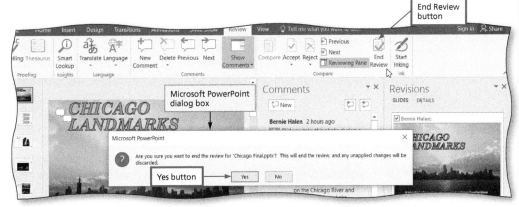

Figure 5–31

2

- Click the Yes button (Microsoft PowerPoint dialog box) to apply the changes you accepted and discard the changes you rejected.

Q&A Which changes are discarded?
You did not apply the aligned WordArt on Slide 1 and did not insert Bernie's proposed Slide 5.

- Click the Show Comments arrow (Review tab | Comments group) to display the Show Comments menu (Figure 5–32).

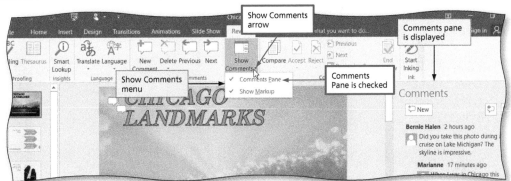

Figure 5–32

3

- Click Comments Pane in the menu to remove the check mark and close the Comments pane.

Q&A Can I also close the Comments pane by tapping or clicking the Close button in that pane?
Yes.

- Click the Show Comments arrow to display the Show Comments menu again (Figure 5–33).

Figure 5–33

4

- Click Show Markup in the menu to hide comments on the slide.

SharePoint

In a business environment, PowerPoint presentations can be stored on a centrally located Slide Library that resides on a server running Office SharePoint. These slide shows can be shared, reused, and accessed by many individuals who then can copy materials into their individual presentations. The Slide Library functions in much the same manner as your community library, for SharePoint time stamps when

BTW
Using a Slide Library
PowerPoint presentations
may be stored on a centrally
located slide library that
resides on a server. These
slide shows may be shared,
reused, and accessed by
many individuals who then
can copy materials into their
own presentations. The
slide library time stamps
when an individual has
borrowed a particular slide
or presentation and then
time stamps the slide or
presentation when it is
returned.

an individual has borrowed a particular slide or presentation and then time stamps the slide or presentation when it is returned. If a particular slide in the Library has been updated, anyone who has borrowed that slide is notified that the content has changed. In this manner, people creating PowerPoint presentations can track the changes to presentations, locate the latest versions of slides, and check for slide updates.

Reusing Slides from an Existing Presentation

Occasionally you may want to insert a slide from another presentation into your presentation. PowerPoint offers two methods of obtaining these slides. One way is to open the second presentation and then copy and paste the desired slides. The second method is to use the Reuse Slides pane to view and then select the desired slides.

The PowerPoint presentation with the file name, Chicago History, has colorful pictures and useful text. It contains three slides, and you would like to insert two of these slides, shown in Figure 5–34, into your Chicago Final presentation. You would also like to use a part of one of the Chicago History slides in Slide 2 of your presentation.

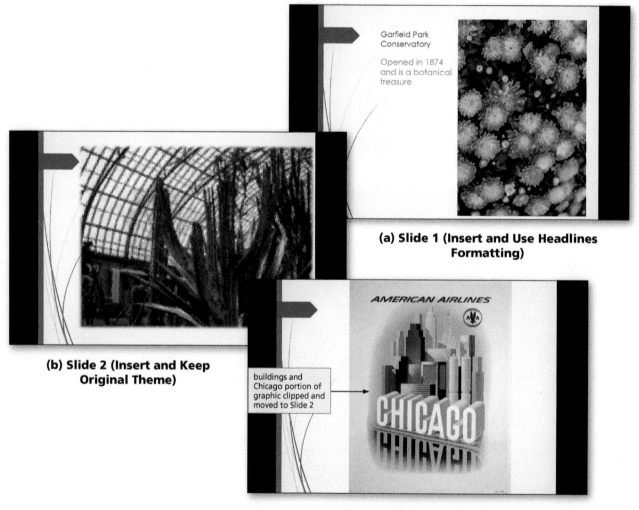

(a) Slide 1 (Insert and Use Headlines Formatting)

(b) Slide 2 (Insert and Keep Original Theme)

(c) Slide 3 (Snip Part of Graphic)

Figure 5–34

To Reuse Slides from an Existing Presentation

You want to insert two slides from the Chicago History presentation in the Chicago Final presentation directly after Slide 3. PowerPoint converts inserted slides to the theme and styles of the current presentation, so the inserted slides will inherit the styles of the current Headlines theme and Chicago Final presentation. However, you want the second slide to keep the source formatting of the Chicago History presentation, which uses the Wisp theme. *Why? The Wisp theme has a plant in the background and uses earthy colors.* You also will need to add the Cube transition to the second slide because you are not applying the Chicago Final formatting. The Chicago History presentation is in your Data Files. The following steps add these two slides to your presentation, and specify that the second slide keep its original (source) formatting.

1

- Display Slide 3 and then display the Home tab.

- Click the New Slide arrow (Slides group) to display the Headlines layout gallery (Figure 5–35).

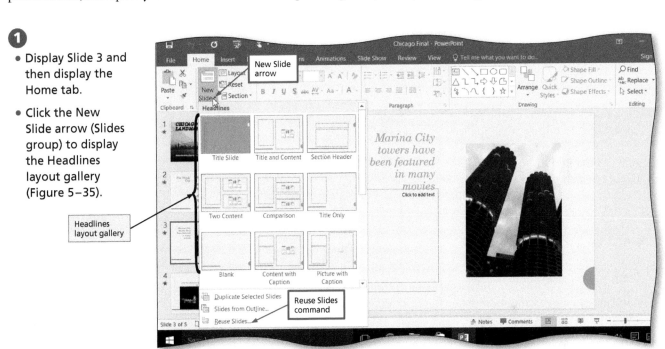

Figure 5–35

2

- Click Reuse Slides in the Headlines layout gallery to display the Reuse Slides pane.

- Click the Browse button (Reuse Slides pane) (Figure 5–36).

Q&A What are the two Browse options shown?
If the desired slides are in a Slide Library on Office SharePoint, then you would click Browse Slide Library. The slides you need, however, are in your Data Files, so you need to click Browse File.

Figure 5–36

3

- Click Browse File to display the Browse dialog box.

- If necessary, navigate to the location of your Data Files and then click Chicago History to select the file (Figure 5–37).

Figure 5–37

4

- Click the Open button (Browse dialog box) to display thumbnails of the three Chicago History slides in the Reuse Slides pane (Figure 5–38).

5

- Click the 'Garfield Park Conservatory' thumbnail to insert this slide into the Chicago Final presentation after Slide 3.

Q&A Can I insert all the slides in the presentation in one step instead of selecting each one individually? Yes. Right-click any thumbnail and then click 'Insert All Slides'.

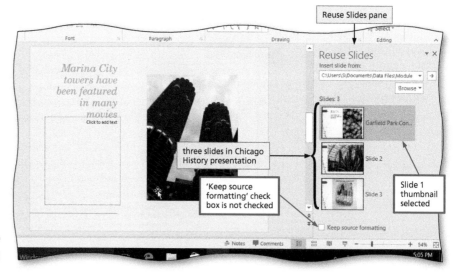

Figure 5–38

6

- Click the 'Keep source formatting' check box at the bottom of the Reuse Slides pane to preserve the Chicago History presentation formatting with the Wisp theme for the next slide that you will insert (Figure 5–39).

Q&A What would happen if I did not check this box?
PowerPoint would change the formatting to the characteristics found in the Headlines theme.

Figure 5–39

7

- Click the Slide 2 thumbnail (Reuse Slides pane) to insert this slide into the presentation as the new Slide 5 in the Chicago Final presentation with the Wisp theme retained (Figure 5–40).

- Click the Close button in the Reuse Slides pane so that it no longer is displayed.

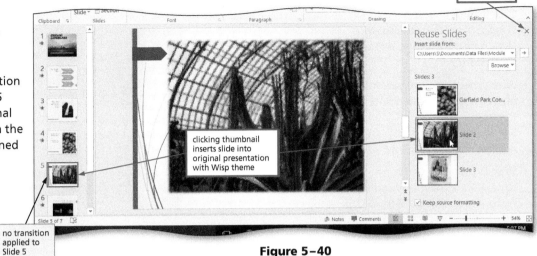

Figure 5–40

- Apply the Cube transition (in the Exciting category) to Slide 5 and change the duration to 2.50.

To Capture Part of a Screen Using Screen Clipping

1 COLLABORATE | 2 FORMAT SLIDES & SET SLIDE SHOW RESOLUTION | 3 SAVE & PACKAGE A PRESENTATION
4 PROTECT & SECURE PRESENTATION | 5 USE PRESENTATION TOOLS

At times you may be developing a presentation and need a portion of a clip or picture in another presentation. You can capture, or **snip**, part of an object on a slide in another presentation that is open. PowerPoint refers to this presentation as being available. The following steps snip part of an image on Slide 3 of the Chicago History presentation and paste it on Slide 2 in the Chicago Final presentation. *Why? This portion of the vintage American Airlines poster has buildings and the word, Chicago, and you desire to place this snip on Slide 2 to reinforce Chicago's rich history.*

- Open the Chicago History file from your Data Files and then display Slide 3 of this presentation.

- Display Slide 2 of the Chicago Final presentation.

- Display the Insert tab and then click the Screenshot button (Insert tab | Images group) to display the Available Windows gallery (Figure 5–41).

Figure 5–41

- Click Screen Clipping (Available Windows gallery) to display Slide 3 of the Chicago History presentation.

- When the white overlay displays on Slide 3, move the pointer to the upper-left edge of the poster below the words, American Airlines.

- Drag downward and to the right to select the buildings and the word, Chicago (Figure 5–42).

Figure 5–42

- Release the mouse button.

- When the snip displays on Slide 2 of the Chicago Final presentation, drag the snip below the title text, The Windy City, using the vertical and horizontal guides to help with positioning (Figure 5–43).

Q&A My clip is a different size than the one shown in Figure 5–43. What should I do?
You can resize the clip in the same manner that you resize pictures.

- Close the Chicago History presentation.

Q&A Why should I close this file?
You no longer need the Chicago History presentation because you have inserted the slides and the screen clip.

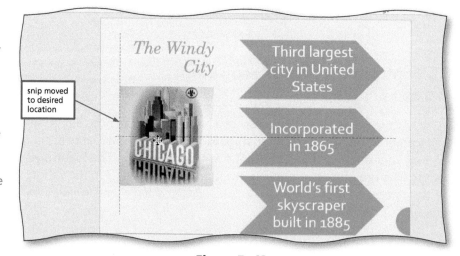

Figure 5–43

Adding a Footer

Slides can contain information at the top or bottom. The area at the top of a slide is called a **header**, and the area at the bottom is called a **footer**. In general, footer content displays along the lower edge of a slide, but the theme determines where these elements are placed. As a default, no information is displayed in the header or footer. You can choose to apply only a header, only a footer, or both a header and footer. In addition, you can elect to have the header or footer display on single slides, all slides, or all slides except the title slide.

Slide numbers are one footer element. They help a presenter organize a talk. While few audience members are cognizant of this aspect of a slide, the presenter can glance at the number and know which slide contains particular information. If an audience member asks a question pertaining to information contained on a slide that had been displayed previously or is on a slide that has not been viewed yet, the presenter can jump to that slide in an effort to answer the question. In addition, the slide number helps pace the slide show. For example, a speaker could have the presentation timed so that Slide 4 is displaying three minutes into the talk.

PowerPoint gives the option of displaying the current date and time obtained from the system or a fixed date and time that you specify. In addition, you can add relevant information, such as your name, your school or business name, or the purpose of your presentation in the Footer area.

To Add a Footer with Fixed Information

1 COLLABORATE | 2 FORMAT SLIDES & SET SLIDE SHOW RESOLUTION | 3 SAVE & PACKAGE A PRESENTATION

4 PROTECT & SECURE PRESENTATION | 5 USE PRESENTATION TOOLS

To reinforce the fact that you visited Chicago, also called Chi-town, in July, you can add this information in the Footer area. You also can add a slide number. The following steps add this text to all slides in the presentation except the title slide. *Why? In general, the footer text should not display on the title slide. In addition, the title slide has a large photo in the background, so you do not want the footer text to overlap this content.*

- Display the Insert tab.

- Click the 'Header & Footer' button (Insert tab | Text group) to display the Header and Footer dialog box.

- If necessary, click the Slide tab to display the Slide sheet (Figure 5–44).

Q&A

Can I use this dialog box to add a header?

The slide theme determines the location of the placeholders at the top or bottom of the slide. The footer elements generally are displayed along the lower edge of the slide. Some themes, however, have the footer elements along the top edge, so they are considered header text.

Figure 5–44

- Click 'Date and time' to select this check box.

- Click Fixed to select this option. Select the existing date and then type **July 31** in the Fixed box.

- Click Slide number to select this check box.

- Click Footer to select this check box.

- Type **Chi-town Summer** in the Footer box.

- If requested by your instructor, type the name of your grade school instead of the word, Summer.

- Click the 'Don't show on title slide' check box to select the box (Figure 5–45).

Q&A What are the black boxes in the Preview section?

The black box in the lower-left placeholder indicates where the footer text and fixed date will appear on the slide; the small black box in the bottom-right placeholder indicates where the page number will appear.

What if I want the current date and time to appear?
Click Update automatically in the 'Date and time' section.

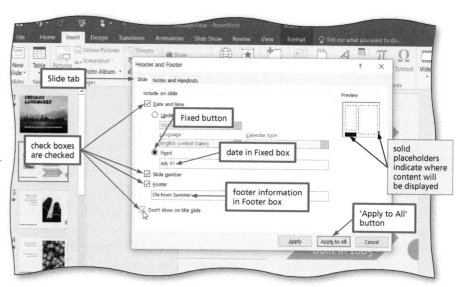

Figure 5–45

3

- Click the 'Apply to All' button to display the date, footer text, and slide number on all slides except Slide 1.

Q&A When would I click the Apply button instead of the 'Apply to All' button?

Click the Apply button when you want the header and footer information to appear only on the slide currently selected.

To Clear Formatting

1 COLLABORATE | 2 FORMAT SLIDES & SET SLIDE SHOW RESOLUTION | 3 SAVE & PACKAGE A PRESENTATION
4 PROTECT & SECURE PRESENTATION | 5 USE PRESENTATION TOOLS

PowerPoint provides myriad options to enhance pictures. You can, for example, format the images by recoloring, changing the color saturation and tone, adding artistic effects, and altering the picture style. After adding various effects, you may desire to reset the picture to its original state. *Why? The Garfield Park Conservatory photo on Slide 5 has several formatting adjustments that obscure the image, and now you want to see the original unformatted picture.* The following steps remove all formatting applied to the Garfield Park Conservatory photo on Slide 5.

1

- Display Slide 5, select the Garfield Park Conservatory picture, and then display the Picture Tools Format tab (Figure 5–46).

Figure 5–46

2

- Click the Reset Picture button (Format tab | Adjust group) to remove all formatting from the picture (Figure 5–47).

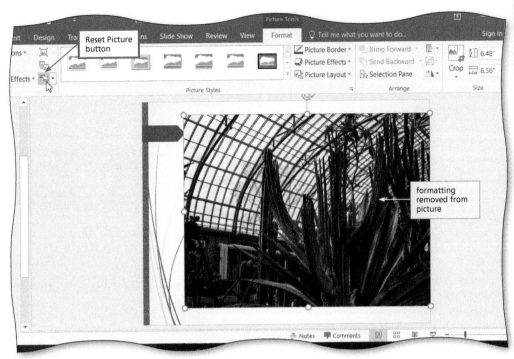

Figure 5–47

Other Ways

1. Right-click picture, click Format Picture, click Picture icon (Format Picture pane), click Picture Corrections, click Reset

Break Point: If you wish to take a break, this is a good place to do so. Be sure to save the Chicago Final file again and then you can exit PowerPoint. To resume at a later time, run PowerPoint, open the file called Chicago Final, and continue following the steps from this location forward.

Changing Slide Size and Slide Show Resolution

Today's technology presents several options you should consider when developing your presentation. The on-screen show ratio determines the height and width proportions. The screen resolution affects the slides' clarity.

To Set Slide Size

1 COLLABORATE | 2 FORMAT SLIDES & SET SLIDE SHOW RESOLUTION | 3 SAVE & PACKAGE A PRESENTATION
4 PROTECT & SECURE PRESENTATION | 5 USE PRESENTATION TOOLS

Prior to PowerPoint 2013, PowerPoint set slides in a 4:3 size ratio, which is the proportion found on a standard monitor that is not widescreen. If you know your presentation will be viewed on a wide screen or you are using a widescreen display, you can change the slide size to optimize the proportions. The following steps change the default setting to 16:9 and then adjust the bulleted paragraphs on Slides 4 and 6. *Why? This 16:9 dimension is the proportion of most widescreen displays. When the slide width is changed, some of the words in the paragraphs are not spaced evenly. A good design principle is to keep all words in a prepositional phrase together on one line.*

- With Slide 5 displaying, display the Design tab and then click the Slide Size button (Design tab | Customize group) to display the Slide Size gallery (Figure 5–48).

- Click Widescreen (16:9) to change the slide size setting.

Figure 5–48

- Display Slide 1 and then drag the right edge of the WordArt placeholder to the right so that the word, Landmarks, is displayed on one line.

- Adjust the size of the Slide 3 photo so that it is approximately 5.21" x 6.97" and then use the vertical and horizontal guides to help with position it to the location shown in Figure 5–49.

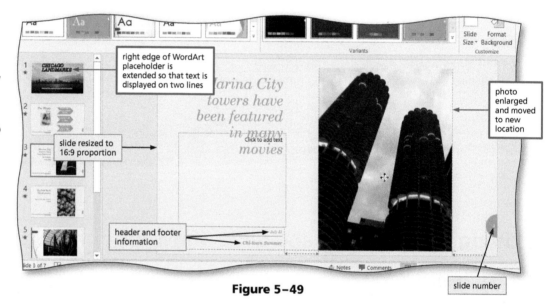

Figure 5–49

To Set Presentation Resolution

1 COLLABORATE | 2 FORMAT SLIDES & SET SLIDE SHOW RESOLUTION | 3 SAVE & PACKAGE A PRESENTATION
4 PROTECT & SECURE PRESENTATION | 5 USE PRESENTATION TOOLS

Screen, or presentation, resolution affects the number of pixels that are displayed on your screen. When screen resolution is increased, more information is displayed, but it is decreased in size. Conversely, when screen resolution is decreased, less information is displayed, but that information is increased in size. Throughout this book, the screen resolution has been set to 1366 x 768. The following steps change the presentation resolution to 800 x 600. **Why?** *You may need to run your presentation on a monitor that has a different resolution.*

- Display the Slide Show tab and then click the 'Set Up Slide Show' button (Slide Show tab | Set Up group) to display the Set Up Show dialog box.

PowerPoint Module 5

• If necessary, click the Slide show monitor arrow in the Multiple monitors section and then choose Primary Monitor.

• Click the Resolution arrow in the Multiple monitors section to display the Resolution list (Figure 5–50).

Figure 5–50

• Click 800 x 600 to change the slide show resolution setting.

• If necessary, click the 'Use Presenter View' check box to clear the check box (Figure 5–51).

Q&A What is Presenter view?
When you use Presenter view, you control the slide show using one screen only you can see, but your audience views the slides on another main screen.

Figure 5–51

• Click the OK button to close the Set Up Show dialog box and apply the new resolution to the slides.

Saving and Packaging a Presentation

PowerPoint 2016, PowerPoint 2013, PowerPoint 2010, and PowerPoint 2007 save files, by default, as a PowerPoint Presentation with a .pptx file extension. You can, however, select other file types that allow other computer users to view your slides if they do not have one of the newer PowerPoint versions installed. You also can save the file as a PowerPoint show so that it runs automatically when opened and does not require the user to have the PowerPoint program. Another option is to save one slide as an image that can be inserted into another program, such as Microsoft Word, or emailed.

If your computer has compact disc (CD) or digital video disc (DVD) burning hardware, the Package for CD option will copy a PowerPoint presentation and linked files onto a CD or DVD. Two types of CDs or DVDs can be used: recordable (CD-R or DVD-R) and rewritable (CD-RW or DVD-RW). You must copy all the desired files in a single operation if you use PowerPoint for this task because you cannot add any more files after the first set is copied. If, however, you want to add more files to the CD or DVD, you can use Windows Explorer to copy additional files. If you are using a CD-RW or DVD-RW with existing content, these files will be overwritten.

The **PowerPoint Viewer** is included when you package your presentation so you can show the presentation on another computer that has Microsoft Windows but does not have PowerPoint installed. The PowerPoint Viewer also allows users to view presentations created with PowerPoint 2003, 2000, and 97.

To Save a File as a PowerPoint Show

1 COLLABORATE | 2 FORMAT SLIDES & SET SLIDE SHOW RESOLUTION | 3 SAVE & PACKAGE A PRESENTATION
4 PROTECT & SECURE PRESENTATION | 5 USE PRESENTATION TOOLS

Why? *To simplify giving a presentation in front of an audience, you may want to start your slide show without having to run PowerPoint, open a file, and then click the Slide Show button.* When you save a presentation as a **PowerPoint show (.ppsx)**, it automatically begins running when opened. The following steps save the Chicago Final file as a PowerPoint show.

- Open the Backstage view, display the Export tab, and then click 'Change File Type' to display the Change File Type section.

- Click PowerPoint Show in the Presentation File Types section (Figure 5–52).

Figure 5–52

- Click the Save As button to display the Save As dialog box.

- Type **Chicago Final Show** in the File name box (Figure 5–53).

- Click the Save button to close the Save As dialog box.

- Close the current Chicago Final Show presentation.

Figure 5–53

Why do I want to close the current Chicago Final Show file?
It is best to use the more current version of the presentation to complete the remaining tasks in this module.

Other Ways

1. Click File on ribbon, click Save As in Backstage view, click Browse button to locate save location, click 'Save as type' arrow, select PowerPoint Show, click Save button

To Save a Slide as an Image

1 COLLABORATE | 2 FORMAT SLIDES & SET SLIDE SHOW RESOLUTION | 3 SAVE & PACKAGE A PRESENTATION
4 PROTECT & SECURE PRESENTATION | 5 USE PRESENTATION TOOLS

To create visually interesting slides, you insert pictures, clips, and video files into your presentation. Conversely, you may want to insert a PowerPoint slide into another document, such as a file you created in Microsoft Word. *Why? A slide may have information that you want to share with an audience and include with other material that is not part of the PowerPoint presentation.* You can save one slide as an image and then insert this file into another document. The following steps save Slide 2 as a JPEG File Interchange Format image.

- Open the Chicago Final presentation and then display Slide 2.

- Open the Backstage view, display the Export tab, and then click 'Change File Type' to display the Change File Type section.

- Click 'JPEG File Interchange Format' in the Image File Types section (Figure 5–54).

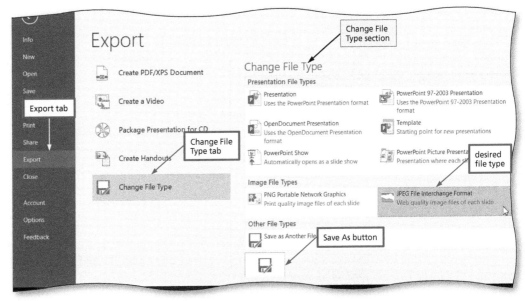

Figure 5–54

2
- Click the Save As button to display the Save As dialog box.
- Type **Chicago SmartArt** in the File name box (Figure 5–55).

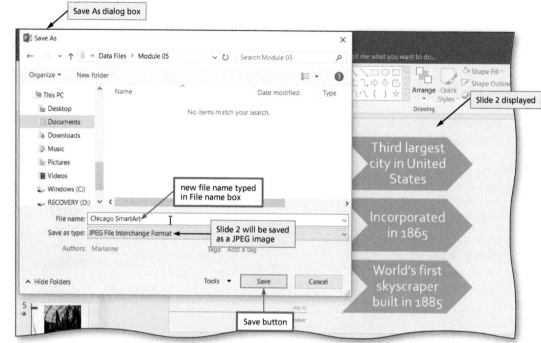

Figure 5–55

3
- Click the Save button (Save As dialog box) to display the Microsoft PowerPoint dialog box (Figure 5–56).

4
- Click the 'Just This One' button to save only Slide 2 as a file in JPEG (.jpg) format.

 What would happen if I clicked All Slides? PowerPoint would save each slide as a separate file in a folder with the file name you specified.

Figure 5–56

Other Ways

1. Click File on ribbon, click Save As in Backstage view, click Browse button to locate save location, click 'Save as type' arrow, select JPEG File Interchange Format, click Save button

To Package a Presentation for Storage on a Compact Disc

1 COLLABORATE | 2 FORMAT SLIDES & SET SLIDE SHOW RESOLUTION | 3 SAVE & PACKAGE A PRESENTATION
4 PROTECT & SECURE PRESENTATION | 5 USE PRESENTATION TOOLS

The Package for CD option will copy a PowerPoint presentation and linked files onto a CD or DVD. The following steps show how to save a presentation and related files to a CD or DVD using the Package for CD feature. *Why? The Package for CD dialog box allows you to select the presentation files to copy, linking and embedding options, and passwords to open and modify the files.*

1

- Insert a CD-RW or DVD-RW or a blank CD-R or DVD-R into your CD or DVD drive.

- Open the Backstage view, display the Export tab, and then click 'Package Presentation for CD' (Figure 5–57).

Figure 5–57

2

- Click the 'Package for CD' button in the Package Presentation for CD section to display the Package for CD dialog box.

- Delete the text in the 'Name the CD' box and then type **Chicago** in the box (Figure 5–58).

Q&A What if I want to add more files to the CD?
Click the Add button and then locate the files you want to add to the CD.

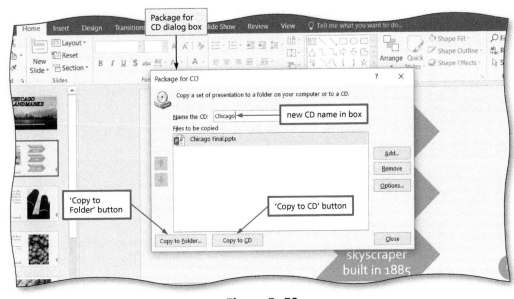

Figure 5–58

3

- Click the 'Copy to CD' button to begin packaging the presentation files and to display the Microsoft PowerPoint dialog box (Figure 5–59).

Q&A When would I copy the files to a folder instead of a CD?
If you want to copy your presentation to a network or to a storage medium other than a CD or DVD, such as a USB flash drive, click the 'Copy to Folder' button, enter a folder name and location, and then click the OK button.

Figure 5–59

- Click the No button (Microsoft PowerPoint dialog box) to not include linked files and to display another Microsoft PowerPoint dialog box (Figure 5–60).

- Click the Continue button (Microsoft PowerPoint dialog box) to continue copying the presentation to a CD without the comments added to the slides.

Figure 5–60

- When the files have been written, click the No button (Microsoft PowerPoint dialog box) to not copy the files to another CD.

- Click the Close button (Package for CD dialog box) to finish saving the presentation to a CD.

To View a PowerPoint Show Using the PowerPoint Viewer

When you arrive at a remote location, you will run the packaged presentation. The following steps explain how to run the presentation using the PowerPoint Viewer.

1 Insert your CD in the CD drive.

2 Accept the licensing agreement for the PowerPoint Viewer to open and run the slide show.

To Save a Presentation in a Previous PowerPoint Format

1 COLLABORATE | 2 FORMAT SLIDES & SET SLIDE SHOW RESOLUTION | **3 SAVE & PACKAGE A PRESENTATION**
4 PROTECT & SECURE PRESENTATION | 5 USE PRESENTATION TOOLS

Prior to Microsoft Office 2007, PowerPoint saved presentations, by default, as a .ppt file type. The earlier versions of PowerPoint cannot open the .pptx type that PowerPoint 2016, 2013, 2010, and 2007 creates by default. The Microsoft website has updates and converters for users of these earlier versions of the program and also for other Microsoft Office software. The Microsoft Office Compatibility Pack for Word, Excel, and PowerPoint will open, edit, and save Office 2016, 2013, 2010, and 2007 documents. The following steps save the Chicago Final file as PowerPoint 97-2003 Presentation. *Why? You cannot assume that people who obtain a .pptx file from you have installed the Compatibility Pack, so to diminish frustration and confusion you can save a presentation as a .ppt type that will open with earlier versions of PowerPoint.*

- Open the Backstage view, display the Export tab, and then click 'Change File Type'.

- Click 'PowerPoint 97-2003 Presentation' in the Presentation File Types section (Figure 5–61).

Figure 5–61

- Click the Save As button to display the Save As dialog box.

- Type **Chicago Final Previous Version** in the File name box (Figure 5–62).

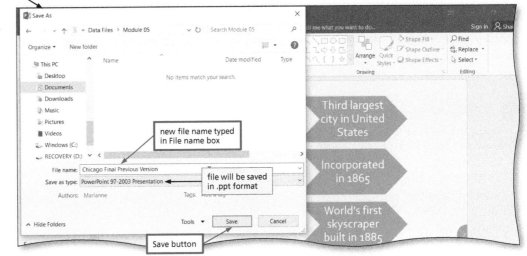

- Click the Save button (Save As dialog box) to save the Chicago Final presentation as a .ppt type and display the Microsoft PowerPoint Compatibility Checker.

Figure 5–62

Q&A Why does this Compatibility Checker dialog box display?
PowerPoint is alerting you that the older file version will not keep some of the features used in the presentation. You will learn more about the Compatibility Checker in the next section of this module.

- Click the Continue button (Microsoft PowerPoint Compatibility Checker) to continue to save the presentation.

- Close the current PowerPoint file and then open your Chicago Final presentation.

Q&A Why do I want to open this presentation instead of using the current file?
The current file is saved in a previous version of PowerPoint, so some features are not available when you run the final version of the slide show. It is best to use the more current version of the presentation to complete the remaining tasks in this module.

Other Ways
1. Click File on ribbon, click Save As in Backstage view, click Browse button to locate save location, click 'Save as type' arrow, select 'PowerPoint 97-2003 Presentation', click Save button

Protecting and Securing a Presentation

When your slides are complete, you can perform additional functions to finalize the file and prepare it for distributing to other users or running on a computer other than the one used to develop the file. For example, the **Compatibility Checker** reviews the file for any feature that will not work properly or display on computers running a previous PowerPoint version. In addition, the Document Inspector locates inappropriate information, such as comments, in a file and allows you to delete these slide elements. You also can set passwords so only authorized people can distribute, view, or modify your slides. When the review process is complete, you can indicate this file is the final version.

To Identify Presentation Features Not Supported by Previous Versions

1 COLLABORATE | 2 FORMAT SLIDES & SET SLIDE SHOW RESOLUTION | 3 SAVE & PACKAGE A PRESENTATION
4 PROTECT & SECURE PRESENTATION | **5 USE PRESENTATION TOOLS**

PowerPoint 2016 has many new features not found in some previous versions of PowerPoint, especially versions older than PowerPoint 2007. For example, WordArt formatted with Quick Styles is an enhancement found only in PowerPoint 2016, 2013, 2010, and 2007. If you give your file to people who have a previous PowerPoint version installed on their computers, they will be able to open the file but may not be able to see or edit some special features and effects. The following steps run the Compatibility Checker. *Why? You can use the Compatibility Checker to see which presentation elements will not function in earlier versions of PowerPoint and display a summary of the elements in your Chicago Final presentation that will be lost if your file is opened in some earlier PowerPoint versions.*

- Open the Backstage view and then click the 'Check for Issues' button in the Info tab to display the Check for Issues menu (Figure 5–63).

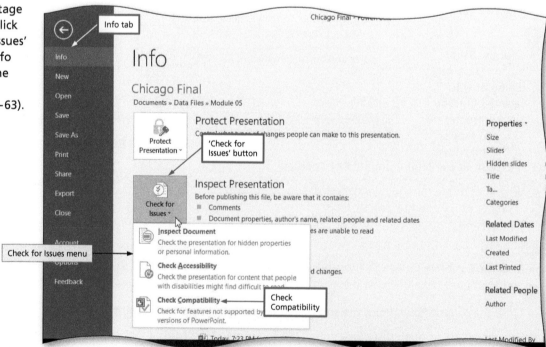

Figure 5–63

2

- Click Check Compatibility to display the Microsoft PowerPoint Compatibility Checker dialog box.

- View the comments in the Summary section regarding the five features that are not supported by earlier versions of PowerPoint (Figure 5–64).

Q&A Why do the numbers 2, 1, 11, 4, and 2 display in the Occurrences column in the right side of the Summary section?
The numbers indicate the number of times incompatible elements, such as the SmartArt graphic, appear in the presentation.

What happens if I click the Help links in the Summary section?
PowerPoint will provide additional information about the particular incompatible slide element.

Figure 5–64

3

- Click the OK button (Microsoft PowerPoint Compatibility Checker dialog box) to close the dialog box and return to the presentation.

To Remove Inappropriate Information

1 COLLABORATE | 2 FORMAT SLIDES & SET SLIDE SHOW RESOLUTION | 3 SAVE & PACKAGE A PRESENTATION
4 PROTECT & SECURE PRESENTATION | 5 USE PRESENTATION TOOLS

As you work on your presentation, you might add information meant only for you to see. For example, you might write comments to yourself or put confidential information in the Notes pane. You would not want other people to access this information if you give a copy of the presentation file to them. You also added a comment and replied to Bernie Halen's questions, and you may not want anyone other than him to view this information. The Document Inspector provides a quick and efficient method of searching for and deleting inappropriate information.

It is a good idea to make a duplicate copy of your file and then inspect this new second copy. *Why? If you tell the Document Inspector to delete content, such as personal information, comments, invisible slide content, or notes, and then decide you need to see those slide elements, quite possibly you will be unable to retrieve the information by using the Undo command.* The following steps save a duplicate copy of your Chicago Final presentation, run the Document Inspector on this new file, and then delete comments.

- Open the Backstage view, click the Save As tab, and then click the Browse button to open the Save As dialog box.

- Type **Chicago Final Duplicate** in the File name box.

- Click the Save button to change the file name and save another copy of this presentation.

Figure 5–65

- Click Inspect Document to display the Document Inspector dialog box (Figure 5–66).

Q&A What information does the Document Inspector check?
This information includes text in the Document Information Panel, such as your name and company. Other information includes details of when the file was last saved, objects formatted as invisible, graphics and text you dragged off a slide, presentation notes, and email headers.

- Open the Backstage view and then click the 'Check for Issues' button to display the Check for Issues menu (Figure 5–65).

Figure 5–66

- Click the Inspect button to check the document and display the inspection results (Figure 5–67).

Figure 5–67

- Click the Remove All button in the Comments and Annotations section of the inspection results to remove the comments from the presentation (Figure 5–68).

Q&A Should I also remove the document properties and personal information?
You might want to delete this information so that no identifying information, such as your name, is saved.

- Click the Close button (Document Inspector dialog box) to close the dialog box.

Figure 5–68

What types of passwords are best for security?
A password should be at least six characters and contain a combination of letters and numbers. Using both uppercase and lowercase letters is advised. Do not use a password that someone could guess, such as your first or last name, spouse's or child's name, telephone number, birth date, street address, license plate number, or Social Security number.

Once you develop this password, write it down in a secure place. Underneath your keyboard is not a secure place, nor is your middle desk drawer.

To Set a Password

1 COLLABORATE | 2 FORMAT SLIDES & SET SLIDE SHOW RESOLUTION | 3 SAVE & PACKAGE A PRESENTATION
4 PROTECT & SECURE PRESENTATION | 5 USE PRESENTATION TOOLS

Why? *You can protect your slide content by using a password.* You can prohibit a user from modifying a file without entering the password. The following steps set a password for the Chicago Final Duplicate file.

- With Backstage view open and the Info tab displaying, click the Protect Presentation button to display the Protect Presentation menu (Figure 5–69).

Figure 5–69

- Click 'Encrypt with Password' to display the Encrypt Document dialog box.
- Type **Chicago4Me** in the Password box (Figure 5–70).

Figure 5–70

- Click the OK button to display the Confirm Password dialog box.
- Type **Chicago4Me** in the Reenter password box (Figure 5–71).

Q&A What if I forget my password?
You will not be able to open your file. For security reasons, Microsoft or other companies cannot retrieve a lost password.

Figure 5–71

- Click the OK button in the Confirm Password dialog box.

Q&A When does the password take effect?
You will need to enter your password the next time you open your presentation.

To Open a Presentation with a Password

To open a file that has been protected with a password, you would perform the following steps.

1. Display the Open dialog box, locate the desired file, and then click the Open button to display the Password dialog box.
2. When the Password dialog box appears, type the password in the Password box and then click the OK button to display the presentation.

To Change the Password or Remove Password Protection

To change a password that you added to a file or to remove all password protection from the file, you would perform the following steps.

1. Display the Open dialog box, locate the desired file, and then click the Open button to display the Password dialog box.
2. When the Password dialog box appears, type the password in the Password box and then click the OK button to display the presentation.
3. Open the Backstage view, click Save As, and then browse to the desired Save location to display the Save As dialog box. Click the Tools button and then click General Options in the Tools list.
4. Select the contents of the 'Password to open' box or the 'Password to modify' box. To change the password, type the new password and then click the OK button. To remove a password, delete the password in the box. If prompted, retype your password to reconfirm it, and then click the OK button.
5. Click the Save button and then click the Yes button to resave the presentation.

To Mark a Presentation as Final

Why? *When your slides are completed, you may want to prevent others or yourself from accidentally changing the slide content or features.* If you use the **Mark as Final** command, the presentation becomes a read-only document. The following steps mark the presentation as a final (read-only) document.

1
- With Backstage view open and the Info tab displaying for the Chicago Final Duplicate file, click the Protect Presentation button to display the Protect Presentation menu again (Figure 5–72).

Figure 5–72

2
- Click 'Mark as Final' to display the Microsoft PowerPoint dialog box indicating that the presentation will be saved as a final document (Figure 5–73).

Figure 5–73

3
- Click the OK button (Microsoft PowerPoint dialog box) to save the file and to display another Microsoft PowerPoint dialog box with information about a final version of a document and indicating that the presentation is final (Figure 5–74).

Figure 5–74

  Can I turn off this read-only status so that I can edit the file?
Yes. Click Mark as Final in the Protect Presentation menu to toggle off the read-only status.

4
- Click the OK button (Microsoft PowerPoint dialog box). If an Information bar is displayed above the slide, click the Edit Anyway button to allow changes to be made to the presentation.

5
- Close the Chicago Final Duplicate file and then open the original Chicago Final presentation.

Using Presentation Tools

When you display a particular slide and view the information, you may want to return to one of the other slides in the presentation. Jumping to particular slides in a presentation is called **navigating**. A set of keyboard shortcuts can help you navigate to various slides during the slide show. When running a slide show, you can press the F1 key to see a list of these keyboard controls. These navigational features are listed in Table 5–1.

Table 5–1 Slide Show Shortcuts	
Keyboard Shortcut	**Purpose**
N ENTER SPACEBAR PAGE DOWN RIGHT ARROW DOWN ARROW	Perform the next animation or advance to the next slide
P BACKSPACE LEFT ARROW UP ARROW PAGE UP	Perform the previous animation or return to the previous slide
NUMBER FOLLOWED BY ENTER	Go to a specific slide number
B	Display a blank black slide
W	Display a blank white slide
S	Stop or restart an automatic presentation
ESC	End a presentation
E	Erase on-screen annotations
H	Go to the next slide if the next slide is hidden
T	Set new timings while rehearsing
R	Rerecord slide narration and timing
CTRL+P	Change the pointer to a pen
CTRL+A	Change the pointer to an arrow
CTRL+E	Change the pointer to an eraser
CTRL+M	Show or hide ink markup

Delivering and Navigating a Presentation Using the Control Bar

When you begin running a presentation in full screen mode and move the pointer, a control bar is displayed with buttons that allow you to navigate to the next slide or previous slide, mark up the current slide, display slide thumbnails, zoom, or change the current display. When you move the mouse, the control bar is displayed in the lower-left corner of the slide; it disappears after the mouse has not been moved for three seconds. Table 5–2 describes the buttons on the control bar.

Table 5–2 Slide Show Control Bar Buttons	
Description	**Function**
Previous	Previous slide or previous animated element on the slide
Next	Next slide or next animated element on the slide
Pen and laser pointer tools	Shortcut menu for laser pointer, pen, highlighter, and eraser
See all slides	View thumbnails of all slides in presentation
Zoom into the slide	Zoom in on specific slide area
Options	Shortcut menu for slide navigation and screen displays. Also displays Presenter View on a single monitor.

To Highlight Items on a Slide

You click the arrow buttons on the left side of the control bar to navigate backward or forward through the slide show. The 'Pen and laser pointer tools' button has a variety of functions, most often to emphasize aspects of slides or to make handwritten notes. The following steps highlight an item on a slide in Slide Show view. *Why?* *You want to call attention to the presentation's featured city.*

- If necessary, display Slide 1 and then run the slide show.

- If the control bar is not visible in the lower-left corner of the slide, move the pointer on the slide.

- Click the 'Pen and laser pointer tools' button on the control bar to display a menu (Figure 5–75).

Q&A Why is the slide displaying smaller than normal? You changed the resolution to 800 x 600, so the slide size is reduced.

Figure 5–75

- Click Highlighter and then drag over the word, Chicago, several times until all the letters are highlighted (Figure 5–76).

Figure 5–76

To Change Ink Color

Instead of Highlighter, you also can click Pen to draw or write notes on the slides. *Why?* *The Pen tool is much thinner than the Highlighter, so you can write words or draw fine lines on the slides.* When the presentation ends, PowerPoint will prompt you to keep or discard the ink annotations. The following steps change the pointer to a pen and then change the color of ink during the presentation.

- Click the Next button to display Slide 2. Click the 'Pen and laser pointer tools' button on the control bar and then click Pen on the menu.

- Click the 'Pen and laser pointer tools' button on the control bar and then point to the color Blue (Figure 5–77).

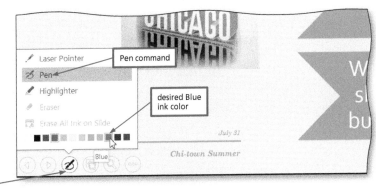

Figure 5–77

2
- Click the color Blue.
- Drag the pointer around the title text to draw a circle around the word, Windy (Figure 5–78).

Figure 5–78

3
- Right-click the slide to display the shortcut menu and then point to End Show (Figure 5–79).

Figure 5–79

4
- Click End Show to display the Microsoft PowerPoint dialog box (Figure 5–80).

5
- Click the Discard button (Microsoft PowerPoint dialog box) to end the presentation without saving the annotations.

Figure 5–80

TO HIDE THE POINTER AND SLIDE SHOW CONTROL BAR

To hide the pointer and the control bar during the slide show, you would perform the following step.

1. Click the Options button on the control bar, click Arrow Options, and then click Hidden.

To Constantly Display the Pointer and Slide Show Control Bar

By default, the pointer and control bar are set at Automatic, which means they are hidden after three seconds of no movement. After you hide the pointer and control bar, they remain hidden until you choose one of the other commands on the Options menu. They are displayed again when you move the mouse.

To keep the pointer and control bar displayed at all times during a slide show, you would perform the following step.

1. Click the Options button on the control bar, click Arrow Options, and then click Visible.

To Save, Reset the Resolution, and Print the Presentation

With the presentation completed, you should save the file and print handouts for your audience. The following steps reset the resolution to 1366 x 768, save the file, and then print a presentation handout.

1 Click the 'Set Up Slide Show' button (Slide Show tab | Set Up group), click the Resolution arrow (Set Up Show dialog box), select 1366 x 768, and then click the OK button.

2 Save the presentation again in the same storage location with the same file name.

3 Print the slides as a handout using the 4 Slides Horizontal layout. If necessary, click 'Print Comments and Ink Markup' on the Print menu to deactivate the command and turn off printing comment pages (Figure 5–81).

4 Because the project now is complete, you can exit PowerPoint, closing all open documents.

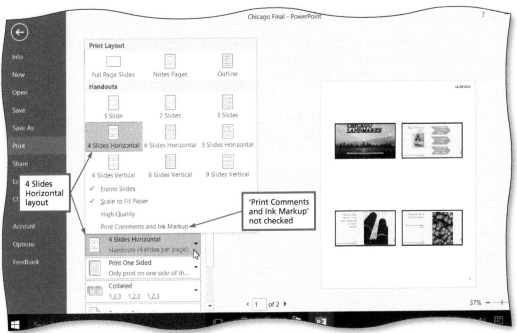

Figure 5–81

BTW

Conserving Ink and Toner
If you want to conserve ink or toner, you can instruct PowerPoint to print draft quality documents by clicking File on the ribbon to open the Backstage view, clicking the Options tab in the Backstage view to display the PowerPoint Options dialog box, clicking Advanced in the left pane (PowerPoint Options dialog box), scrolling to the Print area in the right pane, placing a check mark in the 'Use draft quality' check box, and then clicking the OK button. Then, use the Backstage view to print the document as usual.

BTW

Printing Document Properties
PowerPoint 2016 does not allow you to print document properties. This feature, however, is available in other Office 2016 apps, including Word and Excel.

BTW

Distributing a Document
Instead of printing and distributing a hard copy of a document, you can distribute the document electronically. Options include sending the document via email; posting it on cloud storage (such as OneDrive) and sharing the file with others; posting it on social media, a blog, or other website; and sharing a link associated with an online location of the document. You also can create and share a PDF or XPS image of the document, so that users can view the file in Acrobat Reader or XPS Viewer instead of in PowerPoint.

Summary

In this module you have learned how to merge presentations, review a reviewer's comments, and then review, accept, and reject proposed changes, as well as reply to and insert comments. You reused slides from another presentation, added a footer, cleared formatting from a photo, and changed the slide size and presentation resolution. You also protected and secured the file with a password, checked compatibility, and removed inappropriate information. You then saved the presentation as a PowerPoint show, in a previous PowerPoint format, and packaged on a compact disc. Finally, you ran the presentation and annotated the slides with a highlighter and pen.

CONSIDER THIS: PLAN AHEAD

What decisions will you need to make when creating your next presentation?
Use these guidelines as you complete the assignments in this module and create your own slide show decks outside of this class.

1. Develop a collaboration plan for group members to follow.

　a) Set an overall group goal.

　b) Set long-term and short-term goals.

　c) Identify subtasks that must be completed.

　d) Set a schedule.

2. Accept both positive and negative feedback.

　a) Realize that this criticism helps you to improve yourself and your work.

　b) Oral and written comments from others can help reinforce positive aspects and identify flaws.

　c) Seek comments from a variety of people who genuinely want to help you develop an effective presentation.

3. Give constructive criticism when asked to critique a presentation.

　a) Begin and end with positive comments.

　b) Give specific details about a few areas that can be improved.

　c) Be honest, but be tactful.

4. Select an appropriate password.

　a) A combination of letters and numbers is recommended.

　b) Avoid using words that someone knowing you could guess, such as your child's, best friend's, or pet's name.

　c) Keep your password confidential. Do not write it on a sticky note, place it on a bulletin board, or hide it under your keyboard.

Apply Your Knowledge

Reinforce the skills and apply the concepts you learned in this module.

Inserting and Deleting Comments, Adding a Footer, Saving as a Previous Version, Inspecting a Document, and Marking as Final

Note: To complete this assignment, you will be required to use the Data Files. Please contact your instructor for information about accessing the Data Files.

Instructions: Run PowerPoint. Open the presentation called Apply 5–1 Essay, which is located in the Data Files.

The slides in the presentation present information about steps for writing an essay. The document you open is a partially formatted presentation. You are to insert and reply to comments, add a footer, inspect the document, mark the presentation as final, and save it as a previous Power-Point version. Your presentation should look like Figure 5–82.

Perform the following tasks:

1. On Slide 1 (Figure 5–82a), insert a comment and then type: `I suggest changing the title to: Essay Writing about Nature.` as the text. In the Reply box, type: `That is a good idea. I will edit the slide.` as a reply to the comment.

2. On Slide 2 (Figure 5–82b), select the bulleted list, insert a new comment, and then type `I suggest converting this bulleted list to the Vertical Bullet List SmartArt graphic.` as the text. In the Reply box type `I agree. I will create this graphic.` as a reply to the comment.

3. On Slide 2, convert the bulleted list to the Vertical Bullet List SmartArt graphic (in List area). Change the color to 'Colorful Range - Accent Colors 2 to 3' (in Colorful row) and then change the style to Cartoon (in first 3-D row). Resize the SmartArt graphic to approximately 4.22" × 5.14", as shown in Figure 5–82b.

4. Display the Header and Footer dialog box and then add the slide number and the automatic date and time to only Slide 2. Type your name as the footer text (Figure 5–82a).

5. If requested by your instructor, add your current or previous pet's name in the subtitle placeholder on Slide 1.

6. Apply the Wind transition in the Exciting category to both slides. Change the duration to 3.25 seconds.

7. Save the presentation using the file name, Apply 5–1 Essay Writing. Inspect the document and remove all document properties and personal information. (Do not remove comments and annotations.) Mark the presentation as final.

8. Save the presentation again as a PowerPoint 97-2003 (.ppt) document using the name Apply 5–1 Nature Writing. Submit both presentations in the format specified by your instructor.

9. ✳ In Step 3, you converted the bulleted list to a SmartArt graphic and changed the colors and style of the graphic. How did this improve the presentation?

Continued >

Apply Your Knowledge *continued*

(a) Slide 1

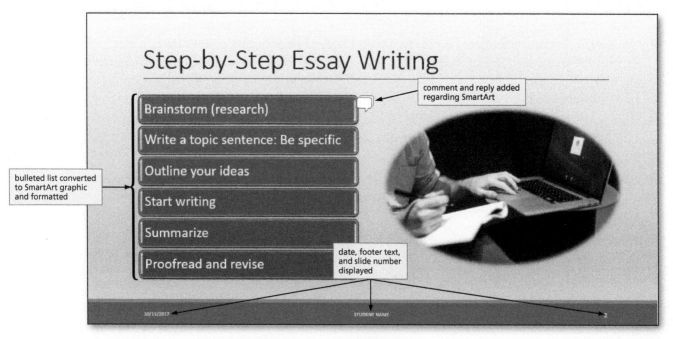

(b) Slide 2

Figure 5–82

Extend Your Knowledge

Extend the skills you learned in this module and experiment with new skills. You may need to use Help to complete the assignment.

Changing Headers and Footers on Slides and Handouts, Inserting and Editing a Comment, and Saving a Slide as an Image

Note: To complete this assignment, you will be required to use the Data Files. Please contact your instructor for information about accessing the Data Files.

Instructions: Run PowerPoint. Open the presentation called Extend 5–1 Lions, which is located in the Data Files. You will change and add information to a footer on a slide and handout. You also will add and change comments and save the slide as an image.

Perform the following tasks:

1. Display the Header and Footer dialog box and then add your next birthday as the fixed date footer text. Type your school's name followed by the words, `Zoology Club - meets every Monday at noon` as the footer text. This footer text will be displayed in the area shown in Figure 5–83.

2. Display the Notes and Handouts tab in the Header and Footer dialog box and then add the text, `Roaring Lions`, as the header text and `Zoology 101` as the footer text.

3. Increase the font size of the footer text to 16 point, bold and italicize this text, and then change the font color to Dark Red (in Standard Colors). *Hint*: Select the footer text boxes and then make the required font changes.

4. Insert a comment on the slide to remind yourself to ask the Zoology Club president if you can post this slide on the organization's website.

5. Edit the existing comment about World Lion Day on the slide by adding this sentence, `This event was founded by Big Cat Rescue, an animal sanctuary in Florida.` to the end of the comment.

6. If requested by your instructor, add the name of your home town after the words, Zoology Club, in the slide footer.

7. Apply the Window transition in the Dynamic Content category to the slide and then change the duration to 2.25 seconds.

8. Save the presentation using the file name, Extend 5–1 Roaring Lions.

9. Save the slide as a .jpg image with the file name, Extend 5–1 Roaring Lions Photo.

10. Submit the revised document in the format specified by your instructor.

11. ✸ In this assignment, you changed the font size and color of the footer text on the slide. How did these changes enhance the slide? You saved the slide as an image. Where could you display this slide other than on the Zoology Club website?

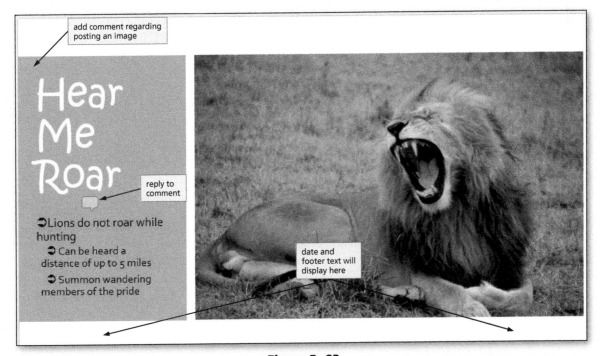

Figure 5–83

Expand Your World

Create a solution that uses cloud or web technologies by learning and investigating on your own from general guidance.

Researching Online Travel Websites

Instructions: You can obtain information about attractions and events worldwide by visiting websites that focus on travel and tourism. Many cities and states have comprehensive websites to promote adventures, events, geography, itineraries, and activities. In this module you learned about a few landmarks in Chicago, and several websites feature detailed information about these and other attractions, tours, and events in this town.

Perform the following tasks:

1. Visit one of the following websites, or locate other websites that contain information about Chicago: Choose Chicago (choosechicago.com), Chicago Traveler (chicagotraveler.com), Chicago Attractions (chicago.org/things-to-do/attraction), or Navy Pier (navypier.com).
2. Locate information on the sites displayed in your Chicago Final slides, tours, attractions, events, sports, architecture, or other activities.
3. Create at least two new slides and then insert them into your Chicago Final presentation. Use SmartArt or WordArt where appropriate.
4. If requested to do so by your instructor, replace the words, Chi-town Summer, in the footer with your high school mascot's name.
5. Save the presentation using the file name, Expand 5 – 1 Chicago Final Travel.
6. Submit the assignment in the format specified by your instructor.
7. ✳ Which features do the websites offer that help you develop content for the two new slides? Who would you ask to review and comment on your revised presentation?

In the Labs

Design, create, modify, and/or use a presentation following the guidelines, concepts, and skills presented in this module. Labs 1 and 2, which increase in difficulty, require you to create solutions based on what you learned in the module; Lab 3 requires you to apply your creative thinking and problem-solving skills to design and implement a solution.

Lab 1: Adding Comments, Protecting a Presentation, and Reusing a Slide

Note: To complete this assignment, you will be required to use the Data Files. Please contact your instructor for information about accessing the Data Files.

Problem: The health food store in your town is planning a series of nutritional seminars, and the first topic concerns choosing products that contain healthy fats. The manager has begun developing PowerPoint slides in two separate files: one regarding beneficial fats and another discussing harmful fats. You agree to help her complete the project by editing the files and then combining slides from both files and creating one presentation. You add a comment and protect the final presentation with a password before sending it to her for approval. When you run the presentation, you add annotations. The annotated slides are shown in Figures 5–84a and 5–84b. Create the slides shown in Figure 5–84.

Perform the following tasks:

1. Run PowerPoint. Open the presentation called Lab 5–1 Good Fats, which is located in the Data Files.

2. On Slide 1 (Figure 5–84a), add a comment on the cookie illustration and then type `You show a cookie, which probably contains bad fats, on this slide. I suggest you add some information about bad fats to this presentation.` as the text.

3. Open the presentation called Lab 5–1 Bad Fats, which is located in the Data Files. Set the slide size to Widescreen (16:9) and then change the slide show resolution to 1366 x 768.

4. On Slide 2 (Figure 5–84b), clear the formatting from the fried food picture. Then, apply the 'Reflected Bevel, Black' picture style to this photo.

5. Save the Lab 5–1 Bad Fats file with the file name, Lab 5–1 Bad Fats Revised, and then close this file.

6. With the Lab 5–1 Good Fats file open, insert Slide 2 from the Lab 5–1 Bad Fats Revised file, keeping the source formatting.

7. On Slide 1, change the title text to, Fats in Our Diet.

8. Run the Compatibility Checker to identify the presentation features not supported in previous PowerPoint versions. Summarize these features in a comment placed on Slide 1.

9. Protect the presentation with the password, fats.

10. If requested by your instructor, add the name of the city in which you were born as the subtitle text on Slide 1.

11. Apply the Peel Off transition in the Exciting category to all slides and then change the duration to 2.50 seconds.

12. Save the presentation using the file name, Lab 5–1 Fats in our Diet.

13. Run the presentation. On Slide 1, use the Pen tool and Blue ink to draw a circle around the word, Fats. When Slide 3 (Figure 5–84c) is displayed, use the Highlighter tool and Light Green ink to highlight the text, Lowers LDL, in both middle boxes, as shown in the figure. Click the Next button to reach the end of the slide show. Save the annotations.

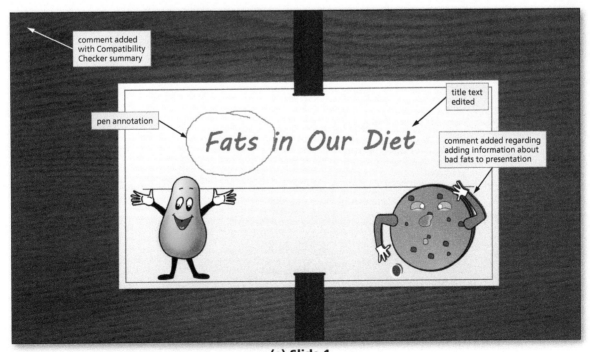

(a) Slide 1

Figure 5–84 (Continued)

Continued >

In the Labs *continued*

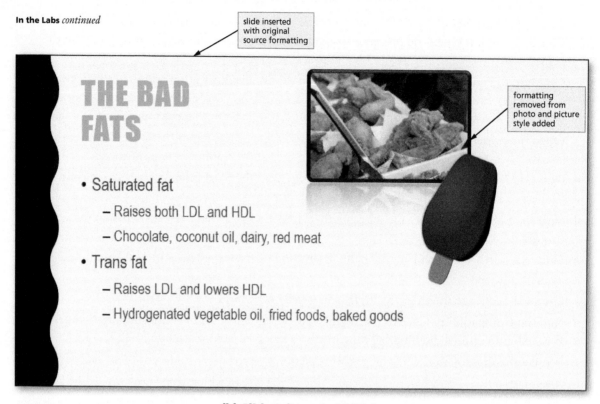

(b) Slide 2 (Inserted Slide)

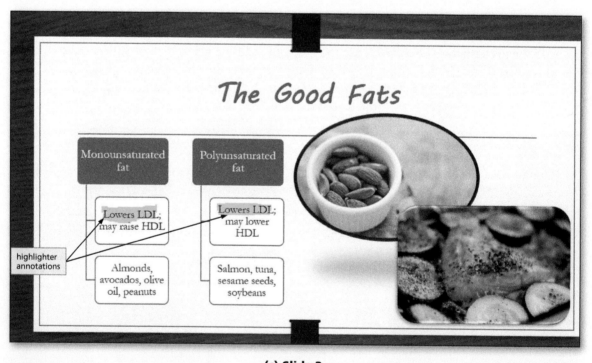

(c) Slide 3

Figure 5–84

14. Submit the document in the format specified by your instructor.

15. ✸ You reused one slide from another presentation. How did combining the slides from the two files help make the presentation more effective for the store manager?

Lab 2: Reviewing and Accepting Comments in a Protected Presentation, Merging Presentations, Using Screen Clipping, and Packaging the Presentation for Storage on a Compact Disc

Note: To complete this assignment, you will be required to use the Data Files. Please contact your instructor for information about accessing the required files.

Problem: Backpackers of all ages and abilities explore the world's exceptional wilderness. They travel on their own, with experienced guides, or with friends and family. Your local sporting goods store is forming a hiking club, and the owner has asked you to help generate interest in the sport. You develop four slides and then ask the owner to review the content. Use her input to create the presentation shown in Figure 5–85. In addition, use the Package for CD feature to distribute the presentation to potential backpacking club members.

Perform the following tasks:

1. Run PowerPoint. Open the presentation called Lab 5–2 Backpacking, which is located in the Data Files. The password is Backpacking.

2. Merge the owner's revised file, Lab 5–2 Backpacking2, located in the Data Files. Accept the theme presentation change so that the transition is added to all slides. Review all of her comments on all four slides. Preview the slides and then print the slides and the comments.

3. On Slide 1 (Figure 5–85a), accept all changes except for the subtitle font color modification.

4. On Slide 2 (Figure 5–85b), accept all the changes.

5. On Slide 3 (Figure 5–85c), accept all the changes.

6. On Slide 4 (Figure 5–85d), accept all changes except for the Text Placeholder 20: National Park Destinations.

7. Search the Internet for National Park Service backpacking guidelines. Insert a screenshot of one of these webpages on Slide 4. You may need to reduce the size of the screenshot on your slide.

8. On Slide 1, enhance the photo by applying the Bevel Perspective Left, White Picture style (in last row).

9. On Slide 4, enhance the photo by applying the Moderate Frame, Black Picture style (in second row).

10. Inspect the document and then remove all document properties and personal information.

11. If requested by your instructor, enter the name of the last TV program you watched as the fourth subtitle paragraph on Slide 1.

12. End the review and hide markup.

13. Save the presentation using the file name, Lab 5–2 Backpacking Basics.

14. Mark the presentation as final.

15. Save the presentation using the Package for CD feature. Name the CD Lab 5–2 Trail Blazers. Submit the revised document and the CD in the format specified by your instructor.

16. ✺ Why would you accept the reviewer's granite texture to the title font on Slide 1? How did converting the bulleted list on Slide 2 to a SmartArt graphic improve the presentation?

Continued >

In the Labs *continued*

(a) Slide 1

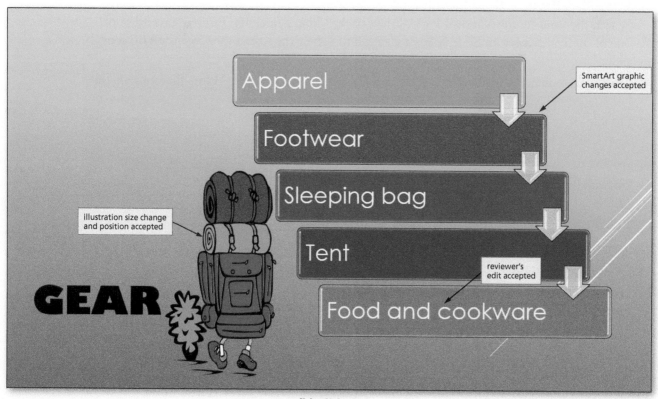

(b) Slide 2
Figure 5–85 (Continued)

(c) Slide 3

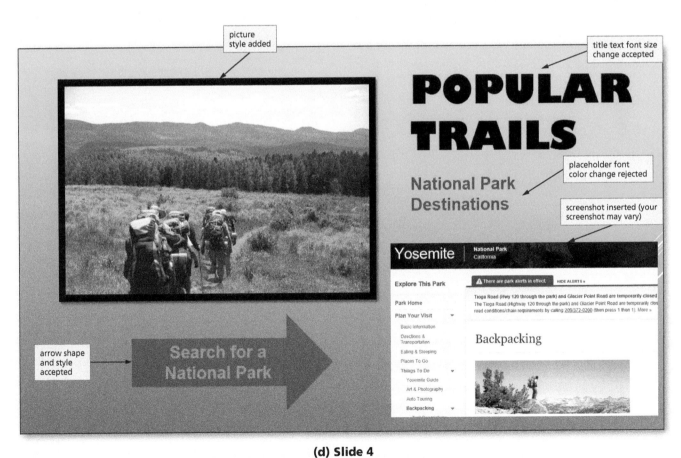

(d) Slide 4

Figure 5–85

Continued >

In the Labs *continued*

Lab 3: **Consider This: Your Turn**

Design and Create a Presentation about Traveling to Cuba

Part 1: You work for a travel agency, and your clients have expressed interest in visiting Cuba now that travel restrictions to that country have been loosened for Americans. Your manager has asked if you would create a PowerPoint presentation about this destination, so you perform some online research to learn about Cuban history and travel regulations. After gathering information, you recommend your travel agency conduct an organized educational program with an itinerary that includes lectures on Spanish colonial architecture, tours to artists' studios, excursions to sandy white beaches and the rolling Sierra Maestra Mountains, and brief community projects in Havana and Santiago de Cuba. Use the concepts and techniques presented in this module to create a presentation. Select a suitable theme, use WordArt and SmartArt graphics where appropriate, insert comments, and ask your manager to review your presentation before you make it final. The presentation could contain photos, illustrations, and videos. The Data Files contains illustrations and a photo called Cuba Flag, Cuba Coat of Arms, Cuba Provinces, and Cuba Coffee Cup. Review and revise your presentation as needed and then save the file using the file name, Lab 5–3 Cuba Travel. Submit your assignment in the format specified by your instructor.

Part 2: ✳ You made several decisions while creating the presentation in this assignment: where to place text, how to format the text (such as font and font size), which graphical image(s) to use, which styles and effects to apply, where to position the graphical images, and which shapes to use to add interest to the presentation. What was the rationale behind each of these decisions? When you reviewed the document, what further revisions did you make and why? Where would you recommend showing this slide show?

6 Navigating Presentations Using Hyperlinks and Action Buttons

Objectives

You will have mastered the material in this module when you can:

- Create a presentation from a Microsoft Word outline
- Add hyperlinks to slides and objects
- Hyperlink to other Microsoft Office documents
- Add action buttons and action settings
- Display guides to position slide elements

- Align placeholder text
- Create columns in a placeholder
- Change paragraph line spacing
- Format bullet size and color
- Change bullet characters to pictures and numbers
- Hide slides

Introduction

BTW

Developing Outlines
A formal outline can help you arrange slide content in multiple levels of major and supporting details. Before you can create this outline, however, you may attempt to develop your ideas by using a scratch outline, which is a rough sketch of the possible major points you would like to showcase and the order in which they might appear.

Many writers begin composing reports and documents by creating an outline. Others review their papers for consistency by saving the document with a new file name, removing all text except the topic headings, and then saving the file again. An outline created in Microsoft Word or another word-processing program works well as a shell for a PowerPoint presentation. Instead of typing text in PowerPoint, as you did in previous projects, you can import this outline, add visual elements such as clip art, photos, and graphical bullets, and ultimately create an impressive slide show. When delivering the presentation, you can navigate forward and backward through the slides using hyperlinks and action buttons to emphasize particular points, to review material, or to address audience concerns.

Project — Presentation with Action Buttons, Hyperlinks, and Formatted Bullet Characters

Speakers may elect to begin creating their presentations with an outline (Figure 6–1a) and then add formatted bullets and columns. When presenting these slides during a speaking engagement, they can run their PowerPoint slides nonsequentially depending

BTW
Defining Outline Levels
Imported outlines can have a maximum of nine outline levels, whereas PowerPoint outlines are limited to six levels (one for the title text and five for body paragraph text.) When you import an outline, all text in outline levels six through nine is treated as a fifth-level paragraph.

upon the audience's needs and comprehension. Each of the three pictures on the Conquer Your Clutter title slide (Figure 6–1b) branches, or hyperlinks, to another slide in the presentation. Action buttons and hyperlinks on Slides 2, 3, and 4 (Figures 6–1c through 6–1e) allow the presenter to jump to Slide 5 (Figure 6–1f), slides in another presentation (Figures 6–1g and 6–1h), or a Microsoft Word document (Figure 6–1i). The four resources on Slide 5 are hyperlinks that, when clicked during a presentation, display webpages of organizations that accept donations of household goods. The slides in the presentation have a variety of embellishments, including a two-column list on Slide 4 that provides tips on organizing a kitchen, formatted graphical bullets on Slides 2 and 5 of a sad face and a question mark, and a numbered list on Slide 3.

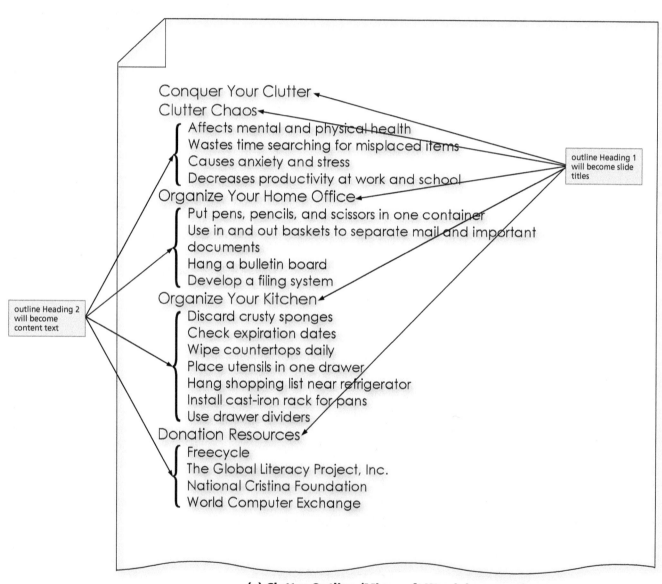

(a) Clutter Outline (Microsoft Word document)

Figure 6–1 (Continued)

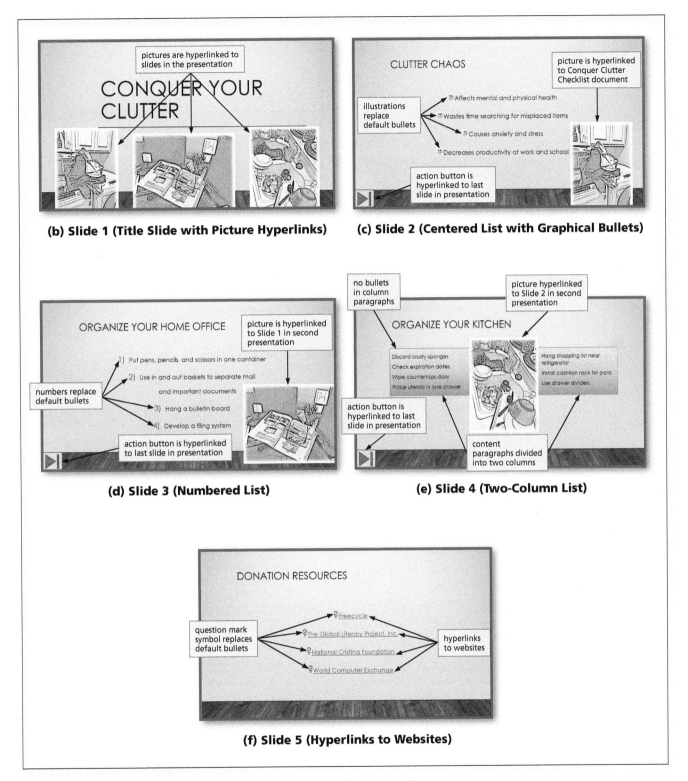

(b) Slide 1 (Title Slide with Picture Hyperlinks)

(c) Slide 2 (Centered List with Graphical Bullets)

(d) Slide 3 (Numbered List)

(e) Slide 4 (Two-Column List)

(f) Slide 5 (Hyperlinks to Websites)

Figure 6–1 (Continued)

(g) Slide 1 (Hyperlinked from First Presentation)   **(h) Slide 2 (Hyperlinked from First Presentation)**

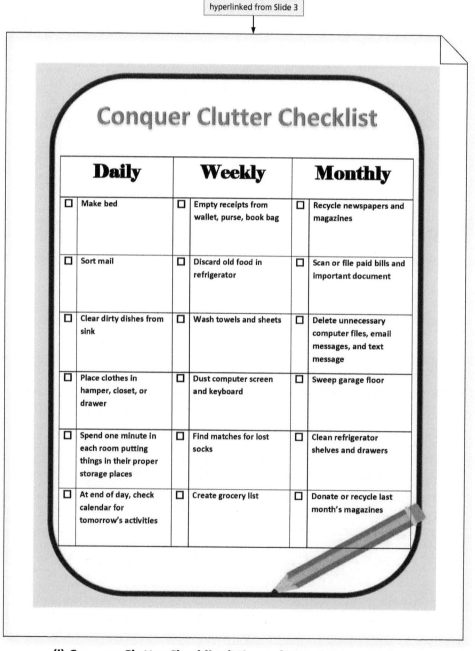

(i) Conquer Clutter Checklist (Microsoft Word document)

Figure 6–1

In this module, you will learn how to create the slides shown in Figure 6–1. The following roadmap identifies general activities you will perform as you progress through this module:

1. OPEN a Microsoft Word OUTLINE.
2. ADD PICTURE and TEXT HYPERLINKS.
3. ADD ACTION BUTTONS and HYPERLINKS.
4. POSITION PICTURES in content placeholders.
5. ALIGN PLACEHOLDER TEXT.
6. CONVERT and FORMAT BULLETS.

Creating a Presentation from a Microsoft Word Outline

An outline created in Microsoft Word or another word-processing program works well as a shell for a PowerPoint presentation. Instead of typing text in PowerPoint, you can import this outline, add visual elements such as pictures and graphical bullets, and ultimately create an impressive slide show.

In the following pages, you will follow these general steps to create a presentation from a Microsoft Word outline:

1. Add hyperlinks to pictures and paragraphs.
2. Insert action buttons and then link them to other slides and files.
3. Align pictures and text.
4. Create columns.
5. Change and format bullet characters.

Converting Documents for Use in PowerPoint

PowerPoint can produce slides based on an outline created in Microsoft Word, another word-processing program, or a webpage if the text was saved in a format that PowerPoint can recognize. Microsoft Word 2016, 2013, 2010, and 2007 files use the **.docx** file extension in their file names. Text originating in other word-processing programs for later use with PowerPoint should be saved in Rich Text Format (.rtf) or plain text (.txt). Webpage documents that use an HTML extension (.htm or .html) also can be imported.

PowerPoint automatically opens Microsoft Office files, and many other types of files, in the PowerPoint format. The **Rich Text Format (.rtf)** file type is used to transfer formatted documents between applications, even if the programs are running on different platforms, such as Windows and Mac OS. When you insert a Word or Rich Text Format document into a presentation, PowerPoint creates an outline structure based on heading styles in the document. A Heading 1 in a source document becomes a slide title in PowerPoint, a Heading 2 becomes the first level of content text on the slide, a Heading 3 becomes the second level of text on the slide, and so on.

If the original document contains no heading styles, PowerPoint creates an outline based on paragraphs. For example, in a .docx or .rtf file, for several lines of text styled as Normal and broken into paragraphs, PowerPoint turns each paragraph into a slide title.

BTW

The Ribbon and Screen Resolution
PowerPoint may change how the groups and buttons within the groups appear on the ribbon, depending on the computer or mobile device's screen resolution. Thus, your ribbon may look different from the ones in this book if you are using a screen resolution other than 1366 × 768.

To Open a Microsoft Word Outline as a Presentation

Why? Instead of typing text for each of the five PowerPoint slides, you can open a Microsoft Word outline and have PowerPoint create the slides automatically. The text for the Conquer Your Clutter presentation is contained in a Word file that is saved in the Rich Text Format (.rtf). The following steps open this Microsoft Word outline located in the Data Files as a presentation in PowerPoint.

1

- Run PowerPoint. If necessary, maximize the PowerPoint window.

- Apply the Blank Presentation theme.

- Open the Backstage view, display the Open dialog box, and then navigate to the Data Files so that you can open the Clutter Outline file in that location.

- Click the File Type arrow to display the File Type list (Figure 6–2).

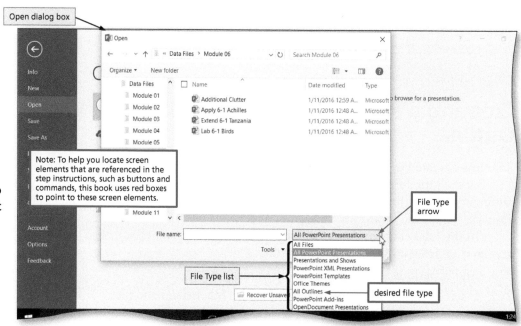

Figure 6–2

2

- Click All Outlines to select this file type.

- Click Clutter Outline to select the file (Figure 6–3).

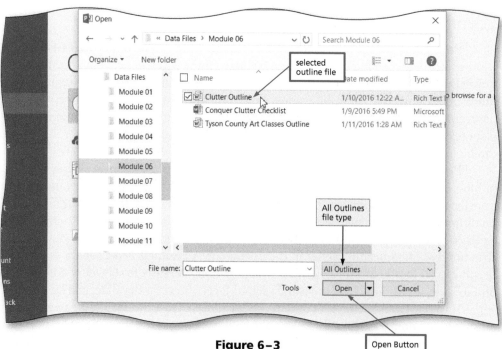

Figure 6–3

3

- Click the Open button to create the five slides in your presentation (Figure 6-4).

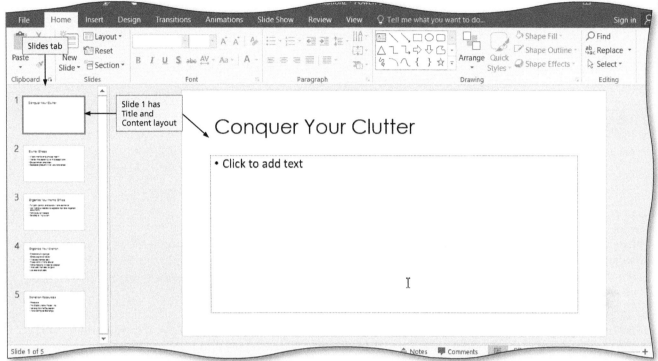

Figure 6-4

4

- Display the View tab and then click the Outline View button (View tab | Presentation Views group) to view the outline in the Slides tab (Figure 6-5).

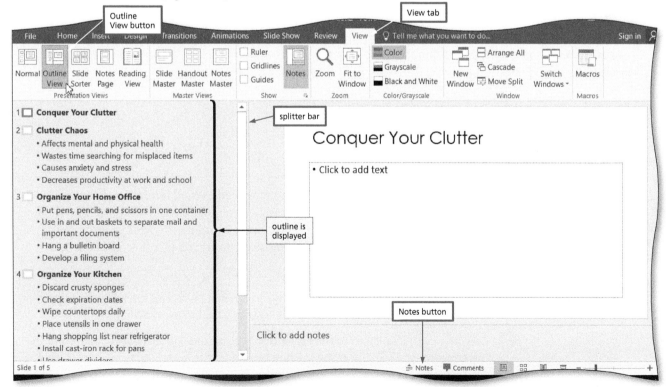

Figure 6-5

Q&A

Do I need to see the text as an outline in the Slides tab now?

No, but sometimes it is helpful to view the content of your presentation in this view before looking at individual slides.

Do I need to change to Normal view to navigate between slides?

No, you can click the slide number in Outline view to navigate to slides.

Can I change the width of the Slides tab?

Yes. Click the splitter bar and drag it to the left or right to reduce or increase the width of the Slides tab.

Other Ways

1. Click New Slide arrow (Home tab | Slides group), click Slides from Outline, click File Type arrow, if necessary click All Outlines, click desired outline, click Insert button, delete first blank slide

---

To Change the Slide 1 Layout and Change the Document Theme

BTW

Benefits of Outline View

Work in Outline view when you want to make global edits, get an overview of the presentation, change the sequence of bullets or slides, or apply formatting changes.

When you created the new slides from the Word outline, PowerPoint applied the Title and Text slide layout to all slides. You want to apply the Title Slide layout to Slide 1 to introduce the presentation. The following steps change the Slide 1 slide layout and change the theme to Gallery.

1 With Slide 1 displaying, display the Home tab, click the Layout button (Home tab | Slides group), and then click Title Slide to apply that layout to Slide 1.

2 Apply the Gallery document theme (shown in Figure 6–6).

3 If necessary, click the Notes button on the status bar to close the Notes pane.

CONSIDER THIS

Think threes.

Speechwriters often think of threes as they plan their talks and PowerPoint presentations. The number three is considered a symbol of balance, as in an equilateral triangle that has three 60-degree angles, the three meals we eat daily, or the three parts of our day — morning, noon, and night. A speech generally has an introduction, a body, and a conclusion. Audience members find balance and harmony seeing three objects on a slide, so whenever possible, plan visual components on your slides in groups of three.

To Insert Pictures

BTW

Touch Screen Differences

The Office and Windows interfaces may vary if you are using a touch screen. For this reason, you might notice that the function or appearance of your touch screen differs slightly from this module's presentation.

Pictures of cluttered areas in the home will add visual interest and cue the viewers to the topic of organizing commonly cluttered areas of the home. The three pictures are located in the Data Files. Later in this module, you will position the pictures in precise locations. The following steps insert the pictures on Slides 1, 2, 3, and 4.

1 On the title slide, insert the pictures called Laundry, Desk, and Kitchen, which are located in the Data Files, in the area below the subtitle box shown in Figure 6–6.

2 Copy the Laundry picture to the lower-right corner of Slide 2, the Desk picture to the lower-center of Slide 3, and the Kitchen picture to the lower-right corner of Slide 4.

3 Save the presentation using Conquer Your Clutter as the file name.

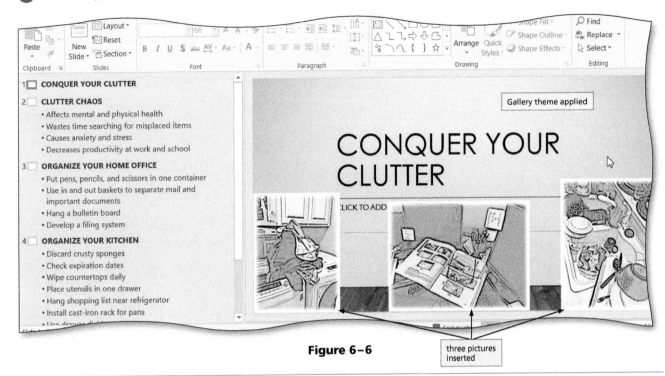

Figure 6–6

three pictures inserted

Choose outstanding hyperlink images or text.
Good speakers are aware of their audiences and know their speech material well. They have rehearsed their presentations and know where the hypertext is displayed on the slides. During a presentation, however, they sometimes need to divert from their planned material. Audience members may interrupt with questions, the room may not have optimal acoustics or lighting, or the timing may be short or long. It is helpful, therefore, to make the slide hyperlinks as large and noticeable to speakers as possible. The presenters can glance at the slide and receive a visual cue that it contains a hyperlink. They then can decide whether to click the hyperlink to display a webpage.

CONSIDER THIS

Adding Hyperlinks and Action Buttons

Speakers sometimes skip from one slide to another in a presentation in response to audience needs or timing issues. In addition, if Internet access is available, they may desire to display a webpage during a slide show to add depth to the presented material and to enhance the overall message. When presenting the Conquer Your Clutter slide show and discussing the information on Slides 1, 2, 3, or 4, a speaker might want to skip to the last slide in the presentation and then access a website for a specific group that accepts donated technology, books, clothes, and other household items. Or the presenter may be discussing information on Slide 5 and want to display Slide 1 to begin discussing a new topic.

One method of jumping nonsequentially to slides is by clicking a hyperlink or an action button on a slide. A **hyperlink**, also called a **link**, connects one slide to a webpage, another slide, a custom show consisting of specific slides in a presentation, an email address, or a file. A hyperlink can be any element of a slide. This includes a single letter, a word, a paragraph, or any graphical image such as a picture, shape, or graph.

BTW
Customizing ScreenTips
You can create a custom ScreenTip that displays when you hover your mouse over a hyperlink. Click the ScreenTip button (Insert Hyperlink dialog box), type the desired ScreenTip text (Set Hyperlink ScreenTip dialog box), and then click the OK button.

To Add a Hyperlink to a Picture

Why? In the Conquer Your Clutter presentation, each picture on Slide 1 will link to another slide in the same presentation. When you point to a hyperlink, the pointer becomes the shape of a hand to indicate the text or object contains a hyperlink. The following steps create the first hyperlink for the Laundry picture on Slide 1.

1

- Display Slide 1, select the Laundry picture, and then display the Insert tab.

- Click the Hyperlink button (Insert tab | Links group) to display the Insert Hyperlink dialog box.

- If necessary, click the 'Place in This Document' button in the Link to area.

- Click '2. Clutter Chaos' in the 'Select a place in this document' area (Insert Hyperlink dialog box) to select and display a preview of this slide (Figure 6–7).

Figure 6–7

Q&A Could I also have selected the Next Slide link in the 'Select a place in this document' area?
Yes. Either action would create the hyperlink to Slide 2.

2

- Click the OK button (Insert Hyperlink dialog box) to insert the hyperlink.

Q&A I clicked the Laundry picture, but Slide 2 did not display. Why?
Hyperlinks are active only when you run the presentation or are in Reading view, not when you are creating it in Normal or Slide Sorter view.

Other Ways
1. Right-click text or object, click Hyperlink, select slide, click OK button   2. Select text or object, press CTRL+K, select slide, press ENTER

To Add Hyperlinks to the Remaining Slide 1 Pictures

The hyperlink for the Laundry picture is complete. The next task is to create the hyperlinks for the other two pictures on Slide 1.

1 On Slide 1, click the Desk picture.

2 Click the Hyperlink button, if necessary click 'Place in This Document', and then click '3. Organize Your Home Office' to select this slide as the hyperlink. Click the OK button.

3 Click the Kitchen picture, click the Hyperlink button, and then click '4. Organize Your Kitchen'. Click the OK button.

To Add a Hyperlink to a Paragraph

If you are connected to the Internet when you run the presentation, you can click each hyperlinked paragraph, and your browser will open a new window and display the corresponding webpage for each hyperlink. By default, hyperlinked text is displayed with an underline and in a color that is part of the color scheme. The following steps create a hyperlink for the first paragraph on Slide 5. *Why? Each second-level paragraph will be a hyperlink to webpage for an organization that accepts donated household and technology products.*

- Display Slide 5 and then select the second-level paragraph that appears first, Freecycle, to select the text.

- Display the Insert Hyperlink dialog box and then click the 'Existing File or Web Page' button in the Link to area (Figure 6–8).

Figure 6–8

- If necessary, delete the text in the Address text box and then type **www .freecycle.org** in the Address box (Figure 6–9).

Q&A | Why does http:// appear before the address I typed?
PowerPoint automatically adds this protocol identifier before web addresses.

Figure 6–9

- Click the OK button to insert the hyperlink.

Q&A | Why is this paragraph now underlined and displaying a new font color?
The default style for hyperlinks is underlined text. The Gallery built-in theme hyperlink color is red, so PowerPoint formatted the paragraph to that color automatically.

Other Ways

1. Right-click selected text, click Hyperlink, click 'Existing File or Web Page', type address, click OK button

2. Select text, press CTRL+K, click 'Existing File or Web Page', type address, press ENTER key

To Add Hyperlinks to the Remaining Slide 5 Paragraphs

The hyperlink for the second-level paragraph that appears first is complete. The next task is to create the hyperlinks for the other second-level paragraphs on Slide 5.

1 Select The Global Literary Project, Inc., which is the second-level paragraph that appears second.

2 Display the Insert Hyperlink dialog box and then type `www.glpinc.org` in the Address box. Click the OK button.

3 Select the third paragraph, National Cristina Foundation, display the Insert Hyperlink dialog box, type `www.cristina.org` in the Address box, and then click the OK button.

4 Select the fourth paragraph, World Computer Exchange, display the Insert Hyperlink dialog box, type `www.worldcomputerexchange.org` in the Address box, and then click the OK button (Figure 6–10).

If requested by your instructor, add a fifth bulleted paragraph with the city or county in which you were born.

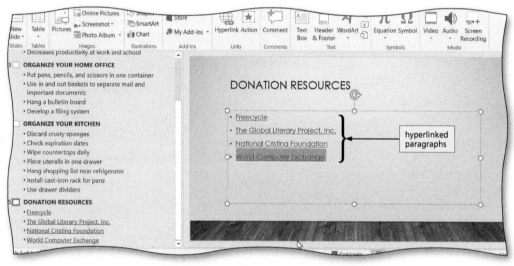

Figure 6–10

Q&A I clicked the hyperlink, but the webpage did not display. Why?
As with the hyperlinks associated with the pictures on Slide 1, hyperlinks associated with text are active only in Reading view or when you run the presentation.

BTW
Using Action Buttons
The action buttons have images representing their functions, such as a right-pointing arrow representing moving forward to the next slide. These buttons are useful when using a touch screen or when a keyboard is not present, such as when a presentation is run at a kiosk. Slide designers also type specific years or descriptive words, such as True or False, on action buttons that link to slides with corresponding information. Be imaginative when developing your own presentations and creating buttons that have a specific meaning for your intended audience.

Action Buttons

PowerPoint provides 12 built-in action buttons. An **action button** is a particular type of hyperlink that has a built-in function. Each action button performs a specific task, such as displaying the next slide, providing help, giving information, or playing a sound. In addition, the action button can activate a hyperlink that allows users to jump to a specific slide in the presentation. The picture on the action button indicates the type of function it performs. For example, the button with the house icon represents the home slide, or Slide 1. To achieve a personalized look, you can customize an action button with a photograph, piece of clip art, logo, text, or any graphic you desire. Table 6–1 describes each of the built-in action buttons.

Table 6–1 Built-In Action Buttons

Button Name	Image	Description
Back or Previous	◁	Returns to the previous slide displayed in the same presentation.
Forward or Next	▷	Jumps to the next slide in the presentation.
Beginning	◁	Jumps to Slide 1. This button performs the same function as the Home button.
End	▷|	Jumps to the last slide in the presentation.
Home	⌂	Jumps to Slide 1. This button performs the same function as the Beginning button.
Information	ⓘ	Does not have any predefined function. Use it to direct a user to a slide with details or facts.
Return	↩	Returns to the previous slide displayed in any presentation. For example, you can place it on a hidden slide or on a slide in a custom slide show and then return to the previous slide.
Movie	▦	Does not have any predefined function. You generally would use this button to jump to a slide with an inserted video clip.
Document	▯	Opens a program other than PowerPoint. For example, you can open Microsoft Word or Microsoft Excel and display a page or worksheet.
Sound	◁:	Does not have any predefined function. You generally would use this button to jump to a slide with an inserted audio clip.
Help	?	Does not have any predefined function. Use it to direct a user to a slide with instructions or contact information.
Custom	☐	Does not have any predefined function. You can add a clip, picture, graphic, or text and then specify a unique purpose.

Customize action buttons for a unique look.

PowerPoint's built-in action buttons have icons that give the presenter an indication of their function. Designers frequently customize these buttons with images related to the presentation. For example, in a grocery store presentation, the action buttons may have images of a coupon, dollar sign, and question mark to indicate links to in-store coupons, sale items, and the customer service counter. Be creative when you develop your own presentations and attempt to develop buttons that have specific meanings for your intended audience.

To Insert an Action Button

1 OPEN OUTLINE | 2 ADD PICTURE & TEXT HYPERLINKS | **3 ADD ACTION BUTTONS & HYPERLINKS**
4 POSITION PICTURES | 5 ALIGN PLACEHOLDER TEXT | 6 CONVERT & FORMAT BULLETS

In the Conquer Your Clutter slide show, the action buttons on Slides 2, 3, and 4 hyperlink to the last slide, Slide 5. You will insert and format the action button shape on Slide 2 and copy it to Slides 3 and 4, and then create a link to Slide 5. *Why? You will be able to display Slide 5 at any point in the presentation by clicking the action button.* When you click the action button, a sound will play. This sound will vary depending upon which slide is displayed. The following steps insert an action button on Slide 2 and link it to Slide 5.

- Display Slide 2 and then click the Shapes button (Insert tab | Illustrations group) to display the Shapes gallery.

- Scroll down and then point to the 'Action Button: End' shape in the Action Buttons area (fourth image) (Figure 6–11).

Figure 6–11

- Click the 'Action Button: End' shape.

- Click the lower-left corner of the slide to insert the action button and to display the Action Settings dialog box.

- If necessary, click the Mouse Click tab (Action Settings dialog box) (Figure 6–12).

Q&A Why is Last Slide the default hyperlink setting?
The End shape establishes a hyperlink to the last slide in a presentation.

Figure 6–12

- Click the Play sound check box and then click the Play sound arrow to display the Play sound list (Figure 6–13).

Figure 6–13

4

- Click Breeze in the Play sound list to select that sound (Figure 6–14).

Q&A I did not hear the sound when I selected it. Why not?
The Breeze sound will play when you run the slide show and click the action button.

5

- Click the OK button to apply the hyperlink setting and sound to the action button and to close the Action Settings dialog box.

Figure 6–14

To Size an Action Button

The action button size can be decreased to make it less obvious on the slide. The following step resizes the selected action button.

1 With the action button still selected and the Drawing Tools Format tab displaying, size the action button so that it is 0.8" x 0.9". If necessary, move the action button to the lower-left corner of the slide, as shown in Figure 6–15.

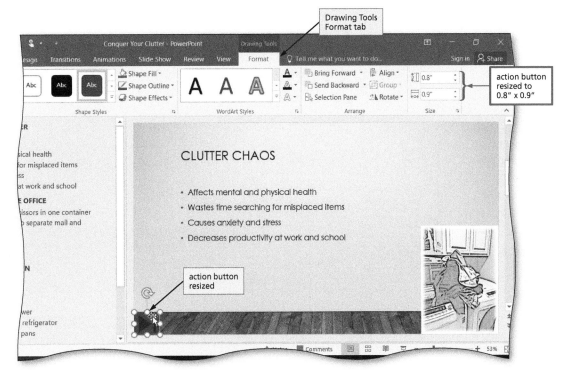

Figure 6–15

To Change an Action Button Fill Color

You can select a new action button fill color to coordinate with slide elements. The following steps change the fill color from Red to Tan. *Why? The action button's red interior color does not coordinate well with the wooden floor on the slide. A tan color will blend with the slide background and complement the dark brown floor.*

- With the action button still selected, click the Shape Fill arrow (Drawing Tools Format tab | Shape Styles gallery) to display the Shape Fill gallery (Figure 6–16).

Figure 6–16

- Point to 'Tan, Background 2' (third color in first Theme Colors row) to display a live preview of that fill color on the action button (Figure 6–17).

Experiment

- Point to various colors in the Shape Fill gallery and watch the fill color change in the action button.

- Click 'Tan, Background 2' to apply this color to the action button.

Figure 6–17

Other Ways

1. Right-click action button, click Format Shape on shortcut menu, click Fill on Shape Options tab (Format Shape pane), click Fill Color button, click desired color
2. Right-click action button, click Shape Fill button on mini toolbar, click desired color

To Copy an Action Button

The Slide 2 action button is formatted and positioned correctly. You can copy this shape to Slides 3 and 4. *Why? Copying the formatted shape saves time and ensures consistency.* The following steps copy the Slide 2 action button to the next two slides in the presentation.

- Right-click the action button on Slide 2 to display a shortcut menu (Figure 6–18).

Q&A

Why does my shortcut menu have different commands?
Depending upon where you pressed or right-clicked, you might see a different shortcut menu. As long as this menu displays the Copy command, you can use it. If the Copy command is not visible, right-click the slide again to display another shortcut menu.

Figure 6–18

- Click Copy on the shortcut menu to copy the action button to the Clipboard.

- Display Slide 3 and then click the Paste button (Home tab | Clipboard group) to paste the action button in the lower-left corner of Slide 3 (Figure 6–19).

- Display Slide 4 and then click the Paste button to paste the action button in the lower-left corner of Slide 4.

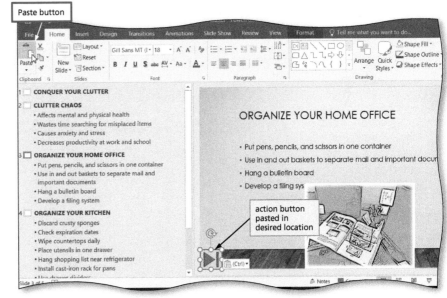

Figure 6–19

Other Ways

1. Copy button (Home tab | Clipboard group), Paste button (Home tab | Clipboard group)

2. CTRL+C to copy, CTRL+V to paste

To Edit an Action Button Setting

When you copied the action button, PowerPoint retained the settings to hyperlink to the last slide and to play the Breeze sound. The following steps edit the Slide 3 and Slide 4 hyperlink sound settings. *Why? For variety, you want to change the sounds that play for the Slide 3 and Slide 4 action buttons.*

• With the action button still selected on Slide 4, display the Insert tab and then click the Action button (Insert tab | Links group) shown in Figure 6–21 to display the Action Settings dialog box.

• Click the Play sound arrow to display the Play sound menu (Figure 6–20).

Figure 6–20

• Click Suction in the Play sound list to select the Suction sound to play when the action button is clicked (Figure 6–21).

• Click the OK button (Action Settings dialog box) to apply the new sound setting to the Slide 4 action button.

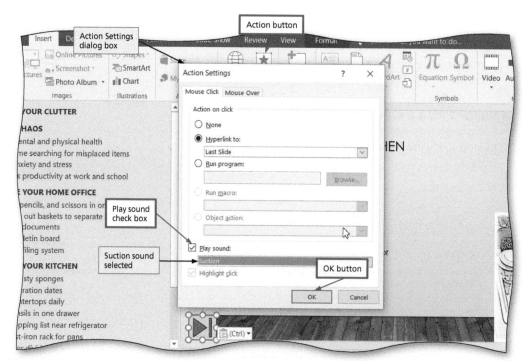

Figure 6–21

3

- Display Slide 3, select the action button, and then click the Action button (Insert tab | Links group) to display the Action Settings dialog box.

- Click the Play sound arrow to display the Play sound menu.

- Click Typewriter in the Play sound list (Figure 6–22).

- Click the OK button (Action Settings dialog box) to apply the new sound setting to the Slide 3 action button.

Figure 6–22

To Hyperlink to Another PowerPoint File

1 OPEN OUTLINE | 2 ADD PICTURE & TEXT HYPERLINKS | 3 ADD ACTION BUTTONS & HYPERLINKS
4 POSITION PICTURES | 5 ALIGN PLACEHOLDER TEXT | 6 CONVERT & FORMAT BULLETS

While hyperlinks are convenient tools to navigate through the current PowerPoint presentation or to webpages, they also allow you to open a second PowerPoint presentation and display a particular slide in that file. Much clutter can arise when paper files are piled on work surfaces and on the floor, so you desire to show your audience some useful information about retaining and disposing paper documents. The first slide in another presentation, Additional Clutter, has a table listing documents to keep and others to shred or discard. The following steps hyperlink the Desk picture on Slide 3 to the first slide in the second presentation. *Why? The hyperlink offers a convenient method of moving from one presentation to another. A speaker has the discretion to use the hyperlink depending upon the audience's interest in the topic and time considerations.*

- Display Slide 3 and then select the Desk picture.

- Display the Insert tab and then click the Action button (Insert tab | Links group) to display the Action Settings dialog box.

- Click Hyperlink to in the 'Action on click' area and then click the Hyperlink to arrow to display the Hyperlink to menu (Figure 6–23).

Figure 6–23

2

- Scroll down and then click 'Other PowerPoint Presentation' to display the Hyperlink to Other PowerPoint Presentation dialog box.

- If necessary, navigate to the location of the Data Files.

- Click Additional Clutter to select this file as the hyperlinked presentation (Figure 6–24).

Figure 6–24

3

- Click the OK button to display the Hyperlink to Slide dialog box (Figure 6–25).

Q&A What are the two items listed in the Slide title area?
They are the title text of the two slides in the Additional Clutter presentation.

Figure 6–25

4

- Click the OK button (Hyperlink to Slide dialog box) to hyperlink the first slide (Documents to Keep, Shred, or Discard) in the Additional Clutter presentation to the Desk picture (Figure 6–26).

5

- Click the OK button (Action Settings dialog box) to apply the new action setting to the Slide 3 picture.

Figure 6–26

Other Ways

1. Select picture, click Hyperlink button (Insert menu | Links group), click 'Existing File or Web Page' (Link to: area), browse to and select desired file, click OK button

2. Right-click picture, click Hyperlink on shortcut menu, click 'Existing File or Web Page' (Link to: area), browse to and select desired file, click OK button

To Hyperlink to a Second Slide in Another PowerPoint File

Another slide in the Additional Clutter presentation gives specific tips on how to begin decluttering a home. This slide might be useful to display during a presentation when a speaker is discussing the information on Slide 4, which describes organizing a kitchen. At this point in the presentation, audience members may be eager to begin the process of organizing, so the techniques shown on this slide could provide a good starting point. If the speaker has time to discuss the material and the audience wants to know these tips, he could click the Kitchen picture on Slide 4 and then hyperlink to Slide 2 in the second presentation. The following steps hyperlink Slide 4 to the second slide in the Additional Clutter presentation.

1 Display Slide 4, select the Kitchen picture, and then click the Action button (Insert tab | Links group) to display the Action Settings dialog box.

2 Click Hyperlink to in the 'Action on click' area, click the Hyperlink to arrow, and then click 'Other PowerPoint Presentation' in the Hyperlink to menu.

3 Click Additional Clutter in the Hyperlink to Other PowerPoint Presentation dialog box to select this file as the hyperlinked presentation and then click the OK button.

4 Click '2. Conquering Clutter Guidelines' (Hyperlink to Slide dialog box) (Figure 6–27).

5 Click the OK button (Hyperlink to Slide dialog box) to hyperlink the second slide in the Additional Clutter presentation to the Kitchen picture.

6 Click the OK button (Action Settings dialog box) to apply the new action setting to the Slide 4 picture.

BTW

Verifying Hyperlinks
Always test your hyperlinks prior to giving a presentation. Web addresses change frequently, so if your hyperlinks are to websites, be certain your Internet connection is working, the websites are active, and that the content on these pages is appropriate for your viewers. If your hyperlinks direct PowerPoint to display specific slides and to open files, click the hyperlinks to verify your desired actions are followed and that the files exist.

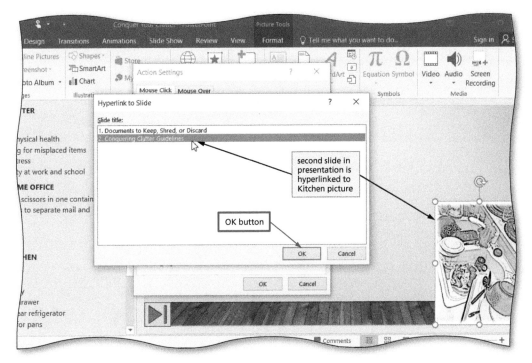

Figure 6–27

To Hyperlink to a Microsoft Word File

Slide 2 in your presentation provides information about problems that can arise from disorganization in the home. Professional organizers recommend keeping a list of reoccurring tasks that should be completed daily, weekly, and monthly. A convenient form for recording these details is located in the Data Files. The file, Conquer Clutter Checklist, was created using Microsoft Word, and it would be useful to display this document when discussing the information on Slide 2 of your presentation. *Why? The checklist can serve as a reminder of which organization tasks have been completed and which need to be done.* PowerPoint allows a speaker to hyperlink to other Microsoft Office documents in a similar manner as linking to another PowerPoint file. The following steps hyperlink the Laundry picture on Slide 2 to the Microsoft Word document with the file name, Conquer Clutter Checklist.

- Display Slide 2, select the Laundry picture, and then click the Action button (Insert tab | Links group) to display the Action Settings dialog box.

- Click Hyperlink to, click the Hyperlink to arrow to display the Hyperlink to menu, and then point to Other File at the end of the Hyperlink to list (Figure 6–28).

Figure 6–28

- Click Other File to display the Hyperlink to Other File dialog box, scroll down, and then click Conquer Clutter Checklist to select this file as the hyperlinked document (Figure 6–29).

Figure 6–29

3
- Click the OK button (Hyperlink to Other File dialog box) to hyperlink this file to the Laundry picture action button (Figure 6–30).

4
- Click the OK button (Action Settings dialog box) to apply the new action setting to the Slide 2 picture.

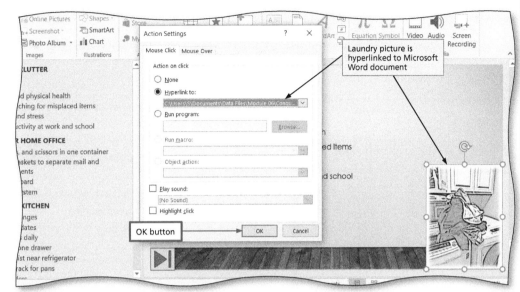

Figure 6–30

To Insert and Format Action Buttons on the Hyperlinked File

The pictures on Slide 3 and Slide 4 hyperlink to slides in the Additional Clutter file. While running the main presentation, if you click an action button or picture link that opens and then displays a slide from another presentation, you may need to review this slide and then return to the previous slide displayed in the first presentation. The Return action button performs this function. The following steps open the Additional Clutter file and then insert and format the Return action button on both slides.

1 In the Backstage view, click the Open command to display the Open pane, navigate to the location of the Data Files, click the File Type arrow to display the File Type list, and then click 'All PowerPoint Presentations' to select this file type.

2 Open the Additional Clutter file located on the Data Files.

3 With Slide 1 displaying, click the Shapes button (Insert tab | Illustrations group) and then scroll down and click the 'Action Button: Return' shape (seventh image).

4 Insert the action button in the lower-right corner of the slide.

5 When the Action Settings dialog box is displayed, select 'Hyperlink to Other PowerPoint Presentation' in the Hyperlink to area to hyperlink the action button to Slide 3 (Organize Your Home Office) in the Conquer Your Clutter presentation.

6 Size the action button so that it is 0.8" x 0.8" and, if necessary, move it to the lower-right corner of the slide.

7 Change the action button fill color to Purple (last color in Standard Colors row).

8 Copy the action button to the same location on Slide 2 (Figure 6–31). Display the Action Settings dialog box and then hyperlink this action button to Slide 4 (Organize Your Kitchen) in the Conquer Your Clutter presentation.

BTW
Showing a Range of Slides
If your presentation consists of many slides, you may want to show only a portion of them in your slide show. For example, if your 30-slide presentation is designed to accompany a 30-minute speech and you are given only 10 minutes to present, you may elect to display only the first 10 slides. Rather than have the show end abruptly after Slide 10, you can elect to show a range of slides. To specify this range, display the Slide Show tab, click the Set Up Slide Show button, and then specify the starting and ending slide numbers in the From and To boxes in the Show slides area (Set Up Show dialog box).

9 Save the Additional Clutter file using the same file name.

10 Close the Additional Clutter file.

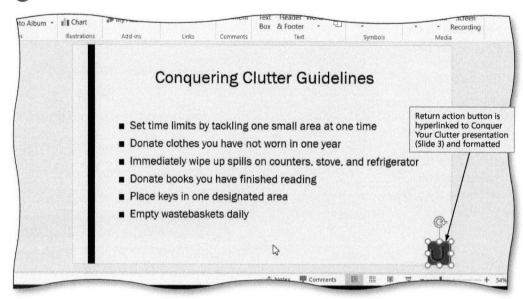

Figure 6–31

Break Point: If you wish to take a break, this is a good place to do so. Be sure to save the Conquer Your Clutter file again and then you can quit PowerPoint. To resume at a later time, start PowerPoint, open the file called Conquer Your Clutter, and continue following the steps from this location forward.

Positioning Slide Elements

BTW

Measurement System
The vertical and horizontal rulers display the units of measurement in inches by default. This measurement system is determined by the settings in Microsoft Windows. You can change the measurement system to centimeters by customizing the numbers format in the 'Clock, Language, and Region' area of the Control Panel. Click Region, click Additional Settings, and then choose the desired measurement system.

At times you may desire to arrange slide elements in precise locations. PowerPoint provides useful tools to help you position shapes and objects on slides. **Drawing guides** are two straight dotted lines, one horizontal and one vertical. When an object is close to a guide, its corner or its center (whichever is closer) **snaps**, or aligns precisely, on top of the guide. You can drag a guide to a new location to meet your alignment requirements. Another tool is the vertical or horizontal **ruler**, which can help you drag an object to a precise location on the slide. The center of a slide is 0.00 on both the vertical and the horizontal rulers.

Aligning and Distributing Objects

If you display multiple objects, PowerPoint can **align** them above and below each other (vertically) or side by side (horizontally). The objects, such as SmartArt graphics, clip art, shapes, boxes, and WordArt, can be aligned relative to the slide so that they display along the top, left, right, or bottom borders or in the center or middle of the slide. They also can be aligned relative to each other, meaning that you position either the first or last object in the desired location and then command PowerPoint to move the remaining objects in the series above, below, or beside it. Depending on the alignment option that you click, objects will move straight up, down, left, or right, and might cover an object already located on the slide. Table 6–2 describes alignment options.

Table 6–2 Alignment Options

Alignment	Action
Left	Aligns the edges of the objects to the left
Center	Aligns the objects vertically through the centers of the objects
Right	Aligns the edges of the objects to the right
Top	Aligns the top edges of the objects
Middle	Aligns the objects horizontally through the middles of the objects
Bottom	Aligns the bottom edges of the objects
to Slide	Aligns one object to the slide

One object remains stationary when you align objects relative to each other by their edges. For example, Align Left aligns the left edges of all selected objects with the left edge of the leftmost object. The leftmost object remains stationary, and the other objects are aligned relative to it. Objects aligned to a SmartArt graphic are aligned to the leftmost edge of the SmartArt graphic, not to the leftmost shape in the SmartArt graphic. Objects aligned relative to each other by their middles or centers are aligned along a horizontal or vertical line that represents the average of their original positions. All of the objects might move.

Smart Guides appear automatically when two or more shapes are in spatial alignment with each other, even if the shapes vary in size. To evenly space multiple objects horizontally or vertically, you **distribute** them. PowerPoint determines the total length between either the outermost edges of the first and last selected object or the edges of the entire slide. It then inserts equal spacing among the items in the series. You also can distribute spacing by using the Size and Position dialog box, but the Distribute command automates this task.

BTW
Displaying Slides
The slides in this presentation have important information about home organization. Your audience needs time to read and contemplate the advice you are providing in the content placeholders, so you must display the slides for a sufficient amount of time. Some public speaking experts recommend each slide in a presentation should display for at least one minute so that audience members can look at the material, focus on the speaker, and then refer to the slide again.

To Display Slide Thumbnails in the Slides Tab

The major slide elements are inserted on all slides, and you next will arrange these essential features. It is easier to move and align these elements when the main Slide pane is large. The following step changes the view from Outline view to Normal view.

1 Display the View tab and then click the Normal button (View tab | Presentation Views group) to display the slide thumbnails in the Slides tab.

2 If the Notes pane is displayed, click the Notes button on the status bar to close the Notes pane.

To Display the Drawing Guides

1 OPEN OUTLINE | 2 ADD PICTURE & TEXT HYPERLINKS | 3 ADD ACTION BUTTONS & HYPERLINKS
4 POSITION PICTURES | **5 ALIGN PLACEHOLDER TEXT** | 6 CONVERT & FORMAT BULLETS

Why? *Guides help you align objects on slides.* Using a mouse, when you point to a guide and then press and hold the mouse button, PowerPoint displays a box containing the exact position of the guide on the slide in inches. An arrow is displayed below the guide position to indicate the vertical guide either left or right of center. An arrow also is displayed to the right of the guide position to indicate the horizontal guide either above or below center. The following step displays the guides.

● Display Slide 2 of the Conquer Your Clutter presentation and then click the Guides check box (View tab | Show group) to display the horizontal and vertical guides (Figure 6–32).

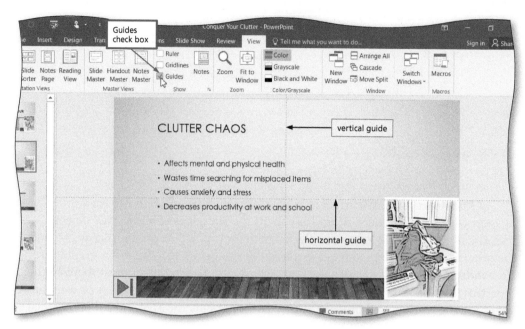

Figure 6–32

Other Ways

1. Right-click area of slide other than a placeholder or object, point to 'Grid and Guides' on shortcut menu, click Guides

2. Press ALT+F9 to toggle guides on/off

To Position a Picture Using Guides

1 OPEN OUTLINE | 2 ADD PICTURE & TEXT HYPERLINKS | 3 ADD ACTION BUTTONS & HYPERLINKS
4 POSITION PICTURES | 5 ALIGN PLACEHOLDER TEXT | 6 CONVERT & FORMAT BULLETS

The upper edge of the three pictures on Slides 2, 3, and 4 should be displayed in precisely the same location, as should the left edge of the pictures on Slides 2 and 4. *Why? They will appear static as you transition from one slide to the next during the slide show.* The following steps position the picture on Slide 2.

● Position the pointer on the horizontal guide in a blank area of the slide so that the pointer changes to a double-headed arrow and then drag the horizontal guide to 0.25 inches below the center. Do not release the mouse button (Figure 6–33).

Q&A Why does 0.25 display when I hold down the mouse button? The ScreenTip

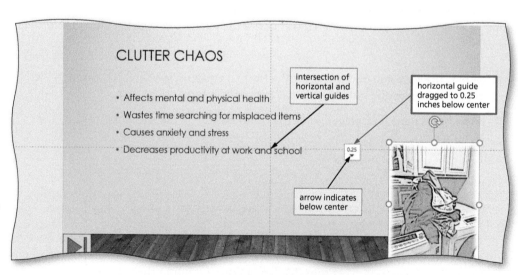

Figure 6–33

displays the horizontal guide's position. A 0.00 setting means that the guide is precisely in the middle of the slide and is not above or below the center, so a .25 setting indicates the guide is 1/4-inch below the center line.

2

- Release the mouse button to position the horizontal guide at 0.25, which is the intended location of the picture's top border.

- Position the pointer on the vertical guide in a blank area of the slide so that the pointer changes to a double-headed arrow and then drag the vertical guide to 2.50 inches right of the center to position the vertical guide.

- Drag the picture so the upper-left corner touches the intersection of the vertical and horizontal guides to position the picture in the desired location (Figure 6–34).

Figure 6–34

Q&A Can I add guides to help me align multiple objects?
Yes. Position the pointer over one guide and then press the CTRL key. When you drag your pointer, a second guide appears.

To Position the Slide 4 and Slide 3 Pictures

The pictures on Slide 4 and Slide 3 should be positioned in the same location as the Slide 2 picture. The guides will display in the same location as you display each slide, so you easily can align similar objects on multiple slides. The following steps position the pictures on Slide 4 and Slide 3.

1 Display Slide 4 and then drag the picture so the upper-left corner of the Kitchen picture touches the intersection of the guides.

2 Display Slide 3 and use the guides to position the Desk picture (Figure 6–35).

BTW
Drawing Guides and Touch Screens
If you are using a touch screen, you may not be able to change the position of the drawing guides. In addition, the measurements indicating the position of the guides are not displayed.

ANIZE YOUR HOME OFFICE

s, pencils, and scissors in one container
nd out baskets to separate mail and important documents
a bulletin board
p a filing system

upper-left corner of picture dragged to guide intersection

Figure 6–35

To Hide Guides

The three pictures on Slides 2, 3, and 4 are positioned in the desired locations, so the guides no longer are needed. The following step hides the guides.

1 If necessary, display the View tab and then click the Guides check box (View tab | Show group) to clear the check mark.

Other Ways

1. Right-click area of slide other than a placeholder or object, click Grid and Guides on shortcut menu, click Guides to turn off Guides

2. Press ALT+F9 to toggle guides on/off

To Display the Rulers

1 OPEN OUTLINE | 2 ADD PICTURE & TEXT HYPERLINKS | 3 ADD ACTION BUTTONS & HYPERLINKS
4 POSITION PICTURES | 5 ALIGN PLACEHOLDER TEXT | 6 CONVERT & FORMAT BULLETS

Why? *To begin aligning the three Slide 1 objects, you need to position either the left or the right object.* The vertical or horizontal **ruler** can help you drag an object to a precise location on the slide. The center of a slide is 0.00 on both the vertical and the horizontal rulers. The following step displays the rulers.

1

- If necessary, display the View tab and then click the Ruler check box (View tab | Show group) to display the vertical and horizontal rulers (Figure 6–36).

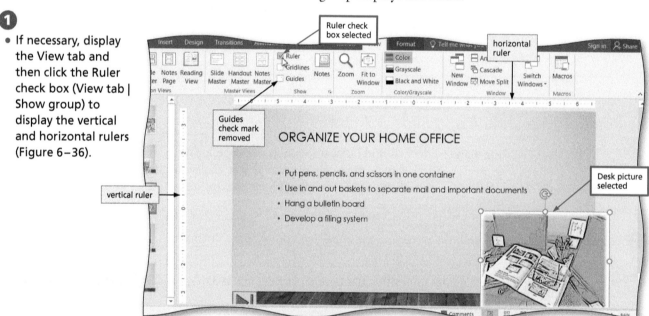

Figure 6–36

Other Ways

1. Right-click area of slide other than a placeholder or object, click Ruler

2. Press SHIFT+ALT+F9 to toggle ruler on/off

To Align Pictures

1 OPEN OUTLINE | 2 ADD PICTURE & TEXT HYPERLINKS | 3 ADD ACTION BUTTONS & HYPERLINKS
4 POSITION PICTURES | 5 ALIGN PLACEHOLDER TEXT | 6 CONVERT & FORMAT BULLETS

Why? *The three pictures on Slide 1 will look balanced if the bottom edges are aligned.* One method of creating this orderly appearance is by dragging the borders to a guide. Another method that is useful when you have multiple objects is to use one of PowerPoint's align commands. On Slide 1, you will position the far left picture of the Laundry and then align its bottom edge with those of the Desk and Kitchen pictures. The following steps align the Slide 1 pictures.

1

- Display Slide 1 and then position the pointer over the clothes pile in the Laundry picture.

- Drag the picture so that the center of the clothes pile is positioned approximately 5½ inches left of the center and approximately 2 inches below the center so that the bottom of the picture aligns with the bottom of the slide (Figure 6–37).

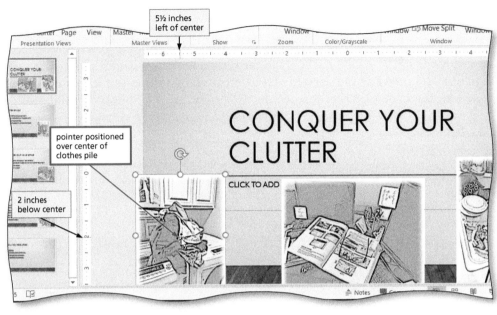

Figure 6–37

2

- Position the pointer over the pencils in the Desk picture.

- Drag the Desk picture so the pencils are positioned approximately 1 inch right of the center and approximately 1½ inches below the center so that the bottom of the picture aligns with the bottom of the slide and the Laundry picture (Figure 6–38).

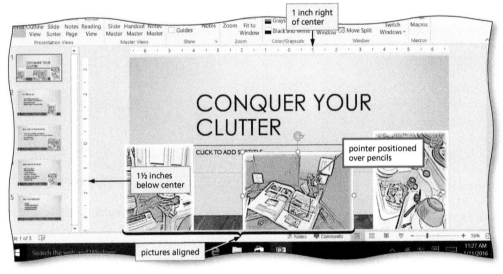

Figure 6–38

3

- Position the pointer over the faucet in the Kitchen picture.

- Drag the Kitchen picture so the faucet is positioned approximately 5 inches right of the center and approximately 3/4 inch below the center bottom of the picture aligns with the bottom of the slide and the other pictures (Figure 6–39).

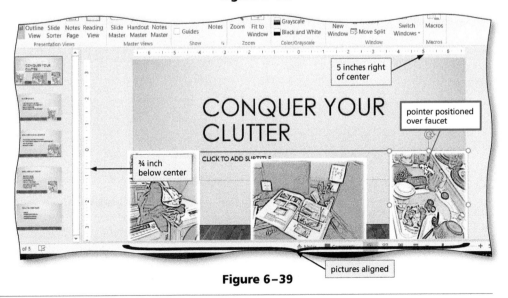

Figure 6–39

To Distribute Pictures

Now that the three Slide 1 pictures are aligned, you can have PowerPoint place the same amount of space between the first and second pictures and the second and third pictures. You have two distribution options: 'Align to Slide' spaces all the selected objects evenly across the entire width of the slide; 'Align Selected Objects' spaces only the middle objects between the fixed right and left objects. The following steps use the 'Align to Slide' option. *Why? This option will distribute the Slide 1 pictures horizontally to fill some of the space along the bottom of the slide.*

1

- Select the three Slide 1 pictures, display the Picture Tools Format tab, and then click the Align Objects button (Picture Tools Format tab | Arrange group) to display the Align Objects menu.

2

- If necessary, click 'Align to Slide' so that PowerPoint will adjust the spacing of the pictures evenly between the slide edges and then click the Align button to display the Align menu again (Figure 6–40).

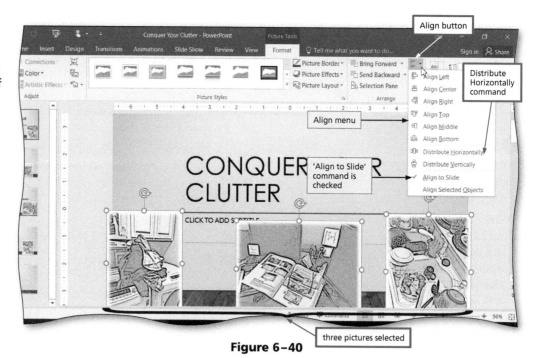

Figure 6–40

3

- Click Distribute Horizontally to adjust the spacing (Figure 6–41).

Figure 6–41

To Hide Rulers

The three pictures on Slide 1 are positioned in the desired locations, so the rulers no longer need to display. The following step hides the rulers.

1 Display the View tab and then click the Ruler check box (View tab | Show group) to remove the check mark.

Other Ways

1. Right-click area of slide other than a placeholder or object, click Ruler
2. Press SHIFT+ALT+F9 to toggle ruler on/off

Hiding a Slide

Slides 2, 3, and 4 present a variety of organizing information with hyperlinks. Depending on the audience's needs and the time constraints, you may decide not to display one or more of these slides. If need be, you can use the **Hide Slide** command to hide a slide from the audience during the normal running of a slide show. When you want to display the hidden slide, press the H key. No visible indicator displays to show that a hidden slide exists. You must be aware of the content of the presentation to know where the hidden slide is located.

When you run your presentation, the hidden slide does not display unless you press the H key when the slide preceding the hidden slide is displaying. For example, if you choose to hide Slide 4, then Slide 4 will not display unless you press the H key when Slide 3 displays in Slide Show view.

To Hide a Slide

1 OPEN OUTLINE | 2 ADD PICTURE & TEXT HYPERLINKS | 3 ADD ACTION BUTTONS & HYPERLINKS
4 POSITION PICTURES | **5 ALIGN PLACEHOLDER TEXT** | 6 CONVERT & FORMAT BULLETS

Slide 4 discusses tips for organizing a kitchen. As the presenter, you decide whether to show Slide 4. *Why?* *If time permits, or if the audience requires information on this subject, you can display Slide 4.* When you hide a slide in Slide Sorter view, a slash appears through the slide number, which indicates the slide is hidden. The following steps hide Slide 4.

- Click the Slide Sorter view button on the status bar to display the slide thumbnails.

- Click Slide Show on the ribbon to display the Slide Show tab and then click the Slide 4 thumbnail to select it (Figure 6–42).

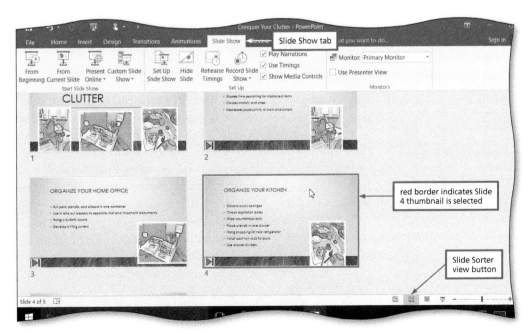

Figure 6–42

2

• Click the Hide Slide button (Slide Show tab | Set Up group) to hide Slide 4 (Figure 6–43).

Q&A How do I know that Slide 4 is hidden?
The slide number has a slash through it to indicate Slide 4 is a hidden slide.

What if I decide I no longer want to hide a slide?
Repeat Step 2. The Hide Slide button is a toggle; it either hides or displays a slide.

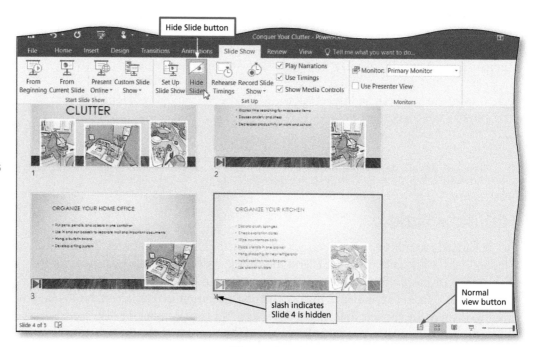

Figure 6–43

3

• Click the Normal view button to display Slide 4.

Other Ways
1. Right-click desired slide in Slide Sorter view or Normal view on Slides tab, click Hide Slide on shortcut menu

Break Point: If you wish to take a break, this is a good place to do so. Be sure to save the Conquer Your Clutter file again and then you can quit PowerPoint. To resume at a later time, start PowerPoint, open the file called Conquer Your Clutter, and continue following the steps from this location forward.

Modifying Placeholder Text Settings

BTW
Saving the Presentation as an Outline
You began this project by opening a Microsoft Word outline, and you can save the presentation as an outline to use in a word processor or another PowerPoint project. An outline is saved in Rich Text Format (.rtf) and contains only text. To save the presentation as an outline, open the Backstage view, click the Save As tab, navigate to the save location and type a file name in the File name box (Save As dialog box), click the 'Save as type' arrow and select Outline/RTF in the 'Save as type' list, and then click the Save button.

The PowerPoint design themes specify default alignment of and spacing for text within a placeholder. For example, the text in most paragraphs is **left-aligned**, so the first character of each line is even with the first character above or below it. Text alignment also can be horizontally **centered** to position each line evenly between the left and right placeholder edges; **right-aligned**, so that the last character of each line is even with the last character of each line above or below it; and **justified**, where the first and last characters of each line are aligned and extra space is inserted between words to spread the characters evenly across the line.

When you begin typing text in most placeholders, the first paragraph is aligned at the top of the placeholder with any extra space at the bottom. You can change this default **paragraph alignment** location to position the paragraph lines centered vertically between the top and bottom placeholder edges, or you can place the last line at the bottom of the placeholder so that any extra space is at the top.

The design theme also determines the amount of spacing around the sides of the placeholder and between the lines of text. An internal **margin** provides a cushion of space between text and the top, bottom, left, and right sides of the placeholder. **Line spacing** is the amount of vertical space between the lines of text in a paragraph, and **paragraph spacing** is the amount of space above and below a paragraph. PowerPoint adjusts the line spacing and paragraph spacing automatically to accommodate various font sizes within the placeholder.

Long lists of items can be divided into several **columns** to fill the placeholder width and maximize the slide space. Once you have created columns, you can adjust the amount of space between the columns to enhance readability.

To Center Placeholder Text

1 OPEN OUTLINE | 2 ADD PICTURE & TEXT HYPERLINKS | 3 ADD ACTION BUTTONS & HYPERLINKS
4 POSITION PICTURES | **5 ALIGN PLACEHOLDER TEXT** | **6 CONVERT & FORMAT BULLETS**

By default, all placeholder text in the Gallery document theme is left-aligned. You want the text to be centered, or placed with equal space horizontally between the left and right placeholder edges, on some slides. *Why? Changing the alignment adds variety to the slide deck.* The following steps center the text in the content placeholders on Slides 2, 3, and 5.

- Display Slide 2 and then select the four paragraphs in the content placeholder (Figure 6–44).

Figure 6–44

- Click the Center button on the mini toolbar (shown in Figure 6–44) to center these paragraphs (Figure 6–45).

- Repeat Steps 1 and 2 to center the paragraph text in the content placeholders on Slides 3 and 5. Do not center the paragraph text on Slide 4.

Figure 6–45

Q&A Why is the Slide 4 text not centered?
Later in this project you will split this text into two columns.

Other Ways

| 1. Click Center button (Home tab \| Paragraph group) | 2. Right-click selected text, click Paragraph on shortcut menu, click Alignment arrow (Paragraph dialog box), click Centered, click OK button | 3. Click Paragraph Dialog Box Launcher (Home tab \| Paragraph group), click Alignment arrow (Paragraph dialog box), click Centered, click OK button | 4. Press CTRL+E |

To Align Placeholder Text

The Gallery document theme aligns the text paragraphs at the top of the content placeholders. This default setting can be changed easily so that the paragraphs are aligned in the center or at the bottom of the placeholder. The following steps align the paragraphs vertically in the center of the content placeholders on Slides 4 and 5. *Why? The slides have a large amount of blank space, so centering the paragraphs vertically will fill some of this area and increase readability.*

1

- With the Slide 5 paragraphs still selected, display the Home tab and then click the Align Text button (Home tab | Paragraph group) to display the Align Text gallery.

- Point to Middle in the Align Text gallery to display a live preview of the paragraphs aligned in the center of the content placeholder (Figure 6–46).

Figure 6–46

 Experiment

- Point to the Bottom option in the gallery to see a preview of that alignment.

2

- Click Middle in the Align Text gallery to align the paragraphs vertically in the center of the content placeholder (Figure 6–47).

Q&A What is the difference between centering the paragraphs in the placeholder and centering the text?
Clicking the Align Text button and then clicking Middle moves the paragraphs up or down so that the first and last paragraphs are equal distances from the top and bottom placeholder borders. The Center button, on the other hand, moves the paragraphs left or right so that the first and last words in each line are equal distances from the left and right box borders.

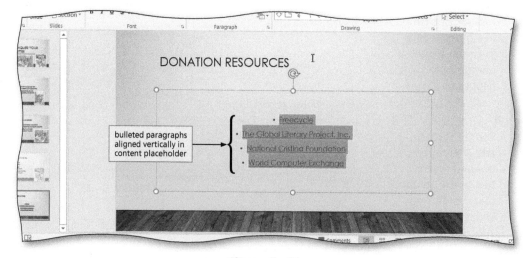

Figure 6–47

3

- Repeat Steps 1 and 2 to center the paragraph text in the middle of the content placeholder on Slide 4.

To Change Paragraph Line Spacing

The vertical space between lines of text is called **line spacing**. PowerPoint adjusts the amount of space based on font size. Default line spacing is 1.0, which is considered single spacing. Other preset options are 1.5, 2.0 (double spacing), 2.5, and 3.0 (triple spacing). You can specify precise line spacing intervals between, before, and after paragraphs in the Indents and Spacing tab of the Paragraph dialog box. The following steps increase the line spacing of the content paragraphs from single (1.0) to double (2.0) on Slides 2, 3, and 5. *Why?* *The additional space helps fill some of the area on the slide and also helps your audience read the paragraph text more easily.*

1
- With the Home tab displayed, display Slide 2 and select the four content paragraphs.

- Click the Line Spacing button (Home tab | Paragraph group) to display the Line Spacing gallery.

- Point to 2.0 in the Line Spacing gallery to display a live preview of this line spacing (Figure 6–48).

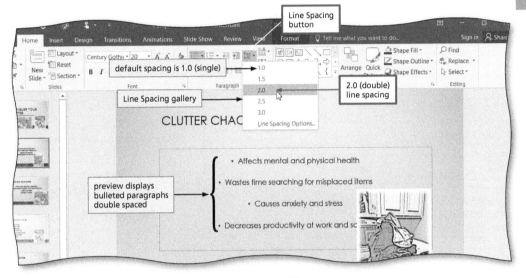

Figure 6–48

Experiment
- Point to each of the line spacing options in the gallery to see a preview of that line spacing.

2
- Click 2.0 in the Line Spacing gallery to change the line spacing to double.

3
- Repeat Steps 1 and 2 to change the line spacing to 2.0 for the paragraph text in the content placeholders on Slides 3 and 5. Do not change the line spacing on Slide 4.

◄ | Why is the line spacing not changing on Slide 4?
Q&A | These content placeholder paragraphs will be changed into columns, so spacing is not a design concern at this time.

4
- Move the Laundry picture on Slide 2 to the right so that it does not overlap the text in the last bulleted paragraph.

Other Ways
1. Right-click selected text, click Paragraph on shortcut menu, click Line Spacing arrow (Paragraph dialog box), click Double, click OK button	2. Click Paragraph Dialog Box Launcher (Home tab | Paragraph group), click Line Spacing arrow (Paragraph dialog box), click Double, click OK button

To Create Columns in a Placeholder

Why? *The list of organizing tips in the Slide 4 placeholder is lengthy and lacks visual appeal.* You can change these items into two, three, or more columns and then adjust the column widths. The following steps change the placeholder elements into columns.

- Display Slide 4 and then click the content placeholder to select it.

- With the Home tab displayed, click the 'Add or Remove Columns' button (Home tab | Paragraph group) to display the Columns gallery (Figure 6–49).

 Experiment

- Point to each of the column options in the gallery to see a preview of the text displaying in various columns.

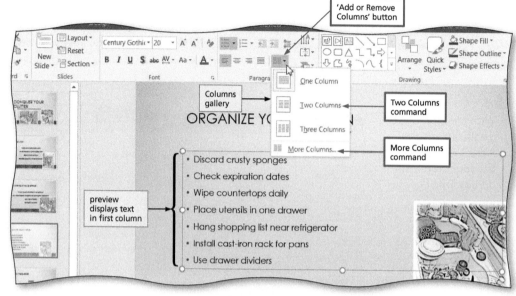

Figure 6–49

Q&A Why doesn't the content display in two columns if I pointed to two columns?
Because all the text fits in the first column in the placeholder.

- Click Two Columns to create two columns of text.

- Drag the bottom sizing handle up to the location shown in Figure 6–50.

Q&A Why is the bottom sizing handle between the fourth and fifth paragraphs?
Seven organization tips are listed in the content placeholder, so dividing the paragraphs in two groups will help balance the layout.

Figure 6–50

- Release the mouse button to resize the content placeholder and create the two columns of text.

Other Ways

1. Right-click placeholder, click Format Shape, click Text Options (Format Shape pane), click Textbox button, click Columns button, enter number of columns in Number box

To Adjust Column Spacing

Why? The space between the columns in the placeholder can be increased to make room for the Kitchen picture, which *you want to move between the columns.* The following steps increase the spacing between the columns.

1

- With the placeholder selected, click the 'Add or Remove Columns' button and then click More Columns.

- Click the Spacing box up arrow (Columns dialog box) until 3.5" is displayed (Figure 6–51).

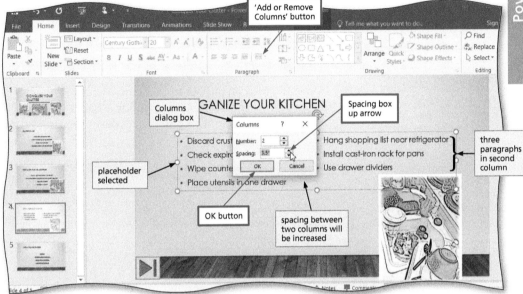

Figure 6–51

2

- Click the OK button to increase the spacing between the columns (Figure 6–52).

 Why did the font size decrease when I increased the spacing between columns? PowerPoint automatically adjusts placeholder text to fit in columns with specified spacing.

Can I change the paragraphs back to one column easily? Yes. Click the Columns button and then click One Column.

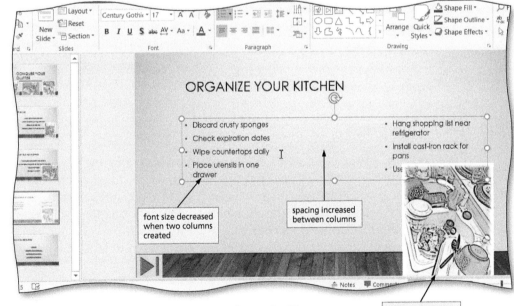

Figure 6–52

Other Ways

1. Right-click placeholder, click Format Shape, click Text Options (Format Shape pane), click Textbox, click Columns button, enter space between columns in Spacing box

To Format the Content Placeholder

BTW

Conserving Ink and Toner
If you want to conserve ink or toner, you can instruct PowerPoint to print draft quality documents by clicking File on the ribbon to open the Backstage view, clicking the Options tab in the Backstage view to display the PowerPoint Options dialog box, clicking Advanced in the left pane (PowerPoint Options dialog box), scrolling to the Print area in the right pane, placing a check mark in the 'Use draft quality' check box, and then clicking the OK button. Then, use the Backstage view to print the document as usual.

To add interest to the Slide 4 content placeholder, apply a Quick Style and then move the Kitchen picture from the lower-right corner to the space between the columns. The following steps apply a purple Subtle Effect style to the placeholder and then change the picture location.

1 With the placeholder selected, click the Quick Styles button (Home tab | Drawing group) to display the Quick Styles gallery.

2 Click 'Subtle Effect – Purple, Accent 4' (fifth style in fourth row).

3 Move the Kitchen picture from the lower-right corner to the area between the two columns so that a vertical Smart Guide is displayed in the center of the picture and a horizontal Smart Guide is displayed below the picture (Figure 6–53).

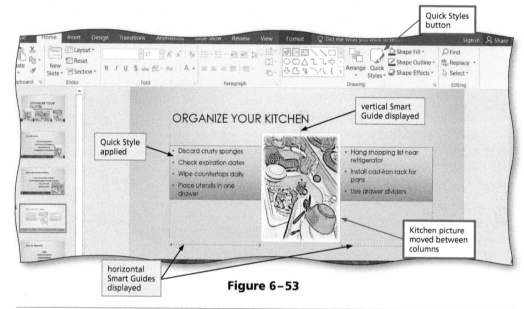

Figure 6–53

To Enter a Line Break

1 OPEN OUTLINE | 2 ADD PICTURE & TEXT HYPERLINKS | 3 ADD ACTION BUTTONS & HYPERLINKS
4 POSITION PICTURES | 5 ALIGN PLACEHOLDER TEXT | 6 CONVERT & FORMAT BULLETS

Why? *The second paragraph in Slide 3 in your presentation is lengthy and extends above the Desk picture. Separating the paragraph after the word, mail, can emphasize the fact that baskets serve two separate functions: one for mail and documents that need attention, and the other for items that have been addressed.* If you press the ENTER key at the end of a line, PowerPoint automatically applies paragraph formatting, which could include indents and bullets. To prevent this formatting from occurring, you can press SHIFT+ENTER to place a **line break** at the end of the line, which moves the insertion point to the beginning of the next line. The following steps place a line break before the word, and, on Slide 3.

- Display Slide 3 and then place the insertion point before the word, and, (after the word, mail) in the second paragraph (Figure 6–54).

Figure 6–54

- Press SHIFT+ENTER to insert a line
break character and move the
words, and important documents,
to the third line in the placeholder
(Figure 6–55).

Figure 6–55

Modifying Bullets

PowerPoint allows you to change the default appearance of bullets in a slide show.
The document themes determine the bullet character. A **bullet character** is a symbol,
traditionally a closed circle, that sets off items in a list. It can be a predefined style, a
variety of fonts and characters displayed in the Symbol gallery, or a picture from a file
or from Office.com. You may want to change a bullet character to add visual interest
and variety. Once you change the bullet character, you also can change its size and color.

If desired, you can change every bullet in a presentation to a unique character.
If your presentation has many bulleted slides, however, you would want to have a
consistent look on all slides by making the bullets a similar color and size.

To customize your presentation, you can change the default slide layout bullets
to numbers by changing the bulleted list to a numbered list. PowerPoint provides a
variety of numbering options, including Arabic and Roman numerals. These numbers
can be sized and recolored, and the starting number can be something other than 1 or I.
In addition, PowerPoint's numbering options include upper- and lower-case letters.

BTW
**Printing Document
Properties**
PowerPoint 2016 does not
allow you to print document
properties. This feature,
however, is available in other
Office 2016 apps, including
Word and Excel.

To Change a Bullet Character to a Picture

1 OPEN OUTLINE | 2 ADD PICTURE & TEXT HYPERLINKS | 3 ADD ACTION BUTTONS & HYPERLINKS
4 POSITION PICTURES | 5 ALIGN PLACEHOLDER TEXT | **6 CONVERT & FORMAT BULLETS**

Why? *The plain bullet characters for the Gallery document theme do not add much visual interest and do not relate
to the topic of chaos that can result from disorganization.* One method of modifying these bullets is to use a relevant
picture. The following steps change the first paragraph bullet character to the Sad Face picture, which is located
in the Data Files.

- Display Slide 2. With the Home
tab still displaying, select all four
content placeholder paragraphs.

Q&A | Can I insert a different bullet
character in each paragraph?
Yes. Select only a paragraph and
then perform the steps below for
each paragraph.

- Click the Bullets arrow (Home tab |
Paragraph group) to display the
Bullets gallery (Figure 6–56).

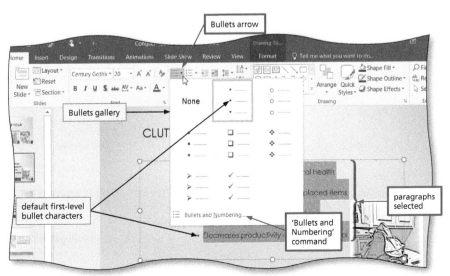

Figure 6–56

Q&A
What should I do if I clicked the Bullets button instead of the Bullets arrow?
If the paragraphs are bulleted, clicking the Bullets button removes the bullets. Click the Bullets button again to display the bullets.

Why is a gray box displayed around the three characters?
They are the default first-level bullet characters for the Gallery document theme.

Experiment

- Point to each of the bullets displayed in the gallery to see a preview of the characters.

2

- Click 'Bullets and Numbering' to display the Bullets and Numbering dialog box (Figure 6–57).

Q&A
Why are my bullets different from those displayed in Figure 6–57?
The bullets most recently inserted are displayed as the first items in the dialog box.

Figure 6–57

3

- Click the Picture button (Bullets and Numbering dialog box) to display the Insert Pictures dialog box (Figure 6–58).

Figure 6–58

- Click the Browse button in the 'From a file' area (Insert Pictures dialog box) to display the Insert Picture dialog box.

- If necessary, navigate to the location of the Data Files.

- Scroll down and then click Sad Face to select the file (Figure 6–59).

Figure 6–59

- Click the Insert button (Insert Picture dialog box) to insert the Sad Face picture as the paragraph bullet character (Figure 6–60).

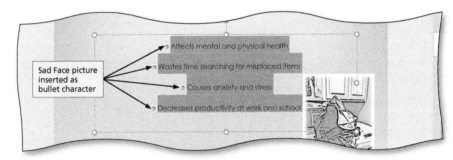

Figure 6–60

Other Ways

1. Right-click paragraph, point to Bullets on shortcut menu, click 'Bullets and Numbering'

To Change a Bullet Character to a Symbol

1 OPEN OUTLINE | 2 ADD PICTURE & TEXT HYPERLINKS | 3 ADD ACTION BUTTONS & HYPERLINKS
4 POSITION PICTURES | 5 ALIGN PLACEHOLDER TEXT | 6 CONVERT & FORMAT BULLETS

Why? *For variety and to add a unique characteristic to the presentation, another bullet change you can make is to insert a symbol as the character.* Symbols are found in several fonts, including Webdings, Wingdings, Wingdings 2, and Wingdings 3. These fonts are available when slides have themes other than the Office theme. The following steps change the bullet character on Slide 5 to a question mark symbol.

- Display Slide 5, select all four hyperlinked paragraphs, click the Bullets arrow (Home tab | Paragraph group), and then click 'Bullets and Numbering' to display the Bullets and Numbering dialog box (Figure 6–61).

Figure 6–61

2

- Click the Customize button (Bullets and Numbering dialog box) to display the Symbol dialog box (Figure 6–62).

Q&A

Why is a symbol selected?

That symbol is the default bullet for the first-level paragraphs in the Gallery document theme.

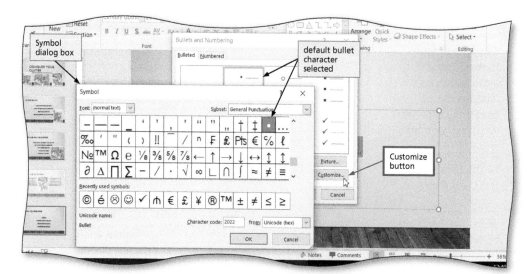

Figure 6–62

3

- Scroll up to locate the question mark symbol.

- Click the question mark symbol to select it (Figure 6–63).

Q&A

Why does my dialog box have more rows of symbols and different fonts from which to choose?

The rows and fonts displayed depend upon how PowerPoint was installed on your system and the screen you are viewing.

Figure 6–63

What is the character code that is displayed in the Symbol dialog box?

Each character in each font has a unique code. If you know the character code, you can type the number in the Character code box to display that symbol. The character code for the question mark symbol is 003F.

4

- Click the OK button (Symbol dialog box) to display the question mark bullet in the Bullets and Numbering dialog box (Figure 6–64).

Figure 6–64

- Click the OK button (Bullets and Numbering dialog box) to insert the question mark symbol as the paragraph bullet (Figure 6–65).

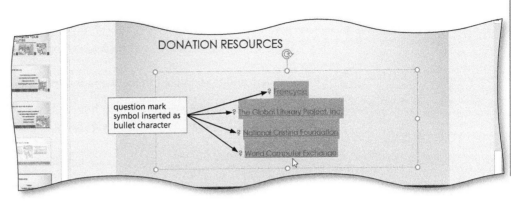

Figure 6–65

To Change Bullet Size

1 OPEN OUTLINE | 2 ADD PICTURE & TEXT HYPERLINKS | 3 ADD ACTION BUTTONS & HYPERLINKS
4 POSITION PICTURES | 5 ALIGN PLACEHOLDER TEXT | 6 CONVERT & FORMAT BULLETS

Bullets have a default size determined by the document theme. **Bullet size** is measured as a percentage of the text size and can range from 25 to 400 percent. The following steps change the question mark symbol size. *Why? It is difficult to see the symbol, so increasing its size draws attention to the visual element.*

- With the Slide 5 paragraphs still selected, click the Bullets arrow (Home tab | Paragraph group) and then click 'Bullets and Numbering' in the Bullets gallery to display the Bullets and Numbering dialog box.

- Set the size in the Size box to 150 (Figure 6–66).

Figure 6–66

- Click the OK button to increase the question mark bullet size to 150 percent of its original size (Figure 6–67).

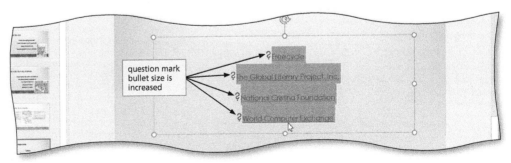

Figure 6–67

To Change the Size of Other Bullet Characters

For consistency, the bullet character on Slide 2 should have a similar size as that on Slide 5. The following steps change the size of the Sad Face bullets.

1 Display Slide 2 and then select the four paragraphs in the content placeholder.

2 Display the Bullets and Numbering dialog box, increase the bullet size to 150% of text size, and then click the OK button (Figure 6–68).

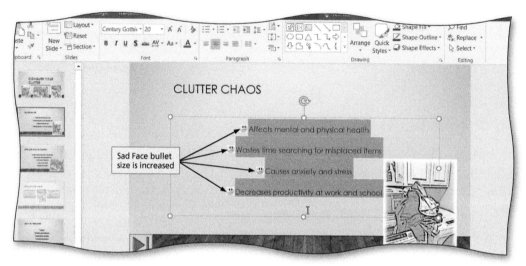

Figure 6–68

To Format Bullet Color

1 OPEN OUTLINE | 2 ADD PICTURE & TEXT HYPERLINKS | 3 ADD ACTION BUTTONS & HYPERLINKS
4 POSITION PICTURES | 5 ALIGN PLACEHOLDER TEXT | **6 CONVERT & FORMAT BULLETS**

A default **bullet color** is based on the eight colors in the design theme. Additional standard and custom colors also are available. The following steps change the question mark bullet color to Purple. *Why? This color coordinates with the action buttons and the Quick Style on Slide 4.*

- Display Slide 5, select the four hyperlinked paragraphs, display the Bullets and Numbering dialog box, and then click the Color button (Bullets and Numbering dialog box) to display the Color gallery (Figure 6–69).

Figure 6–69

2

- Click the color Purple in the Standard Colors area to change the bullet color to Purple (last color in Standard Colors row) (Figure 6–70).

Figure 6–70

3

- Click the OK button (Bullets and Numbering dialog box) to apply the color Purple to the question mark bullets (Figure 6–71).

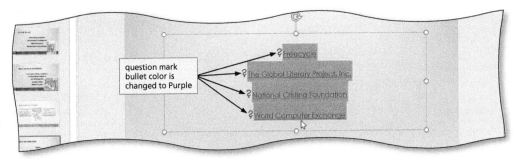

Figure 6–71

Other Ways

1. Right-click paragraph, point to Bullets on shortcut menu, click Bullets and Numbering, select color

To Change a Bullet Character to a Number

1 OPEN OUTLINE | 2 ADD PICTURE & TEXT HYPERLINKS | 3 ADD ACTION BUTTONS & HYPERLINKS | 4 POSITION PICTURES | 5 ALIGN PLACEHOLDER TEXT | **6 CONVERT & FORMAT BULLETS**

PowerPoint allows you to change the default bullets to numbers. The process of changing the bullet characters is similar to the process of adding bullets to paragraphs. The following steps change the first-level paragraph bullet characters on Slide 3 to numbers. *Why? Numbers help to show steps in a sequence and also help guide a speaker during the presentation when referring to specific information in the paragraphs.*

1

- Display Slide 3 and then select all content paragraphs.

- With the Home tab still displaying, click the Numbering arrow (Home tab | Paragraph group) to display the Numbering gallery.

- Point to the 1) 2) 3) numbering option in the Numbering gallery to display a live preview of these numbers (Figure 6–72).

Figure 6–72

Experiment

- Point to each of the numbers in the Numbering gallery to watch the numbers change on Slide 3.

2

- Click the 1) 2) 3) numbering option to insert these numbers as the first-level paragraph characters (Figure 6–73).

Q&A How do I change the first number in the list?
Click 'Bullets and Numbering' at the bottom of the Numbering gallery and then click the up or down arrow in the Start at box to change the number.

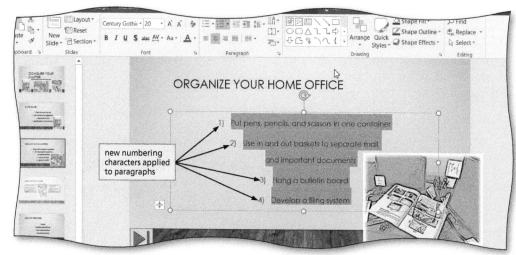

Figure 6–73

Other Ways

1. Right-click paragraph, point to Numbering on shortcut menu, select numbering characters

To Format a Numbered List

1 OPEN OUTLINE | 2 ADD PICTURE & TEXT HYPERLINKS | 3 ADD ACTION BUTTONS & HYPERLINKS
4 POSITION PICTURES | 5 ALIGN PLACEHOLDER TEXT | 6 CONVERT & FORMAT BULLETS

Why? *To add emphasis, you can increase the size of the new numbers inserted in Slide 3.* As with bullets, numbering characters are measured as a percentage of the text size and can range from 25 to 400 percent. The color of these numbers also can change. The original color is based on the eight colors in the design theme. Additional standard and custom colors are available. The following steps change the size and color of the numbers to 125 percent and Purple, respectively.

1

- With the Slide 3 content paragraphs still selected, click the Numbering arrow (Home tab | Paragraph group) to display the Numbering gallery and then click 'Bullets and Numbering' to display the Bullets and Numbering dialog box.

- Change the numbers' size in the Size box to 125% of text size.

2

- Click the Color button (Bullets and Numbering dialog box) to display the color gallery and then click Purple to change the numbers' font color (Figure 6–74).

Figure 6–74

- Click the OK button (Bullets and Numbering dialog box) to apply the new numbers' font size and color.

Other Ways

1. Right-click paragraph, point to Numbering on shortcut menu, click 'Bullets and Numbering', click up or down Size arrow until desired size is displayed, click Color button, select color, click OK button

To Remove Bullet Characters

1 OPEN OUTLINE │ 2 ADD PICTURE & TEXT HYPERLINKS │ 3 ADD ACTION BUTTONS & HYPERLINKS
4 POSITION PICTURES │ 5 ALIGN PLACEHOLDER TEXT │ **6 CONVERT & FORMAT BULLETS**

The organization tips listed in the two Slide 4 columns are preceded by a bullet character. The following steps remove the bullet characters from the items in the two columns on Slide 4. *Why? The slide may appear less cluttered if you remove the bullets.*

- Display Slide 4, select all the text in the two columns, and then click the Bullets arrow (Home tab | Paragraph group).

- Point to the None option in the Bullets gallery to display a live preview of how the slide will appear without bullets (Figure 6–75).

- Click the None option to remove the bullet characters on Slide 4.

Figure 6–75

Q&A | Would I use the same technique to remove numbers from a list?
Yes. The None option also is available in the Numbering gallery.

Other Ways

1. Select bulleted text, click Bullets button to toggle bullets off

Consider the audience's interests.
As audience members start to view your presentation, they often think about their personal needs and wonder, "How will this presentation benefit me?" As you may have learned in your psychology classes, Maslow's hierarchy of needs drives much of your behavior, starting with basic sustenance and moving on to safety, belonging, ego-status, and self-actualization. Audience members cannot move to the next higher level of needs until their current level is satisfied. For example, an individual must first satisfy his needs of hunger and thirst before he can consider partaking in leisure time activities. Your presentations must meet the requirements of your audience members; otherwise, these people will not consider your talk as benefiting their needs. Having hyperlinks and action buttons can help you tailor a presentation to fulfill the audience's satisfaction level.

CONSIDER THIS

Running a Slide Show with Hyperlinks and Action Buttons

The Conquer Your Clutter presentation contains a variety of useful features that provide value to an audience. The graphics should help viewers understand and recall the information being presented. The hyperlinks on Slide 5 show useful websites of organizations that accept donations of household goods and technology. In addition, the action button allows a presenter to jump to Slide 5 while Slides 2, 3, or 4 are being displayed. If an audience member asks a question or if the presenter needs to answer specific questions regarding kitchen organization when Slide 3 is displaying, the information on the hidden Slide 4 can be accessed immediately by pressing the H key.

BTW
**Distributing a
Document**
Instead of printing and
distributing a hard copy of a
document, you can distribute
the document electronically.
Options include sending the
document via email; posting
it on cloud storage (such as
OneDrive) and sharing the
file with others; posting it
on social media, a blog, or
other website; and sharing a
link associated with an online
location of the document.
You also can create and
share a PDF or XPS image of
the document, so that users
can view the file in Acrobat
Reader or XPS Viewer instead
of in PowerPoint.

To Run a Slide Show with Hyperlinks, Action Buttons, and a Hidden Slide

Running a slide show that contains hyperlinks and action buttons is an interactive experience. A presenter has the option to display slides in a predetermined sequence or to improvise based on the audience's reaction and questions. When a presentation contains hyperlinks and the computer is connected to the Internet, the speaker can click the links to display the websites in the default browser. The following steps run the Conquer Your Clutter presentation.

1 Click Slide 1. Click the Slide Show button on the status bar to run the slide show and display Slide 1.

2 Click the Laundry picture to display Slide 2.

3 On Slide 2, click the Laundry picture to run Microsoft Word and open the Conquer Clutter Checklist file. If a PowerPoint Security Notice dialog box is displayed, click the Yes button to continue running the presentation. View the information and then click the Close button on the title bar to exit Word and return to Slide 2.

4 Press the ENTER key to display Slide 3. Click the Desk picture to link to the first slide in the Additional Clutter presentation. If a PowerPoint Security Notice dialog box is displayed, click the Yes button to continue running the presentation.

5 Click the Return action button on the first slide to return to Slide 3 in the Conquer Your Clutter presentation. If a PowerPoint Security Notice dialog box is displayed, click the Yes button to continue running the presentation.

6 Press the H key to display Slide 4. Click the Kitchen picture to link to the second slide, Conquering Clutter Guidelines, in the Additional Clutter presentation. If a PowerPoint Security Notice dialog box is displayed, click the Yes button to continue running the presentation. Click the Return action button on the second slide to return to Slide 4 in the Conquer Your Clutter presentation.

7 Press the ENTER key to display Slide 5. Click the first hyperlink to start your browser and access the Freecycle webpage. If necessary, maximize the webpage window when the page is displayed. Click the Close button on the webpage title bar to close the browser.

8 Continue using the hyperlinks and action buttons and then end both presentations.

To Save, Print, and Exit PowerPoint

The presentation now is complete. You should save the slides, print a handout, and then exit PowerPoint.

1 Save the Conquer Your Clutter presentation again in the same storage location with the same file name.

2 Print the slides as a handout with two slides per page.

3 Exit PowerPoint, closing all open documents.

Summary

In this module you have learned how to open a Microsoft Word outline as a PowerPoint presentation, develop slides with hyperlinks and action buttons, position slide elements using the drawing guides and rulers, align and distribute pictures, center and align placeholder text, and create columns and then adjust the width. You also learned to change a bullet character to a picture or a symbol and then change its size and color, and to format a numbered list. Finally, you ran the presentation using the action buttons and hyperlinks.

What decisions will you need to make when creating your next presentation?
Use these guidelines as you complete the assignments in this module and create your own slide show decks outside of this class.

1. Many aspects of our lives are grouped in threes: sun, moon, stars; reduce, reuse, recycle; breakfast, lunch, dinner. Your presentation and accompanying presentation likewise can be grouped in threes: introduction, body, and conclusion.

2. Make the hypertext graphics or letters large so a speaker is prompted to click them easily during a speaking engagement.

3. Customize action buttons for a unique look. Add pictures and other graphic elements to add interest or make the buttons less obvious to your viewers.

4. Audience members desire to hear speeches and view presentations that benefit them in some way based on their personal needs. A presenter, in turn, must determine the audience's physical and psychological needs and then tailor the presentation to fit each speaking engagement.

Consider This: Plan Ahead

Apply Your Knowledge

Reinforce the skills and apply the concepts you learned in this module.

Aligning Placeholder Text, Changing Paragraph Line Spacing, Revising a Presentation with Action Buttons, Creating Columns in a Placeholder, and Hiding Slides

Note: To complete this assignment, you will be required to use the Data Files. Please contact your instructor for information about accessing the Data Files.

Instructions: Run PowerPoint. Open the presentation called Apply 6–1 Achilles, which is located in the Data Files.

The slides in the presentation present information about the Achilles tendon. The document you open is a partially formatted presentation. You are to change the theme variant, insert action buttons, and hide slides. Your presentation should look like Figure 6–76.

Perform the following tasks:

1. Change the Berlin theme variant from green to blue (the second color variant).
2. On Slide 1 (Figure 6–76a), change the title font to Matura MT Script Capitals and apply the WordArt style, 'Fill - White, Text 1, Outline - Background 1, Hard Shadow - Background 1' (first style in third row), to the title text. Align the title text in the middle of the placeholder and then center the text in the placeholder as shown in the figure. Change the line spacing of the three paragraphs in the black placeholder to 1.0 and then center these paragraphs.
3. On Slide 2 (Figure 6–76b), create a hyperlink for the text, Sports participation, to Slide 5 (Figure 6–76e). On Slide 5, insert a Back or Previous action button in the lower-right corner of the slide to hyperlink to Last Slide Viewed and play the Click sound. Change the color of the action button to 'Black, Background 1'. Size the button so that it is approximately 0.75" × 0.75". Copy and paste this action button to the lower-right corner of Slide 6.
4. On Slide 2 (Figure 6–76b), create a hyperlink for the text, High heels, to Slide 6 (Figure 6–76f).
5. On Slides 2, 3 (Figure 6–76c), and 4 (Figure 6–76d), increase the size of the foot bullets to 125% of text size. Remove the bullet characters on Slide 5.
6. On Slide 4, create two columns in the text placeholder, adjust the column spacing to 1.00", and then adjust the height of the box so that the columns appear as shown in Figure 6–76d.
7. Hide Slides 5 and 6.
8. If requested by your instructor, add the street you grew up on in the subtitle placeholder on Slide 1.
9. Add the Blinds transition for all slides. Change the duration to 2.75 seconds.
10. Run the presentation and verify the links and action buttons are correct. Save the presentation using the file name, Apply 6–1 Achilles Tendon.
11. Submit the revised document in the format specified by your instructor.
12. ✺ In this presentation, you used action buttons between the text on Slide 2 and Slides 5 and 6. Why? When would a presenter want to hide Slides 5 and 6 and when would a presenter want to display them?

(a) Slide 1

(b) Slide 2

(c) Slide 3

(d) Slide 4

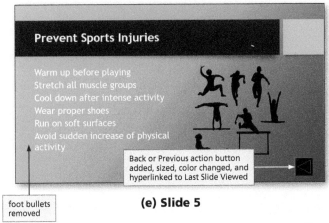

(e) Slide 5

(f) Slide 6

Figure 6–76

Extend Your Knowledge

Extend the skills you learned in this module and experiment with new skills. You may need to use Help to complete the assignment.

Inserting a Photo into an Action Button and Changing a Bullet Character to a Picture

Note: To complete this assignment, you will be required to use the Data Files. Please contact your instructor for information about accessing the Data Files.

Continued >

Extend Your Knowledge *continued*

Instructions: Run PowerPoint. Open the presentation called Extend 6-1 Tanzania, which is located in the Data Files. You will insert hyperlinks on Slide 1, insert action buttons on Slides 2, 3, and 4, and change the bullet characters to pictures on Slides 2, 3, and 4, as shown in Figure 6–77.

Perform the following tasks:
1. On Slide 1 (Figure 6–77a), change the title text font to AR DARLING and then increase the font size to 72 point. Change the subtitle text paragraph alignment to Justified by selecting the text, displaying the Home tab, clicking the Paragraph Dialog Box Launcher (Home tab | Paragraph group), clicking the Alignment arrow in the General area (Paragraph dialog box), and then clicking Justified. Also, change the line spacing to Exactly 40 point by clicking the

(a) Slide 1

(b) Slide 2

Figure 6–77 (Continued)

Line Spacing arrow in the Spacing area (Paragraph dialog box), clicking Exactly, and then increasing the line spacing in the At box.

2. On Slide 1, insert three Custom action buttons (last button in Action Buttons area) on the Africa map. Format these shapes by inserting the pictures called Elephant, Giraffe, and Lion, which are located in the Data Files. Change the size of the elephant shape to approximately 0.8" × 0.8", the giraffe shape to approximately 1.21" × 0.96", and the lion shape to approximately 0.64" × 0.73", and then move the three action buttons to the location shown in the figure. Also remove the shape outline from each action button.

(c) Slide 3

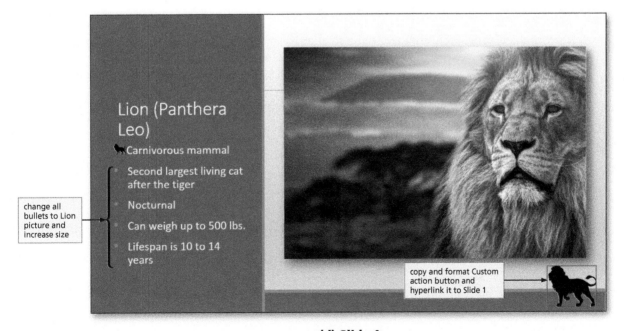

(d) Slide 4

Figure 6–77 (Continued)

Continued >

STUDENT ASSIGNMENTS

Extend Your Knowledge *continued*

3. Hyperlink each picture on Slide 1 to the corresponding slide. For example, the elephant picture should hyperlink to Slide 2 (Figure 6–77b). The other two pictures should hyperlink to Slides 3 and 4 (Figures 6–77c and 6–77d), respectively.

4. On Slide 2 (Figure 6–77b), insert a Custom action button in the lower-right area of the slide and then hyperlink it to Slide 1. Change the size to approximately .75" × .75". Format this shape by inserting the picture called Elephant, which is located in the Data Files. Adjust the transparency of the photo to 80%. Copy and paste this action button on Slides 3 and 4. Change the picture to Giraffe on Slide 3 and Lion on Slide 4.

5. On Slides 2, 3, and 4, change the bullet characters for the paragraphs using the Elephant picture on Slide 2, the Giraffe picture on Slide 3, and the Lion picture on Slide 4. Increase the size of the bullets to 130% for the elephant, 200% for the giraffe, and 118% for the lion.

6. If requested by your instructor, add the year you graduated from high school after the word, Lions, in the subtitle placeholder on Slide 1.

7. Apply the Vortex transition in the Exciting category to all slides and then change the duration to 3.50 seconds.

8. Run the presentation and verify the hyperlinks and action buttons are correct. Save the presentation using the file name, Extend 6-1 Wildlife Experience.

9. Submit the revised document in the format specified by your instructor.

10. ✳ In Step 1, you changed the look of the title and subtitle fonts by changing the font and line spacing. How did this enhance your title slide? How did adding action buttons improve the presentation?

Expand Your World

Create a solution that uses cloud or web technologies by learning and investigating on your own from general guidance.

Using Google Slides to Upload and Edit Files

Instructions: The owner of a dance studio in your town has asked you to create a presentation that encourages potential students to register for lessons. You began working on the slides at the studio but did not have time to finish the slides there and need to complete the slide deck at home. Although you do not have PowerPoint on your home computer, you have an Internet connection and a Google account. You uploaded your PowerPoint presentation to Google Drive so you can view and edit it later from home.

Notes:
- You will use a Google account, which you can create at no cost, to complete this assignment. If you do not have a Google account and do not want to create one, read this assignment without performing the instructions.
- To complete this assignment, you will be required to use the Data Files. Please contact your instructor for information about accessing the Data Files.

Perform the following tasks:

1. In PowerPoint, open the presentation, Expand 6-1 Dancing Lessons in PowerPoint, from the Data Files. Review the slides so that you are familiar with their contents and formats. If desired, print the slides so that you easily can compare them to the Google Slides converted file. Close the presentation.

2. Run a browser. Search for the text, Google Slides, using a search engine. Visit several websites to learn about Google Slides and Google Drive. Navigate to the Google website. If you do not have a Google account and you want to create one, click the Get Started button and follow the instructions. If you do not have a Google account and you do not want to create one, read the remaining instructions without performing them. If you have a Google account, sign in to your account.

3. If necessary, click Drive to display Google Drive. Click the New button, click the File upload, or similar, button, and then follow the instructions to navigate to the location of the file, Expand 6-1 Dancing Lessons in PowerPoint, and upload the file.

4. Rename the file on Google Drive to Expand 6-1 Dancing Lessons in Google. Open the file in Google Slides (Figure 6–78). What differences do you see between the PowerPoint document and the Google Slides converted document? Modify the document in Google Slides so that it looks appealing. If requested by your instructor, replace the name, Stephanie, on Slide 1 with the name of your favorite grade school teacher. Download the revised document to your local storage medium. Submit the document in the format requested by your instructor.

5. What is Google Drive? What is Google Slides? Answer the question posed in #4. If you have an Android smartphone, download the Google Slides app and edit the Expand 6-1 Dancing Lessons file. Do you prefer using Google Slides or PowerPoint? Why?

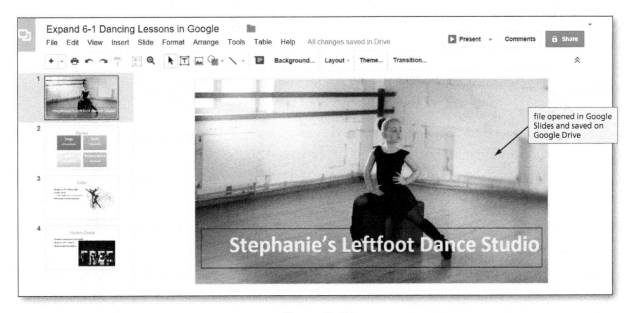

Figure 6–78

In the Labs

Design, create, modify, and/or use a presentation following the guidelines, concepts, and skills presented in this module. Labs 1 and 2, which increase in difficulty, require you to create solutions based on what you learned in the module; Lab 3 requires you to apply your creative thinking and problem-solving skills to design and implement a solution.

Continued >

In the Labs *continued*

Lab 1: Creating Columns in a Box, Increasing the Size of Bullets, Inserting Hyperlinks, Using Guides, and Formatting Bullets

Note: To complete this assignment, you will be required to use the Data Files. Please contact your instructor for information about accessing the Data Files.

Problem: As a member of the Audubon Society, you have enjoyed observing and taking photos of birds. You recently started studying ornithology and would like to share some interesting characteristics you have discovered about our feathered friends with other members of your local Audubon Society chapter. Create the slides shown in Figure 6–79.

Perform the following tasks:

1. Run PowerPoint. Open the presentation called Lab 6-1 Birds, which is located in the Data Files.

2. Create a background for Slides 2 through 5 by inserting the photo called Bird and Sky, which is located in the Data Files. Change the transparency to 50%, as shown in Figures 6–79b through 6–79e.

3. On Slide 1 (Figure 6–79a), change the title text placeholder vertical alignment to Middle. Increase the title text size to 80 point, change the color to Dark Blue (in Standard Colors), and then bold this text. Change the subtitle text placeholder vertical alignment to Middle, increase the subtitle text size to 32 point, and then italicize this text.

4. On Slide 2 (Figure 6–79b), change the title font to AR BLANCA, increase the title text font size to 44 point, change the color to Dark Blue (in Standard Colors), and then bold this text. Use the Format Painter to format the title text on Slides 3, 4, and 5 (Figures 6–79c, 6–79d, and 6–79e) with the same features as the title text on Slide 2.

5. Change the bullet characters for all the level 1 text on Slides 2, 3, and 5 to the illustration called Black Bird, which is available in the Data Files. Increase the size of the bullets to 150% of text size, as shown in Figures 6–79b and 6–79c.

6. On Slide 2, create two columns in the text placeholder and then adjust the column spacing to 1". Change all level 1 text to 32 point and all level 2 text to 24 point. Resize the content placeholder so the paragraphs in the columns display as shown in Figure 6–79b.

7. On Slide 3, create three columns in the text placeholder and then adjust the column spacing to 1.5". Change all level 1 text to 28 point and all level 2 text to 24 point. Resize the content placeholder so the paragraphs in the columns display as shown in Figure 6–79c.

8. On Slide 3, create hyperlinks for the three words in the box, Mantle, Coverts, and Tertials, to Slide 4. (If spell check prompts you to correct the spelling of these three words, ignore the options shown.)

9. On Slide 4, change the color of the shape fill of the 11 callout shapes to Light Blue (in Standard Colors), as shown in Figure 6–79d. Display rulers and guides. With the 11 callout shapes and the bird illustration selected, move these objects so they are centered horizontally and vertically on the slide. Turn off rulers and guides.

10. Insert a Return action button in the lower-right corner of Slide 4 and then hyperlink the button to the Previous Slide, which will be Slide 3 when you run the presentation. Change the color of this action button to 'Gold, Accent 4' (first Theme Colors row) and then change the transparency to 50%, as shown in Figure 6–79d.

(a) Slide 1

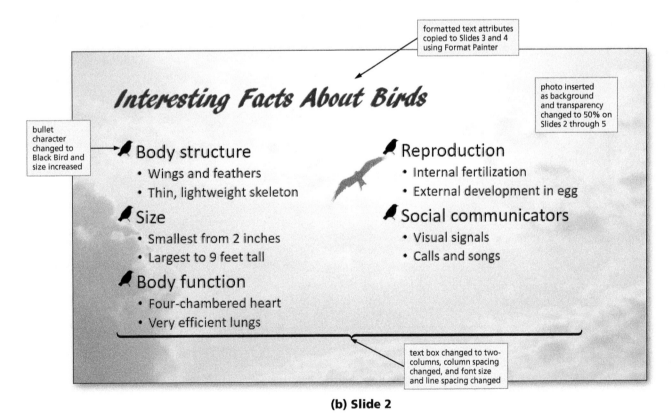

(b) Slide 2

Figure 6–79 (Continued)

11. On Slide 5, increase the size of the title text to 44 point so it appears on two lines, as shown in Figure 6–79e. Increase the size of the photo to 5.76" × 7.3", apply the 'Beveled Oval, Black' picture style, add the Glow Diffused artistic effect (fourth effect in second row), and then move the photo to the location shown in the figure.

Continued >

In the Labs *continued*

(c) Slide 3

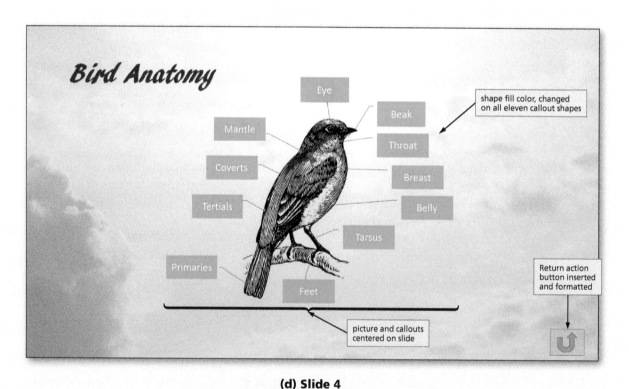

(d) Slide 4

Figure 6–79 (Continued)

12. Create hyperlinks for the three ornithologists shown on Slide 5. Type `www.audubon.org /content/john-james-audubon` for John James Audubon, `www.wilsonsociety .org/society/awilsoninfo.html` for Alexander Wilson, and `www.britannica .com/biography/John-Gould` for John Gould.

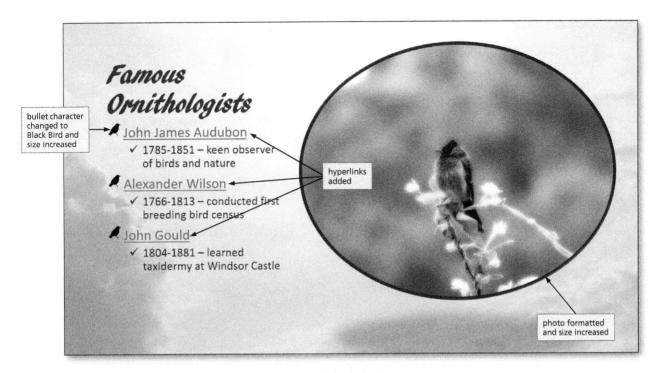

(e) Slide 5

Figure 6–79

13. If requested by your instructor, add your high school mascot as the last line of the subtitle text on Slide 5.

14. Apply the Origami transition in the Exciting Content category to all slides and then change the duration to 3.50 seconds.

15. Run the presentation and verify the hyperlinks and action buttons are correct. Save the presentation using the file name, Lab 6-1 Our Feathered Friends.

16. Submit the document in the format specified by your instructor.

17. ✳ In Step 8, you added hyperlinks to three of the bird anatomy paragraphs on Slide 3 and linked them to Slide 4. Why would a speaker desire to use these hyperlinks? In Step 12, you added hyperlinks to the names of famous ornithologists and linked them to websites. How would a speaker use these hyperlinks during a presentation?

Lab 2: Opening a Microsoft Word Outline as a Presentation, Inserting a Hyperlink to Another Office Document, Using Rulers and Guides, Entering Line Breaks, and Formatting Bullets

Note: To complete this assignment, you will be required to use the Data Files. Please contact your instructor for information about accessing the Data Files.

Problem: Your community center is offering painting classes beginning in January. You received a document outlining the classes that will be offered and a Microsoft Excel file that gives detailed information about the painting classes, schedule, and costs. To help promote the classes, you create the five slides shown in Figures 6–80b through 6–80f.

Continued >

In the Labs *continued*

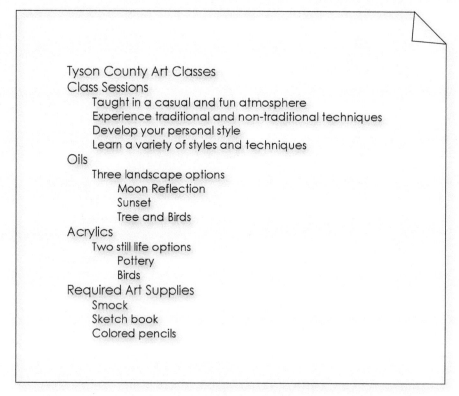

Tyson County Art Classes
Class Sessions
    Taught in a casual and fun atmosphere
    Experience traditional and non-traditional techniques
    Develop your personal style
    Learn a variety of styles and techniques
Oils
    Three landscape options
        Moon Reflection
        Sunset
        Tree and Birds
Acrylics
    Two still life options
        Pottery
        Birds
Required Art Supplies
    Smock
    Sketch book
    Colored pencils

(a) Tyson County Art Classes Outline (Microsoft Word Document)

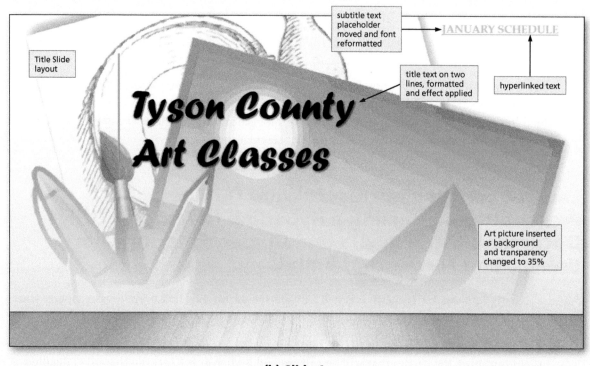

subtitle text placeholder moved and font reformatted

JANUARY SCHEDULE

Title Slide layout

title text on two lines, formatted and effect applied

hyperlinked text

Tyson County Art Classes

Art picture inserted as background and transparency changed to 35%

(b) Slide 1

Figure 6–80 (Continued)

	A	B	C	D	E	F
1	Tyson County Adult Painting Classes Beginning in January					
2	Class and Teacher	Project	Canvas Size	Day and Time	Duration	Cost including all supplies
3	Oils by Erick	Moon Reflection	16 x 20	M,W,F 9 a.m.	6 weeks	$195
4	Oils by Erick	Moon Reflection	8 x 10	Tue & Thur 9 a.m.	5 weeks	$165
5	Oils by Erick	Sunset	16 x 20	M,W,F 2 p.m.	6 weeks	$195
6	Oils by Erick	Sunset	8 x 10	Tue & Thur 2 p.m.	5 weeks	$165
7	Oils by Erick	Trees and Birds	16 x 20	M,W,F 7 p.m.	6 weeks	$195
8	Oils by Erick	Trees and Birds	8 x 10	Tue & Thur 7 p.m.	5 weeks	$165
9	Acrylics by Sandy	Still Life Pottery	11 x 14	Mon & Wed 11 a.m.	6 weeks	$150
10	Acrylics by Sandy	Still Life Pottery	8 x 10	Tue & Fri 2 p.m.	6 weeks	$130
11	Acrylics by Sandy	Still Life Birds	11 x 14	Mon & Thur 2 p.m.	5 weeks	$150
12	Acrylics by Sandy	Still Life Birds	8 x 10	Mon & Thur 7 p.m.	5 weeks	$130
13						

(c) Tyson County Art Classes (Microsoft Excel file)

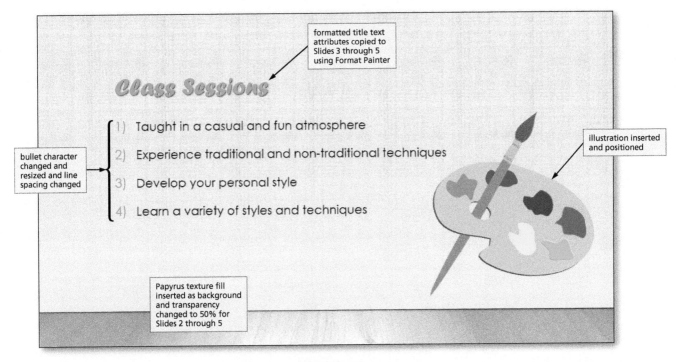

(d) Slide 2

Figure 6–80 (Continued)

Perform the following tasks:

1. Run PowerPoint. Open the Microsoft Word outline, Lab 6-2 Tyson County Art Classes Outline (Figure 6–80a), which is located in the Data Files, as a presentation.

2. Change the Slide 1 layout to Title Slide (Figure 6–80b). Change the title font to Forte and then apply a text shadow to this text. Enter a line break before the word, Art. Change the line spacing for the title to 1.0.

3. Change the theme to Gallery and then select the gold variant. Create a background on Slide 1 only using the illustration called Art, which is located in the Data Files, and then change the transparency to 35%.

Continued >

In the Labs *continued*

(e) Slide 3

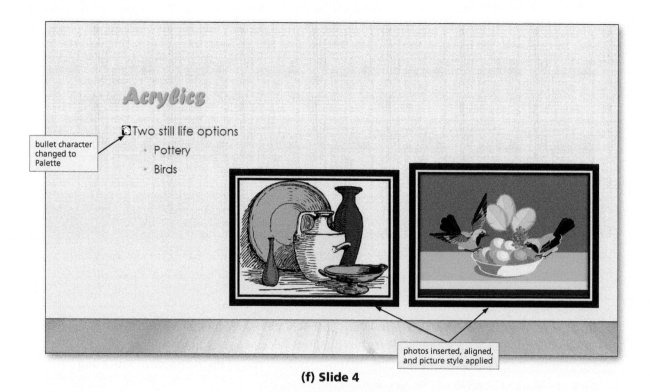

(f) Slide 4

Figure 6–80 (Continued)

4. On Slide 1, move the subtitle placeholder to the upper-right corner of the slide, type
   January Schedule, bold and right-align this text, and then change the color to Green (in
   Standard colors). Create a hyperlink for this text to the Excel document called Tyson County
   Art Classes (Figure 6–80c), which is located in the Data Files.

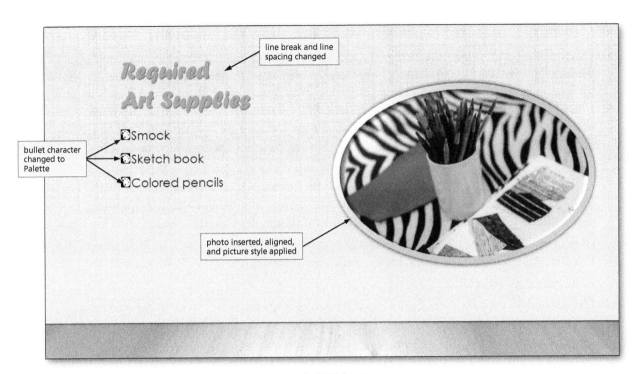

(g) Slide 5

Figure 6-80

5. On Slides 2 through 5, change the background to the Papyrus texture fill (first texture in first row) and then change the transparency to 50%. Display the rulers and guides. Move the horizontal guide to 2.67" below the center and move the vertical guide to 5.75" left of the center. To add a second vertical guide, right-click a blank area of the slide, select Grid and Guides, and then click Add Vertical Guide. Move the new vertical guide to 6.21" right of the center.

6. On Slide 2 (Figure 6-80d), insert the illustration called Pallet and Brush, which is located in the Data Files. Size this illustration to approximately 4.16" × 3.84" and then align it with the horizontal and vertical guides on the right.

7. Change the line spacing to 1.5 for the placeholder text on Slide 2, change the bullet characters to the 1) 2) 3) numbered bullets, increase the bullet size to 110% of text size, and then change the color to Green (in Standard Colors).

8. On Slide 3 (Figure 6-80e), insert the three illustrations called Moon Reflection, Sunset, and Tree and Birds, which are located in the Data Files. Apply the 'Double Frame, Black' picture style to the three illustrations. Size the Moon Reflection illustration to approximately 2.41" × 4", the Sunset illustration to approximately 2.43" × 3.5", and the Tree and Birds illustration to approximately 2.43" × 3.47". Select the Align Bottom alignment for the Sunset and Tree and Birds illustrations and then position them at 2.67" below center and so that the Tree and Birds is against the right guide at 6.21". Center the Moon Reflection illustration above the other two illustrations, as shown in the figure.

9. On Slide 2, change the title font to Forte, increase the font size to 40 point, change the font color to Green (sixth color in Standard colors), and then apply a text shadow to the text. Use the Format Painter to format the title text on Slides 3, 4, and 5 with the same features as the title text on Slide 2.

Continued >

In the Labs *continued*

10. On Slide 4 (Figure 6–80f), insert the two illustrations called Still Life Pottery and Still Life Birds, which are located in the Data Files. Apply the Double Frame, Black picture style to both illustrations. Size the Still Life Pottery illustration to approximately 2.59" × 3.47" and the Still Life Birds illustration to approximately 2.75" × 3.89". Select the Align Bottom alignment for both illustrations and then position them at 2.67" below center and so that the Still Life Birds illustration is against the right guide at 6.21".

11. On Slide 5 (Figure 6–80g), insert a line break before the word, Art. Change the line spacing for the title to 1.0. Insert the illustration called Art Pencils, which is located in the Data Files. Size the illustration to approximately 4.01" × 6.02". Apply the Metal Oval picture style to the illustration. Align the left edge of the illustration at 0" and then align it vertically on the slide.

12. Change the bullet character for all the level 1 text on Slides 3, 4, and 5 to the illustration called Palette, located in the Data Files. Increase the size of the bullets to 120% of text size.

13. Hide the rulers and guides.

14. If requested by your instructor, enter your hair color after the word, style, in the third text paragraph on Slide 2.

15. Apply the Orbit transition in the Dynamic Content category to all slides and then change the duration to 3.25 seconds.

16. Run the presentation and verify the hyperlinks and action buttons are correct. Save the presentation using the file name, Lab 6-2 Tyson County Art Classes.

17. Submit the document in the format specified by your instructor.

18. ✸ Why did you add the art illustration as a background on Slide 1? Did changing the bullet characters to pictures add interest to the presentation?

Lab 3: **Consider This: Your Turn**

Design and Create a Presentation about Interior Design

Part 1: In the project for this module, you developed slides with guidelines for organizing a home, including specific information about arranging items in an office and a kitchen. Once areas of your home are organized, you can create rooms that fit your personality and your budget. One method of beginning a room design from scratch is to look at photos online and in magazines. Lighting, upholstered pieces, wooden cabinets, and accessories help influence the room's style. You want to start shopping for furniture and decide to create a PowerPoint presentation to show to interior decorators at the stores. Use the concepts and techniques presented in this module to create this presentation. Begin by developing a Microsoft Word outline with information about your style preferences and budget. Then, open this outline as a PowerPoint presentation, select a suitable theme, and include hyperlinks to websites that show rooms you admire. Change the bullet characters on at least one slide to a picture or a symbol. You may want to use one or more of the five photos called Lighting, Office, Living Room, Drawers and Ottoman in the Data Files, and you can include your own photos if they are appropriate for this topic. Review and revise your presentation as needed and then save the file using the file name, Lab 6-3 Interior Design. Submit your assignment in the format specified by your instructor.

Part 2: ✸ You made several decisions while creating the presentation in this assignment: where to place text, how to format the text (such as font, font size, and colors), which image(s) to use, formatting bullets, and inserting hyperlinks to add interest to the presentation. What was the rationale behind each of these decisions? When you reviewed the document, what further revisions did you make and why?

7 | Creating a Self-Running Presentation Containing Animation

Objectives

You will have mastered the material in this module when you can:

- Remove a photo background
- Crop and compress a photo
- Animate slide content with entrance, emphasis, and exit effects
- Add and adjust motion paths for animations
- Reorder animation sequences
- Associate sounds with animations

- Control animation timing
- Animate SmartArt graphics and charts
- Insert and animate a text box
- Animate bulleted lists
- Rehearse timings
- Set slide show timings manually

Introduction

BTW

Animation Types
The transitions you have been applying between slides in a presentation are one type of PowerPoint animations. In this module you will use another type of animation to move or change elements on the slide. Animation is effective in adding interest to slide content and to call attention to important content. As a caution, however, resist the urge to add animation simply for the sake of animation when it does not have a purpose on a particular slide.

One method used for disseminating information is a **kiosk**. This freestanding, self-service structure is equipped with computer hardware and software and is used to provide information or reference materials to the public. Some have a touch screen or keyboard that serves as an input device and allows users to select various options so they can browse or find specific information. Advanced kiosks allow customers to place orders, make payments, and access the Internet. Many kiosks have multimedia devices for playing sound and video clips.

Various elements on PowerPoint slides can have movement to direct the audience's attention to the point being made. For example, each paragraph in a bulleted list can fade or disappear after being displayed for a set period of time. Each SmartArt graphic component can appear in sequence. A picture can grow, shrink, bounce, or spin, depending upon its relationship to other slide content. PowerPoint's myriad animation effects allow you to use your creativity to design imaginative and distinctive presentations.

Project — Presentation with Adjusted Pictures, Animated Content, and Slide Timings

Drones are becoming commonplace for personal, commercial, and private ventures. These pilotless aerial vehicles are guided by remote control and can be equipped with such items as cameras, supplies, radar, and sensors. The title slide (Figure 7–1a) has animated title text and a drone that moves and turns in the sky. The second slide (Figure 7–1b) shows drones that are flying across a field. The third slide (Figure 7–1c) uses animated SmartArt to explain the process the Federal Aviation Administration has developed to govern drone registrations. The next slide is an animated chart that shows some of the general drone applications (Figure 7–1d). More specific uses of drones are shown in the last slide (Figure 7–1e).

(a) Slide 1 (Title Slide with Animated WordArt and Photo)

(b) Slide 2 (Animated Photos with Motion Path and Sound)

(c) Slide 3 (Animated SmartArt)

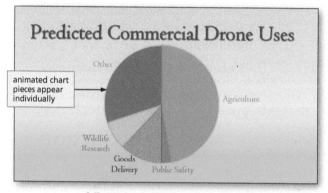

(d) Slide 4 (Animated Chart)

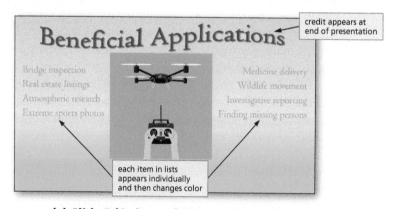

(e) Slide 5 (Animated Lists and Credit)

Figure 7–1

In this module, you will learn how to create the slides shown in Figure 7–1. The following roadmap identifies general activities you will perform as you progress through this module:

1. MODIFY PHOTOS by removing the background, cropping, and compressing.

2. ADD ENTRANCE, EMPHASIS, and EXIT ANIMATIONS to photos and text.

3. ANIMATE BOXES, SMARTART, and CHARTS.

4. CHANGE ANIMATION EFFECTS.

5. SET slide show TIMINGS.

BTW

The Ribbon and Screen Resolution
PowerPoint may change how the groups and buttons within the groups appear on the ribbon, depending on the computer or mobile device's screen resolution. Thus, your ribbon may look different from the ones in this book if you are using a screen resolution other than 1366×768.

Adjusting and Cropping a Photo

At times you may desire to emphasize one section of a photo and eliminate distracting background content. PowerPoint includes formatting tools that allow you to edit photos. The **Remove Background** command isolates the foreground from the background, and the **Crop** command removes content along the top, bottom, left, or right edges. Once you format the photo to include only the desired content, you can **compress** the image to reduce the file size.

To Remove a Background

1 MODIFY PHOTOS | 2 ADD ENTRANCE, EMPHASIS, & EXIT ANIMATIONS
3 ANIMATE BOXES, SMARTART, & CHARTS | 4 CHANGE ANIMATION EFFECTS | 5 SET TIMINGS

The title slide in the Animated Drones presentation has a photo of a yellow drone hovering over a road. You want to eliminate the road and other background from the image. *Why? To direct the viewers' attention to the drone.* The PowerPoint Background Removal feature makes it easy to eliminate extraneous aspects. When you click the Remove Background button, PowerPoint attempts to select the foreground of the photo and overlay a magenta marquee selection on this area. You then can adjust the marquee shape and size to contain all foreground photo components you want to keep. The following steps remove the background from the drone photo.

1
- Run PowerPoint. If necessary, maximize the PowerPoint window.
- Open the presentation, Drones, located in the Data Files.
- Save the presentation using the file name, Animated Drones.

2
- With the title slide displaying, click the drone photo to select it and then click the Picture Tools Format tab (Figure 7–2).

Figure 7–2

- Click the Remove Background button (Picture Tools Format tab | Adjust group) to display the Background Removal tab and a marquee selection area.

- Click and drag the center handle on the bottom of the background removal lines toward the box under the drone and then drag the center handles on the left and right background removal lines outward so that the entire drone is displayed in the marquee selection area.

- Zoom the slide to 150%. Use the vertical and horizontal scroll bars to adjust the slide so the entire yellow drone photo is visible (Figure 7–3).

Figure 7–3

Q&A How does PowerPoint determine the area to display within the marquee?
Microsoft Research software engineers developed the algorithms that determine the portions of the photo in the foreground.

- Click the Keep Changes button (Background Removal tab | Close group) to discard the unwanted photo background.

To Refine Background Removal

1 MODIFY PHOTOS | 2 ADD ENTRANCE, EMPHASIS, & EXIT ANIMATIONS
3 ANIMATE BOXES, SMARTART, & CHARTS | 4 CHANGE ANIMATION EFFECTS | 5 SET TIMINGS

Why? In many cases, the Remove Background command discards all the undesired photo components. When the background is integrated closely with the foreground photo, however, some undesired pieces occasionally remain and other desired pieces are discarded. In the title slide drone photo, part of the white background was not removed, so it is displayed under the right propeller. In contrast, some parts of the propellers were deleted, most notably the left propeller, along with the background. Tools on the Background Removal tab allow you to mark specific areas to remove and to keep. The following steps mark an area to discard and three propeller blades to areas to keep.

- Click the Remove Background button to display the Background Removal tab and the marquee selection area.

- Click the 'Mark Areas to Remove' button (Background Removal tab | Refine group) and then position the pointer in the white area below the right propeller (Figure 7–4).

Figure 7–4

What if different areas were kept/removed in my photo?
Read the steps to Keep or Discard areas of a photo, and keep or remove as appropriate to show just the drone against the sky.

Why did my pointer change shape?
The pointer changed to a pencil to indicate you are about to draw on a precise area of the photo.

I am using a touch screen and am having difficulty positioning the pointer. What should I do?
Zoom your screen to increase the level of detail you need. Using a mouse also might help with this task.

2
• Click and then drag the pointer across the white area to indicate the portion of the photo to discard (Figure 7–5).

Figure 7–5

Why does a circle with a minus sign display on the dotted line?
That symbol indicates that you manually specified the deletion of a portion of the background.

If I marked an area with a line and now want to delete it, can I reverse my action?
Yes. Click the Delete Mark button (Background Removal tab | Refine group) and then click the line to remove it. You also can press CTRL+Z immediately after you draw the line.

3

- Click the Keep Changes button (Background Removal tab | Close group) to review the results of your background refinements.

4

- Click the Remove Background button again to display the Background Removal tab and the marquee selection area.

- Click the 'Mark Areas to Keep' button (Background Removal tab | Refine group) and then position the pointer in the left propeller (Figure 7–6).

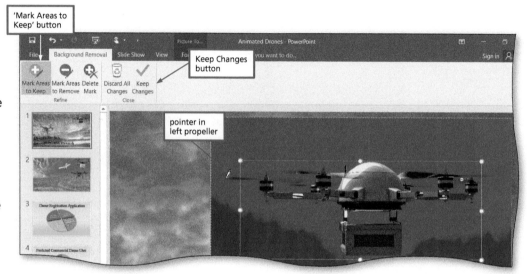

Figure 7–6

5

- Click and then drag the pointer across this propeller. Repeat this process for two other propellers shown in Figure 7–7.

 Why does a circle with a plus sign display on the dotted line?
That symbol indicates that you manually specified the addition of a portion of the background.

Figure 7–7

What if the dotted lines do not cover the desired part of the propellers?
You may need to make several passes to remove all of the unwanted background or add the desired photo elements.

- Click the Keep Changes button (Background Removal tab | Close group) to review the results of your background refinements.

Q&A Why does some of the background remain on my photo?
The location where you drew your background removal line determines the area that PowerPoint modifies.

If I want to see the original photo at a later time, can I display the components I deleted?
Yes. If you click the Discard All Changes button (Background Removal tab | Close group), all the deleted pieces will reappear.

To Crop a Photo

1 MODIFY PHOTOS | 2 ADD ENTRANCE, EMPHASIS, & EXIT ANIMATIONS
3 ANIMATE BOXES, SMARTART, & CHARTS | 4 CHANGE ANIMATION EFFECTS | 5 SET TIMINGS

The Remove Background command deleted the road and trees from your view, but the photo still contains the background even though it is hidden. You can remove the unnecessary elements of the photo and crop it to show just the drone. ***Why?*** *The photo should contain only the element that will be shown.* When you crop a picture, you trim the vertical or horizontal sides so that the most important area of the photo is displayed. Any picture file type except animated GIF can be cropped. The following steps crop the title slide drone photo.

- Zoom the slide to 65%. Use the vertical and horizontal scroll bars to adjust the slide so the entire yellow drone photo is visible.

- With the drone photo still selected, click the Crop button (Picture Tools Format tab | Size group) to display the cropping handles on the photo.

- Position the pointer over the center cropping handle on the bottom of the photo (Figure 7–8).

Q&A Why did my pointer change shape?
The pointer changed to indicate you are about to crop a photo.

Figure 7–8

- Drag the lower center cropping handle inward so that the bottom edge of the marquee is below the box under the drone.

- Drag the center cropping handles on the left, upper, and right edges of the cropping lines inward to frame the photo (Figure 7–9).

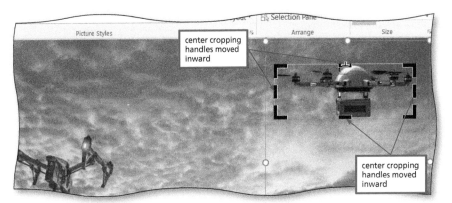

Figure 7–9

Q&A | Does cropping actually cut the photo's edges?
No. Although you cannot see the cropped edges, they exist until you save the file.

Can I crop a picture to exact dimensions?
Yes. Right-click the picture and then click Format Picture on the shortcut menu. On the Crop pane, under Picture position, enter the measurements in the Width and Height boxes.

❸

• Click the Crop button again to crop the edges.

Q&A | Can I press the ESC key to crop the edges?
Yes.

Can I change the crop lines?
If you have not saved the file, you can undo your crops by clicking the Undo button on the Quick Access Toolbar, or clicking the Reset Picture button (Picture Tools Format tab | Adjust group), or pressing CTRL+Z. If you have saved the file, you cannot undo the crop.

Other Ways
1. Right-click photo, click Crop on shortcut menu

BTW
Simultaneous Cropping on Two or Four Sides
To crop equally on two sides simultaneously, press the CTRL key while dragging the center cropping handle on either side inward. To crop all four sides equally, press the CTRL key while dragging a corner cropping handle inward.

TO CROP A PICTURE TO A SHAPE

In addition to cropping a picture, you can change the shape of a picture by cropping it to a specific shape. The picture's proportions are maintained, and it automatically is trimmed to fill the shape's geometry. To crop to a specific shape, you would perform the following steps.

1. Select the picture you want to crop.
2. Display the Picture Tools Format tab and then click the Crop arrow (Picture Tools Format tab | Size group) to display the Crop menu.
3. Point to 'Crop to Shape' and then click the desired shape in the Shape gallery.

To Compress a Photo

1 MODIFY PHOTOS | 2 ADD ENTRANCE, EMPHASIS, & EXIT ANIMATIONS
3 ANIMATE BOXES, SMARTART, & CHARTS | 4 CHANGE ANIMATION EFFECTS | 5 SET TIMINGS

Photos inserted into slides greatly increase the total PowerPoint file size. PowerPoint automatically compresses photo files inserted into slides by eliminating details, generally with no visible loss of quality. You can increase the compression and, in turn, decrease the file size if you instruct PowerPoint to compress a photo you have cropped so you can save space on a storage medium such as a hard disk, USB flash drive, or optical disk. Although these storage devices generally have a large storage capacity, you might want to reduce the file size. *Why? A smaller size reduces the download time from an FTP server or website. Also, some Internet service providers restrict an attachment's file size.*

The photo on the title slide is cropped and displays only the drone. You will not need any of the invisible portions of the photo, so you can delete them permanently and reduce the photo file size. The following steps compress the size of the title slide drone photo.

• With the drone photo selected, click the Compress Pictures button (Picture Tools Format tab | Adjust group) to display the Compress Pictures dialog box (Figure 7–10).

Figure 7–10

Q&A If I want to add an artistic effect, should I apply the effect prior to or after compressing a picture?

Compress a picture and then apply the artistic effect.

2

- Click the OK button (Compress Pictures dialog box) to delete the cropped portions of this photo and compress the image.

Q&A Can I undo the compression?

Yes, as long as you have not saved the file after compressing the photo.

Animating Slide Content

The Slide 1 background photo shows a drone in the sunset sky. When the presentation begins, the audience will view this scene and then see another drone enter from the lower-right corner, move across the slide, pulse slightly at the center of the slide, and then continue moving upward. To create this animation on the slide, you will use entrance, emphasis, and exit effects.

If you need to move objects on a slide once they are displayed, you can define a **motion path**. This predefined movement determines where an object will be displayed and then travel. Motion paths are grouped into the Basic, Lines & Curves, and Special categories. You can draw a **custom path** if none of the predefined paths meets your needs.

BTW
Touch Screen Differences
The Office and Windows interfaces may vary if you are using a touch screen. For this reason, you might notice that the function or appearance of your touch screen differs slightly from this module's presentation.

Use animation sparingly.
PowerPoint audience members usually take notice the first time an animation is displayed on the screen. When the same animation effect is applied throughout a presentation, the viewers generally become desensitized to the effect unless it is highly unusual or annoying. Resist the urge to use animation effects simply because PowerPoint provides the tools to do so. You have options to decide how text or a slide element enters and exits a slide and how it is displayed once it is present on the slide; your goal, however, is to use these options wisely. Audiences soon tire of a presentation riddled with animations, causing them to quickly lose their impact.

CONSIDER THIS

To Animate a Photo Using an Entrance Effect

The drone you modified will not appear on Slide 1 when you begin the presentation. Instead, it will enter the slide from the lower-right corner of the slide to give the appearance it is taking off from ground level. It then will continue moving upward until it reaches near the center of the slide, so you need to move the photo to this location as a resting point of where it will stop moving temporarily, as if it is hovering in mid-air. The following steps apply an entrance effect to the drone photo.

1 With Slide 1 displaying, zoom to 55% and then move the yellow drone photo above the word, research.

2 Display the Animations tab and then click the Fly In animation in the Animation gallery (Animation group) to apply and preview this entrance animation for the drone photo (Figure 7–11).

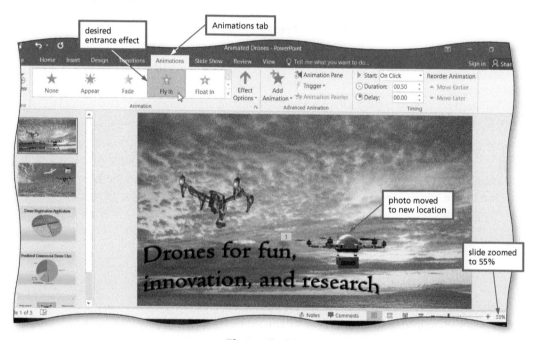

Figure 7–11

To Change Animation Direction

By default, the photo appears on the slide by entering from the bottom edge. You can modify this direction and specify that it enters from another side or from a corner. The following steps change the drone photo entrance animation direction to the bottom-right corner.

1 Click the Effect Options button (Animations tab | Animation group) to display the Direction gallery (Figure 7–12).

2 Click the 'From Bottom-Right' arrow in the Direction gallery to apply this direction to the entrance animation and show a preview.

Figure 7–12

To Animate a Photo Using an Emphasis Effect

The drone will enter the slide from the lower-right corner and stop in the center of the slide. You then want it to fade out and in, or pulse, slightly to give the impression that it is hovering over the water. PowerPoint provides several effects that you can apply to a picture once it appears on a slide. These movements are categorized as emphasis effects, and they are colored yellow in the Animation gallery. You already have applied an entrance effect to the drone photo, so you want to add another animation to this photo. The following steps apply an emphasis effect to the drone photo after the entrance effect.

1 With the drone photo still selected, click the Add Animation button (Animations tab | Advanced Animation group) to expand the Animation gallery (Figure 7–13).

2 Click Pulse in the Emphasis section to apply this emphasis effect to the drone photo.

BTW

Effects for Objects with Text
Some entrance and exit effects (such as Flip, Drop, and Whip) and some emphasis effects (such as Brush Color, Shimmer, and Wave) are available only for objects that contain text. If you want to apply an animation effect that is not available for this reason, add a space inside your object.

Figure 7–13

BTW
Selecting Individual Animations
Selecting individual animations may be difficult when using a touch screen because your finger may be too big to select a small item that is located close to other items. If you encounter this problem, try using a stylus or open the Animation Pane to select an animation.

To Animate a Photo Using an Exit Effect and Change Animation Direction

The animated drone photo will enter the slide from the lower-right corner, stop in the center of the slide, and then pulse. It then will continue flying straight upward. To continue this animation sequence, you need to apply an exit effect. As with the entrance and emphasis effects, PowerPoint provides a wide variety of effects that you can apply to remove a picture from a slide. These exit effects are colored red in the Animation gallery. You already have applied the Fly In entrance effect, so the Fly Out exit effect would give continuity to the animation sequence. The default direction for a photo to exit a slide is To Bottom. In this presentation, you want the drone to exit toward the top of the slide to give the impression it is continuing to fly through the air. The following steps add the Fly Out exit effect to the drone photo after the emphasis effect and then change the exit animation direction from To Bottom to To Top.

1 With the drone photo still selected, click the Add Animation button again to expand the Animation gallery. Scroll down to display the Exit section (Figure 7–14).

2 Click Fly Out in the Exit section to add this exit effect to the sequence of drone photo animations.

3 Click the Effect Options button to display the Direction gallery and then click the To Top arrow to apply this direction to the exit animation effect.

Figure 7–14

BTW
Playing Animations during Previews and Presentations
To be certain that animations play when you present your slide show, click the 'Set Up Slide Show' button (Slide Show tab | Set Up group) to display the Set Up Show dialog box. Check that the 'Show without animation' check box in the Show options area is cleared. If this box is checked, animations will show when you preview your slide show, but not when you present.

To Preview an Animation Sequence

Although you have not completed developing the presentation, you should view the animation you have added. By default, the entrance, emphasis, and exit animations will be displayed when you run the presentation and tap the screen or click the mouse. The following step runs the presentation and displays the three animations.

1 Click the Preview button (Animations tab | Preview group) to view all the Slide 1 animation.

To Modify Entrance Animation Timing

The three animation effects are displayed quickly. To create a dramatic effect, you can change the timing so that the background photo displays and then, a few seconds later, the drone starts to fly through the sky slowly. The default setting is to start each animation with a mouse click, but you can change this setting so that the entrance effect is delayed until a specified number of seconds has passed. The following steps modify the start, delay, and duration settings for the entrance animation.

1 Click the 1 numbered tag on the left side of the drone photo and then click the Start arrow (Animations tab | Timing group) to display the start timing menu.

2 Click After Previous to change the start timing setting.

3 Click the Duration up arrow (Animations tab | Timing group) several times to increase the time from 00.50 second to 03.00 seconds.

4 Click the Delay up arrow (Animations tab | Timing group) several times to increase the time from 00.00 second to 02.00 seconds (Figure 7–15).

5 Click the Preview button to view the animations.

Figure 7–15

To Modify Emphasis and Exit Timings

Now that the entrance animation settings have been modified, you can change the emphasis and exit effects for the drone photo. The emphasis effect can occur once the entrance effect has concluded, and then the exit effect can commence. You will increase the duration of the exit effect compared with the duration of the entrance effect. The animation sequence should flow without stopping, so you will not change the default delay timing of 00.00 second. The following steps modify the start and duration settings for the emphasis and exit animations.

1 Click the 1 sequence number, which now represents the emphasis effect, on the left side of the drone photo, click the Start arrow, and then click After Previous to change the start timing option setting.

BTW
Developing Animations
You can add the parts of the animation in any order and then change the sequence. Many slide designers, however, develop the animation using the sequence in which the elements will display on the slide in an effort to save time and help organize the animation sequence.

2 Increase the duration time to 04.00 seconds.

3 Click the 1 sequence number, which now represents the exit effect, and then change the start timing to After Previous.

4 Increase the duration time to 06.00 seconds (Figure 7–16).

5 Preview the Slide 1 animations.

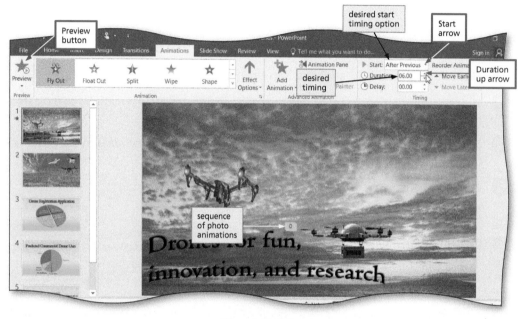

Figure 7–16

BTW
Selecting Paragraph Text Animation Options
Multi-level bulleted list paragraphs can have animation effects that help direct the audience's attention. For example, you can animate the second-level paragraphs so they are displayed individually along with any associated third-level paragraphs. To specify a text animation option, display the Animation Pane, click an animation you want to manipulate in the list, click this animation's list arrow to display a menu, click Effect Options in the list, and then click the Text Animation tab in the dialog box. If desired, you can click the Group Text arrow and select a paragraph level, such as 2nd level, in the list. Click the Automatically after check box and enter a time if you want the next bulleted paragraph to appear after a specific number of seconds. In addition, click the 'In reverse order' check box to build the paragraphs from the bottom to the top of the slide.

To Animate Title Text Placeholder Paragraphs

The drone photo on Slide 1 has one entrance, one emphasis, and one exit animation, and you can add similar animations to the Slide 1 title text placeholder. For a special effect, you can add several emphasis animations to one slide element. The following steps add one entrance and two emphasis animations to the title text paragraph.

1 Click the Slide 1 title text placeholder to select it.

2 Click the border so that it displays as a solid line.

3 Click the More button in the Animation gallery (Animations tab | Animation group) to expand the Animation gallery.

4 Click the Float In entrance effect in the Animation gallery to add this animation.

5 Change the start timing option to With Previous.

6 Change the duration time to 02.00 seconds.

7 Click the Add Animation button and then click the Font Color Emphasis animation effect.

8 Change the start timing option to After Previous.

9 Click the Add Animation button and then click the Wave emphasis animation effect.

⑩ Change the start timing option to With Previous (Figure 7–17).

Figure 7–17

To Change Animation Order

1 MODIFY PHOTOS | 2 ADD ENTRANCE, EMPHASIS, & EXIT ANIMATIONS
3 ANIMATE BOXES, SMARTART, & CHARTS | 4 CHANGE ANIMATION EFFECTS | 5 SET TIMINGS

Two title slide elements have animations: the drone photo and the title text placeholder. PowerPoint applies the animations in the order you created them, so on this slide the drone photo animations will appear first and then the title text placeholder animation will follow. You can reorder animation elements. *Why? You may decide one set of animations should appear before another set or you also can reorder individual animation elements within an animation group.* In this presentation, you decide to display the title text placeholder animation first, and then you decide that the Wave emphasis effect should appear before the Font Color emphasis effect. The following steps reorder the two animation groups on the slide and then reorder the Font Color and Wave emphasis effects.

• If necessary, click the Slide 1 title text placeholder border so that it displays as a solid line. Click the Animation Pane button (Animations tab | Advanced Animation group) to display the Animation Pane (Figure 7–18).

Q&A
Why are the three Rectangle effects shaded in the Animation Pane?
The shading corresponds to the three animation effects that you applied to the title text placeholder. The green star indicates the entrance effect, the A with the multicolor underline indicates the Font Color emphasis effect, and the gold star indicates the Wave emphasis effect.

Why do I see a different number after the Rectangle label?
PowerPoint numbers slide elements consecutively, so you may see a different number if you have added and deleted photos, text, and other graphics. You will rename these labels in a later set of steps.

Figure 7–18

2

- Click the up button in the Animation Pane three times to move the three Rectangle animations above the Picture animations (Figure 7–19).

- Click the Play Selected button (Animation Pane) to see the reordered animations.

Can I click the Move Earlier button (Animations tab | Timing group) on the ribbon instead of the up button in the Animation Pane? Yes. Either button will change the animation order.

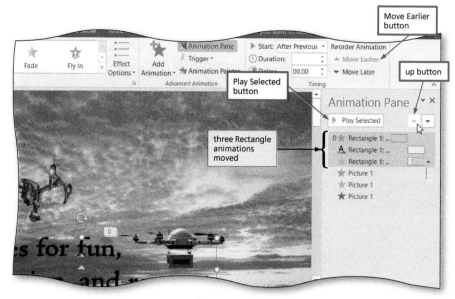

Figure 7–19

3

- In the Animation Pane, click the second Rectangle label representing the Font Color animation to select it and then click the down button to move this animation below the Rectangle label representing the Wave animation (Figure 7–20).

- Click the Play From button (Animation Pane) to see the reordered text placeholder animations beginning with the font color change and the drone animations.

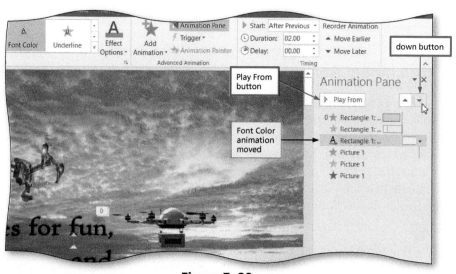

Figure 7–20

Can I click the Move Later button (Animations tab | Timing group) on the ribbon instead of the down button in the Animation Pane? Yes. Either button will change the animation order.

Can I view the Animation Pane at any time when I am adding and adjusting animation effects? Yes. Click the Animation Pane button (Animations tab | Advanced Animation group) to display the Animation Pane.

To Rename Slide Objects

1 MODIFY PHOTOS | 2 ADD ENTRANCE, EMPHASIS, & EXIT ANIMATIONS
3 ANIMATE BOXES, SMARTART, & CHARTS | 4 CHANGE ANIMATION EFFECTS | 5 SET TIMINGS

The two animated title slide elements are listed in the Animation Pane as Rectangle and Picture. You can give these objects meaningful names. *Why? So that you can identify them in the animation sequence.* The following steps rename the animated Slide 1 objects.

1

- Display the Home tab and then click the Select button (Home tab | Editing group) to display the Select menu (Figure 7–21).

- Click Selection Pane in the Select menu to display the Selection pane.

Figure 7–21

2

- Click the Picture label in the Selection pane and then click the label again to place the insertion point in the box (Figure 7–22).

Q&A What does the Picture label represent on three animations?
It indicates that the green entry, yellow emphasis, and red exit animations are applied to a picture, in this case the drone photo.

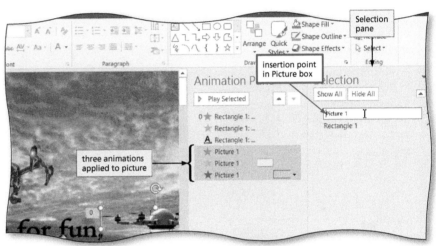

Figure 7–22

3

- Delete the text and then type **Drone** in the Picture box.

- Click the Rectangle label in the Selection pane, click the label again, delete the text, and then type **Title Text** in the Rectangle box (Figure 7–23).

Q&A What does the Rectangle label represent on three animations?
It indicates that the green entry and two emphasis animations are applied to the title text placeholder.

Figure 7–23

4

- Click the Close button on the Selection pane.

- Click the Close button on the Animation pane.

Break Point: If you wish to take a break, this is a good place to do so. Be sure to save the Animated Drones file again and then you can exit PowerPoint. To resume at a later time, run PowerPoint, open the file called Animated Drones, and continue following the steps from this location forward.

To Insert a Text Box and Format Text

1 MODIFY PHOTOS | 2 ADD ENTRANCE, EMPHASIS, & EXIT ANIMATIONS

3 ANIMATE BOXES, SMARTART, & CHARTS | 4 CHANGE ANIMATION EFFECTS | 5 SET TIMINGS

Slide 2 contains three elements that you will animate. First, you will add a text box, format and animate text, and add a motion path and sound. Next, you will add an entrance effect and custom motion path to a drone photo. Finally, you will animate one drone and copy the animations to the other drones using the Animation Painter. The first sequence will be a text box in the lower-left corner of the slide. The following steps add a text box to Slide 2.

- Display Slide 2 and then display the Insert tab.

- Click the Text Box button (Insert tab | Text group).

- Position the pointer in the grass in the lower-left corner of the slide (Figure 7–24) and then click the slide.

Figure 7–24

- Type **Unmanned Aerial Vehicles (UAVs)** in the box (Figure 7–25).

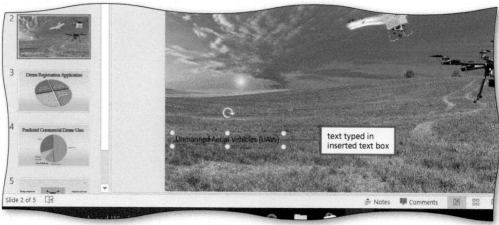

Figure 7–25

3

- Display Slide 1, position the pointer in the second line of the title text placeholder, and then double-click the Format Painter button (Home tab | Clipboard group) (Figure 7–26).

Q&A I am using a touch screen and cannot use the Format Painter for this task. What should I do?
You may need to change the formatting manually.

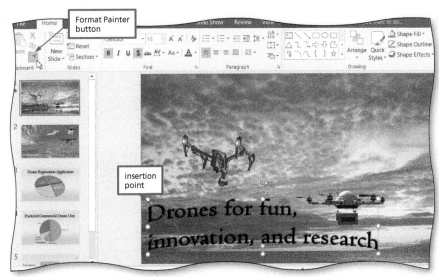

Figure 7–26

4

- Display Slide 2 and then triple-click the inserted box to apply the Slide 1 title text format to the text in the box.

- Press the ESC key to turn off the Format Painter feature.

- Change the font size to 36 point (Figure 7–27).

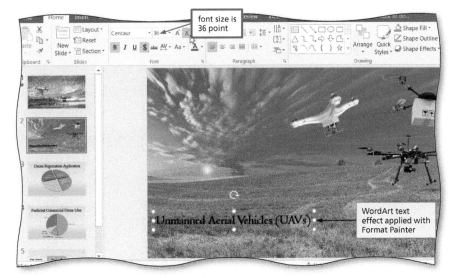

Figure 7–27

5

- Display the Drawing Tools Format tab, click the Text Effects button (Drawing Tools Format tab | WordArt Styles group), point to Transform in the Text Effects menu, and then apply the 'Double Wave 2' WordArt text effect (last effect in fifth row of Warp section) to the words in the box (Figure 7–28).

Figure 7–28

To Animate a Text Box
Using an Entrance Effect

Boxes can have the same animation effects applied to pictures and placeholders, and slide designers often use entrance, emphasis, and exit animations. *Why? These effects can add interest to slides, and the default timings can be changed to synchronize with the slide content.* The 13 effects shown in the Entrance section of the Animation gallery are some of the more popular choices; PowerPoint provides many more effects that are divided into the Basic, Subtle, Moderate, and Exciting categories. The following steps add an entrance effect to the text box.

- If necessary, click the text box to select it and then display the Animations tab.

- Click the More button in the Animation gallery (Animations tab | Animation group) to expand the Animation gallery (Figure 7–29).

- Click More Entrance Effects in the Animation gallery to display the Change Entrance Effect dialog box.

🔍 **Experiment**

- Click some of the entrance effects in the various areas and watch the effect preview in the box on Slide 2.

Figure 7–29

Q&A Can I move the dialog box so that I can see the effect preview?
Yes. Drag the dialog box title bar so that the dialog box does not cover the box.

- Click Expand in the Subtle section (Figure 7–30).

Q&A Why do I see a preview of the effects when I click their names?
The Preview Effect box is selected. If you do not want to see previews, click the box to deselect it.

Figure 7–30

4

- Click the OK button (Change Entrance Effect dialog box) to apply the Expand entrance effect to the text.

- Change the start timing option to With Previous.

- Change the duration to 03.00 seconds (Figure 7–31).

Q&A Can I remove an animation?
Yes. Click None (Animations tab | Animation group). You may need to click the More button to see None.

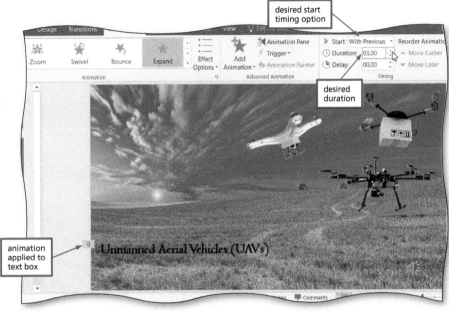

Figure 7–31

To Animate a Text Box by Applying a Motion Path

1 MODIFY PHOTOS | 2 ADD ENTRANCE, EMPHASIS, & EXIT ANIMATIONS
3 ANIMATE BOXES, SMARTART, & CHARTS | **4 CHANGE ANIMATION EFFECTS** | **5 SET TIMINGS**

Why? *One of the more effective methods of animating slide objects is to use a motion path to predetermine the route the object will follow.* In your presentation, the text box will move from the left side of the slide to the right side in an upward curving motion that simulates a drone's flight through the sky. The following steps apply a motion path to the Slide 2 text box and then reverse the direction of the arc.

1

- With the Slide 2 text box still selected, click the Add Animation button (Animations tab | Advanced Animation group) to expand the Animation gallery.

- Scroll down until the Motion Paths section is visible (Figure 7–32).

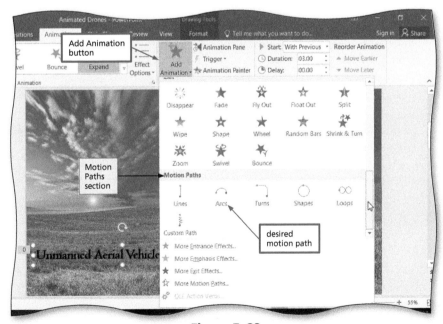

Figure 7–32

2

- Click the Arcs motion path to apply the animation to the box.

- Change the start timing option to After Previous.

- Change the duration to 05.00 seconds (Figure 7–33).

Are more motion paths available in addition to those shown in the Animation gallery? Yes. To see additional motion paths, click More Motion Paths in the lower portion of the Animation gallery. The motion paths are arranged in the Basic, Lines & Curves, and Special categories.

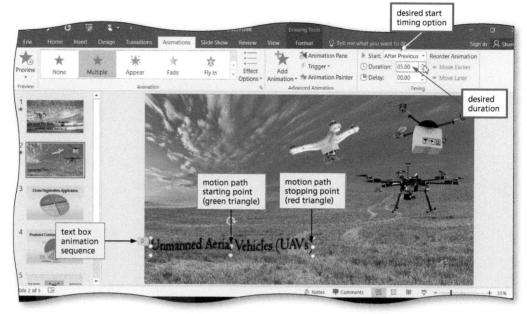

Figure 7–33

3

- Click the Effect Options button (Animations tab | Animation group) to display the Effect Options gallery (Figure 7–34).

4

- Click Up in the Direction section to reverse the direction from Down to Up.

- Click the Preview button (Animations tab | Preview group) to preview the custom animation.

Figure 7–34

To Adjust a Motion Path

1 MODIFY PHOTOS | 2 ADD ENTRANCE, EMPHASIS, & EXIT ANIMATIONS
3 ANIMATE BOXES, SMARTART, & CHARTS | 4 CHANGE ANIMATION EFFECTS | 5 SET TIMINGS

The Arcs motion path moves the box in the correct directions, but the path can be extended to move across the entire width of the slide. The green triangle at the end of the word, Aerial, indicates the starting point, and the red triangle in the right parenthesis indicates the stopping point. You would like to move the stopping point toward the right edge. *Why? The text box is positioned on the left side of the slide, so it does not need to be moved to the left. The stopping point, however, is positioned in the middle of the slide, so it can be moved to the right to increase the distance and provide the maximum animation effect on the slide.* The following steps move the stopping point on the Slide 2 text box animation.

1

- Click the text box to select it. Drag the red stopping point to the location shown in Figure 7–35.

Q&A My entire motion path moved. How can I move only the red stopping point arrow?
Be certain your pointer is a two-headed arrow and not a four-headed arrow.

If I wanted to move the starting point, what would I do?
Drag the green starting point to the desired location.

red stopping point moved to new location

Figure 7–35

2

- Preview the custom animation.

- Click the slide to clear the selected text and view the motion path (Figure 7–36).

Q&A I do not see the motion path on my slide. Where is it?
The white motion path is difficult to see against the green grass. If you look carefully, however, you can see the white line overlaying the first few letters of the word, Vehicles.

Preview button

motion path

sound icon

Unmanned Aerial Vehicles (UAVs)

Figure 7–36

My animation is not exactly like the path shown in Figure 7–36. Can I change the path?
Yes. Continue adjusting the starting and stopping points and playing the animation until you are satisfied with the effect.

To Associate a Sound with an Animation

1 MODIFY PHOTOS | 2 ADD ENTRANCE, EMPHASIS, & EXIT ANIMATIONS
3 ANIMATE BOXES, SMARTART, & CHARTS | **4 CHANGE ANIMATION EFFECTS** | 5 SET TIMINGS

Why? *Sounds can enhance a presentation if used properly, and they can be linked to other animations on the slide.* Slide 2 already has an inserted drone sound. The following step associates the sound with the box on Slide 2.

- Move the pointer to the location where the sound icon is located on Slide 2 (shown in Figure 7–36) and then click the sound icon to display the sizing handles for the sound icon.

- Click the Play button (Animations tab | Animation group).
- Change the start timing option to With Previous (Figure 7–37).

Figure 7–37

- Click the location where the sound icon is located and then display the Audio Tools Playback tab.
- Click 'Loop until Stopped' (Audio Tools Playback tab | Audio Options group) to select the check box (Figure 7–38).

Q&A
How do I know animation has been added to the drone sound?
The 0 in the numbered tag indicates an animation is applied.

Figure 7–38

To Draw a Custom Motion Path

1 MODIFY PHOTOS | 2 ADD ENTRANCE, EMPHASIS, & EXIT ANIMATIONS
3 ANIMATE BOXES, SMARTART, & CHARTS | **4 CHANGE ANIMATION EFFECTS** | 5 SET TIMINGS

Why? Although PowerPoint supplies a wide variety of motion paths, at times they may not fit the precise animations your presentation requires. In that situation, you can draw a custom path that specifies the unique movement your slide element should make. Slide 2 has clips of several drones. You can animate a drone to fly to several areas in the sky. No preset motion path presents the exact motion you want to display, so you will draw your own custom path.

Drawing a custom path requires some practice and patience. A mouse is required to perform this task, and you click the mouse to begin drawing the line. If you want the line to change direction, such as to curve, you click again. When you have completed drawing the path, you double-click to end the line. The following steps draw a custom motion path.

1

• Select the drone carrying a box photo in the upper-right corner of the slide (shown in Figure 7–38). Apply the Fade entrance effect and then change the start timing option to After Previous.

• Click the Add Animation button and then scroll down until the entire Motion Paths section is visible (Figure 7–39).

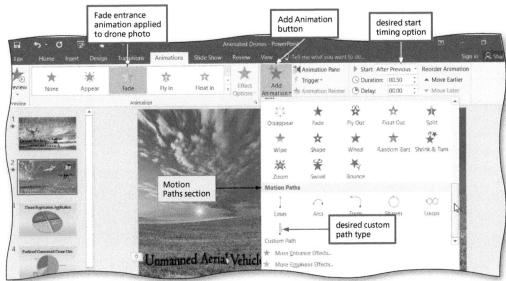

Figure 7–39

◀ | Can I draw a custom motion path when using a touch screen?
Q&A | No. You must use a mouse to perform this task.

2

• Click Custom Path in the Motion Paths gallery to add this animation.

• Click the Effect Options button (Animations tab | Animation group) to display the Type gallery (Figure 7–40).

Figure 7–40

3

• Click Curve in the Type gallery and then position the pointer directly on top of the drone's box.

Figure 7–41

Q&A Why did I need to change the option from Scribble to Curve?

Your custom motion path will select particular locations on the slide, and the Curve type will create rounded edges to connect the lines you draw. The Scribble option would draw only straight lines, so the drone would not have smooth turns as it flew from one location to the next.

- Click to indicate where the curve will start and then move the pointer downward to the location shown in Figure 7–41, which is where the curve will change direction.

- Click to set the bottom of the curve and then position the pointer above the tree near the center of the slide (Figure 7–42).

Figure 7–42

- Click to set the location above the tree where the drone will change direction. Position the pointer on the left side of the white drone, as shown in Figure 7–43, and then click to set the top of the curve in this direction of travel.

Figure 7–43

- Position the pointer on the horizon, as shown in Figure 7–44, and then double-click to indicate the end of the motion path and preview this animation.

- Change the start timing option to After Previous and the duration setting to 07.00 seconds (Figure 7–44).

Figure 7–44

Q&A If my curve is not correct, can I delete it?

Yes. Select the motion path, press the DELETE key, and then repeat the previous steps.

To Use the Animation Painter to Animate a Picture

At times, you may desire to apply the same animation effects to several objects on a slide. On Slide 2, for example, you want to animate the three drones with identical entrance, emphasis, and exit effects. As with the Format Painter that is used to duplicate font and paragraph attributes, the Animation Painter copies animation effects. Using the Animation Painter can save time. *Why? It duplicates numerous animations quickly and consistently.* The following steps animate one drone and then use the Animation Painter to copy these effects to two other drones.

1

- Select the white drone that is located near the center of the slide and then apply the Fly In entrance effect.

- Click the Effect Options button and then change the direction to 'From Top-Left'.

- Change the start timing option to After Previous and the duration to 06.00 seconds (Figure 7–45).

Figure 7–45

2

- Select the white drone, add the Pulse emphasis effect, change the start timing option to After Previous, and then change the duration to 02.00 seconds (Figure 7–46).

Figure 7–46

3

- With the white drone still selected, add the Fade exit effect, change the start timing option to After Previous, and then change the duration to 03.00 seconds (Figure 7–47).

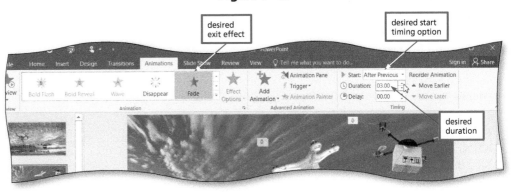

Figure 7–47

Q&A

Can I copy the animation to an object on another slide?

Yes. Once you establish the desired animation effects, you can copy them to any object that can be animated on any slide.

❹

- Click the drone with the box, which has the motion path and other animation effects, to select it and then click the Animation Painter button (Animations tab | Advanced Animation group).

- Position the pointer over the black drone with the camera, which is located beneath the drone with the box (Figure 7–48).

Figure 7–48

◄ Q&A ► Why did my pointer change shape?

The pointer changed shape by displaying a paintbrush to indicate that the Animation Painter function is active.

❺

- Click the black drone to apply the same entrance, emphasis, and exit animation effects as those added to the drone with the box (Figure 7–49).

- Preview the animation effects.

◄ Q&A ► Can I copy the animations to more than one object simultaneously?

Yes. Double-click the Animation Painter button and then apply it to multiple items. The Animation Painter functions in a similar manner as the Format Painter.

Figure 7–49

Other Ways

1. Select animated object, press ALT+SHIFT+C, click target object to copy animation

Break Point: If you wish to take a break, this is a good place to do so. Be sure to save the Animated Drones file again and then you can exit PowerPoint. To resume at a later time, run PowerPoint, open the file called Animated Drones, and continue following the steps from this location forward.

To Animate a SmartArt Graphic

The Federal Aviation Administration (FAA) requires every person who owns a drone weighing more than .55 pounds to file a Drone Registration Application. This online form has four registration components, and they are shown in the Slide 3 SmartArt graphic. You want to add animation to each SmartArt shape. *Why? This animation emphasizes each step in the registration process and helps the audience concentrate on each component.* While you can add a custom animation to each shape in the cycle, you also can use one of PowerPoint's built-in animations to simplify the animation procedure. The following steps apply an entrance animation effect to the Segmented Cycle diagram.

- Display Slide 3, select the SmartArt graphic, and then display the Animation gallery (Figure 7–50).

- Select the Zoom entrance effect.

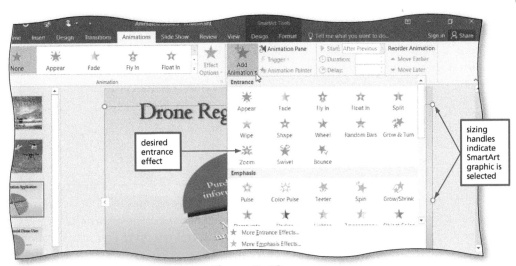

Figure 7–50

To Change a SmartArt Graphic Animation Sequence

By default, all SmartArt graphic components enter the slide simultaneously. You can modify this entrance sequence setting. *Why? Each element will enter one at a time and build a clockwise sequence.* The following steps change the sequence for the SmartArt animation to One by One.

- Click the Effect Options button to display the Effect Options gallery (Figure 7–51).

Q&A
Can I reverse the order of individual shapes in the SmartArt sequence?
No. You can reverse the order of the entire SmartArt graphic but not individual shapes within the sequence.

Figure 7–51

2

- Click 'One by One' in the Sequence section to change the animation order.

- Change the start timing option to After Previous, the duration to 04.00 seconds, and the delay to 01.00 second (Figure 7–52).

- Preview the animations and watch the four SmartArt graphic components enter the slide individually in a clockwise sequence.

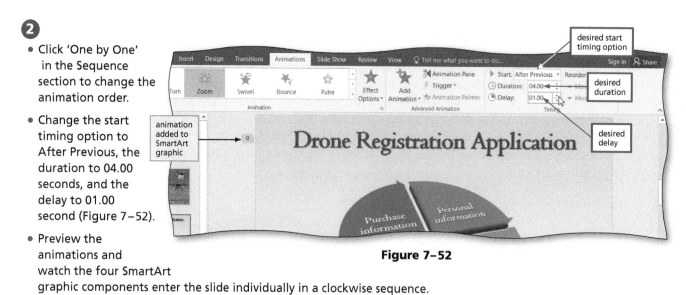

Figure 7–52

To Animate a Chart

1 MODIFY PHOTOS | 2 ADD ENTRANCE, EMPHASIS, & EXIT ANIMATIONS
3 ANIMATE BOXES, SMARTART, & CHARTS | 4 CHANGE ANIMATION EFFECTS | 5 SET TIMINGS

The chart on Slide 4 shows general categories of how drones will be used in the future. You can animate the slices of the pie chart. *Why? So that each slice enters the slide individually and the audience's attention is drawn to each type of drone.* As with the SmartArt animation, PowerPoint gives you many options to animate the chart data. The following steps animate the Slide 4 chart slices.

1

- Display Slide 4 and then click an area outside of the chart so that the frame is displayed.

- Display the Animation gallery and then apply the Fly In entrance effect.

2

- Click the Effect Options button to display the Effect Options gallery. If necessary, scroll down to display both Sequence options (Figure 7–53).

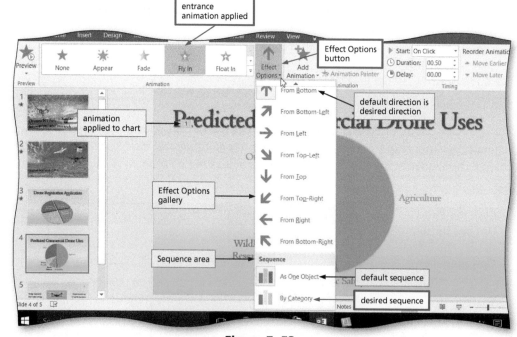

Figure 7–53

3

- Click By Category to change the chart animation so that each slice appears individually and to preview the animations.

4

• Change the start timing option to After Previous, change the duration to 02.00 seconds, and change the delay to 01.50 seconds (Figure 7–54).

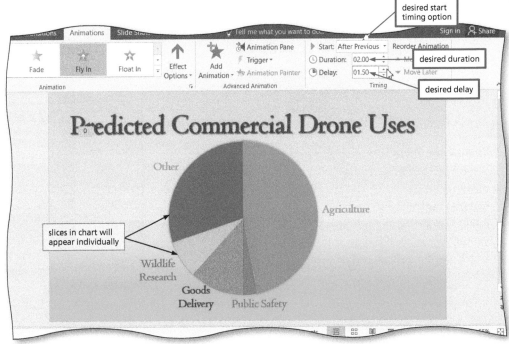

Figure 7–54

To Animate a List

The two lists on Slide 5 give specific applications where drone use has benefited the general public or commercial interests. Each item in the placeholder is a separate paragraph. You can have each paragraph in the left list enter the slide individually. *Why? To add interest during a presentation.* When the entire list has displayed, the list can disappear and then each paragraph in the right list can appear. The following steps animate the Slide 5 paragraph lists.

1

• Display Slide 5 and then select the left text placeholder.

• Apply the Shape entrance animation effect, change the start timing option to After Previous, change the duration to 03.00 seconds, and then change the delay to 01.50 seconds (Figure 7–55).

Figure 7–55

- Click the Effect Options button to display the Effect Options gallery (Figure 7–56).

- Change the Shapes from Circle to Box.

- Click the Effect Options button again and then change the Direction to Out.

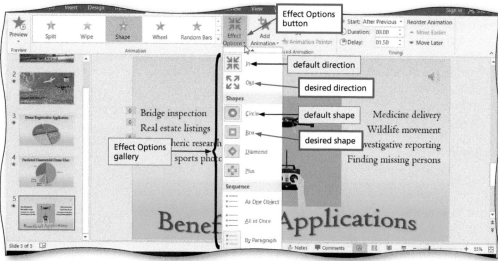

Figure 7–56

CONSIDER THIS

Select colors for dimming text.

After paragraphs of text are displayed, you can change the color, or dim the text, to direct the audience's attention to another area of the slide. Choose the dimming colors carefully. For example, use cool colors, such as blue, purple, and turquoise, as backgrounds so that the audience focuses on the next brighter, contrasting color on the slide. Be certain the color you choose can be seen against the background. In addition, use a maximum of three colors unless you have a compelling need to present more variety.

To Dim Text after Animation

1 MODIFY PHOTOS | 2 ADD ENTRANCE, EMPHASIS, & EXIT ANIMATIONS
3 ANIMATE BOXES, SMARTART, & CHARTS | 4 CHANGE ANIMATION EFFECTS | 5 SET TIMINGS

As each item in the list is displayed, you may desire to have the previous item removed from the screen or to have the font color change, or **dim**. PowerPoint provides several options for you to alter this text by specifying an After Animation effect. The following steps dim each item in the left placeholder list by changing the font color to light blue. *Why? That color is similar to the blue color on the remote control in the illustration.*

- Select the four paragraphs in the left placeholder and then click the Animation Pane button (Animations tab | Advanced Animation group) to display the Animation Pane. Click the double arrow under Content Placeholder to expand the contents and display the four left placeholder paragraphs.

Figure 7–57

- Click 'Extreme sports photos' in the list and then click the Animation Order list arrow to the right of 'Extreme sports photos' to display the Animation Order menu (Figure 7–57).

Q&A Do I need to click the Bridge inspection paragraph, or could I click any of the four paragraphs?

Clicking any of the paragraphs will display the Animation Order menu. When you click the last item, you can see all the paragraphs listed above it.

- Click Effect Options in the Animation Order menu to display the Box dialog box.

- Click the After animation arrow to display the After animation menu (Figure 7–58).

Figure 7–58

- Click the color light blue (fifth color in row of colors) to select this color for the dim effect (Figure 7–59).

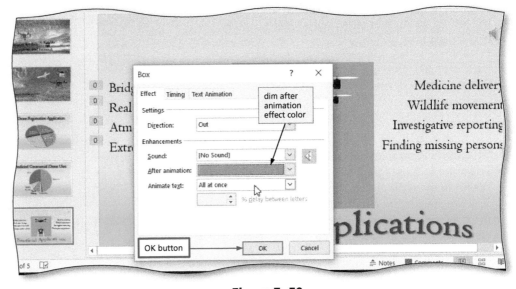

- Click the OK button (Box dialog box) to apply the dim effect to the four items in the left placeholder on Slide 5.

Figure 7–59

To Use the Animation Painter to Animate Text

1 MODIFY PHOTOS | 2 ADD ENTRANCE, EMPHASIS, & EXIT ANIMATIONS

3 ANIMATE BOXES, SMARTART, & CHARTS | **4 CHANGE ANIMATION EFFECTS** | 5 SET TIMINGS

All animations have been applied to the left placeholder paragraphs. You now can copy these animations to the four items in the right text placeholder. The following steps use the Animation Painter to copy the animations. *Why? Copying the animations saves time and ensures consistency between the left and right paragraphs.*

1

- Click the word, Bridge, in the left text placeholder and then click the Animation Painter button (Animations tab | Advanced Animation group) (Figure 7–60).

Q&A Can I place the insertion point in any word in the left text placeholder instead of the first item in the list?

Yes. All the paragraphs have the same animation effects applied, so you can click any word in the list.

Figure 7–60

2

- Click the word, Medicine, in the right list to copy the animations in the left list to the four paragraphs in the right list.

Q&A Can I click any word in the right text placeholder instead of the first item in the list?

Yes. You can click any word in the list to copy the animation effects to all words.

- Select the four paragraphs in the list in the right placeholder, click the Start arrow and change the start timing option to After Previous, change the duration to 03.00 seconds, and then change the delay to 01.50 seconds (Figure 7–61).

- Close the Animation Pane.

Figure 7–61

To Create Credits

1 MODIFY PHOTOS | 2 ADD ENTRANCE, EMPHASIS, & EXIT ANIMATIONS
3 ANIMATE BOXES, SMARTART, & CHARTS | **4 CHANGE ANIMATION EFFECTS** | 5 SET TIMINGS

Many motion pictures use production credits at the end of the movie to acknowledge the people who were involved in the filmmaking process or to provide additional information about the actors or setting. You, too, can use a credit or closing statement at the end of your presentation. *Why? You can use credits to thank individuals or companies who helped you develop your slide show or to leave your audience with a final thought.* The following steps display text as an ascending credit line on Slide 5.

- With Slide 5 displaying, click the placeholder with the words, Beneficial Applications, at the bottom of the slide to select it.

- Display the Animation gallery and then click More Entrance Effects to display the Add Entrance Effect dialog box.

- Scroll down to display the Exciting section (Figure 7–62).

Figure 7–62

- Click the Credits entrance animation effect in the Exciting section to see a preview of the animation effect.

- Click the OK button (Add Entrance Effect dialog box) to apply the effect.

- Change the start timing option to After Previous, the duration to 18.00 seconds, and the delay to 02.00 seconds (Figure 7–63).

- Preview the animation.

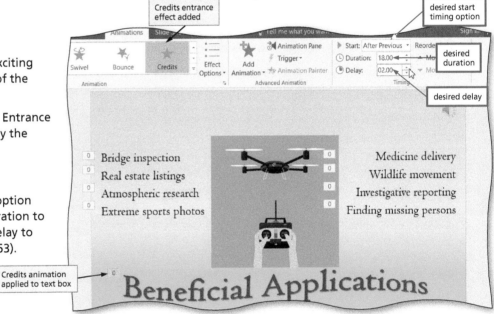

Figure 7–63

To Repeat Credits

To have the credits display more than one time, you would perform the following steps.

1. Display the Animation Pane, click the Animation Order list arrow to the right of the slide element used for the credits, and then click Effect Options in the Animation Order menu.

2. When the Credits dialog box appears, click the Timing tab.

3. Click the Repeat arrow and then select the number of times you desire to have the credits repeat.

To Use the Eyedropper to Format Text

Why? A slide can look cohesive when the shapes, pictures, and text have identical colors. The eyedropper tool can ensure precise color matching. The eyedropper allows you to select any color on the slide to match. The eyedropper is available on several menus, including Shape Fill, Font Color, Shape Outline, Text Outline, Picture Variations, and Glow Colors. After you select the eyedropper, move the pointer to any area of the slide to see a live preview of the color. If you hover over a particular area, a ScreenTip is displayed with the color name and its RGB (red, green, and blue) color coordinates. If many colors are intertwined on the slide, press the ENTER key or the SPACEBAR to select the desired color. The following steps color the text in the text box at the bottom of the slide with the pink color in the drone illustration. Note that the eyedropper tool is not available on touch screens.

1

- Display the Home tab and then select the text, Beneficial Applications.

Q&A Can I select several slide elements to color simultaneously?
Yes. Press CTRL and then click the objects you desire to color.

- Click the Font Color arrow to display the Font Color menu (Figure 7–64).

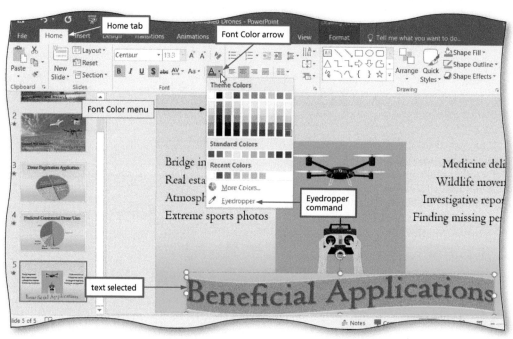

Figure 7–64

2

- Click Eyedropper and then place the pointer over the Pink area of the drone (Figure 7–65).

Q&A Can I cancel using the eyedropper without selecting a color?
Yes. Press the ESC key.

3

- Click the drone to apply the Pink color to the selected text box text.

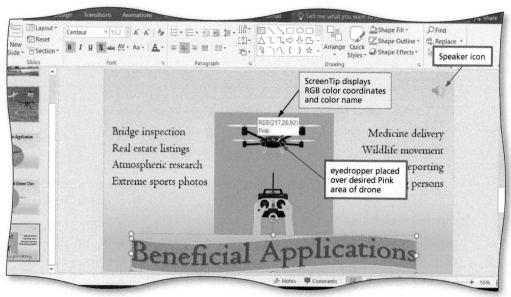

Figure 7–65

To Trigger an Animation Effect

If you select the On Click start timing option and run the slide show, PowerPoint starts the animation when you click any part of the slide or press the SPACEBAR. You may, however, want the option to play an animation in a particular circumstance. *Why? You may have an animated sequence ready to show if time permits or if you believe your audience needs time to understand a process and would understand the concept more readily if you revealed one part of a SmartArt graphic at a time.* A **trigger** specifies when an animation or other action should occur. It is linked to a particular component of a slide so that the action occurs only when you click this slide element. For example, you can trigger an animation effect to start when you click a shape or other object that has the animation applied, or you can trigger an animation effect to begin playing at the start of, or sometime during, an audio or video clip. If you click any other part of the slide, PowerPoint will display the next slide in the presentation. The following steps set the drone illustration on Slide 5 as the trigger to play music, which is an audio clip identified as Closing Music.

1

- Display the Animations tab and then click the speaker icon (shown in Figure 7–65) in the upper-right corner of the slide.

- Click the Play button (Animations tab | Animation group), click the Trigger button (Animations tab | Advanced Animation group) to display the Trigger menu, and then point to 'On Click of' to display the list of Slide 5 elements (Figure 7–66).

Figure 7–66

- Click Picture 1, which is the drone illustration, as the object that will trigger the animation when clicked.

Q&A | How do I know the trigger animation has been added to the Closing Music file?
The tag, with a symbol resembling a lightning bolt, indicates the trigger animation is applied.

To Modify a Transition Effect

The Box transition will be applied to the five slides in this presentation. The default rotation is From Right, so the current slide turns to the left while the new slide appears from the right side of the screen. You can change the Box rotation so that the current slide moves to the top of the screen and the new slide appears from the bottom. *Why? You want the transition effect to emulate a drone taking off from the ground and flying upward.* The following steps apply the Box transition and then modify the transition effect for all slides in the presentation.

- Display the Transitions tab and then apply the Box transition (in Exciting category) to all slides in the presentation.

- Click the Effect Options button (Transitions tab | Transition to This Slide group) to display the Effect Options gallery (Figure 7–67).

Q&A Are the same four effects available for all transitions?
No. The transition effects vary depending upon the particular transition selected.

Figure 7–67

- Click the From Bottom effect to change the rotation.

- Click the 'Apply To All' button (Transitions tab | Timing group) to set the From Bottom transition effect for all slides in the presentation (Figure 7–68).

Figure 7–68

To Apply a Transition to a Single Slide

1 MODIFY PHOTOS | 2 ADD ENTRANCE, EMPHASIS, & EXIT ANIMATIONS
3 ANIMATE BOXES, SMARTART, & CHARTS | 4 CHANGE ANIMATION EFFECTS | **5 SET TIMINGS**

The final slide in the presentation acquaints viewers with specific applications where drones can benefit society and commercial interests. You can change the transition for this one slide. *Why? To emphasize the variety of drone applications.* The following step applies the Wind transition to Slide 5.

- With Slide 5 and the Transitions tab displaying, display the Transitions gallery and then click the Wind transition (in Exciting category) to select this effect for Slide 5 and to see a preview (Figure 7–69).

Figure 7–69

To Run an Animated Slide Show

All changes are complete. You now can view the Animated Drones presentation. The following steps run the slide show.

1 Click the 'Start From Beginning' button in the Quick Access Toolbar to start the presentation and display the title slide.

2 Display each slide, and review the information.

3 When Slide 5 is displayed, click the drone illustration to trigger the music to play while the list of drone applications is displayed.

4 Save the Animated Drones presentation again with the same file name.

Preparing for a Self-Running Presentation

In previous slide shows, you clicked to advance from one slide to the next. Because all animations have been added to the slides in the presentation, you now can set the time each slide is displayed on the screen. You can set these times in one of two ways. The first method is to specify each slide's display time manually. The second method is to use PowerPoint's **rehearsal feature**, which allows you to advance through the slides at your own pace, and the amount of time you view each slide is recorded. You will use the second technique in this module and then adjust the fourth slide's timing manually.

When you begin rehearsing a presentation, the Rehearsal toolbar is displayed. The **Rehearsal toolbar** contains buttons that allow you to start, pause, and repeat viewing the slides in the slide show and to view the times for each slide as well as the elapsed time. Table 7–1 describes the buttons on the Rehearsal toolbar.

Table 7–1 Rehearsal Toolbar Buttons		
Button Name	**Image**	**Description**
Next	➡	Displays the next slide or next animated element on the slide.
Pause Recording	❚❚	Stops the timer. Tap or click the Next or Pause Recording button to resume timing.
Slide Time	0:00:00	Indicates the length of time a slide has been displayed. You can enter a slide time directly in the Slide Time box.
Repeat	↺	Clears the Slide Time box and resets the timer to 0:00:00.
Elapsed Time	0:00:00	Indicates slide show total time.

Give your audience sufficient time to view a slide.
The presentation in this module is designed to run continuously at a kiosk without a speaker's physical presence. Your audience, therefore, must read or view each slide and absorb the information without your help as a narrator. Be certain to give them time to read the slide and grasp the concept you are presenting. They will become frustrated if the slide changes before they have finished viewing and assimilating the material. As you set the slide timings, read each slide aloud and note the amount of time that elapses. Add a few seconds to this time and use this amount for the total time the slide is displayed.

1 MODIFY PHOTOS | 2 ADD ENTRANCE, EMPHASIS, & EXIT ANIMATIONS
3 ANIMATE BOXES, SMARTART, & CHARTS | 4 CHANGE ANIMATION EFFECTS | **5 SET TIMINGS**

To Rehearse Timings

You need to determine the length of time each slide should be displayed. *Why? Audience members need sufficient time to read the text and watch the animations.* Table 7–2 indicates the desired timings for the five slides in the Drones presentation. Slide 1 is displayed and then the title text and animated drone photo appear for 25 seconds. The Slide 2 title text, sound, and clip are displayed for 1:05. Slide 3 has the animated SmartArt, and it takes 45 seconds for the elements to display. The slices in the Slide 4 pie chart can display in 40 seconds, and the two lists and rolling credit on Slide 5 display for one minute, ten seconds.

Table 7–2 Slide Rehearsal Timings		
Slide Number	**Display Time**	**Elapsed Time**
1	0:00	0:25
2	1:05	1:15
3	0:45	2:15
4	0:40	2:50
5	1:10	3:45

BTW

Using the Morph Transition
The Morph transition is a new PowerPoint 2016 feature that helps you animate, move, and emphasize objects smoothly across your slides. To use this transition, you need two consecutive slides with at least one object in common. Place the object on one slide and apply the morph transition to this slide. Then, move the object to a new location on the second slide. When you run the slide show, the object will appear to move seamlessly from one location to the other.

BTW

Conserving Ink and Toner
If you want to conserve ink or toner, you can instruct PowerPoint to print draft quality documents by clicking File on the ribbon to open the Backstage view, clicking the Options tab in the Backstage view to display the PowerPoint Options dialog box, clicking Advanced in the left pane (PowerPoint Options dialog box), scrolling to the Print area in the right pane, placing a check mark in the 'Use draft quality' check box, and then clicking the OK button. Then, use the Backstage view to print the document as usual.

CONSIDER THIS

BTW

Discarding Slide Timings
To remove the slide timings, display the Slide Show tab, click the 'Record Slide Show' arrow (Slide Show tab | Set Up group), point to Clear, and then click 'Clear Timings on All Slides'.

The following steps add slide timings to the slide show.

1

- Display Slide 1 and then click Slide Show on the ribbon to display the Slide Show tab (Figure 7–70).

Figure 7–70

2

- Click the Rehearse Timings button (Slide Show tab | Set Up group) to start the slide show and the counter (Figure 7–71).

Figure 7–71

3

- When the Elapsed Time displays 00:25, click the Next button to display Slide 2.

- When the Elapsed Time displays 01:15, click the Next button to display Slide 3.

- When the Elapsed Time displays 02:15, click the Next button to display Slide 4.

- When the Elapsed Time displays 02:50, click the Next button to display Slide 5.

Figure 7–72

- When the Elapsed Time displays 03:45, click the Next button to display the Microsoft PowerPoint dialog box (Figure 7–72).

4

- Click the Yes button to keep the new slide timings with an elapsed time of 03:45.

- Click the Slide Sorter view button and then, if necessary, zoom the view to display all five thumbnails. Review the timings displayed in the lower-right corner of each slide (Figure 7–73).

Figure 7–73

To Adjust Timings Manually

Why? *If the slide timings need adjustment, you manually can change the length of time each slide is displayed.* In this presentation, you decide to display Slide 4 for 45 seconds instead of 40 seconds. The following step increases the Slide 4 timing.

1

- In Slide Sorter view, display the Transitions tab and then select Slide 4.

- Change the 'Advance Slide After' setting (Transitions tab | Timing group) to 00:45.00 (Figure 7–74).

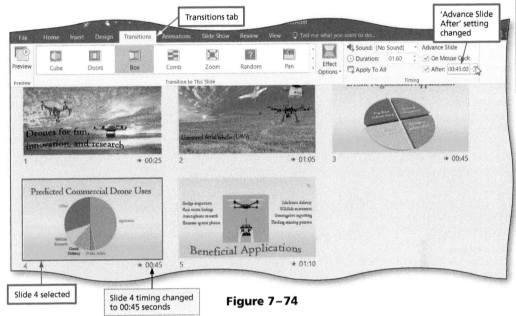

Figure 7–74

To Create a Self-Running Presentation

Why? *The Drones presentation can accompany a speech, but it also can run unattended at hobby shops.* When the last slide in the presentation is displayed, the slide show **loops**, or restarts, at Slide 1. PowerPoint has the option of running continuously until the user presses the ESC key. The following steps set the slide show to run in this manner.

1

- Display the Slide Show tab and then click the 'Set Up Slide Show' button (Slide Show tab | Set Up group) to display the Set Up Show dialog box.

- Click 'Browsed at a kiosk (full screen)' in the Show type section (Figure 7–75).

2

- Click the OK button to apply this show type.

Figure 7–75

BTW

Stopping Slide Shows with a Touch Screen
It may not be possible to stop an animated slide show when using a touch screen, unless you can display a touch keyboard that includes an ESC key.

BTW

Printing Document Properties
PowerPoint 2016 does not allow you to print document properties. This feature, however, is available in other Office 2016 apps, including Word and Excel.

BTW

Distributing a Document
Instead of printing and distributing a hard copy of a document, you can distribute the document electronically. Options include sending the document via email; posting it on cloud storage (such as OneDrive) and sharing the file with others; posting it on social media, a blog, or other website; and sharing a link associated with an online location of the document. You also can create and share a PDF or XPS image of the document, so that users can view the file in Acrobat Reader or XPS Viewer instead of in PowerPoint.

To Run an Animated Slide Show

All changes are complete. You now can view the presentation. The following steps run the slide show.

1 Click the From Beginning button (Slide Show tab | Start Slide Show group) to start the presentation.

2 As each slide automatically is displayed, review the information.

3 When Slide 1 is displayed again, press the ESC key to stop the presentation.

To Save and Exit PowerPoint

The presentation now is complete. You should save the slides with a new file name and then exit PowerPoint.

1 Save the Animated Drones presentation with the file name, Automatic Drones.

2 Exit PowerPoint, closing all open documents.

Summary

In this module you have learned how to remove a background from a photo and then crop and compress the image. You then applied entrance, emphasis, and exit effects to slide content and created a custom animation using a motion path. Also, you inserted and animated a text box and associated a sound with this text. You animated a SmartArt graphic, a chart, and two lists. Then, you set slide timings and created a slide show that runs automatically.

CONSIDER THIS: PLAN AHEAD

What decisions will you need to make when creating your next presentation?
Use these guidelines as you complete the assignments in this module and create your own slide show decks outside of this class.

1. Do not use animation merely for the sake of using animation. Prior to using an animation effect, think about why you need it and how it will affect your presentation.

2. The dimming effect, which changes the color of text paragraphs after they display on a slide, can be used effectively to emphasize important points and to draw the audience's attention to another area of the slide. Select dimming colors that suit the purpose of the presentation.

3. On average, an audience member will spend only eight seconds viewing a basic slide with a simple graphic or a few words. They need much more time to view charts, graphs, and SmartArt graphics. When you are setting slide timings, keep this length of time in mind, particularly when the presentation is viewed at a kiosk without a speaker's physical presence.

Apply Your Knowledge

Reinforce the skills and apply the concepts you learned in this module.

Applying Entrance and Emphasis Effects, Animating a SmartArt Graphic, Renaming a Slide Object, Animating a Text Box by Applying a Motion Path, and Adjusting a Motion Path

Note: To complete this assignment, you will be required to use the Data Files. Please contact your instructor for information about accessing the Data Files.

Instructions: Run PowerPoint. Open the presentation called Apply 7–1 Dogs, which is located in the Data Files. The slides in this presentation present information about your dog walking service. The document you open is a partially formatted presentation. You are to add entrance and emphasis effects to text, an illustration, and a SmartArt graphic. You will adjust a custom motion path, and animate a text box by applying a motion path. Your slides should look like Figure 7–76.

Perform the following tasks:

1. On Slide 1 (Figure 7–76a), increase the size of the dog illustration in the lower-left corner of the slide to 1.75" × 2.21" and remove the 'Simple Frame - Black' picture style from the dog illustration *Hint:* Click the Reset Picture button (Picture Tools Format tab | Adjust group), and then move the picture to the location shown in the figure.

2. Apply the Fly In, From Left entrance effect to the dog illustration, change the start timing option from On Click to After Previous, and then change the duration to 1.75 seconds. Rename the dog illustration from Picture 3 to Dog1.

3. Convert the bulleted text on Slide 1 to the Radial Venn SmartArt graphic (first graphic in fourth Cycle row). Change the font to Arial. Decrease the size of the center circle of the SmartArt graphic to approximately 1.5" × 1.5" and then change the size of the four outer circles of the SmartArt graphic to 1" × 1". Move the four outer circles so they touch the center circle of the SmartArt graphic and then move the graphic to the location shown in the figure. (*Hint:* If needed, use the arrow keys to move the circles in smaller increments and use the guides, if necessary, to keep the circles aligned.) Change the color to 'Transparent Gradient Range - Accent 1' (fifth color in Accent 1 row) and then apply the Cartoon 3-D style (third style in first 3-D row).

4. Apply the 'Grow & Turn' entrance effect to the SmartArt graphic. Add the 'One by One' effect option, change the start timing option to After Previous, and then change the duration to 1.50 seconds.

5. Insert a text box in the center of the Slide 1 and then type **Call 555-555-1234 for more information** in the text box. Change the font to Arial, bold the text, and then change the font color to 'White, Background 1' (first color in first Theme Colors row). If necessary, change the size of the text box so that the text is all on one line. Move the text box to the lower-left corner of the slide. Apply an Arc Up motion path to the text box, change the Start timing option to After Previous, and then change the duration to 2.50 seconds. Adjust the motion path of the text box so that it ends in the lower-right corner of the slide.

6. Open the Animation Pane, select the Dog1 animation object, and then move it down so that it is the last animation on Slide 1. Preview the Slide 1 animations.

7. On Slide 2 (Figure 7–76b), select the title and apply the Random Bars entrance effect, and then change the direction to vertical. Change the start timing option from On Click to After Previous and then change the duration to 2.50 seconds.

Continued >

Apply Your Knowledge *continued*

8. Apply the Bold Reveal emphasis effect to the three paragraphs in the content placeholder. Select the paragraphs, display the Animation Pane, click the Animation Order list arrow to the right of one of the paragraphs, click Effect Options in the Animation Order list, and then click the Animate text arrow in the Bold Reveal dialog box. Choose the By word effect option and then change the delay to 0.5 seconds between words. Click OK to close the Bold Reveal dialog box. Change the start timing option to After Previous and then change the duration to 1.25 seconds.

(a) Slide 1

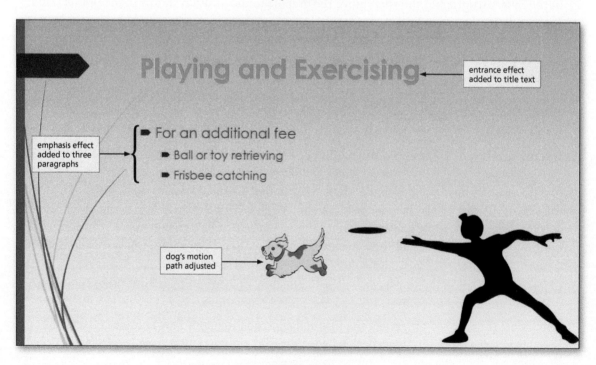

(b) Slide 2

Figure 7–76

9. On Slide 2, adjust the custom motion path for the dog by moving the stopping point (red triangle) to the left edge of the slide. Also, to make the dog jump higher, move the middle sizing handle of the custom motion path box up below the third paragraph of the content placeholder.

10. Open the Animation Pane, and select the title object, and move it up to the first position in the animation. Also, select the Picture 3 object and move it down so it is the last animation on the slide. Close the Animation Pane. Preview the Slide 2 animations.

11. If requested by your instructor, add your grandmother's first name in the lower-left text box after the word, Call, on Slide 1.

12. Run the slide show and then save the presentation using the file name, Apply 7–1 Dog Walking Service.

13. Submit the revised document in the format specified by your instructor.

14. ✳ In this presentation, you converted text to a SmartArt graphic on Slide 1. How will adding this animation to the graphic help focus the audience's attention on this content when you give this presentation?

Extend Your Knowledge

Extend the skills you learned in this module and experiment with new skills. You may need to use Help to complete the assignment.

Changing Animation, Adding Sound to Animation, Copying Animation Using the Animation Painter, Compressing a Photo, and Cropping a Photo to a Shape

Note: To complete this assignment, you will be required to use the Data Files. Please contact your instructor for information about accessing the Data Files.

Instructions: Run PowerPoint. Open the presentation called Extend 7–1 Walking Club, which is located in the Data Files. You will change, reorder, and add sound to animation, copy animations using the Animation Painter, and crop a photo to a shape, as shown in Figure 7–77.

Perform the following tasks:

1. On Slide 1 (Figure 7–77a), add the 'Double Wave 1' Transform text effect (third effect in fifth Warp row) to the title WordArt and then change the color of the text to White, Text 1 (second color in first Theme Colors row). Apply the Wipe entrance effect with the From Left effect option to the title. Change the effect option to By word and then increase the delay between words to 50%. Change the start timing option to After Previous and the duration to 3.00 seconds.

2. Change the Zoom entrance effect on the Explosion 2 shape in the lower right corner of Slide 1 to the 'Grow & Turn' entrance effect. Change the effect option to By word. Change the start timing option to After Previous, change the duration to 3.50 seconds, and then add the Click sound that is included with PowerPoint. (*Hint*: In the Animation Pane, select the Explosion 2 shape, display the Animation Order menu, click Effect Options on the Animation Order menu to display the Grow & Turn dialog box, display the Sound list in the Enhancements section, and then select the sound.) Reorder this entrance effect animation, Explosion 2, so that it follows the title animation. Preview the Slide 1 animation.

3. On Slide 2 (Figure 7–77b), apply the Transparency emphasis effect with the 25% effect option to the SmartArt graphic. Change the sequence to 'One by One'. Change the start timing option to After Previous and then change the duration to 1.50 seconds.

4. Select the female walker illustration on Slide 2 and apply the Fade entrance effect. Change the start timing option to After Previous and then change the duration to 3.75 seconds. Preview the Slide 2 animations.

Continued >

Extend Your Knowledge *continued*

5. On Slide 3 (Figure 7–77c), select the Moonlight walk photo in the upper right corner of the slide and compress it. Crop the picture to fill an oval shape. (Hint: With the picture selected, display the Picture Tools Format tab, click the Crop button arrow, point to 'Crop to Shape', and then click the Oval shape in the Basic Shapes area.) Adjust the size of the shape to approximately 3.25" × 3.43". Change the weight of the border to 3 pt and then change the border color to Orange (third color in Standard Colors).

(a) Slide 1

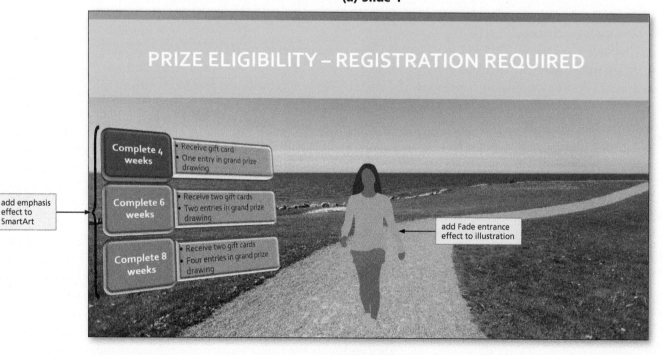

(b) Slide 2

Figure 7–77 (Continued)

Continued >

6. In the orange rectangular text placeholder on Slide 3, select the text 'New Trail Open' and then apply the Fly In, From Right entrance effect. Change the start timing option to After Previous and the duration to 3.00 seconds. Use the Animation Painter to apply same animations to the text 'Join us for a'. Select the text 'Moonlight walk' and then apply the Fly In, From Bottom entrance effect. Change the start timing option to After Previous and the duration to 3.25 seconds. Change the color to green after animation. (*Hint*: In the Fly In dialog box, click the arrow in the After animation box and then select More Colors. In the Colors dialog box, select a

(c) Slide 3

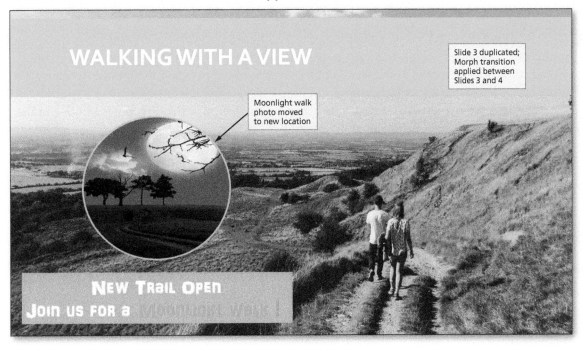

(d) Slide 4

Figure 7–77 (Continued)

Continued >

Extend Your Knowledge *continued*

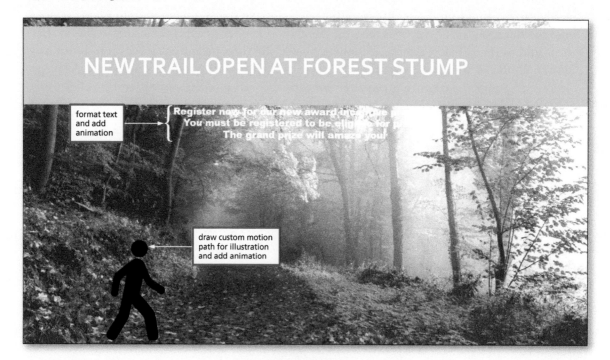

(e) Slide 5

Figure 7–77

green color from the left side of the color chart.) Select the text box with the exclamation point and then add the Bounce entrance effect. Change the start timing option to After Previous and the duration to 3.00 seconds. Preview the Slide 3 animations.

7. Duplicate Slide 3. In the new Slide 4 (Figure 7–77d), move the Moonlight walk photo to the area above the words, New Trail Open, in the orange text placeholder. On Slide 4 only, apply the Morph transition (in Subtle category) and change the duration to 3.00 seconds.

8. On Slide 5 (Figure 7–77e), select the person silhouette illustration and draw a custom motion path so the person moves to the front and center area of the path and then down the path to the end. Change the start timing option to After Previous and the duration to 3.25 seconds. Add a Grow/Shrink emphasis effect to the man and then change the direction to Both and the Amount to Tiny. Change the start timing option to After Previous and the duration to 1.50 seconds. Add a Disappear exit effect to the person. Change the start timing option to After Previous and the duration to 1.50 seconds. Preview the Slide 4 animations.

9. On Slide 5, select the three paragraphs in the placeholder, increase the font size to 24 point, underline the text, and then change the line spacing to 3.0. Move the placeholder to the bottom of the slide, apply the Credits entrance effect, hide after animation, and add the Chime sound (chimes.wav). Change the start timing option to After Previous, and the duration to 16.00 seconds. Repeat the credits 2 times. (*Hint*: Display the Animation Pane, click the Animation Order list arrow to the right of 'Register now…', click Effect Options in the Animation Order menu, click the Timing tab, click the Repeat arrow, and then click 2.)

10. If requested by your instructor, add the name of your current or previous pet as the fourth paragraph of the credits on Slide 5.

11. Run the presentation and then save the file using the file name, Extend 7–1 Four Seasons Walking Club.

12. Submit the revised document in the format specified by your instructor.

13. ☀ In Step 2, you changed the entrance effect for the explosion shape. Is this new entrance effect more effective? Why or why not? In Step 7, did adding the Disappear exit effect to the illustration add visual interest to the slide? Why? Is the Morph transition a beneficial addition to PowerPoint 2016?

Expand Your World

Create a solution that uses cloud or web technologies by learning and investigating on your own from general guidance.

Locating and Inserting Animated GIF Files

Instructions: In this module you animated photos, a SmartArt object, a chart, and text. Some objects, however, already have animation applied when inserted into a PowerPoint slide or other file, such as a website. These animated GIF files generally are simple pictures with a limited number of colors. As noted in this module, animated GIFs cannot be cropped.

GIF, or Graphics Interchange Format, images were introduced in 1987 and are used frequently. They may or may not be animated. Many websites provide a variety of free and low-cost animated GIFs, and some offer information about creating animated GIF files. Care must be taken, however, to visit and download files from reputable sources so that malware is not embedded in the image. You can use a search engine or another search tool to locate recommended or popular resources.

Perform the following tasks:
1. Visit one of the following websites, or locate other websites that contain animated GIFs: Gifs.net, GIFanimations, Giphy, or Animation Factory.
2. Locate files that could enhance your Animated Drones presentation. Some websites have collections of hobbies that could be useful.
3. Download at least two animated GIFs and then insert them into your Animated Drones presentation.
4. If requested to do so by your instructor, insert the name of your favorite grade school teacher in the footer.
5. Save the presentation using the file name, Expand 7 – 1 GIF Animated Drones.
6. Submit the assignment in the format specified by your instructor.
7. ☀ Why did you select these particular images for your slides? Do the animated GIF images enhance or detract from your presentation? Where might you use GIF files other than in PowerPoint slides?

In the Labs

Design, create, modify, and/or use a presentation following the guidelines, concepts, and skills presented in this module. Labs 1 and 2, which increase in difficulty, require you to create solutions based on what you learned in the module; Lab 3 requires you to apply your creative thinking and problem-solving skills to design and implement a solution.

Continued >

In the Labs *continued*

Lab 1: Adding Sound to Animation, Using the Eyedropper to Match Colors, Cropping a Photo, and Animating a SmartArt Graphic

Note: To complete this assignment, you will be required to use the Data Files. Please contact your instructor for information about accessing the Data Files.

Problem: You work as a dietician. In addition to meeting one-on-one with clients, you give group presentations about healthy eating. When you meet with new clients, you use PowerPoint presentations to supplement the nutritional information you discuss. Many of your clients are unfamiliar with the pomegranate, a super food that has many health benefits, so you decide to create a new presentation on that topic. You located a presentation about pomegranates, and now you want to update it by removing and adding animations, adding sounds to an animation, using the eyedropper to match colors, and cropping a photo. You create the slides shown in Figure 7–78.

Perform the following tasks:

1. Run PowerPoint. Open the presentation, Lab 7–1 Pomegranate, from the Data Files.

2. Change the Slice theme variant from green to red (third color variant).

3. On Slide 1 (Figure 7–78a), change the title font text to Arial Black, increase the size to 72 point, center the text, and have it appear on three lines. Decrease the width of the title placeholder to 5.18". Apply the 'Isometric Right Up' 3-D Rotation text effect (second in Parallel group) to the title text. Apply the Fly In, 'From Bottom Right' entrance effect to the text. Change the start timing option to After Previous and then change the duration to 2.50. Add the Laser audio sound. Animate text By word with 50% delay between words. With the title text still selected, use the eyedropper to match the green leaf color in the pomegranate picture.

4. Select the subtitle text on Slide 1 and remove the Swivel entrance effect from the subtitle text. Change the font to Rockwell Extra Bold, increase the size to 54 point, change the line spacing to exactly 40 point, and then align the subtitle in the bottom of the placeholder.

5. On Slide 1, crop the pomegranate picture on the left side to the farthest-left leaf and on the bottom to just below the pomegranate, as shown in Figure 7–78a. Increase the size of the pomegranate picture to approximately 5.77" × 6.71", apply the 'Bevel Perspective Left, White' picture style to the picture, and then if necessary, move it to the location shown in Figure 7–78a.

6. On Slide 2 (Figure 7–78b), change the title text font to Rockwell Extra Bold, increase the font size to 40 point and then change the color to the same color you created with the eyedropper for the title on Slide 1 (Green color in Recent Colors). Add the Zoom entrance effect to the Slide 2 title text, change the start timing option to After Previous, and then change the duration to 2.00 seconds. Animate text By word and then change the delay between words to 100%. Use the Format Painter and Animation Painter to apply these same attributes to the title text on Slide 3.

7. Select the five bulleted paragraphs on Slide 2 and then apply the Pulse emphasis effect. Change the start timing option to After Previous and then change the duration to 2.25 seconds. Change the After animation color to Black, animate text By word, and then add the Suction sound.

8. On Slide 3 (Figure 7–78c), select the four shapes surrounding the pomegranate illustration, apply the Bounce entrance effect, keep the start timing option to On Click, and then change the duration to 2.50 seconds.

9. On the Slide 4 title (Figure 7–78d), change the word, ONE, to the numeral 1. Change the word, GLASS, to SERVING. Change the title text font to Rockwell Extra Bold and then increase the size to 36 point. Increase the size of the numeral 1 to 88 point.

10. Convert the bulleted text on Slide 4 to the Nested Target SmartArt graphic. Change the color to 'Gradient Range - Accent 4' (third in Accent 4 row) and then apply the Cartoon 3-D style (third style in the first 3-D row) to the SmartArt graphic. Change the transparency of the background picture to 25%.

(a) Slide 1

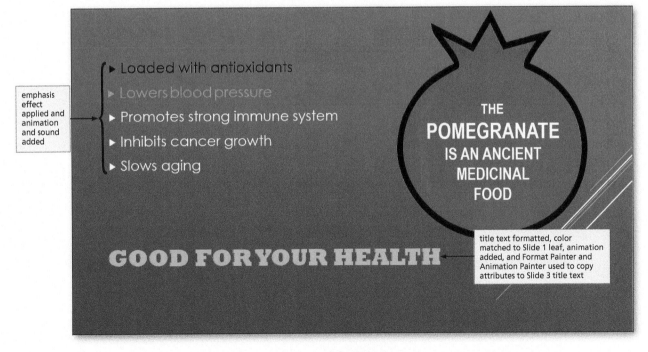

(b) Slide 2

Figure 7–78 (Continued)

Continued >

In the Labs *continued*

(c) Slide 3

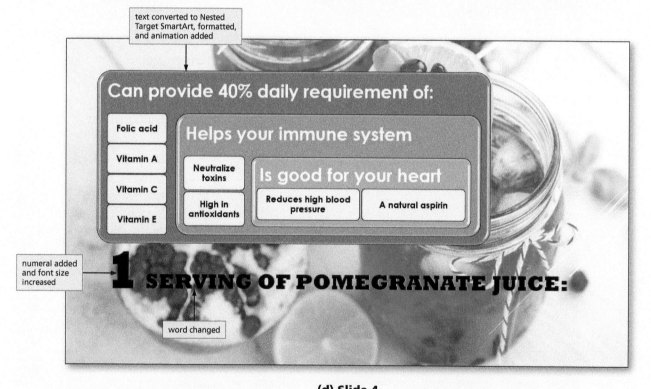

(d) Slide 4

Figure 7–78

11. Apply the Fly In, From Right entrance effect to the SmartArt graphic and then change the sequence to One by One. Change the start timing option to After Previous, change the duration to 0.50 seconds, and then add the chime sound.

12. If requested by your instructor, add the city or county in which you were born as the sixth bulleted paragraph on Slide 2.

13. Run the presentation and then save the file using the file name, Lab 7 – 1 Super Pomegranate.

14. Submit the document in the format specified by your instructor.

15. ✺ Why did you remove the Swivel entrance effect from the subtitle text on Slide 1? Why did you crop the pomegranate picture on Slide 1? How did using the eyedropper tool to match colors help improve the presentation?

Lab 2: Animating a Photo, List, SmartArt, and Chart, Applying a Transition to a Single Slide, and Creating a Self-Running Presentation

Note: To complete this assignment, you will be required to use the Data Files. Please contact your instructor for information about accessing the Data Files.

Problem: Many students have difficulty attempting to find balance in their lives. When juggling the demands of school, family, and work, they feel overwhelmed and exhausted. Your school's Student Life office is offering a seminar with tips for bringing balance to a daily routine, and the director has asked you to develop slides to accompany the presenter, plus a presentation that can be shown at a kiosk. Create the four slides shown in Figure 7 – 79.

Perform the following tasks:

1. Run PowerPoint. Open the presentation, Lab 7–2 Balance, which is located in the Data Files. Add the Berlin theme with the green variant.

2. On Slide 1 (Figure 7–79a), increase the size of the title text placeholder to approximately 3" × 8.6", change the font size to 44 pt, and then center the text. Apply the WordArt style, 'Fill – White, Outline - Accent 1, Shadow' (fourth style in first row). Apply the Glow text effect, 'Lime, 11 pt glow, Accent color 1' (first effect in third Glow Variations row), to this text. Apply the Teeter emphasis effect to the WordArt title. Change the start timing option to After Previous and then change the duration to 4.00 seconds.

3. Remove the background from the key picture, change its size to 4.3" × 4.3", and then move it to the location shown in Figure 7–79a. Apply the Float In entrance effect to this picture with a direction of Float Down. Change the start timing option to After Previous and then change the duration to 2.00 seconds. Open the Animation pane and the Selection pane. Change the name of this picture to Key in the Selection pane. Trigger the key picture to appear on the click of the Subtitle. Close both the Animation and Selection panes.

4. Change the subtitle font size to 36 point and then change the color to Light Blue (seventh color in Standard colors). Apply the Stretch entrance effect (in the Moderate area) to the subtitle. Change the start timing option to After Previous and then change the duration to 1.50 seconds.

5. On Slide 2 (Figure 7–79b), change the title text font size to 40 point, change the font color to Light Blue, and then bold this text. Use the Format Painter to apply these same attributes to the title text on Slides 3 and 4.

6. Remove the background from the scale picture, increase its size to approximately 4.5" × 8.31", and then move it to the location shown in Figure 7–79b. Apply the Fade entrance effect to the photo. Change the start timing option to After Previous, change the duration to 3.25 seconds, and then change the delay to 1.00 seconds.

7. Apply the 'Fill - White, Text 1, Outline - Background 1, Hard Shadow - Background 1' WordArt style (first style in third row) to the word, Work, and the word, Life. Add a Turns motion path for the Work text box so that it curves to the right down to the scale's left tray. To

Continued >

In the Labs *continued*

adjust the motion path, drag the bottom-right sizing handle to the desired location. Change the start timing option to After Previous and change the duration to 2.50 seconds.

8. Add a Turns motion path for the Life text box so that it curves to the left down to the scale's right tray. Change the start timing option to After Previous, change the duration to 2.50 seconds, and then change the delay to 2.00 seconds.

9. On Slide 3 (Figure 7–79c), apply the Float In entrance effect to the photo. Change the start timing option to After Previous and then change the duration to 2.00 seconds.

10. If requested by your instructor, replace the fifth bulleted paragraph on Slide 3 with the name of the last movie you saw.

11. Apply the Fly In, From Top entrance effect to the bulleted text. Change the start timing option to After Previous and then change the duration to 2.00 seconds.

12. On Slide 4, change the chart style to Style 2 and then change the chart color to Color 4 (last row in Colorful area), as shown in Figure 7–79d. Display the Format Data Labels task pane, display the Label Options sheet, and then display only the Category Name labels. Center these labels and then increase the font size to 24 point. Apply the Shape entrance effect to the chart, change the direction to In, and then change the shape to Box. Change the sequence to By Category. Change the timing option to After Previous and then change the duration to 1.50 seconds.

13. Apply the Cube transition in the Exciting section to Slide 4 only, select the From Left effect option, and then change the duration to 1.50 seconds.

14. Run the presentation and then save the file using the file name, Lab 7–2 Balance Life.

15. Rehearse the presentation and then set the slide timings to 15 seconds for Slide 1, 20 seconds for Slides 2 and 3, and 25 seconds for Slide 4. Set the show type as 'Browsed at a kiosk.'

16. Save the presentation again using the file name, Lab 7–2 Balance Life Timings.

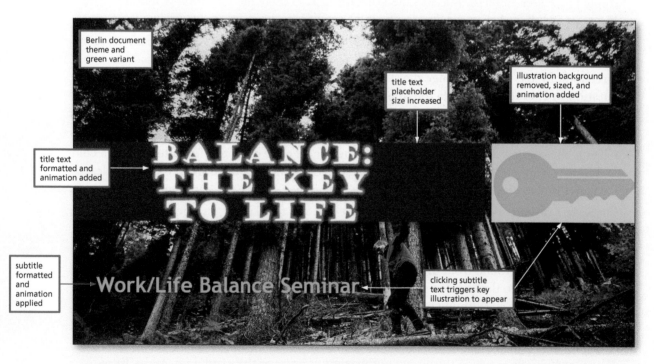

(a) Slide 1

17. Submit the document in the format specified by your instructor.

18. ✳ Did you have difficulty removing the background from the key and scale pictures on Slides 1 and 2? How did removing the backgrounds enhance these two slides? Where would you run the presentation with the slide timings?

(b) Slide 2

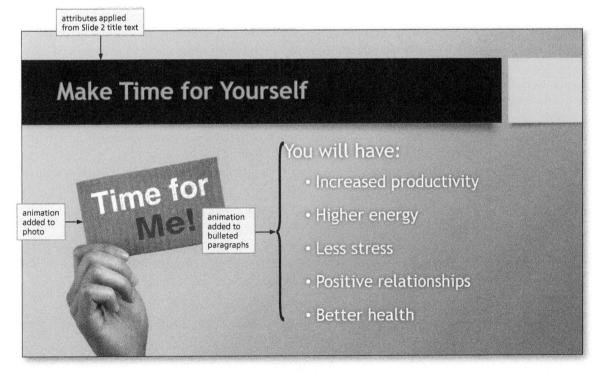

(c) Slide 3

Continued >

In the Labs *continued*

(d) Slide 4

Figure 7–79

Lab 3: **Consider This: Your Turn**

Design and Create a Presentation about Learning to Fly a Drone

Part 1:   The project in this module presents the topic of drones. Learning to fly a drone takes practice, skill, and a knowledge of basic aeronautical principles. Pilots of these unmanned aerial vehicles (UAVs) need to understand how the four aerodynamic forces — lift, gravity, thrust, and drag — interact. Review some websites to learn about the physics involved in flight. Also, research the factors to consider when buying a drone, such as cost, weight, size, battery, and materials. Use the concepts and techniques presented in this module to create a presentation. Select a suitable theme and animate slide content with entrance, emphasis, and exit effects. Include one animated SmartArt graphic showing the four aerodynamic forces. Review and revise your presentation as needed and then save the file using the file name, Lab 7–3 Drone Flying. Submit your assignment in the format specified by your instructor.

Part 2: ☀ You made several decisions while creating the presentation in this assignment: where to place text, how to format the text (such as font and font size), which graphical image(s) to use, where to crop and remove backgrounds from pictures, and which animations to use for graphic elements. What was the rationale behind each of these decisions? When you reviewed the document, what further revisions did you make and why? Where would you recommend showing this slide show?

8 Customizing a Template and Handouts Using Masters

Objectives

You will have mastered the material in this module when you can:

- Apply slide and font themes to a slide master
- Change a slide master background
- Add a background style and graphic to a slide master
- Insert a placeholder into a slide layout
- Apply a Quick Style to a placeholder
- Change text direction and character spacing
- Hide background graphics on individual slides

- Apply a fill to a text box and change transparency
- Rename a slide master
- Save a slide master as a template
- Create handouts using the handout master
- Create speaker notes using the notes master

BTW

Masters Assure Universal Style
Masters are convenient because they allow you to make unique and uniform style changes to every slide in your presentation, including ones added later. Using slide masters saves time because you do not need to format every slide or type the same information repeatedly. You can customize the presentation theme and slide layouts, including the background, color, fonts, effects, and placeholder sizes and location.

Introduction

PowerPoint provides a variety of designs and layouts to meet most presenters' needs. At times, however, you may need a different set of colors, fonts, placeholders, or graphics to display throughout a presentation. PowerPoint allows you to customize the master layouts for slides, handouts, and speaker notes. These masters specify the precise locations and styles of placeholders, pictures, text boxes, and other slide and handout elements.

Once you determine your custom specifications in these masters, you can save the file as a template so that you can reuse these key elements as a starting point for multiple presentations. This unique **template** is a set of special slides you create and then use to create similar presentations. A template consists of a general master slide layout that has elements common to all the slide layouts. One efficient way to create similar presentations is to create a template, save the template, open the template, and then save the slides as a different PowerPoint presentation each time a new presentation is required.

Templates help speed and simplify the process of creating a presentation, so many PowerPoint designers create a template for common presentations they develop frequently. Templates can have a variable number of slide layouts depending upon the complexity of the presentation. A simple presentation can have a few slide layouts; for example, the Zip Line presentation will have three slide layouts. A more complex template can have many slide masters and layouts.

Project — Presentation with Customized Slide, Handout, and Notes Masters

BTW
Multiple Slide Masters
You can insert additional slide masters in one file so that one presentation can have two or more different styles. Each slide master has a related set of layout masters. In contrast, however, one presentation can have only one handout master and one notes master.

Zip lining has grown in popularity in recent years as a tourist and recreational activity throughout the world. Guests are suspended on a cable strung along a slope and propelled downward while gripping a free-moving pulley. Zip lines have been used since the1800s as a method of transporting people and goods over rugged terrain. Facilities offer a wide variety of courses that vary in length and height and are appropriate for people of all ages. The project in this module (Figure 8–1) showcases the amenities at Tree Top Adventures, a park featuring four zip line courses. All three slides are created by starting with a template file that contains two basic slide elements: the park's name on a formatted placeholder and an illustration of a family zip lining. The overall template, called the **slide master** (Figure 8–1a), is formatted with a theme, customized title and text fonts, and customized footer placeholders for the slide layouts. The title slide layout (Figure 8–1b) is used to create Slide 1 (Figure 8–1c), which introduces audiences to the zip line experience. Similarly, the blank slide layout (Figure 8–1d) is used for Slide 2 (Figure 8–1e), which promotes the fun that various groups can share in the park's natural setting. The title and content layout (Figure 8–1f) is used to develop the text describing the four courses and the graphics on Slide 3 (Figure 8–1g). In addition, the custom handout master (Figure 8–1h) is used to create a handout with an illustration of a female zip lining and header and footer text (Figure 8–1i). Likewise, the custom notes master (Figure 8–1j) is used to create speaker notes pages (Figures 8–1k–m).

In this module, you will learn how to create the slides shown in Figure 8–1. The following roadmap identifies general activities you will perform as you progress through this module:

1. CUSTOMIZE SLIDE MASTERS by changing the theme fonts and background.

2. FORMAT and ARRANGE slide master FOOTERS.

3. INSERT and FORMAT GRAPHICS and TEXT BOXES.

4. RENAME and DELETE SLIDE LAYOUTS.

5. CUSTOMIZE HANDOUT and NOTES MASTERS.

6. USE a CUSTOM TEMPLATE to create a new presentation.

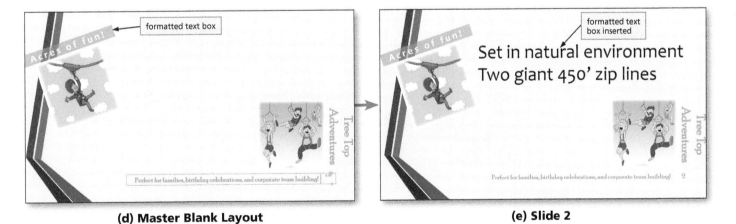

(a) Slide Master

(b) Master Title Slide Layout

(c) Slide 1

(d) Master Blank Layout

(e) Slide 2

Figure 8–1 (Continued)

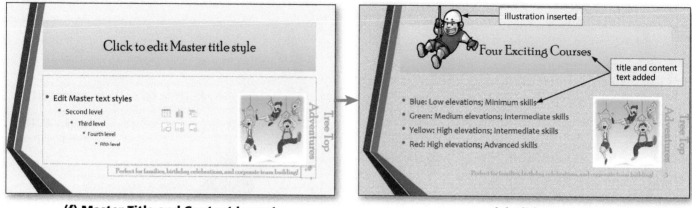

(f) Master Title and Content Layout   **(g) Slide 3**

(h) Handout Master

(i) Handout

Figure 8–1 (Continued)

(j) Notes Master

(k) Speaker Notes – Page 1

(l) Speaker Notes – Page 2

(m) Speaker Notes – Page 3

Figure 8–1

To Run PowerPoint and Save a Presentation with a New File Name

If you are using a computer to step through the project in this module and you want your screens to match the figures in this book, you should change your screen's resolution to 1366 × 768. The following steps run PowerPoint and save a new file.

1 Run PowerPoint. If necessary, maximize the PowerPoint window.

2 Apply the Blank Presentation theme.

3 Save the presentation on your hard drive, OneDrive, or other storage location using the file name, Zip Line.

BTW

The Ribbon and Screen Resolution
PowerPoint may change how the groups and buttons within the groups appear on the ribbon, depending on the computer or mobile device's screen resolution. Thus, your ribbon may look different from the ones in this book if you are using a screen resolution other than 1366 x 768.

Customizing Presentation Slide Master Backgrounds and Fonts

PowerPoint has many template files with the file extension .potx. Each template file has three masters: slide, handout, and notes. A slide master has at least one layout; you have used many of these layouts, such as Title and Content, Two Content, and Picture with Caption, to create presentations. A **handout master** designates the placement of text, such as page numbers, on a sheet of paper intended to distribute to audience members. A **notes master** defines the formatting for speaker's notes.

Slide Master

If you select a document theme and want to change one of its components on every slide, you can override that component by changing the slide master. In addition, if you want your presentation to have a unique design, you might want to create a slide master rather than attempt to modify a current presentation theme. A slide master indicates the size and position of text and object placeholders, font styles, slide backgrounds, transitions, and effects. Any change to the slide master results in changing that component on every slide in the presentation. For example, if you change the second-level bullet on the slide master, each slide with a second-level bullet will display this new bullet format.

One presentation can have more than one slide master. You may find two or more slide masters are necessary when your presentation reuses special slide layouts. In this Zip Line presentation, for example, one slide will have the title slide to introduce the overall concept, another will have a blank slide to showcase the adventure park, and a third slide will have a title and a bulleted list to give specific information about the zip line courses. All slides except the title slide, which has background graphics hidden by default, will have an illustration of a family zip lining and the words, Tree Top Adventures, on the slide master.

BTW

Touch Screen Differences
The Office and Windows interfaces may vary if you are using a touch screen. For this reason, you might notice that the function or appearance of your touch screen differs slightly from this module's presentation.

CONSIDER THIS

Plan the slide master.
Using a new slide master gives you the freedom to specify every slide element. Like an artist with a new canvas or a musician with blank sheet music, your imagination permits you to create an appealing master that conveys the overall look of your presentation.

Before you start developing the master, give your overall plan some careful thought. The decisions you make at this point should be reflected on every slide. A presentation can have several master layouts, but you should change these layouts only if you have a compelling need to change them. Use the concepts you have learned throughout the modules in this book to guide your decisions about fonts, colors, backgrounds, art, and other essential slide elements.

To Display a Slide Master

To begin developing the Zip Line slides, you need to display the slide master. *Why? The slide master allows you to customize the slide components and create a unique design.* The following steps display the slide master.

- Click View on the ribbon to display the View tab (Figure 8–2).

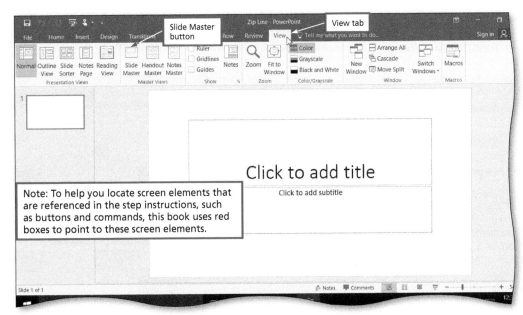

Note: To help you locate screen elements that are referenced in the step instructions, such as buttons and commands, this book uses red boxes to point to these screen elements.

Figure 8–2

- Click the Slide Master button (View tab | Master Views group) to display the Slide Master tab and the slide thumbnails in the Thumbnail pane.

- If necessary, scroll up and then click the Office Theme Slide Master layout (Figure 8–3).

Q&A

What are all the other thumbnails in the left pane below the slide master?

They are all the slide layouts associated with this slide master. You have used many of these layouts in the presentations you have developed in the exercises in this book.

Why is the layout given this name?

The slide layout names begin with the theme applied to the slides. In this case, the default Office Theme is applied. The first slide layout in the list is called the master because it controls the colors, fonts, and objects that are displayed on all the other slides in the presentation.

Figure 8–3

To Apply Slide and Font Themes to a Slide Master

You can change the look of an entire presentation by applying formats to the slide master in the same manner that you apply these formats to individual slides. In this presentation, you will change the slide theme to Parallax and the font colors to blue and green. *Why? The Parallax theme features two lines, which are similar to the zip line cables, along the left edges and colors that match the blue sky.* The following steps apply a theme and change the font theme colors.

1

- With the slide master displaying, click the Themes button (Slide Master tab | Edit Theme group) to display the Themes gallery.

- Scroll down to display the Parallax theme in the gallery (Figure 8–4).

Figure 8–4

2

- Click the Parallax theme to apply this theme to the slide master.

- Click the Theme Colors button (Slide Master tab | Background group) to display the Theme Colors gallery (Figure 8–5).

3

- Click the Blue color scheme in the Theme Colors gallery to change the slide master colors to Blue.

Q&A Can I insert another set of slide masters to give other slides in the presentation a unique look?

Yes. PowerPoint allows you to insert multiple masters into an existing presentation.

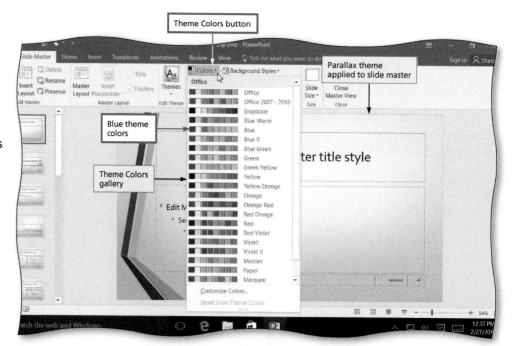

Figure 8–5

To Customize Theme Fonts

Each theme has a heading font and a body font applied to it. At times both fonts are the same, and other times, the heading font differs from the body font, but both fonts coordinate with each other. You can customize theme fonts by selecting your own combination of heading and body font and then giving the new theme font set a unique name. *Why? A particular font may match the tone of the presentation and help convey the message you are presenting.* The following steps apply a new heading font and body font to the Parallax theme.

1

- Click the Theme Fonts button (Slide Master tab | Background group) to display the Theme Fonts gallery (Figure 8–6).

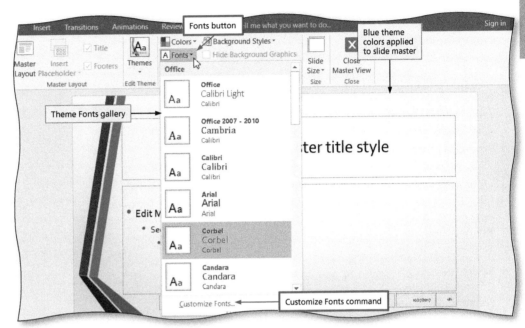

Figure 8–6

2

- Click Customize Fonts in the Theme Fonts gallery to display the Create New Theme Fonts dialog box.

- Click the Heading font arrow and then scroll down to display Poor Richard in the list (Figure 8–7).

Q&A Can I preview the fonts to see how they are displayed on the slide master?

No preview is available when using the Create New Theme Fonts dialog box. Once you select the font, however, PowerPoint will display text in the Sample box.

Figure 8–7

- Click Poor Richard to apply that font as the new heading text font.
- Click the Body font arrow and then scroll up to display Candara in the list (Figure 8–8).

Q&A What if the Poor Richard or Candara fonts are not in my list of fonts?

Select fonts that resemble the fonts shown in Figure 8–8.

Figure 8–8

- Click Candara to apply that font as the new body text font.
- Select the text, Custom 1, in the Name text box and then type **Zip** to name the new font set (Figure 8–9).

Q&A Must I name this font set I just created?

No. If you name the set, however, you easily will recognize this combination in your font set if you want to use it in new presentations. It will display in the Custom area of the Fonts gallery.

Figure 8–9

- Click the Save button (Create New Theme Fonts dialog box) to save this new font set with the name, Zip, and to display the font changes in the slide master.
- Save the presentation again in the same storage location with the same file name.

To Format a Slide Master Background and Apply a Quick Style

1 CUSTOMIZE SLIDE MASTERS | 2 FORMAT & ARRANGE FOOTERS | 3 INSERT & FORMAT GRAPHICS & TEXT BOXES
4 RENAME & DELETE SLIDE LAYOUTS | 5 CUSTOMIZE HANDOUTS & NOTES MASTERS | 6 USE CUSTOM TEMPLATE

Once you have applied a theme to the slide master and determined the fonts for the presentation, you can further customize the slide master. *Why? Adding a unique background and customizing the colors can give your presentation a unique look that matches the message you are conveying.* The following steps format the slide master background and then apply a Quick Style.

1

- Click the Background Styles button (Slide Master tab | Background group) to display the Background Styles gallery (Figure 8–10).

🔍 **Experiment**

- Point to various styles in the Background Styles gallery and watch the backgrounds change on the slide master.

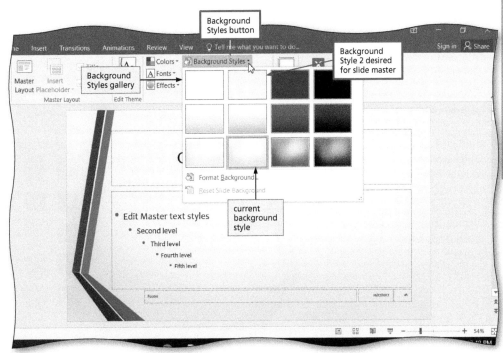

Figure 8–10

2

- Click Background Style 2 (second style in first row) to apply this background to the slide master (Figure 8–11).

Figure 8–11

3

- Click the slide master title text placeholder to select it.

- Display the Home tab and then click the Quick Styles button (Home tab | Drawing group) to display the Quick Styles gallery (Figure 8–12).

Experiment

- Point to various styles in the Quick Styles gallery and watch

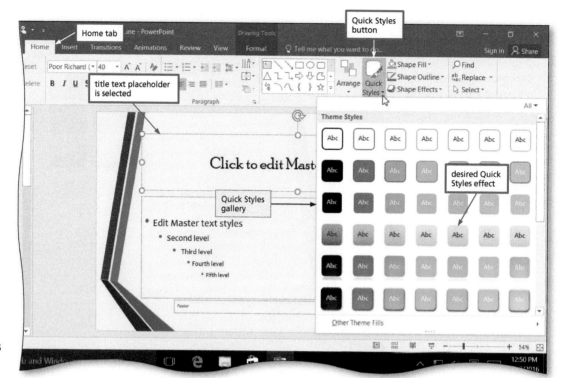

the background and borders change on the slide master title text placeholder.

Figure 8–12

4

- Click the 'Subtle Effect – Bright Green, Accent 4' Quick Style (fifth style in fourth row) to apply this style to the title text placeholder (Figure 8–13).

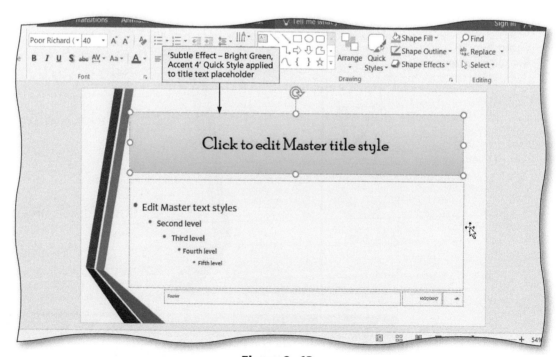

Figure 8–13

To Delete, Move, and Add Text to a Slide Master Footer

Slide numbers, the date and time, and footer text can be displayed anywhere on a slide, not just in the default footer placeholder locations. At times you may want to rearrange or delete these slide elements. *Why? These placeholders might interfere with other slide content, or you might not want to display information, such as a page number or the date.* The following steps delete one footer placeholder, move the footer placeholders, and then add footer text on the slide master.

1

- With the slide master displaying, click the border of the date footer placeholder to select it (Figure 8–14).

2

- Press the DELETE key to delete the date placeholder.

What should I do if the placeholder still is showing on the slide?
Be certain you clicked the placeholder border and not just the text. The border must display as a solid line before you can delete it.

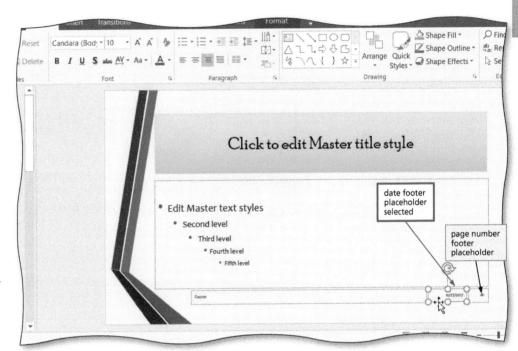

Figure 8–14

3

- Click the content footer placeholder and then drag it to the location where the date placeholder originally appeared (Figure 8–15).

Figure 8–15

- Display the Insert tab, click the Header & Footer button (Insert tab | Text group), and then place a check mark in the Slide number check box.

- Place a check mark in the Footer check box and then type **Perfect for families, birthday celebrations, and corporate team building!** in the Footer text box.

- Place a check mark in the 'Don't show on title slide' check box (Figure 8–16).

Q&A Can I verify where the footer placeholders will display on the slide layout?

Yes. The black boxes in the bottom of the Preview area indicate the footer placeholders' locations.

Figure 8–16

- Click the 'Apply to All' button (Header and Footer dialog box) to add the slide number and footer text to the slide master.

To Format Slide Master Footer Text

1 CUSTOMIZE SLIDE MASTERS | 2 FORMAT & ARRANGE FOOTERS | 3 INSERT & FORMAT GRAPHICS & TEXT BOXES
4 RENAME & DELETE SLIDE LAYOUTS | 5 CUSTOMIZE HANDOUTS & NOTES MASTERS | 6 USE CUSTOM TEMPLATE

You can format slide master footer text using the same font styles and text attributes available to title and subtitle text. **Why?** *Using the same font ensures continuity among the slide elements.* The following steps format the footer text.

- Display the Home tab, select the content footer text, and then click the Font arrow on the mini toolbar to display the Font gallery (Figure 8–17).

Figure 8–17

2

- Click Poor Richard in the Theme Fonts section of the Font gallery to change the footer font.
- Click the Increase Font Size button several times to increase the font size to 20 point.
- Change the font color to Green (sixth color in Standard Colors row).
- Click the Bold button to bold the text.
- Click the Align Right button to move the footer text alignment to the right border of the placeholder.
- Use the Format Painter to apply the content footer placeholder formatting to the page number placeholder (Figure 8–18).

Q&A Why does the page number placeholder now display on two lines?
The increased font size split the placeholder. The page number itself will display on only one line on the slides.

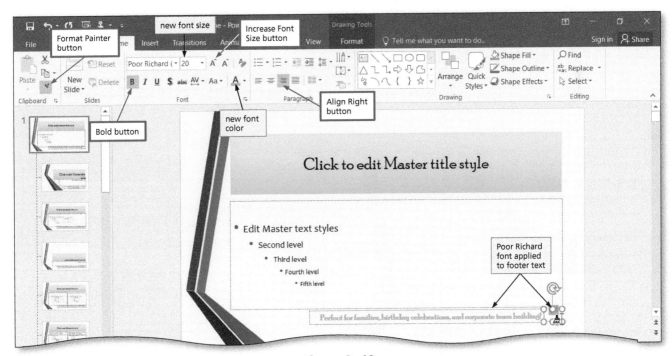

Figure 8–18

To Insert a Background Graphic into a Slide Master

1 CUSTOMIZE SLIDE MASTERS | 2 FORMAT & ARRANGE FOOTERS | 3 INSERT & FORMAT GRAPHICS & TEXT BOXES
4 RENAME & DELETE SLIDE LAYOUTS | 5 CUSTOMIZE HANDOUTS & NOTES MASTERS | 6 USE CUSTOM TEMPLATE

The theme, fonts, footer, and background colors of the slide master are set. The next step is to draw the viewers' attention to the presentation by placing the Family illustration, located in the Data Files, in the same location on every slide. *Why? The repetition of this picture creates consistency and helps reinforce the message.* The following steps insert an illustration of a family zip lining into the slide master.

- With the slide master displaying, click the Insert tab and then click the Pictures button (Insert tab | Images group) to display the Insert Picture dialog box.

- Navigate to the location where your data files are stored and then if necessary, scroll down and click Family to select the file (Figure 8–19).

Figure 8–19

Q&A What if the picture is not in my Data Files folder?

Use the same process, but select the device containing the illustration. Another option is to locate this illustration or a similar one online. You may need to remove the illustration background to call attention to the people zip lining.

- Click the Insert button (Insert Picture dialog box) to insert the illustration into the slide master.

- If necessary, decrease the illustration size to approximately 2.8" × 2.8" and then drag it above the footer and slide number placeholders, as shown in Figure 8–20.

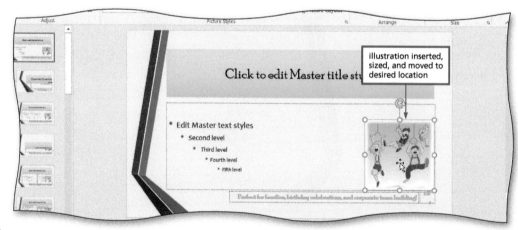

Figure 8–20

Break Point: If you wish to take a break, this is a good place to do so. Be sure to save the Zip Line file again and then you can exit PowerPoint. To resume at a later time, run PowerPoint, open the file called Zip Line, open Slide Master view, and continue following the steps from this location forward.

Adding and Formatting Placeholders

Each design theme determines where placeholders appear on individual layouts. The slide master has placeholders for bulleted lists, title text, pictures, and other graphical elements. At times, you may find that you need a specific placeholder for a design element not found on any of the slide master layouts. You can add a placeholder in Slide Master view for text, SmartArt, charts, tables, and other graphical elements.

To Insert a Placeholder into a Blank Layout

The words, Tree Top Adventures, will appear on the title slide, but you may desire to add these words to every text slide. *Why? Displaying this text in the same location on all slides helps emphasize the name and also provides a consistent, uniform look to the presentation.* One efficient method of adding this text is to insert a placeholder, type the words, and, if necessary, format the characters. The following steps insert a placeholder into the Blank Layout.

1

- In the Thumbnail pane, scroll down and then click the Blank Layout to display this layout.

- If necessary, display the Slide Master tab and then click the Insert Placeholder arrow (Slide Master tab | Master Layout group) to display the Insert Placeholder gallery (Figure 8–21).

Q&A Why does the Insert Placeholder button on my screen differ from the button shown in Figure 8–21? The image on the button changes based on the type of placeholder content that was last inserted. A placeholder can hold any content, including text, pictures, and tables. If the last type of placeholder inserted was for SmartArt, for example, the Insert Placeholder button would display the SmartArt icon.

Figure 8–21

2

- Click Text in the gallery.

Q&A Could I have inserted a Content placeholder rather than a Text placeholder? Yes. The Content placeholder is used for any of the seven types of slide content: text, table, chart, SmartArt, picture, clip art, or media. In this project, you will insert text in the placeholder. If you know the specific kind of content you want to place in the placeholder, it is best to select that placeholder type.

3

- Position the pointer, which is a crosshair, at the upper-right area of the layout (Figure 8–22).

Figure 8–22

4

● Click to insert the new placeholder into the Blank Layout (Figure 8–23).

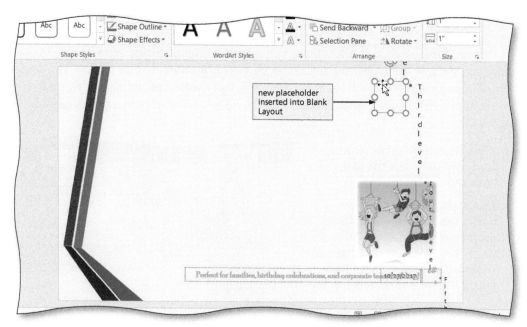

Figure 8–23

To Add and Format Placeholder Text

1 CUSTOMIZE SLIDE MASTERS | 2 FORMAT & ARRANGE FOOTERS | 3 INSERT & FORMAT GRAPHICS & TEXT BOXES
4 RENAME & DELETE SLIDE LAYOUTS | 5 CUSTOMIZE HANDOUTS & NOTES MASTERS | 6 USE CUSTOM TEMPLATE

Now that the text placeholder is positioned, you can add the desired text and then format the characters. You will need to delete the second-, third-, fourth-, and fifth-level bullets in this placeholder. *Why? The placeholders are not used in this presentation.* The following steps add and format the words in the new Blank Layout placeholder.

1

● Display the Home tab and then click inside the new placeholder.

● Click the Select button (Home tab | Editing group) to display the Select menu (Figure 8–24).

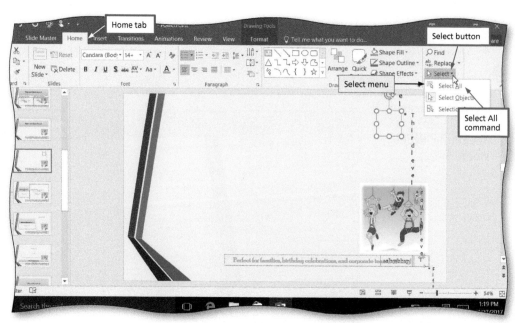

Figure 8–24

2

- Click Select All in the Select menu to select all the text in the placeholder (Figure 8–25).

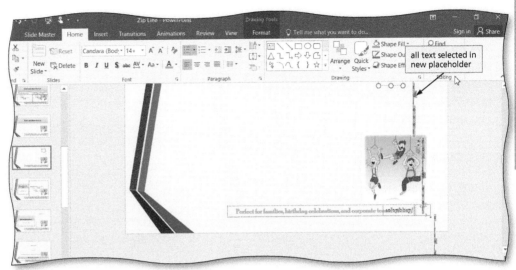

Figure 8–25

3

- Press the DELETE key to delete all the selected text in the placeholder.

- Click the Bullets button (Home tab | Paragraph group) to remove the bullet from the placeholder.

- Type **Tree Top Adventures** in the placeholder.

- Drag the bottom sizing handle down until it is above the Family illustration, as shown in Figure 8–26.

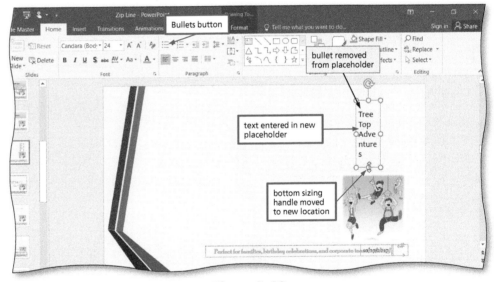

Figure 8–26

4

- Click the Text Direction button (Home tab | Paragraph group) to display the Text Direction gallery (Figure 8–27).

  Experiment

- Point to various directions in the Text Direction gallery and watch the words in the placeholder change direction on the layout.

Figure 8–27

- Click 'Rotate all text 90°' to display the text vertically.

- If necessary, drag the top placeholder border down so the text displays on two lines.

- Click Center (Home tab | Paragraph group) to display the text in the middle of the placeholder (Figure 8–28).

Figure 8–28

Q&A

What is the difference between the Center button in the Align gallery and the Center button in the Paragraph group?

The Center button in the Paragraph group centers the text between the left and right borders. The Center button in the Align gallery positions the text between the top and bottom borders of the placeholder.

6

- Select the text in the placeholder to display the mini toolbar, click the Font arrow, and then select Poor Richard in the Theme Fonts area of the Font gallery.

- Increase the font size to 36 point.

- Click the Bold button to bold the text.

- Click the Font Color button to change the font color to Green (sixth color in Standard Colors row) (Figure 8–29).

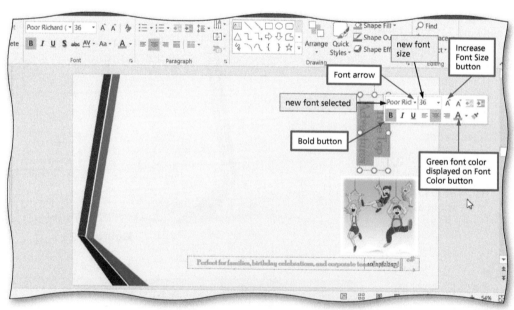

Figure 8–29

To Cut a Placeholder and Paste It into a Slide Master

1 CUSTOMIZE SLIDE MASTERS | 2 FORMAT & ARRANGE FOOTERS | 3 INSERT & FORMAT GRAPHICS & TEXT BOXES
4 RENAME & DELETE SLIDE LAYOUTS | 5 CUSTOMIZE HANDOUTS & NOTES MASTERS | 6 USE CUSTOM TEMPLATE

The new formatted placeholder appears only on the Blank Layout. If you selected any other layout in your presentation, such as Two Content or Title Only, this placeholder would not display. This placeholder should appear on all text slides. ***Why?*** *Repeating this placeholder will provide consistency throughout the presentation.* You are not given the opportunity to insert a placeholder into the slide master, but you can paste a placeholder that you copied or cut from another slide. The following steps cut the new placeholder from the Blank Layout and paste it into the slide master.

1

• With the Home tab displaying, click the new placeholder border and then click the Cut button (Home tab | Clipboard group) to delete the placeholder from the layout and copy it to the Clipboard (Figure 8–30).

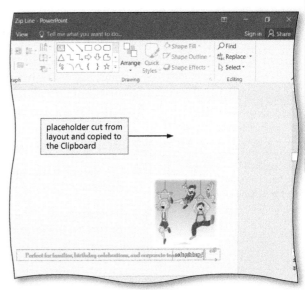

Q&A
Why did I click the Cut button instead of the Copy button?
Tapping or clicking the Cut button deletes the placeholder. Tapping or clicking the Copy button keeps the original placeholder on the slide, so if you paste the placeholder on the slide master, a second, identical placeholder would display on the Blank Layout.

Figure 8–30

2

• Scroll up and then click the Parallax Slide Master thumbnail in the Thumbnail pane to display the slide master.

• Click the Paste button (Home tab | Clipboard group) to copy the placeholder from the Clipboard to the slide master.

• Drag the placeholder to the location shown in Figure 8–31 and then move the Family illustration slightly to the left so that the text does not overlap this picture.

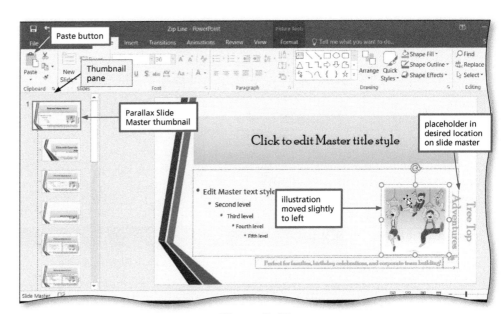

Figure 8–31

Break Point: If you wish to take a break, this is a good place to do so. Be sure to save the Zip Line file again and then you can exit PowerPoint. To resume at a later time, run PowerPoint, open the file called Zip Line, open Slide Master view, and continue following the steps from this location forward.

To Insert an Illustration and a Text Box into a Blank Layout

One slide in the completed presentation will feature Tree Top Adventures' new courses and special events. To ensure continuity when publicizing the Tree Top Adventures promotions and facilities, you can insert another illustration into the Blank Layout and then add and format a text box. This layout includes the Zip Line placeholder you inserted into the slide master. The following steps insert an illustration and a text box into the Blank Layout and then add text in the text box.

BTW

Inserting Objects into the Slide Master
In this project you will add a placeholder, text box, and pictures to the layout. You can, however, insert other objects, including clip art and video and audio files. Corporations often insert their company logos into a slide master.

1 Scroll down and then click the Blank Layout thumbnail in the Thumbnail pane.

2 Display the Insert tab, and then insert the Female illustration from the Data Files into the Blank Layout.

3 If necessary, size the illustration to approximately 2.8" × 2.8" and then drag the picture to the location shown in Figure 8–32.

4 Display the Insert tab and then click the Text Box button (Insert tab | Text group). Insert a new text box in a blank area in the center of the slide layout.

5 Type **Acres of fun!** as the text box text (Figure 8–32).

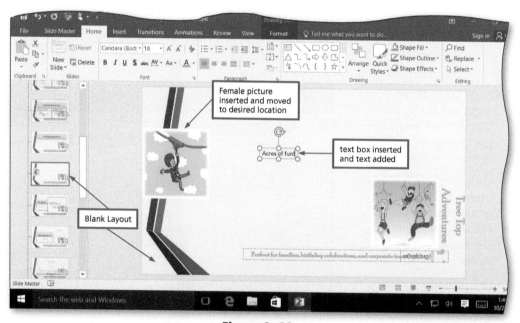

Figure 8–32

To Apply a Fill to a Text Box and Increase Transparency

1 CUSTOMIZE SLIDE MASTERS | 2 FORMAT & ARRANGE FOOTERS | 3 INSERT & FORMAT GRAPHICS & TEXT BOXES
4 RENAME & DELETE SLIDE LAYOUTS | 5 CUSTOMIZE HANDOUTS & NOTES MASTERS | 6 USE CUSTOM TEMPLATE

Now that the text is added, you can format the text box. A **fill** refers to the formatting of the interior of a shape. The fill can be a color, picture, texture, pattern, or the presentation background. If a color fill is desired, you can increase the transparency so that some of the background color or pattern mixes with the fill color. The following steps apply a green fill to the text box on the Blank Layout and increase the transparency. *Why? The green color is part of the Blue theme colors and also coordinates well with the green text.*

● Click the Shape Fill arrow (Home tab | Drawing group) to display the Shape Fill gallery.

🔍 **Experiment**

● Point to various colors in the Shape Fill gallery and watch the placeholder background change.

● Click Green (sixth color in Standard Colors row) to fill the text box.

● Click the Drawing dialog box launcher (Home tab | Drawing group) to display the Format Shape pane (Figure 8–33).

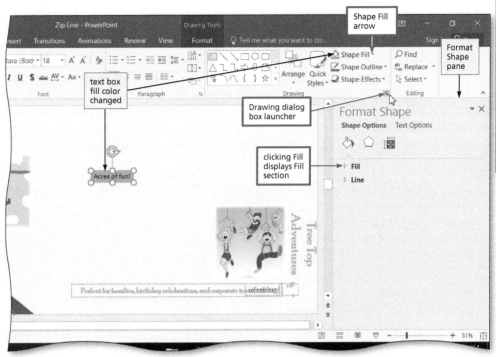

Figure 8–33

②

● If necessary, click Fill to display the Fill section.

● Click the Transparency slider in the Fill section and drag it to the right until 50% is displayed in the Transparency text box (Figure 8–34).

🔍 **Experiment**

● Drag the Transparency slider to the left and right, and watch the text box background change.

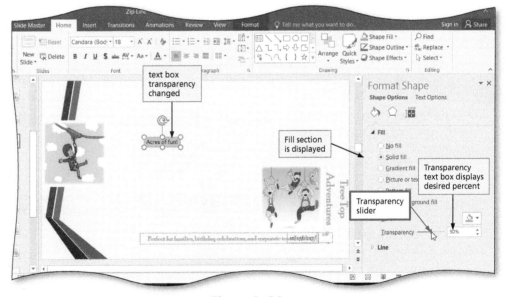

Figure 8–34

Other Ways

1. Enter percentage in Transparency text box   2. Click Transparency up or down arrow

To Change Character Spacing

Now that the text is added and the text box is formatted, you can change the spacing between the letters. The amount of space, called **character spacing**, can be increased or decreased from the Normal default in one of four preset amounts: Very Tight, Tight, Loose, or Very Loose. In addition, you can specify a precise amount of space in the Character Spacing tab of the Font dialog box. In this presentation, you will move the text box above the Female illustration and stretch the letters. *Why? You want to associate the text box with the illustration, so moving them together along the left side of the slide shows the relationship between the female zip liner and the words in the text box. In addition, the letters in the text box can be stretched to fit the length of the illustration.* The following steps increase the character spacing in the text box and then format the text.

1

- Select all the text in the text box. Click the Character Spacing button (Home tab | Font group) to display the Character Spacing gallery (Figure 8–35).

🔍 **Experiment**

- Point to the spacing options in the gallery and watch the characters in the placeholder change.

Figure 8–35

2

- Click Very Loose in the gallery to change the character spacing in the text box.

3

- Increase the font size to 28 point, change the font color to White, Background 1 (first color in first Theme Colors row), and then bold this text.

- Click the text inside the Acres of fun! text box to remove the selection from the letters (Figure 8–36).

Figure 8–36

Other Ways

1. Click Font dialog box launcher (Home tab | Font group), click Character Spacing tab (Font dialog box), select Expanded or Condensed in Spacing box and point size in By box

2. Right-click text, click Font on shortcut menu, click Character Spacing tab (Font dialog box), select Expanded or Condensed in Spacing box and point size in By box

To Change a Text Box Internal Margin

Each placeholder and text box has preset internal margins, which are the spaces between the border and the contents of the box. The default left and right margins are 0.1", and the default top and bottom margins are 0.05". In this project, you will drag the text box above the Female illustration, so you want to change the margins. **Why?** *You want the text to align as closely as possible against the top and bottom borders of the box and the left and right margins to have a slight space between the border and the first and last letters.* The following steps change all four text box margins.

- In the Format Shape pane, click the 'Size & Properties' Shape Option (Format Shape pane).

- If necessary, click Text Box to display the Text Box section.

- Increase the Left margin setting to 0.3".

- Increase the Right margin setting to 0.3".

- Decrease the Top margin setting to 0".

- Decrease the Bottom margin setting to 0" (Figure 8–37).

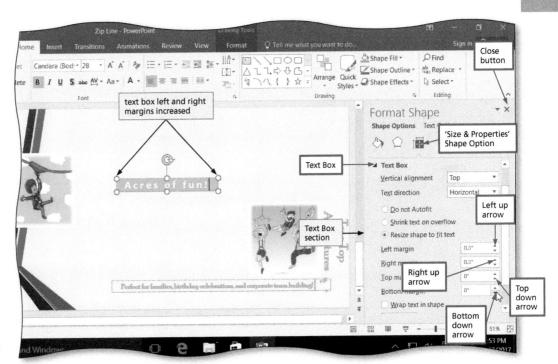

Figure 8–37

Q&A | Must I change all the margins?
No. You can change one, two, three, or all four internal margins depending upon the placeholder shape and the amount of text entered.

- Click the Close button (Format Shape pane).

To Rotate a Picture and a Text Box

Why? *To balance the pictures on the slide, you can move the Female illustration and the Acres of fun! text box. For a dramatic effect, you can change the orientation of the picture and the placeholder on the slide by rotating them.* Dragging the circular rotation handle above a selected object allows you to rotate an object in any direction. The following steps move and rotate the Female picture and the Acres of fun! text box.

- Click the Female illustration to select it.

- Position the pointer over the rotation handle so that it changes to a Free Rotate pointer (Figure 8–38).

Q&A I selected the picture, but I cannot see the rotation handle. Why?
The rotation handle may not be visible at the top of the slide layout. Drag the picture downward, and the rotation handle will appear.

Figure 8–38

- Drag the rotation handle counterclockwise so that it is displayed as shown in Figure 8–39.

Q&A I am using a touch screen and am having difficulty moving the rotation handle. What can I do?
When moving small items on a slide, it may be easier to use a mouse or a stylus instead of attempting to make adjustments using your fingers.

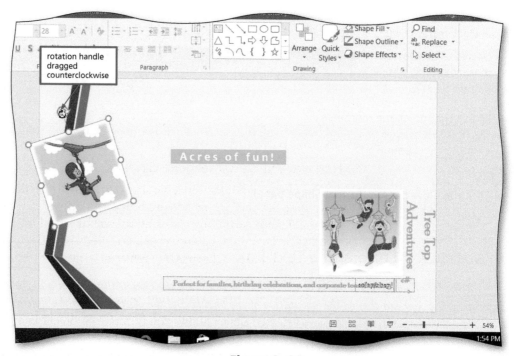

Figure 8–39

3

• Drag the illustration to position it as shown in Figure 8–40.

Can I move the picture in small increments?

Yes. To move or nudge the picture in very small increments, hold down the CTRL key with the picture selected while pressing the UP ARROW, DOWN ARROW, RIGHT ARROW, or LEFT ARROW keys. You cannot perform this action using a touch screen.

4

• Click the Acres of fun! text box to select it. Position the pointer over the rotation handle so that it changes to a Free Rotate pointer.

• Rotate the text box so that it is at the same angle as the Female illustration.

• Drag the text box above the Female illustration, as shown in Figure 8–40.

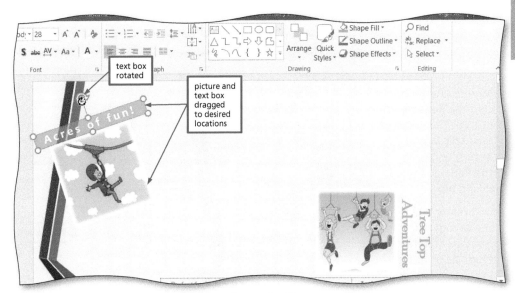

Figure 8–40

Other Ways			
1. For text box, click Rotate button (Drawing Tools Format tab | Arrange group), choose desired rotation	2. For picture, click Rotate button (Picture Tools Format tab | Arrange group), choose desired rotation	3. For picture, right-click picture, click Format Picture on shortcut menu, click Effects icon (Format Picture pane), click 3-D Rotation, set rotation to desired angle	4. For text box, right-click text box, click Format Shape on shortcut menu, click Effects icon (Format Shape pane), click 3-D Rotation, set rotation to desired angle

TO HIDE AND UNHIDE BACKGROUND GRAPHICS

The placeholder, text box, pictures, and other graphical elements are displayed on some slide master layouts and are hidden on others. You have the ability to change the default setting by choosing to hide or unhide the background graphics. The Hide Background Graphics check box is a toggle that displays and conceals the graphics. To hide background graphics on a layout, you would perform the following steps.

1. Display the Slide Master tab, select the desired layout, and then click the Hide Background Graphics check box (Slide Master tab | Background group) to insert a check mark in it.

2. To unhide the graphics, click the same check box to make them appear.

To Rename a Slide Master and a Slide Layout

Once all the changes are made to a slide master and a slide layout, you may want to rename them with meaningful names that describe their functions or features. The new slide master name will be displayed on the status bar; the new layout name will be displayed in the Slide Layout gallery. The following steps rename the Parallax Slide Master, the Title Slide Layout, the Blank Layout, and the Title and Content Layout. *Why? Renaming the layouts gives meaningful names that reflect the purpose of the design.*

1

- Display the Slide Master tab, click the Parallax Slide Master, and then click the Rename button (Slide Master tab | Edit Master group) to display the Rename Layout dialog box.

- Delete the text in the Layout name text box and then type **Zip Line** in the text box (Rename Layout dialog box) (Figure 8–41).

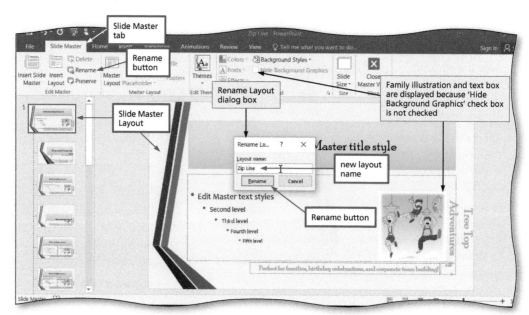

Figure 8–41

2

- Click the Rename button (Rename Layout dialog box) to give the layout the new name, Zip Line Slide Master.

3

- Display the Title Slide Layout, click the Rename button, delete the text in the Layout name text box, and then type **Zip Title** as the new layout name (Figure 8–42).

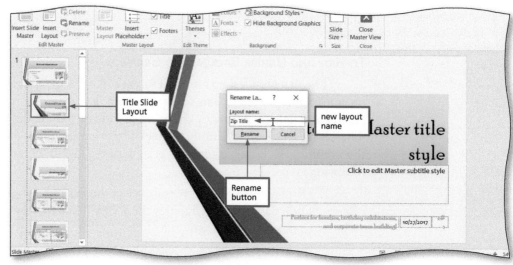

Figure 8–42

4

- Click the Rename button (Rename Layout dialog box) to rename the Title Slide layout.

- Scroll down and then click the Blank Layout to display it, click the Rename button, delete the text in the Layout name text box, and then type **Acres** as the new layout name (Figure 8–43).

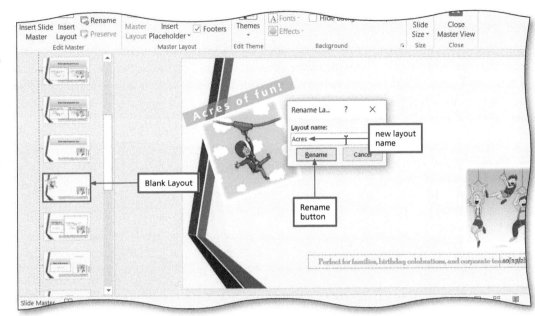

Figure 8–43

5

- Click the Rename button (Rename Layout dialog box).

- Scroll up to display the Title and Content Layout, click the Rename button, delete the text in the Layout name text box, and then type **Miscellaneous** as the new layout name (Figure 8–44).

Figure 8–44

6

- Click the Rename button (Rename Layout dialog box).

To Delete a Slide Layout

You have made many changes to the slide master and two slide layouts. You will use these layouts and the Title and Content Layout, which is now called the Miscellaneous layout, when you close Master view and then add text, graphics, or other content to the presentation in Normal view. You can delete the other layouts in the Thumbnail pane. *Why? You will not use them in this presentation.* The following steps delete slide layouts that will not be used to create the presentation.

- Click the Section Header Layout in the Thumbnail pane to select it (Figure 8–45).

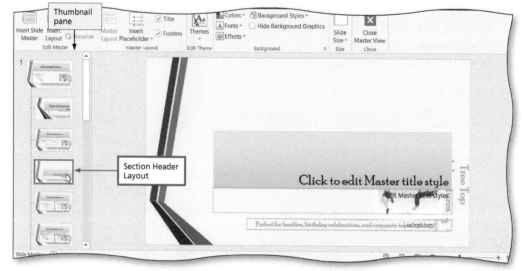

Figure 8–45

2

- Press and hold down the SHIFT key, if necessary scroll down to display the Title Only Layout, and then click the Title Only Layout to select four consecutive layouts (Figure 8–46).

Q&A Why did I select only these four layouts? The layout below the Title Only Layout is the Acres layout, and you will use that layout when you create Slide 2 in your presentation.

Figure 8–46

- Click the Delete button (Slide Master tab | Edit Master group) to delete the four layouts.
- Click the Content with Caption Layout (the layout below the Acres layout) and then select all layouts below it including the last layout, which is the Vertical Title and Text Layout, in the Thumbnail pane (Figure 8–47).

Figure 8–47

- Click the Delete button (Slide Master tab | Edit Master group) to delete the 10 layouts (Figure 8–48).

Q&A

Now that I have created this slide master, can I ensure that it will not be changed when I create future presentations?

Yes. Normally a slide master is deleted when a new design template is selected. To keep the original master as part of your presentation, you can preserve it by selecting the thumbnail and then clicking the Preserve button in the Edit Master group. An icon in the shape of a pushpin is displayed below the slide number to indicate the master is preserved. If you decide to unpreserve a slide master, select this thumbnail and then click the Preserve button.

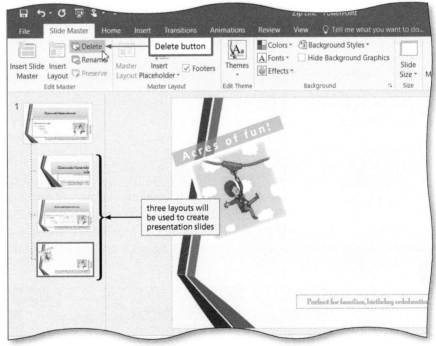

Figure 8–48

Other Ways

1. Click Delete button (Home tab | Slides group)

2. Right-click selected slide, click Delete Layout on shortcut menu

3. Press DELETE key on keyboard

To Add a New Slide Layout

The slide layouts included within each slide master are practical and varied. As you have learned in completing this project, editing these layouts is easy and useful. At times, however, you may desire to create a layout from scratch, especially if your design requires many placeholders and unique design elements. To add a new slide layout, you would perform the following steps.

1. Display the Slide Master tab and then click between the layout thumbnails in the Thumbnail pane to place the pointer where you desire the new slide layout to appear.
2. Click the Insert Layout button to insert a new slide layout with the name, Custom Layout.
3. Click the Rename button (Slide Master tab | Edit Master group) and type a meaningful name for the new layout.

Break Point: If you wish to take a break, this is a good place to do so. Be sure to save the Zip Line file again and then you can exit PowerPoint. To resume at a later time, run PowerPoint, open the file called Zip Line, and continue following the steps from this location forward.

BTW
Formatting the 'Date and time' Placeholder
The 'Date and time' footer can have a variety of formats. If you click the Update automatically arrow, you can choose among formats that display the day, date, and time in a variety of combinations.

Customizing Handout and Notes Masters

You have used PowerPoint's slide master template file to create unique slide layouts for the Zip Line presentation. PowerPoint also has master template files to create handouts and notes. If you are going to distribute handouts to your audience, you can customize the handout master so that it coordinates visually with the presentation slides and reinforces your message. In addition, if you are going to use speaker notes to guide you through a presentation, you can tailor the notes master to fit your needs.

To Customize a Handout Using a Handout Master

1 CUSTOMIZE SLIDE MASTERS | 2 FORMAT & ARRANGE FOOTERS | 3 INSERT & FORMAT GRAPHICS & TEXT BOXES
4 RENAME & DELETE SLIDE LAYOUTS | **5 CUSTOMIZE HANDOUTS & NOTES MASTERS** | 6 USE CUSTOM TEMPLATE

When you created the Zip Line slide master, you specified the background, fonts, theme, and pictures for all slides. You likewise can create a specific handout master to determine the layout and graphics that will display on the printed handout. *Why? You can customize handouts for your audience's needs by moving, restoring, and formatting the header and footer placeholders; setting the page number orientation; adding graphics; and specifying the number of slides to print on each page.* The following steps use the handout master to create a custom handout.

• Display the View tab (Figure 8–49).

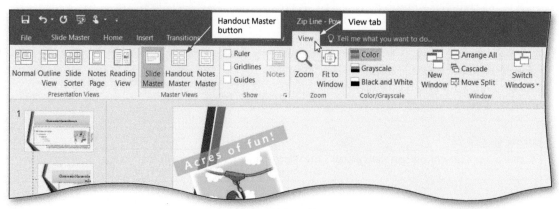

Figure 8–49

2

- Click the Handout Master button (View tab | Master Views group) to display the Handout Master tab.

- If a Microsoft PowerPoint dialog box is displayed, click the Check Out button to close the dialog box.

- Click the 'Slides Per Page' button (Handout Master tab | Page Setup group) to display the Slides Per Page gallery (Figure 8–50).

Q&A Is 6 Slides the default layout for all themes?

Yes. If you have fewer than six slides in your presentation or want to display slide details, then choose a handout layout with 1, 2, 3, or 4 slides per sheet of paper.

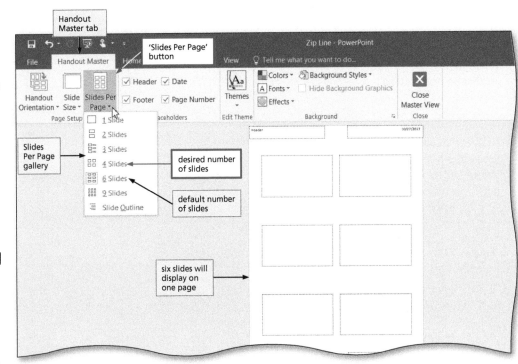

Figure 8–50

3

- Click 4 Slides in the list to change the layout from 6 slides to 4 slides.

- Click the Handout Orientation button (Handout Master tab | Page Setup group) to display the Handout Orientation gallery (Figure 8–51).

Figure 8–51

4

- Click Landscape in the gallery to display the page layout in landscape orientation (Figure 8–52).

Q&A

How do I decide between portrait and landscape orientation? If your slide content is predominantly vertical, such as an athlete running or a skyscraper in a major city, consider using the default portrait orientation. If, however, your slide content has long lines of text or pictures of four-legged animals, landscape orientation may be a more appropriate layout.

Figure 8–52

5

- Click the Header placeholder and then type **Zip Line** as the header text.

- Click the Footer placeholder and then type **Four different color-coded courses open every day.** as the footer text.

- Drag the Footer placeholder above the page number placeholder (Figure 8–53).

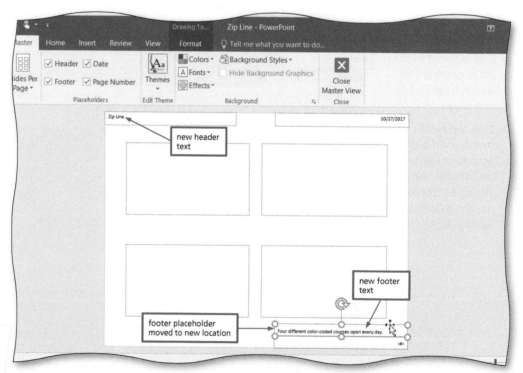

Figure 8–53

6

- Click the Theme Fonts button (Handout Master tab | Background group) to display the Theme Fonts gallery (Figure 8–54).

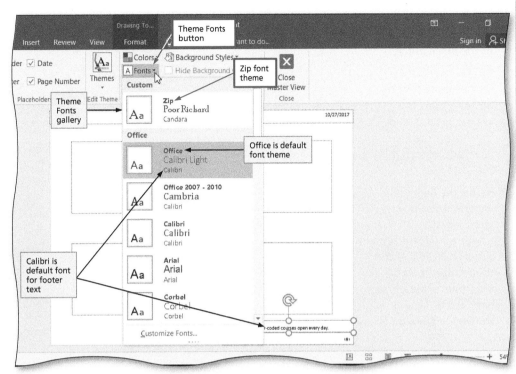

Figure 8–54

7

- Click Zip in the Custom area of the gallery to apply the Candara font to the text in the placeholders.

- Select the footer text, display the Home tab and then click the Align Text button (Home tab | Paragraph group) to display the Align Text gallery (Figure 8–55).

 Experiment

- Point to the Top and Middle icons in the Align Text gallery and watch the words in the placeholder change alignment on the layout.

Figure 8–55

- Click Middle to display the text in the middle of the placeholder.

- Display the Insert tab, click the Pictures button (Insert tab | Images group), and then insert the Female illustration located in the Data Files.

- Resize the Female illustration so it is approximately 2" × 2", rotate this illustration counterclockwise, and then center it along the upper edge of the handout layout, as shown in Figure 8–56.

Figure 8–56

- Display the Insert tab, click the 'Header & Footer' button (Insert tab | Text group), and then place a check mark in the 'Date and time' check box.

- Place a check mark in the Header check box.

- Place a check mark in the Footer check box (Figure 8–57).

Figure 8–57

- Click the 'Apply to All' button (Header and Footer dialog box) to add the header and footer text and date to the handout master.

Q&A | Where will the header and footer display on the handout?
The black boxes in the preview area show where these placeholders are located.

To Customize a Notes Page Using a Notes Master

If you type notes in the Notes pane, you can print them for yourself or for your audience. The basic format found in the Backstage view generally suffices for handouts, but you may desire to alter the layout using the notes master. *Why? You may desire to add graphics and rearrange and format the header, footer, and page number placeholders.* The following steps use the notes master to create a custom handout.

- Display the View tab (Figure 8–58).

Figure 8–58

- Click the Notes Master button (View tab | Master Views group) to display the Notes Master tab.
- If a Microsoft PowerPoint dialog box is displayed, click the Check Out button to close the dialog box.
- Click the Footer placeholder, delete the text, and then type **Challenge your body and your mind.** as the new footer text.

- Click the Theme Fonts button to display the Theme Fonts gallery (Figure 8–59).

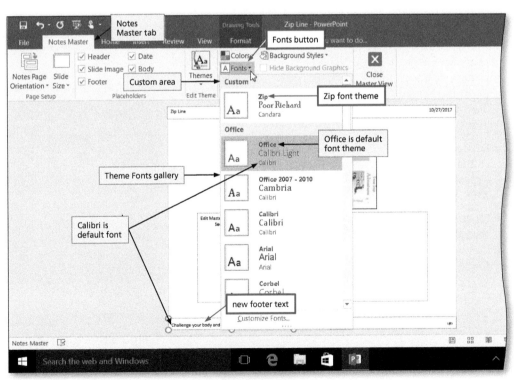

Figure 8–59

4

- Click Zip in the Custom area of the Theme Fonts gallery to apply the Candara font to the text in the header, footer, date, and page number placeholders.

- Click the 'Notes Page Orientation' button (Notes Master tab | Page Setup group) to display the 'Notes Page Orientation' gallery (Figure 8–60).

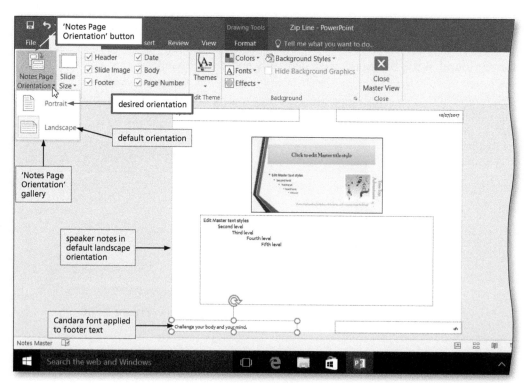

Figure 8–60

5

- Click Portrait in the gallery to display the page layout in portrait orientation.

- Display the Insert tab, click the Pictures button, and then insert the Female illustration located in the Data Files.

- Resize the picture so that it is approximately 2″ × 2″.

- Move the picture so that it is centered between the two footer placeholders, as shown in Figure 8–61.

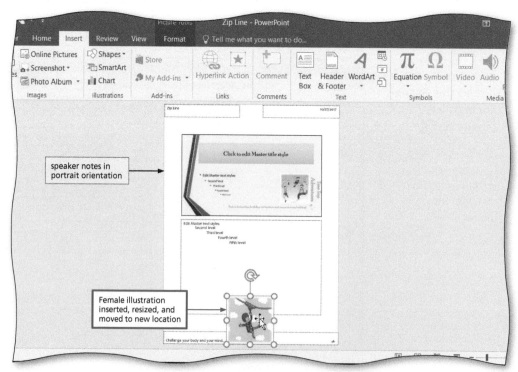

Figure 8–61

To Close Master View

1 CUSTOMIZE SLIDE MASTERS | 2 FORMAT & ARRANGE FOOTERS | 3 INSERT & FORMAT GRAPHICS & TEXT BOXES
4 RENAME & DELETE SLIDE LAYOUTS | 5 CUSTOMIZE HANDOUTS & NOTES MASTERS | 6 USE CUSTOM TEMPLATE

You now can exit Master view and return to Normal view. **Why?** *All the changes to the slide master, handout master, and notes master are complete.* The following steps close Master view.

- Display the Notes Master tab (Figure 8–62).

Figure 8–62

- Click the 'Close Master View' button (Notes Master tab | Close group) to exit Master view and return to Normal view.

To Save a Master as a Template

1 CUSTOMIZE SLIDE MASTERS | 2 FORMAT & ARRANGE FOOTERS | 3 INSERT & FORMAT GRAPHICS & TEXT BOXES
4 RENAME & DELETE SLIDE LAYOUTS | 5 CUSTOMIZE HANDOUTS & NOTES MASTERS | 6 USE CUSTOM TEMPLATE

The changes and enhancements you have made to the Zip Line slide master, handout master, and notes master are excellent starting points for future presentations. The background text and graphics allow users to add text boxes, pictures, SmartArt, tables, and other elements depending upon the specific message that needs to be communicated to an audience. Saving a slide master as a template is convenient when you often reuse and modify presentations. **Why?** *You can save your slide layouts as a template to use for a new presentation and use the revised handout and notes masters to print unique pages.* The following steps save the Zip Line master as a template.

- Display the Save As dialog box.

- Click the 'Save as type' arrow to display the 'Save as type' list (Figure 8–63).

Figure 8–63

• Click 'PowerPoint Template' in the 'Save as type' list to change the save as type.

Why do the file name extensions, such as (*.potx), display after the file type in my 'Save as type' list? These letters identify the file format or type. You can configure Windows to show or hide all common file extensions by opening File Explorer, displaying the View tab, clicking the Options button, clicking the View tab in the Folder Options dialog box, and then either checking or unchecking 'Hide extensions for known file types' in the Advanced settings area.

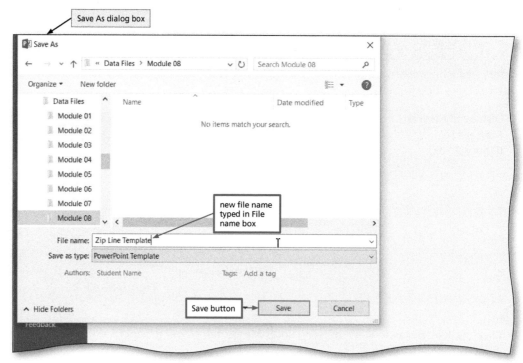

Figure 8–64

• Type **Zip Line Template** in the File name box and then navigate to the desired save location (in this case, the Module 08 folder in the Data Files folder) (Figure 8–64).

• Click the Save button (Save As dialog box) to save the Zip Line presentation as a template.

• Close the Zip Line Template file.

Break Point: If you wish to take a break, this is a good place to do so. You can exit PowerPoint now. To resume at a later time, run PowerPoint and continue following the steps from this location forward.

To Open a Template and Save a Presentation

1 CUSTOMIZE SLIDE MASTERS | 2 FORMAT & ARRANGE FOOTERS | 3 INSERT & FORMAT GRAPHICS & TEXT BOXES
4 RENAME & DELETE SLIDE LAYOUTS | 5 CUSTOMIZE HANDOUTS & NOTES MASTERS | **6 USE CUSTOM TEMPLATE**

The Zip Line Template file you created is a convenient start to a new presentation. The graphical elements and essential slide content are in place; you then can customize the layouts for a specific need, such as a new event or special program. Unless users specify a different location, PowerPoint saves templates they create in a folder called 'Custom Office Templates' in the Documents folder. The steps on the next page open the Zip Line Template file and save the presentation with the Zip Line name.

1

- In Backstage view, click the Open tab to display the Open dialog box (Figure 8–65).

- If necessary, navigate to the save location and then select the file, Zip Line Template.

Q&A If I did not change the default save location, can I select the Zip Line Template from the list of Recent Presentations or by opening the Custom Office Templates folder?
Yes. Either technique will locate the desired template.

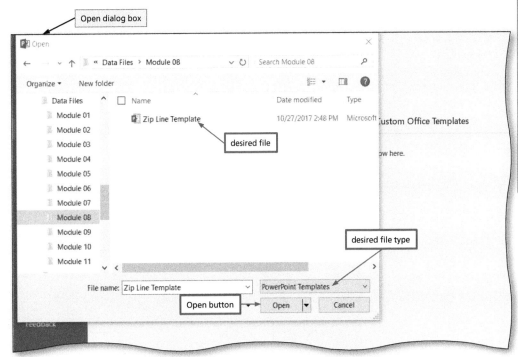

Figure 8–65

2

- Click the Open button to open the file, Zip Line Template.

- In Backstage view, click the Save As tab to display the Save As dialog box.

- Navigate to the location where your files are saved.

- Click the 'Save as type' arrow to display the 'Save as type' list, and then click PowerPoint Presentation in the 'Save as type' list to change the save as type.

- Click Zip Line in the Save As dialog box to select the file (Figure 8–66).

Figure 8–66

- Click the Save button (Save As dialog box) to display the Confirm Save As dialog box (Figure 8–67).

- Click the Yes button to replace the file.

Figure 8–67

BTW
Distributing Notes Text
If you desire to share your notes with your audience, you can print the text with or without thumbnail images of the corresponding slides. Public speaking experts recommend distributing your notes before or after your presentation, not during your speech.

To Add Text and Notes to the Title Slide

By default, the title slide layout, which was renamed Zip Line Title, is applied to the first slide. The following steps add text and speaker notes to Slide 1.

1 With the title slide displaying, type `Tree Top Adventures` as the title text and `The ultimate zip line experience` as the subtitle text. Increase the subtitle text font size to 32 point.

2 If necessary, display the Notes pane. Click the Notes pane and then type `Tree Top Adventures offers tours every 30 minutes and is open from 9 a.m. until dusk.` (Figure 8–68).

If requested by your instructor, change the time in the Notes pane from 9 a.m. to the time of day you were born.

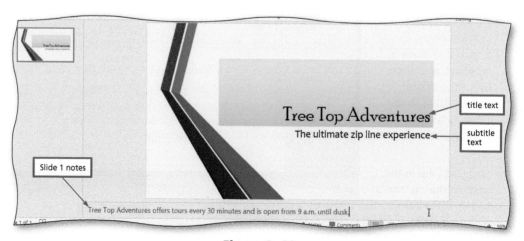

Figure 8–68

To Add Text and Notes to the Blank Layout

The second slide in your presentation will highlight important features. The Acres slide layout, which is the new name for the Blank Layout, is designed so that you can add variable slide content above the Female illustration in the upper-left corner. The following steps add a text box and speaker notes to Slide 2. *Why? The text box will call attention to the features at the Tree Top Adventures, and the speaker notes contain ideas that a presenter may want to discuss during a presentation.*

1 Insert a slide with the Acres layout and then insert a text box between the two illustrations. Type `Set in natural environment` as the first line of text box text and then press the ENTER key. Type `Two giant 450' zip lines` as the second line of text.

2 Increase the text box font size to 54 point. Size the text box as shown in Figure 8–69 and then drag it to the location shown in the figure.

3 In the Notes pane, type `During the training session, you will be fitted into your harness. Your guide will demonstrate how to attach to the safety lines and the zip lines.` (Figure 8–69).

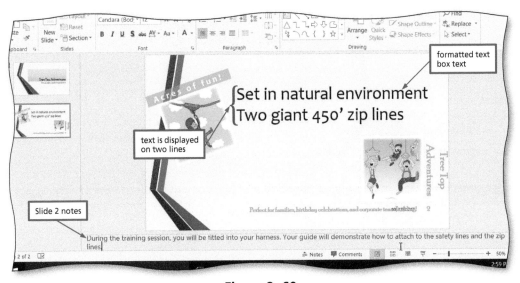

Figure 8–69

To Add Text, Notes, and an Illustration to the Title and Content Layout

The third slide in your presentation will list details about the four courses. In addition, the Notes pane will contain information about clothing requirements. The Miscellaneous layout, which is the new name for the Title and Content slide layout, will allow you to insert text into the content placeholder. The following steps insert a slide and add text and a picture to the title and content placeholder.

1 Insert a slide with the Miscellaneous layout and then type `Four Exciting Courses` as the title text.

2 Type `Blue: Low elevations; Minimum skills` as the first content placeholder paragraph.

3 Type `Green: Medium elevations; Intermediate skills` as the second paragraph.

4 Type `Yellow: High elevations; Intermediate skills` as the third paragraph.

5 Type `Red: High elevations; Advanced skills` as the fourth paragraph.

6 In the Notes pane, type `Clothing requirements: No open-toe shoes; no loose clothes; no necklaces or bracelets. Your clothes will get dirty.`

7 Click anywhere on the blue background without a text box or illustration and then insert the illustration with the file name, Male, located in the Data Files. If necessary, decrease its size to approximately 2.5" × 2.5", and then move the illustration to the upper-left of the slide (Figure 8–70).

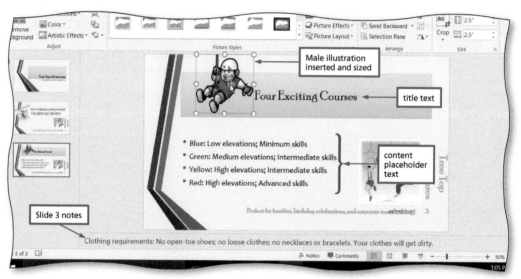

Figure 8–70

To Apply a Fill Color to a Slide

1 CUSTOMIZE SLIDE MASTERS | 2 FORMAT & ARRANGE FOOTERS | 3 INSERT & FORMAT GRAPHICS & TEXT BOXES
4 RENAME & DELETE SLIDE LAYOUTS | 5 CUSTOMIZE HANDOUTS & NOTES MASTERS | **6 USE CUSTOM TEMPLATE**

Earlier in this project, you formatted the interior of the Acres text box by applying a fill. In a similar manner, you can apply a fill to an entire slide by selecting a color from the Shape Fill gallery. If desired, you can increase the transparency to soften the color. The following steps apply a fill to Slide 3 and increase the transparency. *Why? Because the text boxes on Slide 3 have a green font color and the title text placeholder has a green background, you can coordinate the Slide 3 fill color by changing the Slide 3 background to turquoise and decrease the transparency so the letters can be read easily.*

• With Slide 3 displaying, right-click anywhere on the blue background without a text box or illustration to display the shortcut menu (Figure 8–71).

Figure 8–71

2

- Click Format Background on the shortcut menu to display the Format Background pane.

- With the Fill section displaying and the Solid fill option selected, click the Color button to display the Fill Color gallery (Figure 8–72).

Q&A Can I experiment with previewing the background colors?
No live preview feature is available.

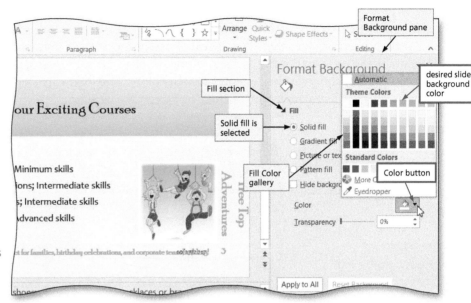

Figure 8–72

3

- Click 'Turquoise, Accent 3' (seventh color in first Theme Colors row) to change the slide background color.

- Click the Transparency slider in the Fill Color area and drag it to the right until 50% is displayed in the Transparency text box (Figure 8–73).

Experiment

- Drag the Transparency slider to the left and right and watch the text box background change.

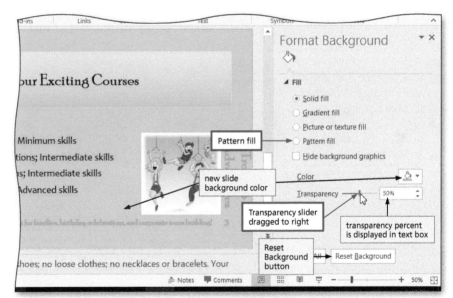

Figure 8–73

Q&A How can I delete a fill color if I decide not to apply one to my slide?
Any fill effect in the Format Background dialog box is applied immediately. If this dialog box is displayed, click the Reset Background button. If you already have applied the fill color, you must click the Undo button on the Quick Access Toolbar.

Other Ways

1. Enter percentage in Transparency text box 2. Click Transparency up or down arrow

To Apply a Pattern to a Slide

You add variety to a slide by making a **pattern fill**. This design of repeating horizontal or vertical lines, dots, dashes, or stripes can enhance the visual appeal of one or more slides in the presentation. If you desire to change the colors in the pattern, PowerPoint allows you to select the fill foreground and background colors by clicking the Color button and then choosing the desired colors. The following steps apply a pattern to Slide 3. *Why? The dots in this pattern coordinate with the Parallax background elements.*

- With the Format Background pane displaying, click Pattern fill to display the Pattern gallery and the 5% pattern on Slide 3 (Figure 8–74).

 Experiment

- Click various patterns in the Pattern gallery and watch the Slide 3 background change.

Q&A How can I delete a pattern if I decide not to apply one to my slide?

If the Format Background pane is displayed, click the Reset Background button. If you already have applied the pattern, you must click the Undo button on the Quick Access Toolbar.

Figure 8–74

- Click the 40% pattern (last color in first row) to apply this pattern to the Slide 3 background (Figure 8–75).

Q&A Can I apply this pattern to all the slides in the presentation?

Yes. You would click the 'Apply to All' button in the Format Background pane.

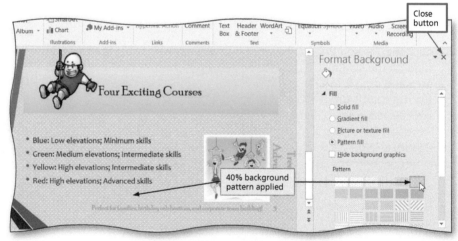

❸
- Click the Close button to close the Format Background task pane.

Figure 8–75

To Add a Slide Transition

A final enhancement you will make in this presentation is to apply the Fly Through transition to all slides and then change the transition speed and effect option. The following steps apply a transition and effect to the presentation.

❶ Display the Transitions tab and then apply the Fly Through transition in the Dynamic Content category to all three slides in the presentation.

❷ Change the duration from 00.80 to 02.00.

❸ Change the Effect Option from In to 'Out with Bounce'.

To Print a Handout Using the Handout Master

The handout master you created has header and footer text using the Candara font, a revised location for the Footer placeholder, and the Family illustration in the lower-left corner. The following steps print a handout using the handout master.

- Open the Backstage view and then display the Print gallery.

- Click the 'Full Page Slides' button in the Settings area to display the gallery (Figure 8–76).

Figure 8–76

- Click '4 Slides Horizontal' in the Handouts area.

- Click Portrait Orientation in the Settings area to display the Orientation gallery (Figure 8–77).

Figure 8–77

- Click Landscape Orientation to change the setting.

- Verify that '4 Slides Horizontal' is selected as the option in the Settings area and that the preview of Page 1 shows the header text, date, footer text, Female illustration, and three slides in landscape orientation.

- Click the Print button in the Print Gallery to print the handout (Figure 8–78).

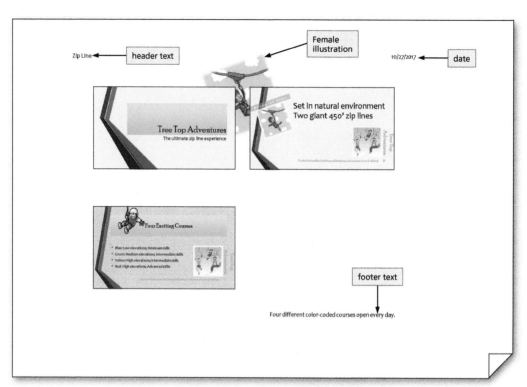

Figure 8–78 Handout in Landscape Orientation

To Print Speaker Notes Using the Notes Master

1 CUSTOMIZE SLIDE MASTERS | 2 FORMAT & ARRANGE FOOTERS | 3 INSERT & FORMAT GRAPHICS & TEXT BOXES
4 RENAME & DELETE SLIDE LAYOUTS | 5 CUSTOMIZE HANDOUTS & NOTES MASTERS | **6 USE CUSTOM TEMPLATE**

You also can print speaker notes while the Backstage view is displayed. The custom notes master you created has the same footer as the handout master, revised footer text using the Candara font, the current date, and the resized Female illustration in the lower center. The following steps print notes pages using the notes master.

- Open the Backstage view, display the Print gallery and then click Notes Pages in the Print Layout area.

- Click Landscape Orientation in the Settings area and then click Portrait Orientation in the gallery to change the setting.

- If necessary, click the Previous Page button to preview Slide 1.

- Verify that the page preview shows the header text, date, speaker notes, revised footer text, Female illustration, and page number in portrait orientation (Figure 8–79).

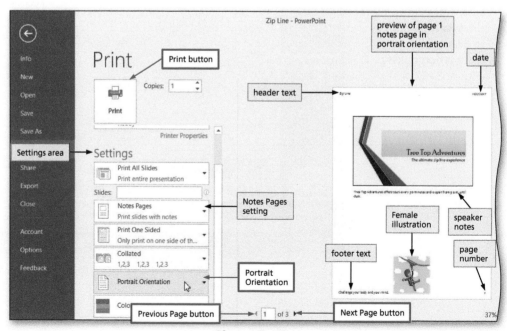

Figure 8–79

2

- Click the Previous Page and Next Page buttons to display previews of the other pages.
- Click the Print button in the Print gallery to print the notes (Figure 8–80).

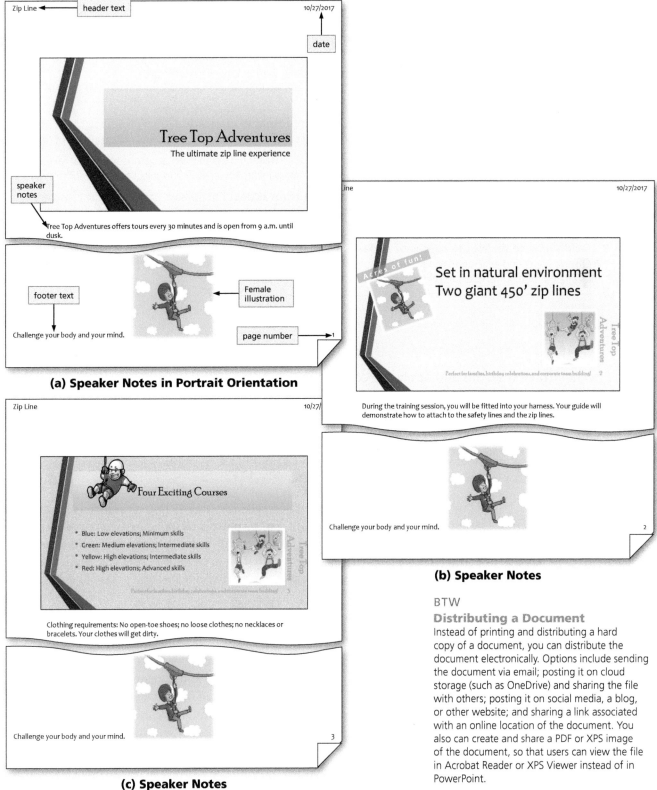

(a) Speaker Notes in Portrait Orientation

(b) Speaker Notes

(c) Speaker Notes

Figure 8–80

BTW

Distributing a Document
Instead of printing and distributing a hard copy of a document, you can distribute the document electronically. Options include sending the document via email; posting it on cloud storage (such as OneDrive) and sharing the file with others; posting it on social media, a blog, or other website; and sharing a link associated with an online location of the document. You also can create and share a PDF or XPS image of the document, so that users can view the file in Acrobat Reader or XPS Viewer instead of in PowerPoint.

3

- Because the project now is complete, you can save the presentation and exit PowerPoint.

Summary

In this module, you learned how to customize master slide layouts by changing the slide and font themes, formatting the background and footers, and adding background graphics. You then inserted a placeholder, added and formatted text, applied a fill, and changed the internal margins. Also, you rotated a picture and a placeholder, displayed the background graphics, and renamed and deleted slide layouts. Then you customized the handout and notes masters by adding a picture and changing the layout orientation. You then saved the slide master as a template, opened this template, added slide content, and printed a handout and speaker notes pages.

What decisions will you need to make when creating your next presentation?
Use these guidelines as you complete the assignments in this module and create your own slide show decks outside of this class.

1. **Plan the slide master.** Using a new slide master gives you the freedom to plan every aspect of your slide. Take care to think about the overall message you are trying to convey before you start PowerPoint and select elements for this master.

2. **Develop the slide master prior to creating presentation slides.** You can save time and create consistency when you design and build your master at the start of your PowerPoint session rather than after you have created individual slides.

3. **Decide how to distribute copies of slides.** Some audience members will desire printed copies of your slides. To conserve paper and ink, you may decide to limit the number of copies you print or to post the presentation electronically in a shared location for users to print the presentation if they so choose.

Apply Your Knowledge

Reinforce the skills and apply the concepts you learned in this module.

Applying a Slide Theme to a Slide Master, Creating a New Theme Font, and Changing the Title Layout

Note: To complete this assignment, you will be required to use the Data Files. Please contact your instructor for information about accessing the Data Files.

Instructions: Run PowerPoint. Open the presentation called Apply 8-1 Pottery, which is located in the Data Files. The three slides in this presentation discuss pottery classes. Instructors at a local art studio will teach you techniques in working with clay to create a ceramic bowl or to paint a molded pottery piece. The document you open is a partially formatted presentation. You will apply a slide theme to a slide master, create a new theme font, and change the slide master background. Your slides should look like Figure 8–81.

Perform the following tasks:
1. Display the Office Theme Slide Master and then apply the Crop theme. Change the theme colors to Blue Warm and then create a customized theme font named Clay using Baskerville Old Face for the heading font and Book Antiqua for the body font. Create a background on all slides by inserting the photo called Pottery, which is located in the Data Files, and then change the transparency to 75%. Make sure the 'Hide background graphics' check box in the Fill section of the Format Background task pane is not checked so that the theme graphics are displayed.

2. Display the Title Slide layout and then decrease the font size of the title text to 60 point and change the color to Dark Red (first color in Standard Colors row). Increase the font size of the subtitle text to 36 point and then apply the Quick Style 'Colored Fill - Teal, Accent 5' Quick Style (sixth style in second row).

3. Display the Two Content Layout and then change the font color of the title text to Dark Red. Display the Picture with Caption Layout and change the font color of the title text also to Dark Red. Close Master view.

4. On Slide 1 (Figure 8–81b), type **Creative Pottery Art Studio** as the title text and **Clay Classes or Pick and Paint** as the subtitle text, as shown in the figure.

5. On Slide 2 (Figure 8–81c), change the layout to Two Content. Increase the size of the hands and clay picture to approximately 2.8" × 4.2" and then apply the Rotated, White picture style. Increase the size of the orange pot illustration to approximately 4" × 4". Move both pictures to the locations shown in the figure.

6. On Slide 3 (Figure 8–81d), change the layout to Picture with Caption. Increase the size of the text in the four paragraphs to 20 point and add the Star Bullets to this text. Decrease the size of the picture to approximately 5" × 4.86", apply the Bevel Perspective picture style, and then move the picture to the location shown in the figure.

7. If requested by your instructor, add the name of your high school mascot as the fifth bulleted paragraph on Slide 3.

8. Apply the Checkerboard transition (Exciting category) and then change the duration to 3.00 for all slides.

9. Run the presentation and then save the file using the file name, Apply 8-1 Creative Pottery.

10. Submit the revised document in the format specified by your instructor.

11. ☀ In this presentation, you created a new theme font in the Slide Master and named it Clay. Is this name appropriate? You also changed the theme colors to Blue Warm. Was this a good choice of theme colors? Would another set of colors been a better complement for the Pottery picture background?

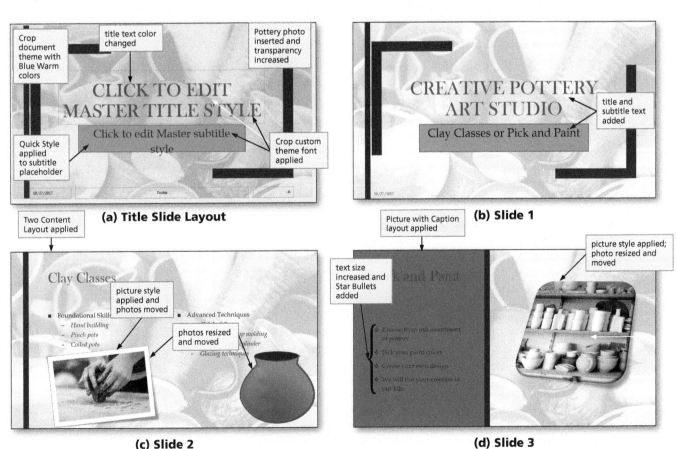

Figure 8–81

Extend Your Knowledge

Extend the skills you learned in this module and experiment with new skills. You may need to use Help to complete the assignment.

Adding a Background to a Slide Master, Hiding a Background Graphic on a Slide, Adjusting Footer Content and Placeholders, Inserting and Renaming a Layout

Note: To complete this assignment, you will be required to use the Data Files. Please contact your instructor for information about accessing the Data Files.

Instructions: Run PowerPoint. Open the presentation called Extend 8-1 Tree, which is located in the Data Files. You will add a background graphic to the slide master, insert a fixed date, adjust content and placeholders, and insert and rename a layout, as shown in Figure 8–82.

Perform the following tasks:

1. Display the Wisp Slide Master. Display the Header and Footer dialog box, click the 'Date and time' check box, click Fixed, and then enter 11/8/17 in the Fixed text box. Apply this fixed date to all slides. Format the date by increasing the font size to 12 point and the font color to 'Black, Text 1' (second color in first Theme Colors row). Insert the illustration called Potted Tree, which is located in the Data Files, in the lower-right corner of the slide near the date, as shown in Figure 8–82a.

2. Display the Two Content Layout. Hide the background graphics. (*Hint:* Click the 'Hide Background Graphics' check box (Slide Master tab | Background group).) Create a background by inserting the illustration called Tree, which is located in the Data Files. Change the transparency to 85%.

3. Select the title text placeholder in the Two Content Layout, change the font size to 40 point and then bold this text. Change the height of the title text placeholder to 1" (Drawing Tools Format tab | Size group), as shown in Figure 8–82b.

4. Display the Title Slide Layout. Apply the Trellis Pattern background fill (fifth pattern in seventh row). If necessary, change the foreground color to 'Orange, Accent 1'.

5. Insert a new layout and rename it Closing Slide. Hide the background graphics. Create a background by inserting the Tree illustration you added to the Two Content Layout in Step 2. Change the transparency to 10%. Close Master view.

6. On Slide 1 (Figure 8–82c), change the layout to Title Slide. Select the subtitle text placeholder and align the text in the middle of the placeholder. Use the eyedropper to color the subtitle text with a dark orange color in the Potted Tree illustration's pot.

7. On Slide 2, change the layout to Two Content. Move the illustration to the right side of the slide and decrease its size slightly so that it does not overlap the placeholder or the date (Figure 8–82d). Convert the bulleted text to the 'Basic Block List' SmartArt graphic (first graphic in first List row). Change the colors to 'Transparent Gradient Range - Accent 2' (fifth color in Accent 2 row), change the style to Powder (fourth style in first 3-D row), change the size of the SmartArt graphic to approximately 5" × 4.72", and then move it to the location shown in the figure.

8. On Slide 3 (Figure 8–82e), apply the Two Content layout. Select the bulleted list placeholder, change its size to approximately 5" × 3", and then apply the Canvas texture fill (second texture in first row). Align the text in the middle of the placeholder.

9. Click the Pictures icon in the right content placeholder and then insert the Three Trees illustration, which is located in the Data Files. Resize the right content placeholder to approximately 5" × 8.75". Move both placeholders to the locations shown in the figure.

10. On Slide 4 (Figure 8–82f), change the layout to Two Content. Select the bulleted list placeholder and then apply Green, Accent 6, Lighter 60% fill (last color in third Theme Colors row). Select the bulleted list and change the bullets to a numbered list with the 1) 2) 3) style. Align the numbered list in the middle of the placeholder. Adjust the size of this placeholder to approximately 4.5" × 5.5" and then move it to the location shown in the figure.

11. Select the photo on Slide 4, adjust the size to approximately 4" × 6.26", change the border color to 'Orange, Accent 1, Lighter 60%' (fifth color in third Theme Colors row), and then move the picture to the location shown.

12. Insert a new slide as Slide 5 and then apply the Closing Slide layout (Figure 8–82g). Copy the subtitle text placeholder from Slide 1 and paste it in Slide 5. Remove the bullet in the subtitle text placeholder and then move the placeholder to the location shown in Figure 8–82g. Delete the title text placeholder.

13. If requested by your instructor, add a sixth bullet with the name of your high school mascot in the bulleted list on Slide 3.

14. Apply the Rotate transition in the Dynamic Content category to all slides and then change the duration to 3.00 seconds.

15. Run the presentation and then save the file using the file name, Extend 8–1 Plant a Tree.

16. Submit the revised document in the format specified by your instructor.

17. ⊛ In this presentation, you changed the background of some slides to a tree illustration. Was this a good choice? Why? In the Slide Master, you inserted a layout, named it Closing Slide, and added the tree illustration as a background. Was this a good choice for a closing slide?

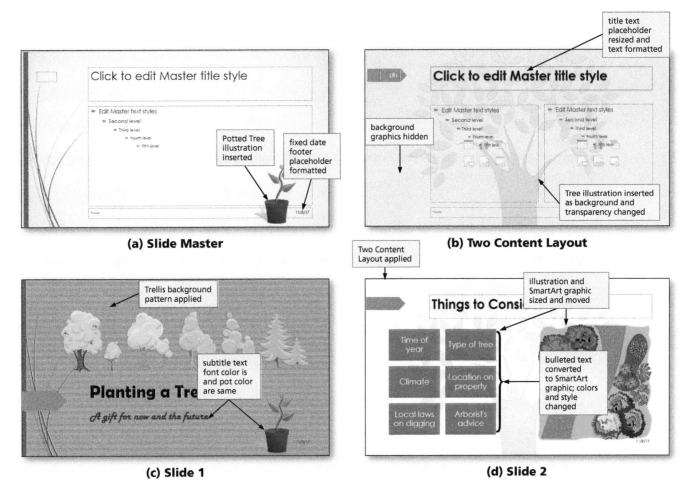

(a) Slide Master

(b) Two Content Layout

(c) Slide 1

(d) Slide 2

Figure 8–82 (Continued)

Continued >

Extend Your Knowledge *continued*

(e) Slide 3

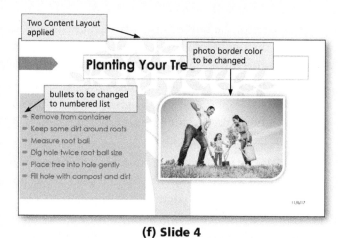

(f) Slide 4

(g) Slide 5

Figure 8–82

Expand Your World

Create a solution that uses cloud or web technologies by learning and investigating on your own from general guidance.

Linking to a YouTube Video

Instructions: You have created a presentation and want to play a video from an online website, such as YouTube or a news or sports organization, while running a slide show. Some websites encourage users to share video clips, while others restrict users from performing this process. The videos are not downloaded and inserted, or **embedded**, in the file; instead, they are **linked** to the presentation so that when the slide show is running and an Internet connection is present, the user can click the Play button to begin watching the video. PowerPoint includes commands on the Insert Video dialog box to insert a video clip from YouTube and from other websites.

Note: You will need Internet access to complete this assignment. If you do not have Internet access, read this assignment without performing the instructions.

Perform the following tasks:
  1. Run PowerPoint and then open the Zip Line presentation you created in this module. At the end of the presentation, insert one slide using the Miscellaneous layout and then add the title text, **Zip Lining Experiences** on Slide 4.

2. With Slide 4 displaying, click the Insert Video icon in the content placeholder to display the Insert Video dialog box.

3. If necessary, click the YouTube icon in the 'Also insert from' area to display the YouTube search box. Click the YouTube search text box, type `zip lining` as the search text, and then click the Search button (the magnifying glass) or press the ENTER key. Watch several videos on the website and then select one you desire to link to your PowerPoint presentation.

4. Click the Insert button (Insert Video dialog box) to display the selected clip on Slide 4. Increase the clip size, and then add a border and an effect. Click the 'Header & Footer' button (Insert tab | Text group) to display the Header and Footer dialog box, click the Footer check box to remove the check mark, and then click the Apply button to hide the footer on this slide. Move the video to the left side of the slide.

5. If requested by your instructor, enter the name of the city or county in which you were born in the Notes pane.

6. Run the presentation and then save the file with the new file name, Expand 8-1 Zip Line with Video.

7. ❀ Do videos add to the audience's ability to retain information presented during a presentation? Do they increase interest in the topic? Why did you select this specific video to display on Slide 4?

In the Labs

Design, create, modify, and/or use a presentation following the guidelines, concepts, and skills presented in this module. Labs 1 and 2, which increase in difficulty, require you to create solutions based on what you learned in the module; Lab 3 requires you to apply your creative thinking and problem-solving skills to design and implement a solution.

Lab 1: Deleting Slide Layouts, Adding a Placeholder, Renaming a Slide Master, and Saving a Slide Master as a Template

Note: To complete this assignment, you will be required to use the Data Files. Please contact your instructor for information about accessing the Data Files.

Problem: You are the president of your bicycle club. Your club plans many events every year for special bike rides. You decide to design a template that can be used for each month's activities. You create the slide master template shown in Figure 8–83a, the title slide layout in Figure 8–83b, and the three slides in Figures 8–83c–e.

Perform the following tasks:
1. Run PowerPoint. Open the presentation, Lab 8-1 Bike Club, which is located in the Data Files.

2. Display Slide Master view. Delete all layouts except the Title Slide Layout and the Blank Layout.

3. Display the Damask Slide Master. Insert the Spokes Logo picture, which is located in the Data Files, and then move it to the upper-left corner. Add the text, `April Events` in the footer placeholder, change the font color to Yellow (fourth color in Standard Colors row), increase the font size to 40 point, and apply the footer to all slides (Figure 8–83a). Delete the date and slide number placeholders. Rename the Slide Master as Spokes Slide Master.

Continued >

In the Labs *continued*

4. Display the Title Slide Layout (Figure 8–83b), insert the photo called Cyclist, which is located in the Data Files, as the new background fill, and then change the transparency to 10%. To display the footer, click the Footers check box (Slide Master | Master Layout group). Delete the title text and subtitle text placeholders.

5. Insert a Right Triangle shape on the left side of the slide. Change the size of the shape to approximately 6" × 6" and then move it to the lower-left area of the slide. Copy this triangle shape, paste it in the slide, and then click the Rotate button (Drawing Tools Format tab | Arrange group) to display the Rotate gallery. Click Flip Horizontal and then move the shape to the lower-right area of the slide.

6. Insert a Text placeholder in the left triangle shape, delete all the sample text, remove the bullet, change the size to approximately 4" × 2", change the font size to 32 point, change the font color to Dark Red (first color in Standard Colors), and then move the text box near the top of the triangle. Copy the Text placeholder, paste it in the right triangle, change the font size to 24 point, and then right align the text. Rename this layout Spokes Title Slide. Close Master view.

7. Save the file as a template with the file name, Lab 8–1 Spokes Spring Events Template.

8. On Slide 1 (Figure 8–83c), reapply the Spokes Title Slide layout to display the changes that were made in the previous steps. Type **First Saturday** in the left triangle Text placeholder and **Sunrise ride along the lake** in the right triangle Text placeholder.

9. Insert the photo called Bikes on Pier, which is located in the Data Files. Resize the photo to approximately 3" × 4.5". Apply the Soft Edge Oval picture style, add the Watercolor Sponge artistic effect (second effect in third row), and then move the photo below the right triangle text box.

10. Insert a new slide (Figure 8–83d) and apply the Spokes Title Slide layout. Type **Second Sunday** in the left triangle Text placeholder and **Ride the resurfaced 24-mile bike path** in the right Text placeholder. Insert the photo called Bike Path, which is located in the Data Files. Change the size of the photo to approximately 2.3" × 3.65", apply the Bevel Rectangle picture style, and then move the photo below the right triangle text box.

11. Insert a new slide (Figure 8–83e) with the Blank layout. Insert the photo called Group of Cyclists, which is located in the Data Files. Adjust the size of the photo to approximately 5" × 7.5" and then apply the Center Shadow Rectangle picture style. Rotate the photo counter-clockwise and then move it to the location shown in the figure.

12. On Slide 3, insert a text box and then type **Last Saturday: New members' meet and greet** in the text box. Change the font size to 32 point and the font color to Dark Red, size the text box to approximately 2" × 3.44", and then apply the Stationery texture fill (fourth texture in fourth row). Rotate the text box counter-clockwise and move it to the location shown in the figure.

13. If requested by your instructor, type the number of bones you have broken in place of the number, 24, in the right text box on Slide 2.

14. Apply the Split transition in the Subtle category to all slides and then change the duration to 2.50 seconds.

15. Run the presentation and then save the template file as a presentation using the file name, Lab 8-1 Spokes Spring Events.

16. Submit the document in the format specified by your instructor.

17. ✳ In Step 7, you saved the presentation as a template. How does creating a template help facilitate updating slides on a monthly or weekly basis? How did adding the triangle shapes and text boxes to the title slide layout enhance your presentation?

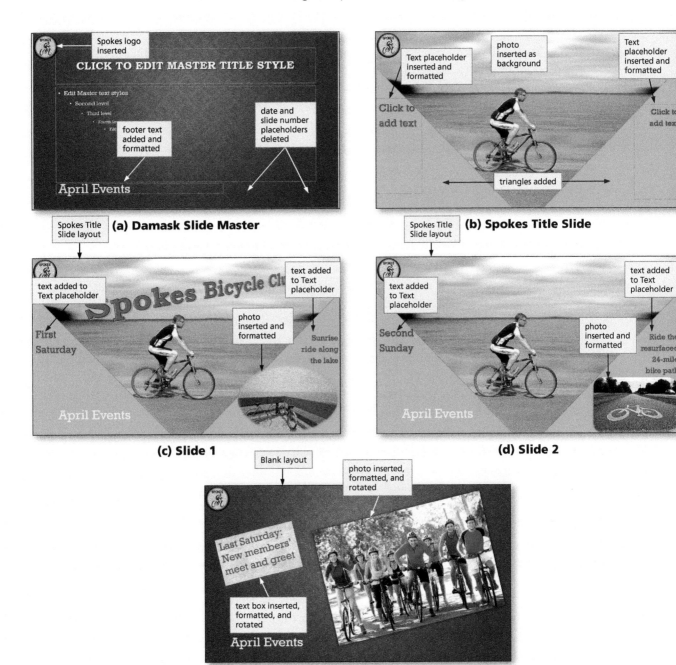

Figure 8–83

Lab 2: Formatting Slide Master Layouts, Inserting Placeholders, and Creating Handouts Using the Handout and Notes Masters

Note: To complete this assignment, you will be required to use the Data Files. Please contact your instructor for information about accessing the Data Files.

Continued >

In the Labs *continued*

Problem: You and your coworkers will be participating in a one-day team-building event at a nearby outdoor adventure center. Your manager made all the arrangements, gave you the details and asked you to put together a presentation for all the employees who will be attending the program. Create the five slides shown in Figure 8–84.

Perform the following tasks:

1. Run PowerPoint and apply the Blank Presentation theme. Display Slide Master view. Delete all layouts except the Title Slide Layout, Title and Content Layout, and Blank Layout.

2. Display the Office Theme Slide Master. Format the Background using a Solid fill, select the color Light Green (fifth color in Standard Colors row), and then change the transparency to 35%. Apply the Wind transition in the Exciting category and then change the duration to 3.25 seconds for all slides. Rename this slide master to Outdoor Adventure.

3. Display the Blank Layout and then insert a Text placeholder in the left side of the slide. Delete all the sample text in the placeholder, remove the bullet, and then type **TEAM** in the placeholder. Click the Text Direction button (Home tab | Paragraph group) to display the Text Direction gallery and then click Stacked. Adjust the size of the text placeholder to 7.5" × 2", change the font to Georgia, increase the font size to 96 point, change the font color to 'Green, Accent 6, Darker 25%' (last color in fifth Theme Colors row), and then align this text in the center of the placeholder. Cut this placeholder and then paste it into the left edge of the Outdoor Adventure Slide Master and then align it with the top, left, and bottom edges of the slide, as shown in Figure 8–84a.

4. Display the Blank Layout again. Insert a Picture placeholder on the slide and then change the placeholder size to 6.5" × 9". With this placeholder selected, click the Shape Outline arrow (Drawing Tools Format tab | Shape Styles group) and then click 'Green, Accent 6, Darker 50%' (last color in last Theme Colors row) to add a border. Click the Shape Effects button (Drawing Tools Format tab | Shape Styles group), point to Glow, and then click 'Green, 18 pt glow, Accent color 6' (last color in last Glow Variations row).

5. Insert a Text placeholder in the right side of the slide, delete all the sample text (but not the bullet), change the size to approximately 6.5" × 2", change the font to Georgia, change the font size to 36 point, change the font color to 'Green, Accent 6, Darker 25%', and then change the Text Direction to 'Rotate all text 90°'. Move the Text placeholder and the Picture placeholders to the locations shown in Figure 8–84b. Rename this layout to Team Picture.

6. Display the Title Slide Layout. Change the title text font to Georgia and then change the font size to 54 point. Apply the 'Subtle Effect - Green, Accent 6' Quick Style (last style in fourth row). Align this text in the middle of the placeholder. Change the subtitle text font to Bradley Hand ITC and then change the font size to 36 point. Align this text in the bottom of the placeholder, as shown in Figure 8–84c. Rename this layout to Team Title.

7. Display the Title and Content Layout. Change the title text font to Georgia, change the font size to 54 point, and then right-align this text. Select the content placeholder and then drag the left-center sizing handle slightly to the right so that the placeholder's new size is approximately 4.76" × 10.5" and it does not overlap the TEAM placeholder, as shown in the Figure 8–84d. Select the five levels of text styles in the content placeholder and then change the font to Bradley Hand ITC. Align the text in the Middle of the placeholder.

8. With the Content placeholder selected, click the Shape Outline arrow (Drawing Tools Format tab | Shape Styles group) and then click 'Green, Accent 6, Darker 50%' (last color in last Theme Colors row) to add a border. Click the Shape Effects button (Drawing Tools Format tab | Shape Styles group), point to Glow, and then click 'Green, 18 pt glow, Accent color 6' (last color in last Glow Variations row). Rename this layout to Team Title and Picture.

9. Display the Handout Master and then change the orientation to Landscape. Type `Outdoor Adventure Day` as the header text. Click the Date check box (Handout Master tab | Placeholders group) to remove the check mark so that the date does not display. Insert the picture called Ant Team, which is located in the Data Files, change the size to approximately 1.3" × 1.61", and then move it to the upper-right area of the handout master, as shown in Figure 8–84e.

10. Display the Notes Master. Type `Outdoor Adventure Day` as the header text, change the font to Bradley Hand ITC, and then increase the font size to 20 point. Delete the Date placeholder. Center the Header placeholder at the top of the page and then align the text in the center and the middle of the placeholder. Display the Header and Footer dialog box and then place a check mark in the Header check box. Insert the picture called Climbing Tower, which is located in the Data Files, change the size to approximately 3" × 2", and then move it between the Footer and Slide Number text boxes, as shown in Figure 8–84f. Select the five master text styles and then change the font to Bradley Hand ITC. Close Master view.

11. With Slide 1 displaying with the Team Title Layout, type `Outdoor Adventure Day` as the title text and then type, `We'll build cohesiveness, restore group morale, and renew workplace energy` as the subtitle text, as shown in Figure 8–84g. Display the Notes pane and then type `Challenging teamwork situations help focus the mind and body.` as the Notes text.

12. Insert a slide with the Team Picture Layout. Insert the picture called Team, which is located in the Data Files. Type `Gain confidence while connecting to and respecting the environment` in the text box, as shown in Figure 8–84h. Type `We'll preserve the natural environment while having fun and staying healthy.` in the Notes pane.

13. Insert a slide with the Team Title and Picture Layout. Type `Event Schedule` as the title text. In the content placeholder, type `Meet Saturday morning at Sandridge Nature Center` as the first paragraph, `Orientation meeting at 8 a.m.` as the second paragraph, `Activities begin at 9 a.m.` as the third paragraph, `Lunch served at noon` as the fourth paragraph, and `Debriefing starts at 4 p.m.` as the last paragraph, as shown in Figure 8–84i. If requested by your instructor, type the name of the last TV program you watched as the sixth bulleted paragraph. Type `Participation in a short program can inspire a substantial, lasting change in attitude and behavior.` in the Notes pane.

14. Insert a slide with the Team Title and Picture Layout. Type `High Ropes Obstacle Course` as the title text. Insert the High Ropes photo, which is located in the Data Files, in the Content placeholder. Increase the photo size to approximately 5.5" × 9.5" and then move it to the location shown in Figure 8–84j. Type `The course has three levels with eight activities each. It starts at 2' above ground and ends at a height of 20'.` in the Notes pane.

15. Insert a slide with the Team Picture Layout. Insert the picture called Tug of War, which is located in the Data Files, in the content placeholder. Type `We saved the best for last!` in the text box (Figure 8–84k). Type `This popular team-building exercise requires brute strength from each side.` in the Notes pane.

16. Run the presentation and then save the file using the file name, Lab 8–2 Team Building.

17. Submit the presentation in the format specified by your instructor.

18. Print the handout (Figure 8–84l) and speaker notes (Figure 8–84m–q).

19. ✸ What are the benefits of creating slide layout masters? Did inserting and formatting Text placeholders and adding the word TEAM and bulleted text add interest to the presentation? Why?

Continued >

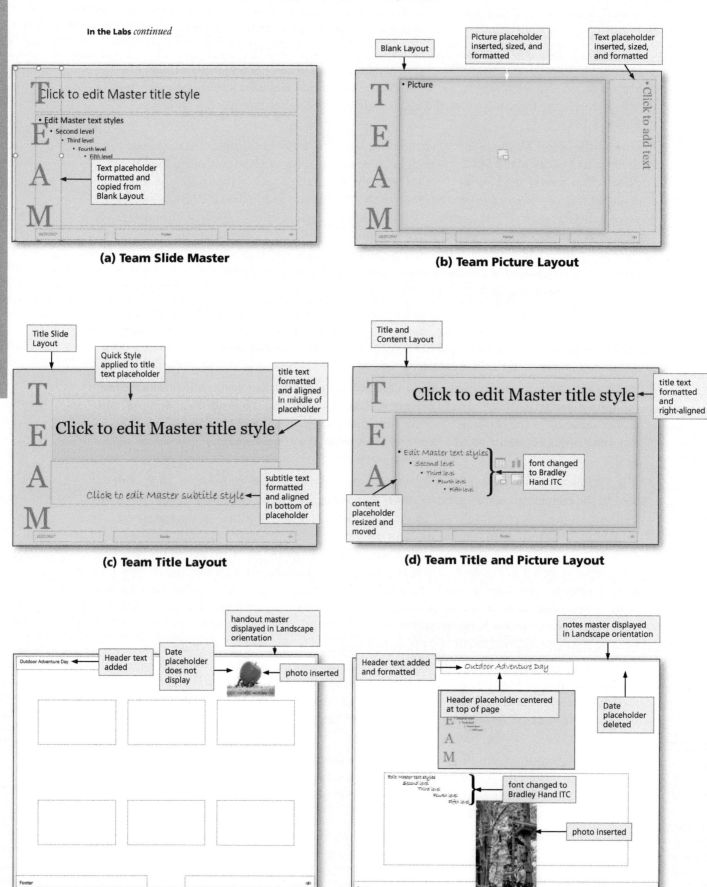

In the Labs *continued*

(a) Team Slide Master

(b) Team Picture Layout

(c) Team Title Layout

(d) Team Title and Picture Layout

(e) Handout Master

(f) Notes Master

Figure 8–84 (Continued)

(g) Slide 1

(h) Slide 2

(i) Slide 3

(j) Slide 4

(k) Slide 5

(l) Handout

Figure 8–84 (Continued)

In the Labs *continued*

(m) Notes Page 1

(n) Notes Page 2

(o) Notes Page 3

(p) Notes Page 4

(q) Notes Page 5

Figure 8–84

Lab 3: **Consider This: Your Turn**

Design and Create a Presentation about Alligators

Part 1:   Alligators are reptiles found primarily in the southeastern areas of the United States and in China. They can weigh more than 1,000 pounds and live approximately 50 years in freshwater swamps, rivers, marshes, and lakes. Males have an average length of 11.2 feet, and females average 8.2 feet. Review some websites to learn about alligators, including their habitat, diet, and anatomy. Use the concepts and techniques presented in this module to create a presentation about this reptile. Develop at least two slide master layouts that include an inserted placeholder, a formatted text box, and picture that displays on all slides, and then rename these layouts. Delete the layouts you do not use. Change the theme colors. Customize the theme fonts. Create a handout master and a notes master with inserted pictures. Three pictures are available in the Data Files: Alligator Drawing, Alligator Head, and Green Alligator. Include information about alligators in the Notes pane. Review and revise your presentation as needed and then save the file using the file name, Lab 8-3 Alligators. Submit your assignment in the format specified by your instructor.

Part 2:   ✵ You made several decisions while creating the presentation in this assignment: where to move the inserted placeholder and formatted text box, which layout masters to use, and where to place the pictures in the slides, notes, and handouts. What was the rationale behind each of these decisions? When you reviewed the document, what further revisions did you make and why?

9 | Modifying a Presentation Using Graphical Elements

Objectives

You will have mastered the material in this module when you can:

- Change a text box outline color, weight, and style
- Set text box formatting as the default for new text boxes
- Apply a gradient, texture, pattern, and effects to a text box
- Convert WordArt to SmartArt
- Reorder SmartArt shapes
- Promote and demote SmartArt text

- Add and remove SmartArt shapes
- Convert a SmartArt graphic to text
- Insert and modify shapes to create custom artwork
- Customize and reset the ribbon
- Create a handout by exporting a file to Microsoft Word
- Save the presentation as a picture presentation

BTW

Identifying Shapes
Most objects in our world are composed of shapes: a circle, square, and triangle. Artists see objects as combinations of these shapes and begin their drawings by sketching these basic forms in proportion to each other. For example, a tree has the form of a circle for the branches and a rectangle for the trunk. A car has the form of a rectangle for the body, a smaller rectangle for the passenger compartment, and four circles for the wheels. Become observant of the relationships between objects in your world as you learn to use PowerPoint's drawing tools.

Introduction

PowerPoint's themes determine the default characteristics of slide objects. Colors, border weights and styles, fills, effects, and other formatting options give the slides a unique character. You can create your own designs for text boxes, shapes, lines, and other slide content, and then reuse these graphical objects throughout the presentation. Once you learn to format one type of object, such as a text box, you can use similar techniques to format other slide objects, such as SmartArt and shapes. One efficient way to create consistent graphical elements is to save your settings as the default. Then, when you insert the same objects later during the presentation design process, they will have the same characteristics as the initial element.

SmartArt graphics have individual layouts, styles, and color schemes. If one of these designs does not meet the specific needs of your slide content, you can modify the graphic by adding shapes, reordering the current shapes, and changing each element's size and location. You also can convert the SmartArt to text or to a shape if SmartArt is not the best method of conveying your ideas to an audience. PowerPoint's myriad formatting options allow you to tailor graphical elements to best fit your unique design needs.

Project — Presentation with Customized Text Boxes, SmartArt, and Shapes

The lure of sailing in tranquil waters near white sandy beaches and tropical paradises has stirred the imagination of experienced sailors and landlubbers alike. The American Sailing Association (ASA) accredits schools that provide training for people to sail safely and confidently, with eight levels of certification. Some schools offer one-week programs where students learn how to maneuver the vessel, communicate with crewmates, navigate, and other skills.

The presentation you create in this module (Figure 9–1) would be useful to show at travel shows and boating stores to promote these classes. All four slides are created by modifying a starting file that has a variety of content. The title slide (Figure 9–1a) contains a colorful picture and a text box that is formatted with an outline style, a weight, and a color. These modifications are saved as the default settings for all other text boxes inserted into other slides. The second slide (Figure 9–1b) features a new picture and a formatted text box. The text on Slide 3 (Figure 9–1c) is converted from WordArt to a SmartArt graphic. The layout, style, color, and shapes are changed and enhanced. The final slide (Figure 9–1d) has bulleted text converted from a SmartArt graphic; it also has a sailboat composed of formatted shapes. After the slides are created, you export the file to Microsoft Word to create a handout (Figure 9–1e, f) and then save the presentation as a picture presentation.

In this module, you will learn how to create the slides shown in Figure 9–1. The following roadmap identifies general activities you will perform as you progress through this module:

1. INSERT and CUSTOMIZE TEXT BOXES by changing the weight, color, and style and by adding an effect, pattern, and fill.

2. CONVERT WORDART TO SMARTART and then FORMAT by changing bullet levels, the layout, and the shape.

3. INSERT and FORMAT SHAPES.

4. DRAW and FORMAT LINES.

5. CUSTOMIZE THE RIBBON by adding a new group and buttons.

6. EXPORT a FILE to Microsoft Word and CREATE a PICTURE PRESENTATION.

(a) Slide 1

(b) Slide 2

Figure 9–1 (Continued)

(c) Slide 3

(d) Slide 4

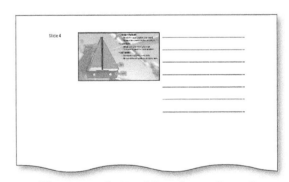

(e) Microsoft Word Handout – Page 1

(f) Microsoft Word Handout – Page 2

Figure 9–1

To Run PowerPoint and Save a File

If you are using a computer to step through the project in this module and you want your screens to match the figures in this book, you should change your screen's resolution to 1366 × 768. The following steps run PowerPoint and then save a file.

1 Run PowerPoint. If necessary, maximize the PowerPoint window.

2 Open the presentation, Sailing, located in the Data Files.

3 Save the presentation using the file name, Sailing Lessons.

CONSIDER THIS

Choose colors wisely.
Color can create interest in the material on your slides, so you need to think about which colors best support the message you want to share with your audience. The color you add to text boxes signals that the viewer should pay attention to the contents. Orange, red, and yellow are considered warm colors and will be among the first colors your viewers perceive on your slide. Blue and green are considered cool colors, and they often blend into a background and are less obvious than the warm colors.

BTW
The Ribbon and Screen Resolution
PowerPoint may change how the groups and buttons within the groups appear on the ribbon, depending on the computer or mobile device's screen resolution. Thus, your ribbon may look different from the ones in this book if you are using a screen resolution other than 1366 x 768.

Formatting Text Boxes

Text boxes can be formatted in a variety of ways to draw attention to slide content. You can apply formatting, such as fill color, gradient, texture, and pattern. You can add a picture; change the outline color, weight, and style; and then set margins and alignment. Once you determine the desired effects for a text box, you can save these settings as a default to achieve consistency and save time. Then, each time you insert another text box, the same settings will be applied.

In the following pages, you will perform these tasks on Slide 1:

1. Insert a text box into Slide 1.
2. Type text into the text box.
3. Change the text box outline weight.
4. Change the text box outline color.
5. Change the text box outline style.
6. Apply a glow effect to the text box.
7. Set the text box formatting as the default for new text boxes.

Once the text box formatting is complete on Slide 1, you then will perform these tasks on Slide 2:

1. Insert a text box and enter text.
2. Apply a pattern to the text box.
3. Change the text box pattern foreground and background colors.

BTW
Touch Screen Differences
The Office and Windows interfaces may vary if you are using a touch screen. For this reason, you might notice that the function or appearance of your touch screen differs slightly from this module's presentation.

You also will perform these tasks on Slide 3:

1. Insert a text box and enter text.
2. Apply a gradient fill to the text box.
3. Align the text box in the center of the slide.
4. Change the Slide 3 picture.

To Insert a Text Box and Text

The default text box for the Office Theme is displayed with the Calibri font and has no border, fill, or effects. To begin customizing the Sailing Lessons presentation, you will insert a text box and then type the text that serves as the title to your presentation. The following steps insert a text box and enter text into the text box.

1 Display the Insert tab, click the Text Box button (Insert tab | Text group), position the pointer in the lower-left corner of Slide 1, and then click to insert the new text box.

2 Type **Learn to Sail in One Week** as the text box text (Figure 9–2).

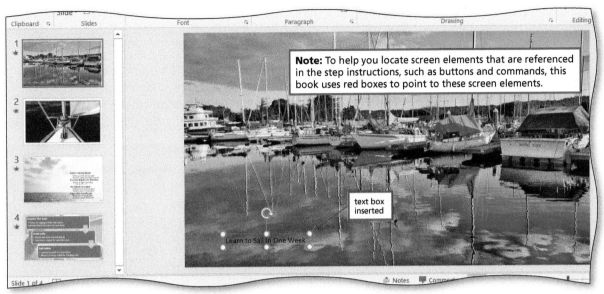

Figure 9–2

Q&A

Do I need to position the text box in the precise location indicated in Figure 9–2?
No. You will reposition the text box later in this module after you have made the formatting changes.

Can I change the shape of the text box?
Yes. By default, a rectangular text box is inserted. If you want to use a different shape, select the text box, display the Drawing Tools Format tab, click the Edit Shape button (Drawing Tools Format tab | Insert Shapes group), point to Change Shape in the list, and then click the desired new shape.

To Format Text Box Text

You now can choose a font and font size that complement the Slide 1 photo. A WordArt style can add visual interest to the text box. The following steps change the text box text to WordArt, change the font size, and center the text in the text box.

1 Select all the text box text, display the Drawing Tools Format tab, click the WordArt Styles More button (Drawing Tools Format tab | WordArt Styles group) to expand the gallery, and then click 'Fill - White, Outline - Accent 2, Hard Shadow - Accent 2' (fourth style in third row) to apply this style.

2 Increase the font size to 66 point.

3 Center the text in the text box. If necessary, drag the text box to the location shown in Figure 9–3.

BTW
Line Spacing Measurements
The lower part of each letter rests on an imaginary line called the baseline. The space between the baseline of one row of type and the baseline of the row beneath it is called line spacing. Typically, the line spacing is 120 percent of the font size. For example, if the font size is 10 point, the line spacing is 12 point so that two points of space are displayed between the lines.

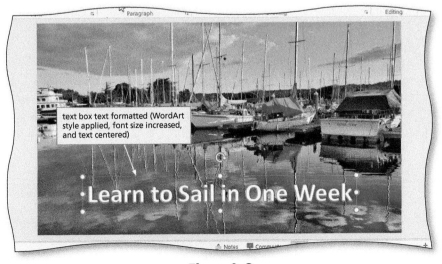

Figure 9–3

To Change a Text Box Outline Weight

The first graphical change you will make to the text box border is to increase the thickness, which is called the outline. ***Why? This thicker line is a graphical element that helps to call attention to the box.*** The weight, or thickness, of the text box border is measured in points. The following steps increase the outline weight.

1

- With the text box still selected, if necessary display the Home tab, and then click the Shape Outline arrow (Home tab | Drawing group) to display the Shape Outline gallery.

- Click Weight in the Shape Outline gallery to display the Weight list (Figure 9–4).

Figure 9–4

2

- Point to 6 pt to display a live preview of this outline line weight (Figure 9–5).

Experiment

- Point to various line weights on the Weight list and watch the border weights on the text box change.

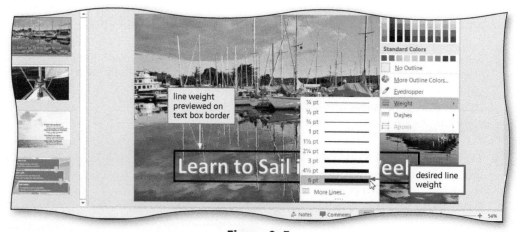

Figure 9–5

3

- Click 6 pt to add an outline around the text box.

Other Ways

1. Click Shape Outline arrow (Drawing Tools Format tab | Shape Styles group), click Weight

2. Right-click text box, click Outline below shortcut menu, click Weight

To Change a Text Box Outline Color

The default outline color in the Office Theme is black. In this project, you will change the outline color to orange. *Why? Orange matches the WordArt text color and contrasts well with the blue water.* The following steps change the text box outline color.

- With the text box still selected, click the Shape Outline arrow again to display the Shape Outline gallery.

- Point to Orange (third color in Standard Colors row) to display a live preview of that outline color on the text box (Figure 9–6).

Experiment

- Point to various colors in the Shape Outline gallery and watch the border colors on the text box change.

- Click Orange to change the text box border color.

Figure 9–6

To Change a Text Box Outline Style

The default outline style is a solid line. You can add interest by changing the style to dashes, dots, or a combination of dashes and dots. The following steps change the text box outline style to Long Dash Dot. *Why? The dashes and dots in this pattern resemble the ripples in the water.*

- Display the Shape Outline gallery and then point to Dashes to display the Dashes list.

- Point to 'Long Dash Dot' to display a live preview of this outline style (Figure 9–7).

Experiment

- Point to various styles in the Shape Outline gallery and watch the borders on the text box change.

- Click 'Long Dash Dot' to change the text box border style.

Figure 9–7

To Apply an Effect to a Text Box

PowerPoint provides a variety of visual effects to add to the text box. They include shadow, glow, reflection, and 3-D rotation. The following steps apply a glow effect to the text box. *Why? The water in the background photo has a soft texture, so you can coordinate with this soft effect by adding a glow effect to the text box.*

- Click the Shape Effects button (Home tab | Drawing group) to display the Shape Effects gallery.

- Point to Glow to display the Glow gallery.

- Point to 'Orange, 18 pt glow, Accent color 2' (second color in last Glow Variations row) to display a live preview of this outline effect (Figure 9–8).

 Experiment

- Point to various effects in the Glow gallery and watch the glow effects change on the text box.

Figure 9–8

- Click the 'Orange, 18 pt glow, Accent color 2' variation to apply the glow effect.

To Set Text Box Formatting as the Default

The text box you inserted and formatted has a variety of visual elements that work well with the sailboat picture and overall theme. You can insert text boxes with the same formatting into other slides in the presentation. *Why? To save time and ensure all the formatting changes are applied consistently, you can set the formatting of one text box as the default for all other text boxes you insert into the presentation.* The following steps set the text box on Slide 1 as the default.

- Right-click the text box outline to display the shortcut menu (Figure 9–9).

- Click 'Set as Default Text Box' on the shortcut menu to set the text box formatting as the default for any new text boxes.

Q&A What should I do if the 'Set as Default Text Box' command is not displayed on the shortcut menu? Repeat Step 1 and be certain to click the text box border, not the interior of the box.

Does setting the default text box affect all presentations or just the current one? Only the current presentation is affected.

Figure 9–9

To Insert a Formatted Text Box and Enter Text

Any new text boxes you insert will have the same formatting you applied to the Slide 1 text box. You want to emphasize to your presentation viewers that sailing lessons are available all year, so a text box on Slide 2 is a good place to state this information. The following steps insert a formatted text box into Slide 2 and enter text.

1 Display Slide 2, display the Insert tab, and then click the Text Box button.

2 Insert the text box into the left side of the slide and then type **Classes** as the first line of the text box text.

3 Press SHIFT+ENTER to insert a line break and then type **held** as the second text box line.

4 Press SHIFT+ENTER to insert a line break and then type **every** as the third text box line.

5 Press SHIFT+ENTER to insert a line break and then type **week** as the fourth text box line.

6 If necessary, drag the text box to the location shown in Figure 9–10.

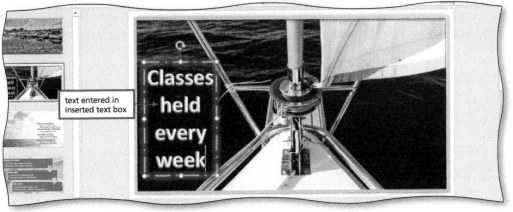

text entered in inserted text box

Figure 9–10

To Apply a Pattern to a Text Box

1 INSERT & CUSTOMIZE TEXT BOXES | 2 CONVERT WORDART TO SMARTART & FORMAT | 3 INSERT & FORMAT SHAPES
4 DRAW & FORMAT LINES | 5 CUSTOMIZE THE RIBBON | 6 EXPORT FILE & CREATE PICTURE PRESENTATION

Why? A pattern fill can call attention to a text box. PowerPoint provides a Pattern gallery, allowing you to change the appearance of the text box with a variety of horizontal and vertical lines, dots, dashes, and stripes. If desired, you can change the default fill foreground and background colors. The following steps apply a pattern to the Slide 2 text box and change the foreground and background colors.

1
• Right-click anywhere on the Slide 2 text box to display the shortcut menu (Figure 9–11).

Format Shape command

Figure 9–11

- Click Format Shape on the shortcut menu to display the Format Shape pane.

- If necessary, click Fill to expand the Fill section. Click Pattern fill to display the Pattern gallery and the 5% pattern on the text box (Figure 9–12).

Q&A Can I experiment with previewing the patterns on the text box?
No, the live preview function is not available.

Can the default pattern gallery color vary?
Yes. You may find that your default color is black rather than the shade of blue shown in the figure.

Figure 9–12

- Click the 'Light upward diagonal' pattern (second pattern in third row) to apply this pattern to the Slide 2 text box.

Q&A How can I delete a pattern if I decide not to apply one to my slide?
If you already have applied the pattern, click the Undo button on the Quick Access Toolbar.

- If necessary, scroll down the Format Shape pane and then click the Foreground button to display the Color gallery (Figure 9–13).

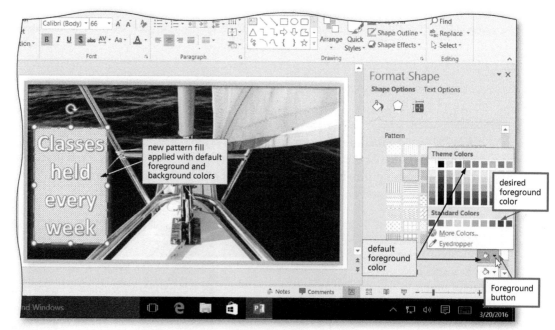

Figure 9–13

Q&A Can the default foreground color vary in the gallery?
Yes. You may find that your default color is black rather than the shade of blue shown in the figure.

4
- Click Dark Blue (ninth color in Standard Colors row) to apply this color to the text box pattern and to display the Pattern gallery with the new foreground color.
- Click the Background button to display the Color gallery (Figure 9–14).

Figure 9–14

5
- Click Light Blue (seventh color in Standard Colors row) to apply this color to the text box background and to display the Pattern gallery with the new background color (Figure 9–15).

6
- Click the Close button to close the Format Shape pane.

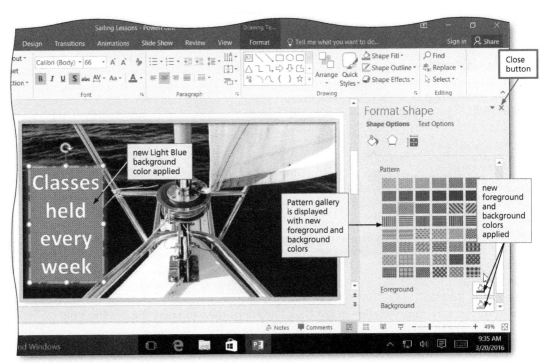

Figure 9–15

To Apply a Gradient Fill to a Text Box

Why? A gradient fill is another type of format you can apply to create interest in a slide element. It blends one color into another shade of the same color or another color. PowerPoint provides several preset gradients, or you can create your own custom color mix. The following steps insert a text box into Slide 3 and then apply a gradient fill.

- Display Slide 3, display the Insert tab, and then insert a text box near the top of the slide.

- Type **Class Highlights** as the text box text, and if necessary, drag the text box to the location shown in Figure 9–16.

Figure 9–16

- Click the Drawing Tools Format tab and then click the Shape Fill arrow (Drawing Tools Format tab | Shape Styles group) to display the Shape Fill gallery.

- Point to Gradient to display the Gradient gallery (Figure 9–17).

🔎 **Experiment**

- Point to various fills in the Gradient gallery and watch the interior of the text box change.

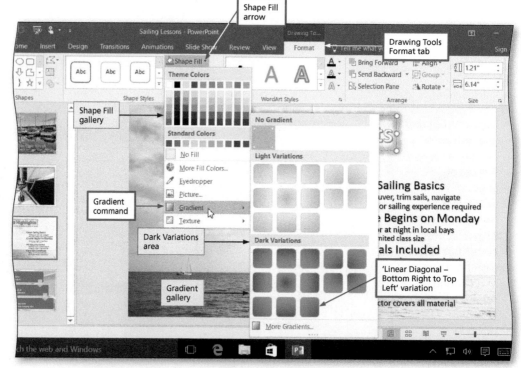

Figure 9–17

3

- Click 'Linear Diagonal - Bottom Right to Top Left' (last variation in last Dark Variations row) to apply the gradient fill.

To Align a Text Box

The text box on Slide 3 will serve as the title. You could attempt to position it horizontally on the slide and use the rulers to aid you in this process. You also can use PowerPoint's Align feature. *Why? Using the Align command is a more efficient method of positioning the text box in the slide.* You can align a slide element horizontally along the left or right sides or in the center of the slide, and you also can align an element vertically along the top, bottom, or middle of the slide. The following steps move the Slide 3 text box horizontally to the left edge of the slide.

- With the Slide 3 text box selected, click the Align button (Drawing Tools Format tab | Arrange group) to display the Align menu (Figure 9–18).

- Click Align Left to move the text box horizontally on the slide.

Figure 9–18

Q&A Can I position a text box in a precise location on a slide?
Yes. With the text box selected, right-click a border of the box to display the shortcut menu and then click Format Shape on the shortcut menu to display the Format Shape pane. Click the Size & Properties icon, click Position, and then enter Horizontal position and Vertical position measurements. Specify if these measurements should be from the Top Left Corner or the Center of the text box and then click the Close button (Format Shape pane).

To Change a Slide Picture

1 INSERT & CUSTOMIZE TEXT BOXES | 2 CONVERT WORDART TO SMARTART & FORMAT | 3 INSERT & FORMAT SHAPES
4 DRAW & FORMAT LINES | 5 CUSTOMIZE THE RIBBON | 6 EXPORT FILE & CREATE PICTURE PRESENTATION

PowerPoint allows you to change a picture on a slide easily. The following steps change the Slide 3 picture. **Why?** *The photograph on Slide 3 features one sailboat that is not prominently featured. A more dramatic photograph of many sailboats is located in the Data Files.*

- With Slide 3 displaying, click anywhere on the picture except the text box to select the picture and then click the Picture Tools Format tab (Figure 9–19).

Figure 9–19

2

- Click the Change Picture button (Picture Tools Format tab | Adjust group) to display the Insert Pictures dialog box and then navigate to the location where your Data Files are stored.

- Click Reflected Sailboats to select the file name (Figure 9–20).

Q&A What if the picture is not in my Data Files folder?
Use the same process, but select the device containing the photograph. Another option is to locate this photograph or a similar one on Facebook, Flickr, and other websites.

Figure 9–20

3

- Click the Insert button (Insert Picture dialog box) to change the Slide 3 picture. If necessary, drag the sizing handles to the borders of the slide (Figure 9–21).

Q&A What if I do not want to use this picture?
Click the Undo button on the Quick Access Toolbar.

Figure 9–21

Break Point: If you wish to take a break, this is a good place to do so. Be sure to save the Sailing Lessons file again and then you can exit PowerPoint. To resume at a later time, run PowerPoint, open the file called Sailing Lessons, and continue following the steps from this location forward.

BTW

SmartArt in Handouts
SmartArt diagrams are composed of individual vector graphics. Some presenters decide to include these diagrams in a handout but not as part of a presentation so that audience members can study the relationships among the shapes after the presentation has concluded.

Manipulating SmartArt

Every SmartArt layout has a unique design and graphical elements. The shapes maximize vertical and horizontal space for text and pictures. When your presentation calls for special design needs or additional shapes, you can change the defaults that specify where each SmartArt element is displayed. You can add, subtract, and reorder shapes; promote and demote text; make a single shape smaller or larger; and change the SmartArt fill, outline, and colors.

In the following pages, you will perform these tasks on Slides 3 and 4:

1. Convert WordArt paragraphs to SmartArt.
2. Reorder two shapes in the SmartArt layout.
3. Reorder two bulleted paragraphs in a SmartArt shape.
4. Promote and demote SmartArt bulleted paragraphs.
5. Change the SmartArt layout, style, and color.
6. Remove a SmartArt shape.
7. Resize the entire SmartArt layout and shapes within the layout.
8. Apply a picture to the text box.
9. Convert the SmartArt graphic to text on Slide 4.

Use keywords in SmartArt graphics.

Most SmartArt shapes have very limited space for text. You must, therefore, carefully choose each word you are going to display in the graphic. The text you select can serve as **keywords**, or a speaking outline. If you glance at the SmartArt when you are presenting the slide show in front of an audience, each word should prompt you for the main point you are going to make. These keywords should jog your memory if you lose your train of thought or are interrupted.

To Convert WordArt to SmartArt

1 INSERT & CUSTOMIZE TEXT BOXES | 2 CONVERT WORDART TO SMARTART & FORMAT | 3 INSERT & FORMAT SHAPES
4 DRAW & FORMAT LINES | 5 CUSTOMIZE THE RIBBON | 6 EXPORT FILE & CREATE PICTURE PRESENTATION

The bulleted paragraphs on Slide 3 are formatted as WordArt. Although WordArt can add visual interest, using a graphical element such as SmartArt can be even more effective in helping the audience to grasp essential concepts. ***Why?*** *SmartArt diagrams are creative means to show processes, lists, cycles, and other relationships.* PowerPoint suggests layouts that might fit the concept you are trying to present and then easily converts WordArt to SmartArt. The following steps convert WordArt to SmartArt.

- With Slide 3 displaying, right-click anywhere in the WordArt bulleted list paragraphs to display the shortcut menu.

- Point to 'Convert to SmartArt' to display the SmartArt gallery (Figure 9–22).

Q&A

Does it matter where I place the cursor?

No. As long as the cursor is placed in the WordArt text, you will be able to convert the paragraphs to SmartArt.

Figure 9–22

- Click 'More SmartArt Graphics' to display the Choose a SmartArt Graphic dialog box.

- Click Matrix in the list of graphic categories and then click Basic Matrix in the gallery to display a picture and a description of this SmartArt layout (Figure 9–23).

Figure 9–23

- Click the OK button (Choose a SmartArt Graphic dialog box) to convert the WordArt to that layout.

Q&A How is the text arranged in the Basic Matrix SmartArt layout?
The four first-level paragraphs are at the top of each shape in the graphic and have a larger font size than the eight bulleted second-level paragraphs.

To Reorder SmartArt Shapes

1 INSERT & CUSTOMIZE TEXT BOXES | 2 CONVERT WORDART TO SMARTART & FORMAT | 3 INSERT & FORMAT SHAPES
4 DRAW & FORMAT LINES | 5 CUSTOMIZE THE RIBBON | 6 EXPORT FILE & CREATE PICTURE PRESENTATION

Now that the SmartArt layout is created, you can modify the graphic. One change you can make is to change the order of the shapes. You decide that two items in the graphic should be displayed in a different order. *Why? The ability to earn a certificate is a desired component of the one-week schools, so it is fitting that the Earn ASA Certificate should be displayed prominently. You also decide that potential students might be interested in cooking onboard, so you want to move that information in the second bulleted paragraph in the All Meals Included shape above the fact that diet restrictions are addressed.* PowerPoint provides tools to move shapes and paragraphs in a vertical layout up or down. The following steps reorder the All Meals Included and Earn ASA Certificate shapes and the two bulleted paragraphs in the All Meals Included shape.

- Position the pointer in the Earn ASA Certificate shape and then click to select it and the two bulleted paragraphs (Figure 9–24).

Is all the text selected in the Earn ASA Certificate shape?
Yes. The words, Earn ASA Certificate, are in a first-level paragraph, and the two bulleted second-level paragraphs are associated with it. When the shape is selected, all related paragraphs are selected with it.

Figure 9–24

2

- With the SmartArt Tools Design tab displaying, click the Move Up button (SmartArt Tools Design tab | Create Graphic group) to reorder the Earn ASA Certificate shape to the left of the All Meals Included shape.

- Position the pointer in the bulleted paragraph, Dietary needs accommodated (Figure 9–25).

Figure 9–25

3

- Click the Move Down button (SmartArt Tools Design tab | Create Graphic group) to reorder the bulleted paragraph, Dietary needs accommodated, below the bulleted paragraph, Students share in preparation.

To Promote a SmartArt Bullet Level

PowerPoint provides tools that allow you to promote and demote bulleted text. These tools function in the same manner as the Increase List Level and Decrease List Level buttons that change the indents for bulleted text.

Another change you want to make on Slide 3 is to promote the bulleted paragraph, Limited class size, to the same level as the bullet above it. *Why? Because this fact may encourage people to register early, and it may be a selling feature of this particular sailing school.* The following steps promote the second bullet in the Course Begins on Monday shape.

- Position the pointer in the bulleted paragraph, Limited class size (Figure 9–26).

Figure 9–26

- Click the Promote button (SmartArt Tools Design tab | Create Graphic group) to decrease the indent of the bulleted paragraph.

To Demote a SmartArt Bullet Level

The two bulleted items in the Learn Sailing Basics shape are second-level paragraphs, but you decide to demote the second paragraph, No prior sailing experience required. You also want to demote the paragraph, Instructor covers all material in the Earn ASA Certificate shape. *Why? The information in these two paragraphs is not as important as the information in the first bulleted paragraphs in each of these shapes.* The following steps demote the second-level bulleted paragraphs.

- Position the pointer in the bulleted paragraph, No prior sailing experience required (Figure 9–27).

Figure 9–27

2

- Click the Demote button (SmartArt Tools Design tab | Create Graphic group) to increase the indent of the bulleted paragraph.

- Position the pointer in the bulleted paragraph, Instructor covers all material, and then click the Demote button to increase the indent of this paragraph (Figure 9–28).

Figure 9–28

To Add a SmartArt Bullet

If you need to add information to a SmartArt shape, you can create a new bulleted paragraph. This text would display below the last bulleted paragraph in the shape. If you wanted to add a SmartArt bullet, you would perform the following steps.

1. Select the SmartArt graphic shape where you want to insert the bulleted paragraph.

2. Click the Add Bullet button (SmartArt Tools Design tab | Create Graphic group) to insert a new bulleted paragraph below any bulleted text.

To Change the SmartArt Layout

1 INSERT & CUSTOMIZE TEXT BOXES | 2 CONVERT WORDART TO SMARTART & FORMAT | 3 INSERT & FORMAT SHAPES
4 DRAW & FORMAT LINES | 5 CUSTOMIZE THE RIBBON | 6 EXPORT FILE & CREATE PICTURE PRESENTATION

Once you begin formatting a SmartArt shape, you may decide that another layout better conveys the message you are communicating to an audience. PowerPoint allows you to change the layout easily. Any graphical changes that were made to the original SmartArt, such as moving shapes or promoting and demoting paragraphs, are applied to the new SmartArt layout. The following steps change the SmartArt layout to Linear Venn. *Why? A Venn diagram has overlapping components. Similarly, the information in the individual Sailing Lessons SmartArt shapes overlaps the information in the other shapes. For example, the basic sailing techniques mentioned in the left shape are needed to earn an ASA certificate, which is the topic of the right shape.*

1

- With the SmartArt Tools Design tab displaying, click the More button (shown in Figure 9–28) in the Layouts group to expand the Layouts gallery (Figure 9–29).

Q&A Can I select one of the layouts displaying in the Layouts group without expanding the layout gallery?
Yes. At times, however, you may want to display the gallery to view and preview the various layouts.

Figure 9–29

• Click More Layouts at the
bottom of the Layouts gallery
to display the Choose a
SmartArt Graphic dialog box,
click Relationship in the list of
graphic categories, and then
click the Linear Venn layout (first
layout in last row) to display a
picture and a description of this
SmartArt layout (Figure 9–30).

Figure 9–30

• Click the OK button (Choose a
SmartArt Graphic dialog box) to
change the layout.

To Remove a SmartArt Shape

1 INSERT & CUSTOMIZE TEXT BOXES | 2 CONVERT WORDART TO SMARTART & FORMAT | 3 INSERT & FORMAT SHAPES
4 DRAW & FORMAT LINES | 5 CUSTOMIZE THE RIBBON | 6 EXPORT FILE & CREATE PICTURE PRESENTATION

Now that the new SmartArt layout is created, you can modify the graphic. One change you can make is
to delete elements. You decide to delete the last shape on Slide 3. **Why?** *The slide contains information about what
students will experience during the lessons, so the facts about meals are a different topic.* The following steps remove a
SmartArt shape.

• Click a border of the right
SmartArt shape, All Meals
Included, to select the entire
shape (Figure 9–31).

• Press the DELETE key to delete
the right SmartArt shape.

How do I delete the shape if I
am using a touch screen?
Press and hold the SmartArt
shape and then tap Delete on
the shortcut menu.

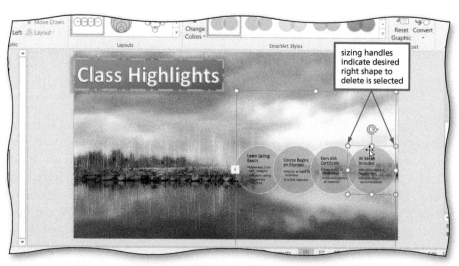

Figure 9–31

To Add a SmartArt Shape

You may add a new SmartArt shape to the layout if you need to display
additional information. PowerPoint gives you the option of adding this shape above or
below a selected shape or to the left or the right side of the shape. If you wanted to add
a SmartArt shape, you would perform the following steps.

1. Select a SmartArt graphic shape near where you want to insert another shape.

2. Click the Add Shape arrow (SmartArt Tools Design tab | Create Graphic
group) to display the Add Shape menu.

3. Click the desired location for the new shape, which would be after, before,
above, or below the selected shape.

To Resize a SmartArt Graphic by Entering an Exact Measurement

Why? *Adequate space exists on the slide to increase all the SmartArt shapes.* You can resize a slide element by dragging the sizing handles or by specifying exact measurements for the height and width. The following steps resize the SmartArt graphic by entering an exact measurement.

- Select the entire SmartArt graphic by clicking an outer edge of the graphic (Figure 9–32).

Q&A How will I know the entire graphic is selected?
You will see the Text pane control and sizing handles around the outer edge of the SmartArt.

Figure 9–32

- Display the SmartArt Tools Format tab, if necessary click the Size button (SmartArt Tools Format tab | Size group) to display the Height and Width boxes, and then change the Height measurement to 9" and the Width measurement to 13" (Figure 9–33).

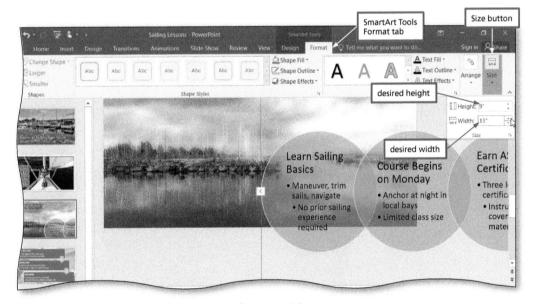

Figure 9–33

- Drag the SmartArt graphic upward so its upper edge is aligned with the top edge of the slide and then center the graphic between the left and right edges of the slide.

Other Ways

1. Right-click graphic, click 'Size and Position' on shortcut menu, if necessary click 'Size & Properties' icon (Format Shape pane), if necessary click Size, enter graphic height and width values in boxes, close Format Shape pane

To Resize a SmartArt Graphic Shape

The entire SmartArt shape and the text box now are the proper proportions to display together on the slide. In addition to changing the height and width of the SmartArt graphic, you also can change the height and width of one individual SmartArt shape in the graphic. *Why? Potential students desire to learn what their lessons will entail and would appreciate knowing they do not need to have sailed prior to enrolling. To emphasize this unique feature, you want to make the center SmartArt shape smaller than the others and, in contrast, emphasize the Learn Sailing Basics shape by increasing its size.* The following steps resize the SmartArt graphic shapes.

- Click the center SmartArt shape, Course Begins on Monday, to select it.

- With the SmartArt Tools Format tab displaying, click the Smaller button (SmartArt Tools Format tab | Shapes group) once to decrease the shape size (Figure 9–34).

Figure 9–34

- Click the left shape, Learn Sailing Basics, to select it and then click the Larger button twice (Figure 9–35).

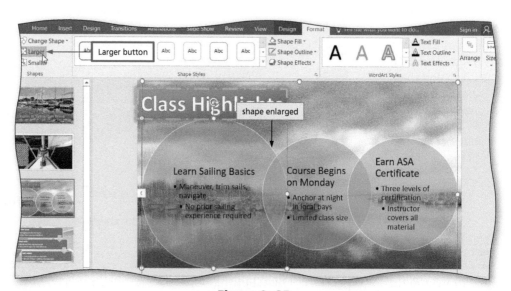

Figure 9–35

Other Ways

1. Right-click graphic, click 'Size and Position' on shortcut menu, if necessary click 'Size & Properties' icon (Format Shape pane), if necessary click Size, enter graphic height and width values in boxes, close Format Shape pane

To Add a SmartArt Style to the Graphic and Change the Color

To enhance the appearance of the circles in the Linear Venn layout, you can add a transparent three-dimensional style that hides some of the background details. You also can add more colors. The following steps add the Powder style and a Colorful range.

1 Select the entire SmartArt graphic, display the SmartArt Tools Design tab, and then click the More button in the SmartArt Styles group to expand the SmartArt Styles gallery.

2 Click Powder in the 3-D area (fourth graphic in first row) to apply this style to the graphic.

3 Click the Change Colors button (SmartArt Tools Design tab | SmartArt Styles group) to display the Change Colors gallery.

4 Click 'Colorful Range – Accent Colors 4 to 5' (fourth graphic in Colorful row) to apply this color variation to the graphic (Figure 9–36).

Figure 9–36

To Apply a Picture to a Text Box

1 INSERT & CUSTOMIZE TEXT BOXES | 2 CONVERT WORDART TO SMARTART & FORMAT | 3 INSERT & FORMAT SHAPES
4 DRAW & FORMAT LINES | 5 CUSTOMIZE THE RIBBON | 6 EXPORT FILE & CREATE PICTURE PRESENTATION

Sufficient space exists on both sides of the text box at the top of the slide to insert a picture. *Why? A picture helps to reinforce the written message and also calls attention to the sailing theme. A sailboat illustration provides contrast with the photograph background.* For consistency with the slide title, you can insert a text box that has the default formatting and then add a picture. The following steps add a text box and then apply a picture.

• Select the Slide 3 title text box, click the Align button (Drawing Tools Format tab | Arrange group), and then click Align Center to move the text box horizontally to the center of the slide.

- Display the Insert tab and then insert a text box to the left of the text box at the top of slide.

- Display the Drawing Tools Format tab and then click the Shape Fill arrow (Drawing Tools Format tab | Shape Styles group) to display the Shape Fill gallery (Figure 9–37).

Figure 9–37

- Click Picture in the Shape Fill gallery to display the Insert Pictures dialog box and then navigate to the location where your Data Files are stored.

- Click Yellow Boat to select the file name (Figure 9–38).

Figure 9–38

- Click the Insert button (Insert Picture dialog box) to insert the Yellow Boat picture into the text box.

- Increase the size of the text box to 1.5" x 1.5" and drag the box so that the right edge of the Yellow Boat text box overlaps the left edge of the title text box. Align the bottom edges of these text boxes (Figure 9–39).

Figure 9–39

To Duplicate and Flip a Text Box Picture

Once the text box and picture are inserted on the left side of the title text box, you can duplicate this slide element and then flip the picture so that the boat is pointed in the opposite direction. *Why? A picture on the right size of the title text box provides symmetry, and both sailboat illustrations will point toward the outer edges of the slide.* The following steps duplicate a text box and then flip the box horizontally.

- With the Yellow Boat text box selected, display the Home tab and then click the Copy arrow (Home tab | Clipboard group) to display the Copy menu (Figure 9–40).

Figure 9–40

- Click Duplicate in the list to create a second text box with the Yellow Boat picture. Drag this new text box to the right side of the title text box and then overlap the left edge of the Yellow Boat text box and right edge of the title text box. Align the bottom edges of the text boxes (Figure 9–41).

Figure 9–41

- Click the Arrange button (Home tab | Drawing group) to display the Arrange menu and then point to Rotate in the Position Objects group to display the Rotate list (Figure 9–42).

Figure 9–42

- Click Flip Horizontal in the Rotate menu to flip the Yellow Boat text box picture (Figure 9–43).

Figure 9–43

To Convert a SmartArt Graphic to Text

1 INSERT & CUSTOMIZE TEXT BOXES | 2 CONVERT WORDART TO SMARTART & FORMAT | 3 INSERT & FORMAT SHAPES
4 DRAW & FORMAT LINES | 5 CUSTOMIZE THE RIBBON | 6 EXPORT FILE & CREATE PICTURE PRESENTATION

Potential students would be curious about specific skills they will learn while sailing. The SmartArt graphic information on Slide 4 explains the basic objectives of the class. In a later portion of this module, you will supplement these details with a graphic pointing out the main components of a sailboat. At times, you may decide that SmartArt is not the optimal method of presenting information to an audience and instead want to depict the same concept using text. *Why? The SmartArt's visual elements may detract from the points being made, so the bulleted list might be useful for instructional purposes. In addition, SmartArt may take up so much room on the slide that other visual elements do not fit.* PowerPoint allows you to remove the shapes and change the text in the graphic to a bulleted list. The following steps convert the SmartArt graphic to text.

- Display Slide 4 and then select the entire SmartArt graphic.

Q&A

If one of the SmartArt shapes is selected, how do I select the entire graphic?
Be certain to click the edge of the graphic. You will see sizing handles and the Text pane control when the SmartArt graphic is selected.

- Display the SmartArt Tools Design tab and then click the Convert button (SmartArt Tools Design tab | Reset group) to display the Convert menu (Figure 9–44).

Figure 9–44

- Click 'Convert to Text' to display the SmartArt text as nine bulleted list paragraphs (Figure 9–45).

- If requested by your instructor, add the word, in, and the city or county in which you were born after the word, safely, in the third first-level paragraph.

Figure 9–45

- Position the bulleted list placeholder in the upper-right corner of the slide. Drag the middle-right sizing handle to the right edge of the slide (Figure 9–46).

Figure 9–46

To Convert a SmartArt Graphic to Shapes

An alternative to changing a graphic to text is changing a graphic to shapes. In this manner, a shape can be moved, resized, or deleted independently of any other shape in the SmartArt. If you wanted to convert a SmartArt graphic to shapes, you would perform the following steps.

1. Select the entire SmartArt graphic.
2. Click the Convert button (SmartArt Tools Design tab | Reset group) to display the Convert menu.
3. Click 'Convert to Shapes'.

Break Point: If you wish to take a break, this is a good place to do so. Be sure to save the Sailing Lessons file again and then you can exit PowerPoint. To resume at a later time, run PowerPoint, open the file called Sailing Lessons, and continue following the steps from this location forward.

Inserting and Modifying Shapes

The items in the Shapes gallery provide a variety of useful shapes you can insert into slides. Diagrams with labels often help audiences identify the parts of an object. Text boxes with clear, large type and an arrow pointing to a precise area of the object work well in showing relationships between components. You also can use items in the Shapes gallery to create your own custom artwork.

A sailboat has several components: They include the hull, which might include a cabin for cooking, sleeping, and other activities. The front of the hull is called the bow and the rear is called the stern. Other components are the sails, called the jib and mainsail; and the mast, which attaches the sails. These parts can be depicted with a variety of items found in the Shapes gallery. You also want to add text boxes and arrows to identify the components. At times, you may be unable to find a shape in the gallery that fits your specific needs. In those instances, you might find a similar shape and then alter it to your specifications.

BTW

Inserting Shapes
The Shapes gallery is displayed on two tabs: the Drawing Tools Format tab (Insert Shapes group) and the Home tab (Drawing group). Shapes also are available if you display the Insert tab and then click the Shapes button (Illustrations group).

To Insert Shapes

You can draw parts of the sailboat with shapes located in the Shapes gallery: two trapezoids for the hull, which contains the cabin; circles for the portholes; right triangles for the sails, called the jib and the mainsail; and a can for the mast. In addition, the Notched Right Arrow shape can be inserted to serve as a leader line for labeling a sailboat part. The following steps insert five shapes into Slide 4.

1 Display the Drawing Tools Format tab. With Slide 4 displaying, click the More button in the Shapes gallery (Drawing Tools Format tab | Insert Shapes group) to display the entire Shapes gallery and then click the Trapezoid shape (sixth shape in first Basic Shapes row).

2 Position the pointer near the lower-left corner of the slide and then click to insert the Trapezoid shape.

3 Display the Shapes gallery and then click the Oval shape (second shape in first Basic Shapes row).

4 Position the pointer to the right of the Trapezoid and then click to insert the Oval shape.

5 Display the Shapes gallery, click the Right Triangle shape (fourth shape in first Basic Shapes row), and then insert this shape above the Trapezoid.

6 Display the Shapes gallery, click the Can shape (eleventh shape in second Basic Shapes row), and then insert this shape above the Right Triangle.

7 Display the Shapes gallery, click the Notched Right Arrow shape (sixth shape in the second Block Arrows row), and then insert this shape in the upper-left corner of the slide (Figure 9–47).

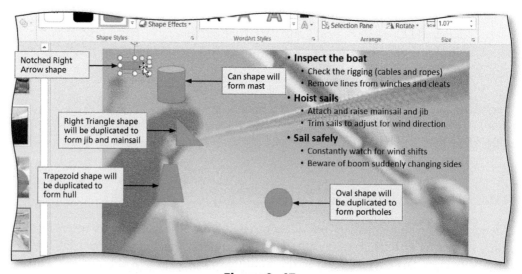

Figure 9–47

BTW

Vector Graphics
Geometric shapes, lines, arrows, and action buttons are vector graphics, which are drawn using mathematical formulas. The size, color, line width, starting and ending points, and other formatting attributes are stored as numeric values and are recalculated when you resize or reformat each shape. Most clip art and video games also use vector graphics.

To Resize and Move Shapes

The five shapes on Slide 4 are the default sizes, and they need to be proportioned to reflect accurate sailboat dimensions. If you are not using a touch screen, you can keep the resized shape proportions identical to the original shape by pressing the SHIFT key while tapping or clicking a sizing handle and then dragging the pointer inward or outward to decrease or increase the size. If you do not hold down the SHIFT key, you can elongate the height or the width to draw an object that is not identical to the shape shown in the Shapes gallery. If you want to alter the shape's proportions, drag one of the sizing handles inward or outward. The following steps resize the shapes and arrow.

1 Select the trapezoid and change the size to 0.2" x 2".

2 With the trapezoid still selected, display the Home tab, click the Copy arrow, and then click Duplicate in the menu. Move the duplicate trapezoid below the first trapezoid, position the pointer over the rotation handle and then turn the shape downward 180 degrees so that it turns upside down. Change the size to 1" x 5" and move the shape toward the bottom of the slide.

3 Drag the small trapezoid to the top of the large trapezoid and use the Smart Guide to center it along the top edge.

4 Select the oval and change the size to 0.5" x 0.5". Duplicate the oval. Drag one oval to the left side of the large trapezoid and the second oval to the right side. If necessary, you may need to bring one of the ovals to the front if it is hidden behind the trapezoid by clicking the Undo button so that this oval is visible and selected, clicking the Bring Forward arrow (Drawing Tools Format tab | Arrange group), clicking 'Bring to Front' in the menu, and then moving the oval back on the trapezoid. Use the Smart Guides to help align the ovals.

5 Select the can and change the size to 5" x 0.2". Drag the can to the smaller trapezoid's upper edge and use the Smart Guides to help you center this shape.

6 Select the right triangle and change the size to 4.2" x 2.4". Drag the shape to the right side of the can, leaving space between these two shapes and between the lower edge of the sail and the upper edge of the smaller trapezoid.

7 Duplicate the right triangle and change the size to 4.5" x 1.7". Flip the shape horizontally, and then drag this shape to left side of the can. The top of the triangle should be even with the top of the can. Leave space between these two shapes (Figure 9–48).

BTW
Displaying Smart Guides
If the Smart Guides are not displayed when you are attempting to align objects, you may need to specify that PowerPoint should show them. Display the View tab, click the Show Group launcher, and then click the 'Display Smart Guides when shapes are aligned' check box to select this option.

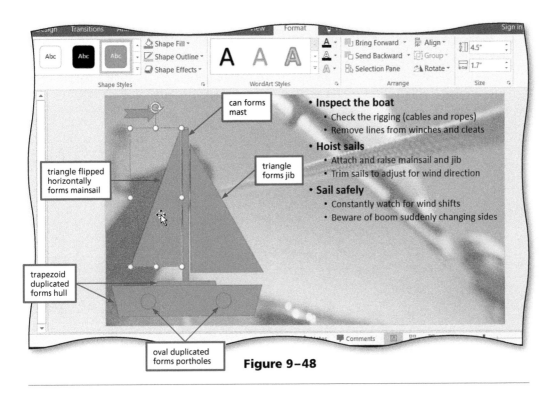

Figure 9–48

To Apply a Fill to a Shape

The shapes on Slide 4 have light blue fill. You can change the shape fill using the same types of fills you used for the text boxes in this presentation. For example, you can apply a gradient, pattern, texture, or picture. *Why? Using similar fills among the slides adds consistency and gives a uniform look to the presentation.* The method of applying these fill effects is similar to the steps you used to format text boxes. The following steps apply fills to the shapes.

- Select the two triangles. With the Drawing Tools Format tab displaying, click the Shape Fill arrow (Drawing Tools Format tab | Shape Styles group) to display the Shape Fill gallery and then point to Gradient to display the Gradient gallery (Figure 9–49).

Experiment

- Point to various gradients in the Gradient gallery and watch the interiors of the two shapes change.

Figure 9–49

- Click More Gradients in the Gradient gallery to display the Format Shape pane.

- Click Gradient fill to expand the gradient options and then click the Preset gradients button to display the Preset gradients gallery (Figure 9–50).

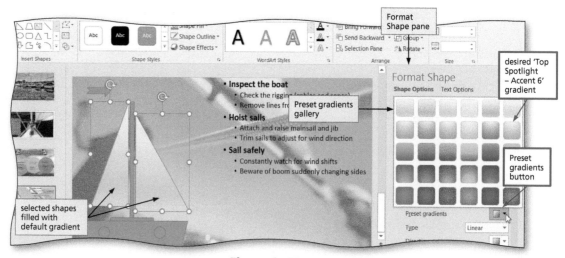

Figure 9–50

Q&A | Can I experiment with previewing the gradient colors?
No, the live preview feature is not available.

• Click 'Top Spotlight - Accent 6' (last color in second row) to apply the gradient fill to the two triangles.

⯇ How can I delete a gradient fill if I decide not to apply one to the shape?
Q&A If you already have applied the pattern, you must click the Undo button on the Quick Access Toolbar.

4

• Select the two trapezoids, click Gradient fill, and then click the Preset gradients button (Figure 9–51).

⯇ Why did these
Q&A two shapes fill with the green gradient fill when I tapped or clicked Gradient fill?
PowerPoint recalls the last gradient you selected.

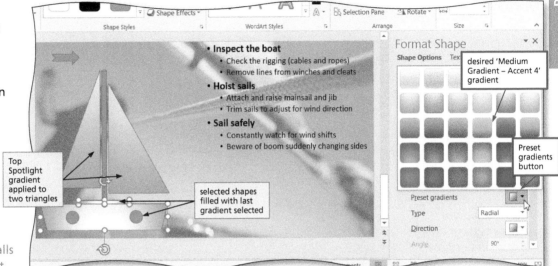

Figure 9–51

5

• Click 'Medium Gradient – Accent 4' (fourth color in third row) to apply this gradient to the shapes.

• Select the can and then click 'Picture or texture fill' to display the ' Picture or texture fill' section (Figure 9–52).

⯇ Why did the can fill
Q&A with a texture?
Depending on previous settings for shape fills, PowerPoint may insert a fill or change the transparency when you click the 'Picture or texture fill' option button.

Figure 9–52

- Click the Texture button to display the Texture gallery (Figure 9–53).

Figure 9–53

- Click the Brown marble texture (first texture in third row) to apply this texture to the can.

- If necessary, set the Transparency slider to 0%.

- Scroll down the Format Picture pane and then, if necessary, click Line to expand the Line section. Click the Color button to display the Color gallery (Figure 9–54).

Figure 9–54

- Click Yellow (fourth color in Standard Colors row) to apply this color to the can edges.

- Click the Close button to close the Format Picture pane.

To Subtract a Shape

1 INSERT & CUSTOMIZE TEXT BOXES | 2 CONVERT WORDART TO SMARTART & FORMAT | 3 INSERT & FORMAT SHAPES
4 DRAW & FORMAT LINES | 5 CUSTOMIZE THE RIBBON | 6 EXPORT FILE & CREATE PICTURE PRESENTATION

The trapezoid hull you drew now has solid blue portholes, but you can easily give the effect of transparent portholes by subtracting the areas of the ovals that overlap the trapezoid. *Why? Your sailboat will look more accurate with this element.* The result is a blank area that displays the slide background. The following steps subtract the ovals.

1

- Click the larger trapezoid, press and hold down the CTRL key, click one oval to select it, and then click the second oval to select all three shapes.

◄ Can I perform this step using a touch screen?
No. You will need to use a keyboard to select multiple shapes.

- With the Drawing Tools Format tab displaying, click the Merge Shapes button (Drawing Tools Format tab | Insert Shapes group) to display the Merge Shapes list (Figure 9–55).

Do I need to select the shapes in this order?
Yes. You first select the shape that you want to keep and then click the shape(s) that you want to delete.

Figure 9–55

Experiment

- Point to the commands in the Merge Shapes list and watch the results of the various merge commands.

2

- Click Subtract in the Merge Shapes list to delete the gold background behind the oval shapes.

To Merge Shapes

1 INSERT & CUSTOMIZE TEXT BOXES | 2 CONVERT WORDART TO SMARTART & FORMAT | 3 INSERT & FORMAT SHAPES
4 DRAW & FORMAT LINES | 5 CUSTOMIZE THE RIBBON | 6 EXPORT FILE & CREATE PICTURE PRESENTATION

The two trapezoids forming the hull and cabin have a common horizontal line where the two shapes intersect. You can eliminate this line if you merge the shapes. ***Why?*** *The two elements will appear seamless as part of the main structure of the sailboat.* The following steps merge the two trapezoids.

1

- Select the two trapezoids. With the Drawing Tools Format tab displaying, click the Merge Shapes button (Drawing Tools Format tab | Insert Shapes group) to display the Merge Shapes list (Figure 9–56).

2

- Click Union (Drawing Tools Format tab | Insert Shapes group) to combine the trapezoid shapes.

When would I use the Union command instead of the Combine command?
The Union command joins the shapes using the formatting of the top shape. The Combine command also joins shapes, but it deletes the area where two shapes overlap.

Figure 9–56

To Draw a Line

Why? The shapes on Slide 4 comprise the main parts of a sailboat. To complete the drawing, you need to add the ropes that connect the sails to the hull. Ropes can be represented by a line shape. One type of rope is a straight bar, and this type of line is included in the Shapes gallery. Some other lines in the gallery are the Elbow Connector, Curve, Freeform, and Scribble. The lines and connectors have zero, one, or two arrowheads. The following steps draw a straight line without arrowheads and position this shape on Slide 4.

1

- Display the Shapes gallery and then point to the Line shape (first shape in the Lines area) (Figure 9–57).

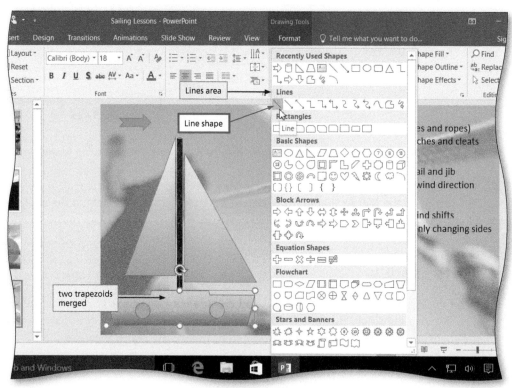

Figure 9–57

2

- Click the Line shape, position the pointer on the top of the left right triangle (the mainsail), and then click to display a line (Figure 9–58).

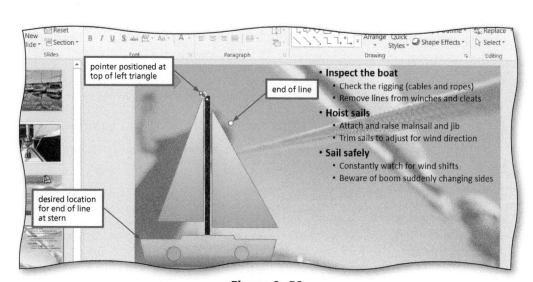

Figure 9–58

3

- Drag the lower sizing handle to the rear (stern) of the boat.

To Change a Line Weight and Color

In this project, you changed a text box and shape outline color and weight. In a similar fashion, you can change line outline formatting. *Why? The line you drew on Slide 4 is thin, and the color does not display well against the slide background.* You can increase the line thickness and change its color to enhance the shape. The following steps change the line thickness and color.

- With the line selected, click the Shape Outline arrow (Drawing Tools Format tab | Shape Styles group) and then point to Weight to display the Weight gallery.

- Point to 1½ pt to see a preview of that weight applied to the line (Figure 9–59).

Experiment

- Point to various weights in the Weight gallery and watch the line thickness change.

Figure 9–59

- Click 1½ pt in the Weight gallery to apply that weight to the line.

- Click the Shape Outline arrow again. Point to 'Gold, Accent 4, Darker 50%' (eighth color in last Theme Colors row) to see a preview of that color applied to the line (Figure 9–60).

Experiment

- Point to various colors in the Theme Colors gallery and watch the line color change.

- Click 'Gold, Accent 4, Darker 50%' to apply that color to the line.

Figure 9–60

To Set Line Formatting as the Default

The line you inserted and formatted is one of two ropes in the sailboat diagram. You can set these line attributes as the default for the other line you will draw in the presentation. *Why? Setting the default characteristics saves time when you add other lines because you do not need to repeat all the formatting steps. It also ensures consistency among the line shapes.* The following steps set the line shape on Slide 4 as the default.

- Right-click the line to display the shortcut menu (Figure 9–61).

- Click 'Set as Default Line' on the shortcut menu to set the line formatting as the default for any new lines.

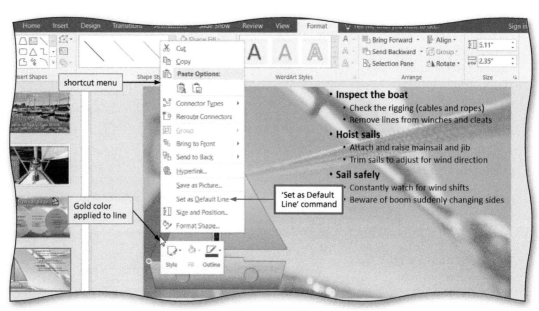

Figure 9–61

To Draw an Additional Line

One more line is needed to connect the jib to the bow (front of the hull). A line with a curve is a good shape to use to connect these two shapes. *Why? This shape has two bends, which can be altered to create one curve.* The following steps draw this curved line.

- Display the Shapes gallery again. Point to the Curved Connector (seventh line in the Lines area) (Figure 9–62).

Figure 9–62

- Click the Curved Connector, position the pointer in the lower-right corner of the jib, and then click to insert one end of the line at this location (Figure 9–63).

Q&A
What is the yellow dot in the middle of the line?
The dot is called a point. Every shape is formed by a series of points connected with lines that are straight or curved. If desired, you can drag a point to alter the shape's form.

Figure 9–63

- Drag the sizing handle at the other end of the line near the front of the hull (Figure 9–64).

Figure 9–64

To Group and Size the Sailboat Objects

All the shapes comprising the sailboat are separate elements on the slide. You will need to move and enlarge the sailboat on the slide. You easily can complete these tasks if you group all the components so they no longer are individual pieces. The following steps group all these shapes and then enlarge the entire sailboat shape.

1. Select all the sailboat shapes and then display the Picture Tools Format tab.

2. Click the Group Objects button (Picture Tools Format tab | Arrange group) to display the Group list and then click Group in the list to combine all the shapes.

3. Size the sailboat object so that it is 6.5" x 5.5" and then move it to the location shown in Figure 9–65.

Figure 9–65

BTW
**Revising Your
Presentation**
If you are going to present
your slide show multiple
times to a variety of
audiences, consider the slides
a work in progress. Each
time you deliver your speech,
you should be able to tweak
the slides to clarify points,
answer questions that arose
during the presentation, and
generate discussion. Revising
a presentation is a positive
step toward communicating
your message clearly and
powerfully.

To Change a Shape Fill and Outline and Apply Effects

Earlier in this project, you changed a text box outline color, weight, and style.
You also applied a glow effect to a text box. Similarly, you can change the outline
formatting and effects for a shape. For consistency, you can enhance the arrow shape
by using some of the same formatting changes that you applied to the text box. The
following steps change the arrow shape outline and apply an effect.

1 Select the Notched Right Arrow, click the Shape Fill arrow (Drawing Tools Format tab
| Shape Styles group), display the Gradient gallery, and then click Linear Right (first
gradient in second Dark Variations row).

2 Click the Shape Outline arrow (Drawing Tools Format tab | Shape Styles group), display
the Weight gallery, and then click 3 pt.

3 Display the Shape Outline gallery again and then click Orange to change the shape
border color.

4 Display the Shape Outline gallery again, display the Dashes gallery, and then click
Square Dot (third style) to change the border style.

5 Click the Shape Effects button to display the Shape Effects gallery, display the Glow
gallery, and then click 'Orange, 5 pt glow, Accent color 2' (second color in first Glow
Variations row) to apply the glow effect (Figure 9–66).

Figure 9–66

To Set Shape Formatting as the Default

1 INSERT & CUSTOMIZE TEXT BOXES | 2 CONVERT WORDART TO SMARTART & FORMAT | 3 INSERT & FORMAT SHAPES
4 DRAW & FORMAT LINES | 5 CUSTOMIZE THE RIBBON | 6 EXPORT FILE & CREATE PICTURE PRESENTATION

The Notched Right Arrow shape you inserted and formatted complements the default text box you
inserted on the slides in the presentation. You will use this shape on several parts of Slide 4 to help identify parts
of the sailboat, so you can set its formatting as a default. **Why?** *To save time and ensure all the formatting changes
are applied, you can set the formatting of one shape as the default for all other shapes you insert into the presentation.* The
following steps set the arrow shape formatting on Slide 4 as the default.

- Right-click the Notched Right Arrow shape to display the shortcut menu (Figure 9–67).

- Click 'Set as Default Shape' on the shortcut menu to set the shape formatting as the default for any new shapes.

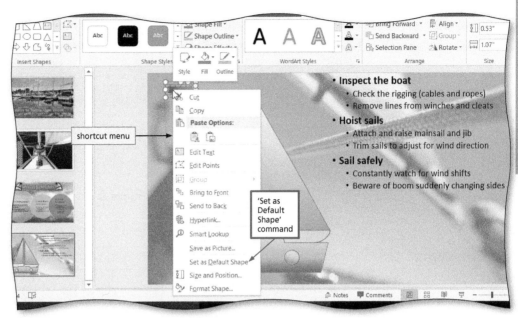

Figure 9–67

To Label the Shapes

The final step in creating Slide 4 is to label the parts of the sailboat. The Notched Right Arrow shape and the text box are formatted as defaults, so the labeling process is easy to accomplish. The following steps insert text boxes and arrows into Slide 4 and then enter text in the text boxes.

1. With Slide 4 displaying, insert a text box into the left side of the slide near the upper hand in the background picture. Type **Mainsail** in the text box and then decrease the font size to 24 point.

2. Duplicate the Mainsail text box, type **Jib** in the box, and then move it under the bulleted list.

3. Drag the Notched Right arrow to the mainsail. Display the Drawing Tools Format tab, click the Bring Forward arrow (Drawing Tools Format tab | Arrange group), and then click 'Bring to Front' to display the arrow on top of the mainsail. Use the arrow keys to move the Mainsail text box to the left of the arrow.

4. Duplicate the Notched Right arrow, rotate it 180 degrees, drag it near the lower-right corner of the jib, and then use the arrow keys to move the Jib text box to the right of this arrow.

5. Select both the Jib text box and arrow, duplicate them, and then type **Hull** in the text box (Figure 9–68).

Figure 9–68

To Customize the Ribbon

Many commands available in PowerPoint are not included on any of the tabs on the ribbon. You can, however, add such commands to the ribbon or to the Quick Access Toolbar. **Why?** *Many of these commands perform tasks you commonly repeat, so it would be convenient to have the buttons accessible in a group on the ribbon.* The following steps customize the ribbon by adding the 'Print Preview and Print' and 'Create Handouts in Microsoft Word' commands to the ribbon and then arranging their order in the group.

1

• With the Home tab displaying, open the Backstage view and then click Options to display the PowerPoint Options dialog box.

• Click Customize Ribbon in the left pane to display the Customize the Ribbon pane (Figure 9–69).

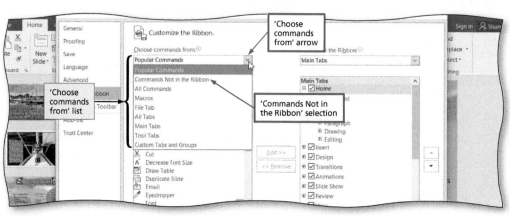

Figure 9–69

2

• Click the 'Choose commands from' arrow to display the 'Choose commands from' list (Figure 9–70).

Figure 9–70

- Click 'Commands Not in the Ribbon' in the 'Choose commands from' list to display a list of commands that do not display in the ribbon (Figure 9–71).

Figure 9–71

- Scroll down and then click 'Create Handouts in Microsoft Word' to select this button.
- Click Editing in the Main Tabs area under Home to specify that the 'Create Handouts in Microsoft Word' button will be added in a new group after the Editing group on the Home tab (Figure 9–72).

Figure 9–72

- Click the New Group button to create a new group.
- Click the Rename button and then type **Handouts** as the new group name in the Display name text box (Rename dialog box) (Figure 9–73).

Figure 9–73

- Click the OK button (Rename dialog box) to rename the new group.
- Click the Add button to add the 'Create Handouts in Microsoft Word' button to the Handouts group.
- Scroll down, click 'Print Preview and Print' in the list of 'Commands Not in the Ribbon', and then click the Add button to add the button to the Handouts group (Figure 9–74).

Figure 9–74

- Click the Move Up button (PowerPoint Options dialog box) to move the 'Print Preview and Print' button above the 'Create Handouts in Microsoft Word' button (Figure 9–75).

- Click the OK button to close the PowerPoint Options dialog box and display the two buttons in the new Handouts group on the Home tab in the ribbon.

Figure 9–75

Work with a buddy.
Although you may believe you create your best work when you work alone, research shows that the work product generally improves when two or more people work together on a creative task. A classmate or team member at work can assist you in many ways. For example, this person can help you gather research for your graphics and bulleted text or provide feedback on the slides' clarity and readability. As you rehearse, a buddy can time your talk and identify the times when the presentation lacks interest. If a buddy attends your actual presentation, he or she can give objective feedback on the components that worked and those that can use revision for the next time you present the material.

To Create a Handout by Exporting a File to Microsoft Word

1 INSERT & CUSTOMIZE TEXT BOXES | 2 CONVERT WORDART TO SMARTART & FORMAT | 3 INSERT & FORMAT SHAPES
4 DRAW & FORMAT LINES | 5 CUSTOMIZE THE RIBBON | **6 EXPORT FILE & CREATE PICTURE PRESENTATION**

The handouts you create using Microsoft PowerPoint are useful to distribute to audiences. Each time you need to create these handouts, however, you need to open the file in PowerPoint and then print from the Backstage view. As an alternative, it might be convenient to save, or export, the file as a Microsoft Word document if you are going to be using Microsoft Word to type a script or lecture notes. *Why? The handout can have a variety of layouts; for example, the notes you type in the Notes pane can be displayed to the right of or beneath the slide thumbnails, blank lines can be displayed to the right of or beneath the slide thumbnails, or just an outline can be displayed.* The following steps use the 'Create Handouts in Microsoft Word' button you added to the new Handouts group on the Home tab to export the presentation to Microsoft Word and then create a handout.

1

- With the Home tab displaying, click the 'Create Handouts in Microsoft Word' button (Home tab | Handouts group) to display the Send to Microsoft Word dialog box (Figure 9–75).

2

- Click 'Blank lines next to slides' to add blank lines next to the slides when the handout is printed (Figure 9–76).

- Click the OK button to save the file with this layout.

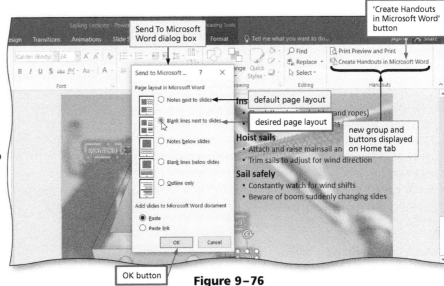

Figure 9–76

3

- If the handout does not display in a new Microsoft Word window, click the Microsoft Word program button on the Windows taskbar to see a live preview of the handout. If you print the handouts, they will resemble the pages shown in Figure 9–77.

(a) Page 1

(b) Page 2

BTW

Conserving Ink and Toner
If you want to conserve ink or toner, you can instruct PowerPoint to print draft quality documents by clicking File on the ribbon to open the Backstage view, clicking the Options tab in the Backstage view to display the PowerPoint Options dialog box, clicking Advanced in the left pane (PowerPoint Options dialog box), scrolling to the Print area in the right pane, placing a check mark in the 'Use draft quality' check box, and then clicking the OK button. Then, use the Backstage view to print the document as usual.

Figure 9–77

- Save the Word file using the file name, Sailboat Word Handout.

- Close the Word file and, if necessary, exit Word.

Other Ways

1. Open Backstage view, display Export tab, click Create Handouts, click Create Handouts button

BTW
Distributing a Document
Instead of printing and distributing a hard copy of a document, you can distribute the document electronically. Options include sending the document via email; posting it on cloud storage (such as OneDrive) and sharing the file with others; posting it on social media, a blog, or other website; and sharing a link associated with an online location of the document. You also can create and share a PDF or XPS image of the document, so that users can view the file in Acrobat Reader or XPS Viewer instead of in PowerPoint.

To Save the Presentation as a Picture Presentation

1 INSERT & CUSTOMIZE TEXT BOXES | 2 CONVERT WORDART TO SMARTART & FORMAT | 3 INSERT & FORMAT SHAPES

4 DRAW & FORMAT LINES | 5 CUSTOMIZE THE RIBBON | **6 EXPORT FILE & CREATE PICTURE PRESENTATION**

Why? *If you are going to share your slides with other presenters and do not want them to alter the slide content, you can save each slide as a picture. When they run the slide show, each slide is one complete picture, so the text and shapes cannot be edited. You also can use an individual slide picture as a graphic on another slide or in another presentation. The following steps save a copy of the presentation as a picture presentation.*

- Open the Backstage view, display the Export tab, and then click 'Change File Type' to display the 'Change File Type' gallery.

- Click 'PowerPoint Picture Presentation' in the Presentation File Types area (Figure 9–78).

Figure 9–78

- Click the Save As button to display the Save As dialog box.

- Type **Sailing Lessons Picture Presentation** in the File name text box (Figure 9–79).

- Click the Save button (Save As dialog box) to save a copy of the presentation as a picture presentation.

- Click the OK button (Microsoft PowerPoint dialog box).

Figure 9–79

To Reset the Ribbon

Why? *Your work with the PowerPoint presentation is complete, so you can delete the group and buttons you added to the ribbon.* The following steps remove the Handouts group and the 'Print Preview and Print' and 'Create Handouts in Microsoft Word' commands from the Home tab.

- Open the Backstage view, click Options to display the PowerPoint Options dialog box, and then click Customize Ribbon in the left pane to display the Customize the Ribbon pane.

- Click the Reset button (PowerPoint Options dialog box) to display the Reset menu (Figure 9–80).

2

- Click 'Reset all customizations'.

- Click the Yes button (Microsoft Office dialog box) to delete all customizations.

- Click the OK button (PowerPoint Options dialog box) to close the dialog box.

Figure 9–80

Q&A | Do I need to remove the group and commands from the ribbon?
No. For consistency, the ribbon is reset after the added group and commands no longer are needed. If you share a computer with others, you should reset the ribbon.

- Because the project now is complete, you can save the presentation again and then exit PowerPoint.

Summary

In this module you have learned how to modify a presentation using text boxes, SmartArt, and shapes. You customized a text box, set it as the default, and then inserted new text boxes and applied formatting, including a texture, gradient, and pattern. You also converted WordArt to SmartArt and then formatted the shapes and bulleted paragraphs. Then you created a diagram from shapes, which had gradients and patterns applied. Finally, you customized and reset the ribbon, created handouts in Microsoft Word, and saved the presentation as a picture presentation.

What decisions will you need to make when creating your next presentation?
Use these guidelines as you complete the assignments in this module and create your own slide show decks outside of this class.

1. **Choose colors wisely.** The appropriate use of color can add interest and help audience members retain information. Used inappropriately, however, mismatched colors will generate confusion and create an impression of unprofessionalism.

2. **Use keywords in SmartArt graphics.** The words you type into your SmartArt graphic can serve as a prompt of the key points you want to make in the presentation.

3. **Use politically correct language.** When you type words into text boxes, be mindful of the terms you are using to identify the images.

4. **Work with a buddy.** As you develop your slide content and then rehearse the presentation, ask a friend or work associate to assist you with various tasks.

Apply Your Knowledge

Reinforce the skills and apply the concepts you learned in this module.

Centering and Formatting Placeholders, Converting WordArt to SmartArt, and Formatting and Reordering Shapes

Note: To complete this assignment, you will be required to use the Data Files. Please contact your instructor for information about accessing the Data Files.

Instructions: Run PowerPoint. Open the presentation called Apply 9–1 Wolves, which is located in the Data Files. The two slides in this presentation are about the hierarchy of wolves in their packs. The document you open is a partially formatted presentation. You will center and format placeholders, convert WordArt to SmartArt, and then format and reorder the shapes. Your presentation should look like Figure 9–81.

Perform the following tasks:

1. On Slide 1 (Figure 9–81a), select the title text placeholder and align it in the center of the slide. With the title text placeholder still selected, apply the 40% pattern fill (last pattern in first row), change the outline color to Blue (eighth color in Standard Colors row), and then change the outline weight to 3 pt.

2. Convert the WordArt text at the bottom of the slide to the Continuous Block Process SmartArt graphic (first graphic in third Process row). Select the rightmost SmartArt shape (Two to twenty per pack) and delete it. Increase the size of the SmartArt graphic

(a) Slide 1

(b) Slide 2

Figure 9–81

to approximately 2.2" × 8". Apply the 'Gradient Range - Accent 5' color (third color in Accent 5 row) to the graphic and then apply the Inset style (second style in first 3-D row). Change the font to Arial, change the font size to 20 point, and then bold this text. Align the SmartArt graphic in the center of the slide to the location shown in Figure 9–81a.

3. On Slide 2 (Figure 9–81b), select the title text placeholder and align it in the center of the slide. With the title text placeholder still selected, apply the 'White, Background 1, Darker 35%' solid fill color (first color in fifth Theme Colors row) and then change the transparency to 50%. Change the shape outline to Square Dot dashed line (third line in Dashes gallery), change the outline weight to 2¼ pt, and then change the outline color to 'White, Background 1' (first color in first Theme Colors row).

4. Change the SmartArt graphic layout to Hierarchy (second style in second Hierarchy row). Select the shape labeled Alpha Male and add a shape after it. Type the text, `Alpha Female` in the added shape. Select the shape labeled Beta Female and demote it. Select the shape labeled Juveniles and Puppies and demote it. Select the shape labeled Omega Males and Females, demote it, and then delete the text, and Females. With this shape still selected, add a shape after it and type, `Omega Females` in the shape.

5. Increase the SmartArt graphic size to 5.5" × 4.7". Change the font in the SmartArt graphic to Arial and then change the font size to 20 point. Select the shapes labeled Alpha Male and Alpha Female and increase the size to approximately 1.3" × 1.6". Move the SmartArt graphic to the location shown in the figure.

6. Change the colors of the SmartArt graphic to 'Gradient Range - Accent 4' (third color in Accent 4 area) and then apply the Cartoon style (third effect in first 3-D row).

7. Apply the 'Reflected Bevel, White' picture style (fifth style in last row) to the wolf picture. Change the picture border color to 'Blue, Accent 5' (ninth color in first Theme Colors row) and then change the border weight to 3 pt.

8. If requested by your instructor, insert a text box in the lower-right corner of Slide 2 and then type your birth year, birth city, and birth state.

9. Apply the Flash transition (Subtle area) and change the duration to 4.00 for both slides.

10. Run the presentation and then save the file using the file name, Apply 9–1 Wolves Ranking Order.

11. Submit the revised document in the format specified by your instructor.

12. ✳ In this presentation, you converted the WordArt to a SmartArt graphic on Slide 1. Was the Continuous Block Process layout an appropriate choice? Would another layout be more suitable for the content? Does the hierarchy chart help your audience comprehend the wolf pack hierarchy? Why or why not?

Extend Your Knowledge

Extend the skills you learned in this module and experiment with new skills. You may need to use Help to complete the assignment.

Setting Default Line Formatting, Applying a Pattern and Outline Style to a Text Box, Modifying Shapes, and Editing SmartArt Shapes

Note: To complete this assignment, you will be required to use the Data Files. Please contact your instructor for information about accessing the Data Files.

Continued >

Instructions: Run PowerPoint. Open the presentation, Extend 9–1 Driving, which is located in the Data Files. You will set line formatting as the default, apply a pattern to a text box, change a text box outline style, change a slide picture, apply a fill to a shape, apply a picture to a text box, and change text box outlines and fills to create the presentation shown in Figure 9–82.

Perform the following tasks:

1. On Slide 1 (Figure 9–82a), change the font for the first line in the title text placeholder to Gill Sans MT, increase the font size to 48 point, change the font color to Red, and then bold this text. Change the font for the second line to Gill Sans Ultra Bold and then increase the front size to 40 point. Apply the 'Wide downward diagonal' pattern fill (fifth pattern in third row) to this placeholder, change the Foreground color to 'Gray-25%, Background 2, Darker 50%' (third color in fourth Theme Colors row), and then change the Background color to 'Gold, Accent 4, Lighter 40%' (eighth color in fourth Theme Colors row).

2. Change the title text placeholder outline weight to 6 pt, change the outline color to 'Gold, Accent 4' (eighth color in Theme Colors row), and then change the outline style to Long Dash Dot (seventh style in Dashes gallery).

3. Select the body of the car that was drawn with the Freeform line and change the fill color to 'White, Background 1, Darker 50%' (first color in last Theme Colors row). Using Figure 9–82a as a guide, place the two window shapes on the car. Select both window shapes and then apply the 'Top Spotlight - Accent 3' gradient (third gradient in second Preset gradients row) to these two shapes.

4. To create the wheels for the car, insert an Oval shape, size the shape to 0.4" × 0.4", change the fill color to 'White, Background 1, Darker 50%' (first color in last Theme Colors row), change the outline color of this shape to 'Black, Text 1', and then change the outline weight (width) to 12 pt. Duplicate the shape and then move the shapes to the car's wheel wells, as shown in the figure.

5. To create the headlight, insert an Oval shape, size it to 0.2" × 0.15", change the shape fill color to Yellow, remove the outline, and then move the shape near the front of the car, as shown in the figure.

6. To create the door handle, insert another Oval shape, size it to 0.1" × 0.2", change the shape fill color to 'Black, Text 1', and then position this shape on the door, as shown in the figure. Select all the car shapes and then group them.

7. On Slide 1, create the goalpost base by inserting a vertical Line shape in the lower-left area of the slide, changing the weight (width) of the line to 12 pt, and then changing the outline color to Gold, Accent 4 (eighth color in first Theme Colors row). Set this line formatting as the default. Change the shape height to 1.5". To form the crossbar, insert a horizontal Line, change the length to 1.86", and then center this line perpendicular to the base. To form the posts, insert a vertical Line, change the height to 1.5", and then move this line to the left side of the crossbar. Duplicate this shape and then move the new line to the right side of the crossbar.

8. Select the four lines, group them, and then move the goalpost to the area shown in the figure.

9. Insert a text box at the bottom of Slide 1 and then type the text shown in Figure 9–82a. Change the font to Arial and then change the font size to 20 pt. Bold, italicize, and underline this text, align it right, and then align it in the middle of the text box. Adjust the size of the text box to approximately 1.35" × 13.33" and then move it to the bottom and side edges of the slide. Apply the 'Gold, Accent 4, Lighter 40%' shape fill color (eighth color in fourth Theme Colors row) to the text box.

10. On Slide 1, select the car, bring it to the front and then move it to the left side of the text box. Change the picture on Slide 1 to the picture called Football Stadium, which is located in the Data Files. Use the sizing handles to increase the size of the picture so that it fills the entire white area of the slide.

11. Change the Up Arrow shape to the Left-Right Arrow shape (fifth shape in Block Arrows group). [*Hint:* Select the shape, click the Edit Shape button (Drawing Tools Format tab | Insert Shapes group), point to Change Shape, and then select the new shape.] Use the rotation and sizing handles to adjust the shape and then move it to the position shown in the figure.

12. On Slide 2 (Figure 9–82b), move the Texting shape in the SmartArt graphic on the left side of the slide up to the top level. Promote the Reading shape one level. Change the SmartArt style from Powder to Inset (second style in first 3-D row).

13. Change the layout of the SmartArt graphic on the right to Trapezoid List (second layout in eighth row of List area). Change the colors to 'Colorful Range - Accent Colors 3 to 4' (third color in Colorful area) and then choose the Cartoon style (third style in first 3-D row). Adjust the size of the SmartArt graphic to approximately 5" × 7" and then move it to the area shown in the figure.

(a) Slide 1

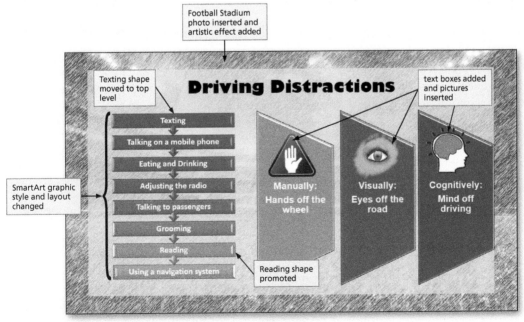

(b) Slide 2

Figure 9–82

Continued >

Extend Your Knowledge *continued*

14. Insert a text box above the text in the first shape of the SmartArt graphic on the right side of Slide 2. In the text box, insert the picture called Hand, which is located in the Data Files, and then adjust the size to 1.5" × 1.5". Insert a text box above the text in the middle shape of the SmartArt graphic, insert the picture called Eye, and then adjust the size to 1.5" × 1.5". Insert a text box above the text in the right shape, insert the picture called Brain, and then adjust the size of the text box to 1.3" × 1.3".

15. On Slide 2, insert a rectangle and then size it to 6.5" × 12". Apply the 'Green, Accent 6, Lighter 60%' shape fill (last color in third Theme Colors row), change the transparency to 20%, and then select no outline. Align the rectangle in the center and middle on the slide, and then send this shape to the back. Insert the Football Stadium picture and then apply the Line Drawing artistic effect to the picture (fifth effect in first row). Using the sizing handles, increase the size of the picture so that it fills the entire area of the slide, and then send this picture to the back.

16. If requested by your instructor, type your mother's maiden name in place of the text, Using a navigation system, in the text box on Slide 2 (Figure 9–82b).

17. Apply the Comb transition in the Exciting category to both slides and then change the duration to 4.00 seconds.

18. Run the presentation and then save the file using the file name, Extend 9–1 Distracted Driving.

19. Submit the revised document in the format specified by your instructor.

20. ✺ Was the pattern fill you applied to the title text placeholder on Slide 1 a good choice of designs? Why or why not? Does the slide content provide sufficient information to persuade people to avoid distracting activities while driving?

Expand Your World

Create a solution that uses cloud or web technologies by learning and investigating on your own from general guidance.

Reviewing Google Images SmartArt

Instructions: You want to add SmartArt to a presentation you have created to accompany a speech you are scheduled to deliver for your local skiing and snowboarding group. You need to add graphical interest to your slides, so you browse Google Images for SmartArt ideas.

Note: You will need Internet access to complete this assignment. If you do not have Internet access, read this assignment without performing the instructions.

Perform the following tasks:
1. Run PowerPoint and then open the file, Expand 9–1 Snowboarding.

2. Open your browser and navigate to Google.com. Click Images at the top of the screen to display the Google Images webpage. Click the Google Images search text box, type `smartart` as the search text, and then click the Search button (the magnifying glass) or press the ENTER key.

3. View several SmartArt images with designs that would be appropriate for the material on Slides 2 and 3. Select two different designs and then convert the bulleted lists in these slides to these designs in PowerPoint. If desired, you can change the SmartArt styles and colors and also arrange the slide elements.

4. If requested by your instructor, add a text box on Slide 1 with the name of your high school mascot.

5. Run the presentation and then save the file with the new file name, Expand 9–1 Snowboarding SmartArt.

6. Submit the revised presentation in the format specified by your instructor.

7. ✳ Which SmartArt images on the Google Images webpage did you use for your presentation? Why did you select these particular examples?

In the Labs

Design, create, modify, and/or use a presentation following the guidelines, concepts, and skills presented in this module. Labs 1 and 2, which increase in difficulty, require you to create solutions based on what you learned in the module; Lab 3 requires you to apply your creative thinking and problem-solving skills to design and implement a solution.

Lab 1: Converting WordArt and SmartArt, Formatting Text Boxes and Shapes, and Combining Shapes

Note: To complete this assignment, you will be required to use the Data Files. Please contact your instructor for information about accessing the Data Files.

Problem: The branch manager of your local bank has asked you to help prepare the slides to accompany her presentation regarding obtaining a car loan. She shows you two slides she has started to create and wants you to put the finishing touches on them. You create the presentation shown in Figure 9–83.

Perform the following tasks:
1. Run PowerPoint. Open the presentation, Lab 9–1 Car Loan, which is located in the Data Files.

2. On Slide 1 (Figure 9–83a), convert the WordArt to SmartArt using the 'Horizontal Bullet List' layout (second layout in third List row). Change the color of the SmartArt graphic to 'Colorful – Accent Colors' (first color in Colorful row) and then apply the Inset style (second style in first 3-D row). Size the SmartArt to approximately 5.8" × 13" and then move it to the location shown in the figure.

3. Insert the illustration, Bank, size it to approximately 1.8" × 2.19", and then move it to the lower area of the left shape. In the middle shape, demote the second bullet (Know your credit score). Insert the illustration, Calendar, size it to approximately 2" × 1.91", and then move it to the lower-right corner of the right shape.

4. Insert a text box in the blue sky area of Slide 1. Type, **Road to Car Loans** as the text box text. Change the text box outline weight to 3 pt, change the outline color to Dark Blue (ninth color in Standard Colors row), change the outline style to Long Dash (sixth style in Dashes gallery), apply the 'Offset Diagonal Top Right' shadow effect (first shadow in third Outer row), increase the font size to 60 point, apply the 'Pattern Fill - Olive Green, Accent 3, Narrow Horizontal, Inner Shadow' WordArt style, and then add the 'Olive Green, Accent 3, Lighter 80%' shape fill (seventh color in second Theme Colors row). Set this text box formatting as the default. Move the text box to the location shown in the figure.

5. On Slide 2 (Figure 9–83b), convert the SmartArt Graphic to text and then increase the font size of the three bulleted paragraphs to 32 point. Reduce the size of the bulleted list placeholder to include only the three bulleted paragraphs and then position the placeholder in the center of the slide.

Continued >

In the Labs *continued*

6. If requested by your instructor, add the name of your grade school or high school as a fourth bulleted paragraph.

7. Create the road shown in the figure by inserting the Curved Connector line and increasing its size to 6" × 6". Right-click the shape and then click Format Shape in the shortcut menu to display the Format Shape pane. Change the color to 'Black, Text 1' and then increase the width to 96 pt. Create the white dashed line by inserting another Curved Connector line and increasing its size to 6" × 6". Change the color to 'White, Background 1', increase the width to 6 pt, and then change the dash type to Dash (fourth dash in the Dash gallery). Close the Format Shape pane. Move the upper edges of the two Curved Connector shapes to the upper-left corner of the slide.

8. Create the car shown in Slide 2 by assembling the shapes on the slide. To begin, make a windshield by centering the yellow shape over the blue shape, selecting the blue shape, holding down the CTRL key and selecting the yellow shape, clicking the Merge Shapes button, and then clicking Subtract in the Merge Shapes list.

9. Make the front end of the car by moving the red headlights and license plate holder over the purple shape, selecting the purple shape, holding down the CTRL key and selecting the three red shapes, clicking the Merge Shapes button, and then clicking Subtract in the Merge Shapes list.

(a) Slide 1

(b) Slide 2

Figure 9–83

10. Move the two black tires up to the lower edge of the car's front end. Move the top of the car down to the upper edge of the car's front end. Select all the shapes, click the Merge Shapes button, and then click Union in the menu to merge all the shapes.

11. Apply a 'Blue, Accent 1' shape fill and the 'Linear Diagonal - Bottom Right to Top Left' gradient fill (last gradient in last Variations row). Size the car to approximately 5" × 5" and then move it to the upper-right corner of the slide.

12. Insert a text box in the lower-right corner. Type, **Negotiate the Loan** as the text box text and then move the text box next to the lower end of the road.

13. Apply the Doors transition in the Exciting category to both slides and then change the duration to 2.00 seconds.

14. Run the presentation and then save the file using the file name, Lab 9–1 Road to Car Loans.

15. Submit the document in the format specified by your instructor.

16. ✷ Is the Horizontal Bullet List a good choice for the SmartArt layout on Slide 1? Why or why not? Did changing the SmartArt graphic to text enhance Slide 2? Why? Did you encounter any difficulties using shapes to assemble the car?

Lab 2: Creating a Picture Background Using Shapes, Combining Shapes, Customizing and Resetting the Ribbon, and Creating a Handout by Exporting a File to Microsoft Word

Note: To complete this assignment, you will be required to use the Data Files. Please contact your instructor for information about accessing the Data Files.

Problem: The number of honey bees is declining. Some researchers think this trend is due to over-use of pesticides on crops and fungicides that contaminate the pollen bees collect for their hives. Tom Wilson is the owner of a local honey farm that has been in business since 1946. He wants community residents to help increase the honey bee population, so he is selling bees and all the equipment needed for a working hive. He recently created a flyer about his farm and asked you to develop a PowerPoint presentation to publicize his efforts. You create the slides shown in Figure 9–84.

Perform the following tasks:

1. Run PowerPoint and then open the presentation, Lab 9–2 Bees, which is located in the Data Files.

2. To begin creating the honeycomb background for Slide 1 (Figure 9–84a), insert a new blank slide. Insert a Hexagon shape (ninth shape in first Basics Shapes row) and resize the shape to 0.9" × 1.1". Change the shape fill color to Orange (third color in Standard Colors row) and then change the outline color to 'Black, Text 1' (second color in first Theme Colors row). Move the shape to the upper-left corner of the slide, as shown in Figure 9–84b.

3. With the hexagon shape still selected, press CTRL+D to duplicate this shape. Move the new shape below the original shape, leaving a small space between them. Press CTRL+D six more times so that you now have a column of eight shapes at the left edge of the slide.

4. Align the shapes horizontally in the column by selecting all eight shapes, clicking the Align arrow (Drawing Tools Format tab | Arrange group), and then clicking Distribute Horizontally in the menu. Align the shapes vertically in the column by clicking the Align arrow again and then clicking Distribute Vertically in the menu.

Continued >

In the Labs *continued*

5. With the eight hexagon shapes still selected, press CTRL+D to duplicate the column and then drag this new column upward and to the right, positioning it as shown in Figure 9–84b. Duplicate this second column of shapes and then it them downward and to the right so that the first shape is at the same height as the first shape in the first column. Repeat these steps until you have 14 columns of shapes. Use the arrow keys to adjust some of the shapes so they are not in perfect alignment.

6. Press CTRL+A to select all the shapes and then group them. Apply the 'Gradient Fill - Gold, Accent 4, No Outline' Shape Quick Style (fifth style in last Presets row) to the grouped shapes. Save the group as a picture with the file name, Honeycomb, using the PNG Portable Network Graphics Format file type. Delete this slide.

7. On Slide 1 (Figure 9–84a), create a background on the slide by inserting the Honeycomb picture you just created. Change the transparency to 50%.

8. To format the text box (Family owned and operated since 1946), select the box, click the Shape Fill arrow, display the Gradient gallery, and then click the Linear Down variation (second variation in first row).

9. To begin creating the beehive on Slide 2 (Figure 9–84c), insert an Oval shape (second shape in first Basic Shapes row), change the shape fill to 'Gold, Accent 4, Lighter 40%' (eighth color in fourth Theme Colors row), change the outline color to 'Gold, Accent 4, Darker 50%' (eighth color in last Theme Colors row), change the outline weight to 1½ pt. Type `We` in the shape and then change the font size to 20 point. Set this shape as the default shape.

10. Insert five Oval shapes under the shape you created. Adjust the size of the first shape to 0.55" × 1", the second shape to 0.8" × 2", the third shape to 0.86" × 2.7", the fourth shape to 1.16" × 3.7", the fifth shape to 1.5" × 4.5", and the sixth shape to 1.5" × 5.8". Type the text shown in the Figure 9–94c in each of the shapes. In the first two shapes, leave the font size at 20 point. In the rest of the shapes, decrease the font size to 16 point. Overlap the shapes and use the SmartGuides to center them under each other.

11. Insert an Oval shape, adjust the size to 0.5" × 0.5", change the shape fill color to 'Black Text 1, no outline', and then move the shape to the bottom-center of the last beehive shape to create the opening for the bees. Select the entire beehive, group the shapes, and then move it to the lower-left area of the slide. Move the bee illustration from the upper-left corner of the slide to the right of the hive opening. If necessary, bring the bee illustration to the front by clicking the Bring Forward button (Picture Tools Format tab | Arrange Group).

12. If requested by your instructor, substitute your mother's name for the word, bees, in the bottom beehive shape on Slide 2.

13. Apply the Honeycomb transition in the Exciting category to both slides and then change the duration to 5.00 seconds.

14. Customize the ribbon by adding the Create Handouts in Microsoft Word button to the Editing group on the Home tab. Click this new button to create a handout in Microsoft Word using the 'Blank lines below slides' page layout, as shown in Figure 9–84d, e. Save the document using the file name, Lab 9–2 Wilson's Honey Farm Word Handout. Close the Word file and then exit Word. Reset the ribbon.

15. Run the presentation and then save the file using the file name, Lab 9–2 Wilson's Honey Farm.

16. Save the presentation as a picture presentation using the file name, Lab 9–2 Wilson's Honey Farm Picture Presentation.

17. Submit the document in the format specified by your instructor.

18. ✺ Did creating a background using shapes on Slide 1 improve the look of the slide? Was saving the formatting as the default for shapes helpful? Why?

(a) Slide 1

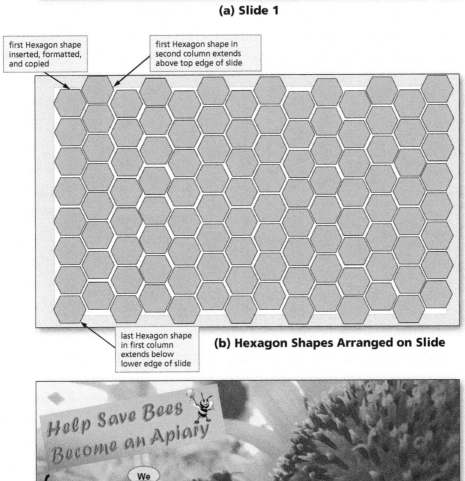

(b) Hexagon Shapes Arranged on Slide

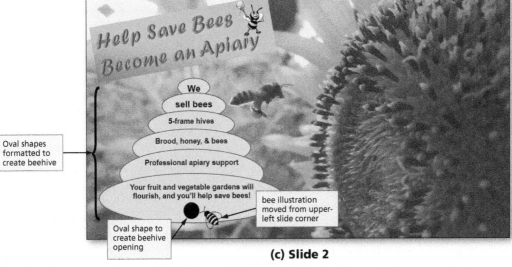

(c) Slide 2

Figure 9–84 (Continued)

Continued >

In the Labs *continued*

Slide 1

Blank
lines
below
slides
option
selected
for
handout

Slide 2

(d) Microsoft Word Handout (Page 1)   **(e) Microsoft Word Handout (Page 2)**

Figure 9–84

Lab 3: **Consider This: Your Turn**

Design and Create a Presentation about Headaches

Part 1:   Headaches are one of the more common nervous system disorders. This pain may occur anywhere in the head, may last from less than one hour to more than one day, and may develop suddenly or gradually. The most common types are migraine, sinus, and tension. They can result from lack of sleep, stress, allergies, exposure to chemicals, head injuries, and many other triggers. Headaches possibly could be prevented by avoiding some foods and beverages, such as caffeine, bananas, nuts, onions, and citrus fruits. Use the concepts and techniques presented in this module to create a presentation with this information and other facts you obtain from online sources. Use at least three objectives found at the beginning of this module to develop the slides, and include shapes, a formatted text box, and SmartArt. Print handouts and speaker notes for the presentation. Review and revise your presentation as needed and then save the file using the file name, Lab 9–3 Headaches. Submit your assignment in the format specified by your instructor.

Part 2:   ✳ You made several decisions while creating the presentation in this assignment: where to insert text boxes and shapes, what fills to use, how to format the text and text box backgrounds (such as font, font size, and colors), which image(s) to use, and which SmartArt graphic(s) to use to make the presentation look professional and consistent. What was the rationale behind each of these decisions? When you reviewed the document, what further revisions did you make and why? Where would you recommend showing this slide show?

10 Developing a Presentation with Content from Outside Sources

Objectives

You will have mastered the material in this module when you can:

- Insert an object from a file
- Embed and edit a file
- Draw and format a table
- Resize, split, distribute, and arrange table columns and rows
- Insert and edit a linked Excel worksheet
- Switch chart rows and columns

- Change a chart type
- Apply a chart style
- Apply effects to chart elements
- Display chart elements
- Edit chart data
- Add a hyperlink to a table

Introduction

BTW

Using Tables and Charts

Charts and tables help audiences understand abstract concepts and the relationships between sets of data. These tools can give meaning to the figures and facts you want to emphasize in your presentation. Present only one main idea in a chart or table. Overloading your slides with data may confuse your audience and defeat the purpose of these graphical elements.

Adding visuals to a presentation could help audience members remember the important facts you want to share. Researchers have found that adding such graphics as tables, charts, graphs, and maps increases retention by more than 50 percent. Audiences also believe that speakers who include visuals in their presentations are more qualified and believable than speakers who do not have accompanying visuals. In addition, studies have shown that meeting times are reduced and decisions are reached more quickly when group members have seen visuals that help them reach a consensus.

PowerPoint has many features that allow you to insert visuals and then modify them directly on the slide. For example, you can embed a Microsoft Word document and then edit its text or replace its graphics. You can link an Excel worksheet with a PowerPoint slide so that when numbers are modified in the slide, the corresponding numbers on the worksheet also are updated. These tools help you work productively and generate slides with graphics that help your audience comprehend and remember your message.

Project — Presentation with Embedded and Linked Files and Formatted Table and Chart

The typical American family spends nearly $2,000 yearly on utility bills. Much of that expense can be reduced by making small changes in the household, such as buying energy efficient appliances, using CFL or LED light bulbs, and installing a programmable thermostat to keep the house a few degrees warmer in the summer and a few degrees cooler in the winter. These and many more energy-efficient improvements can help save natural resources and give long-term financial rewards.

The presentation you create in this module (Figure 10–1) would be useful to show during a workshop at your local home improvement store. You begin Slide 1 (Figure 10–1a) by inserting a flyer with graphics and text (Figure 10–1b). You then decide to emphasize that the workshop focuses on whole-house energy efficiency planning, so you edit the title text by adding the words, at Home, directly onto the slide.

The second slide (Figure 10–1c) includes a chart that you draw and enhance using PowerPoint's tools and graphical features. If you click a cell in the chart when running the presentation, a hyperlinked Adobe PDF file displays with easy, practical advice audience members can use throughout their home, especially pertaining to lighting, heating and cooling, and appliances (Figure 10–1d).

You insert the table on Slide 3 (Figure 10–1e) from a Microsoft Excel worksheet (Figure 10–1f) that contains computations of using incandescent, halogen, CFL, and LED bulbs for one or more hours a day. You will update this table by editing the number of bulbs and the number of hours each day they are turned on. These figures also will update the original Excel worksheet.

Several homeowners in your town took measures during the past winter to reduce their electric consumption, including installing programmable thermostats, adjusting the temperature, and cleaning their furnaces and air ducts. They provided you their electric bills from the summers prior to and after their improvements, and you used this data to average the kilowatts used and then develop the chart that is displayed on Slide 4 (Figure 10–1g) and created in Microsoft Excel (Figure 10–1h). You then obtain the electric bills from a few more community residents who made the heating and cooling enhancements, so you update the worksheet data that generated the chart, which, in turn, modifies the chart automatically.

BTW

Checking for Accessibility Issues
As you develop tables and other slide elements, you may want to check the presentation for content that people with disabilities may be unable to read. To identify possible accessibility problems, display the Info tab in the Backstage view and notice if the message, Content that people with disabilities are unable to read, is displayed next to the 'Check for Issues' button. If so, click the 'Check for Issues' button and then click Check Accessibility in the menu. The Accessibility Checker task pane will display issues that you can address.

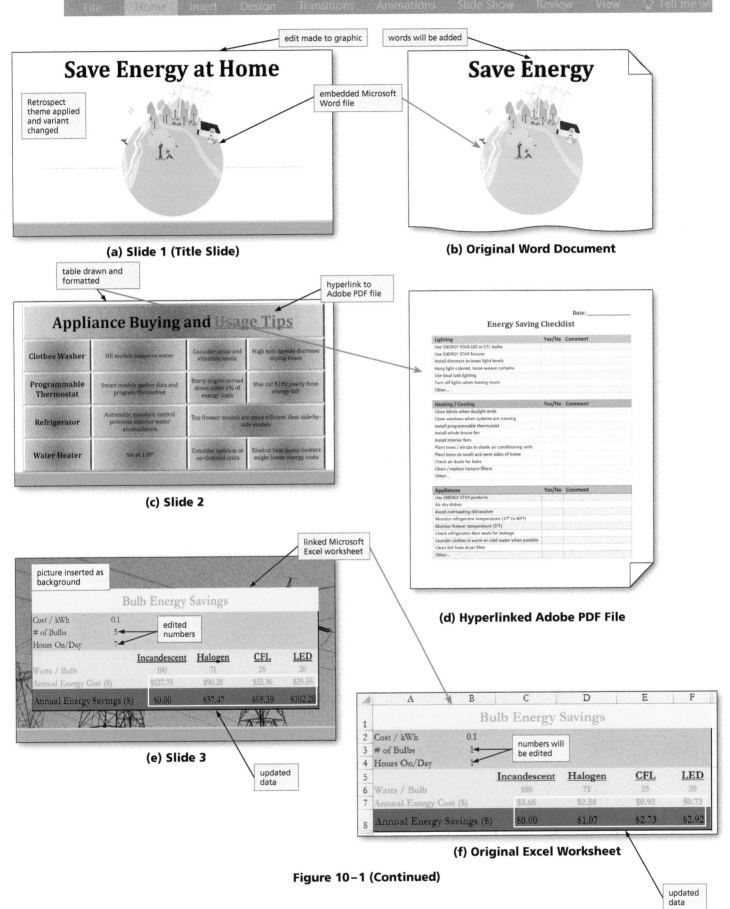

edit made to graphic

words will be added

Save Energy at Home

Save Energy

Retrospect theme applied and variant changed

embedded Microsoft Word file

(a) Slide 1 (Title Slide)

(b) Original Word Document

table drawn and formatted

hyperlink to Adobe PDF file

Appliance Buying and Usage Tips

Clothes Washer	HE models conserve water	Consider noise and vibration levels	High spin speeds decrease drying times
Programmable Thermostat	Smart models gather data and program themselves	Every degree turned down saves 1% of energy costs	May cut $180 yearly from energy bill
Refrigerator	Automatic moisture control prevents exterior water accumulation	Top freezer models are more efficient than side-by-side models	
Water Heater	Set at 120°	Consider tankless or on-demand units	Electric heat pump heaters might lower energy costs

(c) Slide 2

Date: _____

Energy Saving Checklist

Lighting	Yes/No	Comment
Use ENERGY STAR LED or CFL bulbs		
Use ENERGY STAR fixtures		
Install dimmers to lower light levels		
Hang light-colored, loose-weave curtains		
Use local task lighting		
Turn off lights when leaving room		
Other...		

Heating / Cooling	Yes/No	Comment
Close blinds when daylight ends		
Close windows when systems are running		
Install programmable thermostat		
Install whole-house fan		
Install interior fans		
Plant trees / shrubs to shade air conditioning units		
Plant trees on south and west sides of home		
Check air ducts for leaks		
Clean / replace furnace filters		
Other...		

Appliances	Yes/No	Comment
Use ENERGY STAR products		
Air-dry dishes		
Avoid overloading dishwasher		
Monitor refrigerator temperature (37° to 40°F)		
Monitor freezer temperature (5°F)		
Check refrigerator door seals for leakage		
Launder clothes in warm or cold water when possible		
Clean lint from dryer filter		
Other...		

(d) Hyperlinked Adobe PDF File

linked Microsoft Excel worksheet

picture inserted as background

Bulb Energy Savings

Cost / kWh   0.1
# of Bulbs   5
Hours On/Day   7

edited numbers

	Incandescent	Halogen	CFL	LED
Watts / Bulb	100	71	25	20
Annual Energy Cost ($)	$127.75	$90.28	$32.36	$25.55
Annual Energy Savings ($)	$0.00	$37.47	$95.39	$102.20

(e) Slide 3

updated data

	A	B	C	D	E	F
1			**Bulb Energy Savings**			
2	Cost / kWh	0.1				
3	# of Bulbs	1	numbers will be edited			
4	Hours On/Day	1				
5			Incandescent	Halogen	CFL	LED
6	Watts / Bulb		100	71	25	20
7	Annual Energy Cost ($)		$3.65	$2.58	$0.92	$0.73
8	Annual Energy Savings ($)		$0.00	$1.07	$2.73	$2.92

(f) Original Excel Worksheet

Figure 10–1 (Continued)

updated data

(g) Slide 4   **(h) Original Excel Chart**

Figure 10–1

BTW

The Ribbon and Screen Resolution
PowerPoint may change how the groups and buttons within the groups appear on the ribbon, depending on the computer or mobile device's screen resolution. Thus, your ribbon may look different from the ones in this book if you are using a screen resolution other than 1366 × 768.

In this module, you will learn how to create the slides shown in Figure 10–1. The following roadmap identifies general activities you will perform as you progress through this module:

1. INSERT AND EDIT a Microsoft WORD FILE by adding text.

2. CREATE TABLE ROWS AND COLUMNS and then erase lines and split columns and rows.

3. FORMAT a TABLE by adding shading, a gradient fill, and a cell bevel, and then distributing rows and resizing columns and rows.

4. INSERT AND EDIT a LINKED Excel WORKSHEET.

5. COPY, FORMAT and EDIT an Excel CHART by changing the type, colors, legend, labels, background, and data.

To Run PowerPoint, Choose a Theme and Variant, and Save a File

If you are using a computer to step through the project in this module and you want your screens to match the figures in this book, you should change your computer's resolution to 1366 × 768. The following steps run PowerPoint, apply a theme and variant, and then save a file.

1 Run PowerPoint, create a blank presentation, apply the Retrospect theme, and then select the green (second) variant. If necessary, maximize the PowerPoint window.

2 Save the presentation using the file name, Save Energy.

Inserting Graphics or Other Objects from a File

PowerPoint allows you to insert many types of objects into a presentation. You can insert clips, pictures, video and audio files, and symbols, and you also can copy and paste or drag and drop objects from one slide to another. At times you may want to insert content created with other Microsoft Office programs, such as a Word flyer, an Excel table or graph, a Paint graphic, or a document created with another Microsoft Windows-based application. The original document is called the **source**, and the new document that contains this object is called the **destination**. When you want to copy a source document object, such as a Word flyer, to a destination document, such as your PowerPoint slide, you can use one of three techniques.

- **Embedding** — An **embedded object** becomes part of the destination slide, but you edit and modify the contents using the source program's commands and features. In this project, for example, you will embed a Word document and then edit the text using Microsoft Word without leaving PowerPoint.

- **Linking** — Similar to an embedded object, a **linked object** also is created in another application and is stored in the **source file**, the original file in which the object was created. The linked object maintains a connection to its source and does not become part of the destination slide. Instead, a connection, or link, made between the source and destination objects gives the appearance that the objects are independent. In reality, the two objects work together so that when one is edited, the other is updated. If the original object is changed, the linked object on the slide also changes. In this project, for example, you will link a Microsoft Excel table and then edit the data using Excel. As the numbers in the table change, the numbers in the linked table on the PowerPoint slide also are updated to reflect those changes.

- **Copying and pasting** — An object that you copy from a source document and then paste in a destination document becomes part of the destination program. Any edits that you make are done using the destination software. When you paste the object, you have the options of embedding or linking the document. For example, if you copy a picture from a Word document, embed it into your slide, and then recolor or remove the background, those changes are made using PowerPoint's commands and do not affect the source object. In contrast, in this project you will copy an Excel chart and then paste it into a slide by linking the two documents. When you modify the object without leaving PowerPoint, any changes you make to the data in PowerPoint will be reflected in the original Excel source document.

The first two techniques described above are termed **object linking and embedding (OLE,** pronounced o-lay). This means of sharing material developed in various sources and then updating the files within a destination program is useful when you deliver presentations frequently that display current data that changes constantly. For example, your PowerPoint presentation may contain a chart reflecting current fitness center enrollment statistics, or you may include a table with the fitness center's membership totals for the previous year.

BTW
Importing Text Files
In this project you import a Microsoft Word file, but you also can import a text (.txt) file, which has alphanumeric characters with little or no visual formatting. To import a text file, perform the same steps you use to insert the Energy Flyer, but locate a file with the .txt file extension instead of the .docx file extension.

BTW
Touch Screen Differences
The Office and Windows interfaces may vary if you are using a touch screen. For this reason, you might notice that the function or appearance of your touch screen differs slightly from this module's presentation.

To Insert a File with Graphics and Text

1 INSERT & EDIT WORD FILE | 2 CREATE TABLE ROWS & COLUMNS | 3 FORMAT TABLE
4 INSERT & EDIT LINKED WORKSHEET | 5 COPY, FORMAT, & EDIT CHART

The first object you will add to your presentation is a graphical flyer created in Microsoft Word. This flyer contains artwork and text developed as part of an advertising campaign for a previous energy-reduction workshop at the home improvement store. You desire to use this document in your slide show. *Why? The earth image and text fit well with the topic of your presentation.* The following steps insert a Microsoft Word file with a graphic and text.

- Delete both the title and subtitle placeholders.

- Display the Insert tab and then click the Object button (Insert tab | Text group) to display the Insert Object dialog box (Figure 10–2).

Figure 10–2

- Click 'Create from file' (Insert Object dialog box) to display the File box.

- Click the Browse button and then navigate to the location where your Data Files are stored.

- If necessary, scroll down, and then click Energy Flyer to select the Microsoft Word file (Figure 10–3).

Q&A What is the difference between the Create new and the 'Create from file' options?

The Create new option opens an application and allows you to develop an original object. In contrast, the 'Create from file' option prompts you to locate a file that already is created and saved so you can modify the object using the program that was used to create it.

Figure 10–3

- Click the OK button (Browse dialog box) to insert the file name into the File box (Insert Object dialog box) (Figure 10–4).

Figure 10–4

- Click the OK button (Insert Object dialog box) to display the Energy Flyer contents on Slide 1 (Figure 10–5).

Q&A Why did several seconds pass before this flyer was displayed on the slide? PowerPoint takes more time to insert embedded and linked inserted objects than it takes to perform an ordinary cut-and-paste or copy-and-paste action. You must be patient while PowerPoint is inserting the object.

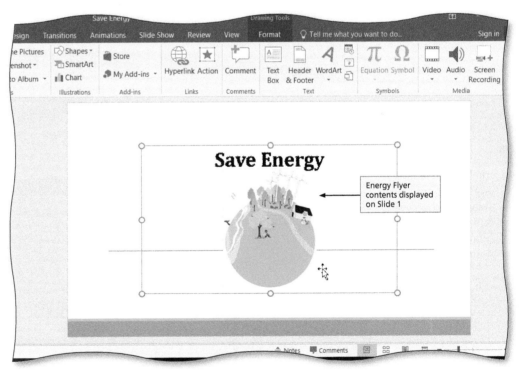

Figure 10–5

To Edit an Embedded File

The flyer provides an excellent graphic and text to use on Slide 1, but you want to edit the text by adding the words, at Home. **Why?** *These words focus the audience's attention on the fact that the presentation emphasizes energy-saving measures that can be taken in the home.* PowerPoint allows you to edit an embedded file easily by opening the source program, which in this case is Microsoft Word. The following steps edit the Microsoft Word text.

- Double-click the embedded earth object to run the Microsoft Word program and open the document on Slide 1 (Figure 10–6).

Figure 10–6

- Edit the document text by adding **at Home** to the flyer title to make it Save Energy at Home (Figure 10–7).

Figure 10–7

3

- Click outside the Word document to close Microsoft Word and display the edited flyer object on Slide 1.

- Display the Drawing Tools Format tab, size the object so that it is approximately 7" x 12", and then position the object as shown in Figure 10–8.

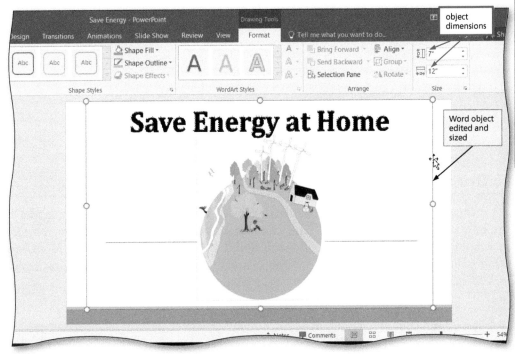

Figure 10–8

Q&A Does PowerPoint take more time to position embedded objects than copied objects?
Yes, you must be patient while PowerPoint responds to your touch, mouse, or arrow key movements.

How can I center the object precisely as shown in Figure 10–8?
Use the Align commands available when you click the Align Objects button (Drawing Tools Format tab | Arrange group). You then can use the ARROW keys to move the object in small increments.

Other Ways

1. Right-click Word object, click Document Object on shortcut menu, click Edit

Drawing and Adjusting a Table

Tables are useful graphical elements to present data organized in descriptive rows and columns. Each cell created from the intersection of a row and column has a unique location name and contains numeric or textual data that you can edit.

In the following pages, you will perform these tasks on Slide 2:

1. Draw a table.
2. Create table rows.
3. Draw table columns.
4. Erase a table line and enter text in a table.
5. Split a table column and row.
6. Add shading to a table.
7. Add a gradient fill to a table.
8. Add a cell bevel.
9. Distribute table rows.
10. Resize table columns and rows and align data in cells.
11. Center the table and format table data.

BTW
Drawing a Table Using a Tablet
In this project, you will create a table using PowerPoint's pencil pointer. This tool allows you to use a mouse and draw rows and columns. On a touch screen, however, the pencil pointer is not available. You may, therefore, use a mouse, stylus, or other pointing device to draw a table. Or, you can create a table by tapping the 'Add a Table' button (Insert tab | Tables group) and then specifying the desired number of rows and columns.

Develop tables that are clear and meaningful.
Use a table to present complex material, but be certain the information makes useful comparisons. Tables generally are used to show relationships between sets of data. For example, they may show prices for grades of gasoline in three states, the number of in-state and out-of-state students who have applied for admission to various college programs, or the rushing and passing records among quarterbacks in a particular league. The units of measurement, such as dollars, specific majors, or yards, should be expressed clearly on the slides. The data in the rows and columns should be aligned uniformly. Also, the table labels should be meaningful and easily read.

To Draw a Table

1 INSERT & EDIT WORD FILE | 2 CREATE TABLE ROWS & COLUMNS | 3 FORMAT TABLE
4 INSERT & EDIT LINKED WORKSHEET | 5 COPY, FORMAT, & EDIT CHART

PowerPoint allows you to insert a table in several ways. You can click the 'Add a Table' button on the Insert tab and click the Insert Table command. You also can click the Insert Table button in a content placeholder. Another method that allows flexibility is to draw the entire table. However, you must use a mouse or other pointing device to use the Draw Table command. The following steps draw a table on Slide 2. *Why? This method allows flexibility to draw the outer edges and then add the columns and rows.*

1

- Insert a new slide with the Blank layout. Display the View tab and then, if necessary, click the Ruler check box (View tab | Show group) to display the horizontal and vertical rulers.

- Display the Insert tab and then click the 'Add a Table' button (Insert tab | Tables group) to display the Insert Table gallery (Figure 10–9).

Figure 10–9

- Click Draw Table and then position the pointer, which has the shape of a pencil, in the upper-left area of the slide.

Q&A If I decide I do not want to draw a table, how can I change the pointer to the block arrow? Press the ESC key.

- Drag the pencil pointer to the lower-right corner of the slide to draw the outer edges of the table (Figure 10–10).

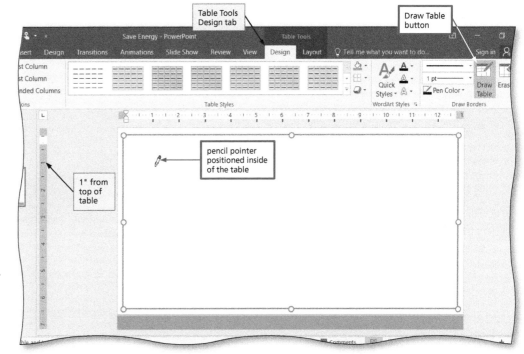

Figure 10–10

3

- Release the mouse button to create the table frame.

Q&A Must my table be the same size or be positioned in the same location shown in the figure? No. You will resize and reposition the table later in this project.

To Draw Table Rows

1 INSERT & EDIT WORD FILE | 2 CREATE TABLE ROWS & COLUMNS | 3 FORMAT TABLE
4 INSERT & EDIT LINKED WORKSHEET | 5 COPY, FORMAT, & EDIT CHART

Once you draw the four sides of the table, you then can use the pointer as a pencil to draw lines for the columns and rows in the positions where you desire them to display. You could, therefore, draw columns having different widths and rows that are spaced in irregular heights. The following steps draw three lines to create four table rows. *Why? The first row will contain the table title, and the remaining rows will list specific appliances: clothes washer, refrigerator, and water heater.* You must use a mouse or other pointing device to draw table rows.

- With the Table Tools Design tab displaying, click the Draw Table button (Table Tools Design tab | Draw Borders group) to change the pointer to a pencil and then position the pencil pointer inside the table approximately 1 " from the top table edge and 1 " from the left table edge (Figure 10–11).

Figure 10–11

• Drag the pencil pointer to the right to draw a horizontal line across the entire table and divide the table into two cells (Figure 10–12).

Q&A

Should I drag the pencil pointer to the right edge of the table?

No. PowerPoint will draw a complete line when you begin to move the pencil pointer in one direction.

If I drew the line in an incorrect location, how can I erase it?

Press CTRL+Z, click the Undo button on the Quick Access Toolbar, or click the Table Eraser button (Table Tools Design tab | Draw Borders group) and then click the line.

Figure 10–12

• Draw two additional horizontal lines, as shown in Figure 10–13. When you start drawing the lines, place your pencil pointer at a location away from the table border, not at a border, to prevent creating a new table.

Q&A

How can I get my pencil pointer to reappear if it no longer is displaying?

Click the Draw Table button again.

Do I need to align the lines in the precise positions shown?

No. You will create evenly spaced rows later in this project.

Figure 10–13

BTW

Displaying Gridlines

Gridlines can help you align charts, shapes, and other objects on slides. To show the gridlines, display the View tab and then select the Gridlines check box (View tab | Show group).

To Draw Table Columns

The pencil pointer is useful to draw table columns with varying widths. Each appliance row has either two or three usage tips. The clothes washer row will be subdivided. *Why? You have three important facts consumers should consider when they are purchasing a clothes washer, so you need to add a cell third in that row.* The following steps draw four vertical lines to create columns. You must use a mouse or other pointing device to draw table columns.

- Position the pencil pointer inside the table approximately 2.5" from the left table edge (Figure 10–14).

Q&A Can I change the line color?
Yes. Click the Pen Color button (Table Tools Design tab | Draw Borders group) and then select a different color.

Figure 10–14

- Drag the pencil pointer down through all the horizontal lines to draw a vertical line that divides the table into eight cells.

- Position the pencil pointer inside the second cell in the second row approximately 6" from the left table edge (Figure 10–15).

Figure 10–15

- Drag the pencil pointer down slightly to draw a vertical line in only that cell (Figure 10–16).

Figure 10–16

- Draw two additional vertical lines, as shown in Figure 10–17.

Q&A
Are vertical and horizontal lines the only types of lines I can draw?
No. You also can draw a diagonal line from one corner of a cell to another corner.

Figure 10–17

To Erase a Table Line

PowerPoint supplies an eraser tool that allows you to delete vertical and horizontal lines in a table. This eraser is useful to delete unnecessary column lines. You must use a mouse or other pointing device to use the eraser tool. The following steps use the eraser to delete one vertical line in a row. *Why? You decide to include only the title text in the first row.*

- Click the Table Eraser button (Table Tools Design tab | Draw Borders group).

- Position the pointer, which has the shape of an eraser, over the vertical line in the first row (Figure 10–18).

Figure 10–18

- Click the vertical line to erase it (Figure 10–19).

- Press the ESC key and then click inside the cell to change the pointer to the I-beam and display the insertion point.

- Display the View tab and then click the Ruler check box (View tab | Show group) to hide the horizontal and vertical rulers.

Figure 10–19

To Enter Text in a Table

Four major appliances will be featured in your table: clothes washer, programmable thermostat, refrigerator, and water heater. The table you created will list these appliances on the left side of each row and give specific buying and usage tips on the right side. The first row will display the table title. To place data in a cell, you click the cell and then type text. The following steps enter text in the cells of the empty table.

1 With the pointer in the first row, type `Appliance Buying and Usage Tips` in the cell. Press the TAB key to advance the insertion point to the first cell in the second row.

2 In the second row, type `Clothes Washer` in the first column, `HE models conserve water` in the second column, `Consider noise and vibration levels` in the third column, and `High spin speeds decrease drying times` in the fourth column. Press the TAB key to advance the insertion point to the first column of the third row.

3 In the third row, type `Refrigerator` in the first column, `Automatic moisture control prevents exterior water accumulation` in the second column and `Top freezer models are more efficient than side-by-side models` in the third column. Advance the insertion point to the first column of the fourth row.

4 In the fourth row, type `Water Heater` in the first column, `Set at 120°` in the second column, and `Consider tankless or on-demand units` in the third column (Figure 10–20).

Q&A How do I insert the degree symbol after 120 in the second cell of the Water Heater row?
Position the insertion point after 120. Click the Symbol button (Insert tab | Symbols group) to display the Symbol dialog box. Scroll down, generally to the sixth or seventh row, to locate the symbol in the gallery and then click the Insert button (Symbol dialog box) to place the degree symbol to the left of the insertion point. Click the Close button to close the Symbol dialog box after inserting the symbol.

Figure 10–20

To Split a Table Column and Row

You easily can create additional table columns and rows by dividing current cells and rows. The following steps split a column and a row. *Why? You want to add information about electric heat pump heaters in the Water Heater row. In addition, the appliances shown in the first column are listed in alphabetical order, and you want to add another appliance, Programmable Thermostat.* To keep the alphabetical order, this new appliance should be inserted between the Clothes Washer and the Refrigerator rows.

1

- With the insertion point in the Consider tankless or on-demand units cell, click the Table Tools Layout tab to display the Table Tools Layout ribbon and then click the Split Cells button (Table Tools Layout tab | Merge group) to display the Split Cells dialog box (Figure 10–21).

Q&A Are the default numbers in the dialog box always 2 columns and 1 row?
Yes, but you can increase the numbers if you need to divide the cell into more than two halves or need to create two or more rows within one cell.

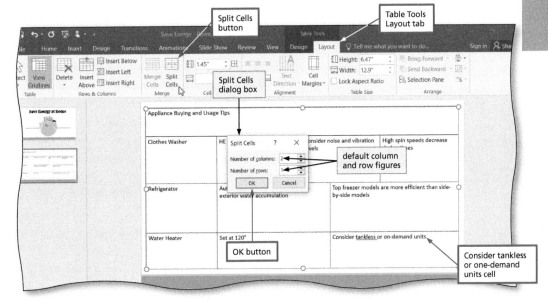

Figure 10–21

2

- Click the OK button (Split Cells dialog box) to create a fourth cell in the Water Heater row.

- Position the insertion point in the Clothes Washer cell.

- Click the Select Table button (Table Tools Layout tab | Table group) to display the Select Table menu (Figure 10–22).

Figure 10–22

- Click Select Row in the Select Table menu to select the Clothes Washer row.

- With the Table Tools Layout tab displaying, click the Split Cells button (Table Tools Layout tab | Merge group) to display the Split Cells dialog box (Figure 10–23).

Figure 10–23

- Decrease the number of columns from 2 to 1.

- Increase the number of rows from 1 to 2 (Figure 10–24).

Q&A How many rows and columns can I create by splitting the cells? The maximum number varies depending upon the width and height of the selected cell.

- Click the OK button (Split Cells dialog box) to create a row below the Clothes Washer row.

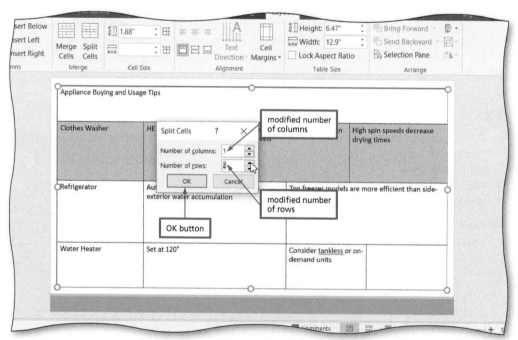

Figure 10–24

Other Ways

1. Right-click table, click Split Cells on shortcut menu, enter number of columns and rows, click OK button

To Enter Additional Text in a Table

With the additional row and column added to the table, you now can add the programmable thermostat information in the inserted row and also add electric heat pump heater information in the new cell in the Water Heater row. The following steps enter text in the new cells.

1 Position the pointer in the first cell of the new row and then type `Programmable Thermostat` in the cell. Advance the insertion point to the adjacent right column cell and then type `Smart models gather data and program themselves` in the second cell, `Every degree turned down saves 3% of energy costs` in the third cell, and `May cut $180 yearly from energy bill` in the last cell in this row.

2 Position the pointer in the new cell in the Water Heater row and then type `Electric heat pump heaters might lower energy costs` in the cell.

3 Drag the edges of the cells so the cell widths are similar to those in Figure 10–25. Use the Smart Guides to help align the cells vertically.

- If requested by your instructor, change the figure, 180, in the Programmable Thermostat row to the year your mother was born.

BTW
Customizing Table Formatting
PowerPoint applies a style to a table automatically based on the theme. To change this format, you can select a style in the Table Styles gallery, which presents several options to give a professional and colorful design and format. You, however, may desire to customize the layout by adding or modifying borders, the background color, or the font. To clear a style from a table, display the Table Tools Design tab, click the More button in the Table Styles group, and then click Clear Table.

Figure 10–25

Use appropriate colors when formatting graphics you want people to remember.
Studies have shown that men and women differ slightly in their recall of graphics formatted with various colors. Men remembered objects colored with shades of violet, dark blue, olive green, and yellow. Women recalled objects they had seen with dark blue, olive green, yellow, and red hues.

To Add Shading to a Table

You can format the table in several ways, including adding shading to color the background. The following steps add shading to the table. *Why? Shading makes the table more visually appealing and helps distinguish each cell.*

- Click the Select Table button (Table Tools Layout tab | Table group) to display the Select Table menu (Figure 10–26).

Figure 10–26

- Click Select Table in the Select Table menu to select the entire table.

- Click the Table Tools Design tab and then click the Shading arrow (Table Tools Design tab | Table Styles group) to display the Shading gallery.

- Point to 'Lime, Accent 1, Lighter 80%' (fifth color in second Theme Colors row) in the Shading gallery to display a live preview of that color applied to the table in the slide (Figure 10–27).

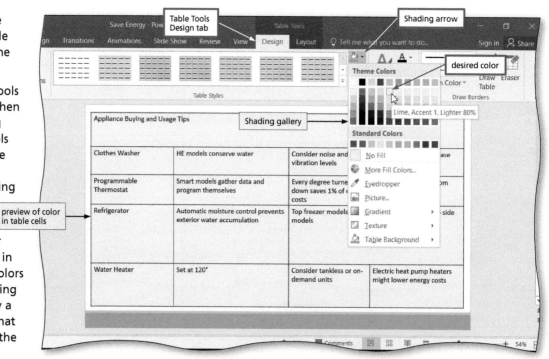

Figure 10–27

Experiment

- Point to various colors in the Shading gallery and watch the background of the table change.

- Click 'Lime, Accent 1, Lighter 80%' in the Shading gallery to apply the selected color to the table.

To Add a Gradient Fill to a Table

Another enhancement you can make to the table is to add a gradient fill so that one shade of the green color gradually progresses to another shade of the same color. The following steps add a gradient fill to the table. *Why? Using a gradient fill is another method of calling attention to each individual table cell.*

- With the table still selected, click the Shading arrow (Table Tools Design tab | Table Styles group) again to display the Shading gallery.

- Point to Gradient to display the Gradient gallery.

- Point to From Center (second gradient in second row of Variations area) to display a live preview of that gradient applied to the table in the slide (Figure 10–28).

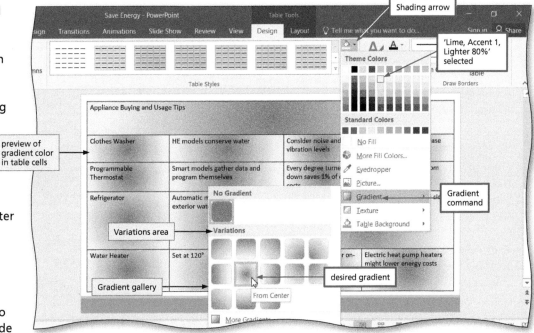

Figure 10–28

Q&A What if my Gradient gallery shows Light and Dark variations?
Select the last gradient in the Light Variations area.

 Experiment

- Point to various gradients in the Gradient gallery and watch the background of the table change.

- Click From Center in the Shading gallery to apply the selected gradient to the table.

To Add a Cell Bevel

Why? Bevels modify the cell edges to give a 3-D effect, which makes each cell stand out. Some bevels give the appearance that the cell is protruding from the table, while others give the effect that the cell is depressed into the table. The steps on the next page add a bevel to the table cells.

- With the table still selected, click the Effects button (Table Tools Design tab | Table Styles group) to display the Effects menu.

- Point to Cell Bevel on the Effects menu to display the Cell Bevel gallery.

- Point to Convex (third bevel in second row) to display a live preview of that bevel applied to the table in the slide (Figure 10–29).

 Experiment

- Point to various bevel effects in the Bevel gallery and watch the table cells change.

- Click Convex in the Bevel gallery to apply the selected bevel effect to the table.

Figure 10–29

To Distribute Table Rows

1 INSERT & EDIT WORD FILE | 2 CREATE TABLE ROWS & COLUMNS | 3 FORMAT TABLE
4 INSERT & EDIT LINKED WORKSHEET | 5 COPY, FORMAT, & EDIT CHART

At times you may desire the row heights to vary. In the Slide 2 table, however, you desire the heights of the rows to be uniform. To make each selected row the same height, you distribute the desired rows. The following steps distribute table rows. *Why? The horizontal lines you drew are not spaced equidistant from each other, and distributing the rows is an efficient manner of creating rows with the same height.*

1

- With the table still selected, display the Table Tools Layout tab and then select the cells in the second, third, fourth, and fifth rows (Figure 10–30).

Figure 10–30

- Click the Distribute Rows button (Table Tools Layout tab | Cell Size group) to equally space these four rows vertically (Figure 10–31).

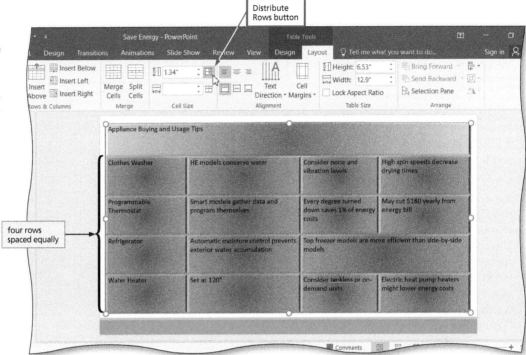

Figure 10–31

To Resize Table Columns and Rows

1 INSERT & EDIT WORD FILE | 2 CREATE TABLE ROWS & COLUMNS | 3 FORMAT TABLE
4 INSERT & EDIT LINKED WORKSHEET | 5 COPY, FORMAT, & EDIT CHART

The first table row should have a height taller than the rows beneath it. In addition, when a row has four cells, each cell should be somewhat narrower than the cells in rows with three cells. *Why? You will increase the heading text font size in a later part of this project, so you need to leave sufficient room for these letters.* The following steps resize the table columns and rows.

- With the Table Tools Layout tab displaying, position the insertion point in the first row.
- Click the 'Table Row Height' up arrow (Table Tools Layout tab | Cell Size group) and set the row height to 1.5" (Figure 10–32).

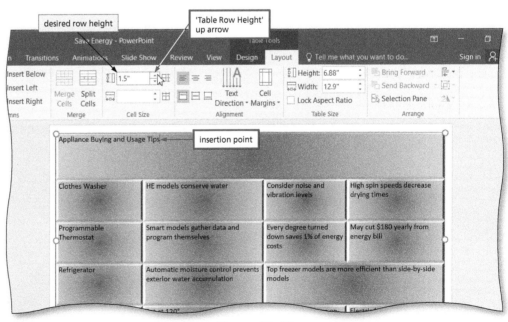

Figure 10–32

2

- Position the insertion point in the third cell in the second row (Consider noise and vibration levels). Click the 'Table Column Width' down arrow (Table Tools Layout tab | Cell Size group) and set the cell width to 2.5".

- Select the cells in the first column, rows 2 – 5 (Clothes Washer, Programmable Thermostat, Refrigerator, and Water Heater). Click the Width down arrow again and then set the width of these cells to 2.5" (Figure 10–33).

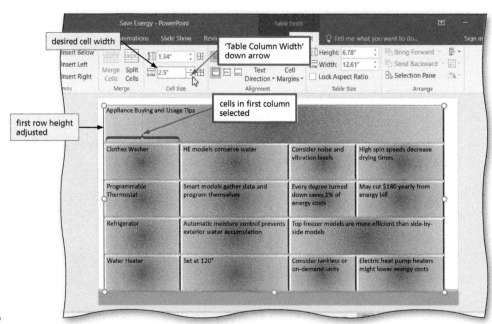

Figure 10–33

To Align Data in Cells

The next step is to change the alignment of the data in all the table cells. In addition to aligning text horizontally in a cell (left, center, or right), you can align it vertically within a cell (top, middle, or bottom). The following steps center data in the table both horizontally and vertically.

1 Select all the table cells and then click the Center button (Table Tools Layout tab | Alignment group) to center the text horizontally in the cells.

2 Click the Center Vertically button (Table Tools Layout tab | Alignment group) to center the contents of the cells vertically (Figure 10–34).

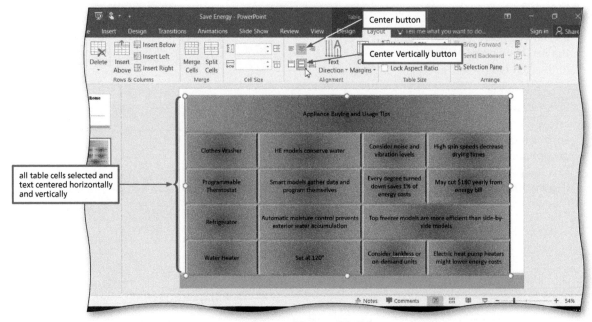

Figure 10–34

To Center a Table

Why? *The table should be positioned an equal distance between the left and right slide edges to balance this object in the slide.* To center the table, you align it in the middle of the slide. The following steps center the table horizontally.

- With the table selected, adjust the table vertically on the slide so that its lower edge is aligned with the top of the green bar at the bottom of the slide. If necessary, move the bottom sizing handle up to adjust the table size.

- Click the Align Objects button (Table Tools Layout tab | Arrange group) to display the Align Objects menu (Figure 10–35).

- Click Align Center on the Align Objects menu, so PowerPoint adjusts the position of the table evenly between the left and right sides of the slide.

Figure 10–35

To Format Table Data

The final table enhancements are to format the text in the table cells. The following steps increase the font size and bold the text in the first row and column and then change the font for all the table data.

1. Select the text in the first row and then increase the font size to 48 point and bold this text.

2. Select the cells in the first column and then increase the font size to 24 and bold this text.

3. Select all the table cells and then change the font to Cambria. If necessary, change the width of the columns so the words display with adequate spacing on the left and right sides (Figure 10–36).

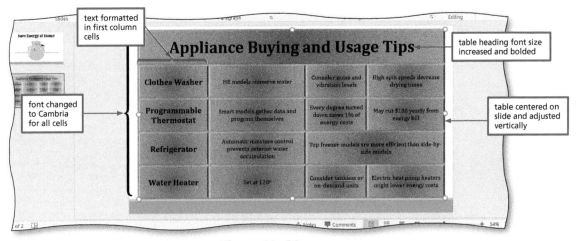

Figure 10–36

Break Point: If you wish to take a break, this is a good place to do so. Be sure to save the Save Energy file again and then you can exit PowerPoint. To resume at a later time, run PowerPoint, open the file called Save Energy, and continue following the steps from this location forward. Note: PowerPoint will prompt you to update any files that you modified.

Inserting a Linked Excel Worksheet

Linked files maintain a connection between the source file and the destination file. When you select the **Link check box** in the Insert Object dialog box, the object is inserted as a linked object instead of an embedded object. Your PowerPoint presentation stores a representation of the original file and information about its location. If you later move or delete the source file, the link is broken, and the object will not be available. Consequently, if you make a presentation on a computer other than the one on which the presentation was created, and the presentation contains linked objects, be certain to include a copy of the source files. The source files must be stored in the exact location as originally specified when you linked them to your presentation.

PowerPoint associates a linked file with a specific application, which PowerPoint bases on the file extension. For example, if you select a source file with the file extension **.docx**, PowerPoint recognizes the file as a Microsoft Word file. Additionally, if you select a source file with the file extension **.xlsx**, PowerPoint recognizes the file as a Microsoft Excel file.

In the following pages, you will insert a linked Excel worksheet, align it on the slide, and then edit three cells.

To Insert a Linked Excel Worksheet

1 INSERT & EDIT WORD FILE | 2 CREATE TABLE ROWS & COLUMNS | 3 FORMAT TABLE
4 INSERT & EDIT LINKED WORKSHEET | 5 COPY, FORMAT, & EDIT CHART

The Bulb Energy Savings Excel worksheet contains a table with data corresponding to computations that determine the cost of using of using incandescent, halogen, CFL, and LED bulbs for one or more hours a day. While the price of electricity can vary in each town and at different times of the year, this worksheet assumes a cost of 10 cents per kilowatt. The initial computations are for one light bulb and one hour of use. The results in the last three rows of the table show that a using an energy-efficient bulb could result in an 80 percent savings. You will update this table by editing the number of bulbs and the number of hours each day they are turned on. These figures also will update the original Excel worksheet. When you insert the Bulb Energy Savings chart, you can specify that it is linked from the PowerPoint slide to the Excel worksheet. **Why?** *Any edits made to specific cells are reflected in both the source and destination files.* The following steps insert and link the Microsoft Excel worksheet.

- Insert a new slide with the Blank layout.
- Click the Format Background button (Design tab | Customize group) to display the Format Background pane. Insert the Wires photo located in the Data Files as a background for the new slide (Figure 10–37).

Figure 10–37

- Close the Format Background pane.
- Display the Insert tab and then click the Object button (Insert tab | Text group) to display the Insert Object dialog box.
- Click 'Create from file' (Insert Object dialog box) to display the File box (Figure 10–38).

Figure 10–38

- Click the Browse button, navigate to the location of your Data Files, and then click Bulb Energy Savings to select the file name (Figure 10–39).

Figure 10–39

4

- Click the OK button (Browse dialog box) to insert the file name into the File box (Insert Object dialog box).
- Click the Link check box (Insert Object dialog box) to select the check box (Figure 10–40).

Figure 10–40

5

- Click the OK button (Insert Object dialog box) to insert the Bulb Energy Savings Excel worksheet into Slide 3.

- Display the Drawing Tools Format tab, click the 'Size and Position Dialog Box Launcher' to display the Format Object pane, click the 'Lock aspect ratio' checkbox to uncheck the box, and then change the worksheet height to 5" and the width to 12" (Figure 10–41).

6

- Close the Format Object pane.

Figure 10–41

To Align a Worksheet

1 INSERT & EDIT WORD FILE | 2 CREATE TABLE ROWS & COLUMNS | 3 FORMAT TABLE
4 INSERT & EDIT LINKED WORKSHEET | 5 COPY, FORMAT, & EDIT CHART

Why? *PowerPoint inserts the table on Slide 3 in a location that is not visually appealing, so you want to center it on the slide.* You can drag the table to a location, but you also can have PowerPoint precisely align the object horizontally in the left, center, or right areas of the slide, and vertically in the top, middle, or bottom of the slide. The following steps align the table horizontally and vertically on Slide 3.

1

- With the Drawing Tools Format tab displaying, click the Align Objects button (Drawing Tools Format tab| Arrange group) to display the Align Objects menu (Figure 10–42).

Figure 10–42

- Click Align Center on the Align Objects menu to position the worksheet evenly between the left and right edges of the slide.

- Click the Align Objects button again to display the Align Objects menu and then click Align Middle to position the worksheet in the center of the slide (Figure 10–43).

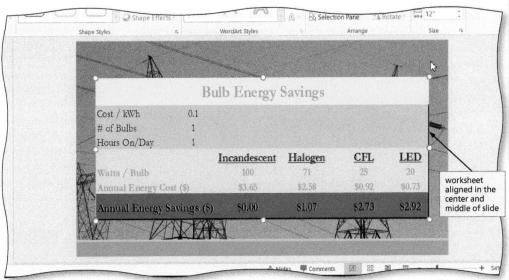

Figure 10–43

To Edit a Linked Worksheet

1 INSERT & EDIT WORD FILE | 2 CREATE TABLE ROWS & COLUMNS | 3 FORMAT TABLE
4 INSERT & EDIT LINKED WORKSHEET | **5 COPY, FORMAT, & EDIT CHART**

Each table or worksheet cell is identified by a unique address, or **cell reference**, representing the intersection of a column and row. The column letter is first and is followed by the row number. For example, cell B3 is located at the intersection of the second column, B, and the third row. Three cells need updating. *Why? Most people use more than one bulb for more than one hour per day, so you want to show realistic figures and the corresponding energy savings.* The following steps edit cells in the linked table.

- Double-click the worksheet to open Microsoft Excel and display the worksheet.

- Click the number 1 to the right of the # of Bulbs cell to make cell B3 the active cell (Figure 10–44).

Figure 10–44

- Type **5** as the new # of Bulbs number and then press the ENTER key to complete the entry and make cell B4 the active cell.

- Type **7** as the new Hours On / Day number and then press the ENTER key to complete the entry and make cell B5 the active cell. (Figure 10–45).

Figure 10–45

- Click the Close button in the upper-right corner of the Microsoft Excel window to exit Excel (Figure 10–46).

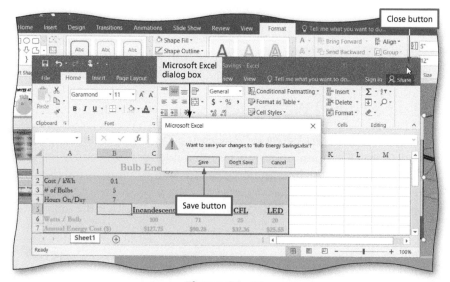

Figure 10–46

- Click the Save button (Microsoft Excel dialog box) to save your edited numbers in the worksheet and display Slide 3 with the two updated figures in the table (Figure 10–47).

Q&A What would occur if I clicked the Don't Save button in the dialog box instead of the Save button? The new figures in cells B3 and B4 would not be updated in the Excel spreadsheet.

Figure 10–47

Break Point: If you wish to take a break, this is a good place to do so. Be sure to save the Save Energy file again and then you can exit PowerPoint. To resume at a later time, run PowerPoint, open the file called Save Energy, and continue following the steps from this location forward.

Copying and Modifying a Linked Excel Chart

The Microsoft Excel table you inserted into Slide 3 is a linked object. You added data to the table using the Microsoft Excel source program, and that change is reflected on the PowerPoint slide and in the original Excel document. Now you will insert and then modify a Microsoft Excel chart on Slide 4. This object will be linked, so any changes you make to the layout, legend, or background will be reflected in the destination object on the slide and in the original Excel worksheet.

Your local home improvement store held seminars this past winter to describe easy low-cost and no-cost methods consumers could take to save energy. Several homeowners attended these seminars and, in turn, made energy-efficient improvements. They gave you their electric bills from the summers prior to and after their improvements, and you averaged their kilowatt consumption and then used this data to develop a Microsoft Excel chart.

In the following pages, you will perform these tasks on Slide 4:

1. Copy a chart from a file.
2. Edit a linked worksheet.
3. Align the chart.
4. Switch rows and columns.
5. Change the chart type.
6. Apply a style.
7. Display and format axis titles.
8. Move and format a legend.
9. Format the background.
10. Edit data.

BTW

Positioning a Chart or Other Slide Object
At times you might desire to place a table, text box, shape, or other element in a precise location on the slide. To specify a position, right-click the object, click Format Shape on the shortcut menu to display the Format Shape pane, click 'Size & Properties' in the Shape Options tab, if necessary click Position, and then enter the precise measurements of the horizontal and vertical distances from either the top-left corner or the center of the slide.

BTW

File Sizes
Files with embedded objects typically have larger file sizes than those with linked objects because the source data is stored in the presentation. In order to keep file sizes manageable, Microsoft recommends inserting a linked object rather than an embedded object when the source file is large or complex.

To Copy an Excel Chart

1 INSERT & EDIT WORD FILE | 2 CREATE TABLE ROWS & COLUMNS | 3 FORMAT TABLE
4 INSERT & EDIT LINKED WORKSHEET | **5 COPY, FORMAT, & EDIT CHART**

The chart you want to insert into your slide show was created in Microsoft Excel. The file consists of two sheets: one for the chart and another for the numbers used to create the chart. The chart is on Sheet1. One method of placing this chart into a PowerPoint presentation is to copy this object from the Excel worksheet and then paste it into a slide. The following steps copy and link a chart from Sheet1 of the Microsoft Excel file using the destination formatting. *Why? Copying and linking allows you to modify the chart content easily. You want to use the destination formatting so the chart uses the Retrospect theme colors and styles.*

• Insert a new
slide with the
Title Only layout.
Type `Kilowatt`
`Comparison` as
the title text, change
the font to Cambria,
and then bold this
text. Center and
align it in the middle
of the placeholder
(Figure 10–48).

Figure 10–48

• Click the File
Explorer app button
on the taskbar
to make the File
Explorer window
the active window.
Navigate to the
location where your
Data Files are stored
and then point to
the kWh Comparison
file in the Name list
(Figure 10–49).

Figure 10–49

3

- Double-click the KWh Comparison file to run Microsoft Excel. If necessary, display the chart on Sheet1.

- Click a blank area above the chart legend in the Chart Area to select the entire chart.

- Click the Copy button (Home tab | Clipboard group) to copy the chart to the Office Clipboard (Figure 10–50).

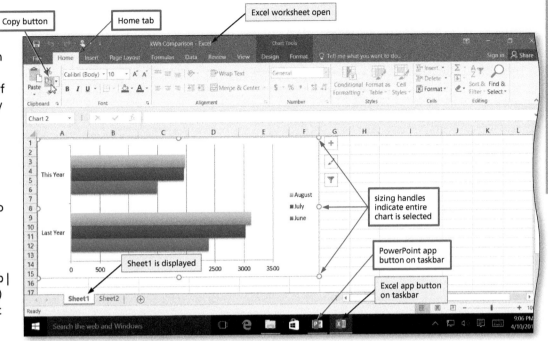

Figure 10–50

4

- Click the PowerPoint app button on the taskbar to make the PowerPoint window the active window. With Slide 4 and the Home tab displaying, click the Paste arrow (Home tab | Clipboard group) to display the Paste Options gallery.

- Point to the 'Use Destination Theme & Link Data' button to display a live preview of the chart in the slide (Figure 10–51).

Q&A
Why did I click the Paste arrow instead of the Paste button?
You want to use the colors and style of Retrospect theme (the destination theme), so you need to display the Paste Options gallery to make that choice and to link the chart to the original Excel worksheet. If you had clicked the Paste button, you would have embedded the chart using the Excel worksheet theme (the source theme).

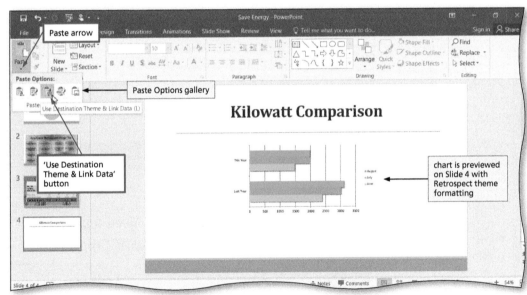

Figure 10–51

🔍 **Experiment**

- Point to the 'Use Destination Theme & Embed Workbook' button in the Paste Options gallery to display a live preview of the chart with the Retrospect theme applied.

5

- Click the 'Use Destination Theme & Link Data' button to paste the chart into Slide 4.

- Display the Chart Tools Format tab and then change the chart size to 4.5" x 11" (Figure 10–52).

Figure 10–52

Other Ways

1. Right-click Excel chart, click Copy, exit Microsoft Excel, click Paste arrow (Home tab | Clipboard group), click 'Use Destination Theme & Link Data'

To Align a Chart

1 INSERT & EDIT WORD FILE | 2 CREATE TABLE ROWS & COLUMNS | 3 FORMAT TABLE
4 INSERT & EDIT LINKED WORKSHEET | 5 COPY, FORMAT, & EDIT CHART

Why? *You aligned the table on Slide 3 horizontally and vertically. Likewise, you want to align the chart on Slide 4 so that it is displayed in an appropriate location on the slide.* Although you can drag the chart on the slide, you also can use PowerPoint commands to align the object horizontally in the left, center, or right areas of the slide, and vertically in the top, middle, or bottom of the slide. The following steps align the chart horizontally and vertically on Slide 4.

1

- With the chart selected and the Chart Tools Format tab displaying, click the Align Objects button (Chart Tools Format tab | Arrange group) to display the Align Objects menu (Figure 10–53).

Figure 10–53

2

- Click Align Right on the Align Objects menu to position the chart along the right edge of the slide (Figure 10–54).

chart aligned on right side of slide

Figure 10–54

To Switch Rows and Columns in a Chart

1 INSERT & EDIT WORD FILE | 2 CREATE TABLE ROWS & COLUMNS | 3 FORMAT TABLE
4 INSERT & EDIT LINKED WORKSHEET | 5 COPY, FORMAT, & EDIT CHART

Excel created the chart on Slide 4 (Sheet1 in the Excel file) based on the values in the worksheet on Sheet2 of the Excel file. The scale is based on the values in the **y-axis**, which also is called the **vertical axis** or **value axis**. The titles along the **x-axis**, also referred to as the **horizontal axis** or **category axis**, are derived from the top row of the Sheet2 worksheet and are displayed along the left edge of the chart. Each bar in the chart has a specific color to represent one of the three months — June, July, and August — grouped by kilowatts used during the two previous summers. You can switch the data in the chart so that a kilowatts used bar is displayed for each of the three months. *Why? In your presentation to consumers, you want to emphasize the lower electricity consumption when energy-reduction measures have been taken.* The following step switches the rows and columns in the chart.

1

- Display the Chart Tools Design tab on the ribbon.

- Click the Switch Row/Column button (Chart Tools Design tab | Data group) to swap the data charted on the x-axis with the data on the y-axis (Figure 10–55).

Q&A
If the Switch Row/Column button is dimmed, how can I switch the data?
Be certain the Excel worksheet is open. The button is active only when the worksheet is open.

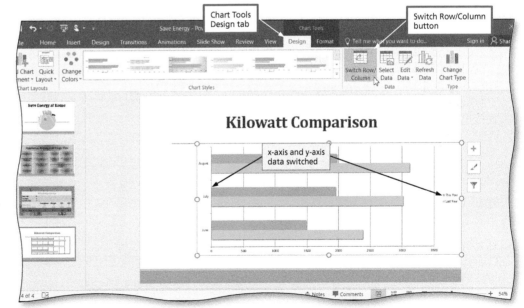

Chart Tools Design tab

Switch Row/Column button

x-axis and y-axis data switched

Figure 10–55

To Change the Chart Type

The bar chart represents data horizontally for each of the three summer months. You can change the chart appearance by selecting another type in the Change Chart Type dialog box. The sample charts are divided into a variety of categories, including column, line, pie, and bar. The clustered column type that you want to use in the presentation is located in the Column area, which has seven layouts. The following steps change the chart to a 3-D Clustered Column chart type. *Why? The vertical bars help show the increase and decrease of kilowatt usage, and the 3-D effect adds an interesting visual element.*

1
- Click the 'Change Chart Type' button (Chart Tools Design tab | Type group) to display the Change Chart Type dialog box.

- Click Column in the left pane (Change Chart Type dialog box) to display a Clustered Column thumbnail (Figure 10–56).

Figure 10–56

2
- Click the '3-D Clustered Column' chart (fourth chart) to select this chart type and display a thumbnail with a 3-D effect (Figure 10–57).

Q&A
Can I see a larger preview of the chart?
Yes. You can point to the chart to enlarge the preview.

3
- Click the OK button (Change Chart Type dialog box) to change the chart type to 3-D Clustered Column.

Figure 10–57

To Exclude Data in a Chart

If you have multiple categories (which display in the x-axis) or series (which display in the legend) of data and want to exclude one or more of them from displaying, you can instruct PowerPoint to exclude data elements. If you wanted to exclude a particular category or series, you would perform the following steps.

1. Click the Chart Filters button (funnel icon) on the right side of the chart to display a pane with each data element.
2. Clear the check boxes of the elements you want to exclude on the chart.
3. To display an excluded data element, select the check box.

To Apply a Style to a Chart

1 INSERT & EDIT WORD FILE | 2 CREATE TABLE ROWS & COLUMNS | 3 FORMAT TABLE
4 INSERT & EDIT LINKED WORKSHEET | **5 COPY, FORMAT, & EDIT CHART**

Why? *You can modify the chart's appearance easily by selecting a predefined style.* The styles available in the Chart Styles gallery have a variety of colors and backgrounds and display in both 2-D and 3-D. The following steps apply a style to the chart.

- Click the Chart Style button (paintbrush icon) on the right side of the chart area to display the Chart Style gallery with the Style tab displayed.

- Scroll down until the eighth style (Style 8) in the Chart Style gallery is displayed and then point to this style to see a live preview on Slide 4 (Figure 10–58).

Figure 10–58

Experiment
- Point to various chart styles and watch the layouts change.

- Click Style 8 in the Chart Style gallery to apply the chart style to the chart.

To Change Chart Colors

You can modify a chart's colors easily by selecting one of the color groups available in the Chart Color gallery. These colors are grouped in two categories: Colorful and Monochromatic. For a unique look, PowerPoint also allows you create a custom color combination. The following steps change the chart colors. **Why?** *The two columns in the chart have very similar colors, so you want to distinguish the kilowatts used during the previous summer from those used this year by changing to a color scheme with more contrast.*

1
- With the Chart Style gallery still displaying, click the Color tab at the top of the pane to display the Chart Color gallery.

Experiment
- Point to various color groups and watch the chart colors change.

2
- Click Color 3 (the third row in the Colorful area) to apply these colors to the chart (Figure 10–59).

- Click the Chart Style button to the right of the chart to close the Chart Color gallery.

- Right-click the Excel app button on the taskbar and then click Close window to exit Excel.

Figure 10–59

Other Ways

1. Click 'Chart Quick Colors' button (Chart Tools Design tab | Chart Styles group)

To Display and Format Axis Titles

The legend below the chart identifies the colors assigned to each of the bars. You can modify the default legend in a variety of ways, including moving its location, changing the fill and outline, adding an effect, and changing the font. The Chart Elements button on the right side of the chart area allows you to display or hide a chart element. When you click this button, the Chart Elements pane is displayed. A check mark appears in the check box for each chart element that is displayed. You can check and uncheck each chart element to display or hide axes, the chart title, labels, gridlines, and the legend. The following steps display the axis titles and then format the text. **Why?** *You want your audience to recognize that the y-axis represents the total number of kilowatts used and the x-axis represents the summer months.*

- Click the Chart Elements button (plus sign icon) on the right side of the chart area to display the CHART ELEMENTS pane.

- Click the Axis Titles check box to display the two default titles for the x and y axes (Figure 10–60).

Figure 10–60

- With the default y-axis title box selected, delete the default text and then type **Total Kilowatts Used** in the text box.

- Select the text and then increase the font size to 18 point and bold the text.

Figure 10–61

- Click the x-axis title to select it, delete the default text, and then type **Month** as the replacement text.

- Select the text and then increase the font size to 18 point and bold the text (Figure 10–61).

Other Ways

1. Click Add Chart Element button (Chart Tools Design tab | Chart Layouts group), click Axis Titles

To Move a Chart Legend

1 INSERT & EDIT WORD FILE | 2 CREATE TABLE ROWS & COLUMNS | 3 FORMAT TABLE
4 INSERT & EDIT LINKED WORKSHEET | 5 COPY, FORMAT, & EDIT CHART

The legend below the chart identifies the colors assigned to each of the bars. You can modify the default legend in a variety of ways, including moving its location, changing the fill and outline, adding an effect, and changing the font. The following steps move the legend to the left side of the chart. *Why? A blank area is available on the left side of the chart, and you believe the legend will be more effective there.*

1

- If necessary, display the CHART ELEMENTS pane by clicking a blank area of the chart beside the legend and then clicking the Chart Elements button (plus sign icon). Position the pointer over the word, Legend, in the list to display an arrow and then click this arrow to display the Legend menu (Figure 10–62).

Figure 10–62

2

- Click Left to display the legend on the left side of the chart.

Other Ways

1. Click Add Chart Element button (Chart Tools Design tab | Chart Layouts group), click Legend arrow

To Format a Chart Legend

1 INSERT & EDIT WORD FILE | 2 CREATE TABLE ROWS & COLUMNS | 3 FORMAT TABLE
4 INSERT & EDIT LINKED WORKSHEET | 5 COPY, FORMAT, & EDIT CHART

You can modify the default legend in a variety of ways, including moving its location, changing the fill and outline, adding an effect, and changing the font. The following steps format the legend. **Why?** *Changing the line color and adding a glow help call attention to the legend.*

1

- With the CHART ELEMENTS pane and Legend menu still displaying, click More Options to display the Format Legend pane. Click the 'Fill & Line' button and then, if necessary, click Border to display the Border area. Scroll down to display the Border area.

- Click Solid line and then, if necessary, scroll down and then click the Color button to display the Color gallery (Figure 10–63).

Figure 10–63

2

- Click Blue (eighth color in Standard Colors row) to change the legend border line color.

- Click the Width up arrow several times to increase the line width to 2 pt (Figure 10–64).

 Q&A Is a live preview available? No, this feature is not offered.

Figure 10–64

3

- Click the Effects button (Format Legend pane) and then, if necessary, display the Glow area (Figure 10–65).

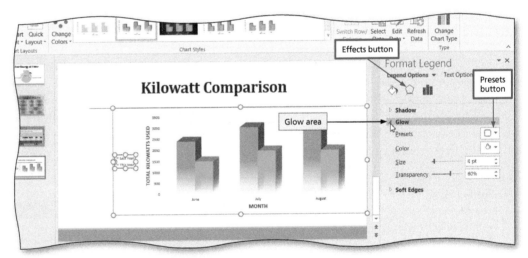

Figure 10–65

4

- Click the Presets button to display the Glow gallery.

- Point to 'Blue, 8 pt glow, Accent color 6' (last variation in second row) (Figure 10–66).

Figure 10–66

5

- Click the 'Blue, 8 pt glow, Accent color 6' variation to apply this formatting to the legend.

- Click the Close button (Format Legend pane).

- With the legend still selected, display the Home tab and then change the font to Cambria and increase the font size to 18 point (Figure 10–67).

Figure 10–67

Other Ways

1. Right-click legend, click Format Legend on shortcut menu

To Format a Chart Background

The background area behind and to the left of the chart bars is called the **chart wall**. You can format this portion of the chart by adding a fill, an outline, and effects such as a shadow. The following steps add a gradient fill to the background chart wall. **Why?** *The gradient adds a visual element and helps call attention to the gridlines.*

1

- Right-click an area of the chart wall to select this chart element and to display a mini toolbar and shortcut menu. If necessary, click the Chart Elements arrow and then click Walls in the list (Figure 10–68).

Q&A How will I know if this piece of the chart is selected? You will see six small blue circles, each one located at the upper or lower gridline corner.

Figure 10–68

- If necessary, display the shortcut menu again and, if necessary, click Fill to expand the Fill section of the Format Walls pane (Figure 10–69).

Figure 10–69

- Click Gradient fill to display options related to the gradient colors in the pane. Click the Preset gradients button to display a palette of built-in gradient fill colors (Figure 10–70).

Figure 10–70

- Click 'Medium Gradient – Accent 6' (last gradient in third row) to apply this gradient to the chart walls (Figure 10–71).

- Click the Close button (Format Walls pane).

Figure 10–71

Other Ways

1. Click the Chart Elements arrow (Chart Tools Format tab | Current Selection group), click Walls, click Format Selection (Chart Tools Format tab | Current Selection group), if necessary click Fill & Line button, if necessary click Fill, click Gradient fill (Format Walls pane)

To Edit Data in a Chart

The data in Sheet2 of the worksheet is used to create the chart on Slide 4. If you edit this data, the corresponding bars in the chart change height to reflect new numbers. The chart is a linked object, so when you modify the data and close the worksheet, the chart will reflect the changes and the original file stored in your Data Files also will change. The following steps edit three cells in the worksheet. *Why? You have obtained electric bills from additional homeowners who made energy-reduction improvements this past year, and you want to update your chart and the Excel worksheet with this information.*

- Display the Chart Tools Design tab and then click the Edit Data button (Chart Tools Design tab | Data group) to display Sheet2 of the worksheet.

Q&A

Why might I want to click the Edit Data arrow instead of the Edit Data button? You would be given the option to run Microsoft Excel and then edit the worksheet using that app. More options would be available using Excel. If you simply need to edit data, you can perform that task easily using PowerPoint.

- Position the pointer in the lower-right corner of the worksheet (Figure 10–72).

Figure 10–72

- If necessary, drag the pointer downward so that all cells with data in the worksheet are visible.

- Click cell B2 (June of Last Year) to make cell B2 the active cell (Figure 10–73).

Figure 10–73

- Type **2401** as the replacement number and then press the DOWN ARROW key to make cell B3 (July of Last Year) the active cell.

- Type **2993** as the replacement number and then press the RIGHT ARROW key to make cell C3 (July of This Year) the active cell.

- Type **1861** as the replacement number and then press the ENTER key (Figure 10–74).

Figure 10–74

- Click the Save button on the spreadsheet toolbar to save the data to the Excel spreadsheet.
- Click the Close button on the spreadsheet to close the window.

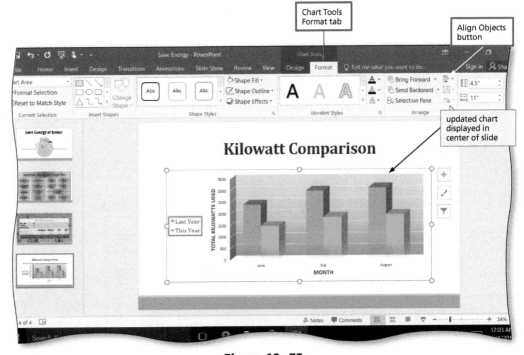

Figure 10–75

- Display the Chart Tools Format tab, click the Align Objects button (Chart Tools Format tab | Arrange group), and then click Align Center to position the chart in the center of the slide (Figure 10–75).

Q&A The Align Center command is dimmed. What should I do? Click the chart area so that the chart walls are not selected and then click the Align Objects button again.

To Add a Hyperlink to a Table

A hyperlink connects one element on a slide to another slide, presentation, picture, file, webpage, or email address. Presenters use hyperlinks to display these elements to an audience. In this Save Energy presentation, you will create a hyperlink from a cell in the table on Slide 2 to an Adobe PDF file. *Why? You want to show your audience a simple form they can use to analyze the measures they can take to save energy in lighting, heating and cooling, and appliances.* When you click this particular table cell during a slide show, Adobe Acrobat starts and then opens this PDF file. The following steps hyperlink a table cell to a PDF file.

1

- Display Slide 2 and then select the words, Usage Tips, in the first row.

- Display the Insert tab and then click the 'Add a Hyperlink' button (Insert tab | Links group) to display the Insert Hyperlink dialog box.

- If necessary, click the 'Existing File or Web Page' button in the Link to area.

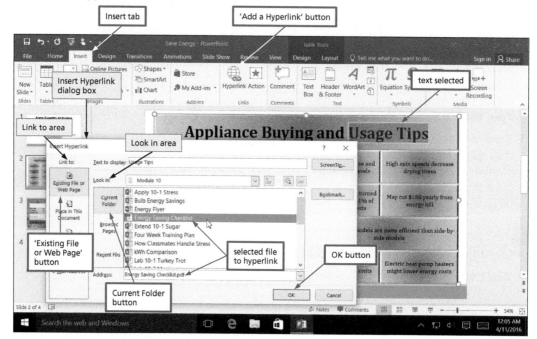

- If necessary, click the Current Folder button in the Look in area and then navigate to the location where your Data Files are stored.

- Click Energy Saving Checklist to select this file as the hyperlink (Figure 10–76).

Figure 10–76

2

- Click the OK button (Insert Hyperlink dialog box) to insert the hyperlink.

BTW
Distributing a Document
Instead of printing and distributing a hard copy of a document, you can distribute the document electronically. Options include sending the document via email; posting it on cloud storage (such as OneDrive) and sharing the file with others; posting it on social media, a blog, or other website; and sharing a link associated with an online location of the document. You also can create and share a PDF or XPS image of the document, so that users can view the file in Acrobat Reader or XPS Viewer instead of in PowerPoint.

To Add a Transition between Slides

The final enhancements you will make in this presentation are to apply a transition, change the transition effect option, and change the transition speed. The following steps apply these transition effects to the presentation.

1 Apply the Blinds transition in the Exciting category to all slides.

2 Change the effect option to Horizontal.

3 Change the transition speed from 1.40 to 3.00 seconds.

To Run, Print, Save, and Exit PowerPoint

The presentation now is complete. You should run the presentation, view the hyperlinked file, print the slides, save the presentation, and then exit PowerPoint.

1 Run the Save Energy presentation. When Slide 2 is displayed, click Usage Tips in the first row of the table to display the Energy Saving Checklist document as the hyperlinked file. If the Microsoft PowerPoint Security Notice dialog box is displayed, click the Yes button, then click OK in the Microsoft Office dialog box, to open the PDF file.

2 Review the contents of the Energy Saving Checklist. Point to the PowerPoint app button on the taskbar to see the PowerPoint window and a live preview of Slide 2.

3 Click the thumbnail of Slide 2 to display that slide and then display Slides 3 and 4.

4 End the slide show. Close the Energy Saving Checklist.

5 Print the Save Energy presentation as a handout with two slides per page.

6 Save the Save Energy presentation again with the same file name.

7 Because the project now is complete, you can exit PowerPoint, closing all open documents.

BTW
Conserving Ink and Toner
If you want to conserve ink or toner, you can instruct PowerPoint to print draft quality documents by clicking File on the ribbon to open the Backstage view, clicking the Options tab in the Backstage view to display the PowerPoint Options dialog box, clicking Advanced in the left pane (PowerPoint Options dialog box), scrolling to the Print area in the right pane, placing a check mark in the 'Use draft quality' check box, and then clicking the OK button. Then, use the Backstage view to print the document as usual.

Summary

In this module you have learned how to develop a presentation using information you inserted from a Microsoft Word flyer and Microsoft Excel worksheet and chart. These documents were either embedded or linked, and you edited each of them to update words or numbers. You also drew a table, enhanced and formatted it, and linked an Adobe PDF file to the table. You then altered a Microsoft Excel object by changing the chart type, background, gridlines, and legend.

What decisions will you need to make when creating your next presentation?
Use these guidelines as you complete the assignments in this module and create your own slide show decks outside of this class.

1. **Use powerful words to accompany the text on your slides.** The slides are meant to enhance your talk by clarifying main points and calling attention to key ideas. Your speech should use words that explain and substantiate your visuals.

2. **Develop tables that are clear and meaningful.** Tables are extremely useful vehicles for presenting complex relationships. Their design plays an important part in successfully conveying the information to the audience.

3. **Use appropriate colors when formatting graphics you want people to remember.** Numerous studies have shown that appropriate graphics help audiences comprehend and remember the information presented during a speech. Color has been shown to increase retention by as much as 80 percent. When choosing colors for your graphics, use hues that fit the tone and objective of your message.

CONSIDER THIS

Apply Your Knowledge

Reinforce the skills and apply the concepts you learned in this module.

Copying a Chart from an Excel file, Changing a Chart Type, and Drawing a Table

Note: To complete this assignment, you will be required to use the Data Files. Please contact your instructor for information about accessing the Data Files.

Instructions: Run PowerPoint. Open the presentation called Apply 10-1 Stress, which is located in the Data Files. You conducted a survey of your freshman class to find out how they handle stress and entered the results in an Excel worksheet. The document you open is a partially formatted presentation highlighting the results of your survey and information on reactions to stress. You will copy a chart from an Excel file, change the chart type, and draw a table. Your presentation should look like Figure 10–77.

Perform the following tasks:

1. Open the Microsoft Excel file called How Classmates Handle Stress, which is located in the Data Files, and then copy the doughnut pie chart located on Sheet1. Paste the chart onto Slide 1 (Figure 10–77a) with the ' Use Destination Theme & Link Data' option. Change the chart style to Style 7 and then change the chart type to Sunburst.

2. Increase the size of the chart to 4.5" × 6". Hide the legend. Change the font color of the data labels to 'Black, Background 1' and then bold this text. Change the chart colors to Color 4. Add a 6 pt black border. Move the chart to the lower-right corner of the slide.

3. On Slide 2 (Figure 10–77b), draw a table with four columns and three rows. Adjust the size of the table to 2.5" × 10.5". Set the height of the first row to 0.83" and the second and third rows to 0.75". Set the width of the first column to 3" and the width of the second, third, and fourth columns to 2.5". Merge the four cells in the first row. Enter the data shown in the figure. Center the data vertically in the cells.

4. If requested by your instructor, add your birth year after the word, Stress, in the table title.

5. Increase the font size of the table title to 32 point, change the font color to 'Green, Accent 6' (last color in first Theme Colors row), and then bold and center the text. Increase the font size of the text in the second and third rows to 20 point. Underline and bold the words, Emotional and Physical, in the first column and then center these words in the cells.

6. With the table still selected, click the Pen Weight arrow (Table Tools Design tab | Draw Borders group) and then click 3 pt in the Pen Weight gallery. Click the Pen Color button (Table Tools Design tab | Draw Borders group) and then change the pen color to 'Green, Accent 6'. Click the Borders arrow (Table Tools Design tab | Table Styles group) and then click All Borders in the Borders gallery to change all borders to this new weight and color. Add 'Dark Blue, Background 2, Darker 50%' (third color in last Theme Colors row) shading to the entire table. Move the table to the area shown in Figure 10–77b.

7. Apply the Fracture transition (Exciting category) and then change the duration to 3.25 seconds for both slides.

8. Run the presentation and then save the file using the file name, Apply 10-1 Stress Symptoms.

9. Submit the revised document in the format specified by your instructor.

10. ☀ Is the Sunburst chart type appropriate for the chart on Slide 1? Can you suggest other formatting changes to make for the Slide 2 table?

(a) Slide 1

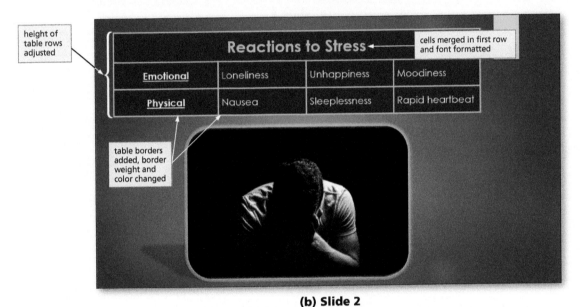

(b) Slide 2

Figure 10–77

Extend Your Knowledge

Extend the skills you learned in this module and experiment with new skills. You may need to use Help to complete the assignment.

Inserting a Linked Object and Drawing a Table

Note: To complete this assignment, you will be required to use the Data Files. Please contact your instructor for information about accessing the Data Files.

Instructions: Run PowerPoint. Open the presentation called Extend 10-1 Sugar, which is located in the Data Files. You will edit a table from a linked document and then draw and format a second table, as shown in Figure 10–78.

Continued >

Extend Your Knowledge *continued*

(a) Slide 1

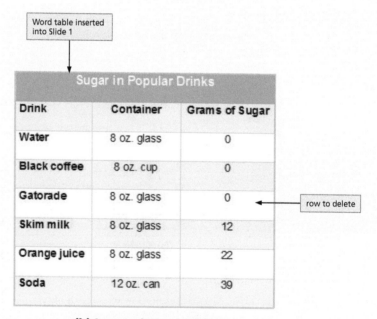

(b) Inserted Word Table

Figure 10–78 (Continued)

Perform the following tasks:

1. Display Slide 1 (Figure 10–78a). Insert the table object from the Microsoft Word file called Sugar in Popular Drinks (Figure 10–78b), which is located in the Data Files.

2. Delete the fourth row of the table, which contains the text, Gatorade, 8 oz. glass, and 0, by double-clicking the table to open Microsoft Word, double-clicking the table, placing the insertion point in the Gatorade row, displaying the Table Tools Layout tab (Microsoft Word), clicking the Delete Table button (Table Tools Layout tab | Rows & Columns group), and then clicking Delete Rows in the Delete Table menu. Exit Word by clicking the Close button in the upper-right corner of the screen. The edited table object is displayed on Slide 1.

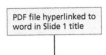

PDF file hyperlinked to word in Slide 1 title

Watermelon Breeze

Ingredients:

2 cups chopped seedless watermelon, chilled

½ cup pomegranate juice, no sugar added

Juice of ½ lemon

1 mint leaf

Directions:

Add all ingredients to the blender and blend until smooth. Pour over ice and garnish with additional mint if desired.

This recipe makes 2 servings and yields about 2 cups

(c) Hyperlinked Adobe PDF File

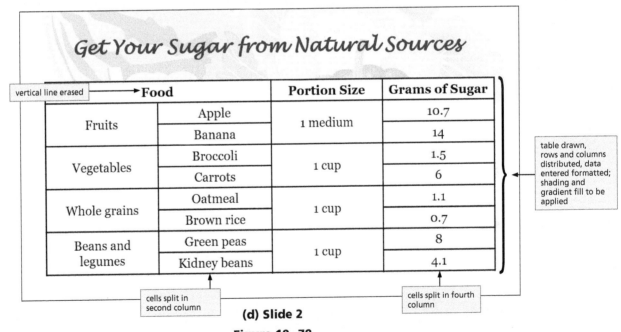

Get Your Sugar from Natural Sources

vertical line erased

Food		Portion Size	Grams of Sugar
Fruits	Apple	1 medium	10.7
	Banana		14
Vegetables	Broccoli	1 cup	1.5
	Carrots		6
Whole grains	Oatmeal	1 cup	1.1
	Brown rice		0.7
Beans and legumes	Green peas	1 cup	8
	Kidney beans		4.1

table drawn, rows and columns distributed, data entered formatted; shading and gradient fill to be applied

cells split in second column

cells split in fourth column

(d) Slide 2

Figure 10–78

Continued >

Extend Your Knowledge *continued*

3. Click outside the table object on Slide 1. If necessary, click the table object to select it. Display the Drawing Tools Format tab, click the Size and Position Dialog Box Launcher, and then unlock the aspect ratio. Change the table size to 5" × 5.5" and then move it to the lower-left corner of the slide.

4. Select the word, Drink, in the title text placeholder and then and hyperlink it to the PDF file called Watermelon Breeze (Figure 10–78c), which is located in the Data Files. (*Hint:* You might need to click the 'Existing File or Web Page' button in the Link to area.)

5. Display Slide 2 (Figure 10–78d) and then draw a table with five rows and four columns. Erase the vertical line between the first and second cells in the first row and then type, **Food,** in that cell as the column heading. Type **Portion Size** as the second column heading and **Grams of Sugar** as the third column heading.

6. Split each of the cells in the second and fourth columns so that they are displayed as one column and two rows. Distribute the rows and the columns. *Hint:* To distribute the columns, display the Table Tools Layout tab and then click the Distribute Columns button (Table Tools Layout tab | Cell Size group).

7. With the table selected, click the Pen Weight arrow (Table Tools Design tab | Draw Borders group) and then click 2 1/4 pt in the Pen Weight gallery. Click the Pen Color button (Table Tools Design tab | Draw Borders group) and then change the pen color to 'Gold, Accent 4, Darker 25%' (eighth color in fifth Theme Colors row). Click the Borders arrow (Table Tools Design tab | Table Styles group) and then click All Borders in the Borders gallery to apply the new border settings.

8. Enter the data in the table using Figure 10–78d as a guide. Select all text in the table and then change the font to Georgia and the font size to 24 point. Center the text vertically in each cell and then align the text in the middle of the cells. Bold the three column headings in the first row of the table.

9. If requested by your instructor, insert your grandfather's first name after the word, Food, in the first column heading.

10. Change the size of the table to 5" × 12". Change the shading color to 'Gold, Accent 4, Lighter 60%' (eighth color in third Theme Colors row) and then apply the Linear Down gradient (second gradient in first Variations row). Align the table in the center of the slide.

11. Apply the Flip transition in the Exciting category to both slides and then change the direction to Left. Change the duration to 3.00 seconds.

12. Run the presentation and then save the file using the file name, Extend 10-1 Sugar in Our Diet.

13. Submit the revised document in the format specified by your instructor.

14. ✷ In this presentation, you added borders to the table on Slide 2. Do these borders help separate the cells and make the data easier to read? Do the shading and gradient choices complement the slide background and overall presentation topic? Why or why not?

Expand Your World

Create a solution that uses cloud or web technologies by learning and investigating on your own from general guidance.

Creating a Slide with SmartArt Using PowerPoint Online

Instructions: You are at your local library waiting for your study partner to arrive. You notice that the computers in the library's Tech Link Lab can access the Internet, but they do not have Microsoft Office 2016 installed. To make the best use of your time, you decide to begin working on a project for your economics class about saving money when buying and using appliances. You use

PowerPoint Online and the data in Slide 2 of the Save Energy presentation in this module to create a SmartArt graphic (Figure 10–79). This graphic can be used as a replacement for Slide 2 if you decide to present the same information in an alternate manner. When you have access to Microsoft Office 2016, you open the file containing this slide and edit the slide contents using this software.

Perform the following tasks:

1. Run a browser and navigate to the Office Online website. You will need to sign in to your Microsoft account. Run PowerPoint Online.

2. Create a new presentation using the Ion Boardroom theme. Save the file using the file name, Expand 10-1 Appliance Energy Savings.

3. Change the layout to Title and Content layout and then change the Ion Boardroom variant to Variant 2.

4. Type **Appliance Buying and Usage Tips** as the title text. If requested by your instructor, type, **for** and your grandmother's or grandfather's first name or middle name. Change the font to Century Schoolbook, increase the font size to 40 point, and then center this text.

5. To begin creating the SmartArt graphic, click the SmartArt icon in the content placeholder, click the More Layouts arrow (SMARTART TOOLS DESIGN tab | Layouts group), and then select the Hierarchy List in the Layouts gallery (last design in third row).

6. Enter the data from Slide 2 of the Save Energy presentation, which is shown in Figure 10–1c. When you have typed all the data, click a blank area of the slide to display the graphic. If some of the data does not display properly in the individual graphic boxes, delete that text and continue performing the remaining steps in this assignment.

7. Select the SmartArt graphic and then right-click to display the mini toolbar. Click the Style button in the mini toolbar and then apply the Inset style (second style in second row). Click the Color button and then change the colors to Colorful – Accent Colors (first color in Colorful row). Change the font of all SmartArt text to Tahoma. Use the SmartArt corner sizing handles to increase the graphic's size, as shown in Figure 10–79.

8. Click the 'OPEN IN POWERPOINT" button and then click the Yes button (Microsoft Office dialog box) to open the document in the PowerPoint desktop app. If necessary, sign in to your Microsoft account when prompted. Note: You may need to respond to security warnings regarding viruses. If you are using a browser other than Microsoft Edge, you may need to respond to questions in that browser's dialog box.

Figure 10–79

Continued >

Expand Your World *continued*

9. In the PowerPoint desktop app, apply the Metallic Scene SmartArt style to the graphic and bold the four column headings (Clothes Washer, Programmable Thermostat, Refrigerator, and Water Heater). Save the slide on your OneDrive account with the file name, Expand 10-1 Appliance Energy Savings Modified.

10. Submit the Expand 10-1 Appliance Energy Savings and the Expand 10-1 Appliance Energy Savings Modified documents in the format requested by your instructor. Sign out of your OneDrive account. Sign out of the Microsoft account in PowerPoint.

11. ✷ Which SmartArt features that are available in the PowerPoint desktop app are not available in PowerPoint Online? Is the information presented more clearly in the Save Energy chart or in the SmartArt graphic? Why?

In the Labs

Design, create, modify, and/or use a presentation following the guidelines, concepts, and skills presented in this module. Labs 1 and 2, which increase in difficulty, require you to create solutions based on what you learned in the module; Lab 3 requires you to apply your creative thinking and problem-solving skills to design and implement a solution.

Lab 1: Inserting Content from Word Documents and Excel Worksheets, Switching Rows and Columns in a Chart, and Entering Data in a Table

Note: To complete this assignment, you will be required to use the Data Files. Please contact your instructor for information about accessing the Data Files.

Problem: The town of Midland is hosting its ninth annual Thanksgiving Day Turkey Trot. More than 20,000 runners are expected to participate. In previous years, the runners have come from the five neighboring towns. The director of the Turkey Trot has asked for your help in publicizing the event. She gives you the Microsoft Word file with the logo she used for last year's event and wants you to update it for this race. You create the presentation shown in Figure 10–80.

Perform the following tasks:

1. Run PowerPoint. Open the presentation, Lab 10-1 Turkey Trot, which is located in the Data Files.

2. On Slide 1 (Figure 10–80a), insert the Word object, Midland Turkey Trot Logo (Figure 10–79b), which is located in the Data Files. Move it to the lower-right area of the slide. Edit the text in the flag by placing the insertion point before the number 8, typing **9,** and then deleting the number 8. Click outside the object to close the editing window.

3. On Slide 2, copy and paste the table from the Microsoft Word file called Reasons to Run (Figure 10–80c), which is located in the Data Files (Figure 10-80d) using the destination styles. Change the size of the table to 4" × 8" and then move the table to the area shown in the figure. Center the text vertically and then increase the font size of the four cells in the first column to 24 pt. Bold the text in the second column. Edit the text in the third row, right column, by typing **and scenic Downtown** after the word, parks. Add the Cool Slant cell bevel effect (fourth effect in first row) and then add the Linear Right gradient to the table.

4. If requested by your instructor, add your home address in the last row, first column of the table on Slide 2.

(a) Slide 1

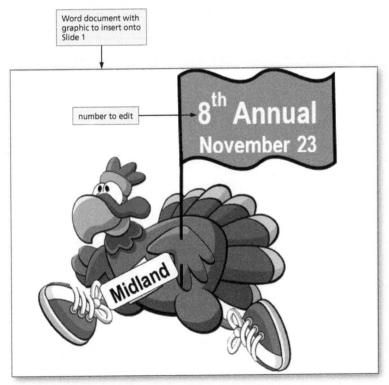

(b) Original Word Graphic

Figure 10–80 (Continued)

Continued >

In the Labs *continued*

(c) Original Word Document

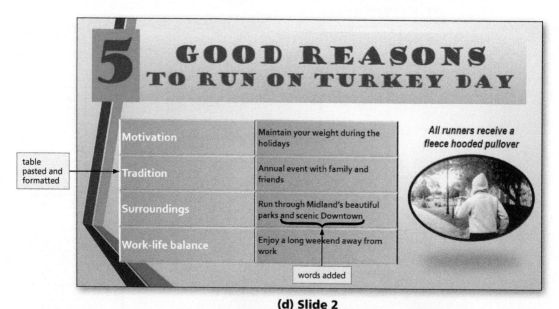

(d) Slide 2

Figure 10–80 (Continued)

5. On Slide 3 (Figure 10–80e), insert and link the Microsoft Excel table called Four Week Training Plan (Figure 10–80f), which is located in the Data Files. Unlock the aspect ratio, change the size to 4.5" × 11.5", and move it to the location shown in Figure 10–80e. For Week 4, change the running times in the Monday and Friday columns from 45 min to 50 min. Save the changes in the Excel worksheet.

6. Open the Microsoft Excel file called Last Year's Participants, which is located in the Data Files, and then copy the chart located on Sheet1 (Figure 10–80g). Paste the chart onto Slide 4 (Figure 10–80h) with the 'Use Destination Theme & Link Data' option and then resize it to 6" × 10". Switch the chart's rows and columns so the town names are listed at the bottom of the chart. Change the chart type to 3-D Column, the chart style to Style 11, the colors to Color 1.

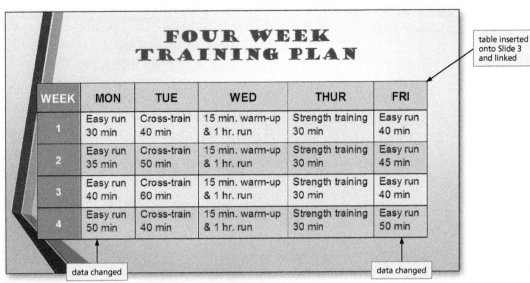

table inserted onto Slide 3 and linked

data changed

data changed

(e) Slide 3

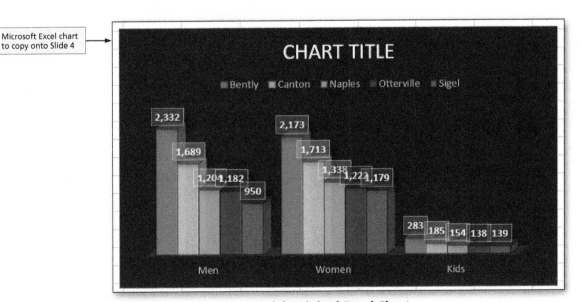

Microsoft Excel table to insert onto Slide 3

data to change

data to change

(f) Original Excel Table

Microsoft Excel chart to copy onto Slide 4

(g) Original Excel Chart

Figure 10–80 (Continued)

Continued >

In the Labs *continued*

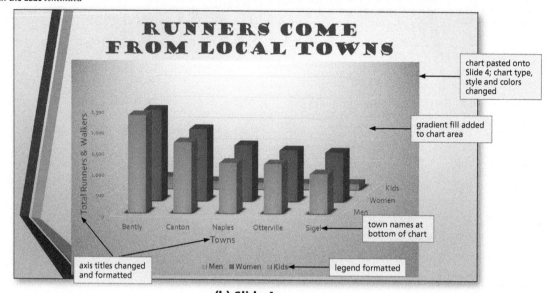

(h) Slide 4

Figure 10–80

7. Type **Total Runners & Walkers** as the vertical axis title and **Towns** as the horizontal axis title. Change the font size for both axis titles to 20 pt. Delete the chart title by displaying the CHART ELEMENTS pane and then clicking the Chart Title check box and the Data Labels check box to remove the check marks.

8. Format the chart area with the 'Top Spotlight - Accent 3' preset gradient fill (third gradient in second row). Click one of the depth axis labels (Men, Women, Kids) to select all three words, display the Home tab, and then increase the font size to 16 pt. Then, select a horizontal axis label and increase the font size to 16 point. Select all the legend items, increase the font size to 16 point, and then bold this text.

9. Align the chart in the center of the slide.

10. Apply the Clock transition in the Exciting category and then change the duration to 3.50 seconds for all slides.

11. Run the presentation and then save the file using the file name, Lab 10-1 Midland Turkey Trot. Close any open Microsoft Excel or Word files.

12. Submit the document in the format specified by your instructor.

13. ❋ Were the formatting changes you made to the Slide 2 table appropriate choices? What other changes could make the table more visually appealing? Would you choose a different chart type, chart style, or colors for the Slide 4 chart? Which Microsoft Word or Excel files would you find useful to insert in a PowerPoint presentation that you would create for your job or at school?

Lab 2: Copying and Pasting Graphics from PowerPoint and Excel Documents, Formatting a Table and a Chart, Adding a Hyperlink to a Table, and Editing Linked Files

Note: To complete this assignment, you will be required to use the Data Files. Please contact your instructor for information about accessing the Data Files.

Problem: You work for a moving and storage company, and your boss asked you to prepare a presentation to run on kiosks at both office locations. Some of the slides also will be added to the company's website. While developing content for your presentation, you learn that the most popular days to move are Friday and Saturday. You also find that approximately 40 percent of your customers moved to a new home that was located 100 miles or more from their current home. A smaller percentage of your customers — about 14 percent — moved 25 miles or less. You create the presentation shown in Figure 10–81.

Perform the following tasks:
1. Run PowerPoint. Open the presentation called Lab 10-2 Moving, which is located in the Data Files.
2. Display Slide 1 (Figure 10–81a). Open the PowerPoint presentation called, Why People Move, which is available in the Data Files, select the graphic on Slide 1, and then copy and paste it on Slide 1 of the Moving presentation. Use the SmartGuides to center the graphic below the title text.
3. On Slide 2 (Figure 10–81b), increase the table size to 5" × 11". Distribute all rows and columns. Select all text in the table and then change the font to Arial. Increase the font size of the column headings in the first row to 20 point. Increase the font size of the text in the five rows below the column headings to 18 point. Align the table in the center of the slide.
4. Change the table background shading to 'Red, Accent 2, Lighter 40%' (sixth color in fourth Theme Colors row) and then apply the Relaxed Inset cell bevel (second bevel in first Bevel row) to the table.

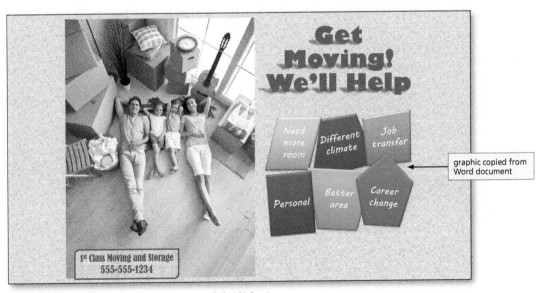

(a) Slide 1

Figure 10–81 (continued)

Continued >

In the Labs *continued*

hyperlink to display
Moving Checklist
Word document

text formatted,
background
shaded, and cell
bevel applied

(b) Slide 2

Word file hyperlinked to
word in Slide 2 table

Moving Checklist

8 to 10 weeks before

- ☐ Set a moving date
- ☐ Get estimates from 3 professional movers
- ☐ Go through the house and make a list of what you are taking
- ☐ Decide what items you can donate or discard
- ☐ Get new-resident information from your new town

6 weeks before

- ☐ Get change-of-address forms from your post office
- ☐ If moving long distance, get medical, dental, and vet records
- ☐ If necessary, transfer school records

4 weeks before

- ☐ Get packing materials, including boxes, labels, markers, tape, and bubble wrap
- ☐ Start packing and labeling items you won't need (holiday decorations & off-season clothing, etc.)
- ☐ Decide what items you may want to store in a storage facility
- ☐ Arrange baby and dog sitters for moving day

3 weeks before

- ☐ Confirm delivery of new appliances and furnishings
- ☐ Contact electric, gas, and other utilities at both locations to set off/on dates
- ☐ Take packed items to storage facility

2 weeks before

- ☐ Contact local newspaper to set up new delivery address
- ☐ Give mail and/or email change-of-address forms to post office and creditors
- ☐ Contact bank and/or credit union with change of address

1 week before

- ☐ Sort and pack legal and valuable documents that you will move personally
- ☐ Notify family and friends of your new address
- ☐ Pack and label clearly other items except for clothing and kitchen items you may need

1 day before

- ☐ Label boxes "open first" with items such as tools, cleaning supplies, and lights
- ☐ Check and replenish cash needed for payments (movers, helpers, meals, etc.)
- ☐ Clean out refrigerator and donate perishable items

(c) Hyperlinked Word File

Figure 10–81 (Continued)

(d) Excel Worksheet

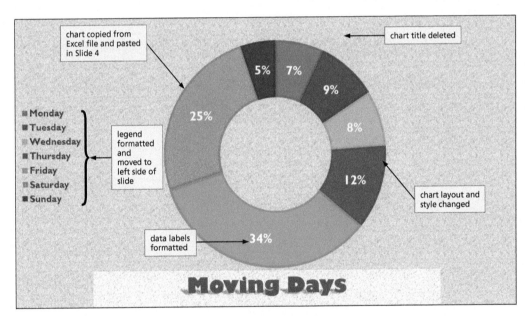

(e) Slide 3

Figure 10 – 81 (Continued)

5. On Slide 2, select the column heading, Personal, and then insert a hyperlink to the Microsoft Word file called Moving Checklist (Figure 10–81c), which is located in the Data Files.

6. If requested by your instructor, type the name of your current or previous pet after the word, Veterinarian, in the last row of the table.

7. Open the Microsoft Excel file called Moving Days, which is located in the Data Files, and then copy the chart (Figure 10–81d) located on Sheet1. Paste the chart onto Slide 3 (Figure 10–81e) with the 'Keep Source Formatting & Link Data' option and then resize

Continued >

In the Labs *continued*

(f) Original Excel Chart

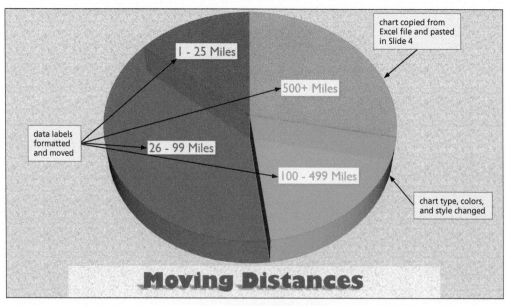

(g) Slide 4

Figure 10 – 81 (Continued)

it to 7.1" × 12". Click the Quick Layout button (Chart Tools Design tab | Chart Layouts group) and then change the layout to Layout 6. Change the chart style to Style 8.

8. Delete the chart title. Move the legend to the left side of the slide, change the font to Gill Sans MT, increase the font size to 18 point, and then bold this text. Select the data labels in the doughnut chart, change the font to Gill Sans MT, and then increase the font size to 24 point. Align the chart in the left and the top of the slide.

	A	B	
1	Distance	Customers	
2	500+ Miles	28	cell B2 figure edited
3	100 - 499 Miles	20	
4	26 - 99 Miles	38	
5	1 - 25 Miles	14	cell B3 figure edited
6			

Excel Sheet1

(h) Excel Worksheet
Figure 10–81

9. Edit the chart in Microsoft Excel by changing the figure in cell B6 (customers moving on Saturday) to 25 and the figure in cell B7 (customers moving on Sunday) to 5. Save the new values in the Moving Days worksheet.

10. Open the Microsoft Excel file called Moving Distances, which is located in the Data Files, and then copy the chart located on Sheet2 (Figure 10–81f). Paste the chart onto Slide 4 (Figure 10–81g) with the 'Keep Source Formatting & Link Data' option and then resize it to 7" × 11". Change the chart type to 3-D Pie, change the colors to Color 4 (last row in Colorful group), and then change the style to Style 2.

11. Edit the chart in Microsoft Excel by displaying Sheet1 and changing the figure in cell B2 (customers moving 500 or more miles) to 28 and the figure in cell B3 (customers moving 100 – 499 miles) to 20 (Figure 10–81h). Save the new values in the Moving Distances worksheet.

12. Change the font of the data labels to Gill Sans MT and then increase the font size to 24. Move the data labels to the locations shown in the figure. Align the chart in the center and the top of the slide.

13. Apply the Fade transition in the Subtle category and then change the duration to 2.50 seconds for all slides.

14. Run the presentation and then save the file using the file name, Lab 10-2 1st Class Moving and Storage. Close any open Microsoft Excel or Word files.

15. Submit the document in the format specified by your instructor.

16. ✸ On Slide 2, you distributed rows and columns in the table and added a shading and a bevel to the background. Did this improve the look of the table? Would a different chart type on Slide 3 better represent the moving days?

Continued >

In the Labs *continued*

Lab 3: **Consider This: Your Turn**

Design and Create a Presentation about Sodium in the Diet

Part 1:   The Extend Your Knowledge exercise in this module discusses sugar levels in popular drinks and natural sources. Nutritionists recommend monitoring sugar intake because excessive sugar can negatively affect overall health. Eating foods with high sugar levels can lead to an impaired immune system, diabetes, and obesity. High sodium levels, likewise, may cause health issues, including high blood pressure and osteoporosis. Review the tables in Figure 10–78 and then use the concepts and techniques presented in this module to create a similar presentation on the topic of sodium in your diet. Obtain information about foods with high sodium contents. Also, explore healthier alternatives, and then present this information in a table. Use at least three objectives found at the beginning of this module to develop the slides, and include at least one table. Review and revise your presentation as needed and then save the file using the file name, Lab 10-3 Sodium. Submit your assignment in the format specified by your instructor.

Part 2:   ✳ You made several decisions while creating the presentation in this assignment: where to research nutritional guidelines on sodium content, how to present this information in a table, how to format a table, and how to make the presentation look professional and consistent. What was the rationale behind each of these decisions? When you reviewed the document, what further revisions did you make and why? Where would you recommend showing this slide show?

11 | Organizing Slides and Creating a Photo Album

Objectives

You will have mastered the material in this module when you can:

- Create a section break
- Rename and reorder a section
- Create a custom slide show
- Create a photo album and add captions
- Reorder pictures in a photo album
- Adjust the quality of pictures in a photo album

- Look up information
- Change slide orientation
- Set up a custom size slide
- Copy and compress a video file
- Email a presentation
- Create a video from a presentation

Introduction

BTW
Using Photographs
A carefully selected image can convey an engaging message that your audience will remember long after the presentation has ended. One picture can evoke emotions and create a connection between the speaker and the listeners. The adage, "A picture is worth a thousand words," is relevant when audience members view PowerPoint slides.

Sharing photographs and videos has become a part of our everyday lives. We often use smartphones, digital cameras, and mobile devices, and we visit online social media websites to share our adventures, special occasions, and business activities. The presentations can be organized into sections so that particular slides are shown to specific audiences. For example, one large presentation created for freshmen orientation can be divided into one section for registration, another for financial aid, and a third for campus activities; each section could be shown to different audiences.

In addition, PowerPoint's ability to create a photo album allows you to organize and distribute your pictures by adding interesting layouts, vibrant backgrounds, and meaningful captions. These photo albums can be emailed, published to a website, or turned into a video to distribute to friends and business associates, who do not need PowerPoint installed on their computers to view your file.

Project — Presentation with Sections and a Photo Album

Iceland is a stunning country known as "The Land of Fire and Ice." Its diverse geographical regions feature forests, farmlands, volcanoes, lagoons, hot springs, and major towns. Whale watching excursions are plentiful, and visitors are apt to view a variety of marine mammals. The small Icelandic horse is a descendent of an ancient breed that lived more than one thousand years ago. Tourists also enjoy relaxing in geothermally heated water, the most famous being the Blue Lagoon. Many travel groups plan group vacations, and they welcome experts and vacationers who share insights and photos of travel destinations. Members of the Travel Club in your community have asked you to present highlights of that country during their monthly meeting at the library.

The presentation you create in this module (Figure 11–1) contains photos of Icelandic highlights. You divide the slide show into sections for Lagoons and Geysers (Figure 11–1a), Cities and Countrysides, Animals, and Glaciers. You then create a photo album, add pictures, make adjustments to brightness and contrast, and edit captions (Figures 11–1b and 11–1c). You also create a second photo album with black-and-white images (Figure 11–1d). In addition, you create two slides with a custom size to use as a marketing tool to promote your presentation at the library and insert a video file on one of the slides (Figure 11–1e). You then email the announcement file to a member and also convert another file to a video so that Travel Club members who do not have PowerPoint installed on their computers can view the Eyjafjallajokull volcano that erupted in 2010.

In this module, you will learn how to create the slides shown in Figure 11–1. The following roadmap identifies general activities you will perform as you progress through this module:

1. CREATE and ORGANIZE SECTIONS in a presentation.
2. Select specific slides to CREATE a CUSTOM SLIDE SHOW.
3. CREATE a PHOTO ALBUM and ENHANCE photo album ELEMENTS.
4. SPECIFY a CUSTOM SLIDE SIZE and ADD a VIDEO CLIP.
5. SHARE and DISTRIBUTE a PRESENTATION by emailing and creating a video.

To Run PowerPoint and Save a File

If you are using a computer to step through the project in this module and you want your screens to match the figures in this book, you should change your computer's resolution to 1366 × 768. The following steps run PowerPoint and then save a file.

1 Run PowerPoint. If necessary, maximize the PowerPoint window.

2 Open the presentation, Iceland, located in the Data Files.

3 Save the presentation using the file name, Discover Iceland.

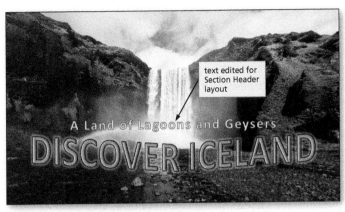

(a) Discover Iceland Section Slide

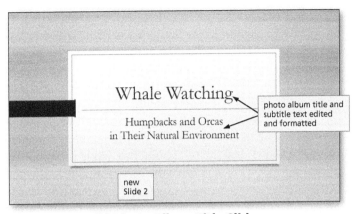

(b) Photo Album Title Slide

(c) Photo Album Slide

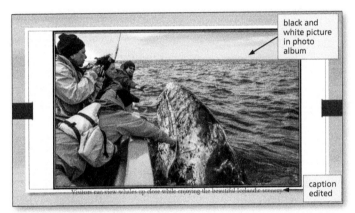

(d) Black-and-White Photo Album Slide

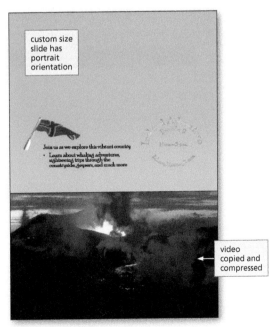

(e) Custom Size Slide

Figure 11–1

Creating Sections and a Custom Slide Show

Quality PowerPoint presentations are tailored toward specific audiences, and experienced presenters adapt the slides to meet the listeners' needs and expectations. Speakers can develop one slide show and then modify the content each time they deliver the presentation. In the Discover Iceland slide show, for example, a speaker may decide to place the slides that showcase spectacular glaciers at the end of the presentation to build suspense. Or, these slides can appear at the beginning of the presentation to generate interest.

You can divide the slides into **sections** to help organize the slides. These sections serve the same function as dividers in a notebook or tabs in a manual: They help the user find required information and move material in a new sequence. In PowerPoint, you can create sections, give them unique names, and then move slides into each section. You then can move one entire section to another part of the slide show or delete the section if it no longer is needed. Each section can be displayed or printed individually.

A **custom show** is an independent set of slides to show to a specific audience. These slides can be in a different order than in the original presentation. For example, you may desire to show a title slide, the last nine slides, and then Slides 2, 5, and 8, in that order. One PowerPoint file can have several custom shows to adapt to specific audiences.

To Insert Slides with a Section Layout

1 CREATE & ORGANIZE SECTIONS | 2 CREATE CUSTOM SLIDE SHOW | 3 CREATE PHOTO ALBUM & ENHANCE ELEMENTS | 4 SPECIFY CUSTOM SLIDE SIZE & ADD VIDEO CLIP | 5 SHARE & DISTRIBUTE PRESENTATION

Your presentation will have four sections: Lagoons and Geysers, Cities and Countrysides, Animals, and Glaciers. One of PowerPoint's layouts is named Section Header, and it is similar to the Title Slide layout because it has a title and a subtitle placeholder. To ensure consistency and save time, you can create one slide with a Section Header layout and then duplicate and modify it for each section. *Why? You can help your audience understand the organization of your slide show if you have one slide announcing the content of each section.* The following steps insert the four section slides.

1

- With Slide 1 selected and the Home tab displaying, click the New Slide arrow (Home tab | Slides group) to display the Office Theme gallery (Figure 11–2).

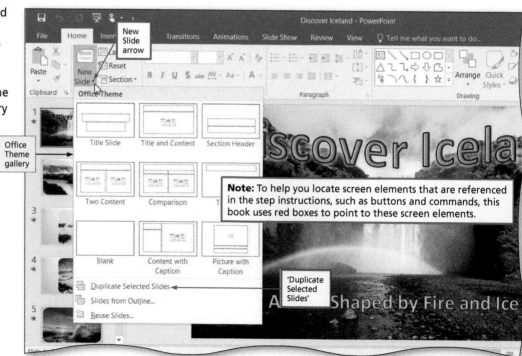

Figure 11–2

2

- Click 'Duplicate Selected Slides' in the Office Theme gallery to create a new Slide 2 that is a duplicate of Slide 1.

- Click the Slide Layout button (Home tab | Slides group) to display the Office Theme layout gallery (Figure 11–3).

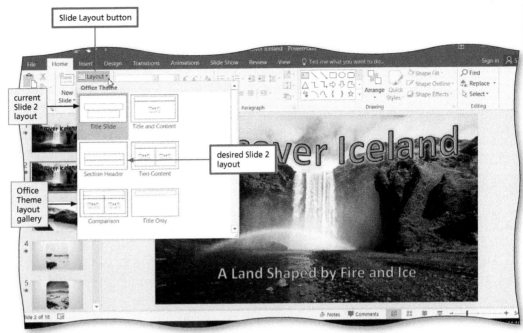

Figure 11–3

3

- Click the Section Header layout to apply that layout to the new Slide 2 (Figure 11–4).

Figure 11–4

Other Ways

1. Right-click Slide 1, click Duplicate Slide on shortcut menu; then right-click Slide 2, click Layout on shortcut menu

To Edit the Subtitle

The slide with the Section Header layout should have characteristics similar to the title slide to give the presentation continuity. One method of slightly altering the title slide is to change the text to reflect the next set of slides in the presentation. The following steps edit the subtitle text.

1 With Slide 2 displaying, select the words, Shaped by Fire and Ice, in the subtitle text placeholder and then type `of Lagoons and Geysers` as the replacement text.

2 Select all the subtitle text, change the font size to 36 point, click the Character Spacing button (Home tab | Font group), and then change the character spacing to Loose.

3 Center this text in the placeholder and then change the subtitle text font color to 'Tan, Background 2' (third color in first Theme Colors row) (Figure 11–5).

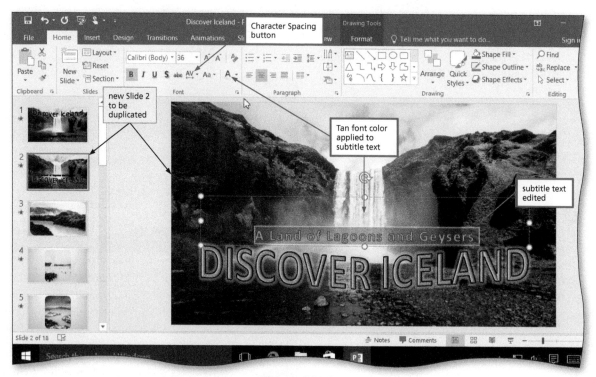

Figure 11–5

To Duplicate and Edit the Section Slides

Slide 2 is formatted appropriately to display at the beginning of the Lagoons and Geysers section of the slide show. A similar slide should display at the beginning of the Cities and Countrysides, Animals, and Glaciers sections. The following steps duplicate Slide 2 and edit the title text.

1 With Slide 2 selected and the Home tab displaying, click the New Slide arrow and then click 'Duplicate Selected Slides'.

2 Repeat Step 1 twice to insert two additional duplicate slides.

3 Display Slide 3, select the words, Lagoons and Geysers, and then type `Cities and Countrysides` in the subtitle text placeholder.

4 Display Slide 4, select the words, Lagoons and Geysers, and then type `Animals` in the subtitle text placeholder.

5 Display Slide 5, select the words, Lagoons and Geysers, and then type `Glaciers` in the subtitle text placeholder (Figure 11–6).

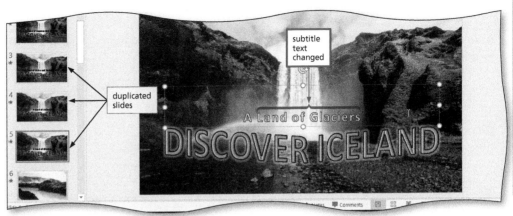

Figure 11–6

To Arrange Slides in Slide Sorter View

1 CREATE & ORGANIZE SECTIONS | **2 CREATE CUSTOM SLIDE SHOW** | **3 CREATE PHOTO ALBUM & ENHANCE ELEMENTS**
4 SPECIFY CUSTOM SLIDE SIZE & ADD VIDEO CLIP | **5 SHARE & DISTRIBUTE PRESENTATION**

The four slides with a Section Header layout currently are displayed after the title slide. They are followed by 16 slides grouped into four categories, each of which has a distinct photo style or effect and background. The Lagoons and Geysers slides have photos with a rounded border and a green background, the Cities and Countrysides slides have photos with a green border and a patterned background, the Animal photos have soft edges and a grass photo background, and Glaciers photos have a bevel effect and a water background. One of the four section slides you formatted should be positioned at the beginning of each category. When the presentation has only a few slides, you easily can drag and drop the slide thumbnails in the Slides pane. Your Discover Iceland presentation, however, has 21 slides. The following steps arrange the slides in Slide Sorter view. *Why? To easily arrange the slides, you can change to Slide Sorter view and drag and drop the thumbnails into their desired locations.*

1
- Click the Slide Sorter view button to display the slides in Slide Sorter view and then click the Slide 3 thumbnail (A Land of Cities and Countrysides) to select it.

- Drag the Zoom slider to the left to change the zoom percentage to 30% so that all the slides are displayed (Figure 11–7).

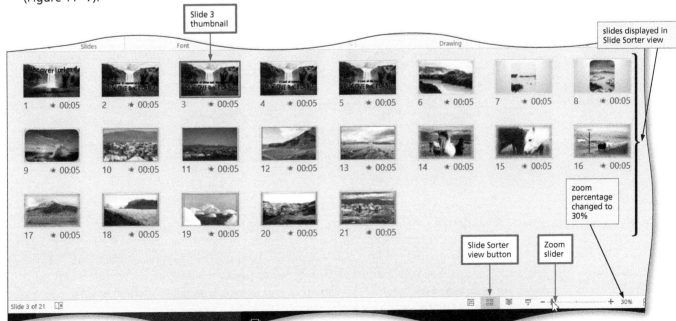

Figure 11–7

②

• Drag the Slide 3 thumbnail between the Slide 9 and Slide 10 thumbnails so that it is positioned in the desired location between these two slides (Figure 11–8).

Figure 11–8

③

• Release the mouse button to display the Slide 3 thumbnail in a new location as Slide 9.

• Select the new Slide 3 (A Land of Animals) and drag it between Slide 13 and Slide 14.

• Select the new Slide 3 (A Land of Glaciers) and drag it between Slide 17 and Slide 18 (Figure 11–9).

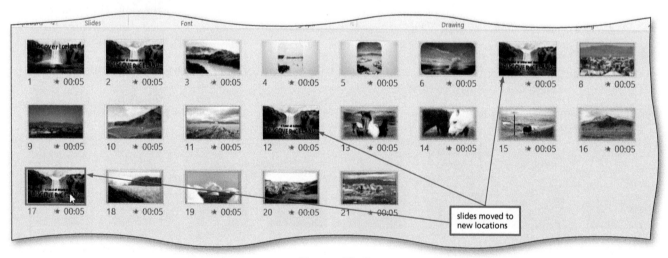

Figure 11–9

To Create a Section Break

1 CREATE & ORGANIZE SECTIONS | 2 CREATE CUSTOM SLIDE SHOW | 3 CREATE PHOTO ALBUM & ENHANCE ELEMENTS
4 SPECIFY CUSTOM SLIDE SIZE & ADD VIDEO CLIP | 5 SHARE & DISTRIBUTE PRESENTATION

The slides in the presentation are divided into four categories: Lagoons and Geysers, Cities and Countrysides, Animals, and Glaciers. You can create a section break to organize slides into a particular group. *Why? At times, you may want to display slides from one particular category or move a section of slides to another part of the presentation.* The following steps create five sections in the presentation.

1

• In Slide Sorter view, position the pointer between Slide 1 and Slide 2 and then click once to display the vertical bar (Figure 11–10).

Q&A I am using a touch screen. When I tap between the slides to display the vertical bar, a shortcut menu also displays with an Add Section button. Can I just tap that button instead of using the Home tab Section button?

Yes.

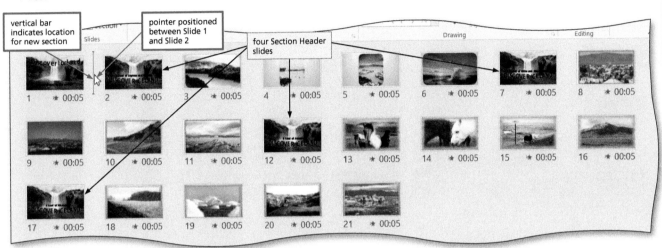

Figure 11–10

2

• With the Home tab displaying, click the Section button (Home tab | Slides group) to display the Section menu (Figure 11–11).

Figure 11–11

3

• Click Add Section in the menu to create a section with the name, Untitled Section.

• Position the pointer between Slide 6 and Slide 7, which is the start of the slides with the Cities and Countrysides photos, and then click once to display the vertical bar (Figure 11–12).

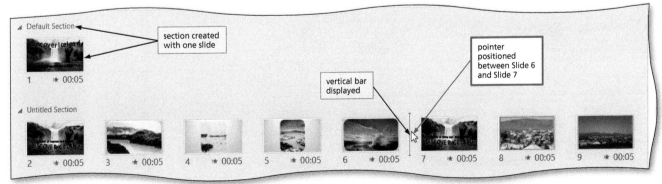

Figure 11–12

4

- Click the Section button (Home tab | Slides group) to display the Section menu and then click Add Section in the menu to create a section with the name, Untitled Section.

- Position the pointer between Slide 11 and Slide 12, which is the start of the slides with animal photos, and then click once (Figure 11–13).

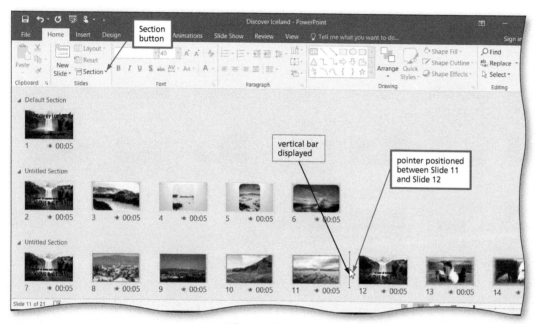

Figure 11–13

5

- Click the Section button and then click Add Section in the menu to create a section with the name, Untitled Section.

- Scroll down to display the final slides in the presentation, position the pointer between Slide 16 and Slide 17, and then create a section (Figure 11–14).

Figure 11–14

To Rename a Section

The default section names, Untitled and Default, do not identify the content of the slides in the group. The following steps rename each of the five sections in the presentation. *Why? Giving each section a unique name helps to categorize the slides easily.*

1

• With the last section featuring the glacier photos selected and the Home tab displaying, click the Section button (Home tab | Slides group) to display the Section menu (Figure 11–15).

Q&A

If the Glaciers section is not highlighted, how can I select it? Click the divider between the sections. You will know the section is selected when the thumbnails have a red border and the text and slide numbers have a red font color.

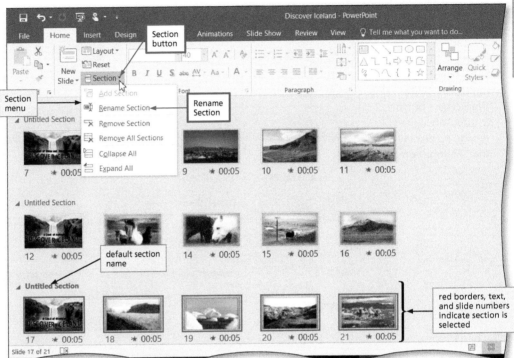

Figure 11–15

2

• Click Rename Section in the menu to display the Rename Section dialog box.

• Type **Glaciers** in the Section name box (Figure 11–16).

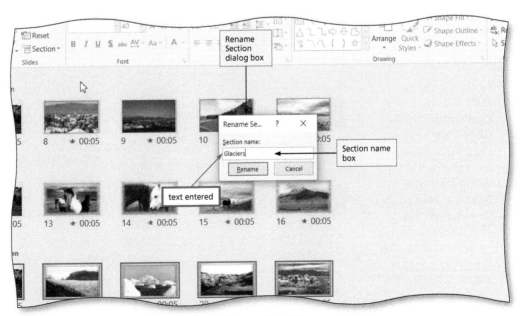

Figure 11–16

3

- Click the Rename button (Rename Section dialog box) to change the section name.

- Click the Untitled Section divider for the Animals section (Slide 12 through Slide 16) to select it and then click the Section button (Home tab | Slides group) to display the Section menu (Figure 11–17).

Figure 11–17

4

- Click Rename Section to display the Rename Section dialog box, type **Animals** in the Section name box, and then click the Rename button to change the section name.

- Select the divider for the Cities and Countrysides section (Slide 7 through Slide 11), display the Rename Section dialog box, type **Cities and Countrysides** as the new section name, and then click the Rename button (Figure 11–18).

Figure 11–18

⑤

- Scroll up to display the first two sections, select the divider for the Lagoons and Geysers slides (Slide 2 through Slide 6), display the Rename Section dialog box, type `Lagoons and Geysers` as the new section name, and then click the Rename button.

- Select the Default Section divider for Slide 1, display the Rename Section dialog box, type `Discover Iceland Title` as the new section name, and then click the Rename button (Figure 11–19).

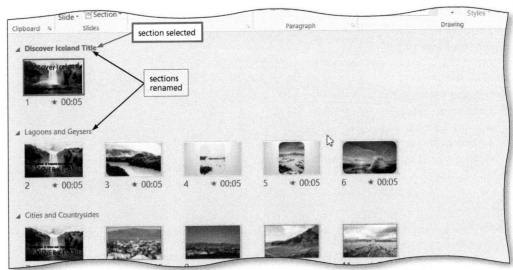

Figure 11–19

Other Ways

1. Right-click section divider, click Rename Section on shortcut menu

---

To Collapse and Reorder Sections

1 CREATE & ORGANIZE SECTIONS | 2 CREATE CUSTOM SLIDE SHOW | 3 CREATE PHOTO ALBUM & ENHANCE ELEMENTS
4 SPECIFY CUSTOM SLIDE SIZE & ADD VIDEO CLIP | 5 SHARE & DISTRIBUTE PRESENTATION

Why? *Travel Club members have expressed much more interest this year in animals than the cities and countryside landscape, so you want to change the order of these two sets of slides in your presentation.* When slides are organized into sections, it is easy to change the order in which the sections display. Because your presentation consists of multiple sections, you can collapse the sections so that only the section titles are displayed. You then can reorder the sections and expand the sections. The following steps collapse the sections, reorder the Animals and Cities and Countrysides sections, and expand the sections.

①

- With the first section, Discover Iceland Title, selected and the Home tab displaying, click the Section button (Home tab | Slides group) to display the Section menu (Figure 11–20).

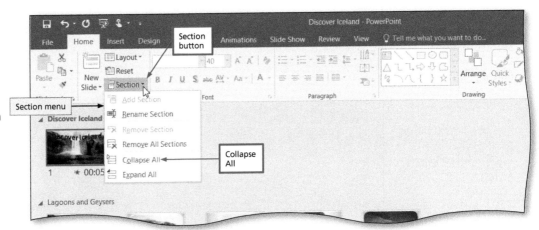

Q&A

Can I remove a section?

Yes. To delete one section, select the section title and then click Remove Section in the Section menu. To remove all sections, display the Section menu and then click 'Remove All Sections'.

Figure 11–20

2

- Click Collapse All in the Section menu to display only the section names.

- Click the Animals section name to select it and then drag the section upward between the Lagoons and Geysers and the Cities and Countrysides sections (Figure 11–21).

Figure 11–21

3

- Release the mouse button to move the Animals section between the Lagoons and Geysers and Cities and Countrysides sections.

- Click the Section button (Home tab | Slides group) to display the Section menu (Figure 11–22).

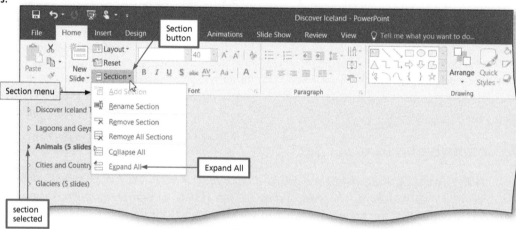

Figure 11–22

4

- Click Expand All in the Section menu to display all the slides in their corresponding sections (Figure 11–23).

5

- Run the presentation to display all the slides in the desired order.

Figure 11–23

Other Ways

1. Right-click section name, click Move Section Up, Move Section Down, Collapse All, or Expand All on shortcut menu

To Show a Presentation with Manual Timing

The Discover Iceland slides are set to display for specified times. If you desire to override the automatic timings and advance the slides manually, you would perform the following steps.

1. Display the Slide Show tab and then click the 'Set Up Slide Show' button (Slide Show tab | Set Up group) to display the Set Up Show dialog box.

2. Click Manually in the Advance slides area (Set Up Show dialog box) and then click the OK button.

Break Point: If you wish to take a break, this is a good place to do so. Be sure to save the Discover Iceland file again and then you can exit PowerPoint. To resume at a later time, run PowerPoint, open the file called Discover Iceland, and continue following the steps from this location forward.

To Create a Custom Slide Show

1 CREATE & ORGANIZE SECTIONS | 2 CREATE CUSTOM SLIDE SHOW | 3 CREATE PHOTO ALBUM & ENHANCE ELEMENTS
4 SPECIFY CUSTOM SLIDE SIZE & ADD VIDEO CLIP | 5 SHARE & DISTRIBUTE PRESENTATION

Many presenters deliver their speeches in front of targeted audiences. For example, the director of human resources may present one set of slides for new employees, another set for potential retirees, and a third for managers concerned with new regulations and legislation. Slides for all these files may be contained in one file, and the presenter can elect to show particular slides to accompany specific speeches. PowerPoint allows you to create a **custom show** that displays only selected slides. The following steps create a custom show. *Why? You want to create a smaller file in case your speech time at the library is less than planned and you need to shorten your talk.*

- Click the Normal view button to display the slides in Normal view and then display the Slide Show tab.

- Click the 'Custom Slide Show' button (Slide Show tab | Start Slide Show group) to display the Custom Slide Show menu (Figure 11–24).

Figure 11–24

- Click Custom Shows to open the Custom Shows dialog box (Figure 11–25).

Figure 11–25

- Click the New button (Custom Shows dialog box) to display the Define Custom Show dialog box.

- Click '1. Discover Iceland' in the 'Slides in presentation' area to place a check mark in the check box and select this slide (Figure 11–26).

Figure 11–26

- Click the Add button (Define Custom Show dialog box) to add this slide to the 'Slides in custom show' area.

- Scroll down and then click the check boxes for Slide 3, Slide 6, Slide 9, Slide 11, Slide 13, Slide 14, Slide 19, and Slide 21 in the 'Slides in presentation' area.

- Click the Add button (Define Custom Show dialog box) to add these slides to the 'Slides in custom show' area (Figure 11–27).

Figure 11–27

• Select the text in the 'Slide show name' text box (Define Custom Show dialog box) and then type **Popular Iceland Attractions** as the new name (Figure 11–28).

Figure 11–28

• Click the OK button (Define Custom Show dialog box) to create the new Popular Iceland Attractions custom show and display the Custom Shows dialog box (Figure 11–29).

• Click the Close button (Custom Shows dialog box) to close the dialog box.

Figure 11–29

To Open and Edit a Custom Slide Show

1 CREATE & ORGANIZE SECTIONS | 2 CREATE CUSTOM SLIDE SHOW | **3 CREATE PHOTO ALBUM & ENHANCE ELEMENTS**
4 SPECIFY CUSTOM SLIDE SIZE & ADD VIDEO CLIP | 5 SHARE & DISTRIBUTE PRESENTATION

A PowerPoint file can have several custom slide shows. You can elect to display one of them at any time depending upon the particular needs of your audience. If you need to reorder the slides, you can change the sequence easily. The following steps open a custom show and edit the slide sequence.

1

- With the Slide Show tab displaying, click the 'Custom Slide Show' button (Slide Show tab | Start Slide Show group) to display the Custom Slide Show menu (Figure 11–30).

Q&A Why does 'Popular Iceland Attractions' display in the Custom Slide Show menu?

The names of any custom shows will be displayed in the menu. If desired, you could click this custom show name to run the slide show and display the selected slides.

Figure 11–30

2

- Click Custom Shows to display the Custom Shows dialog box (Figure 11–31).

Figure 11–31

3

- With the Popular Iceland Attractions custom show selected in the Custom shows area, click the Edit button (Custom Shows dialog box) to display the Define Custom Show dialog box.

- Click '8. Slide 19' in the 'Slides in custom show' area to select it (Figure 11–32).

Figure 11–32

- Click the Up button six times to move Slide 19 below Slide 1 as the second slide in the custom show (Figure 11–33).

Figure 11–33

- Click '9. Slide 21' in the 'Slides in custom show' area to select it and then click the Up button six times to move Slide 21 below Slide 19 as the third slide in the custom show.

- Click '6. Slide 9' in the 'Slides in custom show' area to select it and then click the Down button once to move Slide 9 below Slide 11 as the seventh slide in the custom show (Figure 11–34).

Q&A Can I move the slides so they display later in the custom show? Yes. Select the slide you want to reorder and then click the Down button.

Figure 11–34

- Click the OK button (Define Custom Show dialog box) to create the revised Popular Iceland Attractions custom show and display the Custom Shows dialog box (Figure 11–35).

Figure 11–35

- Click the Show button (Custom Shows dialog box) to run the Popular Iceland Attractions custom show.

- When all the slides have displayed, exit the custom show.

- Save the Discover Iceland file. Do not close this file because you are going to use it later in this project.

Use photographs with sharp focus and contrast.

Clear, sharp pictures provide details that draw an audience into your presentation. High-quality photographs impress your audience and state that you have an eye for detail and take pride in your work. When your slides are projected on a large screen, any imperfection is magnified, so you must take care to select photographs that are in focus and have high contrast.

Creating a Photo Album

A PowerPoint **photo album** is a presentation that contains pictures to share with friends and business colleagues. It can contain a theme, a vibrant background, custom captions, a specific layout, frames around pictures, and boxes. You can enhance the quality of the pictures by increasing or decreasing brightness and contrast, and you can rotate the pictures in 90-degree increments. You also can change color pictures to display in black and white.

You can share your photo album in a variety of ways. You can, for example, email the file, publish it to the web, or print the pictures as handouts.

BTW

Printing in Grayscale

In this project you will convert your photos from color to black and white. If you desire to keep your images in color but you do not have a color printer or do not require a color printout, choosing Grayscale will print all the slide objects in shades of gray. In grayscale, some objects on the slides will appear crisper and cleaner than if you choose the Color option on a non-color printer. Click File on the ribbon to open the Backstage view, click the Print tab in the Backstage view to display the Print pane, click the Color button in the Settings area, click Grayscale, and then click the Print button. If you then want to print in color, click the Grayscale button and then click Color.

To Start a Photo Album and Add Pictures

1 CREATE & ORGANIZE SECTIONS | 2 CREATE CUSTOM SLIDE SHOW | **3 CREATE PHOTO ALBUM & ENHANCE ELEMENTS**
4 SPECIFY CUSTOM SLIDE SIZE & ADD VIDEO CLIP | 5 SHARE & DISTRIBUTE PRESENTATION

Why? Once you have gathered files of digital pictures, you can begin building a photo album. You initially create the album and then later enhance its appearance. The following steps start a photo album and add pictures.

- Display the Insert tab and then click the 'New Photo Album' button (Insert tab | Images group) to display the Photo Album dialog box (Figure 11–36).

Why am I viewing a menu with the 'New Photo Album' and 'Edit Photo Album' commands instead of the Photo Album dialog box?
You mistakenly clicked the 'New Photo Album' arrow instead of the 'New Photo Album' button.

Figure 11–36

2

- Click the File/Disk button to display the Insert New Pictures dialog box.

- If necessary, navigate to the location where your Data Files are stored (Figure 11–37).

Figure 11–37

3

- If necessary, click the 'Change your view.' arrow, which has the ScreenTip, More options, on the toolbar (Insert New Pictures dialog box) to display the view settings (Figure 11–38).

Figure 11–38

BTW

Selecting Slides or Other Items

To select sequential or adjacent files or items, select the first item, press and hold down the SHIFT key, and then select the last item. All items between the first and last item will be highlighted. To select nonadjacent files or items, select the first item and then press and hold down the CTRL key. While holding down the CTRL key, select additional items.

- If necessary, click List in the view settings to change the view setting and display only the picture file names.

- Click on the left side of the Whale Head icon to select the file name and then select the file names Whale Mouth, Whale Pectoral, Whale Sunset, Whale Tail, Whale Town, and Whale Watching as additional files to insert (Figure 11–39).

Figure 11–39

If I mistakenly select a file name, how can I remove the selection?
Click the file name again to remove the check mark.

I'm using a touch screen and am having trouble selecting multiple files. What can I do?
You may need to use a mouse in combination with the onscreen keyboard CTRL key, or you can select and insert each file individually.

- Click the Insert button (Insert New Pictures dialog box) to add the pictures to the album.

To Reorder Pictures in a Photo Album

PowerPoint inserted the pictures in alphabetical order, which may not be the desired sequence for your album. You easily can change the order of the pictures in the same manner that you change the slide order in a custom show. The following steps reorder the photo album pictures. *Why? Showing the town of Husavik at the beginning of the presentation orientates your audience members to the area where many of the whaling excursions begin.*

- Click the check box for the sixth picture, Whale Town, to select it (Figure 11–40).

Figure 11–40

2

- Click the Move Up button five times to move the Whale Town photo upward so that it now is the first picture (picture 1) in the album.

Q&A I clicked the Move Up button, but the photo is not moving. What should I do?
Be patient. The photo eventually will move.

- Click the Whale Town check box to remove the check mark.

3

- Select the fifth picture, Whale Sunset, and then click the Move Down button two times to move this picture downward so that it now is the last picture (picture 7) in the album.

- Click the Whale Sunset check box to remove the check mark (Figure 11–41).

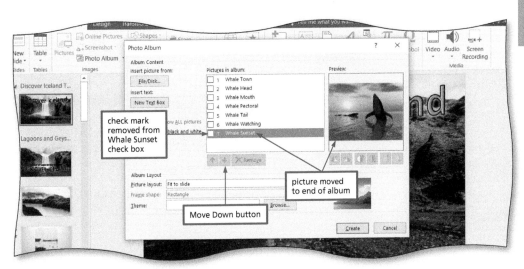

Figure 11–41

To Adjust the Rotation of a Photo Album Image

1 CREATE & ORGANIZE SECTIONS | 2 CREATE CUSTOM SLIDE SHOW | 3 CREATE PHOTO ALBUM & ENHANCE ELEMENTS
4 SPECIFY CUSTOM SLIDE SIZE & ADD VIDEO CLIP | 5 SHARE & DISTRIBUTE PRESENTATION

Digital images have either a portrait (vertical) or landscape (horizontal) orientation. If a picture is displayed in your album with the wrong orientation, you can rotate the image in 90-degree increments to the left or the right. The following steps rotate a photo album picture. *Why? The photo of the whale will be more dramatic if the mouth is facing the audience members.*

- Click the check box for the third picture, Whale Mouth, to select it and display a preview (Figure 11–42).

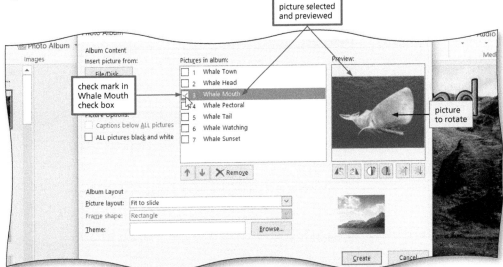

Figure 11–42

2

- Click the 'Rotate Right 90°' button (Photo Album dialog box) to turn the picture to the right (Figure 11–43).

3

- Click the Whale Mouth check box to remove the check mark.

Figure 11–43

To Adjust the Contrast of a Photo Album Image

1 CREATE & ORGANIZE SECTIONS | 2 CREATE CUSTOM SLIDE SHOW | 3 CREATE PHOTO ALBUM & ENHANCE ELEMENTS
4 SPECIFY CUSTOM SLIDE SIZE & ADD VIDEO CLIP | 5 SHARE & DISTRIBUTE PRESENTATION

A picture you insert may need correcting to enhance its visual appeal. You can adjust the difference between the darkest and lightest areas of the picture by increasing or decreasing the contrast. The following steps adjust the contrast of a photo album picture. **Why?** *The Whale Head photo lacks contrast and has many light areas. It would be more dramatic if it had a wide variety of dark and light regions.*

1

- Click the check box for the second picture, Whale Head, to select it and display a preview (Figure 11–44).

2

- Click the Increase Contrast button (Photo Album dialog box) four times to increase the contrast of this picture.

Figure 11–44

To Adjust the Brightness of a Photo Album Image

If a picture in the photo album is too light or too dark, you can adjust its brightness to enhance its appearance. The following step adjusts the brightness of a photo album picture. *Why? The Whale Head photo is somewhat light, so decreasing the brightness would help the colors stand out on the slide and give more depth to the image.*

- With the Whale Head picture selected, click the Decrease Brightness button (Photo Album dialog box) two times to intensify the colors in the picture (Figure 11–45).

- Click the Whale Head check box to remove the check mark.

Figure 11–45

To Change a Photo Album Layout

PowerPoint inserts each photo album picture so that it fills, or fits, one entire slide. You can modify this layout to display two or four pictures on a slide, display a title, or add white space between the image and the slide edges. You also can add a white or black frame around the perimeter of each picture. The following steps change an album layout. *Why? The photos are spectacular, so you want to display only one on each slide. Adding a frame provides contrast between the photos and the background.*

- With the Photo Album dialog box displayed, click the Picture layout arrow in the Album Layout area (Photo Album dialog box) to display the Picture layout list (Figure 11–46).

Figure 11–46

- Click 1 picture in the Picture layout list to change the layout so that one picture is displayed on each slide and a rectangular frame is displayed around each picture.

- Click the Frame shape arrow in the Album Layout area (Photo Album dialog box) to display the Frame shape list (Figure 11–47).

Figure 11–47

- Click 'Simple Frame, White' in the Frame shape list to add a white frame around the picture.

To Add a Photo Album Theme

1 CREATE & ORGANIZE SECTIONS | 2 CREATE CUSTOM SLIDE SHOW | 3 CREATE PHOTO ALBUM & ENHANCE ELEMENTS
4 SPECIFY CUSTOM SLIDE SIZE & ADD VIDEO CLIP | 5 SHARE & DISTRIBUTE PRESENTATION

The themes that are used to design a presentation also are available to add to a photo album. These themes determine the colors and fonts that complement each other and increase the visual appeal of the slides. The following steps add a theme to the photo album. *Why? The photos feature outdoor scenes, so you want to select a theme that has natural colors and a simple layout and font that will complement the majestic photos.*

- Click the Browse button in the Album Layout area (Photo Album dialog box) to display the Choose Theme dialog box.

- Click Organic in the theme list to select this theme (Figure 11–48).

- Click the Select button (Choose Theme dialog box) to apply this theme to the presentation.

Figure 11–48

To Add Captions below All Pictures

If you desire a caption below each picture, you can request PowerPoint add this feature to the slides. The file name is displayed as the caption text, but you can edit and add effects to this text. The following step selects the option to add a caption below all pictures in the photo album. *Why? The audience members will see the text on the slide and hear you describe the images. Because they are using these two senses, they should be able to recall the information you are presenting. In addition, absent Travel Club members could view the presentation during their free time and learn the names of the places and objects presented on the slides.*

- In the Picture Options area (Photo Album dialog box), click the 'Captions below ALL pictures' check box to select the check box (Figure 11–49).

Figure 11–49

To Create a Photo Album

Once you have inserted the pictures, determined the picture sequence, layout, and frame shape, you are ready to make the photo album. *Why? You have specified all the information PowerPoint needs to create this album.* The following step creates the photo album.

- Click the Create button (Photo Album dialog box) to close the dialog box and create a photo album with a title slide and seven pictures (Figure 11–50).

Figure 11–50

Why does a particular name display below the Photo Album title?

PowerPoint displays the user name that was entered when the program was installed. To see this name, display the Backstage view, click Options to display the PowerPoint Options dialog box, and then view or change the name entered in the User name box in the Personalize your copy of Microsoft Office area.

To Edit a Photo Album

1 CREATE & ORGANIZE SECTIONS | 2 CREATE CUSTOM SLIDE SHOW | 3 CREATE PHOTO ALBUM & ENHANCE ELEMENTS
4 SPECIFY CUSTOM SLIDE SIZE & ADD VIDEO CLIP | 5 SHARE & DISTRIBUTE PRESENTATION

Once you review the photo album PowerPoint creates, you can modify the contents by adding and deleting pictures, changing the layout and frames, and adding transitions. The following steps edit the photo album. *Why? You want to change the frame style and color, add a text box on a new slide, and add a transition to add interest and to give additional information to your audience members.*

1

- Display the Insert tab and then click the 'New Photo Album' arrow (Insert tab | Images group) to display the New Photo Album menu (Figure 11–51).

Figure 11–51

2

- Click 'Edit Photo Album' in the menu to display the Edit Photo Album dialog box.

- Click the Frame shape arrow to display the Frame shape list and then click 'Compound Frame, Black' in the list to change the frame from a single white border to a double black border.

- Click the 'New Text Box' button (Edit Photo Album dialog box) to insert a new slide in the album with the name, Text Box.

- Click the Text Box check box and then click the Move Up button once to move this picture upward as the first slide in the 'Pictures in album' list (Figure 11–52).

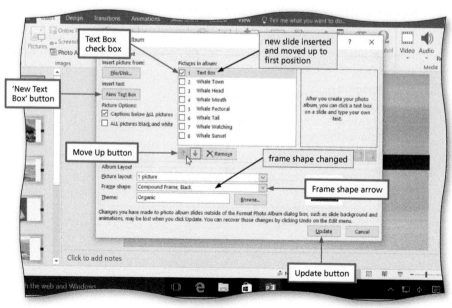

Figure 11–52

Q&A Can I insert a text box on a slide that already has a picture?

Yes. Click the Text Box button (Insert tab | Text group) and then click the slide where you want to insert the box. You then can arrange the box and picture on the slide.

3

- Click the Update button (Edit Photo Album dialog box) to make the changes to the photo album.

- Apply the Cube transition and then change the duration to 03.00 seconds for all slides.

To Insert and Format Text in a Photo Album

PowerPoint inserts text into the slides, such as the file name for captions and the user name associated with the Microsoft Office installation as the subtitle text on the title slide. You can revise and format this text by changing the font, font size, color, and any other font styles and effects. The following steps edit text in the photo album.

1 With Slide 1 displaying, select the title text, Photo Album, and then type **Whale Watching** as the replacement text.

2 Select the subtitle text, by [Student Name], type **Humpbacks and Orcas** as the first paragraph, press the SHIFT+ENTER keys, and then type **in Their Natural Environment** as the second paragraph replacement text.

3 Increase the font size of the subtitle text to 32 point.

4 Display Slide 2, select the words, Text Box, and then type **Husavik is Iceland's whale watching capital. Guests board traditional oak ships and sail into Skjalfandi Bay.** as the replacement text.

5 Press the ENTER key two times and then type **The best time to see the marine mammals in the cold Arctic waters is from April through September.** as the second paragraph.

6 Display Slide 3, select the caption text, and then type **Silica once was a major export of the whaling town, Husavik.** as the new caption.

7 Display Slide 8, select the caption text, and then type **Visitors can view whales up close while enjoying the beautiful Icelandic scenery.** as the new caption.

8 Display Slide 1 and then run the slide show.

9 Save the presentation with the file name, Whale Watching Photo Album (Figure 11–53).

BTW

Resetting Placeholders
You can reset all customization changes to the preset options. Click the Reset button (Home tab | Slides group) or right-click the slide or thumbnail and then click Reset Slide on the shortcut menu. To retain custom formatting changes and move the placeholders to their original locations, click the Layout button (Home tab | Slides group) or right-click the slide or thumbnail and then click Layout on the shortcut menu. Then, reapply the active layout from the Layout gallery.

BTW
Distributing a Document
Instead of printing and distributing a hard copy of a document, you can distribute the document electronically. Options include sending the document via email; posting it on cloud storage (such as OneDrive) and sharing the file with others; posting it on social media, a blog, or other website; and sharing a link associated with an online location of the document. You also can create and share a PDF or XPS image of the document, so that users can view the file in Acrobat Reader or XPS Viewer instead of in PowerPoint.

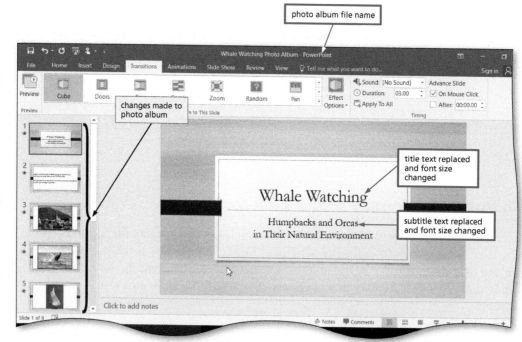

Figure 11–53

To Create Black-and-White Images in a Photo Album

1 CREATE & ORGANIZE SECTIONS | 2 CREATE CUSTOM SLIDE SHOW | 3 CREATE PHOTO ALBUM & ENHANCE ELEMENTS
4 SPECIFY CUSTOM SLIDE SIZE & ADD VIDEO CLIP | 5 SHARE & DISTRIBUTE PRESENTATION

Why? *Black-and-white pictures often generate interest and give a unique version of the color photographs. The series of shades ranging from black to white, or grayscale, provide a different perspective of our world.* The following steps edit a photo album to use black-and-white images.

1

- Display the Insert tab, click the 'New Photo Album' arrow, and then click 'Edit Photo Album'.

- Click the 'ALL pictures black and white' check box to select the check box (Figure 11–54).

Q&A Can I change the view to see my slides in grayscale or black and white?
Yes. Display the View tab and then click the Grayscale or the 'Black and White' button (Color /Grayscale group). The Grayscale option shows a variety of shades ranging from white to black whereas the 'Black and White' option displays only black-and-white objects.

Figure 11–54

2

- Click the Update button (Edit Photo Album dialog box) to change the photographs from color to black-and-white images on the slides.

- Run the slide show.

- Save the presentation with the file name, Whale Watching Photo Album Black and White.

- Print the presentation as a handout with three slides per page (Figure 11–55).

(a) Handout Page 1

(b) Handout Page 2

(c) Handout Page 3

Figure 11–55

BTW

Conserving Ink and Toner

If you want to conserve ink or toner, you can instruct PowerPoint to print draft quality documents by clicking File on the ribbon to open the Backstage view, clicking the Options tab in the Backstage view to display the PowerPoint Options dialog box, clicking Advanced in the left pane (PowerPoint Options dialog box), scrolling to the Print area in the right pane, placing a check mark in the 'Use draft quality' check box, and then clicking the OK button. Then, use the Backstage view to print the document as usual.

To Look Up Information

You can search for information regarding a wide variety of topics using PowerPoint's reference materials. If you are connected to the Internet, you can use the Insights task pane. The Explore tab provides reference information, including images and articles. The Define tab displays a definition and word origin. The following steps use the Insights task pane to locate material about a word. **Why?** *You want to know more about the word, silica, which you typed as part of the Slide 3 caption text.*

1

- Display Slide 3 and then select the word, Silica, in the caption.

- Display the Review tab and then click the Smart Lookup button (Review tab | Insights group) to display the Insights task pane.

- If necessary, click the Got it button in response to the "We value your privacy" message to allow Microsoft to send information to Bing regarding your search.

- If necessary, click the Explore tab (Figure 11–56).

Q&A Why does my Insights task pane look different?
Depending on your settings, your Insights task pane may appear different from the figure shown here.

What is Bing?
It is the name of Microsoft's search engine, which is a program that locates websites, webpages, images, videos, news, maps, and other information related to a specific topic.

Figure 11–56

2

In the Insights task pane, read the Wikipedia opening paragraphs about silica, also called silicon dioxide, and then scroll down to see photos of this chemical compound and to view articles discussing this material (Figure 11–57).

Q&A Can I view additional articles and images?
Yes. Click the More link at the end of each research section to locate more information on the search topic.

Figure 11–57

- Click the Define tab in the Insights task pane and then scroll up to display the definition and the origin of the word, silica.

- Click the speaker icon to hear the correct pronunciation of this word (Figure 11–58).

Q&A Can I copy information from the Insights task pane into my slides? Yes, you can use the Copy and Paste commands to insert the text. Be certain, however, that you do not plagiarize this material.

Figure 11–58

- Click the Close button in the Insights task pane.

To Close a Presentation

The second photo album with the black-and-white pictures is complete. The following step closes the Whale Watching Photo Album Black and White file.

1 Open the Backstage view and then click Close to close the open Whale Watching Photo Album Black and White file without exiting PowerPoint.

Break Point: If you wish to take a break, this is a good place to do so. You can exit PowerPoint now. To resume at a later time, run PowerPoint and continue following the steps from this location forward.

Sharing and Distributing a Presentation

Many people design PowerPoint presentations to accompany a speech given in front of an audience, and they also develop slide shows to share with family, work associates, and friends in a variety of ways. For example, they can print a slide on thick paper and send the document through the mail. They also can email the file or create a video to upload to a website or view on a computer. Video files can become quite large in file size, so PowerPoint allows you to reduce the size by compressing the file.

Use hyperlinks to show slides with landscape and portrait orientations.
When you are creating your presentation, you have the option to display all your slides in either the default landscape orientation or in portrait orientation. You may, however, desire to have slides with both orientations during a single presentation. Using hyperlinks is one solution to mixing the orientations. Apply a hyperlink to an object on the last slide in one orientation and then hyperlink to another presentation with slides in the other orientation. If you desire to hyperlink to one particular slide in a second presentation, click the Bookmark button in the Insert Hyperlink dialog box and then select the title of the slide you want to use as your link. Once you have displayed the desired slides in the second presentation, create another hyperlink from that presentation back to a slide in your original presentation.

CONSIDER THIS

To Change the Slide Orientation

By default, PowerPoint displays slides in landscape orientation, where the width dimension is greater than the height dimension. You can change this setting to specify that the slides display in portrait orientation. *Why? In portrait orientation, the height dimension is greater than the width dimension, so it is useful to display tall objects, people who are standing, or faces.* The following steps change the slide orientation.

- Open the presentation, Iceland Travel, located in the Data Files.

- Display the Design tab and then click the Slide Size button (Design tab | Customize group) to display the Slide Size gallery (Figure 11–59).

Figure 11–59

- Click 'Custom Slide Size' to display the Slide Size dialog box and then click Portrait in the Slides area of the Orientation section to change the slide orientation from Landscape to Portrait (Figure 11–60).

Figure 11–60

To Set Up a Custom Size

Why? To announce your presentation at the library and encourage Travel Club members to attend, you want to mail postcards to their homes. To simplify the process, you can create a PowerPoint slide that is the precise measurement of a postcard, print the card on heavy paper stock, and mail the card to Travel Club members. You can specify that your PowerPoint slides are a precise dimension. The following steps change the slide size to a custom size.

- With the Slide Size dialog box displaying, click the 'Slides sized for' arrow to display the size list (Figure 11–61).

Figure 11–61

- Click Custom in the size list.
- Change the slide width to 5 inches in the Width box.
- Change the slide height to 7 inches in the Height box (Figure 11 – 62).

Q&A Can I type the width and height measurements in the boxes instead of clicking the down arrows repeatedly?

Yes. You also can click and hold down the mouse button instead of repeatedly clicking the arrows until the desired dimensions are displayed.

Figure 11–62

- Click the OK button (Slide Size dialog box) to display the Microsoft PowerPoint dialog box (Figure 11–63).

- Click the Ensure Fit button (Microsoft PowerPoint dialog box) to apply the custom sizes and close the dialog box.

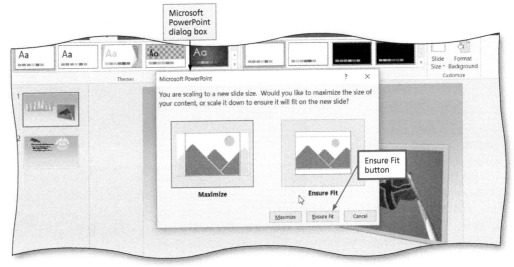

Figure 11–63

To Display Multiple Presentation Windows Simultaneously

Why? *When you are reviewing elements of several presentations, it often is efficient and convenient to open and display them simultaneously on the screen.* The following steps display three open presentations simultaneously.

1

- Open the presentation, Other Attractions, located in the Data Files and then display the View tab (Figure 11–64).

- If necessary, open the Discover Iceland file if you closed it earlier in this project.

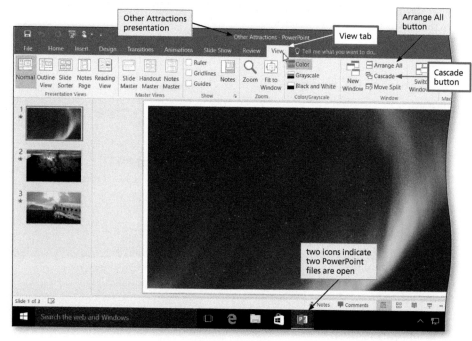

Figure 11–64

2

- Click the Cascade button (View tab | Window group) to display the three open presentations – Other Attractions, Iceland Travel, and Discover Iceland – from the upper-left to the lower-right corners of the screen.

Q&A What is the difference between the Cascade button and the Arrange All button?
When you click the Cascade button, the open windows display overlapped, or stacked, on each other. Tapping or clicking the Arrange All button tiles all the open windows side by side on the screen. Each window may display narrower than in Normal view so that all the open windows are visible simultaneously.

- If necessary, click the Other Attractions presentation title bar to display that presentation in the front of the screen (Figure 11–65).

Q&A The Other Attractions title bar is not visible on my screen. Can I move the presentation windows so that it is visible?
Yes. You can drag the presentation title bars to arrange the windows.

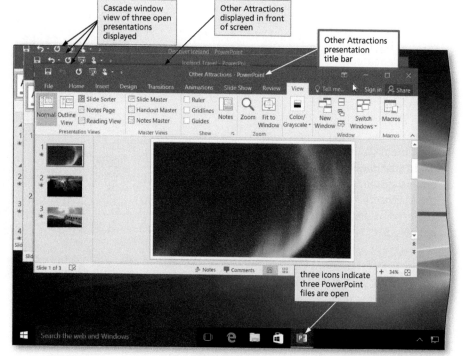

Figure 11–65

Organizing Slides and Creating a Photo Album **PowerPoint Module 11 PPT** 629

1 CREATE & ORGANIZE SECTIONS | 2 CREATE CUSTOM SLIDE SHOW | 3 CREATE PHOTO ALBUM & ENHANCE ELEMENTS
4 SPECIFY CUSTOM SLIDE SIZE & ADD VIDEO CLIP | 5 SHARE & DISTRIBUTE PRESENTATION

PowerPoint Module 11

To Copy a Video File

Why? *Slide 2 in the Other Attractions presentation contains a video clip of the Eyjafjallajokull volcano that you want to insert at the bottom of Slide 2 in the Iceland Travel file.* With multiple presentations open simultaneously on your screen, you can view all the slides quickly and decide which elements of one presentation you desire to copy to another. The following steps copy the video file from Slide 2 of the Other Attractions presentation to Slide 2 of the Iceland Travel presentation.

1
- Click the Slide 2 thumbnail of the Other Attractions presentation to display that slide.

- Right-click the video image in the center of the slide to select it and to display the shortcut menu (Figure 11–66).

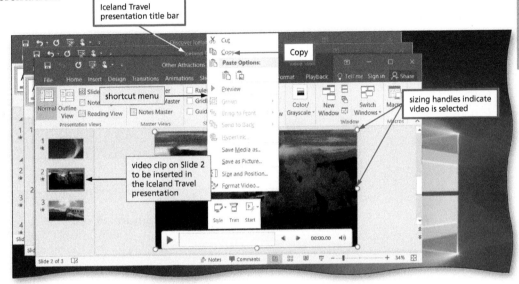

Figure 11–66

2
- Click Copy on the shortcut menu.

- Click the Iceland Travel presentation title bar to display that presentation in the front of the screen.

- Click the Slide 2 thumbnail of the Iceland Travel presentation to display that slide.

- Right-click the slide to display the shortcut menu and then point to the 'Use Destination Theme' button under Paste Options to display a preview of the video clip on that slide (Figure 11–67).

Figure 11–67

- Click the 'Use Destination Theme' button in the Paste gallery to insert the video into the slide.

- If necessary, drag the Iceland Travel presentation title bar downward so the Other Attractions title bar is visible (Figure 11–68).

Figure 11–68

4

- Click the Other Attractions title bar and then click that presentation's Close button to close that presentation.

- Click the Maximize button in the Iceland Travel presentation to maximize the PowerPoint window.

- Select the video, display the Video Tools Format tab, size the video to 2.8" x 4.98", and then move the clip to the location shown in Figure 11–69.

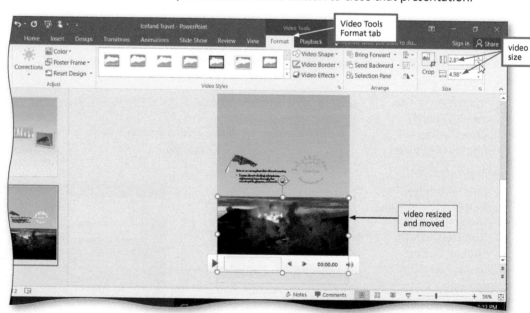

Figure 11–69

BTW

Screen Recording

You can include screen recordings in your PowerPoint presentations if you have a sound card, microphone, and speakers. Display the slide you would like to record at the beginning of the presentation, display the Insert tab, click the Screen Recording button (Insert tab | Media area), select an area of your screen to record, and then click the Record button. Capture the desired information, including voice narrations, slide timings, and ink and laser pointer gestures. Then, insert the recording directly into your presentation.

To Compress a Video File

Why? *The file size of videos can be quite large. This size can pose a problem if you desire to email a presentation or if the space on a storage device is small.* PowerPoint includes a feature that will compress your file to reduce its size. You can specify one of three compression qualities: Presentation, Internet, or Low. In this project, you are going to email the Iceland Travel file, so you desire to keep the file size as small as possible without sacrificing too much resolution quality. The following steps compress the video file.

- With the video clip selected on Slide 2, display the Backstage view and then click the Compress Media button (Info tab | Media Size and Performance section) to display the Compress Media menu (Figure 11–70).

Q&A

Why am I seeing an error message stating that the media could not be compressed?
Graphics cards have acceleration capabilities that allow video, animation, transitions, and other graphics to display smoothly. Your PowerPoint file may have too many graphics that are consuming the resources of your graphics card. If so, you may need to disable hardware graphics acceleration. These settings are found in the Display section of the PowerPoint Options Advanced tab.

Figure 11–70

- Click Low Quality to display the Compress Media dialog box and compress the file (Figure 11–71).

- When the video file has been compressed, click the Close button (Compress Media dialog box) to return to the Backstage view.

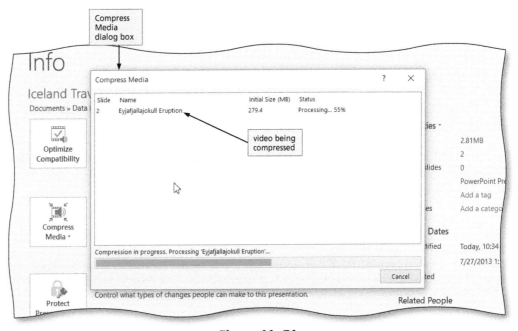

Figure 11–71

BTW
Turn Off Slide Timings
If you recorded narration with slide timings, you might decide to play the comments for your audience but want to advance the slides manually. PowerPoint gives you the option to turn slide timings off and then turn them back on without having to recreate them. Click the 'Set Up Slide Show' button (Slide Show tab | Set Up group) and then click Manually in the Advance slides area (Set Up Show dialog box). To turn the slide timings back on, click 'Using timings, if present' in the Advance slides area (Set Up Show dialog box).

BTW
Restricting Permissions
You can allow PowerPoint users to see your presentation but not allow them to change the slide content, copy the slides, or print the presentation. To protect your presentation, click File on the ribbon to open the Backstage view, display the Info tab in the Backstage view, click the Protect Presentation button, click the Restrict Access button, and then click 'Connect to Rights Management Servers and get templates'.

TO RECORD NARRATION

In some situations, you may want your viewers to hear recorded narration that accompanies slides. You can record narration separately and then add this file to the slide. You also can record narration while the slide show is running. To record this narration, you would perform the following steps.

1. Display the Slide Show tab and then click the 'Record Slide Show' arrow (Slide Show tab | Set Up group).
2. Click 'Start Recording from Beginning' if you want to begin with the first slide or click 'Start Recording from Current Slide' if you want to begin with the slide that is displaying on your screen.
3. Click the 'Narrations, ink, and laser pointer' check box (Record Slide Show dialog box) and, if appropriate, click the 'Slide and animation timings' check box ('Record Slide Show' dialog box) to select or remove the check mark.
4. Click the Start Recording button (Record Slide Show dialog box).
5. When you have finished speaking, right-click the slide and then click End Show on the shortcut menu.

TO PREVIEW NARRATION

Once you have recorded narration, you can play the audio to review the sound. To preview this narration, you would perform the following steps.

1. In Normal view, click the sound icon on the slide.
2. Display the Audio Tools Playback tab and then click the Play button (Audio Tools Playback tab | Preview group).

TO SHOW A PRESENTATION WITH OR WITHOUT NARRATION

If you have recorded narration to accompany your slides, you can choose whether to include this narration when you run your slide show. You would perform the following steps to run the slide show either with or without narration.

1. Display the Slide Show tab and then click the Play Narrations check box (Slide Show tab | Set Up group) to remove the check from the box.
2. If you have chosen to show the presentation without narration and then desire to allow audience members to hear this recording, click the Play Narrations check box (Slide Show tab | Set Up group) to check this option.

To Email a Slide Show from within PowerPoint

1 CREATE & ORGANIZE SECTIONS | 2 CREATE CUSTOM SLIDE SHOW | 3 CREATE PHOTO ALBUM & ENHANCE ELEMENTS
4 SPECIFY CUSTOM SLIDE SIZE & ADD VIDEO CLIP | 5 SHARE & DISTRIBUTE PRESENTATION

Why? *Presenters often email their presentations to friends and colleagues to solicit feedback and share their work.* PowerPoint offers a convenient method of emailing a presentation directly within PowerPoint. The following steps create a message, attach a presentation, and send a slide show to Victoria Halen.

BTW
Optimize Media Compatibility
To help ensure your audio or video files will play correctly on other computers or devices, you can optimize these files. Click File on the ribbon to open the Backstage view and then display the Info tab in the Backstage view. If the media in your presentation was inserted in a format that might have compatibility issues when played on another device, the Optimize Media Compatibility option will appear. Click the Optimize Compatibility button to have PowerPoint improve any media file that needs optimization. If the Optimize Compatibility option does not appear, you do not have compatibility issues.

1

- With the Backstage view displaying, display the Share gallery.

- Click the Email button to display the Email options (Figure 11–72).

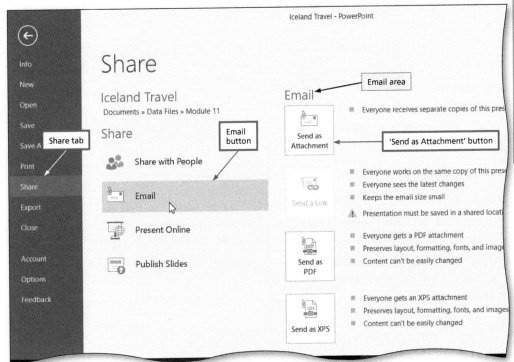

Figure 11–72

2

- Click the 'Send as Attachment' button in the Email area to open the Iceland Travel.pptx – Message (HTML) window in Microsoft Outlook (Figure 11–73). If necessary, enter your user name or password in the Windows Security dialog box.

Q&A Must I use Microsoft Outlook to send this email message?

No, you do not have to have Outlook installed; however, you need to have an email program installed in Windows to send the email. If you don't use Outlook, you could use Windows Mail or another email program.

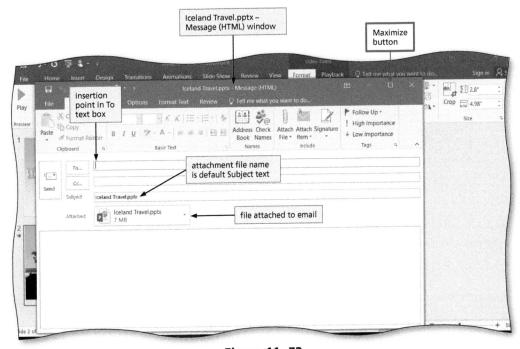

Figure 11–73

❸

- If necessary, click the Maximize button in the Iceland Travel.pptx – Message (HTML) window to maximize the window.

- With the insertion point in the To box, type `victoria_halen@hotmail.com` to enter the email address of the recipient.

- Click to position the insertion point in the Subject box, select the file name that is displaying, and then type `Travel Club Meeting` as the subject.

- Press the TAB key two times to move the insertion point into the message area.

❹

- Type `Miss Halen,` as the greeting line.

- Press the ENTER key to move the insertion point to the beginning of the next line.

- Type `The announcement for our next Travel Club meeting at the library is attached. I hope you will be able to attend.` to enter the message text.

- Press the ENTER key twice to insert a blank line and move the insertion point to the beginning of the next line. Type `Charlotte Wilson` as the signature line (Figure 11–74).

   If requested by your instructor, type your name instead of Charlotte Wilson's name followed by your current or previous pet's name.

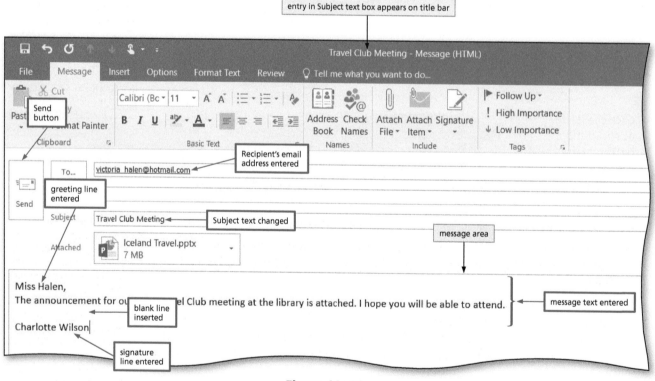

Figure 11–74

❺

- Click the Send button in the message header to send the email message and to close the message window.

Rehearse, rehearse, rehearse.
Speakers should spend as much time practicing their presentations as they do preparing their PowerPoint slides. Frequently, however, they use the majority of their preparation time designing and tweaking the slides. Audience members expect to see a presenter who is prepared, confident, and enthusiastic. Practicing the presentation helps convey this image. As you rehearse, focus on a strong introduction that grasps the audience's attention and previews the main points of your talk. You have only one chance to make a good first impression, so begin the speech by establishing eye contact with audience members in various parts of the room. Resist the urge to stare at the slides projected on the screen. Your audience came to your presentation to hear you speak, and rehearsing will help you deliver a high-quality talk that exceeds their expectations.

To Run and Save the Presentation

When you run the Iceland Travel presentation, the video will play automatically because the file had that setting in the Other Attractions presentation. The following steps run the slide show and then save and close the document.

1 Display Slide 1 and then run the presentation.

2 Save the presentation with the file name, Iceland Travel Mail.

3 Display the Backstage view and then click Close to close the Iceland Travel Mail file without exiting PowerPoint.

To Present a Slide Show Online

Microsoft's Office Presentation Service feature allows you to share your presentation remotely with anyone having an Internet connection. As you display your slides, they see a synchronized view of your slide show in their web browser, even if they do not have PowerPoint installed on their computers. To present your presentation online, you would perform the following steps.

1. Click the Present Online arrow (Slide Show tab | Start Slide Show group) to display the Present Online menu.

2. Click 'Office Presentation Service' to display the Present Online dialog box.

3. Click the CONNECT button to agree to the service terms, then, if necessary, sign in to your Microsoft account, and then click the Next button (Sign in dialog box).

4. After PowerPoint has connected to the service and completed preparing the presentation, share the presentation link with up to 50 remote viewers and then click the START PRESENTATION button (Present Online dialog box). People visiting the website can view your presentation with any annotations you make.

5. When you have displayed the last slide, click the 'End Online Presentation' button (Present Online tab | Present Online group) and then click the 'End Online Presentation' button (Microsoft PowerPoint dialog box).

BTW
Use Your Mouse as a Laser Pointer
When you are presenting, you can emphasize an important point in your slide by using your mouse as a laser pointer. In Slide Show view, click either the From Beginning or the 'From Current Slide' button (Slide Show tab | Start Slide Show group), press and hold the CTRL key, and then click and drag the left mouse button to point to specific slide contents. To change the laser pointer color, click the 'Set Up Slide Show' button (Slide Show tab | Set Up group) to display the Set Up Show dialog box. In the Show options area, click the 'Laser pointer color' button, select the desired color in the gallery, and then click the OK button.

BTW
Configuring Slide Show Resolution
You can change the resolution you want to use to display your presentation. This feature is valuable when your computer is connected to two different monitors, when you are delivering your presentation using a computer other than the one used to create the slides, or when the projector does not support the resolution you specified when you saved the presentation. To configure the resolution, click the 'Set Up Slide Show' button (Slide Show tab | Set Up group), click the Resolution arrow in the Multiple monitors area (Set Up Show dialog box), and then select the new resolution.

To Create a Video

Why? *Watching video files is a common activity with the advent of easy-to-use recording devices and websites that host these files.* You can convert your PowerPoint presentation to a video file and upload it to a video-sharing website or burn the file to a CD or DVD to distribute to people. You can include your narrations, timings, animations, transitions, and laser pointing gestures in the file, which can be saved in MPEG-4 or WMV format. The following steps create a video of the Discover Iceland presentation.

1

- Display the Discover Iceland file and, if necessary, click the Maximize button in the title bar to maximize the window.

- Display the Backstage view and then display the Export gallery.

- Click the 'Create a Video' button to display the Create a Video section.

- Click the Presentation Quality button in the Create a Video section to display a list of file sizes and screen resolutions (Figure 11–75).

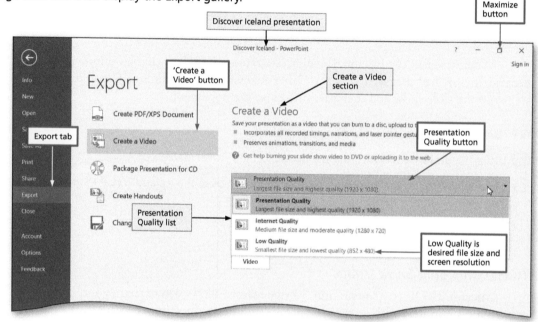

Figure 11–75

2

- If Low Quality is not the selected option, click Low Quality to select the smallest file size and 852 × 480 resolution.

- Change the 'Seconds spent on each slide' time to 10 seconds (Figure 11–76).

 Is 5 seconds always the default slide display time?
Yes. If you have not set transitions in your file, PowerPoint will display each slide for this amount of time in the video.

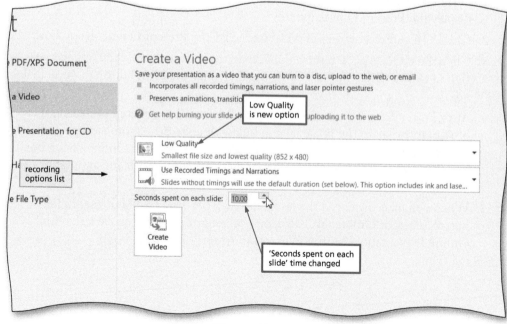

Figure 11–76

3

• Click the 'Use Recorded Timings and Narrations' button in the Create a Video section to display a list of recording options (Figure 11–77).

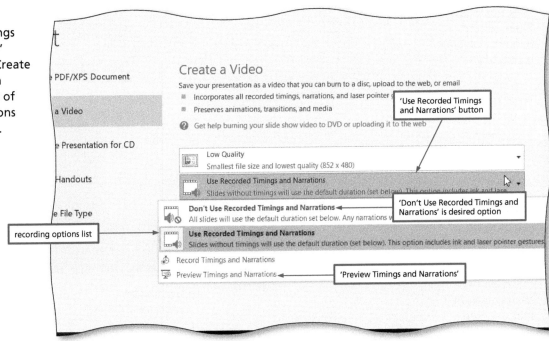

Figure 11–77

4

• Click 'Preview Timings and Narrations' to run the slide show.

• When all the slides in the presentation have displayed, end the slide show.

• Click the 'Use Recorded Timings and Narrations' button in the Create a Video section and then click the 'Don't Use Recorded Timings and Narrations' option (Figure 11-78).

Figure 11–78

 When would I select the 'Use Recorded Timings and Narrations' option?
If you had recorded and timed narrations and also had turned you mouse into a laser pointer, then you would want to include these features in your video.

- Click the Create Video button to open the Save As dialog box.

- Change the video file name to Discover Iceland Video (Figure 11–79).

- Click the Save button (Save As dialog box) to begin creating the Discover Iceland Video file.

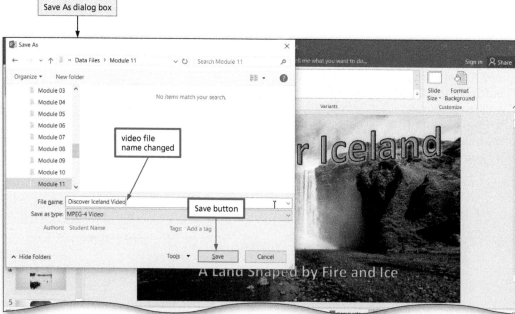

Figure 11–79

Q&A
Does PowerPoint take a long period of time to create the video?
Yes. It may take several minutes to export the presentation to a video. Do not attempt to open the video file while it is being created.

- When the video has been created, save the presentation again.

BTW

Practice Using Presenter View
Presenter view allows a speaker to use dual monitors: one that displays what the audience is seeing, and another with controls to aid the presenter. You can rehearse using Presenter view with one monitor so that you are comfortable using the features. Be certain that 'Use Presenter View' is selected (Slide Show tab | Monitors group) and then press ALT+F5. You will not be able to edit the slides while using Presenter view.

TO SET UP PRESENTER VIEW

Speakers often deliver a presentation using two monitors: one to display their speaker notes privately, and a second to display the slides and project them on a large screen for the audience to view. PowerPoint's **Presenter view** supports the use of two monitors connected to one computer so presenters can view the slide currently being projected while viewing the slide thumbnails, seeing a preview of the next slide or animation, reading their speaker notes, viewing the elapsed time, lightening or darkening the audience's screen, or customizing the presentation by skipping the next slide or reviewing a slide previously displayed. A computer must support the use of multiple monitors and must be configured to use this feature. To use Presenter view, you would perform the following step.

1. Display the Slide Show tab and then click the 'Use Presenter View' check box (Slide Show tab | Monitors group).

To Run and Print the Presentation

The presentation now is complete. You should run the slide show, print handouts, and then exit PowerPoint.

1 Run the slide show.

2 Print the presentation as a handout with six horizontal slides per page (Figure 11–80).

3 Because the project now is complete, you can exit PowerPoint, closing all open documents.

BTW

Printing Selections
When you are developing slides or creating handouts for a particular audience, you may not want to print every slide in your presentation. To print specific slides, select the desired slides in the Thumbnail pane. Then, click File on the ribbon to open the Backstage view, display the Print tab in the Backstage view, click the first button in the Settings area, click Print Selection in the list to specify you want to print the slides you have selected, and then click the Print button in the Print gallery to print these slides.

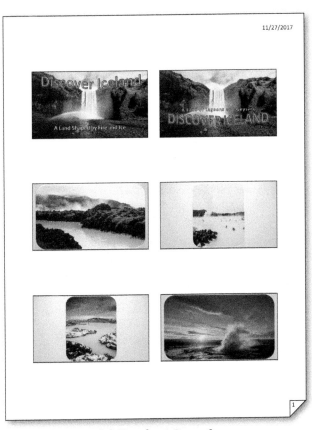

(a) Handout Page 1

(b) Handout Page 2

(c) Handout Page 3

(d) Handout Page 4

Figure 11–80

Summary

In this module you have learned how to organize a presentation into sections and then rename and move entire sections in the file. You then created a photo album, added and organized pictures, selected a theme and layout, adjusted a photo's contrast and brightness, and edited captions. You also changed the images to black and white in a separate photo album. Then, you specified a custom size and modified two slides by changing the slide orientation to portrait and inserting and compressing a video file. You then emailed the file and converted another file to video.

CONSIDER THIS: PLAN AHEAD

What decisions will you need to make when creating your next presentation?
Use these guidelines as you complete the assignments in this module and create your own slide show decks outside of this class.

1. **Use photographs with sharp focus and contrast.** The adage, "A picture is worth a thousand words," is relevant in a PowerPoint presentation. When your audience can see a visual representation of the concept you are describing during your talk, they are apt to understand and comprehend your message. Be certain your pictures are sharp and clear.

2. **Use hyperlinks to show slides with landscape and portrait orientations.** All slides in one presentation must be displayed in either landscape or portrait orientation. If you want to have variety in your slide show or have pictures or graphics that display best in one orientation, consider using hyperlinks to mix the two orientations during your presentation.

3. **Rehearse, rehearse, rehearse.** Outstanding slides lose their value when the presenter is unprepared to speak. Always keep in mind that the visual aspects are meant to supplement a speaker's verbal message. Practice your presentation before different types of audiences to solicit feedback, and use their comments to improve your speaking style.

Apply Your Knowledge

Reinforce the skills and apply the concepts you learned in this module.

Creating Sections and Custom Slide Shows

Note: To complete this assignment, you will be required to use the Data Files. Please contact your instructor for information about accessing the Data Files.

Instructions: Run PowerPoint. Open the presentation called Apply 11-1 Golf, which is located in the Data Files. The slides in this presentation provide information about golf lessons at the Harper Valley Golf Academy. Instructors at the golf academy teach all ages and skill levels, and they have developed programs for beginners, intermediate, and advanced skill levels. The manager mentioned that most students from last year are returning and probably will enroll in the intermediate or advanced classes. The beginners program may be eliminated, and classes may be changed to intermediate or advanced to accommodate the returning students. The document you open is a partially formatted presentation. You will insert slides, insert section breaks, rename and reorder sections, and create two custom slide shows. Your presentation should look like Figure 11–81.

Perform the following tasks:
1. Select Slide 1 (Figure 11–81a), and create a new Slide 2 that is a duplicate of Slide 1. Resize the golf ball illustration in the lower-right corner of Slide 2 to 2.5 × 2.46 and then move it by the sand trap, as shown in Figure 11-81b. Select the words, 'and skill levels', in the rectangle shape and then type **at beginner level** as the replacement text.

(a) Slide 1

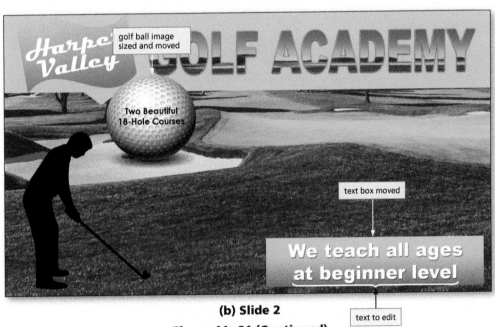

(b) Slide 2

Figure 11–81 (Continued)

2. If requested by your instructor, add the city where you were born as the third line of the rectangle shape text.

3. Move the rectangle shape to the lower-right area of the slide, as shown in Figure 11-81b. Create a new Slide 3 that is a duplicate of Slide 2. Select the word, beginning, in the rectangle shape and then type **intermediate** as the new text. Duplicate Slide 3 and then replace the word, intermediate, with the word, **advanced,** in the new Slide 4.

4. In Slide Sorter view, add a section break after Slide 1 and the rename the new (Untitled) section, Beginners.

Continued >

Apply Your Knowledge *continued*

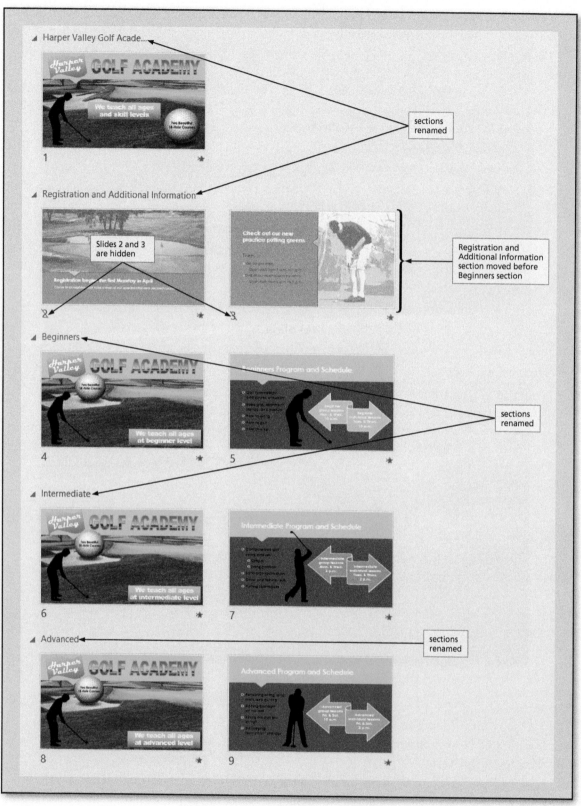

(c) Presentation in Slide Sorter View

Figure 11–81

5. Rename the Default Section divider (before Slide 1), Harper Valley Golf Academy.

6. Add a section break before Slide 3 and then rename it, Intermediate. Add a section break before Slide 4 and then rename it, Advanced.

7. Adjust the zoom so that all slides are visible. Move Slide 5 (Beginners Program and Schedule) to the Beginners section so that it becomes the second slide of that section and Slide 3 in the presentation. Move Slide 6 (Intermediate Program and Schedule) to the Intermediate section so that it becomes the second slide of that section and Slide 5 in the presentation. Slide 7 should remain as the second slide in the Advanced section.

8. Add a section break before Slide 8 and then rename it, Registration and Additional Information. Slide 9 should remain as the second slide in this section.

9. Collapse all sections and then move the Registration and Additional Information section before the Beginners section. Hide both slides in this section.

10. Apply the Wind transition (Exciting category) and change the duration to 03.50 for all slides.

11. Expand all the sections and then change the view to Normal. Create a custom slide show called Intermediate Golf Lessons. Include only Slides 1, 2, 3, 6, and 7 in this custom slide show. Show the custom presentation.

12. Create a second custom slide show called Advanced Golf Lessons. Include only Slides 1, 2, 3, 8, and 9 in this custom slide show. Show the custom presentation.

13. Run the Golf presentation and then save the file using the file name, Apply 11-1 Golf Lessons.

14. Submit the documents in the format specified by your instructor.

15. ✳ In this presentation, you duplicated the title slide and then created three new slides that served as the first slide of each section. How does this common element help guide audience members through the presentation? Is it more effective to display the Registration and Additional Information section at the beginning or the end of the presentation? Why? When might a presenter want to hide one or both slides in the Registration and Additional Information section?

Extend Your Knowledge

Extend the skills you learned in this module and experiment with new skills. You may need to use Help to complete the assignment.

Renaming Sections, Removing a Section, Using the Smart Lookup Tool to Find Information, and Setting Up a Custom Size

Note: To complete this assignment, you will be required to use the Data Files. Please contact your instructor for information about accessing the Data Files.

Instructions: Run PowerPoint. You volunteer at the local wildlife reserve where people can observe many kinds of birds. The lake on the reserve had been home to large colonies of flamingos and herons, but the heron colony no longer is present. You locate a presentation about these birds that was used at the visitors' center kiosk several years ago, and now you will revise it. You also will create a banner from the title slide that will be printed and posted near the path to the lake. Open the presentation called Extend 11-1 Flamingos and Herons, which is located in the Data Files. Create the presentation shown in Figure 11–82.

Continued >

Extend Your Knowledge *continued*

Perform the following tasks:

1. On Slide 1 (Figure 11–82a), delete the heron picture on the left side of the slide. Increase the size of the flamingo picture to 6.4" × 9.91" and then align it in the center and the middle of the slide. Delete the words, and Heron, from the text box and then change the text box shape fill color to Red (in Recent Colors row).

2. Use Smart Lookup to find the etymology (origin) of the word, flamingo. Copy and paste this information in the Notes pane on Slide 1.

3. Using Slide Sorter view (Figure 11–82b), remove the Heron Colony section and the three slides in this section. (*Hint:* You may need to use Help to learn how to remove a section and associated slides.)

4. Move the Flamingo Habitats section up so that is below the Flamingo - General Information section.

5. Remove the Flamingo Breeding section and slide.

6. Rename the first section, Flamingo Colony - Entry Sign.

7. Create a custom slide show called Flamingos. Include only Slides 2, 3, and 4 in this custom slide show. Move Slide 3 (Diet) up so that it becomes the second slide and displays after Slide 1 (FLAMINGO). Show the custom show.

8. If requested by your instructor, add the number of bones you have broken after the word, feathers, on Slide 2.

9. Change the transition from Fade to Uncover in the Subtle category, change the duration to 03.50 seconds, and then apply the transition to all slides.

10. Run the presentation and then save the file using file name, Extend 11-1 Flamingo Reserve.

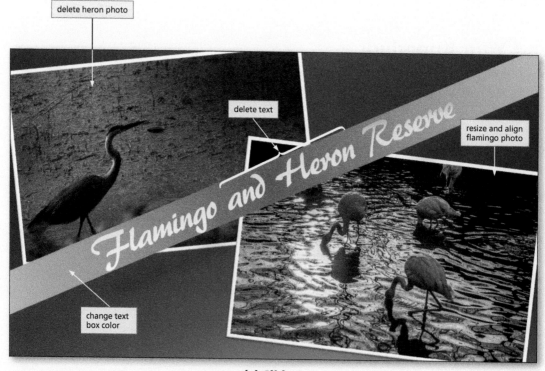

(a) Slide 1

Figure 11–82 (Continued)

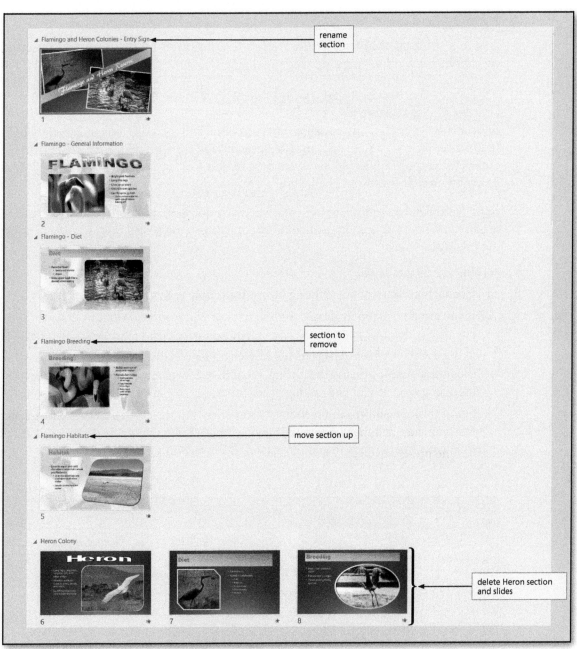

(b) Presentation in Slide Sorter View

Figure 11–82

11. Display Slide 1 and create a custom slide size for a banner. [*Hint:* Click the Slide Size button (Design tab | Customize group), click Custom Slide Size, click the 'Slides sized for' arrow (Slide Size dialog box), and then click Custom.] Change the banner width to 48" and the height to 32". Ensure the banner will fit on the new slide.

12. Delete Slides 2, 3, and 4 and the associated sections.

13. Save Slide 1 using the file name, Extend 11-1 Flamingo Reserve Banner.

14. Submit the revised documents in the format specified by your instructor.

15. ✺ In this presentation, you removed the section with the herons. Why? Which reference did you use to find the etymology for the word, flamingo? What other information about this bird is available in the Insights task pane's Explore tab?

Expand Your World

Create a solution that uses cloud or web technologies by learning and investigating on your own from general guidance.

Exploring Add-Ins for Office Apps

Instructions: You regularly use apps on your phone and tablet to look up a variety of information. In Office apps, you can use add-ins, which essentially are apps that work with PowerPoint and the other Office apps. You would like to investigate some of the add-ins available for PowerPoint to determine which ones would be helpful for you to use.

Note: You will be required to use your Microsoft account to complete this assignment. If you do not have a Microsoft account and do not want to create one, read this assignment without performing the instructions.

Perform the following tasks:

1. Use Help to learn about Office add-ins. If necessary, sign in to your Windows account.

2. If you are not signed in already, sign in to your Microsoft Account in PowerPoint.

3. Display the Insert tab and then click the 'Insert an Add-in' button (Insert tab I Add-Ins group) to display the Office Add-ins dialog box. (If a menu is displayed, click the See All link to display the Office Add-ins dialog box.) Click the Office Store button or the STORE tab (Office Add-ins dialog box) to visit the online Office Store.

4. Scroll through add-ins in the various categories (Figure 11–83). Locate a free add-in that you feel would be helpful to you while you use PowerPoint, click this desired add-in, and then follow the instructions to add the add-in to PowerPoint.

Figure 11–83

5. In PowerPoint, click the 'Insert an Add-in' button again to display the Office Add-ins dialog box. Click the add-in you added and then click the Insert button to use the add-in. Click the 'Insert an Add-in' arrow to see the added add-in in the list.

6. Practice using the add-in. Does the add-in work as you intended? Would you recommend the add-in to others?

7. ✲ Which add-ins, if any, were already on your computer or mobile device? Which add-in did you download and why? Answer the questions in #6.

In the Labs

Design, create, modify, and/or use a presentation following the guidelines, concepts, and skills presented in this module. Labs 1 and 2, which increase in difficulty, require you to create solutions based on what you learned in the module; Lab 3 requires you to apply your creative thinking and problem-solving skills to design and implement a solution.

Lab 1: Working with Multiple Presentation Windows Simultaneously, Setting Manual Timings, and Creating a Video

Note: To complete this assignment, you will be required to use the Data Files. Please contact your instructor for information about accessing the Data Files.

Problem: You are preparing a presentation about jellyfish for your marine biology class and are working with two PowerPoint presentations simultaneously. One has basic facts about jellyfish and their life cycle. The second one contains information about different species of jellyfish and a video that you want to use in your presentation. You create a video of your final combined presentation, and email the presentation.

Perform the following tasks:
1. Run PowerPoint. Open the presentation, Lab 11-1 Jellyfish Facts, which is located in the Data Files. Remove all sections (but not the slides).

2. Open the presentation, Lab 11-1 Jellyfish with Video, which is located in the Data Files, and then cascade the two open document windows on the screen.

3. Copy the video on Slide 3 of the Jellyfish with Video presentation to Slide 4 of the Jellyfish Facts presentation using the destination theme. Change the video style to Reflected Bevel, White (fourth style in first Intense row). Increase the size of the video frame to 5.4" × 9.6 and then align it on the middle and the right side of the slide.

4. Display Slide 3 of the Jellyfish with Video presentation. Select the text box with the two bulleted paragraphs, copy it, and then paste it on Slide 4 of the Jellyfish Facts presentation using the 'Keep Source Formatting' option. Align the text box in the middle and the left side of the slide (Figure 11–84).

5. If requested by your instructor, add the name of your grade school or high school as a third paragraph in the bulleted text box on Slide 4.

6. Close the Jellyfish with Video presentation without saving changes.

7. Apply the Ripple transition in the Exciting category to Slide 4 and then change the duration to 03.50 seconds.

Continued >

In the Labs *continued*

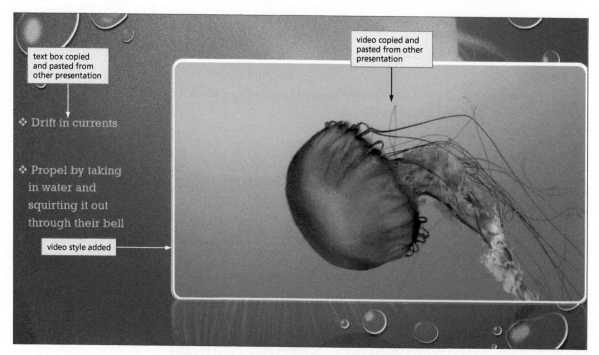

Figure 11–84 Remarkable Jellyfish Slide 4

8. Set up the slide show to advance slides manually. Run the presentation using Presenter View.

9. Save the presentation using the file name, Lab 11-1 Remarkable Jellyfish.

10. Create a video of the Lab 11-1 Remarkable Jellyfish presentation. Select Internet Quality, do not record timings and narrations, and then change seconds spent on each slide to 10.00. Save the video using the file name, Lab 11-1 Remarkable Jellyfish Video.

11. Email the presentation to your instructor.

12. ✳ You copied the video on Slide 4 from another presentation. Was the video style you added to it appropriate, or can you recommend another style that is more suitable? What other videos and photos would enhance this presentation?

Lab 2: Creating Photo Albums in Color and Black-and-White, Adjusting Brightness and Contrast of an Image, Copying and Compressing a Video File, and Recording a Narration

Note: To complete this assignment, you will be required to use the Data Files. Please contact your instructor for information about accessing the Data Files.

Problem: You recently vacationed in Australia and have decided to create a photo album to share your experiences. To add interest to the color photo album, you want to add a short video you took of a kangaroo with a beautiful sunset in the background. You will copy the video into your color photo album. Then, you will create a black-and-white photo album with narration. You create the slides shown in Figure 11–85.

Perform the following tasks:

Part 1:

1. Run PowerPoint. Apply the Blank Presentation theme. Insert a new photo album.

2. Insert the Australia1, Australia2, Australia3, Australia4, Australia5, Australia6, Australia7, and Australia8 pictures, which are located in the Data Files.

3. Move the Australia7 picture in the album above the Australia2 picture.

4. Move the Australia4 picture in the album to the end of the album after the Australia8 picture.

5. Change the album picture layout to 2 pictures, select the 'Simple Frame, White' frame shape, and then select the 'Captions below ALL pictures' option.

6. Create the photo album. Apply the Vapor Trail theme. Save the presentation using the file name, Lab 11-2 Australia Color Album.

7. On Slide 1, type, `Visit Australia` as the new title text and then, if necessary, type your name in the subtitle placeholder (Figure 11–85a).

8. If requested by your instructor, type the time of day you were born after the word, Australia.

9. On Slide 2, type, `Sydney Opera House` as the caption for the left picture and `Cathedral Range State Park` as the caption for the right picture (Figure 11–85b).

10. On Slide 3, type, `Melbourne` as the caption for the left picture and `Spectacular dive site` as the caption for the right picture. Edit the photo album and then rotate the right picture clockwise (Figure 11–85c).

11. On Slide 4, type `Mount Oberon` as the caption for the left picture and `Lake Eldon` as the caption for the right picture (Figure 11–85d).

12. On Slide 5, edit the photo album by removing the Australia8 picture. Increase the size of the beach picture to 6" × 8.25" and then align the picture in the center and the middle of the slide. Type the caption, `7-Mile Beach` (Figure 11–85e).

14. Insert a new slide after Slide 5 and select the Blank layout.

(a) Slide 1

Figure 11–85 (Continued)

Continued >

In the Labs *continued*

(b) Slide 2

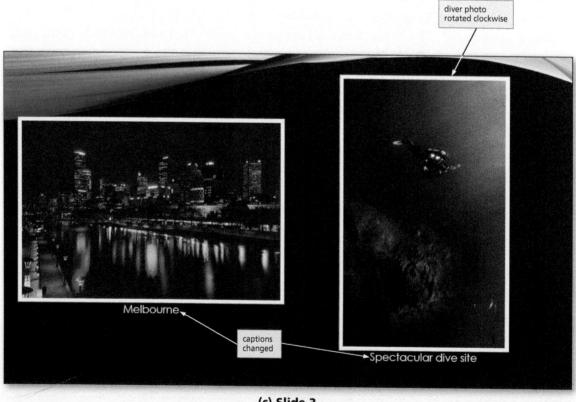

(c) Slide 3

Figure 11–85 (Continued)

(d) Slide 4

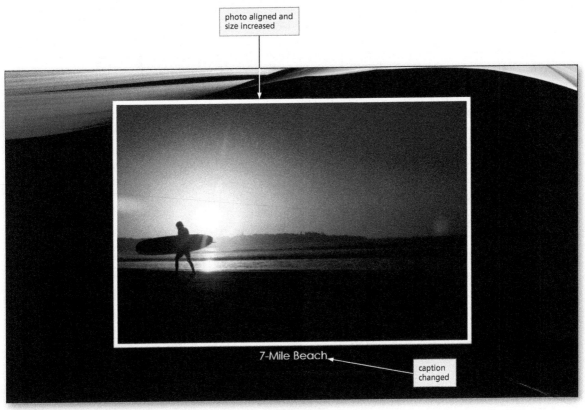

(e) Slide 5

Figure 11–85 (Continued)

Continued >

In the Labs *continued*

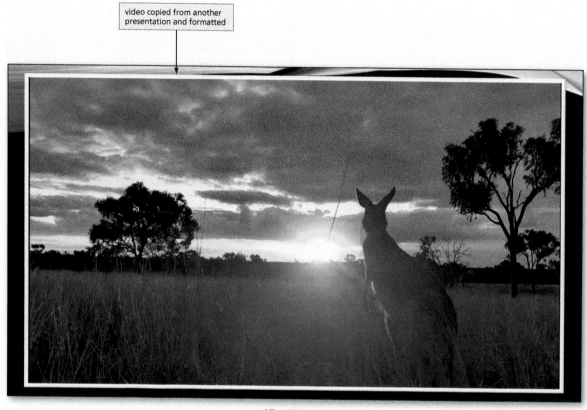

video copied from another presentation and formatted

(f) Slide 6

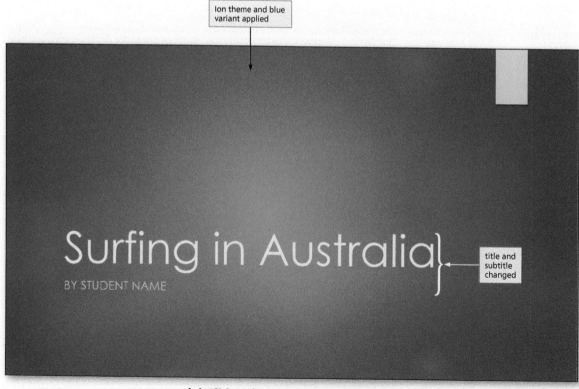

Ion theme and blue variant applied

title and subtitle changed

(g) Slide 1 (Narrated Presentation)
Figure 11–85 (Continued)

photo contrast increased

(h) Slide 2 (Narrated Presentation)

photo brightness
decreased

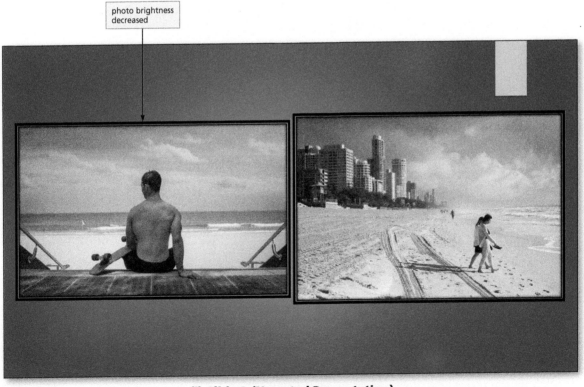

(i) Slide 3 (Narrated Presentation)

Figure 11–85

Continued >

In the Labs *continued*

15. Open the presentation, Lab 11-2 Australia Sunsets, which is located in the Data Files. Cascade the two open document windows on the screen. Copy the video from Slide 2 and paste it into Slide 6 of the Lab 11-2 Australia Color Album using the destination theme.

16. Close the Lab 11-2 Australia Sunsets presentation. Maximize the Lab 11-2 Australia Color Album presentation. Adjust the size of the video to 7" × 12.44" and then align it in the center and the middle of the slide. Change the start option to Automatically and then change the video style to 'Simple Frame, White' (sixth style in first Subtle row) (Figure 11–85f).

17. Apply the Comb transition (Exciting category), change the duration to 03.50 seconds, and then apply to all slides.

18. Set up the show to run in Presenter View.

19. Compress the media files in the presentation using the Low Quality setting. Save the presentation again using the same file name.

20. Run the presentation. Submit the revised document in the format specified by your instructor.

Part 2:

1. Insert a new photo album.

2. Insert the Australia9, Australia10, Australia11, and Australia12 pictures, which are located in the Data Files.

3. Change the album picture layout to 2 pictures, select the 'Compound Frame, Black' frame shape, select the 'ALL pictures blank and white' option, and then add the Ion theme.

4. Select the Australia10 picture and increase the contrast two times.

5. Select the Australia11 picture and decrease the brightness of the picture two times.

6. Create the photo album and then apply the Ion theme's blue variant.

7. Edit the album by removing the Australia9 picture. Insert the Australia4 picture and then move it to the beginning of the album. Update the slides.

8. On Slide 1, type, **Surfing in Australia** as the new title text and then, if necessary, type your name in the subtitle placeholder (Figure 11–85g).

9. If requested by your instructor, type the year you started college after the word, Australia.

10. Select Slide 2 (Figure 11–85h). Record the slide show from the current slide. Note: The following steps contain narration that you will read while progressing through the slides. Read the following narration: **"Australia has many great surfing spots to explore."** for this slide.

11. Advance to Slide 3 (Figure 11–85i) and then read the following narration: **"Whether you are a beginner or an experienced surfer, you can find your surfing spot somewhere in Australia."** for this slide.

12. Stop the presentation so that the recording session ends.

13. Display Slide 1 and then run the slide show to view the presentation and to hear the narration you just recorded.

14. Apply the Fall Over transition, change the duration to 03.00 seconds, and then apply to all slides.

15. Preview the presentation and then save the file using the file name, Lab 11-2 Surfing in Australia Narration.

16. Submit the revised document in the format specified by your instructor.

17. ✸ When you created the color and black-and-white photo albums of Australia pictures, you set up the albums with two photos per slide. Would another picture layout be more dramatic? Why or why not? Did changing the contrast and brightness of the photos enhance the quality? In the black-and-white photo album, you used the Ion design with the blue variant. Was this a good choice? Why?

Lab 3: **Consider This: Your Turn**

Design and Create a Presentation about Snakes

Part 1:   Naturalists at the nature center in your community work with teachers to bring environmental education into the classroom. One of the traveling exhibits features snakes. The outreach coordinator has asked you to develop a presentation to accompany her talk and then create a video from the presentation. She provides a video, called Garter Snake, and tells you that this reptile is non-venomous and grows to between 1 foot (0.3048 m) and 2 feet (0.6096 m) long. It eats bugs and small rodents, so it can help control mice or insects. While developing the slides, you use the Smart Lookup feature to gather more information about snakes, including their habitat, diet, and anatomy. Use the concepts and techniques presented in this module to create a presentation with sections and that includes the garter snake video. The Data Files contains the Garter Snake video and seven snake illustrations called Snake 1 - Cobra, Snake 2 - Copperhead, Snake 3 – Diamondback Water, Snake 4 – Eastern Coral, Snake 5 – Rattlesnake, Snake 6 – Timber Rattlesnake, and Snake 7 – Cartoon Snake. You also can add photos you found using Smart Lookup, as long as you cite the source of these photos in the caption or in the Notes pane. Create section breaks and format the background. Compress the video. Review and revise your presentation as needed and then save the file using the file name, Lab 11-3 Snakes. Then, create a video and save that file using the file name, Lab 11-3 Snakes Video. Submit your assignment in the format specified by your instructor.

Part 2:   ✸ You made several decisions while creating the presentation: how to organize the sections, how to order the photos and video, which photo enhancements to use, and which layout and theme to apply. What was the rationale behind each of these decisions? When you reviewed the document, what further revisions did you make and why?

Index

Note: **Boldfaced** page numbers indicate
key terms

A

account, signing in, OFF 6–8
action button(s), **PPT 300**
  built-in, PPT 301
  changing fill color, PPT 304
  copying, PPT 305
  editing, PPT 306–307
  formatting on hyperlinked file, PPT 311–312
  inserting, PPT 301–303
  inserting on hyperlinked file, PPT 311–312
  sizing, PPT 303
  slide show running with, PPT 336
active tab, **OFF 19**
add-in, **PA-10**
adding
  borders to table, PPT 208–209
  captions, photo album, PPT 619
  effects to table, PPT 209–210
  gradient fill to table, PPT 549
  hyperlinks, linked Excel chart, PPT 574
  hyperlinks to paragraphs, PPT 299–300
  hyperlinks to pictures, PPT 298
  image in table, PPT 215–216
  new slide layout, PPT 440
  notes, blank layout, PPT 451
  notes, title slide, PPT 450
  photo album, PPT 612–614
  placeholders text, PPT 426–428
  shading to table, PPT 548
  slide transition, PPT 454
  SmartArt bullet, PPT 491
  SmartArt shapes, PPT 492
  SmartArt style to graphics, PPT 189–190,
    PPT 495
  table cell bevel, PPT 549–550
  text, blank layout, PPT 451
  text, notes, illustration to title/content layout,
    PPT 451–452
  text, slide master footer, PPT 421–422
  text, title slide, PPT 450
  themes, photo album, PPT 618
  transition between slides in table, PPT 219
address bar, **OFF 30**
Adobe Reader, OFF 26
aligning, **PPT 312**
  data in cells, table, PPT 552
  linked Excel chart, PPT 562–563
  linked Excel worksheet, PPT 556–557
  objects, PPT 312–313
  options, PPT 313
  paragraph, **PPT 320**
  pictures, PPT 316–317
  text box, PPT 484–485
American Sailing Association (ASA),
    PPT 474
animation
  adjusting motion path, PPT 374–375
  associating sound with, PPT 375–376
  changing direction, PPT 362–364
  changing entrance direction, PPT 151
  changing exit direction, PPT 154
  changing orders, PPT 367–368

changing SmartArt graphics sequence,
    PPT 381–382
  chart, PPT 382–383
  content placeholder paragraphs, PPT 157–158
  creating credits, PPT 386–387
  custom, PPT 150–158
  dim text after, PPT 384–385
  drawing custom motion path, PPT 376–378
  effect icon colors, PPT 150
  eyedropper for formatting text, PPT 388
  formatting text, PPT 370–371
  inserting text box, PPT 370–371
  list, PPT 383–384
  modifying emphasis timing, PPT 156,
    PPT 365–366
  modifying entrance timing, PPT 155–156,
    PPT 365
  modifying exit timing, PPT 156, PPT 365–366
  modifying transition effects, PPT 389–390
  photos using emphasis effect, PPT 363
  photos using entrance effect, PPT 362
  photos using exit effect, PPT 364
  presentation with, PPT 121–122
  previewing sequence, PPT 154, PPT 364
  renaming slide objects, PPT 368–369
  repeating credits, PPT 387
  running slide show, PPT 390–391
  slide content, PPT 150–158
  SmartArt graphic, PPT 381
  text box applying motion path, PPT 373–374
  text box using entrance effect, PPT 372–373
  title text placeholder paragraphs, PPT 366–367
  triggering effects, PPT 389
  using Animation Painter, animating picture,
    PPT 379–380
  using Animation Painter, animating text,
    PPT 385–386
  using emphasis effect, PPT 152
  using entrance effect, PPT 150–151
  using exit effect, PPT 153
animation emphasis effects, **PA-8**
app(s), **OFF 2**
  exiting Office, OFF 42, OFF 53
  Office Mix, PA-12
  running and using. See running apps
  switching between, OFF 32
Apply to All button vs. Apply button, PPT 99
ASA. See American Sailing Association
audio
  adding options, PPT 145–146
  inserting file, PPT 143–145
  presentation with, PPT 121–122
  trimming file, PPT 146
augmented reality with Office Mix, teaching,
    PA-13
automatic spelling correction, PPT 17
automatically updated properties, **PPT 44**
axis titles
  displaying, linked Excel chart, PPT 566–567
  formatting, linked Excel chart, PPT 566–567

B

backgrounds, slide
  formatting background picture fill
    transparency, PPT 88

inserting picture to create, PPT 87–88
  in specific order, PPT 86
BACKSPACE key, error correction, OFF 23
Backstage view, **OFF 24**
  closing, OFF 33
  closing Office using, OFF 49–50
  creating new documents from, OFF 48
  Info tab in, OFF 24
  opening recent files using, OFF 50
Berlin theme, PPT 4–5, PPT 9
bevel effects, PPT 71
black slide, **PPT 37**
blank layout
  adding notes, PPT 451
  adding text, PPT 451
  inserting illustration and text box into, PPT 430
  inserting placeholders into, PPT 425–426
blinking bar, OFF 23
brightness, **PPT 66**
  photo album image, PPT 617
Bring Forward, **PPT 126**
Bring to Front, **PPT 126**
bullet character(s), **PPT 327**
  changing bullet size, PPT 331
  changing size of other, PPT 332
  changing to numbers, PPT 333–334
  changing to pictures, PPT 327–329
  changing to symbols, PPT 329–331
  formatting numbered list, PPT 334–335
  removing, PPT 335
bullet color, **PPT 332**
  formatting, PPT 332–333
bulleted list, **PPT 13**
  adding new text slide with, PPT 12–13
  creating text slide with multilevel, PPT 13–19
  deleting bullets on slide, PPT 16
  presentation with pictures and, PPT 2–3
  removing extra, PPT 17

C

card, **PA-6**
category axis, **PPT 563**
cell reference, **PPT 557**
cells, **PPT 192**
  aligning text in, PPT 217–218
  displaying text in, PPT 214–215
  merging, PPT 212–213
centering table, PPT 553
centering text, **PPT 128**
characters
  in file name, OFF 34
  formatting in presentation, PPT 9–12
  inserting special, PPT 71
character spacing, **PPT 432**
chart(s). See also linked Excel chart
  aligning, PPT 562–563
  animation, PPT 382–383
  changing layout, PPT 198
  changing shape outline color, PPT 197
  changing shape outline weight, PPT 196–197
  font size changing, PPT 199
  formatting background, PPT 570–571
  formatting text, PPT 201–202
  inserting, PPT 193–194
  inserting text box, PPT 201–202